Light at the End of the Tunnel

Light at the End of the Tunnel

A Vietnam War Anthology

Revised Edition

Edited by
Andrew J. Rotter

A Scholarly Resources Inc. Imprint
Wilmington, Delaware

© 1999 by Scholarly Resources Inc.
All rights reserved
First published 1991 by St. Martin's Press
Printed and bound in the United States of America

Scholarly Resources Inc.
104 Greenhill Avenue
Wilmington, DE 19805-1897

Acknowledgment of permission to reprint copyrighted material appears within the List of Sources.

Library of Congress Cataloging-in-Publication Data

Light at the end of the tunnel : a Vietnam War anthology / edited by Andrew J.
  Rotter. — Rev. ed.
    p.   cm.
   ISBN 0-8420-2712-2 (cloth: alk. paper)— ISBN 0-8420-2713-0 (paper: alk.
paper)
    1. Vietnamese Conflict, 1961–1975—United States. 2. Vietnam—Politics and
government—1945–1975. I. Rotter, Andrew Jon.
DS558.L54   1999
959.704'3373—dc21   98-40989
                                                  CIP

To my students

Acknowledgments

My thanks go to Matthew Hershey and Linda Pote Musumeci at Scholarly Resources, who handled this book (and its editor) with professionalism and grace. Dozens of scholars made valuable suggestions for improving this edition; David Anderson and George Herring read the revised manuscript in its entirety and were particularly helpful and supportive. Marci Brennan at Corbis-Bettmann found many of the photographs, Julia Meyerson drew the map that appears on page xx, and Noam Chomsky, Gloria Emerson, and William Shawcross were generous in allowing me to reprint their words without charge. Jane L. Pincin, Provost and Dean of Faculty at Colgate University, provided a significant publication subvention and thus made the book happen. Padma Kaimal bailed me out again and again. I am most grateful to my students at Colgate University, who amaze me, year after year, with their dedication to History 317: The United States and Vietnam. This one's for them.

Contents

Preface

The Preface to the first edition of this book began with a quotation from Michael Herr's *Dispatches*: "Vietnam Vietnam we've all been there." Those of us who grew up during the 1960s and 1970s knew what Herr meant, but I suspected that his meaning would escape most of the college students who read the quotation, and I wanted to try to explain these words before the Vietnam War disappeared from public memory. As it turned out, I need not have worried. What I saw as an encouraging but probably ephemeral surge of interest in Vietnam during the late 1980s has shown no sign of diminishing; and, indeed, it may have swelled. Bookstore shelves are packed with volumes, both fiction and nonfiction, on the war, and more are published each year. In the summer of 1997, the Public Broadcasting Service reran the powerful thirteen-part series *Vietnam: A Television History*. Dozens of colleges and universities offer courses on the Vietnam War, and colleagues tell me that these are among the most popular courses on campus, thereby confirming my experience at Colgate University.

Why is there still so much interest in the Vietnam War? This is a question I ask my students even as they jostle for seats on the first day of class. Some answer that they are curious about current relations between the United States and Vietnam: the controversy over American (never Vietnamese) servicemen missing in action, President Bill Clinton's decision to extend diplomatic recognition to Vietnam, or the prospects for U.S. investment. Others are frustrated by what they think they do not know about the war, what they think they have not learned in high school. (When I was growing up, the popular lament was that high-school U.S. history classes never got past World War II. Now, the election of John F. Kennedy seems to have become a frequent terminus, although some students report that teachers skip Vietnam on their way to Watergate, or rush through the war, having become bogged down earlier in the New Deal.) Students tell me that they are fascinated by the 1960s generally and know that the war played an important role in the history of that decade. A few want to know why the United States lost the war in Vietnam, given the military's previous string of successes. And, more and more, although it often takes some gentle prodding, students are reporting a personal interest in Vietnam because a father was an officer there, or an aunt was a nurse, or the school guidance counselor was wounded there. Why won't my dad talk to me about his war? Why does my aunt cry when she watches reruns of *China Beach*? How did the guidance counselor get wounded? To an even greater extent, the 1960s shibboleth, "The personal is political," applies to students of the Vietnam War today.

In 1991 I put together the first edition of *Light at the End of the Tunnel* primarily for my students. I never imagined that a second edition would be necessary, but here we are. I have made a number of changes, in both scope and content, to strengthen the anthology and bring it up to date. The book is divided into twelve chapters, the first four of which provide a chronological survey of the U.S. war in Vietnam. Each chapter contains two or three scholarly or journalistic accounts of the war and, with the exception of Chapter 1, a passage or two from personal accounts of participants. Chapters 5 through 7 focus on the war itself, examining the Vietnamese who fought the Americans, the Vietnam battlefield, and the exertions of the U.S. military. The overflow of the Vietnam War into neighboring Laos and Cambodia is the subject of Chapter 8. Chapters 9, 10, and 11 treat the consequences of the war, especially for the United States. They cover, respectively, the scholarly controversy over the sources of the war, the emergence of the antiwar movement and its impact on American society, and the legacy of the war for the United States and Vietnam.

Chapter 12, an "Afterword," is an excerpt from a book by Le Ly Hayslip, a Vietnamese woman. It is included not only because it is a moving piece of writing but also in order to leave the reader with the testimony of someone who lived in Vietnam while the war was going on. This collection of readings focuses on the U.S. experience, for which I make no apology. But we misunderstand the nature of that experience if we look upon Vietnam merely as a venue for war rather than as a country with a history and a culture. At least occasionally I have tried to make this distinction, both in the Introduction and in the selection of readings.

Beyond that, I have worked to choose readings that are diverse, interesting, provocative, and intellectually responsible. Teachers, of course, may edit the collection by assigning only certain selections or reorganizing the book to suit their needs. I suggest that this book be used with a collection of documents on the war, such as William Appleman Williams et al., *America in Vietnam: A Documentary Collection*; George Donelson Moss, ed., *A Vietnam Reader: Sources and Essays*; or excerpts from Gareth Porter, ed., *Vietnam: The Definitive Documentation of Human Decisions*, the *Pentagon Papers*, or the appropriate volumes in the State Department series *Foreign Relations of the United States*. I hope above all that this book will be of use to students, mine and others, who continue to look for answers to their questions about the Vietnam War.

Introduction

For years, most westerners who studied Vietnam depicted it as a geopolitical empty space into which periodically came migrants or invaders from bigger places. The Vietnamese, scholars claimed, got their religion, their notions about statecraft and economics, their system of agriculture, and their art and architecture from China and India, whose peoples "diffused" into Southeast Asia or imposed their culture through conquest. The Vietnamese thus created nothing; they simply absorbed the ideas their neighbors brought.

Recent investigations by historians and anthropologists have pointed to different conclusions. Although there is no question that traditional Vietnamese culture was syncretic—that is, blended from various forms, some of them external to Vietnam—the country was not simply a cultural sponge, indiscriminately soaking up every idea with which it came in contact. For example, sometime in the first century A.D., a kingdom called Funan was established in southern Vietnam, near the delta of the Mekong River. It was a strong and prosperous place; two hundred years after Funan's founding, a Chinese visitor noted the kingdom's walled cities and grand palaces and, according to historian G. C. Bentley, observed that Funan's people "paid their taxes in pearls, gold, and perfumes." Scholars have determined that Funan's political and religious institutions were indigenous, not the products of other peoples' cultures. Religious rituals and political practices elsewhere in Vietnam were also based on internally created forms.

Historically, most Vietnamese have lived in small villages and grown rice. Because they rely on the land for sustenance, peasants are powerfully bonded to the soil, to a particular place. These peasants define themselves according to their position in their families, presenting themselves not as "I" but as "my parents' second son" or "your father's sister," a participant in a kinship network. Respect for one's elders and one's social betters is the source of stability for the family, the village, and the state. At the same time, however, respect is a reciprocal obligation. Those who are socially and politically powerful must demonstrate qualities of leadership; they must live virtuously, worship the gods properly, and protect their villages and families from harm. In other words, they must be effective and behave themselves. Inability or unwillingness to abide by these obligations is ground for popular dissatisfaction.

Comfortable with their culture and their place in the cosmos, the Vietnamese have never suffered invasion gladly. The Chinese were the first to discover their resistance. They came to northern Vietnam late in the third century B.C., and ultimately the Han dynasty (106 B.C.–A.D. 222) extended its control into what is now central Vietnam. For centuries the Vietnamese gave their conquerors no peace. Vietnam gained its independence in 967 and fought off repeated Chinese efforts to repossess it, only to be reabsorbed once more late in the fourteenth century, when it was weakened by its own bullying of its smaller neighbors. The end of Chinese rule finally came in 1428, after Emperor Le Loi decisively defeated Chinese forces near Hanoi. The Chinese went

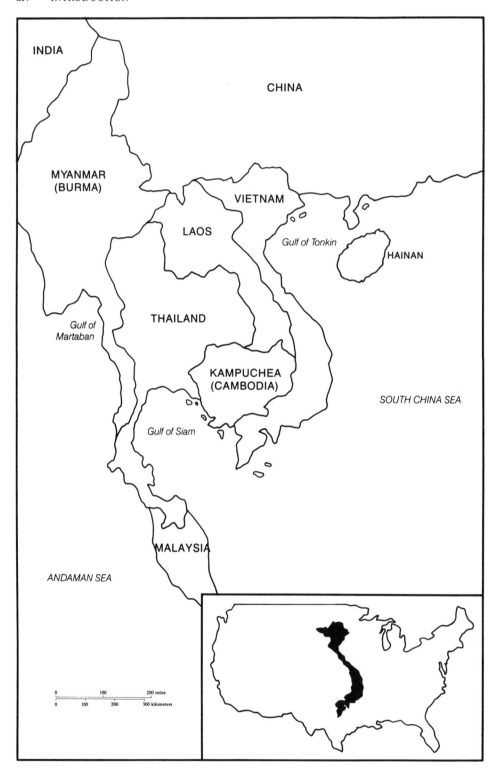

Map 1. Southeast Asia; (*insert*) Vietnam in scale with the United States.

home; the Vietnamese, to be safe from future invasions, agreed to pay a yearly tribute to China.

The independence of Vietnam was not threatened again for four hundred years. By the nineteenth century, weakened by internal warfare, the country again fell prey to outsiders. The interlopers this time were the French. They came because they had a *mission civilisatrice*—to lift the shroud of heathenism that covered the Vietnamese and replace it with the gilded robe of Christianity. They hoped to protect their position in the emerging China market to the north and to secure Vietnamese resources; moreover, in the last half of the nineteenth century, the prestige of a nation was measured by the number of dependencies it held. The French divided Vietnam into three states: Tonkin, in the north; Annam, in the narrow waist of the country; and Cochin China, encompassing the Mekong River delta in the south. The last state they made a colony in 1867; in 1884 they established a protectorate over Tonkin and Annam. The French improved sanitation and started new schools. They also institutionalized the production and consumption of opium (despite the *mission civilisatrice* this was good money), insulted the Vietnamese with their arrogance, threw the social structure into chaos, and horribly mistreated the Vietnamese who worked for them on their rubber plantations, in their factories, and in their mines. The French frequently disrupted time-honored patterns of authority in the villages and created an educated urban elite, many of whom would come to oppose the control of their country by another. As the old order came unstuck, the people were left angry and confused, and the way was opened to resistance. By the early twentieth century, sporadic tax revolts indicated an incipient Vietnamese nationalism.

The man who would finally give direction to the anti-French sentiment in the country was Ho Chi Minh. A man of many pseudonyms and nearly as many identities, Ho traveled widely, to the United States, Great Britain, and France. In post-World War I Paris, he experienced a political epiphany. Rejected by the Allies when he pleaded that President Woodrow Wilson's idea of self-determination should apply to the Vietnamese, Ho moved quickly through the halfway house of European socialism and became a Communist. The reason for this affiliation was simple: the Communists were unequivocally anticolonialist, and they alone, with their base in Moscow, might help him remove the French from his country. (Years later, U.S. foreign policymakers would sneer at the claim made by American liberals that Ho was a nationalist first and a Communist second. In fact, the claim was literally true.) Ho went to the Soviet Union and China. In 1929 he founded the Indochinese Communist Party.

In Vietnam, resistance to the French had intensified. A variety of organizations sought in their own ways to mobilize the people. The Vietnam Nationalist Party, or the Viet Nam Quoc Dan Dang (VNQDD), staged an abortive revolt in 1930. There were persistent rebellions by dislocated farmers and strikes by unhappy workers. A quasireligious sect, the Cao Dai, gained the support of thousands of poor peasants and became a powerful force in the south, but it was politically unpredictable. By the late 1930s the Communists were in the best position to rally the nationalists. Early in 1941, Ho Chi Minh returned to Vietnam and announced the formation of the Vietnam Independence League, or Vietminh. All nationalists were to join; the Communists would lead it, and Ho was its General Secretary.

At this point, Japan forcefully entered Southeast Asian political affairs. Intent on creating an Asian empire euphemistically called the Greater East Asia Co-Prosperity Sphere, the Japanese had seized Manchuria in 1931 and six years later expanded the conflict to China proper. By late 1939, when the war in Europe broke out, the Japanese were bombing targets in south China and thinking seriously about the raw materials of

Southeast Asia, including tungsten, tin, rubber, and, above all, oil. French Indochina—Laos and Cambodia as well as Vietnam—was a gateway to these natural riches. When France surrendered to Germany in June 1940, the Japanese asked the French collaborationist, or Vichy, government for permission to place military observers in Hanoi; in July they demanded the right to build military bases throughout Indochina. The French were not in a position to refuse.

The Japanese threat to Southeast Asia caught the attention of the United States. In 1940 few Americans even knew where Vietnam was, and few felt any motivation to find out. The level of sophistication in government circles was scarcely higher: some years later, when a State Department officer wrote a profile of "Ho Chi Mink," the error went undetected. The Americans, however, came to see the connection between the colonial economies of Southeast Asian nations and the fighting capabilities of the colonies' European owners. Specifically, they understood that the British, who faced Nazi Germany virtually alone after the summer of 1940, would be in deep trouble if Japan cut off their supply of Malayan rubber and tin and their oil from the Dutch East Indies. The United States decided to draw the line against Japanese expansion at Indochina. When the Japanese moved to construct military installations in Indochina in July 1940, the State Department embargoed exports of aviation fuel and high-quality scrap iron and steel to Japan. Negotiations between the two powers over the next year proved fruitless, and the Japanese, running out of fuel for their war machine, demanded in July 1941 that the Vichy regime permit their troops to occupy southern Indochina. This decision apparently resulted from Japan's misapprehension of American concern for southeast Asia, and it cost Tokyo dearly. The Americans then embargoed all exports to Japan, save those of food and cotton, and froze that nation's assets in the United States, a move immediately imitated by Great Britain and the Dutch East Indies. These steps persuaded Japanese militants that their country was trapped and that the only way out was military action. On December 7 the Japanese attacked the U.S. military base at Pearl Harbor. On that same day they moved against the Philippines, Hong Kong, and Malaya.

The Japanese quickly conquered most of Southeast Asia. They occupied Vietnam but decided to leave the Vichy French government in place with nominal powers of control. Thus, the Vietminh had two different colonial powers to battle. Ho Chi Minh directed what military efforts he could against the Japanese; the two sides skirmished frequently until 1945. The Vietnamese leader also planned for the eventual independence of his nation. He drafted a platform calling for representative government, a balanced economy, the eight-hour day, and a minimum wage. In March 1945, in retreat throughout Asia and witnessing the liberation of France, the Japanese overthrew the Vietnamese Vichy government and took charge. When they themselves surrendered in August, the way seemed open at last for the Vietminh. On September 2, 1945, Ho Chi Minh, speaking to a cheering crowd in Hanoi, declared Vietnam independent. "We hold these truths to be self-evident: that all men are created equal," he began. He believed this to be true. He also knew that France would want his country back and that only the United States could prevent Vietnam from being reclaimed.

Ho had some reason to hope that Washington would support him. In August 1941, President Franklin D. Roosevelt had endorsed (with a reluctant Winston Churchill, the British prime minister) the Atlantic Charter, a statement that declared, among other things, that people had the right to determine their own form of government. Even though Roosevelt died in April 1945, the Vietnamese continued to take this declaration seriously. In the last days of the war, operatives of the U.S. Office of Strategic Services (OSS) had worked with Ho in the Tonkin jungle. In return for help in finding downed American pilots, some of the OSS officers proffered advice and support. The Americans on the scene believed that Ho was sincerely interested in their assistance and thus could be influenced by the United States. "We had Ho Chi Minh on a silver platter," one of them said later.

Roosevelt's views on colonialism are worth considering, largely because both the OSS men and the Vietminh turned out to be naive about the president's intentions. In an ideal world, FDR thought, all nations would be democracies and would trade with each other freely and openly. But the postwar world would be a troubled place, not instantly susceptible to utopian solutions. Although it was good to have the Atlantic Charter on the books, defining as it did the ideal world, it would be necessary to compromise its philosophy temporarily to achieve peace and stability. This conclusion had particular implications for colonialism. Not all nations were ready for independence. Places such as Algeria, Palestine, and Vietnam might require tutelage by a Great Power—instruction in the practices of liberalism and capitalism—for some time. FDR imagined a world divided into four blocs, each one overseen by a powerful "policeman": the United States, Great Britain, the Soviet Union, and China. Gradually, the president hoped, these blocs would dissolve and a world system based on the principle of self-determination would emerge, but until that time nationalist aspirations threatened order and so must be put on hold.

Roosevelt concluded that Vietnam, Laos, and Cambodia were not ready for self-rule. At the same time, France did not figure prominently in the president's plans for the postwar system. The French, FDR told British officials, were "hopeless." They were bad colonialists, both cruel and shortsighted. They had capitulated to Germany with shocking speed and then had collaborated much too easily with the Nazis and the Japanese to be considered trustworthy. FDR was suspicious of even the courageous resistance movement, for it was led by Charles de Gaulle, whom he regarded as an arrogant opportunist. Instead of reverting to French control, then, Indochina should be given in trust to China, under the leadership of Generalissimo Chiang Kai-shek (Jiang Jieshi).

Those who consider Franklin Roosevelt a realist might ponder the practicality of this plan. Certainly there were many at the time who believed that it was unworkable. The British feared that FDR's hostility toward French colonialism might soon come to rest upon them. (The British ambassador to Washington worried that "one of these days" FDR "might have the bright idea that the Netherlands East Indies or British Malaya would go under international trusteeships.") Officials in London were also skeptical that China would become a Great Power—and a worthy policeman—after the war. Even Chiang Kai-shek had doubts about tutoring Indochina. The Vietnamese would object, to put it mildly. Most compelling, however, was the opposition to the Chinese trusteeship scheme by officials in the Roosevelt administration. By 1944 most State Department experts anticipated trouble with the Soviet Union in Europe. Because defeated Germany would not provide a bulwark against Soviet expansion into western Europe, it was essential that France be made strong enough at least to forestall a Soviet invasion. To strip France of its Indochina colony would shatter French pride, weaken the nation's economy, and destroy the French will to resist Soviet incursions. State Department officials, joined by military leaders, pressured Roosevelt to give up the scheme altogether.

Early in 1945, FDR changed his mind. The first indication of this shift came at Yalta at the Big Three Conference (Roosevelt, Churchill, and Joseph Stalin) in February, when the president reluctantly agreed that nations need not place their colonies under trusteeships unless they wanted to. Even more revealing was a conversation that

FDR had with an adviser in mid-March, when he expressed concern for "the brown people in the East" and stated that the U.S. "goal must be to help them achieve independence." When the adviser asked specifically about Indochina, FDR "hesitated a moment and then said—'well, if we can get the proper pledge from France to assume for herself the obligations of a trustee, then I would agree to France retaining these colonies with the proviso that independence was the ultimate goal.'" By the time of Roosevelt's death on April 12, hopes for self-determination had not quite disappeared from U.S. policy toward Indochina, but they had been overmatched by sympathy for the return of French colonialism.

This policy was left to Harry S. Truman, a former senator from Missouri who had been vice president for only two and one-half months when the death of FDR elevated him to the presidency. Truman's experience with foreign affairs was limited, and, like most Americans, he did not know who Ho Chi Minh was. Relations with French Indochina were handled largely by Truman's secretaries of state—James F. Byrnes (1945–1947), George C. Marshall (1947–1949), and Dean Acheson (1949–1953)— and their staffs in the State Department, with assistance from civilian and military officials in other departments. The president, however, provided the fundamental principles of foreign policy and set its tone. Truman came to believe that the Soviet Union was determined to spread communism across the globe through military and political means. Only the United States, acting in concert with other free nations, could prevent Russian expansion. Truman likened the Soviets to the Nazis: "There isn't any difference in totalitarian states. I don't care what you call them, Nazi, Communist, or Fascist." The administration implemented the containment strategy in an effort to stop the Russians. With the Truman Doctrine speech in March 1947, the president divided the world into two armed camps, one for the Communists and the other for everyone else, and offered economic and military assistance to Turkey and Greece, two anti-Communist governments with no claim to democracy. Less than three months later, Secretary of State Marshall announced the plan that would bear his name: a massive grant of economic aid to the war-devastated countries of Western Europe in order to provide the United States with trade partners and diminish the appeal of communism. Then came the signing of the North Atlantic Treaty in April 1949, which created a military alliance between the United States, Canada, and various Atlantic and Western European nations. These policies left no room for accommodation with Communists such as Ho Chi Minh.

In Vietnam, meanwhile, matters had taken a serious turn. The Great Powers ignored Ho's declaration of independence and instead fabricated a stunted version of Roosevelt's trusteeship plan. Vietnam was divided at the sixteenth parallel, with China occupying the north and Great Britain the south. All parties acknowledged that this scheme would soon give way to French repossession of both sectors, and indeed that is what happened. In September 1945 the British military commander in Saigon obediently armed fourteen hundred French troops who had been imprisoned by the Japanese. The soldiers, acting with appalling brutality, forced the Vietminh government to flee and recaptured Saigon. In the north, on March 6, 1946, Ho Chi Minh managed to get the Chinese out by accepting, under duress, an agreement to make Vietnam a free state within the French Union—not an independent nation—and the return of French troops to Vietnamese soil.

The French soon demonstrated their determination to keep all of Vietnam in the fold. In negotiations they dithered or threatened; outside the conference room they gathered their forces. The March 6 agreement was never implemented. During the summer of 1946, Ho went to Paris, seeking greater French flexibility. He came away with the Fontainebleau agreement of September, which offered, again, almost nothing. In the meantime, the French separated Cochin China from the rest of Vietnam and placed it by fiat under the French Union. Ho, under rising pressure to act from more radical members of the Vietminh, begged the French to make concessions that would give him "a weapon against the extremists." The French were unyielding.

Ho and the Vietminh were not dewy-eyed pacifists. They were quite capable of brutality and shrank not at all from the use of military means to gain their objectives. By the fall of 1946 there was open warfare in the south, and tensions ran high in the northern cities of Hanoi, where the Vietnamese Assembly convened in late October, and especially in Haiphong, where there were armed clashes in early November. The French bore primary responsibility for starting the violence. On November 23 their artillery opened up on the Vietnamese quarter of Haiphong, killing at least six thousand people. Ho pleaded for calm, but it was no good. On the night of December 19, 1946, the Vietnamese in Hanoi, probably acting without Ho's orders, attacked the French with a full array of weapons. Fighting erupted throughout the countryside, and, by the dawn of the Western new year, there was no turning back. "Before all, order must be reestablished," said the French premier, Léon Blum. "The war will be long and difficult," said Ho Chi Minh.

The French soldiers who fought the Vietminh soon came to appreciate Ho's words. Confident of quick victory, French authorities discovered instead that the Vietnamese desire for independence would not be easily denied. They decided, therefore, to fabricate a new government that would prove more cooperative; for its leader they selected the former emperor and erstwhile collaborator with the Japanese, Bao Dai. It took some doing to persuade Bao Dai to take the job. The former emperor was not without sympathy for the nationalists' position, and in 1947 he was leading a safe and comfortable life, dividing his time between Hong Kong and the French Riviera. The French cajoled him with various promises of self-government, and Bao Dai ultimately found the attractions of partial power irresistible. In April 1949 he returned to Vietnam as head of state "within the French Union."

The Bao Dai government held no interest for the Vietminh or for the majority of Vietnamese, who regarded the new regime as a sham. The war intensified. The French, for their part, introduced their protégé around, in particular to the Americans, who alone had the wherewithal to bankroll the former emperor. When Bao Dai returned to Vietnam, the French formally asked the Truman administration to offer diplomatic recognition and financial and military assistance to the new government.

The Americans hesitated. There were many questions about Bao Dai. Did he have popular support? Assuming that he did not, could he get it if the United States helped him? Was he essentially a playboy, involved in politics only for prestige or financial gain? What was his relationship with the French? Was he merely their stooge, a useful way for the French to maintain colonial control? Or was he another Chiang Kai-shek, the Chinese leader whose government at that moment was crumbling before the Communists? The evident answers to these questions were not reassuring to policymakers. Many of the Asian experts within the Truman administration counseled caution. At least, these experts warned, the French should promise that they were moving toward independence for Vietnam.

However, 1949 and 1950 were years of crisis in U.S. foreign policy, and patience became increasingly difficult to find in Washington. America's allies were still struggling to recover from the war. Japan and Germany—really the Allied occupation zone in the western part of Germany—had moved quickly from being wartime enemies to being peacetime friends, but both nations depended heavily on U.S. economic aid, and

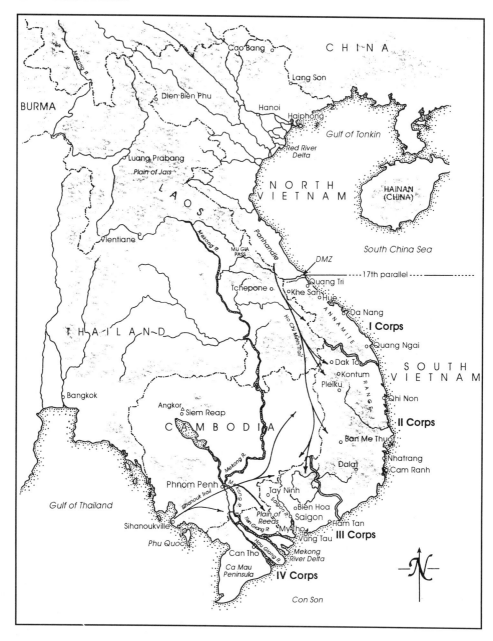

Map 2. Indochina, circa 1965.

West Germany seemed an imperiled frontline state in the Cold War between Western and Eastern Europe. The economy of Great Britain had shown signs of life in 1948, the first year of the Marshall Plan, but, by the summer of 1949, British exports and dollar reserves dropped dramatically, and officials in London pleaded for help. France's economy was staggering too. Production and wages remained depressed, thereby burdening workers especially, and many turned to communism. The French government claimed that it could do little to help labor because of the country's costly obligations in Vietnam. To make matters worse, the Other Side, the Communist world that most believed was monolithic, seemed by the end of 1949 to be enjoying remarkable success. Communist parties had political clout in Italy and France, and Ho Chi Minh had the French on the run in Vietnam. Late in the summer the Soviet Union detonated its first atomic bomb, years before Western experts believed that Moscow would have such capability. In October the Chinese Communist leader, Mao Tse-tung (Mao Zedong), announced the formation of the People's Republic of China, and soon after Chiang Kai-shek retreated to Taiwan.

The Truman administration tried to regain the initiative both militarily and diplomatically. It pressed forward with efforts to ensure the recovery of its Allies in Europe and the Pacific. In January 1950 the president authorized a program to build a hydrogen bomb and asked for a reassessment of U.S. "objectives in peace and war" and "the effect of these objectives on our strategic plans." The result was the National Security Council (NSC) document number 68, which called for an enormous increase in defense spending. Policymakers talked of arming West Germany. Of lesser magnitude but with equally profound implications, in the spring Truman decided to give $10 million in military aid and a small quantity of economic assistance to the French-backed Indochina government. The administration hoped that the limited commitment represented by the aid would strengthen the anti-Communist forces in Southeast Asia, secure regional markets for the Japanese, protect key British investments in Malayan raw materials, and offer some relief to the French, who had domestic problems (and now German rearmament) to worry about. It was too much to expect of $10 million— much too much, as it turned out. Outside of a small group of statesmen and area specialists, few noticed that the outlay had been made.

On June 25, Communist North Korea attacked non-Communist South Korea, its peninsular neighbor south of the thirty-eighth parallel. Although North Korea was a Soviet client and had Stalin's permission to launch the assault, the timing and nature of the invasion had as much to do with Korean politics as Cold War conditions. The Truman administration was convinced, however, that the North Korean attack represented a Soviet thrust by proxy, and in the week following the invasion sent American forces (under United Nations auspices) to defend the besieged ally. Ultimately, the Americans stemmed the tide, pushed the North Koreans back across the thirty-eighth parallel, and then joined South Korean troops in a drive to liberate North Korea. This move came to a halt in the late fall of 1950, when the Chinese intervened and forced the Americans to retreat south. By mid-1951 the Americans had rallied and stabilized their lines near the thirty-eighth parallel. On the battlefield a bloody stalemate ensued, while acrimonious negotiations between the two sides dragged on fruitlessly.

The Korean War had important implications for U.S. policy in Southeast Asia. For one thing, it became for policymakers a model of how Asian conflicts broke out during the Cold War: small Communist states, acting on behalf of the Soviet Union or the People's Republic of China, invaded their weak, non-Communist neighbors. Regarding Indochina this was a misplaced analogy, for it assumed that the two states in question were equally legitimate, which was never the case in Vietnam. Immediately following the North Korean attack, the Americans, who along with the French expected the next major Communist thrust to come in Vietnam, significantly increased their aid for Indochina; by 1952 they were covering nearly one-third of the cost of the conflict. This support partly bolstered French confidence, but it also made the French wary of displacement by the United States; after all, wasn't this still a French fight? To show their mettle, they now decided to take the offensive against the Vietminh. In late 1953 the French commander, General Henri Navarre, decided to try to lure the enemy into a set-piece battle in the northwest part of Vietnam, near the village of Dienbienphu. The Vietminh general, Vo Nguyen Giap, accepted the challenge. By early 1954 the French garrison, ensconced in a valley, found itself surrounded by Vietnamese soldiers and artillery. Disaster loomed for the French. They now urgently requested U.S. military intervention to rescue Dienbienphu.

There was a new administration in Washington: the Republican Dwight D. Eisenhower had been elected president in 1952. Eisenhower certainly allowed himself to be represented as a tough-minded realist on the Cold War, a president who would not shrink from confronting the Russians and the Chinese. His secretary of state, John Foster Dulles, a gimlet-eyed lawyer from upstate New York, rejected the containment strategy as "futile and immoral" and proposed instead the "liberation" of Communist countries by any means. Dulles also endorsed a policy of "massive retaliation" against perceived aggressors, a term with patently awful implications.

Because Eisenhower never publicly repudiated Dulles's pronouncements, most people assumed that he shared them. But recent scholarship on the Eisenhower period has demonstrated that the president's thinking about foreign policy was not nearly as virulent as Dulles's statements might suggest. The president was not the passive, rather slow-witted bungler that liberals labeled him, but rather a shrewd man who played the foreign policy bureaucracy with the precision of a concert pianist. (Some have argued that the hopelessly tangled sentences that Eisenhower offered up during press conferences were deliberately designed to confuse or mislead the public.) Eisenhower used Dulles's public posture to ensure for the administration the support of the Republican right wing. Massive retaliation, which effectively replaced expensive conventional weapons with a few efficient nuclear missiles, was a cost-cutting measure. Ike's broad grin and golf swing concealed a mind of energy and subtlety.

Unlike his immediate predecessors, President Eisenhower had been a career military man. As commander of the Allied forces in Europe during World War II, he understood both war's horrors and its limitations. He believed that the stalemate in Korea was a disaster, so he had brought the conflict to a speedy conclusion in 1953—in part by threatening privately to drop atomic bombs on China. When the French approached the administration seeking military help at Dienbienphu, Eisenhower was dubious. He allowed the proposal a serious hearing by the Joint Chiefs of Staff and mused out loud about the possibility of a U.S. air strike against Vietminh positions, as long as the planes were disguised as French ones. In the long run, however, because the president believed that U.S. military intervention would serve no useful purpose, he made it conditional on congressional acquiescence, the cooperation of the British, and French willingness to accept the eventual independence of Vietnam. It was unlikely that even one of these conditions would be met; that all three would be met was impossible, as Eisenhower surely knew. Despite some embarrassing public blustering by Dulles and Vice President Richard Nixon, Eisenhower kept his "hidden hand" firmly on the decision-making process. Thus, when Dienbienphu fell on May 7, 1954, it did not take American prestige with it.

Even before the debacle, the French sensed that their time in Vietnam was grow-ing short. They had already asked for discussion of the Indochina problem at a confer-ence on Far Eastern issues that opened in Geneva in late April. If the French had any leverage when the conference began, their influence disappeared with the collapse of Dienbienphu. On June 17 a new government in Paris, led by Socialist Premier Pierre Mendès-France, promised to resign unless it could reach a negotiated solution to the war within thirty days.

At last, Ho Chi Minh must have thought, the years of struggle would be rewarded by a diplomatic victory over France. It was not to be, for the Great Powers had their own interests to pursue in Vietnam. Stalin's death the previous year had caused tumult in the Russian political elite but had removed a major obstacle to change in Soviet foreign policy. The British worried that persistent instability in Indochina, or a Com-munist triumph there, would jeopardize their position in the economically valuable and unstable colony of Malaya. The Chinese, for whom the Vietnamese had no love, hoped that the annoying upheaval on their southern frontier would not bring U.S. inter-vention—the truce in Korea was not yet a year old—and therefore sought a political solution in Vietnam that would not humiliate the West. Just offstage the Americans glowered, as if daring the Vietminh to appear intractable.

The result was a remarkable arm-twisting session in the last hours before Mendès-France's self-imposed deadline, in which V. M. Molotov, the Soviet foreign minister, and the Chinese premier, Chou En-lai (Zhou Enlai), forced the Vietminh to accept a series of proposals that seemed to disregard the latter's superior military position on the ground. A cease-fire was proclaimed for Vietnam, Laos, and Cambodia. (Commu-nist forces enjoyed a military advantage in the latter two states as well.) Vietnam was partitioned at the seventeenth parallel. The northern part of the country, the Demo-cratic Republic of Vietnam, would be governed by the Vietminh, and the south, called the State of Vietnam, would remain under the nominal control of Bao Dai, backed by the French, who would remain in place. The two zones were by no means to be perma-nent: elections were to be held throughout the country in 1956 to choose a single government. These elections would be overseen by an international commission that would guarantee their fairness.

The Vietminh had hoped for more territory and quicker elections, but Ho Chi Minh was willing to wait for the 1956 referendum, certain that he and his political allies would win. Thousands of southern Vietminh fighters were summoned north of the seventeenth parallel to await reunification. Ho, meanwhile, tried to whip the north-ern economy into shape—no easy task, given that most of Vietnam's food was grown in the south—and carried out a draconian land-reform policy in which thousands of landlords were killed. In the south, Bao Dai found himself outmaneuvered politically by Ngo Dinh Diem, whom Bao Dai had appointed prime minister in June 1954. Diem was a Catholic mandarin who was in his own mind a patriot and a would-be despot. Westerners who met Diem found him a fascinating bundle of contradictions—alternately puzzling, magnetic, and infuriating as he talked compulsively about Viet-namese philosophy and statecraft. Whatever Diem may have been, he had more back-bone than Bao Dai. With the help of Col. Edward G. Lansdale, head of the U.S. military advisory mission in Saigon, Diem asserted himself against the powerful Vietnamese sects and his other political rivals. By early 1955 he had established himself in Ameri-can circles as a Vietnamese George Washington. The French could not abide him, and by the spring of 1955 they had pulled out.

That withdrawal left the United States as Vietnam's sole outside support. The Eisenhower administration was hostile to the agreements reached at Geneva, believing that the French had conceded too much by allowing the Vietminh to control the area north of the seventeenth parallel. U.S. representatives had difficulty understanding the complexities of Vietnamese politics: at Geneva, Undersecretary of State Walter Bedell Smith said that "one-third of the Vietnamese people supported Bao Dai, one-third supported Ho Chi Minh, and two-thirds were on the fence," but the Americans were resolved to prevent the Vietminh from taking control of the whole country. The administration decided to support Diem as head of government in a South Vietnam that was not just an artificial construct created as an expedient at Geneva but a nation with an independent future. Dulles found a way to tie South Vietnam to a regional defense association, the Southeast Asia Treaty Organization (SEATO), although this arrangement was specifically prohibited by the Geneva accords. Washington backed Diem when he refused to hold the 1956 elections, and by 1961 it had subsidized his regime to the tune of $1 billion. Under the foreboding rubric "black psywar," U.S. intelligence agents and their Vietnamese trainees conducted subversive operations against the Vietminh in the north. Typical activities included gunrunning, distributing phony leaflets, and contaminating the gas tanks of North Vietnamese buses. Occasionally, matters got out of hand: the *Pentagon Papers*, a secret Defense Department study of the war written in the late 1960s, disclosed that an alleged Communist prisoner was "interrogated by being handcuffed to a leper, both [men were] beaten with the same stick to draw blood, [the prisoner was] told he would now have leprosy, and both [were] locked up in a tiny cell together."

Although these policies enraged Ho and the government in Hanoi, they resisted making a response to Diem's actions. Not so the Communist Party members who had remained in the south, in their home villages, after 1954. They and their families were the victims of intimidation, arrest, torture, and murder by the Saigon government. Restrained by Hanoi's policy of patience, the Southern Party, according to historian Gabriel Kolko, lost at least two-thirds of its membership to arrest or execution during 1957–58. Many struck back. The chief tactic of the southern Vietminh was to assassinate Diem's officials along with uncooperative village leaders. Finally, in January 1959 the North Vietnamese government acceded to its southern allies; by midyear, arms and advisers had begun to flow south. The National Liberation Front (NLF), a collection of Communists, angry peasants, and disgruntled former sectarians, was formed in 1960 to carry out the armed struggle. The NLF was called by Diem the Vietcong, or Vietnamese "Commies."

In the United States, President Eisenhower was succeeded by the Democrat John F. Kennedy, who defeated Richard Nixon in 1960 after a hard-fought campaign. As a senator from Massachusetts, JFK had been a champion of Diem; and during the presidential campaign he had attacked the Eisenhower administration for letting the Communists push the United States around, especially in Cuba and on two islands off the coast of China, Quemoy and Matsu. Kennedy charged that the Republican strategy of massive retaliation—the threat of nuclear attack—had paralyzed American foreign policy, robbing it of the flexibility it needed to respond to small conflicts in the so-called Third World. It was not always credible to threaten a country with nuclear annihilation because nuclear weapons were inefficient in rural areas, unable to discriminate between soldiers and civilians, and provocative, to say the least. JFK's solution to this strategic conundrum was "flexible response," which promised to fashion for policymakers an instrument that was somewhere between the penknife of CIA subversion and the battle axe of atomic weaponry.

Everything about Kennedy suggested motion. Eisenhower played golf; Kennedy and his brothers played touch football, with undisguised brio. During the campaign,

JFK had said, "It's time to get the country moving again." Where the country was to move and why movement was important were not so clear. It was a bit like the dialogue in Jack Kerouac's "beat" novel, *On the Road*: "We gotta go and never stop going till we get there." "Where are we going, man?" "I don't know, but we gotta go." Or, more to the point, as a Kennedy staffer put it: "The United States needs a *Grand Objective*. We behave as if . . . our real objective is to sit by our pools contemplating the spare tires round our middles. . . . The key consideration is not that the *Grand Objective* be exactly right, it is that we *have* one and that we start moving toward it." In fairness, it must be said that JFK pointed toward "a new frontier," one with a variety of dimensions. Among them was Southeast Asia.

Kennedy was determined to "oppose any foes," as he put it in his inaugural address, and very quickly he found an opportunity to do that. Cuba had a Communist government led by Fidel Castro. From the Eisenhower administration, JFK had inherited a plan mandating an invasion of Cuba by a group of anti-Castro exiles, trained in Guatemala by the CIA. Kennedy gave the scheme the go-ahead, and on April 16, 1961, the attack began. The invaders never had a chance: they were vastly outnumbered, American air support was inadequate, and the people of Cuba, most of them reasonably content with their lot, failed to rise against the government when the exiles splashed ashore at the Bay of Pigs. Everyone knew, or soon found out, that the CIA had been involved in the scheme. Kennedy blamed "the experts" for giving him bad advice, and he fired Allen Dulles, head of the CIA and brother of the late John Foster. But it was the president who suffered the humiliation of failure. He had swung hard at communism and missed.

Laos offered another chance. When Eisenhower briefed Kennedy on Southeast Asia in January 1961, he warned the incoming president that serious trouble was brewing in Laos, where an insurgency threatened to topple the Royalist government of Phoumi Nosavan. It might be necessary, Ike suggested, to intervene unilaterally to salvage the situation. (About Vietnam, Eisenhower said little, although it must have been clear that prospects were not encouraging.) Phoumi's regime was in good part the creature of the CIA, which was one of the largest employers in the country, and was financed by a vigorous opium trade. It was besieged by a coalition of parties that ran the gamut from moderate (a group led by Prince Souvanna Phouma) to Communist (the Pathet Lao). The coalitionists seemed close to victory by early 1961.

Even before the Bay of Pigs fiasco, Kennedy's inclination was to use military force to protect the Royalist government in Laos. Robert McNamara, the new secretary of defense, suggested air strikes. The Joint Chiefs of Staff went further, calling for an invasion of Laos by 250,000 American troops, with tactical nuclear strikes held in reserve. It seemed likely that the United States would intervene. Then, in late April, the administration's "roving ambassador," W. Averell Harriman, weighed in strongly for a negotiated solution to the conflict. At the eleventh hour Harriman and others, especially John Kenneth Galbraith, the U.S. ambassador in India, achieved a ceasefire in Laos and an agreement by both sides to reconvene the Geneva Conference to discuss a joint Laotian government. It was a victory for diplomacy, some would argue, but on one level the president was disappointed. Negotiations with Communists were neither vigorous nor "manly," both important values in Kennedy's Camelot. JFK had started a second swing against communism, then checked it and fouled one off.

The third swing came in Vietnam. When JFK took office, the United States was committed to Diem. Most of the $1 billion that South Vietnam had received from Washington had gone to the military. There were over fifteen hundred American military advisers in Vietnam, and the CIA was still conducting its "psywar" north of the seventeenth parallel. In the late spring, following the Bay of Pigs and the decision to negotiate in Laos, Kennedy took several small but symbolically meaningful steps toward greater involvement in the war. He sent in one hundred more advisers and recalled his ambassador, Elbridge Durbrow, who had urged the administration to make further aid to Diem conditional on genuine social reform; Durbrow was replaced by Frederick Nolting. Most critically, the president secretly sent four hundred Special Forces troops to teach the South Vietnamese how to fight guerrilla warfare. The Special Forces, the best known of whom were the Green Berets, were avatars of flexible response and great favorites of JFK. The Special Forces were not combat troops in the technical sense, but they often found themselves on the front lines anyway because of the realities of counterinsurgency warfare and the inexperience (or cowardice) of their South Vietnamese hosts.

Kennedy did not do as much as some officials in the administration would have liked. He was not sure how many soldiers it would take to defeat the Communists, and he was aware that if he sent thousands of troops to Vietnam, as adviser Walt W. Rostow urged, they would surely take casualties and involve the United States further in the war. Still, retreat was unthinkable. The "defeats" in Cuba and Laos drove Kennedy to seek victory in Vietnam. The president was also convinced that Nikita Khrushchev, the Soviet premier who had emerged from the power struggles following Stalin's death, respected only toughness: the Russian baited JFK mercilessly during their first summit conference, at Vienna in June 1961. And there was the commitment itself. Kennedy believed that American credibility was at stake in Vietnam. If the United States abandoned its charge, no one, either friend or enemy, would ever again respect America's word.

The decision to deepen the Kennedy administration's commitment collided with the increasing popularity of the NLF in the countryside, the willingness of the North Vietnamese to fight indefinitely for the unification of the country on their terms, the persistence of Soviet and Chinese support for the Communists, and, most of all, the alarming degradation of the Diem government. Diem was a poor administrator, incapable of incisiveness and grudging on the matter of delegating authority, except to members of his immediate family. He was unsuited for leadership, and as his self-doubts increased, he more and more allowed himself to come under the influence of his opium-addict brother, Ngo Dinh Nhu, and Nhu's peculiar wife, Madame Nhu. The main reason for Diem's failure was his lack of a political base beyond certain neighborhoods in Washington. He was not of the people. When the South Vietnamese voted for him in periodic desultory elections, it was because there was no choice, or he was no worse than anyone else on the ballot, or he hated communism, or they were afraid not to vote for him. Frances FitzGerald called Diem "the sovereign of discord" and observed that peasants defined his government by the behavior of its representatives, the " 'arrogant' officials who took bribes" and the soldiers who "drank too much, stole food, and raped the village girls." Diem hoped he had secured the Confucian "mandate of Heaven." It was his only hope, for he ruled without the true consent of the governed.

A crisis involving South Vietnam's Buddhists led to Diem's downfall. Buddhist leaders believed that Diem, a Catholic with a quasi-Confucian ideology, had no respect for their religion, a view apparently confirmed on May 8, 1963, when government soldiers fired on a Buddhist gathering in Hue. The following month, in protest, a Buddhist monk sat down at an intersection in Saigon and allowed himself to be burned to death. The world was shocked, but the Diem government responded harshly. Madame Nhu spoke sadistically of "bronze barbecues," and in August the regime's own version of the Special Forces, trained by Americans, raided Buddhist pagodas throughout the country and carted protesting citizens off to jail. There were many injuries and some deaths.

Some members of the Kennedy administration now decided that Diem must go. With the latest ambassador in Saigon, the strong-minded Henry Cabot Lodge, Jr., leading the effort, the administration seemed to flash a green light before a group of Diem's disgruntled generals who were known to be planning a coup. The generals, led by Duong Van ("Big") Minh, were a skittish bunch who sought guarantees of American support for their efforts. The administration responded by tightening ever so slightly the aid conduit to Diem. This was signal enough. The coup took place on November 1, 1963. Diem and Nhu, left friendless, escaped to a Catholic church. They surrendered early the following morning, having been promised safe passage, but Big Minh had them both killed. (He later claimed that the brothers had committed suicide, although he could not explain the multiple entry wounds, some of them made with a knife.) Kennedy was appalled by the murders and may have experienced a flicker of doubt about his Vietnam policy. We will never know. Just three weeks later, ironically and tragically, he himself was assassinated in Dallas.

In later years, many of the slain president's advisers did indeed claim that Kennedy was contemplating a withdrawal from Vietnam before the killings of Diem and Nhu. Some pointed to a White House policy statement of October 2, 1963, that described the planned withdrawal of 1,000 men by December and implied that the rest would be home by the end of 1965. Read closely, however, the statement makes clear that withdrawal would be contingent on victory, which the authors of the statement assumed would be at hand within two years. It is also true that most of Kennedy's key advisers on Vietnam—Robert McNamara, Walt Rostow, Secretary of State Dean Rusk, and national security adviser McGeorge Bundy—stayed on with the next administration, which increased the U.S. commitment. We know only that in November 1963 there were 16,000 U.S. troops in Vietnam, and that seventy Americans had died there.

Kennedy's successor, Lyndon Baines Johnson, was a shrewd politician from Texas. There is evidence that Johnson was insecure in his new office. He hated to be alone or understimulated, so he surrounded himself with television sets, spent hours on the telephone cajoling members of Congress to support one bill or another, and even briefed aides while he sat on the toilet. Added to this apparent insecurity was the burden of his predecessor's legacy. Kennedy's luster shone brighter with his death, and LBJ never escaped the feeling that he was a usurper, an awkward Southerner who had rudely stumbled into the sanctum of the Harvard Club and who would not be forgiven for having done so.

Vietnam—"that bitch of a war," in LBJ's colorful phrase—would come to obsess the new president. As vice president, Johnson had been to Vietnam, and he had concluded upon his return that the United States must fight communism in Southeast Asia or face a threat to its own security. Like his predecessors, and like most Americans in the 1960s, LBJ feared and loathed communism. He also believed in the importance of the U.S. commitment to South Vietnam. Beyond that, Johnson came to regard Vietnam as a personal test of manhood. He likened the war to a hunt—a rite of passage for Southern men. With victory in Vietnam, he said he would "nail the coonskin to the wall." Defeating the enemy would stop communism, reassure the allies, and establish LBJ's reputation as president.

Johnson had the misfortune to take office as the military situation was worsening. Following the overthrow of Diem, Vietnam "went on an emotional binge," in Douglas Pike's phrase. Big Minh and his generals proved incompetent; the government ceased to govern. The NLF took the offensive in the countryside, and when North Vietnamese regulars joined their comrades in the south in ever-increasing numbers, the killing escalated. In January 1964 there was another coup in Saigon, this one led by General Nguyen Khanh and a group of young officers. Khanh tried to walk the line between U.S. demands for stability and pacification of the countryside and the expectations of his people for peace and justice, but he ended up pleasing no one. Khanh was an anti-Communist general, not a national leader. By the end of 1964, the Americans deduced, the NLF controlled 40 percent of the territory and 50 percent of the population in South Vietnam, estimates that were probably conservative. Khanh had temporarily re-signed, to be replaced by a months-long power struggle.

From Lyndon Johnson's viewpoint, this turmoil simply would not do. Frustrated below the seventeenth parallel, the president contemplated carrying the war to what he believed was its source. Early in the summer of 1964, his advisers drew up plans for U.S. bombing attacks on targets in North Vietnam. To implement these plans would require a good deal of discretionary power for the president, who had no desire to consult Congress each time a bombing sortie seemed necessary. Johnson got his op-portunity in August, when a series of dubious incidents in the Tonkin Gulf brought from an obedient Congress a resolution authorizing the president to take "all the nec-essary measures to repel any armed attacks against the forces of the United States and to prevent further aggression." It was not a declaration of war, but for years it was the functional equivalent.

The administration stayed its hand, but not for long. On February 6, 1965, the NLF attacked the American barracks at Pleiku, in the central highlands, killing nine men. That evening, Johnson ordered retaliation bombings north of the seventeenth parallel. Four days later, he decided reprisals were not enough, and Operation Rolling Thunder, a systematic program of bombing, was begun. (Actually, it joined a program of bombing in Laos, Operation Barrel Roll, already in progress.) The bombing was the brainchild of the U.S. Air Force, and particularly of General Curtis LeMay, who was famous for the ruthless effectiveness of American strategic bombing in World War II. LeMay promised "to bomb them back to the Stone Age."

The rejoinder was that the Vietnamese were still in the Stone Age, a culturally arrogant reply, but one that contained a germ of truth. The bombings, although terribly destructive, failed to demoralize the North Vietnamese. Indeed, the closed system in which bombing times and targets were selected leaked badly. "It was uncanny," wrote General Bruce Palmer, Jr., "how the Viet Cong and the North Vietnamese were able to defeat our security precautions." The North Vietnamese also responded with alacrity to the bombing. As quickly as bridges or roads were destroyed, mass labor reconstructed them. And the North Vietnamese economy was readily decentralized, denying the Americans large, tempting targets. Within a couple of years, the pilots in their power-ful B-52s were reduced to targeting bicycle repair shacks in the Vietnamese jungle.

Johnson made another fateful decision later in February 1965. Responding to a request from General William Westmoreland, commander of U.S. forces in Vietnam since the middle of 1964, the president sent two Marine battalions—about 3,500 men—to defend the U.S. air base at Danang. They arrived on March 8. These were neither advisers nor "support troops," as their predecessors were called, but plain combat troops whose job description called for them to kill the Vietcong. As some people predicted, the presence of the Marines in Vietnam made it easy to justify the military's requests for more, if only to protect those who were already there. LBJ authorized 40,000 addi-tional troops in April. By December there were 185,000 American soldiers in Viet-nam; two years later the total was 500,000, and the generals were clamoring for 200,000 more. But growing U.S. troop strength failed to bring stability to the government of

South Vietnam. From the power struggle of early 1965 emerged a rakish air marshal named Nguyen Cao Ky. Like his predecessors, Ky tried hard to live up to the image that his American backers had fashioned for him and, like them, he failed. Ky was deeply involved in the lucrative heroin trade, and association with him was embarrassing for the Americans. He was eased aside in September 1967 in favor of Nguyen Van Thieu, who won a rigged election with Ky as his running mate.

The decisions to bomb and send combat troops in early 1965 brought indignation and anger from many Americans, especially college students. There were rallies, marches, and "teach-ins," in which faculty members and students discussed the history of the war and its implications. Disturbed, if not yet alarmed, by the unrest on campus, LBJ dispatched administration "truth squads" to many universities, hoping to set the record straight. Confrontations occurred. Some protestors saw Vietnam as the latest and most brutal exercise in American imperialism, and they demanded fundamental changes in the political and economic system so as to make imperialism impossible. Many who opposed the war were veterans of the black civil rights movement who instinctively mistrusted the liberal administration's commitment to social change and in some cases felt racial solidarity with the Vietcong. The leading radical organization for white college students was the Students for a Democratic Society, or SDS. At its national convention in June 1965 the SDS decided to take up the antiwar cause. From that point onward, the movement grew: 100,000 people marched on the Pentagon (and a few tried to levitate it) in October 1967; in November 1969 more than 500,000 protestors came to Washington, thus constituting the largest demonstration to that point in the capital.

Despite what many on the left said of him, Lyndon Johnson did not revel in the expanded war. Between 1965 and 1968 he did flirt occasionally with the possibility of negotiations. LBJ continued to insist, however, on attaining goals in Vietnam that were incompatible with the aspirations of the North Vietnamese, the NLF, and their peasant supporters. Johnson viewed the war as a case of aggression by the North Vietnamese against a legally constituted state in the south. Thus, before there could be peace, the North Vietnamese would have to withdraw NLF troops from South Vietnam and recognize the legitimacy of the South Vietnamese government. The Communists and their allies countered that the Americans, not the Vietnamese, were the aggressors, that it was absurd to talk of removing indigenous forces (the NLF) from South Vietnam, and that the government of South Vietnam was a fabrication of the United States and had no popular support. Potential talks were further complicated by Thieu, the South Vietnamese president, who gambled that his hawkish sponsors in Washington would support him even if he objected to sitting down with the Communists. For a time, he was not far wrong.

Then came Tet 1968. Beginning on the night of January 30, 1968—the night of the lunar new year, or Tet—thousands of NLF and North Vietnamese troops attacked U.S. strongholds throughout South Vietnam. The provincial capital of Hue was taken, followed by the horrific slaughter of civilians by the Vietcong. Just outside Saigon, the Tan Son Nhut air base, then the world's busiest airport, came under intense fire. Most shocking to the Americans, a handful of Vietcong entered the compound of the U.S. embassy in Saigon. They killed two guards and held the grounds for over six hours.

In the ensuing days, every Communist thrust was parried. Hue was retaken in bloody, house-to-house fighting. Tan Son Nhut did not fall. Every Vietcong who entered the embassy compound was slain; the building was secured in time for business the morning after its siege. The North Vietnamese command confessed to making serious mistakes in planning and executing the Tet offensive, and the NLF, whose soldiers had been used as shock troops by Hanoi, was badly damaged. But Tet did not seem like a victory to politicians, opinion makers, and ordinary people in the United States. It is possible, as Peter Braestrup has argued, that the media unfairly represented Tet as a military defeat for the United States and South Vietnam. More to the point, however, the administration had raised hopes that the enemy was on its last legs and presumably incapable of launching such a powerful assault as the Tet offensive. Victory "lies within our grasp—the enemy's hopes are bankrupt," Westmoreland had said on a visit back home the previous November. The offensive also seemed to exhibit, and exacerbate, the special ugliness of the war. Americans witnessed the summary execution of a suspected Vietcong terrorist by the chief of South Vietnam's national police. The officer, America's ally, placed his pistol to the prisoner's head and squeezed the trigger; a photographer caught the spray of blood and the man's death grimace. Walter Cronkite, anchor of the *CBS Evening News* and to many the most trusted man in America, was visibly shaken by the events of Tet and soon became a doubter.

Johnson's Vietnam policy had been tottering near the abyss, and the Tet offensive pushed it over the edge. Defense Secretary McNamara, disillusioned by his own failures, had already announced his intention to resign and actually left within a month of the Tet offensive. His replacement was Clark Clifford, a political veteran and a Johnson loyalist. Within days, however, Clifford had reached the same conclusions as McNamara: despite its insatiable appetite for more soldiers, the military could not promise that increased force would bring success in Vietnam. Clifford thus refused to endorse a request for 200,000 more troops, a position consistent with that of the apostate McNamara. On March 12 the president, bidding for reelection, suffered a stunning blow in the New Hampshire Democratic primary, when antiwar Senator Eugene McCarthy came within a few hundred votes of defeating him. Johnson had had enough. On March 31 he told the American people that he unilaterally had stopped the bombing of most of North Vietnam and that he sought negotiations toward a peace settlement. He closed with a surprise: he would not seek another term as president.

The Democratic Party split wide open. The antiwar Robert Kennedy, JFK's attorney general and brother of the slain president, joined the fray. When Robert Kennedy was assassinated in June, on the night of his victory in the California primary, George McGovern tried to take up his mantle. During a tumultuous convention in Chicago, in which demonstrators were confronted by Mayor Richard Daley's ill-tempered police and lost, Vice President Hubert Humphrey secured the nomination. He showed touching loyalty to LBJ by refusing to criticize the administration's Vietnam policy, but Humphrey's discretion was not the best politics. Although he did become more dovish as the campaign went along, it was too late to save the Democrats. The Republican Richard Nixon, unsuccessful in previous campaigns for president and for governor of California and now rising like the phoenix from the political ash heap, narrowly defeated Humphrey and inherited the war.

What all this meant for those actually fighting in Vietnam was unclear. The North Vietnamese put a brave face on the Tet offensive and were pleased by the dramatic shift in American public opinion, but they admitted that their strategy had "many deficiencies and weak points" that "limit our successes." The death of Ho Chi Minh in September 1969 was also sobering. The troops of South Vietnam—the Army of the Republic of Vietnam, or ARVN—had frequently fought well during the Tet engagement. Nevertheless, the ranks continued to suffer high rates of corruption and desertion. The strain was beginning to show on the Americans, too. Eager volunteers such as future author Philip Caputo, who went ashore at Danang in March 1965, increasingly were replaced by draftees. These men, who were disproportionately poor, black, and undereducated, were sent to the "front"—really on patrols into the jungle and rice paddies. Derided by other military units and often treated as cannon fodder by their officers, these "grunts" turned sullen and dangerous. By 1969 the troops routinely dulled their fears by using drugs, and the incidence of "fragging," or killing one's own officers, climbed steeply.

Nixon promised to end the suffering. The new president was a vengeful and profane man, given to secrecy and duplicity, yet he had some advantages his predecessors had not enjoyed. Nixon's credentials as an anti-Communist were impeccable. He had cut his political teeth on the sensational Alger Hiss case in the late 1940s, in which Hiss, a former high-ranking official in the State Department, had been found guilty of lying about his past associations with the Communist Party. Nixon hated bureaucracy and had no compunction about circumventing it, openly or with stealth, and he was not constrained by any scruples about morality in international affairs. Following his national security adviser, Henry Kissinger, the president believed himself a realist. It did no good to pursue a moralistic foreign policy, he argued, because morals were relative: one nation's morality was another nation's high crime. Above all, Kissinger and Nixon agreed that stability among the Great Powers was essential for the maintenance of world peace. Different ideologies, presumably based on different perceptions of morality, should not stand in the way of dialogue between nations. Thus, the Nixon administration would open serious talks with the Soviets and make an astonishing overture to the Chinese Communists. Because it prevented détente, a measure of understanding between the Great Powers, the war in Vietnam must be liquidated, one way or another.

What followed was an exercise in contradiction. On the one hand, Nixon and Kissinger moved to reduce American troop commitments. Without waiting for any change in Hanoi's position, the president began to order withdrawals: 65,000 in 1969, 140,000 in 1970, and 160,000 in 1971. This move was consistent with the Nixon Doctrine, announced in July 1969, which implied that Asians should fight Asians, albeit with help from their Great Power patrons. The administration also moved to revitalize negotiations with the other side. Initiated by the Johnson administration, the Paris peace talks had thus far proved unproductive. In February 1970, Kissinger began secret negotiations with North Vietnamese representatives. At first as fruitless as the Paris discussions, these "back channel" negotiations ultimately achieved some success: by the spring of 1971, Kissinger and Hanoi's negotiator, Le Duc Tho, were snarling and hissing toward a kind of accommodation.

The other side of the Nixon-Kissinger policy was the intensification of the war. Vietnamization meant arming the ARVN to the teeth to protect the retreating Americans and to hold up the Thieu government once the Americans were gone. South Vietnam's troops were augmented by over 15 percent, and its air force was made the fourth largest in the world. The Nixon administration also expanded the war to Cambodia and Laos. Both nations provided sanctuaries, without enthusiasm, to the NLF and North Vietnamese. The leaders of both countries, Prince Norodom Sihanouk in Cambodia and Prince Souvanna Phouma in Laos, desperately hoped to avoid a wider war. They could not avoid it. Early in 1969, during the first months of his administration, Nixon authorized the bombing of enemy sanctuaries in Cambodia. These attacks, which continued for over a year, were concealed from Congress and the American people—although they were, of course, no secret to the Cambodian peasant families whom they decimated and displaced. In April 1970, U.S. and South Vietnamese troops invaded Cambodia. Laos had been bombed for years; its turn for invasion came in February 1971, when the ARVN crossed the border in the first serious test of the Nixon Doctrine, known locally as Vietnamization. The invasion was a disaster, with the ARVN taking casualties at a rate of 50 percent. All the while, American planes dropped their bombs on targets inside North Vietnam.

Nixon's dual policy of sweet reason and deadly force failed to placate the antiwar movement at home. Some, it should be said, were mollified by the troop withdrawals. On the whole, however, the left mistrusted Nixon and Kissinger, and protestors correctly pointed out that the killing in Vietnam had not diminished under the Nixon Doctrine. The antiwar demonstrations grew larger and angrier. News of the invasion of Cambodia in the spring of 1970 sent thousands into the streets. On college campuses across the country, students denounced the invasion and the institutional complicity of their universities in the war. At Kent State University the Ohio National Guard killed four students on May 4; later that month, two students were slain at Jackson State, in Mississippi. The ranks of the demonstrators were swelled by housewives who had been touched by the war, blacks angered by the conflict's racism, disgruntled veterans, even high-school and grade-school students. Public opinion polls indicated widespread disenchantment with Nixon's policy. The president called the protestors "bums" and instructed his subordinates to spy on his critics, a decision that led to the Watergate scandal and to Nixon's eventual downfall.

In Vietnam the North Vietnamese had been rather subdued since the failures of the Tet offensive; they were content, it seemed, to harass the departing Americans and blunt any ARVN initiatives. In the spring of 1972, however, the Communists launched a massive offensive. If the Communists hoped that the attacks would end U.S. support for the Thieu regime, they were disappointed. But the Eastertide offensive achieved several other objectives. It exposed once more the folly of Vietnamization. The ARVN, writes James William Gibson, "went into immediate shock," taking 140,000 casualties and surrendering hundreds of allegedly secure villages. Again, as in the Tet offensive, an American-inspired counterattack rolled back the northern forces. A furious Nixon warned the Soviet Union that détente would be jeopardized unless the Russians could make their clients behave, and then he escalated the war. Again, B-52 bombers were unleashed to pound the enemy in the north and south. The president established a naval blockade of North Vietnam and authorized the mining of Haiphong Harbor.

The new bloodshed seemed to have had a sobering effect on both sides, and in May there were at last signs of movement in the talks. Speaking for Hanoi, Le Duc Tho proposed a tripartite coalition government for the south, to include representatives of North Vietnam, the NLF, and the existing Saigon regime, although Thieu himself was unacceptable. Kissinger rejected the idea of coalition, but he sensed flexibility on the Communist side and bore down. By September the North Vietnamese had dropped their demand that Thieu be replaced and transformed the coalition scheme into an all-parties council that would administer free elections in the south. Both sides squabbled and fine-tuned a bit; then, on October 1, they achieved substantial agreement on the text of the peace agreement. Kissinger was triumphant and flew off to Saigon to get Thieu's approval.

No one should have been surprised when Thieu balked at the agreement. He had previously objected to a number of the provisions to which Kissinger had just agreed, and he argued that the language of the treaty was sufficiently vague to permit the Communists dangerously wide latitude in interpreting it. Kissinger raged at Thieu, threatening to halt aid for his government and even hinting that the United States might make peace without him. He then returned home and announced: "We believe that peace is at hand."

Nixon was not as willing as his national security adviser to abandon Thieu. A week after he was overwhelmingly reelected to the presidency—his opponent, the dove

George McGovern, won only seventeen electoral votes—Nixon reassured Thieu of his full support and told Kissinger to take Thieu's objections to the North Vietnamese. Reluctantly, Kissinger did so. Le Duc Tho was indignant, and after a month of pointless bickering between the sides, he broke off the talks and went home. This was Nixon's signal to renew the air war over North Vietnam. Thirty-six thousand tons of bombs were dropped there during the 1972 Christmas season, more than had been dropped in the period from 1969 to 1971. The pilots did not try to hit civilians, but with all the ordnance, precision was impossible: a bomb fell on Hanoi's Bach Mai Hospital, killing eighteen people and wounding dozens more. The North Vietnamese air defense took its toll on the Americans, who lost twenty-six planes and had ninety-three fliers killed or captured. The administration's critics reacted with anger. It was a bleak and ghastly time for everyone. It did, however, usher in the final phase of the war. An apparently chastened Nixon now decided to press Thieu to go along with the Paris accords. Without the president's backing, Thieu believed that he had no choice, and so at last he acquiesced. Smiling tightly, Kissinger and Le Duc Tho signed on January 27 what was substantially the same agreement they had made the previous October.

There followed what Gareth Porter has called "the cease-fire war" as both sides jostled for advantage. The Nixon administration claimed that the Communists were responsible for most of the violations, but it did not look that way to outsiders, who recorded numerous ARVN transgressions and pointed out that the Communists seemed more aggressive because their moves were more successful. Nixon tried hard, within the constraints placed on him by the Paris agreement and an impatient Congress, to bolster Thieu by providing extensive aid, moral support, and threats directed at the North Vietnamese. Ultimately, none of it worked. Congress cut off funds for U.S. military activity in or over Indochina as of August 15, 1973. By that time, Nixon had been implicated in the Watergate affair, and his power to pursue an unpopular foreign policy dropped dramatically as he fought to keep his office. Kissinger, now secretary of state, moved into the breach, reviving the argument that the allies would be demoralized if the United States let South Vietnam go. Congress refused to accept this claim. The North Vietnamese sensed that their time had come, and early in 1975 they began a massive offensive, which they hoped would bring victory by the following year. It would not take that long.

South Vietnam fell during the brief presidency of Gerald Ford, who had succeeded Nixon upon the latter's resignation in August 1974. Ford was widely regarded as a decent man, but there was not much he could do about the situation in Southeast Asia. Alarmed at the collapse of ARVN forces during the spring of 1975, the president asked Congress for more military aid for Thieu, perhaps hoping that his own obvious integrity would change some minds on Capitol Hill. The efforts were unavailing. Thieu resigned on April 21 and left the country four days later. By the 29th the Communists had reached the outskirts of Saigon and were making plans to share their rice with starving Saigonese, if necessary. Amid the panic of those South Vietnamese who had worked closely with the United States and who feared what was to come, the last Americans departed the U.S. embassy by helicopter. The next day the Communists captured the presidential palace. For the Americans, the war was over.

The end of the war did not instantly have a profound effect on the United States. There was a vigorous debate about what came to be called by conservatives "the Vietnam syndrome," the alleged reluctance of the U.S. government to assert itself in foreign policy for fear of public criticism. The controversies over Americans still missing in action in Southeast Asia, the treatment of veterans, the construction of the Vietnam Veterans' Memorial in Washington, and the meaning of the war for American culture would emerge in the 1980s. Ultimately, passions would cool enough in the 1990s to allow the administrations of George Bush and Bill Clinton to move toward normalizing relations with Vietnam. The United States extended diplomatic recognition to Vietnam in 1995, by which time several American corporations and entrepreneurs were champing at the bit to get at the Vietnamese market.

In Vietnam, the problems were greater and more immediate. Hundreds of thousands of people had been killed, millions bore wounds, and millions more were refugees. The land was devastated and the economy was wrecked. Relations with neighboring nations quickly soured: Vietnam invaded Cambodia in 1978, overthrowing its atrocious and truculent Communist government; early the following year, Vietnam itself was attacked by China, which had supported the Cambodian regime. Domestically, Hanoi's rigid policies prevented any reconciliation between north and south. Industry was nationalized, agriculture collectivized, and southerners who had opposed the revolution were subjected to rigorous political "reeducation." Millions of southerners, many of them ethnic Chinese, fled Vietnam; many settled in the United States. On the other hand, there was no bloodbath in Vietnam, and by the early 1980s grain production and industrial output had increased. Today, the revolutionary generation is growing old. Like the People's Republic of China, Vietnam seems on a quest to achieve a dynamic economy under authoritarian political control. At this writing, the country's future is unclear, but one can say that once more, as in traditional times, Vietnam has been restored to itself. It is no longer a cockpit of empires.

ONE

A CHRONOLOGY OF
U.S. INTERVENTION

CHAPTER 1

Getting In
1945–1952

Although American involvement in Vietnam began before 1945, Franklin D. Roosevelt's decision early in that year to permit the return of French colonialism to Indochina provides a convenient starting point for this account. The readings in this chapter describe relations between the United States, France (and its Vietnamese clients), and the Communist-nationalist Vietminh, led by Ho Chi Minh, through the end of the Truman administration. Robert Shaplen, the distinguished reporter who covered Vietnam for *The New Yorker* for many years, details Ho's efforts to cultivate American representatives of the Office of Strategic Services (OSS) during the mid-1940s. Historian George Herring places U.S. decision making on Vietnam in the context of the intensifying Cold War with the Soviet Union and, after 1949, with the People's Republic of China; he reminds us that Vietnam, small and remote though it may have seemed to many Americans, nevertheless appeared at the juncture of important strategic and economic issues by 1950. The security of France—and thus all of continental Western Europe—as well as the economic viability of Great Britain and Japan and the preservation of Southeast Asia against Communist imperialism seemed to U.S. policymakers to be at stake. While Shaplen argues that the United States missed a chance to work with Ho in establishing an independent Vietnam, Herring shows that such an overture was always unlikely, and by 1947 it was plainly out of the question.

New York. General Vo Nguyen Giap (left), commander in chief of the Vietminh Armed Forces, and Ho Chi Minh, president of Vietnam, are shown as they study a military operations map, presumably in General Giap's headquarters. The picture was photographed from a 1953 Soviet booklet on Vietnam. UPI/BETTMANN NEWSPHOTOS

1
Ho Chi Minh: The Untried Gamble
ROBERT SHAPLEN

If the relationship between the Americans and the Vietminh in Cochin China was never more than a tentative one, it was much closer in the north, both in the months preceding the end of the war and in the period immediately afterward. There are moments in history when certain events, however obscure and fragmentary they may seem in retrospect, nevertheless serve as an endless source of speculation: *if* they had been approached in another way, *if* they had been allowed to run their course, would the whole chain of events that followed have perhaps been different? There is certainly some reason to believe that this might have been true about the relations between Ho Chi Minh and a number of Americans in 1945 and 1946, and, more significantly, about Ho's relations with a small group of French politicians and diplomats. It is easy now to dismiss these events and their meaning as unimportant if one assumes that the Communists, and Ho in particular, never had any other intention than to create a Communist state in Vietnam. However, in the opinion of those who, with varying degrees of political sophistication, lived through this early postwar period and helped form part of its history, such broad assumptions are over-simplifications of what was a highly tenuous and complicated set of political circumstances.

I have always shared the belief of many, if not most, observers who were in Indochina at the time that a serious mistake was made by both the French and the Americans, especially by the dominant French policymakers in Paris, in not dealing more realistically with Ho in 1945 and 1946, when there was a strong possibility that he might have been "Titofied" before Tito and Titoism were ever heard of; that the whole course of events might thereby have been altered and a great deal of bloodshed averted; and that today a unified Vietnam, even under some form of left-wing leadership, might have been the bulwark of a neutral bloc of Southeast Asian states seeking, above all, to avoid Chinese Communist domination. Some of the highest American officials have privately told me, in recent years, that they now believe the gamble with Ho should have been taken; in fact, a considerable number of them are again talking about Vietnam becoming a Southeast Asian Yugoslavia, a possibility that seems to me now rather remote. History, contrary to the popular belief, seldom does repeat itself, and second chances are seldom offered. It is one of the particular tragedies of American postwar policy that so many first chances have been missed.

There are many facets to the story of Ho's relations with the West during and after the Second World War. Let us start with the somewhat naïve but at the same time revealing account of a former young lieutenant in the United States Army—I shall have to refer to him only as John—who in May, 1945, parachuted into Ho's jungle headquarters near the village of Kim Lung in northern Tonkin on a mission to establish an underground that would help Allied personnel escape to freedom. Kim Lung lies on the edge of a heavy rain forest, thickly underlaid by brush. Amid sugar-loaf formations of mountains lie tiny valleys, and it was in one of these, near a small stream halfway up a tall hill, that Ho Chi Minh's camp, consisting of four huts, lay sequestered. Each of the huts was twelve feet square, set four feet off the ground on bamboo stakes, and Ho's was as bare as the others.

In this crude revolutionary cradle, deep in Japanese territory, John had the unique experience of living and working with Ho for several months. He found Ho completely cooperative in lending the support of his guerrillas for scouting and raiding parties, including one to rescue some French internees near the China border. John used his portable radio to put Ho in preliminary touch with French negotiators who were in Kunming, China, and who would soon be debating Indochina's postwar future with Ho in Hanoi, but John himself played a more immediate role in Vetnamese affairs by informally helping Ho frame a Declaration of Independence.

"He kept asking me if I could remember the language of our Declaration," John says. "I was a normal American, I couldn't. I could have wired up to Kunming and had a copy dropped to me, of course, but all he really wanted was the flavor of the thing. The more we discussed it, the more he actually seemed to know about it than I did. As a matter of fact, he knew more about almost everything than I did, but when I thought his demands were too stiff, I told him anyway. Strange thing was he listened. He was an awfully sweet guy. If I had to pick out one quality about that little old man sitting on his hill in the jungle, it was his gentleness."

He and John exchanged toasts and shared stewed tiger livers. John now admits his naïveté in being ready to believe that Ho was not a Communist. But even if he was, John felt certain that Ho was sincere in wanting to co-operate with the West, especially with France and the United States. Some of Ho's men impressed John less. "They go charging around with great fervor shouting 'independence,' but seventy-five per cent of them don't know the meaning of the word," he wrote in his diary. John still has two letters in English Ho sent him in the jungle. One of them, written soon after the Japanese surrender, when the Vietminh was about to seize control of the nationalist movement, reads as follows:

Dear Lt. [John],
I feel weaker since you left. Maybe I'd have to follow your advice—moving to some other place where food is easy to get, to improve my health. . . .
I'm sending you a bottle of wine, hope you like it.
Be so kind as to give me foreign news you got.

. . . Please be good enuf to send to your H.Q. the following wires.

1. Daiviet [an anti-Vietminh nationalist group] plans to exercise large terror against French and to push it upon shoulder of VML [Vietminh League]. VML ordered 2 millions members and all its population be watchful and stop Daiviet criminal plan when & if possible. VML declares before the world its aim is national independence. It fights with political & if necessary military means. But never resorts to criminal & dishonest act.

Signed—NATIONAL LIBERATION COMMITTEE OF VML

2. National Liberation Committee of VML begs U.S. authorities to inform United Nations the following. We were fighting Japs on the side of the United Nations. Now Japs surrendered. We beg United Nations to realize their solemn promise that all nationalities will be given democracy and independence. If United Nations forget their solemn promise & don't grant Indochina full independence, we will keep fighting until we get it.

Signed—LIBERATION COMMITTEE OF VML

Thank you for all the troubles I give you. . . . Best greetings!
Yours sincerely, Hoo [*sic*]

What spells the difference between 1945 and 1965, between John's jungle love feast with Ho Chi Minh—the vast prestige America then enjoyed in Asia—and the complex tragedy of the war in Vietnam today, in which Americans are engaged in bombing Ho's country? Those who insist that we should have tried to win Ho to our side maintain this even though they were aware of the fact that he had never wavered from a straight Marxist-Leninist course. Despite his orthodox ideological convictions (or perhaps because they were so orthodox), and because Indochina was a long way from Stalin's Moscow, Ho had already written his own unique revolutionary case history. He was, at this time, less a potential apostate than a kind of old Bolshevik maverick, a last Marxist Mohican in the anti-colonial wilderness of Southeast Asia. If it appears that he simply bewitched a handful of Americans in an atmosphere of dangerous and rollicking camaraderie late in the war and the months afterward, there is considerably more evidence than John's alone to substantiate the theory that Ho meant what he said, that he very much wanted the friendship of liberal Americans and liberal Frenchmen, with whose help he hoped to steer a moderate course to Vietnamese freedom. Was it only a game he was playing, as a superb actor, and did he just use this small group of foreign friends to further his own burning cause in Moscow's image? There is enough proof of his sincerity to doubt this over-simplified conclusion. Not only was Moscow far off, with a record of having done little to help Ho concretely in the difficult years gone by, but, significantly, Communist China did not yet exist. Who, then, more than the Americans, professing themselves to be ardently against colonialism in the projected postwar world, were in a position to help him win liberty from France and simultaneously ward off Chinese penetration?

Official wartime American policy had been alternately positive and vague about Indochina. President Roosevelt had obtained the tentative approval of Stalin and Chiang Kai-shek for a postwar Indochina trusteeship, though both had expressed themselves as favoring ultimate independence for the Vietnamese. Churchill's reaction to the trusteeship proposal had been negative, and Roosevelt had chided him as an old imperialist. Roosevelt had been somewhat ambivalent himself, however, when it came to doing anything to pave the way for Vietnam's independence. In October, 1944, he had told Secretary of State Cordell Hull that "we should do nothing in regard to resistance groups in Indochina," and when a Free French mission to Kandy, Ceylon, sought help from the Allied Southeast Asia Command, Roosevelt gave orders that "no American representatives in the Far East, whether civilian or military, are authorized to make any decisions on political questions with the French or anyone else."

The "anyone else" presumably included Ho Chi Minh, although Roosevelt may never even have heard of him. Ho had long been a man of mystery and many names. For the moment, one need only go back to 1939, when Ho was still known as Nguyen Ai Quoc (Nguyen, the Patriot). In that year, following the fall of the Popular Front in France, the Indochina Communist Party Ho had welded together was disbanded and went underground. When the Japanese swept into Tonkin in September, 1940, the Communists and the non-Communist nationalists launched uprisings against both the French and the Japanese, but they were quickly crushed. In May, 1941, after the Japanese had established their puppet regime of Vichy Frenchmen, Ho and other Vietnamese Communists met with other nationalists at Tsin-li, just across the Tonkinese border in China. They reorganized their scattered ranks into the Vietnam Doc Lap Dong Minh—Vietminh for short—and the guiding spirit, the man selected as General Secretary, was bearded little Nguyen Ai Quoc, who had unexpectedly shown up at the meeting, though many had thought he had died of tuberculosis years before in the jungle. Without any flexing of Communist muscles, Ho and his friends concentrated on creating a common nationalist front to continue the fight against both Japan and France and to gain Vietnamese freedom.

At the end of 1941, Nguyen Ai Quoc was arrested by the Kuomintang secret police. They knew he was a Communist but chose to describe him as "a French spy" and threw him into jail at Liuchow. Eying Tonkin, as the Chinese had for many years, the Kuomintang had its own plans to build an anti-French "independence" movement around picked pro-Chinese Vietnamese. They soon discovered, however, that it was Nguyen Ai Quoc's Communist guerrillas of the Vietminh front who had the only real experience in Indochina. No one else, with one exception, had a network of agents there. The exception, oddly enough, was a civilian group headed by a dozen Allied businessmen, each of whom had his private organization of French, Chinese, and Vietnamese operatives; their original purpose had been to do what could be done to protect Allied assets and property in the Far East, and after Pearl Harbor this unique group had started working with Ho's guerrillas to gather intelligence for Allied air forces based in China and in India.

Early in 1943, Nguyen Ai Quoc sent a message from his prison cell to the southern Chinese warlord, Chang Fa Kwei, who, while an important leader of the Kuomintang, had frequently fought for power with Chiang Kai-shek and had his own ideas about Indochina. Nguyen Ai Quoc told Chang Fa Kwei that if he were set free, he would regather his intelligence network in Indochina and, presumably, work on Chang's behalf. Chang thereupon ordered his release from the Liuchow jail, and did so without telling Chiang Kai-shek. It was at this point that Nguyen Ai Quoc adopted the name Ho Chi Minh (He Who Shines), primarily to hide his identity from Chiang Kai-shek's secret-police chief, Tai Li. As Ho, he became the directing head of the umbrella organization of Vietnamese revolutionary groups called the Dong Ming Hoi, which the Kuomintang was sponsoring and of which the Communist-dominated Vietminh was at first simply a part.

Ho received and disbursed a hundred thousand Chinese Nationalist dollars a month to carry on espionage and sabotage in Indochina. During 1943 and 1944, the Vietminh built up its own political strength at the expense of the other Dong Minh Hoi organizations, and by the end of 1944 it had an independent army of ten thousand rebels under the command of the young lawyer and teacher, Vo Nguyen Giap, who had already begun to demonstrate a remarkable military talent. Inevitably, as a result of the Vietminh's growing independence, relations between Ho and the Kuomintang in Chungking and Kunming became strained; under the circumstances, there was little his guardian angel, Chang Fa Kwei, could do about it. Equally unhappy about Ho were both the Vichy and the Free French, who buried their differences long enough to exchange secret information about him.

In the second half of 1944, Ho began to look to the Americans; what took place over the next two years, including the strange jungle romance between Ho and young soldiers like John, had overtones of comic opera, although the story had a sad ending. Ho, on four separate occasions, came secretly to the Office of Strategic Services in Kunming, late in 1944 and early in 1945, seeking arms and ammunition in return for intelligence, sabotage against the Japanese, and continued aid in rescuing shot-down Allied pilots. He was rejected each time. According to Paul E. Helliwell, who was O.S.S. intelligence chief in China at the time and who has since denied that O.S.S. in any way "managed" Ho, "O.S.S. China was at all times consistent in its policy of giving no help to individuals such as Ho, who were known Communists and therefore obvious postwar sources of trouble." At the same time, however, and despite President Roosevelt's expressed policy of hands off the Indochina resistance movement—Helliwell says he was personally unaware of any direct orders—the decision not to help Ho was principally based, he adds, on Ho's refusal to pledge that any arms he received would be used only against the Japanese and not against the French.

Ho kept on trying. Helliwell finally gave him six .38-caliber revolvers and twenty thousand rounds of ammunition, but this was simply a token of appreciation for Vietminh assistance in bringing out three American pilots. Later, Ho wrote to Richard Heppner, who was chief of O.S.S. in China late in the war, requesting the help of the United States, which had already pledged the Philippines their freedom, in pressuring the French to grant Indochina independence. The fact is Ho did get some assistance from O.S.S. and from other American and Allied agencies over and above Helliwell's six pistols, although the material aid he received was not as great as the inspirational encouragement he was unofficially accorded. As a subsequent American intelligence chief in the Far East put it, "Ho offered to be our man, and we never grabbed his hand because we couldn't bankroll him."

Ho tried several Allied sources. Major General Claire Chennault, head of the 14th Air Force, who was warned by his Kuomintang friends to steer clear of him, at one point unwittingly had Ho introduced to him as "an old Vietnamese guide." Nothing came of that, but the British were somewhat more helpful and dropped some supplies to Free French and Vietminh guerrillas in November, 1944, after Ho had secretly moved back into Tonkin with about two hundred of his Vietminh followers. With him came a representative of the civilian group of former American businessmen in Indochina, who had for some time been cooperating with Ho's men. This hush-hush group had been under the wing of the O.S.S. at first but was now unofficially attached to another American Army group, the Air Ground Aid Service (AGAS). The arms that Ho and his handful of Vietnamese carried with them into Tonkin at this point are known to have come partly from O.S.S. supplies, although they had not been initially distributed for that purpose, and partly from some other American arsenals.

In the northern Tonkin jungle, in a mixed-up area where Chinese bandits, Free French and American paratroopers, and various groups of nationalists were all active, Ho Chi Minh set up his revolutionary headquarters. Vietminh troops, under young Giap, successfully harassed the Japanese, proselytized in behalf of Vietnamese freedom, and helped rescue additional Allied pilots. An American who was with Ho at his forest headquarters during this period remembers above all "his strength of character and his single-mindedness." His appraisal of Ho was as follows: "You've got to judge someone on the basis of what he wants. Ho couldn't be French, and he knew he could fight the French on his terms. He was afraid of the Chinese, and he couldn't deal with them because they'd always demand their pound of flesh. Moscow, so far away, was good at blowing up bridges, but not much good at building them again. If it weren't for the war, of course, Ho wouldn't have had a chance against the long background of French colonialism. But now he was in the saddle, although it wasn't clear what horse he was riding. For the moment, surely, he was helping us, on the ground. We and the French were in a position to help him in the future. I think he was ready to remain pro-West."

Ho Dickers with France

In the light of the above summary of Ho's career as a long-time trusted worker in Communist vineyards, let us return to the jungle and to the months, just before the end of the war in 1945, when he sounded out the French in Kunming over the radio of the young American lieutenant, John.

The messages John sent out for Ho reached Léon Pignon, a political career man of the French who was later to be High Commissioner of Indochina, and Major Jean Sainteny, a Free French Army officer who became the chief French representative in North Vietnam. After reading Ho's demands for guaranteed independence from France in five to ten years, Pignon and Sainteny replied that they were willing to negotiate, but no time or place was set. The Americans by this time were posing a new problem for the French. When Roosevelt's orders against helping the underground in Indochina were lifted, early in April, the Office of Strategic Services had begun to retrain and equip some two thousand French soldiers who had made their way to Kunming after the Japanese takeover. The plan was to drop Franco-American teams back into Indochina, with supplies to follow if guerrilla resistance bands could be organized. In point of fact, while willingly taking any material help they could get, the French wanted to avoid any direct American involvement. Helliwell, the former O.S.S. intelligence head, later said: "It was perfectly obvious by June of 1945 that the French were infinitely more concerned with keeping the Americans out of Indochina than they were in defeating the Japanese or in doing anything to bring the war to a successful conclusion in that area."

Not too many Americans did get into Tonkin, but several O.S.S. teams were dropped into the jungle, and with their help Ho's forces managed to augment their supplies with a small number of tommy guns and carbines. At the war's end, replenishing their arsenal with captured or surrendered Japanese equipment, Vietminh troops moved swiftly to carry out Ho's orders of a general insurrection. All over Indochina, there was rising support for the independence movement. Under Giap, now a self-styled General, the Vietminh troops moved into Hanoi on August 17, 1945. A week later, Major Sainteny parachuted into the city from a Free French bomber, with Major Archimedes Patti, of the O.S.S. Patti's mission was to liberate war prisoners, for which he had to obtain the cooperation of the Japanese, since the Chinese occupation forces had not yet arrived. Sainteny found himself immediately hamstrung by the Vietminh and by the Japanese, who, with Patti's apparent blessing, completely restricted his movement, on the grounds of his personal safety, and kept several hundred French citizens virtually locked up in the Hotel Metropole. Sainteny was incensed, and five days after his arrival he telegraphed Calcutta: "We are before a collusive Allied maneuver with the purpose of throwing the French out of Indochina." He had a point, but it was far more accidental than collusive.

Within a period of weeks, other American officers arrived in Hanoi, among them some top officers of the China Combat Command. At the same time came a number of American correspondents. Their open sympathies, in typical American fashion of supporting the underdog, were clearly with the Vietminh, and especially with Ho. Major Patti made no bones about favoring Vietnamese independence; French sources say he even offered to help Ho get arms, and that an American general on the scene indicated he had some business connections back home that would sell the new regime heavy equipment for rebuilding the country. That Ho needed help was obvious. My *Newsweek* associate, Harold Isaacs, saw Ho in November, and Ho expressed his readiness to permit the French to maintain their economic position in Vietnam if they recognized Vietnamese independence. "Why not?" Ho asked. "We've been paying out our life's blood for decades. Suppose it costs us a few hundred million more piastres to buy our freedom?"

Recalling his long struggles, his years in Chinese and British prisons, Ho was full of humility and neither looked nor played the part of a head of government. He wore a faded khaki jacket and trousers, a white shirt, and old slippers. "They call me 'Excellency.' Funny, eh?" he remarked.

The sympathy Americans had for Ho late in 1945 and early in 1946 found expression in the formation of the Vietnam-American Friendship Association. Its first meeting in Hanoi was attended by an American general and his officers. After listening to Vietnamese professions of esteem and fondness for America, the general returned the compliments and looked forward to such things as student exchanges. Major Sainteny, who had suffered the further indignity of being arrested by the Japanese while riding in his jeep, which carried a French flag, and having an American colonel obtain his release, later referred to the Americans' "infantile anticolonialism, which blinded almost all of them." Despite his dismay, it was Sainteny who, more than any other Frenchmen, was to sympathize with Ho Chi Minh and try to promote a real policy of cooperation with him.

After two meetings with Ho, late in September and early in October, Sainteny felt that he was "a strong and honorable personality." Subsequently, in his book, *The Story of a Lost Peace, 1945–1947*, Sainteny wrote that "this ascetic man, whose face revealed at once intelligence, energy, cleverness, and fineness, was a personality of the highest order who would not be long in placing himself in the foreground of the Asian scene." Pignon, who was more interested in building up other nationalists than in adopting Ho, was also impressed but was less sure of his sincerity. From the outset, Pignon had no illusions about "Ho's Communist face" and considered him "a great actor." Nevertheless, both Frenchmen regarded Ho as "a man of peace," and Pignon's reservations about Ho's honesty did not include skepticism about Ho's preference for moderation and for compromise over killing. The two French negotiators differed most strongly perhaps on their assessment of Ho's humility and pride: Sainteny was always impressed with the first; Pignon flashed warning signals about the second.

Sainteny did most of the negotiation with Ho that led to the agreement of March 6, 1946, whereby the Republic of Vietnam was recognized as an independent part of the French Union, with French troops permitted to return to Tonkin. During the period of the negotiations, Sainteny has written, Ho "aspired to become the Gandhi of Indochina." Ho is quoted as saying: "While we want to govern ourselves. . . . I need your professional men, your engineers, and your capital to build a strong and independent Vietnam." Ho, says Sainteny, wanted the French Union to be constructed with "a Vietnamese cornerstone. . . . He wanted independence for his country, but it was to France herself that he wanted to owe it. . . . It is certainly regrettable that France minimized this man and was unable to understand his value and the power he disposed of." Sainteny points out that China was Vietnam's age-old enemy, that Ho's overtures to the Americans had already proved "rather disappointing," and that, "against the wishes of an important faction of his party," Ho was not inclined to look for aid in Moscow, "which he knew too well." Sainteny, nevertheless, was realistic enough to admit that Ho's preference for French backing was partly predicated on the expectations of a Communist victory in France.

When the Communists in France lost out, Sainteny says, Ho felt he needed the support of French liberals and moderates more than ever if he was successfully to "muzzle his opposition" in Vietnam, which had begun to cause him some trouble. This particularly included some of the old Chinese Dong Minh Hoi groups, which Ho had subjugated in the late-war jungle days, when the Vietminh had become the dominant part of the underground front. The Chinese in Hanoi sought to reactivate these organizations, notably the Dong Minh Hoi and the more important Vietnam Quoc Dan Dang

(VNQDD), the leading Vietnamese national party; they specifically wanted Ho to include representatives of these groups in his government.

The Chinese in the northern part of Vietnam had several objectives. In the first place, they were there for profit, if not for outright loot, and they succeeded—by inflating the Chinese dollar at the expense of the Indochina piastre; by making off with huge amounts of opium, which they seized both in Laos and in Vietnam; and by engaging in heavy black-market operations in Hanoi and Haiphong, where there was a large Chinese mercantile population. In the second place, the Chinese had no use for the French or the Vietnamese, and they did not hesitate to terrorize the local French and Vietnamese citizens. The fact that many of their occupation troops were more ragtail than professional encouraged this, and in the winter of 1945 things became so bad that Sainteny cabled Paris to ask for a United Nations investigation of the conduct of the Chinese forces; both the British and the American representatives in Hanoi supported him. As events turned out, this was not necessary, since the French finally managed to get the Chinese out of the north by renouncing their extraterritorial and other rights in China and by granting numerous concessions to the Chinese in Vietnam, including a free zone for Chinese goods at Haiphong and certain customs exemptions for goods shipped in over the railroad from Kunming.

Though the Chinese agreed to leave by mid-March, 1946, they actually didn't pull out the bulk of their troops until the summer. In the meantime, they kept up their political offensive, and they obtained some advantage from the fact that initially the Vietminh's strength was largely concentrated in Hanoi itself and in a few other cities but not yet in the countryside, where both the Dong Minh Hoi and the VNQDD had previously built up considerable support, especially in the areas near the Chinese border. Much of the Vietminh's support, despite its Communist leadership, came from non-Communist Vietnamese, whose passionate desire for independence was a powerful factor in enabling Ho Chi Minh to form his original broad front in his own dynamic image. In order to stress his nationalist feelings more than his Communist background and doctrine, and also as a result of the orders that had come from the French Communist Party, Ho, in mid-November, 1945, dissolved the Indochina Communist Party in the north. (A small group of Communist extremists, including Giap and Dang Xuan Khu—better known today as Truong Chinh, the strongest pro-Peking man among the Hanoi Communists—formed what they called Marxist Study Groups, which later became the nucleus of the Laodang, or Workers, Party, the successor of the old Communist Party in Indochina.)

To obtain the support of as many groups as possible for the agreement he was about to sign with Sainteny, Ho selected the chief of the Dong Ming Hoi to be his Vice-president, and he gave three top Cabinet jobs to VNQDD men, including the Ministry of Foreign Affairs. At the same time, to pacify the Chinese further, he dropped Giap and one other leading Communist from the Cabinet. As the Vietminh began organizing People's Committees to replace the old Councils of Notables in the villages, it made further temporary concessions to the Chinese parties, promising the VNQDD fifty seats and the Dong Minh Hoi twenty out of a total of three hundred and fifty in the assembly elections that were to be held in January, 1946. The vote took place on a limited basis only, in some parts of the country, and about half of those elected, as it turned out, were nonpolitical-party people, though the Vietminh did well by controlling the vote in many villages, and in Hanoi Ho received an alleged ninety-eight percent of the ballots. Ho had other reasons for wanting to go slow politically. He had an extremely difficult economic situation on his hands. There had been a famine early in 1945, followed by floods that had swept over the broken dikes of the Red River Delta.

Then came a severe drought. The breakdown of the Vietnamese transportation system had made it impossible to ship rice from the south, which was having its own troubles. In 1945 and through the early part of 1946, it was estimated that a million Vietnamese died of starvation in the north.

Modus Vivendi Is Signed

In the face of all these difficulties, Ho's eagerness in wanting to conclude the March, 1946, agreement with Sainteny can better be understood. When he signed it, he made a direct and dramatic appeal to the Vietnamese people at a big outdoor meeting in Hanoi. "Fellow countrymen, who have followed me up to now," he asked, "follow me once more. I would prefer death a hundred times to betraying my country."

Two months later, as the French were doing their best to sabotage Ho by holding the separatist conference at Dalat, in the south, and by getting ready to set up their independent puppet regime in Cochin China, Ho left for France with a small delegation to negotiate what he hoped would be a full implementation of the March contract he had made with Major Sainteny. During the summer, while he was away, and with both Sainteny and Pignon out of Hanoi, too, the extremist group among the Communists, led by Giap and Dang Xuan Khu, rode roughshod over the non-Communist nationalists. As in the south, terror also struck the country, and many pro-French Vietnamese as well as Frenchmen were assassinated. There are those who say that this was all part of the game, that Ho went to France and remained there as the pretender of peace, tortuously seeking an agreement, while the extremists were given a free hand back in Vietnam. Sainteny, among others, vehemently denies that this was the case.

In Biarritz, where he first rested, in Paris and then at the conference in Fontainebleau, Ho enjoyed huge personal success. He charmed everyone, especially the press. He distributed roses to women reporters, signed his name in blood for an American male correspondent. He was widely compared to Confucius, to the Buddha, to St. John the Baptist, to anyone's doting grandfather, and it was noted that he was an ascetic, since, among other things, he refused to take a drink. Everywhere he went, whether to the opera, to a fancy reception, to a picnic, or to a press conference, he appeared in his simple, high-buttoned linen work suit. "As soon as one approaches this frail man, one shares the admiration of all men around him, over whom he towers with his serenity acquired from wide experience," wrote one reporter. Noting his "tormented face and his eyes of blue which burn with an inner light," another declared that he "hides a soul of steel behind a fragile body." His wit, his Oriental courtesy, his *savoir-faire*, his mixed profundity and playfulness in social intercourse, his open love for children, above all his seeming sincerity and simplicity, captured one and all.

Unfortunately, in point of accomplishment Ho's trip was far less successful. The fault, now generally admitted, was chiefly that of the French, who, while the conference went on, continued to violate its spirit by further fostering the idea of the separate south and central federation in Indochina. In Paris, the shakiness of the national government delayed the start of the sessions with Ho. He stayed at Biarritz to wait and go fishing. "The conference was fishy from the start," one of his delegates remarked. Sainteny later wrote that Ho was "reticent and nervous," but after playing pelota, roaming the countryside, and visiting Lourdes, he "found his smile again" and was "as affable and simple as before." When three leading Communists, including the Minister of Air, paid him a visit and commented, for propaganda purposes, about the "indescribable conditions" in which Ho was quartered at Biarritz, Ho announced that, on the contrary, he was "enchanted" by his stay on the Basque coast.

When he and Sainteny finally flew up to Paris for the start of the talks, Sainteny described him as "pale, eyes brilliant, and tight-throated," and he quoted Ho as saying, when the plane was settling down, "Above all, don't leave me, whatever you do." As the conference dawdled in the shadow of defeat, by now the result of the activities of the Vietminh extremists in Hanoi as well as of the French maneuvers in Cochin China, Ho grew more and more restless. Sainteny agreed he ought to return to Hanoi as soon as possible. "What would I be able to do if I went home emptyhanded?" Ho asked. "Don't let me leave this way," he begged Sainteny and Marius Moutet, the Socialist Minister of Overseas Territories. "Arm me against those who would seek to displace me. You will not regret it." It was a significant plea, as significant as what Ho said on another evening to Sainteny and Moutet, "If we have to fight, we will fight. You will kill ten of our men and we will kill one of yours, and in the end it will be you who will tire of it."

At midnight on September 14, 1946, the frail figure of Ho Chi Minh, in its military tunic, walked out of the Hotel Royal-Monceau in Paris (the Fontainebleau sessions had ended) and strolled to Moutet's house nearby. There Ho and Moutet signed a *modus vivendi*, which, while it underlined Vietnamese (and some French) concessions for safeguarding French rights in Indochina, only postponed agreement on basic political questions; it at least placed upon the French the responsibility for restoring order in Cochin China. This was nothing more than had been agreed to in the spring and been vitiated since, but Ho publicly called the *modus vivendi* "better than nothing." He murmured to a security officer who accompanied him back to the hotel early in the morning, however, "I have just signed my death warrant."

Despite the failure of his mission, Ho, in his true cosmopolitan fashion, had enjoyed his stay in Paris, a city he had always loved. Years before, standing on a bridge across the Seine, he had remarked to a Communist comrade, "What a wonderful city, what a wonderful scene!" When his friend had replied that Moscow was also beautiful, Ho had said, "Moscow is heroic, Paris is the joy of living." During the 1946 conference, Ho had revisited some of his former haunts and, mixing socially with several foreign correspondents, had talked freely about himself and his politics. "Everyone has the right to his own doctrine," he had said. "I studied and chose Marx. Jesus said two thousand years ago that one should love one's enemies. That dogma has not been realized. When will Marxism be realized? I cannot answer. . . . To achieve a Communist society, big industrial and agricultural production is necessary. . . . I do not know when that will be realized in Vietnam, where production is low. We are not yet in a position to meet the conditions."

Ho's self-analysis, in relation to Indochina's development, is a markedly honest one, in Marxist terms. From the outset, Marxism was far more than a blueprint for him. It was a *logique*, and as one of the keenest Indochina scholars, Paul Mus, has pointed out, it was acquired by Ho as a vital Western weapon, an arsenal in fact, with which, as an Asian, he could combat his French masters. Ho, as a Marxist, was quick to appreciate how his country was being robbed, kept in economic penury by a purposefully unimaginative colonial power. While the French took out rubber or rice or whatever else they wanted and sold it in the world market at a high profit, the Vietnamese lived under a system in which only human labor and not money, in any international sense, counted; goods were in effect bartered for subsistence. Such an economic condition became the fulcrum of Ho's anger and drove him way back, almost inevitably, to Marxism and thence to Communism. "Ho had to build on what every Asian must build *per se*," Mus says, "a Western logic to deal with us Europeans. Whether it be a profession such as the law or medicine or what have you, an Asian must find this *logique* or be lost. Ho found it first in Marxism and he became a Leninist, since Lenin was faced in Russia with the same problem of the vacuum at the village level. Ho was successful because he remained true to Leninism and Marxism. In this sense, straightforward according to *his* view, he belongs to a proper fraternity."

Along with Sainteny, Mus is one of those Frenchmen who admit that France and the Western world missed a proper opportunity with Ho in 1946. Mus himself, as a French negotiator, met Ho a year later, and he has the same queer fondness for him most men who knew him have retained. "I have no reason, as a Frenchman, to like Ho for what he has done," Mus told me long afterward, "but still I like him. I am not afraid to say so. I like him for his strong mind. Although he is a great actor—one cannot afford to be naïve with him—he does not go back on his word. He believes in the truth as he sees it. But he is a Marxist, and that is where we part company." He quotes Ho as telling him, in 1947, "My only weapon is anger. . . . I won't disarm my people until I trust you." Ho's willingness to deal with the French, Mus believes, was largely predicated on his need for French advice, above all for financial advisers. "Marxist doctrine calls for the proletarian state to use, at least temporarily, the accountancy of the bourgeois-capitalist countries," Mus says. Because of the inbred economy imposed by the Bank of Indochina, Ho knew that Vietnam could not stand on its own feet, either in terms of money or trade. He also knew he could not rely on the colonial French. His political approach was through metropolitan France. He wasn't convinced that this was his only chance, but he was determined to play the possibilities. He wavered between his affection and regard for France, which had given him his self in the Marxist image, and his new disillusion of 1946. "If we had supported him more strongly then," Mus added, "we might have won. . . . We thought we could crush him if it came to war. We did not appreciate how hard he could fight. But we must not forget that he really wanted an agreement with France at the time of Fontainebleau because it would have served him. That part of his motivation afterward died, of course, but we should understand that it existed at the time and that he was truly disappointed."

When Ho returned to Vietnam from France at the end of that sad 1946 summer, he was confronted with a difficult internal political situation. While the conflict between himself and the extremists was perhaps exaggerated, there is no doubt that the younger men around Ho, especially Giap and Dang Xuan Khu, had disapproved of his moderation and patience at Fontainebleau. They almost certainly wanted to move on to violence at once. Considerable conjecture about Ho's troubles with this group soon arose, and then shifted to speculation that ranged from rumors of Ho's retirement into mere figurehead status to the increasingly heard report, of which the French sporadically claimed proof, that he was dead. It is a fact that for many months he was not seen and was hardly mentioned, but what seems to have happened was this:

Ho became quite ill when he arrived back in Hanoi. He stayed in bed for several weeks. During this period, he may have been under some protective form of house arrest (British sources insist this was so); apparently he was surreptitiously moved in and out of a nearby jungle headquarters. Various elements within the Vietminh and out—among them the old pro-Chinese groups, for their own obvious purposes—openly accused Ho of having sold out to France with the *modus vivendi*, and tracts distributed in the Hanoi area bitterly attacked him. "When a man remains in foreign countries for a long while, he becomes their slave," one of them read. These were probably nothing more than the dying gasp of the pro-Chinese Vietnamese leaders, some of whom had already fled to China when Giap, with the departure of Chinese Troops, unrestrainedly cracked down on them.

If Ho was temporarily and perhaps deliberately kept in the background, his eclipse did not last long. His policy of moderation was surely in evidence once more in the fall of 1946, when a constitution of surprising temperance, by Communist terms, was adopted. Two months later, in December, following the incident over customs control in Haiphong harbor and the outbreak of Vietminh terror and French Army reprisals in Hanoi, the war between the French and the Vietminh began. Both sides by then seemed not only ready but anxious to fight. Ho and his government fled into the jungle. However, by April, 1947, Ho's position as the commanding figure in the Vietminh was again supreme. It was in that month that Paul Mus traveled through the forest as a French emissary to meet Ho and offer him what amounted to terms of unconditional surrender. When Ho asked Mus if he—were he in Ho's place—would accept them, Mus admitted he wouldn't. "In the French Union there is no place for cowards," Ho then declared. "If I accepted those conditions, I should be one." Mus says it was completely obvious to him that Ho was running his own show, and that he had the power to reject the French offer without even having to consult the Tong Bo, the five-man Vietminh "politburo."

Even if Ho had had trouble with the extremists, if he had still at that time been a moderate hoping for a *rapprochement* with France, this would not have meant that he was not also, as he always has been in the final analysis, Moscow's man; the two Ho's were not incompatible, and much of what has since happened in the postwar world would seem to corroborate this. Moscow, as a matter of fact, may very well have intervened secretly to restore fully Ho's power and prestige; in substantiation of this theory is the belief that some of the other Vietminh leaders, notably Dang Xuan Khu, have always been under the influence of the Chinese Communists rather than Moscow-orientated. If Ho was torn, within himself and with relation to his followers, a little Moscow glue may have put him together again.

An interesting comment on Ho came at this time from none other than Bao Dai, whose brief tenure as Ho's adviser ended when he fled to Hong Kong, from which place the French would soon resurrect him to head an opposition government in the south. "During the few months I was in Hanoi as Supreme Counselor," Bao Dai said, "I saw Ho Chi Minh suffer. He was fighting a battle within himself. Ho had his own struggle. He realized Communism was not best for our country, but it was too late. Ultimately, he could not overcome his allegiance to Communism."

After Paul Mus's 1947 visit, no non-Communist Westerner is believed to have seen Ho in the jungle until late in 1954. On several occasions, however, he replied telegraphically to questions sent him by Western correspondents. What gradually evolved was a somewhat altered version of him. While he became more cynical and coy, he also became more folksy. "Uncle Ho," the patriarch, emerged. And as he increasingly became more anti-American, he hewed closer than ever to the Communist line, as handed down by Moscow and later by Peking as well. He continued, however, to speak the truth about himself, in his own peculiar lights. "When I was young, I studied Buddhism, Confucianism, Christianity, as well as Marxism," he once told a United Press questioner. "There is something good in each doctrine." Asked his opinion of American intentions in Asia, Ho snapped back, "Marshallization of the world." The Russians, he said, were "against Marshallization of the world." In the next breath, with sad truth, he declared that American aid "is a good thing if it goes directly to the people," thereby touching a sore spot inasmuch as the United States aid to the Vietnamese became a sensitive issue with the French in the south. Ho denied vehemently that Vietnam was or could become Russia's or anyone else's "satellite." He kept insisting he could remain neutral, "like Switzerland," in the world power struggle. "If the Chinese Communists offer you artillery and heavy mortars, would you accept them?" he was subsequently asked. Ho fell back on coyness. "What friendly advice would you give us in that case?" he wired back to his questioner. To a Siamese journalist who inquired, "Is there any truth in the rumors that Mao Tse-tung and you have set up a close relationship and that you favor Communism of the Moscow kind?" Ho replied—with an odd quality of dishonesty vis-à-vis his Asian questioner—"What is astonishing is that many intelligent foreigners believe these French slanders."

Events themselves belied Ho's last answer. There was no doubt that after 1950 he moved swiftly and snugly into the Moscow-Peking ideological camp.

As it evolved, the Vietminh emphasized the dominant role of the working class, in accordance with the decisions of the Asian and Australian Trade Union Conference held at Peking in November and December, 1949. Ho and Mao exchanged cables at that time, and soon thereafter eight hundred Vietnamese labor leaders met in rebel Indochina territory and, among panoplied pictures of Stalin, Mao, and Ho, demonstrated their total allegiance to Communism. Titoism was attacked, although when Yugoslavia quickly recognized Ho's regime, along with Soviet Russia and China, Ho had some embarrassing moments; he solved them typically, by pointing out that he had announced his readiness to establish relations with "any government" while at the same time continuing to blast Tito on the Vietminh jungle radio.

Early in 1951, when the Communists resumed their open leadership of the Vietminh movement, Ho lapsed into another period of silence. It was then that rumors of his death in the jungle again were heard. From time to time, Dang Xuan Khu, who became General Secretary of the new party, or someone else in the hierarchy, would publicly extol him. The tone grew reverential; a Ho myth in the milder image of a Stalin myth was reared, and a much tougher, more rigid Ho than he had ever made himself out to be slowly emerged. In 1953, Joseph Starobin, correspondent of the *Daily Worker* in New York, met Ho in the Tonkin jungle. He was not unexpectedly charmed by "the legendary president" who wore such simple peasant clothes and who knew so much about the world. Starobin rhapsodized: "As we sat there that first evening, these facets of the president's personality emerged. He was the world traveler, in whom each recollection of a crowded past was still vivid. He was the old-timer, the Communist leader of an older generation, for whom the lamps of memory needed only the reburnishing of conversation to become shiny and bright. There was also the Uncle Ho who works his own garden, types his own messages, teaches the four virtues—industriousness, frugality, justice and integrity—to the youth." Starobin was with Ho when Stalin died. He described the rapt jungle scene: "Crude benches illumined by candles set in a makeshift candelabra made out of bamboo; at the front was a portrait of Stalin wreathed in flowers . . . two violins played softly."

This touching bit of pastoral Stalinoidism was real enough in the context of the time, or real enough, at least, for so stalwart a Stalinist as Starobin; but it seems somehow doubtful that Ho took it quite so seriously or regarded it so poignantly. He was far too clever for that, and he had seen far too many of his old comrades purged by Stalin to render such an unqualifiedly touching response to the old tyrant's death. Nevertheless, it was certainly true that by this time the die had been cast, and that Ho, rejected by the West, no longer had any option—if one may assume that he had one earlier—but to attach himself firmly to the Communist camp. The wandering minstrel of Southeast Asia was home again, but there were to be many moments in the future when his relationship to the Communists, especially after the Sino-Soviet split, would once again be tenuous and difficult to define. Perhaps no one anywhere in the world would be called upon to perform such a unique balancing act between Moscow and Peking as the adroit old guerrilla, Nguyen Ai Quoc. For the moment, however, it is sufficient to reemphasize "what might have been" in that crucial year between August, 1945, when the big war ended, and July–September, 1946, when the abortive conference at Fontainebleau preceded by a few months the start of the Indochina war. This was the first important turning point in the unfortunate history of Indochina, and this, perhaps more than any other time, was when "the lost revolution" was actually lost.

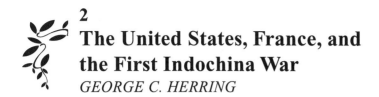

2
The United States, France, and
the First Indochina War
GEORGE C. HERRING

By the outbreak of World War II, the United States had come to regard Vietnam as important to its global interests. A relative newcomer to the region, America established itself as a power in the Southwest Pacific with the acquisition of Hawaii and the Philippines in 1898. Eager for new markets and investments in East Asia, it had also promoted an "open-door" policy in China while working within the prevailing imperial system. French monopolies sharply limited trade and contact with Indochina, but in the interwar years the United States established increasingly important economic interests in the resource-rich Dutch and British East Indies. Southeast Asia provided about 90 percent of America's crude rubber and 75 percent of its tin, and U.S. oil companies produced about 27 percent of the sizable output of the East Indies. Support for China, concern for the Philippines, and a considerable stake in Southeast Asian raw materials put the United States on a collision course with Japan in the 1930s, and Americans grew increasingly alarmed by Japanese designs for a Greater East Asia Co-Prosperity Sphere. Tokyo's move into Indochina in 1941 first impressed on U.S. officials the strategic importance of the French colonies as a gateway to China, the Philippines, and Southeast Asia, leading to the imposition of sanctions and eventually to the attack on Pearl Harbor.

For a time during World War II, the United States actively opposed the return of Indochina to France. Some U.S. officials perceived the growth of nationalism in Vietnam and feared that a French attempt to regain control of its colony might provoke a long and bloody war, bringing instability to an area of economic and strategic significance. Even if France should succeed, they reasoned, it would restore monopolistic controls that would deny the United States access to raw materials and naval facilities. President Franklin D. Roosevelt seems instinctively to have recognized that colonialism was doomed and that the United States should identify with the forces of nationalism in Asia. Roosevelt profoundly disliked France and its leader, Charles de Gaulle, moreover, and he regarded the French as "poor colonizers" who had "badly mismanaged" Indochina and exploited its people.[1] Roosevelt therefore advocated placing Indochina under international trusteeship in preparation for independence.

In 1945, however, Roosevelt retreated sharply from his earlier forthright stand. Fearing for their own colonies, the British had strenuously opposed his trusteeship scheme, and many of Roosevelt's top advisers urged him not to antagonize an important ally by forcing the issue.[2] At Yalta in February 1945, the President endorsed a proposal under which colonies would be placed in trusteeship only with the approval of the mother country. In view of France's announced intention to return to its former colony, this plan implicitly precluded a trusteeship for Indochina.

After Roosevelt's death in April 1945, the United States adopted a policy even more favorable to France. Harry S. Truman did not share his predecessor's personal interest in Indochina or his concern about colonialism. American thinking about the postwar world also underwent a major reorientation in the spring of 1945. Military and civilian strategists perceived that the war had left the Soviet Union the most powerful nation in Europe and Asia, and the subjugation of Eastern Europe raised growing fears that Joseph Stalin had broader, perhaps global, designs. Assigning top priority to the promotion of stable, friendly governments in Western Europe that could stand as bulwarks against Russian expansion, the Truman administration concluded that the United States "had no interest" in "championing schemes of international trusteeship" that would weaken and alienate the "European states whose help we need to balance Soviet power in Europe."[3] France assumed special importance in the new scheme of things, and the State Department insisted that the United States must repair the rift that had opened under Roosevelt by cooperating "wholeheartedly" with France and allaying "her apprehensions that we are going to propose that territory be taken away from her."[4] The Truman administration quickly scrapped what remained of Roosevelt's trusteeship plan and in the summer of 1945 assured de Gaulle that it would not stand in the way of restoration of French sovereignty in Indochina.

The United States viewed the outbreak of war in Indochina with concern. Along with revolutions in Burma, Malaya, and Indonesia, it underscored the explosiveness of nationalism in Southeast Asia. France's stubborn pursuit of outmoded colonial goals seemed to preclude anything except a military solution, but the State Department's Far Eastern Office doubted that France had the capacity to subdue the revolution and feared that a French defeat would eliminate Western influence from an area of economic and strategic importance. The State Department's Asian experts warned of the dangers of identifying with French colonialism and pressed the administration to force France to come to terms with Vietnamese nationalism.

American skepticism about French policy in Asia continued to be outweighed by European concerns. In the spring of 1947, the United States formally committed itself to the containment of Soviet expansion in Europe, and throughout the next two years attention was riveted on France, where economic stagnation and political instability aroused grave fears of a Communist takeover. Warned by moderate French politicians that outside interference in colonial matters would play into the hands of the French Communist party, the United States left France to handle the Indochina question in its own way. An "immediate and vital interest" in retaining a "friendly government to assist in the furtherance of our aims in Europe," the State Department concluded, must "take precedence over active steps looking toward the realization of our objectives in Indochina."[5]

By early 1947, moreover, the Truman administration had drawn conclusions about Ho's [Ho Chi Minh] revolution that would determine U.S. policy in Vietnam for the next two decades. From the outset, the Vietminh and United States viewed each other through badly distorted lenses. Isolated in the northern mountains of Vietnam and cut off from the outside world, Vietminh leaders clung to hopes that the friendly demeanor of the OSS [Office of Strategic Services] representatives might reflect official American views toward their revolution. On numerous occasions, therefore, Ho appealed for U.S. support, even suggesting that Vietnam would be a "fertile field for American capital and enterprise" and raising the possibility of a naval base at Cam Ranh Bay.[6] In April 1947, the Vietminh dispatched an emissary to Bangkok to convince the United States of their moderation and seek political and economic support. In meetings with lower-level Americans, the Vietnamese diplomat stressed that his people sought primarily independence from France. Speaking language he thought capitalists wanted to hear, he offered tax-free monopolies for American imports and for the rice export trade.

Such arguments and inducements had no impact in Washington. American political reporting about Vietnam was devoid of expertise and based on racial prejudices and stereotypes that reflected deep-seated convictions about the superiority of Western culture. In U.S. eyes, the Vietnamese were a passive and uninformed people, totally unready for self-government. The "Annamites" were not "particularly industrious," said one diplomat, nor were they noted for "honesty, loyalty, or veracity."[7] U.S. officials thus concluded that even if the Vietnamese were to obtain independence from France, they would be susceptible to the establishment of a Communist police state and vulnerable to external control.

Ho's long-standing ties with Moscow reinforced such fears. U.S. diplomats in Vietnam could find no evidence of direct Soviet contact with the Vietminh and stressed that regardless of ideology, Ho had established himself as the "symbol of nationalism and the struggle for freedom to the overwhelming majority of the population."[8] Stalin was also preoccupied with Europe, and there are indications that ideological conflicts with Ho dating to the 1920s influenced his aloofness toward the Vietminh revolution. Such subtleties were lost on Americans increasingly obsessed with the Communist menace in Europe. Intelligence reports stressed that Ho had remained loyal to Moscow throughout his career. The lack of close ties with the Soviet Union simply meant that he was trusted to carry out Stalin's plans without supervision. In the absence of irrefutable evidence to the contrary, the State Department concluded, the United States could not "afford to assume that Ho is anything but Moscow-directed." Unwilling, as Secretary of State George C. Marshall put it, to see "colonial empires and administrations supplanted by philosophies and political organizations emanating from the Kremlin," the administration refused to do anything to facilitate a "Communist" triumph in Indochina.[9]

Thus, during the first three years of the Indochina war, the United States maintained a distinctly pro-French "neutrality." Fearful of antagonizing its European ally and of assisting the Vietminh even indirectly, the United States refused to acknowledge Ho's appeals for support and to use its leverage to end the fighting. After several unproductive meetings, the contact in Thailand was quietly terminated. Unwilling to support colonialism openly, the Truman administration provided "indirect" financial and military aid. Ships turned over to France under the war-time lend-lease program transported French troops to Vietnam, and the United States extended credits for the purchase of additional transports. Washington provided weapons for use in Europe that were, in fact, employed in Vietnam, and Marshall Plan funds enabled France to divert its own resources to the war in Indochina.[10]

Internationalization of the War

Chinese Communist assistance to the Vietminh and U.S. aid for France transformed by 1950 an anticolonial struggle into a major and increasingly dangerous theater in the emerging Cold War. Isolated diplomatically and desperately in need of external assistance, the Vietminh finally turned to Mao Tse-tung's Chinese Communists for help. Recently triumphant in their own civil war, the Chinese proudly viewed their revolution as a model for other nations in the region, and they appear to have been encouraged by Stalin to take the lead in Asia. China thus leaned toward the Vietminh out of its "glorious internationalist duty." The Chinese also viewed with growing alarm the threat posed by the United States, and they saw support for the Vietminh as a means of securing their southern border. In early 1950, Mao created a Chinese Military Advisory Group and sent some of his best officers to help organize and train the Vietminh armies and plan strategy. He committed increasing volumes of military and nonmilitary equipment, provided sanctuaries for training troops, and took a keen personal interest in the planning and execution of Vietminh military operations. Not surprisingly, the two ancient and often hostile neighbors eyed each other suspiciously, and relations between them were frequently tense. But aid from China was vital to the survival of the Vietminh at this crucial point in the war and to its military success thereafter.[11]

The possibility of a French defeat, along with the Communist victory in China, brought forth in early 1950 a U.S. decision to support France in Indochina, the first step toward direct involvement in Vietnam. The collapse of Chiang Kai-shek's government in China in 1949 and the southward advance of Mao Tse-tung's army raised the ominous possibility of Chinese Communist collaboration with the Vietminh. From late 1949 on, French officials urgently warned that without direct American military aid, they might have to withdraw from Indochina.

The French appeals came at a time when Washington, already gripped by near panic, was frantically reassessing its global Cold War strategy. The fall of China and Russia's successful testing of a nuclear device persuaded many U.S. officials that the Communist threat had assumed even more menacing proportions than that posed by the Axis nations a decade earlier. Any doubts about the direction of Stalin's foreign policy had long since been waved aside: the Soviet Union, "animated by a new fanatic faith," was determined to "impose its absolute authority on the rest of the world." Recent successes seemed to have spurred the Soviet leadership to a new level of confidence and militancy, and Communist expansion, in the eyes of American policymakers, had reached a point beyond which it must not be permitted to go. Any further "extension of the area under the domination of the Kremlin," the National Security Council (NSC) warned, "would raise the possibility that no coalition adequate to confront the Kremlin with greater strength could be assembled."[12] Facing a world divided into two hostile blocs, a precarious balance of power, and the possibility, if not likelihood, of global war, the Truman administration initiated plans to increase American military capabilities, shore up the defense of Western Europe, and extend the containment policy to East Asia.

In the dramatically altered strategic context of 1950, support for France in Indochina was considered essential for the security of Western Europe. Massive expenditures for the war against the Vietminh had retarded France's economic recovery and the attainment of political stability. Certain that Europe was vulnerable to the Soviet threat, American policymakers in early 1950 formulated plans to raise the military forces necessary to defend against the Red Army. Preliminary proposals required France to contribute sizable numbers of troops and provided for West German rearmament, measures the French were likely to resist. The administration thus feared that if it did not respond positively to its ally's appeals for aid, France might refuse to cooperate with its strategic design for Western Europe.

American willingness to support France in Indochina also reflected a growing concern about the future of Southeast Asia. The raging conflict in Indochina and insurgencies in Burma, Malaya, and Indonesia all sprang from indigenous roots, but in a seemingly polarized world their mere existence and leftist orientation persuaded Americans that Southeast Asia was the "target of a coordinated offensive directed by the Kremlin." The European colonial powers and the fragile, newly independent governments of the region seemed incapable of subduing the revolutions, and the presence of a hostile China to the north added enormously to the danger.

In the aftermath of the fall of China, American strategists concluded that Southeast Asia was vital to the security of the United States. Should the region be swept by communism, the NSC warned, "we shall have suffered a major political rout the repercussions of which will be felt throughout the world." The loss of an area so large and populous would tip the balance of power against the United States. Recent Communist triumphs had already aroused nervousness in Europe, and another major victory might tempt the Europeans to reach an accommodation with the Soviet Union. The economic consequences could be equally profound. The United States and its European allies would be denied access to important markets, and the Europeans would lose a major source of the dollars they desperately needed to rebuild their shattered economies. Southeast Asia was the world's largest producer of natural rubber and an important source of oil, tin, tungsten, and other strategic commodities. Should control of these vital raw materials suddenly change hands, the Soviet bloc would be enormously strengthened at the expense of the West.

American policymakers also feared that the loss of Southeast Asia would irreparably damage the nation's strategic position in East Asia. Control of the offshore island chain extending from Japan to the Philippines, America's first line of defense in the Pacific, would be endangered. Air and sea routes between Australia and the Middle East and the United States and India could be cut, severely hampering military operations in the event of war. Japan, India, and Australia, those nations where the West retained predominant influence, would be isolated and vulnerable.

The impact on Japan, America's major east Asian ally and the richest economic prize in the area, would be disastrous. Even before China fell, the United States was pushing for the reintegration of Japan with Southeast Asia, its rice bowl and breadbasket and an essential source of raw materials and markets. With China having fallen to communism, U.S. officials concluded, the loss of Southeast Asia would leave Japan no choice but to accommodate with the adversary. The United States thus set out to defend a region perceived to be the "vital segment" of the "great crescent" of containment extending from Japan to India, ironically seeking to preserve for Japan in 1950 the sphere of economic influence it had attempted to thwart in 1941.[13]

American officials agreed that Indochina, and especially Vietnam, was the key to the defense of Southeast Asia. Soviet recognition of the Vietminh on January 30, 1950, confirmed long-standing beliefs about Ho's allegiance, revealing him, in Secretary of State Dean Acheson's words, in his "true colors as the mortal enemy of native independence in Indochina." It was also misinterpreted as a "significant and ominous" portent of Stalin's intention to "accelerate the revolutionary process" in Southeast Asia.[14] Ho's well-organized guerrillas had already scored major gains against France, and with increased Soviet and Chinese backing they might now be able to force a French withdrawal, removing the last military bulwark between China and the rest of Southeast Asia. Indochina was in the "most immediate danger," the State Department concluded, and was therefore "the most strategically important area of Southeast Asia."[15]

Indochina was considered intrinsically important for its raw materials, rice, and naval bases, but it was deemed far more significant for the presumed effect its loss would have on other areas. By early 1950, American policymakers had firmly embraced what would become known as the "domino theory," the belief that the fall of Indochina would cause in rapid succession the collapse of the other nations of Southeast Asia. Acceptance of this concept reflected the perceived fragility of the region in 1950, as well as the experience of World War II, when Hitler had overrun Western Europe in three months and the Japanese had seized much of Southeast Asia in even less time. First employed to justify aid to Greece in 1947, the idea, once applied to Southeast Asia, quickly became an article of faith. Americans were certain that if Indochina fell, the rest of Southeast Asia would be imperiled. The strategic reassessment of 1950 thus ended American "neutrality" and produced a commitment in early

March to furnish France with military and economic assistance for the war against the Vietminh. It also established principles that would form the basis for U.S. policy in Vietnam for years to come and would eventually lead to massive involvement.

The Bao Dai Solution

The creation of nominally independent governments in Indochina made it easier for the United States to rationalize support of France. Unable to defeat the Vietminh militarily, the French had attempted to undercut it politically by forming "free states" within the French Union in Laos, Cambodia, and Vietnam, the latter headed by the former Emperor of Annam, Bao Dai. Many U.S. officials were rightly skeptical of the so-called Bao Dai solution, warning that it was only a smoke screen for continued French domination and could not succeed. The State Department acknowledged the strength of these arguments, but Bao Dai seemed the only alternative to "Commie domination of Indochina," as Acheson put it, and while American support did not guarantee his success, the lack of it would ensure his failure.[16] By backing Bao Dai, moreover, the United States would at least avoid the appearance of being an accomplice of French imperialism. In February 1950, the Truman administration formally recognized the Bao Dai government and the free states of Laos and Cambodia and initiated plans to support them with economic and technical assistance.

The assumptions on which American policymakers acted in 1950 were misguided. The Southeast Asian revolutions were not inspired by Moscow, and although the Soviet Union and China at times sought to direct and control them, their capacity to do so was limited by their lack of military and especially naval power and by the strength of local nationalism. American assessment of the situation in Vietnam was well off the mark. Although a dedicated Communist, Ho was no tool of the Soviet Union, and while he was willing to accept help from the major Communist powers—indeed, he had no choice but to do so—he was not prepared to subordinate Vietnamese independence to them. Vietnam's historic fears of its larger northern neighbor made submission to China especially unlikely. "It is better to sniff French dung for a while than eat China's all our life," Ho once said, graphically expressing a traditional principle of Vietnamese foreign policy.[17] Perhaps most important, regardless of his ideology, Ho by 1950 had captured the standard of Vietnamese nationalism, and by supporting France, even under the guise of the Bao Dai solution, the United States attached itself to a losing cause.

U.S. policymakers were not unaware of the pitfalls. Should the United States commit itself to Bao Dai and he turn out to be a French puppet, a State Department Asian specialist warned, "we must then follow blindly down a dead-end alley, expending our limited resources . . . in a fight that would be hopeless."[18] Some officials even dimly perceived that the United States might get sucked into direct involvement in Vietnam. But the initial commitment seemed limited and the risks smaller than those of inaction. Caught up in a global struggle reminiscent of World War II, with Russia taking Germany's place in Europe and China Japan's place in Asia, U.S. officials were certain that if they did not back France and Bao Dai, Southeast Asia might be lost, leaving the more awesome choice of a "staggering investment" to recover the losses or a "much contracted" line of defense in the western Pacific.[19]

By the time the United States committed itself to assist France, the Vietminh had gained the military initiative in Indochina. Ho Chi Minh controlled an estimated two-thirds of the countryside, and Vietminh regulars and guerrillas numbered in the hundreds of thousands. The Chinese provided sanctuaries and large stocks of weapons. With Chinese encouragement, [Vo Nguyen] Giap, by early 1950, felt sufficiently confident to take the offensive. The French maintained tenuous control in the cities and the major production centers, but at a very high cost, suffering 1,000 casualties per month and in 1949 alone spending 167 million francs on the war. Even in the areas under nominal French control, the Vietminh spread terror after dark, sabotaging power plants and factories, tossing grenades into cafes and theaters, and brutally assassinating French officials. "Anyone with white skin caught outside protected areas after dark is courting horrible death," an American correspondent reported.[20]

The Bao Dai solution, Bao Dai himself ruefully conceded, was "just a French solution."[21] The much-maligned "playboy Emperor" was in fact a tragic figure. An intelligent man, genuinely concerned about the future of his nation, he had spent most of his life as a puppet of France and then Japan, whiling away the years by indulging an apparently insatiable taste for sports cars, women, and gambling. The agreement of February 1950 gave him little to work with. Under this impossibly complex document of 258 pages, the French retained control of Vietnam's treasury, commerce, and foreign and military policies. They refused even to turn over Saigon's Norodom Palace as the seat of the new government. The government itself was composed largely of wealthy southern landowners, many of them more European than Vietnamese and in no sense representative of the people. Nationalists of stature refused to support Bao Dai, and the masses either backed the resistance or remained aloof. The emperor may have wished to become a leader, but he lacked the experience and temperament to do so. Introverted and given to moods of depression and indolence, he lived in isolation in one of his palaces or aboard his 600-ton air-conditioned yacht or escaped to the French Riviera, all the while salting away large sums of money in Swiss bank accounts. Not "the stuff of which Churchills are made," U. S. Ambassador Donald Heath lamented with marvelous understatement.[22]

The onset of the Korean War in the summer of 1950 added new dangers. North Korea's invasion of South Korea confirmed U.S. suspicions that the Soviet Union sought to conquer all of Asia, even at the risk of war, and the defense of Indochina assumed even greater importance. By the end of the year, however, the United States and France had suffered major reversals. Chinese intervention in Korea forced General Douglas MacArthur into headlong retreat from the Yalu River. In the meantime, Giap had inflicted upon France its "greatest colonial defeat since Montcalm had died at Quebec," trapping an entire army at Cao Bang in northeastern Vietnam and costing the French more than 6,000 troops and enough equipment to stock an entire Vietminh division.[23] Chinese intervention in Korea raised fears of a similar plunge into Vietnam, and American policymakers were increasingly concerned that growing defeatism in France would raise demands for withdrawal from Indochina.

The Franco-American Partnership in Vietnam

Against this background of stunning defeat, the Truman administration struggled to devise a workable policy for Indochina. With large numbers of U.S. troops committed to Korea and Europe vulnerable to a possible Soviet invasion, the Joint Chiefs of Staff (JCS) agreed that even should the Chinese invade Indochina, the United States could not commit military forces to its defense. France must bear primary responsibility for that war. More certain than ever that Indochina was essential to American security, the administration had to rely on military assistance to bolster French defenses. In late 1950, the United States committed more than $133 million for aid to Indochina and ordered immediate delivery of large quantities of arms and ammunition, naval vessels, aircraft, and military vehicles.

Most Americans agreed, however, that military equipment would not be enough. As early as May, Acheson complained that the French seemed "paralyzed, in a state of moving neither forward or backward."[24] A fact-finding mission dispatched to Indochina before the Cao Bang disaster reported that the French state of mind was "fatuous, even dangerous," and warned that unless France prosecuted the war with greater determination, used native manpower more effectively, and moved boldly and generously to win over the Vietnamese, the United States and its ally might be "moving into a debacle which neither of us can afford."[25] The JCS proposed that the United States condition its military aid on French pledges to take drastic measures, including the promise of eventual independence.

The administration approached this question with great caution. Acheson conceded that if the United States supported France's "old-fashioned colonial attitudes," it might "lose out." But the French presence was essential to defend Indochina against communism, he quickly added, and the United States could not press France to the point where it would say, "All right, take over the damned country. We don't want it." Admitting the inconsistency of American policy, he saw no choice but to encourage the French to remain until the crisis had eased but at the same time persuade them to "play with the nationalist movement and give Bao Dai a chance really to get the nationalists on his side."[26] The administration would go no further than to gently urge France to make symbolic concessions and build a Vietnamese army, in the meantime holding Bao Dai's "feet to the fire" to get him to assert effective leadership under French tutelage.[27]

To strengthen the governments of Indochina and increase their popular appeal, the United States between 1950 and 1952 spent more than $50 million for economic and technical assistance. American experts provided fertilizer and seeds to increase agricultural production, constructed dispensaries, developed malaria-control programs, and distributed food and clothing to refugees. To ensure achievement of its objectives, the United States insisted that the aid go directly to the native governments. To secure maximum propaganda advantage, zealous U.S. aid officials tacked posters on pagoda walls and air-dropped pamphlets into villages indicating that the programs were gifts of the United States and contrasting the "real gains" with "Communism's empty promises."[28]

The Truman policy brought limited results. Their hopes of victory revived by the prospect of large-scale American assistance, the French in late 1950 appointed the flamboyant General Jean de Lattre de Tassigny to command the armed forces in Indochina and instructed him to prosecute the war vigorously. A born crusader and practitioner of what he called *dynamisme,* de Lattre announced upon arriving in Vietnam that he would win the war within fifteen months, and under his inspired leadership French forces repulsed a major Vietminh offensive in the Red River Delta in early 1951. But when de Lattre attempted to follow up his success by attacking Vietminh strongholds just south of Hanoi, France suffered its worst defeat of the war. De Lattre himself would die of cancer in early 1952, and the French military position was more precarious at the time of his death than when he had come to Vietnam.

In other areas as well there was little progess. Desperately short of manpower, the French finally put aside their reluctance to arm the Vietnamese, and de Lattre made determined efforts to create a Vietnamese National Army (VNA). The Vietnamese were understandably reluctant to fight for a French cause, however, and by the end of 1951 the VNA numbered only 38,000 men, far short of its projected strength of 115,000. Responding to American entreaties, the French vaguely promised to "perfect" the independence of the Associated States, but the massive infusion of American supplies and de Lattre's early victories seemed to eliminate any compelling need for real concessions. The French were unwilling to fight for Vietnamese independence and never seriously considered the only sort of concession that would have satisfied the aspirations of Vietnamese nationalism. France transferred to the "free states" some additional responsibilities, but their governments remained shadow governments lacking in real authority and popular support.

By 1952, the United States was bearing roughly one-third of the cost of the war, but it was dissatisfied with the results and with its inability to influence French military policy. A small Military Assistance and Advisory Group (MAAG) had been sent to Vietnam in 1950 to screen French requests for aid, assist in the training of Vietnamese soldiers, and advise on strategy. By going directly to Washington to get what he wanted, however, de Lattre reduced the MAAG to virtual impotence. Proud, sensitive, and highly nationalistic, he ignored the American "advisers" in formulating strategy, denied them any role in training the Vietnamese, and refused even to inform them of his current operations and future plans.[29]

Deeply suspicious of American intrusion into their domain, the French expressed open resentment against the aid program and placed numerous obstacles in its way. De Lattre bitterly complained that there were too many Americans in Vietnam spending too much money, that the U.S. aid program was making France "look like a poor cousin in Vietnamese eyes," and that Americans were "fanning the flames of extreme nationalism." At a dinner for the U.S. consul in Hanoi in the spring of 1951, he launched into an anti-American tirade that lasted until 1:00 A.M. , raving like a "madman," according to a British diplomat, and accusing the United States of trying to replace France in Vietnam. French officials attempted to block projects that did not contribute directly to the war and encouraged Vietnamese suspicions by warning that American aid contained "hidden traps" to subvert their "independence." Largely as a result of French obstructionism, the aid program touched only a small number of people. American officials conceded that its "beneficial psychological results were largely negated because the United States at the same time was pursuing a program of [military] support to the French." America was looked upon "more as a supporter of colonialism than as a friend of the new nation."[30]

While firmly resisting U.S. influence, France demanded additional military assistance, and the United States could do little but comply. By early 1952, the domino theory was firmly rooted as a principle of U.S. foreign policy. Policymakers agreed that Southeast Asia must not be permitted to "fall into the hands of the Communists like a ripe plum" and that a continued French presence in Indochina was essential to that end.[31] Aware that the threat to Indochina had increased since 1950, and fearful that the French might pull out if their requests were not met, the administration in June 1952 approved $150 million in military assistance. Although thoroughly dissatisfied with France's performance in the war and deeply annoyed by its secretiveness and obstructionism, Truman and Acheson rejected Defense Department proposals to use the leverage afforded by aid to force France to adopt a "dynamic program" to "produce positive improvement in the military and political situation." The State Department feared that if it "pressed the French too hard they would withdraw and leave us holding the baby."[32]

America's Indochina policy continued to be a hostage to its policy in Europe. Since 1951, the United States had been pressing for allied approval of the European Defense Community, a plan for the integration of French and German forces into a multinational army originally put forward by France to delay German rearmament. The French repeatedly warned that they could not furnish troops for European defense without generous American support in Indochina, a ploy Acheson accurately described as "blackmail." The European Defense Community had also become a volatile political issue in France, where there was strong resistance to surrendering the identity of the French army and collaborating with a recent, and still despised, enemy. With the question awaiting ratification by the French parliament, Acheson later recalled, no one "seriously advised" that it would be "wise to end, or threaten to end, aid to Indochina unless an American plan of military and political reform was carried out."[33]

Despite a considerable investment in Indochina, Truman and Acheson left to their successors a problem infinitely more complex and dangerous than the one they had taken on in 1950. What had begun as a localized rebellion against French colonialism had expanded into an international conflict of major proportions. The United States was now bearing more than 40 percent of the cost of the war and had established a stake in its outcome. Chinese aid to the Vietminh had increased from 400 tons [of equipment] per month to more than 3,000, and Chinese advisers trained the Vietminh army and helped plan its major campaigns. The war had spilled over into neighboring Laos and Thailand, where China and the Vietminh backed insurgencies against governments supported by the United States and France. In Vietnam, itself, French control had been reduced to enclaves around Hanoi, Haiphong, and Saigon, and a narrow strip along the Cambodian border, and France faced a new and much more ominous type of military threat. "The enemy, once painted as a bomb-throwing terrorist or hill sniper lurking in night ambush," American journalist Theodore White observed, "has become a modern army, increasingly skillful, armed with artillery, organized into divisional groups."[34]

French military operations had settled into a frustrating and debilitating pattern. The Vietminh by this time were deeply entrenched in the Red River Delta, using the rugged terrain and exceptional skills at camouflage to conceal themselves. In late 1952, the French high command launched Operation Lorraine, its largest operation of the war, mobilizing nearly 30,000 troops plus tanks and artillery to attack the Vietminh's delta strongholds. The hope was to draw the enemy into a set-piece battle where superior firepower could chew them up. French forces plunged deep into Vietminh territory without meeting significant resistance. When the roadbound French convoys sought to withdraw, however, they were caught in a series of deadly ambushes and chopped to pieces. Not for the last time, the French would not get their set-piece battle. Operation Lorraine cost nearly a battalion in casualties and tied up large-scale forces desperately needed elsewhere.[35]

The French had naively hoped that American aid might be a substitute for increased sacrifice on their own part, but they had come to realize that it only required more of them. Fearful of their nation's growing dependence on the United States and aware that victory would require an all-out effort, in late 1952 some French political leaders outside the Communist party began for the first time to recommend withdrawal from Indochina. The "real" problem, Acheson warned the incoming administration, was the "French will to carry on the . . . war."[36]

Notes

1. Edward R. Stettinius, Jr., Diary, March 17, 1944, Edward R. Stettinius, Jr., Papers, University of Virginia Library, Charlottesville, Va. For Roosevelt and Indochina, see Walter LaFeber, "Roosevelt, Churchill, and Indochina, 1942–1945," *American Historical Review*, 80 (December 1975), 1277–1295; Garry R. Hess, "Franklin D. Roosevelt and Indochina," *Journal of American History*, LIX (September 1972), 353–368; and Christopher Thorne, "Indochina and Anglo-American Relations, 1942–1945," *Pacific Historical Review*, XLV (February 1976), 73–96.

2. Significantly, some Vietminh officials were also wary of Roosevelt's trusteeship scheme, considering it only one step removed from colonialism. See Robert K. Brigham, "Cautious Allies: The Vietminh and the O.S.S., 1945," paper delivered at the annual meeting of the Society for Historians of American Foreign Relations, June 1991.

3. Office of Strategic Services, "Problems and Objectives of United States Policy," April 2, 1945, Harry S. Truman Papers, Harry S. Truman Library, Independence, Mo., Rose Conway File, Box 15.

4. James Dunn memorandum, April 23, 1945, 851G.00/4-2345, Department of State Records, National Archives, Washington, D.C. See also George C. Herring, "The Truman Administration and the Restoration of French Sovereignty in Indochina," *Diplomatic History*, I (Spring 1977), 97–117.

5. Department of State, "Policy Statement on Indochina," September 27, 1948, in Department of State, *Foreign Relations of the United States* (Washington, D.C., 1974), VI, 48. Hereafter cited as *FR* with date and volume number.

6. Robert Blum, "Ho Chi Minh and the United States, 1944–1946," in U.S. Senate, Committee on Foreign Relations, *The United States and Vietnam, 1944–1947* (Washington, D.C., 1972), p. 13.

7. Quoted in Mark Bradley, "An Improbable Opportunity: America and the Democratic Republic of Vietnam's 1947 Initiative," in Jayne S. Werner and Luu Doan Huynh (eds.), *The Vietnam War: Vietnamese and American Perspectives* (New York, 1993), pp. 13–14.

8. "Policy and Information Statement on Indochina," July 1947, Philippine and Southeast Asia Branch File, Department of State Records, Box 10.

9. George C. Marshall to U.S. Embassy Paris, February 3, 1947, *FR, 1947*, VI, 67–68.

10. George McT. Kahin, *Intervention: How America Became Involved in Vietnam* (New York, 1986), pp. 7–8.

11. Qiang Zhai, "Transplanting the Chinese Model: Chinese Military Advisers and the First Vietnam War, 1950–1954," *Journal of Military History, 57* (October 1993), 689–715; Jian Chen, "China and the First Indochina War, 1950–1954," *China Quarterly* (March 1993), 85–110.

12. NSC 68, April 14, 1950, printed in *Naval War College Review* (May–June 1975), 51–108.

13. NSC 48/I, "The Position of the United States with Respect to Asia," December 23, 1949, U.S. Congress, House, Committee on Armed Services, *United States–Vietnam Relations, 1945–1967: A Study Prepared by the Department of Defense* (Washington, 1971), Book 8, 226–272; Michael Schaller, "Securing the Great Crescent: Occupied Japan and the Origins of Containment in Southeast Asia," *Journal of American History, 69* (September 1982), 392–413; Ronald McGlothen, *Controlling the Waves: Dean Acheson and U.S. Foreign Policy in Asia* (New York, 1993), 191–201.

14. *Department of State Bulletin* (February 13, 1950), 244; Charles Yost memorandum, January 31, 1950, *FR, 1950*, VI, 710–711.

15. Dean Rusk to James H. Burns, March 7, 1950, U.S. Congress, Senate Subcommittee on Public Buildings and Grounds, *The Pentagon Papers (The Senator Gravel Edition)* (4 vols.; Boston, 1971), I, 363. Hereafter cited as *Pentagon Papers (Gravel)*.

16. Dean Acheson to U.S. Embassy Manila, January 7, 1950, *FR, 1950*, VI, 692; Gary R. Hess, "The First American Commitment in Indochina: The Acceptance of the Bao Dai Solution," *Diplomatic History*, 2 (Fall 1978), 331–350.

17. Quoted in Jean Lacouture, *Ho Chi Minh: A Political Biography* (New York, 1968), p. 119.

18. Charles Reed to C. Walton Butterworth, April 14, 1949, 851G.00/4–1449, Department of State Records.

19. Acheson to Truman, May 14, 1950, Truman Papers, Confidential File. For an excellent discussion of the initial commitment in Indochina, see Robert M. Blum, *Drawing the Line: The Origin of the American Containment Policy in East Asia* (New York, 1982), especially pp. 198–213.

20. Tilman Durdin, "War 'Not for Land but for People,' " *New York Times Magazine* (May 28, 1950), 48.

21. Robert Shaplen, *The Lost Revolution: The U.S. in Vietnam, 1946–1966* (New York, 1966), p. 64.

22. Heath to John Foster Dulles, April 28, 1953, *FR, 1952–1954*, XIII, 523; Ellen Hammer, "The Bao Dai Experiment," *Pacific Affairs*, 23 (March 1950), 58.

23. Bernard Fall, *Street without Joy* (New York, 1972), p. 33.

24. Minutes of meeting. National Security Council, May 4, 1950, Truman Papers, President's Secretary's File.

25. Melby Mission Report, August 6, 1950, *FR, 1950*, VI, 843–844; Policy Planning Staff Memorandum, August 16, 1950, ibid., 857–858.

26. U.S. Congress, Senate, *Reviews of the World Situation: 1949–1950 Hearings Held in Executive Session before the Committee on Foreign Relations* (Washington, D.C., 1974), pp. 266–268, 292–293.

27. Livingston Merchant to Dean Rusk, October 19, 1950, *FR, 1950*, VI, 901–02.

28. Mutual Security Agency, *Dateline Saigon—Our Quiet War in Indochina* (Washington, D.C., 1952). The United States Information Service even prepared a Vietnamese-language edition of the *Outline History of the United States* with an introduction by President Truman expressing hope that an "account of the progress of the American people toward a just and happy society can be an inspiration to those Vietnamese who today know something of the same difficulties as they build a new nation." Roger Tubby to Joseph Short, March 8, 1951, Truman Papers, Official File 203-F. The French dismissed as the "height of national egotism" the fact that this first book translated by Americans into Vietnamese was a history of the United States. Heath to Secretary of State, June 14, 1951, *FR, 1951*, VI, 425–427.

29. Ronald H. Spector, *Advice and Support: The Early Years, 1941–1960* (Washington, D.C., 1983), pp. 115–121.

30. Shaplen, *Lost Revolution*, pp. 86–89; Embassy Saigon to Secretary of State, May 15, 1951, *FR, 1951*, VI, 419; Frank Gibbs to R. H. Scott, April 28, 1951, FO 371/92420, Foreign Office Records, Public Record Office, London.

31. NSC 124/2, June 24, 1952, *Pentagon Papers (Gravel)*, I, 385–386; "Pacific Security Pact," January 2, 1952, Truman Papers, President's Secretary's File, Churchill-Truman Meetings, Box 116.

32. Quoted in John M. Allison, *Ambassador from the Prairie, or Allison Wonderland* (New York, 1976), pp. 191, 194.

33. Dean G. Acheson, *Present at the Creation* (New York, 1969), p. 676.

34. Theodore H. White, "France Holds On to the Indo-China Tiger," *New York Times Magazine* (June 8, 1952), 9.

35. Fall, *Street Without Joy*, pp. 61–106.

36. Henry Cabot Lodge, Jr., *As It Was* (New York, 1976), p. 36.

CHAPTER 2

Fighting Shy
1953–1961

President Truman's modest commitment of aid to the French-backed government in Vietnam proved a snare from which the United States never extricated itself. The readings in this section suggest why. Truman's successor, Dwight Eisenhower, was unwilling to commit American power and prestige to salvage the dismal French military position in Vietnam, but that did not mean that he was giving up on the place: Ike ultimately intensified the American commitment, as David Anderson demonstrates. The Americans were dismayed when the French, in the aftermath of their defeat at Dienbienphu in 1954, agreed to partition Vietnam. Ellen Hammer shows why, describing in some detail the diplomatic maneuvering that occurred at the Geneva Conference during that spring and summer.

Col. Edward Lansdale picks up the story in 1955, when he was formally assigned to the U.S. Military Assistance Advisory Group (MAAG) in Saigon. Lansdale, who was reputed to have elevated counterinsurgency to the level of an art form in the Philippines, now worked to help South Vietnamese leader Ngo Dinh Diem gain control of the southern part of Vietnam. Through Lansdale, the Eisenhower administration endeavored to build a nation from a temporary cease-fire zone, subverting the intent of the Geneva accords. Although President Eisenhower for the most part kept the United States out of a shooting war in Vietnam, one may legitimately ask whether the administration's opposition to the Geneva accords set the stage for deeper U.S. involvement in the future.

The U.S. delegation at the beginning of the Geneva Conference on May 8, 1954. The United States was unhappy with the settlement that temporarily partitioned Vietnam at the seventeenth parallel and promised only that it would not disturb the agreement by force. At center foreground is Gen. Walter Bedell Smith, head of the delegation. COURTESY UPI/BETTMANN NEWSPHOTOS

3
Dwight D. Eisenhower and
Wholehearted Support of Ngo Dinh Diem
DAVID L. ANDERSON

"The loss of South Vietnam would set in motion a crumbling process that could, as it progressed, have grave consequences for us and for freedom," President Dwight D. Eisenhower declared in an April 1959 speech.[1] This statement reaffirmed the famous "falling domino" analogy that he had used five years earlier to explain the strategic importance of Indochina. If the states of Southeast Asia fell under "the Communist dictatorship," he asserted in April 1954, the result would be a "disintegration" with the "most profound influence" for "millions and millions and millions of people."[2] Throughout his eight years as president, Eisenhower never wavered in his conviction that the survival of an independent, noncommunist government in southern Vietnam was a vital strategic imperative for the United States. This objective, which Eisenhower's successors in the White House would also support, was the cornerstone of his policies in Southeast Asia, but it left open the question of the means of achieving that goal.

Eisenhower and his foreign policy advisers went through two stages in attempting to devise a successful method of securing U.S. interests in Vietnam. The first approach, which lasted through 1954 and into 1955, was to continue the Truman tactic of working with and through the French and other Western allies to contain communism in Southeast Asia. During this early phase, Eisenhower showed remarkable restraint considering the administration's Cold War rhetoric about the global danger of communist expansionism. He managed to avoid involving the United States militarily in Indochina as France suffered a humiliating defeat at Dienbienphu at the hands of the communist-led Vietminh army. After the French surrender at Dienbienphu, an international conference at Geneva, Switzerland, arranged a Franco-Vietminh cease-fire in July 1954. In the following months, the Eisenhower administration tried to maintain an allied strategy in Indochina. It established the Southeast Asia Treaty Organization (SEATO) and sent a special mission to Vietnam headed by General J. Lawton Collins to attempt, among other things, to continue a joint U.S.-French program in the region.

By the spring of 1955, however, the administration had begun a second, essentially unilateral approach in which the United States sought to protect its strategic interests in Southeast Asia by building a new Vietnamese nation around a reclusive autocrat named Ngo Dinh Diem. For the remainder of the Eisenhower presidency, the United States pegged its Vietnam policy on the questionable ability of Diem. In contrast to the cautious good judgment of the first phase that limited U.S. risks in Southeast Asia, the second phase exhibited a tragic irresponsibility by enmeshing the United States in the tangled web of Vietnamese politics and exposing Americans and American interests to considerable danger.

Eisenhower brought with him to the White House the conviction that the areas of the world "in which freedom flourishes" were under assault from a "Communist-regimented unity."[3] In his first State of the Union address in February 1953, he described France's struggle against the Vietminh as holding "the line of freedom" against "Communist aggression throughout the world."[4] As he prepared to leave office eight years later, his bipolar perception of the world divided between freedom and tyranny—

with Southeast Asia at the center of that conflict—had not altered. Eisenhower's farewell address to the nation is remembered primarily for its warning against the dangerous influence of the military-industrial complex in America, but the speech opened with the stern reminder that the nation had faced and would continue to confront "a hostile ideology—global in scope, atheistic in character, ruthless in purpose, and insidious in method."[5] The next day, on January 19, 1961, he warned president-elect John Kennedy that the civil war then raging in Laos threatened to spread communism throughout the entire region.

Besides his commitment to no compromise with world communism, the other hallmark of Eisenhower's policies in Indochina and elsewhere was cost reduction. In a strategy labeled the New Look, his administration sought the most economical ways to protect U.S. security. Commonly associated with the threat to use nuclear force for "massive retaliation," the New Look also called for a greater reliance on military alliances and covert operations.[6]

The New Look was apparent during the initial phase of the administration's Indochina policies in the effort to work with France to defeat the Vietnamese communists. Although they shared the Truman administration's displeasure at the French intent to recolonize Indochina, the Republicans decided that the Cold War required them to stand with their North Atlantic Treaty Organization (NATO) ally. Secretary of State John Foster Dulles candidly admitted to the Senate Foreign Relations Committee that U.S. choices in this situation were distasteful, but in "the divided spirit" of the world today, the United States would have to tolerate the colonialists a bit longer to help block Soviet and Chinese infiltration of Southeast Asia.[7] Dulles also felt compelled to cooperate with France in Indochina because he wanted French officials to accept a rearmed West Germany (a frightening prospect for many in France) as part of a U.S.-backed plan for NATO called the European Defense Community. To bolster French resolve in both Indochina and Europe, the Eisenhower administration increased U.S. aid to the point that it accounted for almost 80 percent of France's military expenditures in Southeast Asia by January 1954.[8]

As the Eisenhower administration observed its first anniversary in office, however, Paris's perseverance was waning. The French public and politicians were tiring of the seven-year burden of the Indochina war. The resilient Vietminh, under the charismatic leadership of Ho Chi Minh, continued to exact a heavy price in blood and treasure from their would-be masters. To the regret of Washington, French leaders accepted a Soviet proposal for a multinational conference at Geneva, set to begin in April, that would attempt to structure a diplomatic settlement in Indochina. Then, in March, the Vietminh assaulted an entrenched French garrison at Dienbienphu with such overwhelming force that a French military disaster appeared possible on the eve of the truce talks. The French might decide at Geneva to capitulate to their communist foes.

The prospect of a socialist ally of the Soviet Union and the People's Republic of China (PRC) emerging triumphant over a member of NATO that had been openly aided by the United States deeply troubled U.S. leaders, who began serious consideration of the New Look's trump card—massive retaliation. Although this option implied the possibility of using nuclear weapons, few U.S. planners believed that the atomic bomb was necessary to balance the military scales at Dienbienphu. In this case, the proposal involved a staggering conventional bombardment of the attacking force using as many as 350 planes from U.S. aircraft carriers and from bases in Okinawa and the Philippines.[9]

Throughout March and April, Eisenhower, Dulles, and other top administration officials weighed the air strike idea but never used it. In early May, the French garrison surrendered after sustaining heavy losses, and this outcome set the stage for the signing of a cease-fire agreement between France and the Vietminh at Geneva. This turn of events has long fascinated observers of Eisenhower's foreign policies. The president and his secretary of state encouraged the image that their hands were tied by congressional and allied reluctance to countenance a risky and perhaps unwarranted rescue of France's failed ambitions. Although this characterization made the White House appear passive, it paid excellent political dividends. It helped shield Eisenhower from personal attacks that he had "lost" something in Vietnam, as Truman had been excoriated for allegedly losing China.

While in office, Eisenhower was beloved by many Americans who admired his leadership of the Allied forces that defeated Nazi tyranny during World War II and who appreciated his humble demeanor and engaging grin. At the same time, however, he seemed to be a rather lackadaisical chief executive who presided over but did not propel his administration. The later declassification of confidential White House files reversed this picture dramatically. The record revealed Eisenhower to be directly and often decisively involved in key decisions such as those on Indochina in 1954. His management of the Dienbienphu crisis has become something of a centerpiece of the rehabilitation of his presidential image in recent years. He utilized the skills of talented subordinates such as Dulles and let them absorb some of the public pressure produced by controversial actions, but the president kept a firm, if hidden, hand on the administration's helm.[10]

The origin of Eisenhower's leadership ability is clear. His rise to the pinnacle of the nation's military structure as a five-star general provided him with a wealth of experience that prepared him to be president. The military had been his leadership laboratory, and his advancement up the ranks in competition with other extremely able officers revealed that he was an adept student of management theory. His method of handling subordinates, for example, was carefully considered. During World War II, he delegated extensive responsibility to such forceful commanders as George Patton and Omar Bradley, but he retained the authority to call them to account when necessary. Similarly, his approach to public relations, contingency planning, and other areas of executive responsibility demonstrated active leadership and effective management style.[11]

The details of the Dienbienphu decision have especially enhanced Eisenhower's reputation. Confronted with a military-diplomatic problem that corresponded to his personal experience, he confidently shaped the policy deliberations. Neither Dulles nor Vice-President Richard M. Nixon, both of whom often spoke out publicly and stridently on foreign policy, fashioned the administration's actions. The president made the decisions that kept U.S. ground and air forces out of combat. "It would be a great mistake for the United States to enter the fray in partnership only with France," Eisenhower believed; "united action by the free world was necessary, and in such action the U.S. role would not require use of its ground troops."[12] The prudence of his course appears statesmanlike in contrast to the steps of later presidents who plunged U.S. forces into hostile action in Southeast Asia.[13]

Yet praise for the decision can easily be overdrawn. Eisenhower's restraint had more to do with the immediate predicament of the French and the perception that Paris had lost the will to fight than with any careful reassessment of U.S. purposes in Vietnam. He was willing to accept a tactical setback in the Cold War at Dienbienphu but was not prepared to question the proclaimed importance of Indochina in the global balance of power. Also, it is a mistake to conclude that Eisenhower was an energetic leader just because the career soldier chose to involve himself personally in a national security issue. A few days after the French garrison surrendered, for example, the U.S. Supreme Court issued its momentous school desegregation decision, *Brown v. the Board of Education of Topeka*. On the matter of racial injustice, which burdened millions of American citizens every day, the president chose to stay uninvolved, declaring that he would express neither "approbation nor disapproval" of the Court's action.[14]

When the Court ruled on the *Brown* case, U.S. delegates were sitting at the Geneva Conference deliberating the fate of Vietnam. The Vietminh victory at Dienbienphu made it likely that the French would accept a compromise with the communists. The Eisenhower administration took a largely passive role in the proceedings to avoid any responsibility for the outcome, but the United States maintained a presence there because the president and his advisers were not willing to embark on a separate, solitary course in the region. With Britain, the USSR, and the PRC mediating, the French and Vietminh reached a cease-fire agreement that temporarily partitioned the country at the 17th parallel. The communist-led Democratic Republic of Vietnam (DRV) would control the North, and France would regroup its military forces in the South. An all-Vietnam election was to be held in two years to determine the future political structure of the nation. The U.S. delegation publicly acknowledged these terms but did not sign or verbally endorse any of them.[15]

Determined to salvage the southern part of Vietnam from communist domination and to do so by collective defense if possible, the Eisenhower administration championed the creation of SEATO in September 1954. Comprising the United States, France, Britain, Australia, New Zealand, the Philippines, Thailand, and Pakistan, this alliance was not a binding security pact like NATO, but it did provide a mechanism for possible joint action in future crises like Dienbienphu and especially in the event of overt aggression by the DRV or PRC. Under the terms of the Geneva Accords, Vietnam and neighboring Laos and Cambodia could not enter into military agreements, but the SEATO pact extended a vague commitment to their security in an attached protocol. Despite the treaty's weaknesses, Dulles hailed it as a "no trespassing" sign to warn away potential communist aggressors, and Eisenhower and his successors in the White House cited SEATO as the authority for U.S. intervention in the region's affairs.[16]

Eisenhower's handling of Dienbienphu, Geneva, and SEATO, taken together, highlighted the strengths and weaknesses of his leadership style. He was managing the Vietnam issue politically but not solving it substantively. Using Dulles as his primary spokesman, Eisenhower had urged "united action" during the siege of Dienbienphu to counter the communist threat in Southeast Asia. With the formation of SEATO, such allied unity seemed possible. Opinion polls indicated that the American public favored this kind of multilateral approach over unilateral action. Similarly, Eisenhower's decision to maintain a discreet distance from the negotiations and final settlement at Geneva avoided a charge that he had accepted a compromise with communists—an allegation that critics had made against Franklin Roosevelt after the Yalta Conference of 1945. The American people wanted toughness in U.S. policy without the risk of war, and the administration's coolness toward the Geneva Accords and its creation of SEATO suited this public mood. In terms of policy, however, toughness alone was not a solution. The true alternatives were either to use force to break DRV power or to accept DRV success. The administration would do neither and hence only deepened the U.S. commitment in Southeast Asia with no realistic prospect for resolving the dilemma of how to protect U.S. interests without war.[17]

Although France entered SEATO, U.S.-French cooperation in Southeast Asia after the Geneva Conference was strained almost to the breaking point. Eisenhower and many of his aides believed that Paris had essentially forfeited its influence on Western policies in Indochina with its weak performance against the Vietminh. The president complained that he was "weary" of the French and their "seemingly hysterical desire to be thought such a 'great power.' "[18] Still, many of the French had strong economic and personal ties with Indochina and were loath to surrender what remained of their position.

In an effort to reestablish a working relationship with French officials in South Vietnam, Eisenhower sent General J. Lawton Collins, a trusted World War II colleague and former army chief of staff, to Saigon in November 1954 as his personal representative. "Lightning Joe" Collins was also to formulate "a crash program to sustain the Diem government and establish security in Free Vietnam." The president thought that French officials in Saigon would cooperate, but, if not, "we ought to lay down the law to the French," he told the National Security Council. "It is true that we have to cajole the French with regard to the European area," Eisenhower added, "but we certainly didn't have to in Indochina."[19]

Collins had some success with military training programs and bureaucratic changes, but eventually his mission and U.S. policy in general reached an impasse with the French over the internal political structure of the South. At issue was the leadership of Ngo Dinh Diem. While the Geneva Conference was under way, Emperor Bao Dai had made Diem prime minister of the State of Vietnam, the vacuous regime that French officials had created as a Vietnamese nationalist alternative to the Vietminh and their alien Marxist ideology. It was this government, currently under the protection of the French in their regroupment zone south of the 17th parallel, that would face the DRV and its president Ho Chi Minh in the Geneva-mandated elections. Not all Vietnamese approved of the Vietminh, who had often ruthlessly silenced their political rivals, but the leaders of the DRV enjoyed the advantage of having forced the capitulation of the colonialists. Diem's regime would have to prove its ability and its patriotism if it was going to shake the appearance of dependence on the Westerners. Some Americans thought Diem might be able to meet this challenge, but only if the French allowed him the true independence to do so.

Diem himself was a complex individual. He was personally honest and courageous and had a well-established record of resistance to French domination of his homeland. These qualities were assets for a Vietnamese politician. He had genuine liabilities, though, that the French were quick to emphasize. He had no political base except his own large family, which had a well-earned reputation for clannish self-interest. His Catholic religion may have pleased the French but only served to isolate him from his predominantly Buddhist countrymen. His personality was aloof, even monkish—the opposite of the modern politician. In addition, he had lived briefly in the United States and knew some influential American politicians and church leaders, such as Senator Mike Mansfield (D-Mont.) and Francis Cardinal Spellman. In fact, it may have been Diem's ties to the United States that prompted Bao Dai to name him prime minister, in a move to court official U.S. support as French power waned in Vietnam.[20]

How Bao Dai came to appoint Diem, a man whom he disliked immensely, is not known with certainty. Some accounts have speculated that the CIA or some other secret U.S. influence was behind the selection. There is no particular evidence available for this scenario, however, and Bao Dai may well have had his own reasons. Clandestine American contact with Diem after he became prime minister has become well known. Covert initiatives were an explicit element of the New Look, and CIA Director Allen W. Dulles (the secretary of state's brother) sent a special agent to Saigon at the same time that Diem assumed office. Allen Dulles's choice was Air Force Colonel

Edward G. Lansdale, an unconventional warfare officer who had aided the Philippine government's successful resistance of a communist rebellion. Lansdale quickly became Diem's confidant and an ardent advocate for firm U.S. support of the prime minister.[21]

Despite endorsement of Diem from Lansdale and others, Eisenhower had given explicit instructions to Collins to evaluate Diem's leadership qualities.[22] After five months of close observation, Collins reported that he judged Diem incapable of providing South Vietnam with the dynamic leadership it needed. Diem and his brothers were running a "practically one-man government," the general informed Washington, and they were stubbornly resistant to helpful advice. Collins recommended other Vietnamese officials whom he thought could better organize a broad-based coalition to compete with the communists. Collins's report shocked Secretary of State Dulles. Although initially dubious of Diem's prospects, the secretary had come to accept the argument of Diem's American friends that the prime minister was the best hope for a nationalist alternative to Ho and that all Diem needed was the confidence that he had the "*wholehearted* backing" of the United States.[23]

Unlike the Dienbienphu discussions of the previous year, debate on the Diem issue in the spring of 1955 did not directly engage the president, Eisenhower chose to stand aside and let Secretary Dulles and General Collins reach a conclusion. The president was preoccupied with the Taiwan Straits crisis and the approach of his first summit conference with Soviet leaders. Meeting with Dulles and other State Department officials in Washington on April 25, Collins maintained his position that Diem was not indispensable, and the secretary reluctantly agreed. Literally at the moment these decisions were being made, street fighting erupted in Saigon. Probably instigated by Diem himself in a desperate demonstration to Washington, the violence enabled the prime minister to obtain enough backing from the fledgling South Vietnamese armed forces to quell the unrest. As Collins rushed back to Saigon to oversee U.S. interests in the unstable situation, Dulles's Asian advisers convinced him to reverse himself and to make wholehearted support of Diem the basis of U.S. policy. The aides argued that the violent outbreak proved that it was an inopportune time to tamper with Saigon's internal politics.[24]

Once the Eisenhower administration had determined that it would stick with Diem, the task remained to convince the French to accept this course. In early May, exactly a year after the surrender of Dienbienphu, Dulles met several times with French premier Edgar Faure. The sessions were stormy, but Faure finally acquiesced to Dulles's insistence on Diem.[25] It was clear that Paris no longer wished to contest Washington over the direction of Western policy in Vietnam. Through the rest of 1955, the French rapidly withdrew the remainder of their forces in South Vietnam and left the fate of the would-be nation to the Americans and their client Diem.

In the long-term history of U.S. involvement in Southeast Asia, Washington had turned an important corner. SEATO had provided a semblance of collective sanction to the U.S. intent to bolster South Vietnam, but the departure of the French demonstrated that the effort actually would be a unilateral U.S. program. The feasibility of the plan hinged on the questionable judgment that Diem could make it work. The administration entered a new and perilous policy phase.

With the basic decision having been made to build a nation around Diem, the implementation now fell to the foreign policy bureaucracy with little additional input from the president or Dulles. After Eisenhower suffered a heart attack in September 1955, many issues that his staff deemed routine, such as Vietnam, were kept from his schedule. The following year, Dulles developed abdominal cancer, and although he remained in office almost until his death in 1959, his personal agenda too became more restricted.[26] Yet the course that Eisenhower and Dulles had set in Vietnam remained the administration's policy until the end of Eisenhower's presidency, and occasionally the two men would publicly reaffirm the concept of wholehearted support for Diem.

The task of nation building loomed large before the administration. The legitimacy of Diem's regime rested only on his appointment by the heir of Vietnam's last royal dynasty, and Sa Majesté Bao Dai had taken up permanent residence on the French Riviera. The State of Vietnam had a small army of 150,000 led by an inexperienced officer corps that, under the French, had never been allowed to have any command or staff authority. The civil bureaucracy consisted only of *fonctionnaires* trained to take orders, not to solve problems. Industry was virtually nonexistent in South Vietnam, and the agricultural base of rice and rubber, although potentially valuable, had been wrecked by exploitative landlords who had impoverished much of the peasantry. Diem himself had no political following that could compete with the regimented and motivated cadre in the DRV.[27]

Diem's political weakness seemed especially important because of the national reunification elections that were supposed to occur in 1956. Although many observers of all ideological perspectives believed that Ho Chi Minh would win any truly free countrywide election, the chances of a referendum occurring were slim from the beginning. The Geneva conferees had drafted a vague proposal for elections because they could not fashion any workable political formula themselves. How the Vietnamese were to vote and on what was never specified. No official in North or South Vietnam had ever organized or conducted a free election, and there was no reason to expect that the Vietnamese would do so now under these strained circumstances. In the months following the Geneva Conference, it was clear that Diem and his American patrons had no enthusiasm for an election, but there was also no pressure for a vote from China, the Soviet Union, Britain, or France. None of these governments was inclined to assume any risk to itself to champion elections in Vietnam for the benefit of the DRV. The Eisenhower administration can be given little credit or blame for the failure of the election provisions of the Geneva agreements.[28]

Even without the serious possibility of a reunification vote, Diem's specious political legitimacy posed grave difficulties for U.S. objectives. Kenneth T. Young, the State Department officer in charge of Southeast Asian affairs, saw the problem as a paradox. He believed that if South Vietnam did not become a republic the anachronistic State of Vietnam would be easy prey for the revolutionary line of the DRV. At the same time, though, he feared that voting for a representative assembly in the South might open the door to political anarchy.[29] While Young and other Americans worried, Diem acted. He staged a lopsided referendum in October 1955 to depose Bao Dai and to make himself president of a newly created Republic of Vietnam (RVN). In March 1956, Diem organized an election of a constituent assembly, heavily stacked in his favor, to draft a constitution. The voting was not an exercise in democracy, but it was impressive evidence of the ability of the Ngo family, especially Diem's brothers Ngo Dinh Nhu and Ngo Dinh Can, to manipulate ballots. The RVN provided a facade of popular government for an ambitious family aspiring to centralized authority.[30]

Evidence of the emerging Ngo family dictatorship mounted. Nhu and Can operated a secret organization, the Can Lao, that used bribery and intimidation to garner personal support for Diem from key members of the military and bureaucracy. Vietminh "suspects," that is, persons thought disloyal to the regime, were arrested and sent to "reeducation camps." An RVN ordinance abolished elected village councils and substituted government appointees to run local affairs. Some U.S. officials, including Secretary Dulles, excused this authoritarianism as typical of Asia and even saw it as prudent because it provided a measure of stability in a nation still developing its institutional structure. Among his criticisms of Diem, Collins had warned that the Ngos' penchant for self-protection would only isolate Diem from the people and weaken the regime. That caution had been rejected, however, in favor of wholehearted support for Diem. As Collins had predicted, the Ngos increasingly behaved as if they could take U.S. aid for granted regardless of how they acted.[31]

The level of U.S. assistance to South Vietnam was high, almost $250 million annually through the end of the Eisenhower years. Some of these funds were designated for economic development. Very little aid went to the agricultural sector, but after U.S. urging, the Diem government announced some rent controls and land transfer plans, which went largely unimplemented. In the urban areas, a U.S.-designed Commercial Import Program made U.S. dollars available to subsidize imports. Rather than stimulate economic activity, however, the plan produced an influx of consumer goods, such as refrigerators and motorbikes, that created an appearance of prosperity but masked the lack of real economic growth.[32]

The bulk of U.S. aid, about 80 percent of it, went directly to the South Vietnamese armed forces. During the Eisenhower presidency, the number of U.S. military personnel in the RVN never exceeded 700, but the large percentage of U.S. aid that went for military purposes revealed the high priority placed on the military security of the new nation. Eighty-five percent of the funds for paying, equipping, and training the RVN's 150,000-man force came from the U.S. Treasury.[33]

Eisenhower and his advisers chose to declare Diem's leadership of South Vietnam a grand success, despite the repressive nature of the Saigon regime and its heavy dependency on aid. On May 8, 1957, the president himself stood on the hot parking apron at Washington National Airport to greet Diem as the RVN leader arrived for a highly publicized state visit. During the next four days, among lavish receptions and private meetings, Diem conferred with Eisenhower, Dulles, and other officials and addressed a joint session of Congress. This pageantry was part of a series of such events hosted by the administration for a number of Asian and African dignitaries. The purpose was to improve U.S. relations with the Third World, which, as Washington had learned during the Suez Canal crisis of 1956, could be vitally important. Diem was a beneficiary of this administration initiative in personal diplomacy.[34]

Eisenhower and other American speakers hailed Diem as a "tough miracle man" and the "savior" of South Vietnam.[35] The administration congratulated Diem and itself on his survival since 1954 and characterized the RVN as a stalwart ally in the struggle against world communism. Behind closed doors the rhetoric was friendly but somewhat more restrained. When Diem asked for an increase in U.S. aid, for example, Eisenhower rebuffed him with the explanation that U.S. global aid commitments prevented greater assistance. The Eisenhower-Diem summit reconfirmed the administration's earlier decisions to treat South Vietnam as strategically important and to give wholehearted endorsement to Diem's regime. It also showed that, even in a region of vital interest, the New Look principle of fiscal restraint still applied.[36]

In the late 1950s, Congress too was determined both to contain foreign aid budgets and to continue assistance to the Diem regime. Only once during the decade did congressional committees hold hearings specifically on Indochina, and that occasion was an investigation of alleged corruption in the management of the aid program in Saigon. Although both Democratic and Republican members questioned the amounts and uses of some funds, the probe uncovered no serious misconduct. At no time during the Eisenhower presidency did Congress as a body challenge the goals of the administration's policies in Vietnam. During the Dienbienphu crisis, some congressional leaders, including Senator Lyndon B. Johnson (D-Tex.), urged the White House to avoid a unilateral U.S. intervention in the French war, but that position was already preferred by the president. Later, as the U.S. commitment to Diem grew, a bipartisan alignment of lawmakers—many of them in an interest group called the American Friends of Vietnam that included Senator John F. Kennedy (D-Mass.)—staunchly defended U.S. involvement in the region.[37]

During Eisenhower's second term, two pressures largely shaped the conduct of U.S. policy in Southeast Asia: (1) the proclaimed value of South Vietnam to U.S. security and (2) the need to manage economically the United States' global obligations. These twin concerns often exasperated the diplomats and military officers charged with devising and implementing appropriate actions. The problem was how to do more with less. With his attention on Sputnik, Cuba, and elsewhere, the president provided no additional direction to U.S. policymakers as conditions within Vietnam worsened.

By 1957 and 1958, terrorism and armed insurrection were on the rise in South Vietnam. This violence often represented retaliation and resistance to Diem's increasingly repressive regime. Most of these incidents occurred without the instigation of Hanoi. The DRV had not given up its objective of reuniting Vietnam under its rule, but its leaders had ordered their southern cadres to be patient. Hanoi preferred to try propaganda and other destabilizing techniques first rather than to plunge into an armed conflict that could prompt a U.S. military attack on the North. Southern resistance leaders, who faced being jailed and even executed, refused to wait, however, and began acting on their own with assassinations, firebombings, and small attacks on RVN military units and outposts.[38]

Both Vietnamese and American officials in Saigon shared a mounting feeling of crisis, but the instructions from Washington remained clear that the nation-building program would have to make do with what it was already receiving, or likely even less, as the total foreign aid budget shrank.[39] The result was a bitter and debilitating battle between American diplomats and the Ngo family and among the Americans themselves over how to utilize the available resources. The issue was whether to increase the already high percentage of U.S. funds that went to military use or to place more emphasis on economic development and political reform.

U.S. Ambassador in Saigon Elbridge Durbrow took the lead in arguing that the RVN government would remain under attack from within as a neocolonialist dependent as long as it failed to take genuine steps toward improving the economic and social welfare of its citizens. He even went so far as to suggest to Washington that helicopters and other military items that Diem desired be withheld until the RVN president demonstrated progress on land reform, civil rights, and other abuses—urgent problems that were fueling the hostility toward his regime. Meanwhile, Diem and Nhu vehemently demanded more military aid of all types with which to increase the size and armament of their forces.[40]

Lieutenant General Samuel T. Williams, the chief of the U.S. Military Assistance Advisory Group in Vietnam, took sharp exception to Durbrow's views and sided with the Ngos. He argued that economic and political reforms remained impossible until the partisan violence had been crushed militarily. He also considered it deplorable that Durbrow would propose threatening to deny matériel to Diem at a time when the RVN government was under attack by armed and ruthless opponents. The general complained privately that the ambassador was better suited to be a salesman in a ladies' shoe store than a diplomat in Asia. Williams got support from Lansdale, now a brigadier general in the Pentagon, who advised his Defense Department superiors that Durbrow was "insulting, misinformed, and unfriendly" toward Diem.[41]

Lansdale's and Williams's personal attacks on the ambassador demonstrated that there was more to the policy debate than just the merits of military versus economic aid. In question was the long-standing Eisenhower administration commitment to whole-hearted support of Diem. The generals contended that rather than criticism and pres-sure, Diem needed Washington's acceptance and reassurance. With the backing of the State Department's Southeast Asia specialists, Durbrow maintained that no one, in-cluding Diem, was indispensable. In a pointed comment to his diplomatic colleagues, the ambassador recalled his Pentagon critic's past association with Diem: "We have to recognize that we are dealing with a somewhat more complicated situation in the case of the GVN [Government of Vietnam]," Durbrow declared, "and that we have left the 'Lansdale days' behind."[42] The intensity with which both sides argued revealed how important these officials considered Vietnam to be to the United States. The debate also gave no indication that any of these policymakers thought of doing nothing and simply leaving the outcome in Vietnam up to the Vietnamese.

In January 1961, a few days before John Kennedy took the oath of office as Eisenhower's successor, Lansdale returned from an inspection visit to South Vietnam with a dire report. The RVN was in "critical condition," he declared, and the Vietcong (Washington's new term for Vietnamese communists) "have started to steal the coun-try and expect to be done in 1961."[43] His urgent tone may have derived in part from his ongoing debate over tactics with State Department officers, but it also revealed that the time had come for either reaffirmation or reassessment of the United States' whole-hearted support of Diem and the RVN.

As Lansdale delivered his evaluation to the Pentagon, Eisenhower was briefing the president-elect on current world conditions. With a civil war under way in Laos in which the United States and the Soviet Union were supplying weapons to the contend-ing sides, their discussion turned to Southeast Asia. The retiring chief executive claimed that the SEATO treaty obligated the United States to defend the region from commu-nist encroachment. The United States should protect the area's security in cooperation with the SEATO allies if possible, but if not, Eisenhower advised, "then we must go it alone."[44] The next day, January 20, Eisenhower's constitutional authority over the di-rection of U.S. foreign policy expired, but the course that he had charted in Vietnam would continue.

A review of the long-term significance of the two phases of Eisenhower's Vietnam policies reveals that the second or post-1955 stage with its unilateral and assertive commitment to South Vietnam prevailed over the original multilateral and cautious approach. The goal during both periods was the same: to deny Vietnam or as much of it as possible to the Vietnamese communists. Phase one was a setback to this objective because it ended with de facto acceptance of communist control of the northern half of the country. Eisenhower's negative decision—to avoid taking overt action to resist this outcome—appears as a wise, statesmanlike acceptance of the reality of the Vietminh's success in resisting French colonialism. It was a caution dictated by the immediate circumstances, however. The second phase was also based upon a negative decision—to avoid acceptance of an internal Vietnamese resolution of political authority in the country.[45] This decision was far from statesmanlike. It failed to acknowledge Diem's neocolonial dependence on U.S. support. It placed U.S. actions in conflict with the manifest Vietnamese desire for national independence. Yet Washington's wholehearted support of Diem continued. By the time Eisenhower left office in 1961, the goal of a noncommunist South Vietnam and the means of obtaining that objective—nation building premised on the survival of the Diem regime—were so deeply embedded in U.S. global strategy as to be virtually unassailable.

Eisenhower's personal strengths served him well during the first phase. His knowledge of military affairs and the politics of war enabled him to perceive clearly the military and political costs inherent in U.S. intervention in the French war. His talent for utilizing a good staff organization also enhanced his analysis of policy options and enabled him to present the outcome as a bureaucratic decision. This maneuvering mitigated potential criticism about being pusillanimous in Vietnam.[46] During the second phase, these same strengths failed him. Once the Geneva cease-fire took effect, the issue in Vietnam was not one of military strategy but of the internal political and economic development of a new nation. Although his experience on General Douglas MacArthur's staff in the Philippines in the 1930s made Eisenhower sensitive to the aspirations of Asian nationalists and familiar with the frustrations of dealing with them, he had no personal acquaintance with any Vietnamese leaders and little grasp of the complex sociopolitical realities of the Asian communism that Diem faced.[47] His one meeting with Diem was largely ceremonial. Similarly, his system of having his staff sift through options did not help alleviate this problem of comprehending complexity. Indeed, the key staff member upon whom he relied for foreign policy advice, Secretary Dulles, generally accepted the single-minded fixation on Diem. It could be argued that Eisenhower's 1955 heart attack made him excessively dependent on his staff, but even after his recovery and return to a rather heavy work load, he gave little personal attention to the details of Vietnam, which his staff presented to him as an issue that was being managed well.[48] He accepted their optimistic assessments and, during Diem's 1957 visit, lent his voice to the chorus of praise for the RVN's achievements. Beneath the miracle facade, however, were serious problems: Diem's narrow political base, his regime's weak military structure, South Vietnam's weak economy, and the growing insurgency. When Eisenhower yielded the White House to Kennedy, the policy of wholehearted support of Diem remained in place not because it was achieving U.S. objectives but because to waver even slightly could risk collapse of the administration's eight-year effort to keep the dominoes from falling. Eisenhower's accomplishments in Vietnam were negative: no war, but no peace. It was a record of nonsolution and ever-narrowing options.

Notes

1. *Public Papers of the Presidents of the United States: Dwight D. Eisenhower, 1959* (Washington, D.C.: GPO, 1960), 311–13.
2. *Public Papers: Eisenhower, 1954* (Washington, D.C.: GPO, 1958), 382–84.
3. Dwight D. Eisenhower, *Crusade in Europe* (Garden City, N.Y.: Doubleday, 1948), 476.
4. *Public Papers: Eisenhower, 1953* (Washington, D.C.: GPO, 1958), 16.
5. *Public Papers: Eisenhower, 1960* (Washington, D.C.: GPO, 1961), 1035–40. See also Clark Clifford memorandum to Lyndon Johnson, September 29, 1967, U.S. Department of Defense, *The Pentagon Papers: The Defense Department History of United States Decision Making on Vietnam*, Senator Gravel edition, 4 vols. (Boston: Beacon Press, 1971), 2:635–37.
6. John L. Gaddis, *Strategies of Containment: A Critical Appraisal of Postwar American National Security Policy* (New York: Oxford University Press, 1982), 145–61.
7. U.S. Senate, *Executive Sessions of the Senate Foreign Relations Committee (Historical Series)*, vol. 5, 83d Cong., 1st sess., 1953 (Washington, D.C.: GPO, 1977), 385–88.

8. George McT. Kahin, *Intervention: How America Became Involved in Vietnam* (New York: Knopf, 1986), 42; George C. Herring, *America's Longest War: The United States and Vietnam, 1950–1975*, 2d ed. (New York: Knopf, 1986), 25–29.

9. Arthur W. Radford, *From Pearl Harbor to Vietnam: The Memoirs of Admiral Arthur W. Radford*, ed. Stephen Jurika, Jr. (Stanford, Calif.: Hoover Institution Press, 1980), 391–95; Ronald H. Spector, *The United States Army and Vietnam: Advice and Support: The Early Years, 1941–60* (Washington, D.C.: GPO, 1983), 199–202; John Prados, *The Sky Would Fall: Operation Vulture: The Secret U.S. Bombing Mission to Vietnam, 1954* (New York: Dial Press, 1983), 152–56.

10. For examples of this Eisenhower revisionism, see Fred I. Greenstein, *The Hidden-Hand Presidency: Eisenhower as Leader* (New York: Basic Books, 1982); John P. Burke and Fred I. Greenstein, *How Presidents Test Reality: Decisions on Vietnam, 1954 and 1965* (New York: Russell Sage Foundation, 1989); Stephen E. Ambrose, *Eisenhower*, 2 vols. (New York: Simon & Schuster, 1983–84); and Robert A. Divine, *Eisenhower and the Cold War* (New York: Oxford University Press, 1981). For an appraisal of this revisionism, see Chester J. Pach, Jr., and Elmo Richardson, *The Presidency of Dwight D. Eisenhower*, rev. ed. (Lawrence: University Press of Kansas, 1991), 237–39.

11. Fred I. Greenstein, "Dwight D. Eisenhower: Leadership Theorist in the White House," in Fred I. Greenstein, ed., *Leadership in the Modern Presidency* (Cambridge, Mass.: Harvard University Press, 1988), 76–107.

12. Arthur Minnich memorandum of conversation, no date, U.S. Department of State, *Foreign Relations of the United States, 1952–1954*, vol. 13, *Indochina* (Washington, D.C.: GPO, 1982), 1413 (hereafter cited as *FRUS*).

13. Melanie Billings-Yun, *Decision against War: Eisenhower and Dien Bien Phu, 1954* (New York: Columbia University Press, 1988); Richard E. Neustadt, *Presidential Power and the Modern Presidents: The Politics of Leadership from Roosevelt to Reagan* (New York: Free Press, 1990), 295–302; Richard H. Immerman, "Between the Unattainable and the Unacceptable: Eisenhower and Dienbienphu," in Richard A. Melanson and David Myers, eds., *Reevaluating Eisenhower: American Foreign Policy in the Fifties* (Urbana: University of Illinois Press, 1987), 120–21, 142–44.

14. Quoted in Harvard Sitkoff, *The Struggle for Black Equality, 1954–1980* (New York: Hill & Wang, 1981), 25. See also Robert Burk, *The Eisenhower Administration and Black Civil Rights* (Knoxville: University of Tennessee Press, 1984); George C. Herring and Richard H. Immerman, "Eisenhower, Dulles, and Dienbienphu: 'The Day We Didn't Go to War' Revisited," *Journal of American History* 71 (September 1984): 343–63; and Robert J. McMahon, "Eisenhower and Third World Nationalism: A Critique of the Revisionists," *Political Science Quarterly* 101 (Fall 1986): 453–73.

15. Herring, *America's Longest War*, 37–40; Lloyd C. Gardner, *Approaching Vietnam: From World War II through Dienbienphu, 1941–1954* (New York: Norton, 1988), 248–56, 281–84.

16. Memorandum of conversation, June 29, 1954, *FRUS, 1952–54*, vol. 12, *East Asia and the Pacific* (Washington, D.C.: GPO, 1984), 588. See also U.S. Department of State, *Bulletin* (September 20, 1954): 394–96; and Immerman, "Between the Unattainable and the Unacceptable," 145–46.

17. Burke and Greenstein, *How Presidents Test Reality*, 269–70; David L. Anderson, "China Policy and Presidential Politics, 1952," *Presidential Studies Quarterly* 10 (Winter 1980): 79–90.

18. Eisenhower to Alfred M. Gruenther, June 8, 1954, *FRUS, 1952–54*, 13: 1667–69.

19. Discussion at the 218th NSC meeting, October 22, 1954, ibid., 2157.

20. For various interpretations of Diem's appointment. see Herring, *America's Longest War*, 49; Kahin, *Intervention*, 78; Chester L. Cooper, *The Lost Crusade: America in Vietnam* (New York: Dodd, Mead, 1970), 20–21; Bui Diem and David Chanoff, *In the Jaws of History* (Boston: Houghton Mifflin, 1987), 71–72, 86; William C. Gibbons, *The U.S. Government and the Vietnam War: Executive and Legislative Roles and Relationships*, part 1,

1945–1960 (Princeton, N.J.: Princeton University Press, 1986), 266–67; and Robert Scheer, *How the United States Got Involved in Vietnam* (Santa Barbara, Calif.: Center for the Study of Democratic Institutions, 1965), 13–15.

21. Edward G. Lansdale, *In the Midst of Wars: An American's Mission to Southeast Asia* (New York: Harper & Row, 1972).

22. Eisenhower to Collins, November 3, 1954, *FRUS, 1952–54*, 13:2207; Andrew J. Goodpaster memorandum of conference with the president, November 3, 1954, box 3, Diary series, Ann Whitman File, Dwight D. Eisenhower Papers, Dwight D. Eisenhower Library, Abilene, Kans.

23. Dulles to Collins, April 20, 1955, *FRUS, 1955–57*, vol. 1, *Vietnam* (Washington, D.C.: GPO, 1985), 270–72 (Dulles's italics), See also Collins to Dulles, March 31, 1955, and April 7, 1955, ibid., 168–71, 218–21.

24. J. Lawton Collins, *Lightning Joe: An Autobiography* (Baton Rouge: Louisiana State University Press, 1979), 405–7.

25. John Foster Dulles, "An Historic Week—Report to the President," May 17, 1955, pp. 4–5, box 91, John Foster Dulles Papers, Princeton University Library.

26. Pach and Richardson, *Eisenhower*, 113–14, 203–4.

27. For a good description of Diem's Vietnam, see Robert Scigliano, *South Vietnam: Nation under Stress* (Boston: Houghton Mifflin, 1963).

28. William J. Sebald memorandum to Dulles, May 10, 1956, *FRUS, 1955–57*, 1:680–82; Kahin, *Intervention*, 88–92; Gibbons, *U.S. Government and the Vietnam War*, 1:299–300.

29. Kenneth T. Young memorandum to Walter S. Robertson, October 5, 1955, Young to G. Frederick Reinhardt, October 5, 1955, *FRUS, 1955–57*, 1:550–54.

30. Reinhardt to Dept. of State, November 29, 1955, ibid., 589–92; Reinhardt to Dulles, March 3, 1956, file 751G.00/3–356, and Reinhardt to Dulles, March 8, 1956, file 751G.00/3–856, U. S. Department of State General Records, Record Group 59, National Archives, Washington, D.C. (hereafter cited as RG 59).

31. Reinhardt to Dulles, December 6, 1955, file 751G.00/12–655, RG 59; G. Frederick Reinhardt interview by Philip A. Crowl, October 30, 1965, John Foster Dulles Oral History Project, Princeton University Library; Bernard B. Fall, *The Two Viet-Nams: A Political and Military Analysis*, rev. ed. (New York: Praeger, 1964), 246–68.

32. Arthur Z. Gardiner to Dept. of State, August 2, 1956, file 751G.5–MSP/8–256, and C. E. Lilien memorandum of conversation, December 10, 1957, file 751G.131/12–1057, RG 59; Kahin, *Intervention*, 84–88.

33. Scigliano, *South Vietnam*, 193; Fall, *Two Viet-Nams*, 289–306.

34. Program for Ngo Dinh Diem Visit, May 3, 1957, box 73, Subject series, White House Central Files (Confidential File), Eisenhower Library; Burton I. Kaufman, *Trade and Aid: Eisenhower's Foreign Economic Policy* (Baltimore: Johns Hopkins University Press, 1982), 99–110.

35. United States Department of State, *Bulletin* (May 27, 1957): 851; *Public Papers: Eisenhower, 1957* (Washington, D.C.: GPO, 1958), 417.

36. Elbridge Durbrow memorandum of conversation, May 9, 1957, *FRUS, 1955–57*, 1:794–99; Ambrose, *Eisenhower*, 2:376–81.

37. Gibbons, *U.S. Government and the Vietnam War*, 1:301–5, 320–27; John D. Montgomery, *The Politics of Foreign Aid: American Experience in Southeast Asia* (New York: Praeger, 1967), 221–35; Eisenhower, *Crusade in Europe*, 347; Dulles memorandum for the file, April 5, 1954, *FRUS, 1952–54*, 13:1224–25.

38. Kahin, *Intervention*, 109–15; Jeffrey Race, *War Comes to Long An: Revolutionary Conflict in a Vietnamese Province* (Berkeley: University of California Press, 1972), 105–22; William J. Duiker, *The Communist Road to Power in Vietnam* (Boulder, Colo.: Westview, 1981), 187–99.

39. Dulles to Durbrow, November 19, 1957, *FRUS, 1955–57*, 1:863–64.

40. Durbrow to Christian Herter, May 3, 1960, Durbrow to Daniel V. Anderson, July 18, 1960, *FRUS, 1958–60*, vol. 1, *Vietnam* (Washington, D.C.: GPO, 1986), 433–37, 514–15.

41. Lansdale to Edward J. O'Donnell, September 20, 1960, ibid., 580. See also memorandum prepared in Dept. of Defense, May 4, 1960, ibid., 439–41; and Samuel T. Williams to R. E. Lawless, May 15, 1962, box 8, Samuel T. Williams Papers, Hoover Institution Archives, Stanford, Calif.

42. Durbrow to Richard E. Usher, April 18, 1960, *FRUS, 1958–60*, 1:394.

43. Lansdale to Williams, January 17, 1961, box 8, Williams Papers. See also Lansdale to secretary of defense and deputy secretary of defense, January 17, 1961, box 49, Edward G. Lansdale Papers, Hoover Institution Archives.

44. Clifford to Johnson, September 29, 1967, *Pentagon Papers*, 2:635–37.

45. See James David Barber, *The Presidential Character: Predicting Performance in the White House,* 3d ed. (Englewood Cliffs, N.J.: Prentice-Hall, 1985), 134, 148, for a description of Eisenhower as a "passive-negative" president. For a favorable view of Eisenhower's negative achievements, see Divine, *Eisenhower*, 154–55.

46. Billings-Yun, *Decision against War*; Burke and Greenstein, *How Presidents Test Reality*, 268; Ambrose, *Eisenhower*, 2:185.

47. Burke and Greenstein, *How Presidents Test Reality*, 263–64; Ambrose, *Eisenhower*, 1:104–18.

48. Neustadt, *Presidential Power*, 133–34, 301.

4
Geneva, 1954: The Precarious Peace
ELLEN J. HAMMER

In 1954 a precarious peace came to Indochina. It came because Frenchmen had lost any desire to continue a fight which they could not possibly win against the Viet Minh; because the United States was not prepared to take over the war alone; because for the Soviet Union an Indochinese cease-fire seemed consistent with Communist international strategy; because the Chinese, finally, courting public opinion in neutral Asia and the free world, urged concessions on the Viet Minh. Even so, peace came only with difficulty.

Making peace was such a complex task because it had been so long neglected. More than ten years before, Franklin D. Roosevelt, who was concerned about the future of Indochina, had expressed the belief that the Vietnamese people merited a regime under which they could achieve their freedom, and that it was the responsibility of the United States and its allies to establish such a regime. In the years that followed, the American people and the leaders of both parties, Democrats and Republicans alike, often forgot the meaning of these objectives even though they sometimes paid lip service to them. It was only in 1954 that an American delegation arrived in Geneva to consider how to stop a war which should never have been allowed to start; and then the bargaining power of the United States' friends in Indochina was so slight that American officials were not at all sure that the timing or the circumstances were right for negotiations.

This was an awkward time for American policy-makers; they were forced to recognize the unpalatable fact that practically all of the assumptions underlying United States policy in Indochina were simply not true.

First, there was the assumption that the American Government had been helping the French and the peoples of Indochina not only to fight Communism but also to win freedom for Viet Nam, Laos, and Cambodia. In Viet Nam, this would have made sense if the people knew something of the nature of political freedom and understood the oppressive nature of international Communism; some American officials seemed to have confused the Vietnamese peasant masses with the sophisticated German workers who rose in open revolt against Communism in East Berlin. The only freedom that most Vietnamese wanted was not from Communism, about which they knew little and understood less, but from France; and Communist-dominated though it was, the Viet Minh was the only force in the country fighting for an independence which the French were persistently unwilling to grant. This was the reason why so many Vietnamese supported the Viet Minh and why the neutralist nations of Asia, with their aversion for colonialism, no matter how anti-Communist their own internal policies, would not take an open stand against the Viet Minh. Only in Laos and Cambodia was the independence issue fairly clear-cut; and the people of both those countries, although determined to oppose any Viet Minh encroachments on their territory, were primarily interested in achieving their independence from France—which they did by means of diplomacy, exploiting in their own interests French difficulties with the Viet Minh.

Second, there was the assumption that the Bao Dai regime, put into power by the French and recognized by the United States, had substantial popular support. This corrupt, ineffectual government had been instituted by French officials in 1949 not to oppose Communism, for the Vietnamese were not alone in making the Communism of the Viet Minh a secondary issue (the French have never felt so intensely as the United States about the Communist menace in Asia), but to enable France to divide and win control over the Vietnamese independence movement. There was never any secret that this was French strategy and the Vietnamese did not have to be particularly intelligent to realize it. It is true that there were honest Nationalists anxious to set up a truly independent and representative regime which could compete effectively with the Viet Minh for popular support but they received little help from the United States and, not unnaturally, none at all from France. As a result, most Vietnamese withheld their active support from Bao Dai, with grave political and military consequences for American policy.

It is not surprising that American officials did not wish to probe too deeply into the validity of their assumptions; it was naturally painful to have to recognize that by choosing to oppose Vietnamese Communism almost entirely by military means, the United States had failed to win the friendship of the Vietnamese people. This does not mean that the Vietnamese wanted to be Communists and that the Americans tried in vain to stop them. What it does mean is that they wanted to be independent under their own leaders, with American aid, and that the United States refused them. Even when the American Government started pouring money into the military effort against the Viet Minh, the United States refused to give meaning to that military effort by helping the men around Bao Dai to stand on their own feet and make an honest bid for popular support.

American policy was based on still a third and equally erroneous assumption. This was that the French military position in Indochina was strong and growing stronger. For seven and a half years France and the United States had been fed on illusions and half-truths about the Vietnamese situation; they regarded Indochina through a thick fog of unreality. The American Government continued to give the French Union forces substantial aid but failed to give the Vietnamese who supported the Viet Minh, or were asked to go to war against it, a reason for fighting alongside the French; and by 1954 the most important single fact in Indochina was the grave deterioration of the French military position in the north. If French officials were reluctant to admit this fact before French public opinion, they were even more reluctant to admit it before their American allies. The result was a widening gap between the two countries. As the French spoke of the need for negotiations, the Americans called for a war to the end; when the French talked of necessary concessions to the Communists, the Americans warned against appeasement and capitulation.

Foreign Minister Georges Bidault carried home a diplomatic success from the four-power conference in Berlin, in February 1954, when Secretary of State John Foster Dulles and Soviet Foreign Minister Molotov, as well as British Foreign Secretary Anthony Eden, agreed to the holding of a conference in Geneva not only to discuss Korean problems but also to try to reach a peace settlement in Indochina. But that was not to meet until April 26 and in the meantime the war went on, on the political front as well as the military one.

The problem for the West was that it had little with which to bargain at Geneva. The obvious method of trying to moderate the demands of the Communist powers by promising American recognition of Communist China or its admission to the United Nations would have been rejected by the American Senate under the leadership of Senator [William] Knowland; the Senate would not accept at any price even the appearance of conciliation of the Chinese, nor would most of the American public at that time. There remained the bargaining strength of military force, but this, it was soon clear, would have to be American force; the French were hardly in a position to bargain. The first official intimation that the United States received of French military weakness came when General Paul Ely arrived in Washington in March and described the difficult situation of the French forces in the strong terms which French generals had used privately for years. French sources, in fact, reported General Ely's mission to be a request by the French Government, hitherto firmly opposed to more open American intervention in the war, for such intervention, although it does not appear to have been treated as such by the United States.

Highlighting General Ely's gloomy report was the military situation itself. General Vo Nguyen Giap had opened an all-out offensive after the announcement of the forthcoming Geneva Conference, and on March 13 he launched an attack on Dien Bien Phu. This was no guerrilla maneuver, as so many previous Viet Minh actions had been; backed by substantially increased Chinese aid, it was a major action that speedily developed into a nutcracker movement as the Viet Minh slowly and mercilessly closed in on the highly vulnerable French positions.

Under other circumstances this could have been just one battle among many, with a Viet Minh victory or defeat at Dien Bien Phu of no determining importance for the outcome of the war; although some attempt was made by Frenchmen to explain the action as defending Laos, it had no overriding strategic importance. But it rapidly assumed enormous political meaning as the imminence of the Geneva Conference turned a high-powered lens upon each event of these March and April weeks.

For the Viet Minh, Dien Bien Phu had a crucial significance. This was the last opportunity before the Geneva Conference for the Viet Minh to show its military strength, its determination to fight until victory. And there were those who thought that General Giap was resolved on victory, no matter the cost, not only to impress the enemy but also to convince his Communist allies that the Viet Minh by its own efforts had earned a seat at the conference table and the right to a voice in its own future.

For the French people, who watched the siege of Dien Bien Phu with a strained attention they had not shown any previous event of the war, it became a symbol of their will to fight. Upon the outcome of the battle depended much of the spirit in which they would send their representatives to Geneva.

Dien Bien Phu was a poorly chosen place in which to make a stand, a valley exposed on all sides to the enemy artillery in the hills and impossible to supply except by air. And having chosen it, General Navarre was later accused by well-informed critics of failing to give the embattled garrison the total support it needed. Certainly French Intelligence underestimated the effectiveness of the heavy artillery supplied by the Chinese which the Viet Minh was able to bring against Dien Bien Phu.

For fifty-six days Viet Minh troops pounded at the beleaguered fortress. In desperation, the Laniel-Bidault government, taking literally Washington's frequent affirmations of the importance of the American stake in Indochina, appealed for American air intervention. They made one appeal early in April and another more urgent one later that month.

At one point in these tense days high American military authorities considered seriously dropping some atomic bombs on the Viet Minh but decided against it. The United States did not only decide against using atomic bombs; it also announced that it was not prepared to undertake any military intervention of its own in Indochina. An astonishing attempt was made at one point by State Department spokesmen to place the responsibility on the refusal of the British to join in any military action on the eve of Geneva, but in fact the decision not to intervene was an American one. Put to the test, the American Government, with Congress lacking support from a public disillusioned over the Korean war, was not prepared to give the all-out help that the belligerent declarations of American officials had led the French Government to expect.

Secretary Dulles tried to create a position of strength through diplomacy. Even before the April 3rd request of the French for aid, he had issued a call for "united action" against the Communists in Southeast Asia, and he hurried off to London and Paris in an effort to bring his allies into a formal Southeast Asian alliance of ten anti-Communist nations which would have had the effect of including Viet Nam, Laos, and Cambodia in a Southeast Asian defense system guaranteed by the Western powers. But this maneuver did not work. Even when Mr. Dulles said that the Chinese were "awful close" to intervention, he could not persuade the British and the French to join him in a move which seemed to them inevitably to give the impression that the United States had no intention of taking the Geneva Conference seriously. Eventually the British and the French were prepared to consider a Southeast Asian alliance but, having committed themselves to the principle of negotiation, they were determined first to give that a fair trial, and they pointedly noted that the Americans had done the same in Korea after a much shorter war.

The weeks leading up to the Geneva Conference were thus a record of failure for the West. The American diplomatic barrage of threats and warnings directed against increasing Chinese aid to the Viet Minh proved to signify nothing more than Washington's quite understandable dissatisfaction with the state of affairs in Southeast Asia, and contrasted sharply with its evident reluctance to undertake any concrete action. From the viewpoint of Western solidarity and American prestige, it was unfortunate that the French Government had been allowed to get to the point of asking for an intervention which the United States had no intention of undertaking, and that "united action" had been proclaimed only to spotlight disunity and inaction in the West.

From some of the neutralist Asian governments came proposals for a cease-fire in Indochina. Prime Minister Nehru took the lead in this peace drive and India was followed by its fellow members of the Colombo bloc, Indonesia, Burma, Pakistan, and Ceylon. The importance of these well-intentioned gestures was underscored by the course of the military struggle. On May 8, the anniversary of the end of the Second World War in Europe, France mourned the fall of Dien Bien Phu. It was a poor omen for the outcome of the conference already in session in Geneva. Frenchmen saw it as a symbol of the tragedy and mismanagement of the eight-year struggle and in France there was despair and final disillusionment.

In Geneva, the fall of Dien Bien Phu came as a body blow to the West.

Few international conferences have begun in an atmosphere of greater uncertainty than the Far Eastern Conference which opened in Geneva on April 26, 1954. Its discussions on Korea will not be dealt with here; it is enough to state that, to no one's surprise, they proved fruitless. The Korean situation remained unchanged. For a while it seemed that the Indochinese conversations might also be deadlocked, there was so little initial agreement among the great powers. But as the weeks passed it became evident that the Geneva Conference was going to be a tremendous victory for China, Russia, and the Viet Minh.

The conference marked wide international acceptance, outside the United States, of Communist China as one of the five great powers, although American officials made a great point of avoiding even the most casual contacts with the Chinese during the time they spent at Geneva.

The Chinese and Russians insisted on the presence of the Viet Minh at the conference table, and out of the jungles and mountains of northern Viet Nam came the delegation of the Viet Minh or, more accurately, "the Democratic Republic of Viet Nam."[1] Three of the four delegates were no strangers to negotiations with France; in 1946, when they found that they were getting nowhere with their demands, they had broken off their talks with the French at Fontainebleau. Now they came to Geneva determined to force far more drastic terms on France and this time with the strength to back them up. Heading the delegation, as he had formerly headed the delegation at Fontainebleau, was Pham Van Dong, Vice President and Acting Foreign Minister, and with him were two other Fontainebleau veterans, Phan Anh, Minister of Economy, and Ta Quang Buu, Vice Minister of National Defense. The fourth delegate was the Viet Minh ambassador to Peking, Hoang Van Hoan.

The French Government had not demonstrated much interest in consulting the Associated States but at the last moment delegations from Laos, Cambodia, and Viet Nam also arrived in Switzerland. It was part of the tragic irony of the Vietnamese war that the key figures in the Vietnamese Nationalist delegation, Nguyen Quoc Dinh and Nguyen Dac Khe, had last seen members of the Viet Minh delegation when acting as legal advisors to them during the Fontainebleau Conference.

Behind the scenes were certain prominent figures on the Nationalist side, like former Prime Minister Tran Van Huu, who also came to Geneva to investigate the intentions of the Viet Minh and to advocate a united Viet Nam, neutralized politically and strategically, and independent of China. Even the Cao Dai pope, Pham Cong Tac, went there to try to evaluate Viet Minh intentions.

Foreign Minister Bidault, who attacked the problem from a different angle, had long been counting on opening negotiations with Communist China to strike a bargain under which the Chinese would have ended their considerable aid to the Viet Minh, leaving it an easy prey to the French Union forces. Bidault had never sought or even believed in the usefulness of direct negotiations with the Viet Minh, but his exaggerated expectations of American military aid backfired and for the first time he had to try to reach a compromise with the enemy.

In this effort he found himself quite alone. The American delegates, divided among themselves and highly sensitive to domestic political pressures against any concessions to the Communists, having nothing to offer either to their allies or to their enemies in the direction of conciliating their opposing positions, could hardly take over leadership at Geneva. It was left to Foreign Secretary Anthony Eden, who attempted to link the Colombo Powers to the Geneva Conference, to act as mediator between the Communists and the French. The Indian Government, which was well intentioned if not always well informed on Indochina, although not officially a member of the conference, also played a certain role, directly through Krishna Menon, Nehru's personal representative in Geneva, and indirectly by means of the influence which India as a key member of the Commonwealth exerted on the British.

Unlike the United States, the British came to Geneva with a plan for peaceful settlement; and their plan, which called for a partition of Viet Nam, was in the end accepted by the conference. But what kind of partition? A division of the country by which at least a part of Viet Nam could be saved from the Communists? Or just a face-saving device for giving the entire country to the Viet Minh?

The Russians had come to Geneva because they were ready to negotiate on Indochina. And if Chou En-lai was there, it was obviously because he was prepared to make some concessions, or at least to make the Viet Minh consent to them. This was particularly the case after Chou, during a recess in the conference, made flying visits to Nehru in New Delhi and U Nu in Rangoon, and then conferred with Ho Chi Minh in northern Viet Nam, reportedly to convince him of the opposition of non-Communist Asia to Viet Minh insistence on French capitulation.

The French, for their part, were in Geneva because they had to negotiate; they had no other choice since they now knew finally that the United States was not willing to intervene in the war. Evidently the French would have to give up something, and it was soon clear that this would be northern Viet Nam, where the Communists were most firmly entrenched.

None of the Western governments liked this. The "State of Viet Nam" (the Nationalist government), which was most directly affected, was very unhappy about it, but did not help the situation when it insisted at all costs on unifying Viet Nam under Bao Dai. This was a preposterous demand at a time when the intrinsic failure of his regime was more obvious than ever. And the insistence on a unified Viet Nam was a dangerous one. If military and political necessity dictated partition, an intelligent diplomacy should have recognized this, however unpleasant it was, and fought to safeguard whatever region was granted to the Nationalists. Above all, it was essential to construct a juridical wall at the northern limits of the Nationalist zone which the Communists could not penetrate under any pretext; but that would have required a political realism which was absent from Geneva. Instead, the Nationalist delegates, supported by the United States, insisted righteously and unrealistically on unity, which led inevitably to their acceptance of the principle of national elections to determine the future even of their own zone. And any elections, in view of the political chaos in the non-Communist areas of Viet Nam, threatened to open the entire country to the highly organized Communists.

Cambodia, though a small state, demonstrated that it was possible to make an independent policy even at a great power conference like Geneva. With Laos, it received Western help in successfully opposing Viet Minh claims on behalf of the Laotian and Cambodian dissident movements and in rejecting Viet Minh demands on the territories of the two states. But at the eleventh hour, with all the powers against it, Cambodia stood alone. It declared that it would not be neutralized and insisted on its right to self-defense. And the great powers gave way.

The Cambodian delegates followed the spirited precedent laid down by their King Norodom Sihanouk, standing up for their own rights when these were challenged. But the Vietnamese Nationalists had only Bao Dai, who had long since given up any hope of independent action, relying on foreigners to save himself.

Bidault, struggling to salvage something for France, tried to separate the arrangements for a cease-fire in Viet Nam from those for a political settlement, reasoning soundly enough that he could get better terms once the fighting had ceased. He tried to avoid even a temporary partition, which would come about if the opposing military forces were regrouped in separate zones, suggesting instead that the cease-fire be imposed on pockets of French and Viet Minh troops scattered throughout the country. But the obvious advantages to France of such proposals made them naturally unacceptable to the Communists.

To all the weaknesses of the French position was now added the instability of the French Government itself. Within the period of a month the Cabinet of Premier Laniel had twice had to ask the French Assembly for votes of confidence on its Indochina policy. It had won them but not easily, and by June Bidault was under bitter attack in the Assembly. Having continually to fight on two fronts, in Paris as well as Geneva, while the military situation deteriorated daily in Viet Nam, he was badly placed to carry on effective negotiations.

The Laniel government finally fell after a smashing attack on the Indochina issue led by Pierre Mendès-France, who on June 17 succeeded Laniel as Premier. He carried the Assembly by an impressive majority when he promised that in thirty days (by July 20) he would either achieve peace terms ending the Indochina war or resign.

As his own Foreign Minister, Mendès-France hurried off to Geneva to take up where Bidault had left off. The bitter personal enmity between the two men and the widespread personal antagonisms which afflicted French internal politics had the effect of obscuring many of the realities of the Indochinese situation. It is little wonder that foreign governments and the French public experienced such difficulty in arriving at a correct estimate of the French position. If his predecessors had painted the French military position in too rosy a light, Mendès-France now had his own reasons for darkening it.

Whereas Bidault had long since been identified with a "tough" policy toward the Viet Minh grounded on internationalizing the peace and the war, Mendès-France had consistently favored a negotiated peace, achieved by direct talks with the Viet Minh; and soon after he assumed office he proceeded to initiate conversations with Pham Van Dong. American suspicions of this policy were highlighted rather overdramatically when Mr. Dulles decided to withdraw the official American representation at Geneva, thereby undercutting the Western position by underlining the general impression that the United States had washed its hands of the conference.

Bowing to urgent French and British requests, however, Dulles dashed over to Paris and, after consultations with Mendès-France and Eden, announced that he did after all have confidence in the intentions of the French Premier to conclude an honorable peace. Under Secretary of State Walter Bedell Smith, who for a time had replaced Dulles at the conference, was sent back to Geneva.

But this byplay did not really alter the situation. The United States had in fact washed its hands of the conference, thereby facilitating the task of the Communists at Geneva. It would seem that the Communists, suspecting premeditated organization against them even when it did not exist, had placed an unwarranted faith in the unity of the Western powers and had believed, at first, that they might be called upon to make substantial concessions. There is some evidence that at a time when they were insisting publicly on Vietnamese unity, they would actually have been prepared to accept a Korean-type settlement, namely, partition of the country for an indefinite period.[2] However, as the conference proceeded, they saw that the unified Western front which they dreaded did not exist; and so the negotiations revolved around, not the maximum concessions which the Communists would make, but their maximum demands which, with some modifications, were finally accepted. By failing to take a leading role in the discussions once it became clear that the West had no choice but to surrender at least a part of Viet Nam to the Communists, the American delegation withheld from Mendès-France the only real bargaining strength he had left, that of diplomacy, making it impossible for him to salvage intact even southern Viet Nam from the Geneva debacle. Instead, he had to agree that national elections be held in Viet Nam in the near future, even though there was good reason to fear that such elections would give the entire country to the Communists.

If the conference moved faster after Mendès-France replaced Bidault, it was partly because of the thirty-day limit he had set for himself, which, given the willingness of the Communists to make peace terms, undoubtedly speeded up the proceedings considerably. Also the Communists were aware that Mendès-France would give them the best terms they could expect from France; if he failed it was fairly certain that the conference would break down and that he would be replaced by a government determined to continue the war, doubtless with increased American military backing.

To these political advantages, Mendès-France tried to add a third when he announced that if the conference failed, French conscripts would be sent for the first time to Indochina to reinforce the expeditionary corps. This was a move so unpopular among the French public that hitherto no French politician had dared to advocate it. But even this announcement did not counteract the devastating news of the sudden withdrawal of French Union forces from the southern part of the Tonkinese Delta, where they were under strong Viet Minh pressure, in order to strengthen what remained of the French military position in the rest of the country. The evacuation left the French in control of a small area around Hanoi (which almost certainly would fall to the Communists anyway in a partition agreement), but abandoned to the Viet Minh important non-Communist areas, notably the Catholic bishoprics of Phat Diem and Bui Chu.

On the diplomatic front, once Mendès-France had accepted the basic Communist demands—not only that the Viet Minh be given immediate control over northern Viet Nam, but also that national elections be held fairly soon—final agreement could hardly be in doubt. It was then only a question of deciding where the partition line would be drawn (the Communists had asked for the thirteenth parallel but finally agreed on the seventeenth[3]); when the Vietnamese elections were to be held to reestablish national unity (the Viet Minh had asked for six months but finally accepted two years); and what international controls were to be set up.

In the meantime, discussions between the military authorities of both sides on a cease-fire agreement began in Geneva, then were transferred to Trung Gia in Viet Minh territory in North Viet Nam. In Geneva, the nine delegations, making no genuine attempt to negotiate real political problems, worked out a series of face-saving devices, avoiding the basic issues involved. The result was the Geneva Accord (finished just in time to meet the deadline set by Mendès-France) which divided Viet Nam at the seventeenth parallel.[4] All of north Viet Nam and part of central Viet Nam—from the Chinese frontier almost down to the old imperial capital of Hué, and including the important cities of Hanoi and Haiphong—were recognized as under the control, no longer of "rebels," as they had been described for years by the French, but of the Democratic Republic of Viet Nam. The south was left under the control of the State of Viet Nam.

Other provisions of the agreement called for the grouping of the military forces of one side which remained in the territory of the other into specified areas, which were to be evacuated in stages over a period of three hundred days; a broad political amnesty throughout the country and a ban on reprisals against citizens for their wartime activities; the safeguarding of democratic liberties; and a free option for all Vietnamese to choose in which zone they wished to live.

Neither zone was permitted to receive reinforcements of foreign troops, arms, or military supplies, or to establish new military bases. Nor could either government have foreign bases in its territory nor enter military alliances. The French Union forces in southern Viet Nam were the exception to this rule; they were to remain, to be withdrawn only at the request of the southern Vietnamese government.

Responsibility for the carrying out of these terms was, in the first instance, recognized as that of the French and the Viet Minh. They in turn were made subject to the surveillance of an international commission (composed of Canadian, Indian, and Polish representatives, under Indian chairmanship) which was generally to vote by majority, although on certain important questions unanimity was required.

The independence of Viet Nam, as of Laos and Cambodia, and also the principle of Vietnamese unity, were formally recognized by the conference.[5] In July 1956 the future of Viet Nam was to be decided by free and secret elections under the control of the international commission constituted by Canada, India, and Poland. And consultations between the Democratic Republic of Viet Nam and the State of Viet Nam about the elections were scheduled to begin a year in advance, on July 20, 1955.

For Laos and Cambodia, the peace arrangements, although on paper not unlike the Vietnamese settlement, were in practice very different. They also were to have national elections—the Cambodians in 1955, the Laotians in September 1956—and the carrying out of the accords was to be under the surveillance of the same three nations as in Viet Nam. But while elections in Viet Nam looked like a convenient way of giving the entire country to the Communists, in Cambodia and Laos they seemed certain to constitute popular endorsement of the royal governments which were recognized by the Communist powers as well as by the West as the only legitimate authorities in both countries.

The agreement on Laos, which recognized the right of the Laotians to keep two French military bases and French military instructors, as the Laotians had requested, offered a general amnesty to the Viet Minh-controlled Laotian dissidents known as Pathet Lao. However, this did not finally settle the Communist problem in Laos. Alien military troops were to be evacuated within four months, but the Laotian rebels who did not choose to be reintegrated into the Laotian community were given two northern provinces of Laos, Phang Saly and Sam Neua, where they were to have special representation under the royal administration. This arrangement was supposed to last only until the elections.

The agreement on Cambodia made no provision for setting up regrouping areas. Within three months all French and other foreign troops were to have evacuated Cambodia. Although until the last hours of the conference it had been accepted that Laos and Cambodia would be neutralized, thanks to Tep Phan, Cambodian Foreign Minister, both countries won recognition of their right to ask for foreign aid in men and matériel if it became necessary to do so to defend themselves, to allow foreign military bases on their territory if their security was menaced, and to enter into alliances which were not contrary to the United Nations Charter.

On July 21 the official documents were signed, which brought peace to Indochina. The United States maintained its strong reservations on the accord and, like the State of Viet Nam, which protested hopelessly against the agreement, did not join the other seven countries in accepting the final declaration of the conference. General Bedell Smith, who thanked Eden and Molotov, the two presidents of the conference, for their good will and tireless efforts in reaching an agreement, issued a separate American declaration. It declared that the United States would abstain from any threat to modify the accords, and that it would regard any resumption of aggression in violation of the accords with grave concern and as a serious menace to international peace and security.

The Viet Minh may not have won all that it wanted at Geneva but it had every reason to be pleased. Its Communist dictatorship was reinforced by international recognition. And not only was its control recognized over the northern and more populous half of Viet Nam, but excellent opportunities were opened to the Viet Minh to take over the south as well, by infiltration. In large part at least, this was the inevitable result of the disastrous political and military policy pursued over the years by the French Government in Indochina, supported by the United States.

In any case, peace, however controversial its form and dubious its content, had come to Viet Nam. On August 11, after nearly eight years of war, the cease-fire was operating throughout all Indochina.

Notes

1. In deference to popular usage, the less accurate term, "the Viet Minh," has been and will continue to be used here to designate the Ho Chi Minh regime, even though, technically, the Viet Minh as a national front movement has been absorbed into the Lien Viet.
2. According to a report of Colonel (now General) de Brebisson, who negotiated military questions with the Viet Minh at Geneva, the Viet Minh took the initiative to propose a private discussion at which, on June 10, the French were told that "for the Viet Minh, Tonkin was the essential and vital region, and that it was necessary to concentrate on two large regroupment zones, one in the north, for the Viet Minh, the other in the south, where the forces of the French Union would be regrouped. The dividing line between the two zones should be established somewhere near Hué." *Journal Officiel*, Assemblée Nationale, December 17, 1954, p. 6517.
3. M. Mendès-France reported to the National Assembly that the Viet Minh had first asked for the thirteenth parallel. (*Journal Officiel*, Assemblée Nationale, July 23, 1954, p. 3580.) Yet the line mentioned above, in the previous footnote, proposed by the Viet Minh some six weeks before the conclusion of the conference, was actually the seventeenth, the one finally agreed upon. It can be seen that the Viet Minh altered its strategy between June 10, when it offered concessions, and the following period when it found it more profitable to make demands.
4. For British and French texts of these accords, see British White Paper, Cmd. 9239, *Further Documents Relating to the Discussion of Indochina at the Geneva Conference June 16– July 21, 1954*. And *Notes et Etudes Documentaires* No. 1901, *Documents relatifs à la Conférence de Genève sur l'Indochine (21 juillet 1954)*; and *ibid.*, No. 1909, *Accords sur la cessation des hostilités en Indochine (Genève, 20 juillet 1954)*.
5. The independence of Viet Nam had been formally recognized by France on June 4. . . . And in December 1954 the three Associated States signed agreemeets with France giving them full financial and economic independence. (See *Notes et Etudes Documentaires* No. 1973, *Accords et Conventions signés lors de la conférence quadripartite entre le Cambodge, la France, le Laos, et le Viet-Nam, Paris 29 et 30 décembre 1954*.

5
The CIA Comes to Vietnam
EDWARD GEARY LANSDALE

After months of doing business out of my hip pocket in Vietnam, I was delighted to be assigned a formal office of my own in January 1955. Perhaps "formal" is too elegant a term. It actually was a little shed in the yard of MAAG headquarters in Cholon. Duckboards covered the dirt floor. Two bare lightbulbs, dangling from their cords, lit the interior. Folding chairs and field tables, and some open crates to hold files, completed the furnishings. The shed was one of several clustered around the main building of the headquarters, which was an old French colonial schoolhouse of cement and stucco noted principally in the neighborhood for having once been a whorehouse set up by the Japanese for the convenience of their troops. The French had assigned this place to the Americans as one of their many "in" jokes. I never did find out the genesis of my own particular shed.

My move to a daily stint in this shed at MAAG came after I volunteered for the Franco-American organization that had been agreed upon in December as the instrument for training the Vietnamese Army. While details of just how the French and the Americans were to work together were being thrashed out, General [John] O'Daniel gathered together the Americans selected to staff the new organization and put us in the only available space at his headquarters, the sheds in the yard, to do some advance planning for the work ahead. There were four staff divisions: army, navy, air force, and pacification. I headed pacification, which was to guide the Vietnamese Army in its moves to reoccupy former Vietminh zones as well as to oversee any security operations in areas where guerrillas were still terrorizing the population.

The next couple of weeks saw most of our basic planning done, including suggested directives for the Vietnamese whenever they were ready to start the program. Although my own planning drew heavily upon the lessons I had learned in the Philippines and from my travels around the Vietnamese countryside, it also was tailored and shaped by the Vietnamese. I discussed each step with the prime minister, the minister of national defense, and the leaders of the Vietnamese Army, whom I was continuing to see almost daily. This Vietnamese input was the most important element in the planning. We Americans and French would be guiding the Vietnamese into taking control of their own affairs. If they were to succeed, the proposed operations would have to be wholly understood and accepted by the Vietnamese.

The first change they made was in the name of our program. They objected to the word *pacification*, saying that it denoted a French colonial practice devised by General Lyautey in North Africa and applied to Vietnam by GAMOs (Mobile Administrative Groups) which had set up local governments and home guards in areas cleared by French Union forces. (I had seen the work of the GAMOs and thought that much of it was excellent.) The Vietnamese leaders did agree with the concept of using the Vietnamese Army to help and to protect the people, so I insisted that if they didn't like *pacification*, they pick a name themselves. After much head-scratching, the leaders chose a Vietnamese term for the work, which translated into English as *national security action*. We adopted this name promptly. Amusingly enough, the Vietnamese themselves (along with the French and Americans) continued to speak of the work as *pacification*. Years later, despite other official changes of name, it still is spoken of as *pacification*. Habit dies hard.

Toward the end of January, the new Franco-American training organization, TRIM, became a reality. The French command made the Cité Lorgeril, a walled compound in Cholon, consisting of a collection of pleasant villas around a courtyard, available as headquarters. Its organization was balanced, with scientific precision, between the Americans and the French. General O'Daniel was the chief of TRIM but acted under the authority of the top French commander, General Ely. TRIM's chief of staff (and my immediate boss) was [the] French briefing officer, Colonel Jean Carbonel. . . . His deputy was an American, Lieutenant Colonel Bill Rosson. Under them were the chiefs of the four staff divisions (army, navy, air, and national security), two of whom were French and two American, each with a deputy of the other nationality. I was chief of the national security division. My deputy was a French paratrooper, Lieutenant Colonel Jacques Romain-Defosses. Our staff division had equal numbers of French and American officers.

There was too little amity in TRIM for me. The French chief of staff who was my immediate boss seemed perpetually piqued at me and showed his feelings by refusing to speak to me directly. Instead, he would position his adjutant, a French officer, next to him and, while looking at me, would ask the adjutant to relay such and such a message to me. When the adjutant had finished, I would reply directly to the chief of staff, who promptly would ask the adjutant, "What did he say?" My reply would be repeated. It was lugubrious, since we all were being stiffly correct in military fashion and were speaking English face-to-face. He carried this practice into our official social life. At receptions he would stamp his feet and turn his back when I approached. I hardly endeared myself to him by my own behavior. I would put an arm across his shoulders familiarly and announce to those standing nearby in a grating American manner, "This guy is my buddy. You treat him right, you hear?" This made him explode, angrily shaking my arm off his shoulders.

Most of the French officers in my staff division let me know openly that they were from various intelligence services. Once in a while, they would have the grace to blush when I came upon them as they were busy writing reports of my daily activities, presumably for a parent service. On the other hand, all of them had served in Vietnam for periods of six years or more and were exceptionally well-informed about Vietnamese life and geography. Thus, my problem was to divert them from an unduly psychotic suspicion of everything I did and toward genuine help in the Vietnamese preparation for the serious and complex national security operations then underway. I was only partially successful.

For example, one of the French officers was from a clandestine service. He sat at a desk facing me, busied himself with paper work for a time, and then just sat there, staring. I noticed that his stare became more and more fixed on a telephone near me which was designated for English-language use. Even the telephones at TRIM were evenly divided between the two nationalities, although the execrable service was impartial. Both the French- and English-speaking phones were subject to sound effects apparently from outer space, additional voices picked up in midsentence or in shouts of "Allo, allo!" and dead silences. Nearly every incoming call would begin with blasphemous complaints about the long delays and frustrations involved in getting the call through to us. Then the caller would hurriedly shout his message before he was cut off. Knowing the performance record of the telephone, I assumed that the French officer staring at it was simply giving it a silent hate treatment.

But one morning, this English-language telephone rang. The French officer, who had been scribbling on a piece of paper and referring frequently to his French-English dictionary, jumped to his feet, snatched up the piece of paper, and rushed over to the ringing telephone before an American could reach it. Holding up the paper and reading from it, he spoke carefully into the mouthpiece, "I do not speak English, goodbye." Then he hung up. He looked at me to see if I had noticed his zany prank. I laughed aloud. He looked a bit surprised at my reaction and then grinned himself.

I went back to his desk with him. The French officer at the next desk was fluent in English and I asked if he would mind interpreting for the two of us. It was time that we all became better acquainted. We embarked upon a session of mutual talk. The prankster admitted that he had only three months longer to stay in Vietnam and frankly was sitting out the time until departure. I confessed that I didn't have all the answers on how to help the Vietnamese at the present moment. Since he had served many years among them, surely there must be at least one thing that he had long wanted to do for the Vietnamese that the war had prevented him from doing? If he named it, and if it could be fitted into our work, he could spend all of his remaining time at such a self-chosen task and have all the support I could muster.

He replied thoughtfully that he had long wanted to assist Vietnamese children and would like to draft an explicit proposal for a youth program to fit in with the national security concept. This sounded good, I said, worthy of backing, and his eyes lighted up. With such work to do, he told me that he would put in for further service in Vietnam, although he did want some brief home leave first because he had been away from his family for years. We parted on this agreeable note. The next day, at TRIM, he stood at attention before my desk, saluted, and informed me in formal tones that he had been ordered rotated back to France. His departure was set for the next day. Did he ask for an extension of duty in Vietnam, as we had discussed? He answered brusquely, "Yes, sir," his eyes showing a silent inner hurt. He told me that he would have to go. We said farewell.

Other French officers in my division also had deep feelings about ways in which they would really like to help the Vietnamese. I dug patiently for their ideas and put them to work on self-projects whenever I could. Abrupt departures continued. The staff division gradually settled into an atmosphere of surface civility, marred occasionally by outbursts pinned up on the bulletin board anonymously by both nationalities. We tackled a heavy workload of operational and logistical planning with the Vietnamese. Two large-scale national security campaigns and scores of other activities were enough to keep us all busy for a time.

The preoccupation of the French establishment in Vietnam with my presence led to a confrontation in this period. Apparently the various stories about my doings had been collected by the French clandestine service, whose officers made complaints about me to the CIA, their normal liaison. They claimed they had a long list of charges against my conduct. I learned of this from the ambassador, who said that the French wanted to confront me, make the charges one by one, and record my answers. Although he warned me that he objected to such a confrontation, because of the star-chamber aspect of the proceedings, I was eager to accept. I had had my fill of attempts at character assassination by so many of the French, and it was time to meet them head-on.

When this was being discussed in the ambassador's office, the CIA chief, a smug smile on his face, offered to host the meeting with the French at a luncheon at his home, saying that this would be acceptable to the French. He seemed to be relishing the meeting, apparently expecting me to get a severe verbal mauling or worse from his French associates. The French, he added, would let him sit in as an observer of the interrogation, and he promised to give the ambassador a complete report for forwarding to Washington. I said quickly that I would submit a report also, which could be forwarded concurrently. I felt like Daniel about to enter the lion's den.

So, one noon soon afterward, I met with the French at the home of the CIA chief in Saigon. The local director of the French clandestine service, a colonel with whom I had had a most friendly association in my work with the O'Daniel mission to Indochina in 1953, sat at a card table, papers spread out before him, face stern, back rigidly erect, and started the meeting by formally requesting that I respond as I wished to any of the charges which were listed in the papers before him. Since the list was very long, it was doubtful that all the items could be taken up before luncheon. We could break the meeting long enough to dine and then return to the inquisition. There were several of his officers present who were thoroughly knowledgeable about the incidents on his list, and did I mind their presence, since they would be advising him on the correctness of any answers I gave? I assured him that I was pleased to have them present.

The first item charged me with supplying arms to Ba Cut, the Hoa Hao rebel, by an airdrop on a specific date. I could hardly believe my ears. I broke out laughing. The French officers glared. My laughter offended them. When I caught my breath again, I explained to them that on the specific date they had named, an airdrop indeed had been made to Ba Cut (who had been made a colonel in the Vietnamese Army by General Hinh just before his departure for Paris, although Ba Cut remained antagonistic toward the Saigon government). However, the operation demonstrably wasn't mine.

The Vietnamese Army, I informed them, had observed this airdrop and had investigated it. The Vietnamese Army had recovered three of the parachutes and traced them by their markings to a French military unit. French officers had been present with Ba Cut when he received the airdrop. The tail markings of the delivery aircraft had been noted, and a check with flight operations records and personnel at Tan Son Nhut airport had revealed the names of the French pilots and crew who had been aboard the aircraft at the time the delivery was made to Ba Cut. The Diem government had lodged a formal complaint to the French command about this incident, thoroughly documented. Whatever made them feel that, by some magic, I had had a hand in this purely French operation?

My inquisitors were shaken. The colonel turned aside and whispered urgently to the panel of "informed experts" who were sitting in. Then he gamely read off the second item. I was charged with supplying arms to Trinh Minh Thé, thus assisting him in his fight against the French who, after all, were allies of the Americans. I answered this assertion in as quiet a tone as I could. Trinh Minh Thé and his Lien-Minh troops were on their way to Saigon to be integrated into the regular Vietnamese Army and were certainly not about to fight the French unless the French tried to stop this move and thus interfere with the best interests of the Vietnamese Army—which they had asserted formally that they would aid. The fighting had ended *after* I had visited Trinh Minh Thé in Tay Nihn, and I trusted that the significance of this fact, along with the safe return of three French prisoners whom the Lien-Minh had held, wasn't lost on them.

However, I continued, speaking of weapons, I had noticed several U.S. machine guns which the Lien-Minh had captured from French forces sent against them, and I had copied down the serial numbers of these guns to have them checked against U.S. lists in Saigon. They had been supplied originally by the U.S. to the French in Hanoi in 1951, to support French actions against the Communists. I had some sharp questions in my mind about how these weapons had been switched from use against the Communists to use by French forces against a Vietnamese officer who was known to be fighting the Communists, since he had captured the weapons in question from the French.

At this point in the proceedings, luncheon was announced. The French officers told our host that they couldn't stay for lunch. As a matter of fact, they couldn't continue the meeting any longer because they had urgent business to attend to elsewhere. They rose, gathered up their papers, and prepared to depart. Their faces were flushed with embarrassment. The first two items had blown up against them like exploding cigars, and they didn't want to sit there and be exposed to further humiliation. I insisted that they stay and finish the inquisition, whether they ate lunch or not, since the whole business was their idea, not mine. Reluctantly, they sat down again and we worked our way through the whole list. It was clear that the French officers thoroughly regretted having to go through with the farce they had begun.

All but one of the charges were patently inventions, easily destroyed fictions. The exception was the charge that my team in Haiphong was planning "to blow up the harbor of Haiphong." I admitted that they had talked about this subject and then explained the background. The French admiral commanding in Haiphong was an older man who lived next door to the house where my team and other Americans lived. The Americans had noticed that the French admiral's water closet was only a few feet from their house and that he spent an unusually long time seated on the toilet every morning; and whimsy had seized them. How could they give the old gentleman a thrill while he sat there of a morning? Should they throw firecrackers through the window? No, his heart might not stand the strain. They had hit instead upon the idea of talking loudly about blowing up the whole harbor, water and all, before it had to be turned over to the Vietminh. The admiral, overhearing this, bolted out of the bathroom to send an urgent message to General Ely. I had been informed of the incident promptly and had told these American officers to stop scaring French admirals. They had promised to behave. However, if the French Navy officers were still frightened, I would take further measures. The French officers told me curtly that that wouldn't be necessary.

The meeting ended. Presumably, the French command received a report of these proceedings. I gave my own summary report to our ambassador, to forward to Washington with whatever information the local CIA chief was reporting. The whole business should have ended there. Of course it didn't, the perversity of human nature being what it is. French attempts at character assassination continued, reaching their peak some weeks later in the spring of 1955. The fictions invented by French circles in Saigon found their way into the French press and eventually into the lurid journalism of weekend supplements in newspapers of other European countries. Well-meaning people would clip these stories and send them to me. They added a Mad Hatter touch to the events I was living through.

The whistle could have been blown on me for other activities in early 1955, though. For example, I passed along some psywar ideas to a group of Vietnamese nationalists who were getting ready to leave North Vietnam for the South. They described the long barrage of Communist propaganda which they had suffered for years. They were burning to strike a final blow in return before they departed from their northern homes. Did I have any suggestions? Indeed I did. I gave them two, which they promptly adopted.

The first idea was used just before the French quit the city of Hanoi and turned over control to the Vietminh. At the time, the Communist apparatus inside the city was busy with secret plans to ready the population to welcome the entry of Vietminh troops. I suggested that my nationalist friends issue a fake Communist manifesto, ordering everyone in the city except essential hospital employees to be out on the streets not just for a few hours of welcome but for a week-long celebration. In actuality this would mean a seven-day work stoppage. Transportation, electric power, and communication services would be suspended. This simple enlargement of plans already afoot should give the Communists an unexpectedly vexing problem as they started their rule.

An authentic-looking manifesto was printed and distributed during the hours of darkness on the second night before the scheduled entry of the Vietminh. The nationalists had assured me that they could distribute it safely because the chief of police in Hanoi was a close friend of theirs and would rescue any of them who might be caught and arrested. The next day the inhabitants of Hanoi read the fake manifesto and arranged to be away from homes and jobs for a one-week spree in the streets. The manifesto looked so authentic that the Communist cadre within the city bossily made sure, block by block, that the turnout would be 100 percent. A last-minute radio message from the Communists outside the city, ordering the Communists inside to disregard this manifesto, was taken to be a French attempt at counterpropaganda and was patriotically ignored. When the Vietminh forces finally arrived in Hanoi, their leaders began the touchy business of ordering people back to work. It took them three days to restore public services. A three-day work stoppage was a substantial achievement for a piece of paper.

When the nationalists saw me later in Saigon, however, they were woebegone. One arrest had been made when the manifesto was distributed. Their friend, the chief of police, became so imbued with the spirit of the affair that he had taken a stack of the manifestoes out in his car to help directly in the distribution. The French caught him in the act and, with the evidence of the copies of the manifesto in his possession, were convinced that he was a Communist agent. They had arrested him and put him in his own prison. He begged to be taken south as a prisoner. The French had done so and had turned him over to the Vietnamese government in Saigon. Nobody believed his story that the manifesto was a fake. He was being held in jail. Would I help? I explained what had happened to Prime Minister Diem. It took me until January to overcome his skepticism and obtain the release.

The second idea utilized Vietnamese superstitions in an American form. I had noted that there were many soothsayers in Vietnam doing a thriving business, but I had never seen any of their predictions published. Why not print an almanac for 1955 containing the predictions of the most famous astrologers and other arcane notables, especially those who foresaw a dark future for the Communists? Modestly priced—gratis copies would smack too much of propaganda—it could be sold in the North before the last areas there were evacuated. If it were well done, copies would probably pass from hand to hand and be spread all over the Communist-controlled regions.

The result was a hastily printed almanac filled with predictions about forthcoming events in 1955, including troubled times for the people in Communist areas and fights among the Communist leadership. To my own amazement, it foretold some things that actually happened (such as the bloody suppression of farmers who opposed the poorly-executed land reforms and the splits in the Politburo). The almanac became a best seller in Haiphong, the major refugee port. Even a large reprint order was sold out as soon as it hit the stands. My nationalist friends told me that it was the first such almanac seen in Vietnam in modern times. They were embarrassed to discover that a handsome profit had been made from what they had intended as a patriotic contribution to the nationalist cause. Unobtrusively, they donated this money to the funds helping the refugees from the North.

South Vietnam. Marines maneuvering a 105-mm howitzer, a weapon that was especially effective for striking at a target in a trench or behind cover. OFFICIAL U.S. MARINE CORPS PHOTO

CHAPTER 3

Digging In
1961–1968

The U.S. presence in Vietnam escalated steadily during the administrations of two Democrats, Presidents Kennedy and Johnson. In 1961, Americans thought of Vietnam as someone else's skirmish, if they thought of it at all; by 1968 it had become the Vietnam War, in which thousands of Americans fought and died. Historians and political scientists have been curious about the seeming recklessness of decisions made by these bright and savvy men. Kennedy's most momentous decision was to send waves of Special Forces to train and support the Army of the Republic of Vietnam (ARVN). The selection from Herbert Parmet's book on the Kennedy presidency offers a possible explanation for this step. In August 1964, President Johnson used an alleged North Vietnamese attack on U.S. ships in the Gulf of Tonkin to win from Congress a resolution giving him enough latitude to intensify the war. Robert McNamara, who was secretary of defense at the time, here looks back at the Gulf of Tonkin incident in an excerpt from his 1995 memoir. (The piece—the whole memoir—is highly self-critical, although some readers found it disingenuous.)

Historian Lloyd Gardner picks up the story in late 1964, following Johnson's landslide electoral victory over Barry Goldwater. Johnson agonized as his advisers debated the merits of escalating the conflict by bombing North Vietnam or sending in U.S. combat troops, but early in 1965 he decided to go ahead with both moves. Quoting extensively from the documentary record, political scientist Larry Berman analyzes events leading up to and including Lyndon Johnson's Waterloo: the Communist Tet offensive in 1968. Finally, George Ball, undersecretary of state in the Johnson administration, offers the perspective of an in-house dissenter from July 1965 to early 1968. In light of what happened in Vietnam, Ball's views seem startling in their prescience.

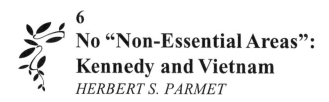

6
No "Non-Essential Areas":
Kennedy and Vietnam
HERBERT S. PARMET

The presidential summer retreat that year [1963] was not at Hyannis Port but at the nearby Squaw Island cottage that [President Kennedy] rented from his father's friend Morton Downey, the tenor. There, just a few miles to the west of the family compound, was the possibility of more seclusion for himself, Jackie, and the children.

While Jackie was there, she had to be rushed to the nearby Otis Air Force Base Hospital for an emergency cesarean operation. The President heard the news while meeting with his Citizens Committee for a Nuclear Test Ban. By the time his plane landed at Otis at 1:30 that afternoon, their baby had already arrived. Five weeks premature and weighing just four pounds, ten and a half ounces, he had to struggle against a burden not uncommon among infants born so early, hyaline membrane disease. A coating of the air sacs was making breathing so difficult that although he seemed to be doing well at first, emergency assistance soon became necessary. He was rushed from Otis to the Children's Hospital Medical Center in Boston and placed in a chamber where oxygen was administered under pressure. But the infant, who was baptized as Patrick Bouvier Kennedy before leaving Otis, still couldn't overcome the condition. At 4:04 A.M. on August 9, just thirty-nine hours after his birth, his heart gave out under the strain.

The President was with his wife almost constantly during those hours. After the death he stayed at Squaw Island with Caroline and little John until their mother returned from the hospital. Patrick was originally buried near the President's birthplace, at Holyhood Cemetery in Brookline. [Kenneth] O'Donnell and [David] Powers have written that "the loss of Patrick affected the President and Jackie more deeply than anybody except their closest friends realized."[1]

By the late afternoon of Monday, August 12, the President was back in the Oval Office for a meeting on the situation in the Far East. With the ratification of the test ban treaty at the center of his attention, and with Cuba remaining as a potentially vulnerable spot politically, there were new dangers to his position emanating from deteriorating conditions in South Vietnam. After a long period of relative stability, one in which Kennedy had been able to maneuver between those advocating stronger American commitments to the government in Saigon and others, such as Averell Harriman and Chester Bowles, who had opposed any major involvement, the "limited partnership" with [Ngo Dinh] Diem was becoming less tenable. North Vietnamese support for the Vietcong had been stepping up. By the end of 1962 there was a tenfold increase in the number of Americans killed and wounded over the previous year. In December, Mike Mansfield had gone there at the President's request and in effect confirmed what such American correspondents as David Halberstam and Neil Sheehan were filing from the war zone. Just as had the French, Mansfield warned, the United States was in danger of being sucked into a futile conflict. "It wasn't a pleasant picture I depicted for him," said the senator afterward.[2] Diem had resisted having American combat troops. He did not want the U.S. to take over his war and his country. Moreover, he continued to defy the Kennedy administration's insistence that he make internal reforms.

Kennedy's "limited partnership," as General [Maxwell] Taylor called the enterprise, was characteristic of his approach. He increased the level of American "advisers," and the numbers of helicopters and other equipment. The CIA, under Station Chief John Richardson, worked actively to provide intelligence support. Diem meanwhile adopted the strategic-hamlet program of Sir Robert Thompson. Thompson, a British counterinsurgency expert, had experimented with the plan in Malaya and the Philippines. In South Vietnam, it was hoped, the guerrillas could in effect be starved out by preventing peasant villages from becoming sanctuaries, and that meant regrouping the villages into hamlets under the protection of the army with such barriers as moats and stake fences. At the same time, the number of Americans there under the Military Assistance and Advisory Group headed by General Paul Harkins escalated to some eleven thousand by the end of 1962.[3]

Later on it would become almost inconceivable to realize that the Vietnamese situation did not capture major attention from the American press until after the start of 1963. Only then did stories from that part of Southeast Asia command steady front-page coverage. Nor was it at the center of the President's own interest. Such matters as the Congo, Berlin, and Cuba had taken far more of his time.

In December, in addition to the Mansfield trip and the gloomy dispatches about the Diem government's inability to make much progress, further discouragement came from a State Department intelligence report. There was, in short, little room for optimism. Instead of giving more emphasis to nonmilitary means of counterinsurgency, reorganizing his government, and sharing some of his authority, Diem was moving too slowly in that direction and relying too much on the strategic-hamlet program and military measures. The adjustments he had been tentatively making in response to Washington's pressures had slowed down the Vietcong somewhat, but neither had their forces weakened nor the "national liberation war" abated. The guerrilla force was estimated at about twenty-three thousand elite fighting personnel, in addition to another 100,000 irregulars and sympathizers. The enemy still controlled about one fifth of the villages, had varying degrees of influence among an additional forty-seven percent, and was thought to be dominant over some nine percent of the population. Furthermore, "Viet Cong influence has almost certainly improved in urban areas not only through subversion and terrorism but also because of its propaganda appeal to the increasingly frustrated non-Communist anti-Diem elements," reported Roger Hilsman in an intelligence memorandum to Dean Rusk.[4]

There was increasing internal discontent among important military and civilian officials, who were participating in plots to overthrow Diem. If the fight against the Communists should deteriorate much further, Hilsman also warned, a "coup could come at any time."[5] Diem himself had been responding by turning inward and relying more on his brother, Nhu. "The two men," George Herring has written, "personally controlled military operations in the field and directed the strategic hamlet program, and they brooked no interference from their American advisers."[6] Nhu's wife had become the government's chief spokesman. Her insensitivity to the Buddhist critics of the Catholic family oligarchy ruling the government gradually brought increasing unpopularity to the regime.

Kennedy meanwhile feared the consequences of negotiating an American way out. His position had not altered from the off-the-record press briefing he gave on August 30, 1961, in which he said, "It is probably true in hindsight that it was not wise to become involved in Laos, but how do we withdraw from South Korea, from Viet-Nam. I don't know where the non-essential areas are. I can't see how we can withdraw from South Korea, Turkey, Iran, Pakistan. Over-extended commitments is a phrase with a lot of appeal, including to some at Harvard."[7] Holding fast in each area had long since become a test of American credibility. To yield in one would mean signaling susceptibility to withdrawal everywhere. As late as September 9, 1963, he was asked by David Brinkley on an NBC television program whether he subscribed to the domino theory. "I believe it," he replied. "I think that the struggle is close enough. China is so large, looms so high just beyond the frontiers, that if South Viet-Nam went, it would not only give them an improved geographic position for a guerrilla assault on Malaya, but would also give the impression that the wave of the future in Southeast Asia was China and the Communists. So I believe it."[8]

At the start of the year Roger Hilsman and Michael Forrestal went to Saigon for the President. Kennedy wanted still another view. This time he knew it would come from two critics of Diem. Considering their outlook, a glowing report would have relaxed him.

Forrestal and Hilsman had separate sessions with Diem and his brother. From Diem, Forrestal heard about the importance of strength rather than reforms for maintaining loyalty from the peasants. The long conversation left the American visitor convinced that the South Vietnamese president was not only immovable but had rationalized the rule exerted by his own family as one that was consistent with the family structure of the society itself. Forrestal left without many doubts that Diem was a serious obstruction to any kind of settlement. Hilsman himself was an experienced guerrilla fighter. During World War II he had served with the famed Merrill's Marauders in Asia and with the Office of Strategic Services. When he met with Diem's brother, he thought that Nhu had been on drugs. He seemed devious, unattractive, harsh, and very explicit about his own ambitions. He also boasted about his connections with the northerners and some of their leaders. His attitude toward the problem of relocating the peasants in the delta was far more brutal than Diem's. Nhu also supported the use of chemical warfare and defoliants. Both Americans, Hilsman explained afterward, discovered that the war was "a fraud, a sham. The American military are still chasing Viet Cong and advising the Vietnamese to chase Viet Cong. They're not adopting the program the President has recommended, our own military are not. Diem has turned the strategic-hamlet program over to Nhu, who's taken the title, the name of it, and nothing else. And in fact, what Diem signed, what we persuaded him to, had not been adopted."[9]

Their report was less critical than Mansfield's, but still disturbing. Conceding that some progress had been made over the past year, it pointed out that the negatives were still "awesome." Even the officially supplied figures were disturbing. Despite U.S. urgings, it said, "there is still no single country-wide plan worthy of the name but only a variety of regional and provincial plans," and they seemed to be "both inconsistent and competitive." The strategic-hamlet program was mostly a sham, "inadequately equipped and defended," or "built prematurely in exposed areas." But the real question Forrestal and Hilsman raised was "whether the concentration of power in the hands of Diem and his family, especially Brother Nhu and his wife, and Diem's reluctance to delegate is alienating the middle and higher level officials on whom the government must depend to carry out its policies." The government had to be pushed harder for an overall plan.[10]

Meanwhile the Joint Chiefs of Staff came up with a plan for the possible withdrawal of American advisers starting in late 1963 and ending in 1965.[11] It was, however, one plan among many, and Kennedy's own reevaluation of the situation offered little evidence for believing that he was ready to negotiate and begin pulling out. He knew that falling back would leave him wide open to American conservatives. "If I tried to pull out completely now from Vietnam," he explained to Mansfield, "we would have another Joe McCarthy red scare on our hands, but I can do it after I'm reelected. So we had better make damned sure that I am reelected."[12]

Then came a sharp setback, an entirely new phase, and the upgrading of the war on the President's list of priorities. On May 8 a crowd gathered in Hué to celebrate the anniversary of Buddha's birth was fired into by government troops. Protesting against religious persecution and demanding a reversal of such policies, Buddhist priests went on hunger strikes. Far more startling to the world was the subsequent photograph of a monk seated in the middle of a downtown Saigon street totally enveloped in flames. That picture of his self-immolation in protest against the government became the most graphic evidence of the dissension. It was only the first in a series of such suicides and helped raise new questions about the entire American commitment.[13]

The division within Kennedy's administration was centered around whether or not support for Diem should be withdrawn. Those who argued against undermining the regime held that there was no adequate replacement in sight. Meanwhile, Kennedy had sent several emissaries to Saigon to try to get Diem and the Buddhists together, but each side was immovable. When Ambassador Frederick Nolting's tour of duty expired that summer, the President replaced him by sending Henry Cabot Lodge, Jr., to Saigon.

Why Lodge? He spoke French, he had had experience in international affairs as Eisenhower's representative to the United Nations, but most of all, as Dean Rusk's biographer explains, Kennedy was persuaded by his secretary of state that "Lodge was to the Republican Party of 1963 what Dulles had been in 1950: the personification of its liberal internationalist wing. . . . Rusk sought to coopt part of the Republican Party, to outmaneuver . . . [Barry] Goldwater. . . ."[14]

Actually the Lodge appointment was entirely consistent with Kennedy's placement of people like John McCloy and John McCone in positions of potential partisan conflict. In his 1964 interview Bob Kennedy explained that "Lodge was interested in going someplace where there was a difficult problem, they needed somebody who would work with the military, spoke French, had some diplomatic experiences. So he fitted into it."[15]

The most intriguing possibility eventually raised is that Lodge was sent to effectuate the overthrow of Diem by working with the generals who hoped to bring about a coup.[16] Lodge has explained that Kennedy was very much disturbed by the picture of the monk on fire. He talked about the overall reportage of what was going on in Saigon and said that the Diem government was entering a terminal phase. The American embassy had also had poor press relations. "I suppose that there are worse press relations to be found in the world today," Lodge remembered that the President told him, "and I wish you would take charge of press relations." As far as helping to overthrow Diem, Kennedy said that the "Vietnamese are doing that for themselves and don't need any outside help."[17]

Almost immediately after that, Diem helped to speed his own downfall. Just before Lodge's arrival, in complete contradiction of a promise made to Ambassador Nolting, Nhu's American-trained Special Forces went on a rampage against Buddhist pagodas in Hué, Saigon, and other cities. More than fourteen hundred Buddhists were arrested. Right after that American intelligence also reported that Diem was actively engaged in trying to work out a deal with the Hanoi regime of North Vietnam.[18]

If Lodge had been sent with an understanding that he might have to support the generals wanting to get rid of Diem, his actions appeared to confirm that purpose. He showed as little outward support toward the South Vietnamese president as possible, disassociating himself almost completely.[19] On August 24, with Kennedy at Hyannis

Port and, "by a strange coincidence, most of the other senior members of the administration" out of town for the weekend, word arrived that South Vietnamese generals knew that Ngo Dinh Nhu was negotiating with the Communists. The information was relayed to Washington via long-distance telephone by Admiral Harry Felt.[20]

Quickly on that Saturday, after a series of consultations and telephone calls—including to the President, Forrestal, and Hilsman—Harriman sent a cable to Lodge in the name of the State Department. Its message was clear: The U.S. could no longer tolerate a situation where power remained in Nhu's hands. "We wish to give Diem reasonable opportunity to remove Nhus, but if he remains obdurate, then we are prepared to accept the obvious implication that we can no longer support Diem. You may also tell appropriate military commanders we will give them direct support in any interim period of breakdown central government mechanism." Lodge cabled back that it was most unlikely that Diem would get rid of both his brother and sister-in-law and that Nhu was in control of the combat forces in Saigon. "Therefore," he replied, "propose we go straight to Generals with our demands, without informing Diem. Would tell them we prepared to have Diem without Nhus but it is in effect up to them whether to keep him."[21]

For a time it almost seemed that it was the American State Department, in the absence of Dean Rusk, Robert McNamara, John McCone, or McGeorge Bundy, that had undertaken its own coup against those who continued to believe that there was little choice but to back Diem. General Maxwell Taylor first heard about the cable when Ros Gilpatric called him that evening at Fort Myer with the information that clearance from the President had already been obtained and that, in Rusk's absence, George Ball had consented while playing golf. Gilpatric has since observed that "I frankly thought it was an end run. I didn't see why it had to be done Saturday night with the President away, with Rusk away, with McNamara away, Bundy away. I was suspicious of the circumstances in which it was being done. . . . In other words the Defense and military were brought in sort of after the fact."[22] To General Taylor it seemed somewhat of a *fait accompli.* Even if Diem wanted to comply, the telegram to Lodge was obviously an open encouragement "to plotters to move against him at any time."[23]

Mike Forrestal agrees that the circumstances indeed were suspicious. Harriman had originated the cable. The senior diplomat, by then undersecretary of state for political affairs, wanted to take advantage of the weekend conditions because he knew how much trouble he would have getting support if everybody were present.[24] Still, the most important—and often the least noticed element—was the endorsement that came from the President himself, not at the center of action in the Oval Office, but at the other end of a wire in Hyannis Port.

But there was no immediate result. The cable had advised the Voice of America radio people to publicize only that part of the message that would prevent the Vietnamese army from being associated with any plot. Hilsman tried to work that out by briefing a news correspondent so the information could be fed to the Voice, thereby maintaining the usual procedure according to which the propaganda network operated. But the people who actually made the broadcast failed to check their instructions with a telegram sent to guide them. The entire story then went out on the airwaves, "not only," as Hilsman wrote, "that the United States had proof that the Vietnamese Army was innocent of the assault on the pagodas and that Nhu's secret police and Special Forces were to blame," but about the threatened sharp American reduction of aid to Diem.[25]

At a meeting in the embassy in Saigon, Lodge was furious. "Jack Kennedy would never approve of doing things this way," he shouted. "This certainly isn't his way of running a government."[26]

When the President returned from the Cape and met with his staff that Monday, he found more opposition to the Harriman cable than he had evidently expected. "And so the government split in two," the attorney general later said. "It was the only time really, in three years, the government was broken in two in a very disturbing way."[27] In Saigon the generals were unable to get the backing of key army units and remained uncertain, despite CIA assurances, of what American intelligence would do, and withheld any actions.[28]

When the coup came, it resulted from the appropriate opening, which was a combination of the muffled hand from Washington and changed circumstances in Saigon. In the interim Kennedy's customary indecision made the entire process seem more diabolical than it was. First of all the failed move of August provided an opportunity to reassess the situation. At the end of the month Lodge cabled that there was "no turning back" from the overthrow. American prestige was already too committed.[29] Kennedy sent him a personal and private message that pledged his full support to enable his ambassador to "conclude this operation successfully," and, with the clear memory of what happened at the Bay of Pigs, added, "I know from experience that failure is more destructive than an appearance of indecision."[30] On September 2, after [French President Charles] De Gaulle had criticized the American involvement in Vietnam, Kennedy was interviewed by Walter Cronkite on a CBS television news program. At that point, in response to a question about Diem changing his pattern, the President answered in a matter that has too often been quoted incompletely. What he said at that point was: "We hope that he comes to see that, but in the final analysis it is the people and the government itself who have to win or lose this struggle. All we can do is help, and we are making it very clear, but I don't agree with those who say we should withdraw. That would be a great mistake."[31] It was not immediately evident that, in reality, he was talking just as much about the Vietnamese choice of a leader as about the American commitment. On the same day that he talked to Cronkite, Kennedy called Hilsman and asked whether his undersecretary of state had done any thinking about "selective cuts in aid that would not hurt the war effort but still make Diem and Nhu understand that we mean business."[32] Encouragement was also given to Senator [Frank] Church's threat to introduce a resolution calling for the suspension of aid to South Vietnam unless it ended its repressive policies.[33] During this period, however, the President had no way of knowing that things in Saigon would be better without Diem. But his hand was being pushed. An Alsop story in *The Washington Post* on September 18, evidently based on interviews with Diem and Nhu, gave further information about their dealings with Hanoi.[34] Reacting to such stories, Kennedy sent McNamara and General Taylor to Saigon. Once again Diem was immovable, contending that the war was going well, pointing with pride to favorable results from just completed rigged elections, and, as McNamara wrote, offering "absolutely no assurances that he would take any steps in response to the representations made to American visitors. . . . His manner was one of at least outward serenity and of a man who had patiently explained a great deal and who hoped he had thus corrected a number of misapprehensions." The McNamara-Taylor report, however, cautioned that it was not the time to take the initiative in trying to change the government. "Our policy should be to seek urgently to identify and build contacts with an alternative leadership if and when it appears." Mainly the suggestion of the mission was to apply selective pressures on the regime.[35]

On October 2 the White House announced that a thousand men would be withdrawn by the end of the year. Gilpatric later stated that McNamara did indicate to him that the withdrawal was part of the President's plan to wind down the war, but that was too far in the future. They were still, at that moment, deeply divided about what to do about the internal situation in Saigon.[36] At just that point the recall of John Richardson, the CIA station chief who was close to the regime, seemed to be another signal, although it may not have been intended for that purpose.[37] Still, it is hard to believe that the move, along with the talk about reductions of American aid to the government, lacked the purpose of giving further encouragement to the anti-Diem generals.

During a series of meetings that were held from August 23 through October 23 between Lodge, General Harkins, and the anti-Diem plotters, including Duong Van Minh (Big Minh), there was agreement on what had to be done: The U.S. agreed that Nhu had to go and that the disposition of Diem ought to be left to the generals. There could be no American help to initiate the action, but support would come during the interim period in case of a breakdown of the central government's mechanism. What was also clear was that if they did not get rid of the Nhus and the Buddhist situation were not redressed, the United States would end economic and military support.[38]

Lodge later reported that he had advised the President "not to thwart" a coup. That act, rather than initiating one, would have constituted interference.[39] Yet even at that point Kennedy wavered, suffering a recurrence of earlier doubts. He told Bundy that the U.S. should be in a position to blow the whistle if it looked as though the coup was failing.[40] Bundy cabled Lodge that there should be no American action that would reveal any knowledge that a coup was even possible. The "burden of proof" must be on the plotters "to show a substantial possibility of quick success; otherwise we should discourage them from proceeding since a miscalculation could result in jeopardizing U.S. position in Southeast Asia."[41] Indeed, the Americans in Saigon behaved as though things were normal.

On the morning of November 1 Admiral Felt paid a courtesy call on Diem at the presidential palace. In the afternoon Diem called Lodge to ask about the American attitude toward the coup. Lodge was evasive, but admitted he was worried about Diem's personal safety. That night, the president and Nhu escaped from the palace to a hideout in the Chinese quarter of Saigon. From there Diem contacted the generals and asked for safe conduct back so he could make a graceful exit from power. On his return, however, according to a prearranged plan, he and his brother were shot and killed by Big Minh's personal bodyguard.[42]

The news of Diem's death outraged Kennedy. General Taylor wrote that he "leaped to his feet and rushed from the room with a look of shock and dismay on his face which I had never seen before."[43] George Smathers remembered that Jack Kennedy blamed the CIA, saying "I've got to do something about those bastards"; they should be stripped of their exorbitant power.[44] Mike Forrestal called Kennedy's reaction "both personal and religious," and especially troubled by the implication that a Catholic President had participated in a plot to assassinate a coreligionist.[45] Every account of Kennedy's response is in complete agreement. Until the very end he had hoped Diem's life could be spared.

It has now become clear that however futile his efforts Kennedy tried to prevent the murder. He told Francis Cardinal Spellman that he had known in advance that the Vietnamese leader would probably be killed, but in the end he could not control the situation.[46] At least one attempt, and possibly three, came from a direct attempt to communicate with Diem by using a personal emissary, someone completely loyal to

Jack Kennedy, someone totally without any other obligation, his intimate friend, Torby Macdonald, the Massachusetts congressman.

As far as is known, there are no written records. It was completely secret. Mike Forrestal remembers briefing Macdonald for the trip.[47] Torbert Macdonald, Jr., recalls that his father told him about it.[48] The congressman's widow is certain that he made at least three trips to Saigon for the President.[49] Torby's closest friend during his final years, who desires to remain anonymous, has a photograph of him posing before the ancient temple at Angkor Wat in Cambodia, indicating that he went through that country while traveling to South Vietnam as a private citizen.[50]

Macdonald himself explained why Kennedy sent him. The President had begun to develop personal sources of information from FBI men who were bypassing J. Edgar Hoover and going directly to him. Some CIA people were following a similar route and avoiding the Agency. By that time the President was learning. When he first came into offfice, he had been intimidated by the Pentagon and the CIA, but he had begun to find out how to get around them. When he heard that Big Minh and his group were planning to assassinate Diem, he wanted to make a direct contact. He was hesitant about using the embassy in Saigon because he could not trust his own people there. Nor did he have enough confidence in Lodge, who had maintained a distant relationship with Diem. Finally, there was no South Vietnamese he could trust. So he called on Torby, who then carried the President's personal plea, which was to get rid of his brother and take refuge in the American embassy. As Macdonald later explained it, he told Diem: "They're going to kill you. You've got to get out of there temporarily to seek sanctuary in the American embassy and you must get rid of your sister-in-law and your brother." But Diem refused. "He just won't do it," Macdonald reported to the President. "He's too stubborn; just refuses to."[51]

Diem's death preceded Jack Kennedy's by just three weeks. What JFK would have done about American involvement in South Vietnam can never be known for certain. It is probable that not even he was sure.

Ken O'Donnell has been the most vigorous advocate of the argument that the President was planning to liquidate the American stake right after the completion of the 1964 elections would have made it politically possible. The withdrawal of those thousand advisers, he said, was but a first step in that process.[52] At the time the Joint Chiefs asked for an increase of American strength to seventeen thousand, Kennedy told his military aide, Ted Clifton, that he would go along with the request but had warned that he would approve no more.[53]

At that moment Kennedy could not have anticipated the shape of either the domestic political climate or the situation in Southeast Asia. Still, for him to have withdrawn at any point short of a clear-cut settlement would have been most unlikely. As Sorensen has said in an oral-history interview, Kennedy "did feel strongly that for better or worse, enthusiastic or unenthusiastic, we had to stay there until we left on terms other than a retreat or abandonment of our commitment."[54] The remarks he had planned to deliver at the Trade Mart in Dallas on the afternoon of November 22 contained the following statement of purpose: "Our assistance to these nations can be painful, risky and costly, as is true in Southeast Asia today. But we dare not weary of the test."[55] "I talked with him hundreds of times about Vietnam," said Dean Rusk, "and on no single occasion did he ever whisper any such thing to his own secretary of state." In addition, and what was more important, Rusk pointed out, was that a decision in 1963 to take troops out in 1965 following the election of 1964 "would have been a decision to have Americans in uniform in combat for domestic political reasons. No President can do that and live with it."[56] When Ken O'Donnell was pressed about whether the President's decision to withdraw meant that he would [not] have undertaken the escalation that followed in 1965, the position became qualified. Kennedy, said O'Donnell, had not faced the same level of North Vietnamese infiltration as did President Johnson, thereby implying that he, too, would have responded in a similar way under those conditions.[57] As Bobby Kennedy later said, his brother had reached the point where he felt that South Vietnam was worth keeping for psychological and political reasons "more than anything else."[58]

Notes

1. Kenneth P. O'Donnell and David F. Powers, *"Johnny, We Hardly Knew Ye":* Memories of *John Fitzgerald Kennedy* (Boston, 1972), p. 378; cf. Travell, *Office Hours*, p. 421; Lincoln, *Twelve Years*, pp. 349–354; Gallagher, *My Life*, pp. 283–289.
2. George C. Herring, *America's Longest War: The United States and Vietnam, 1950–1975* (New York, 1979), p. 92.
3. Walt W. Rostow, JFK Symposium Remarks, Los Angeles, California, November 14, 1980.
4. Gravel, *Pentagon Papers*, v. 2, pp. 690–691.
5. Ibid., p. 691.
6. Herring, *America's Longest War*, p. 90.
7. Memorandum, Chalmers Roberts, August 30, 1961, Roberts Personal Papers.
8. Kennedy, *Public Papers, 1963*, p. 659.
9. Michael Forrestal, interview, February 17, 1981; Roger Hilsman, JFKL-OH (Dennis J. O'Brien interview).
10. Gravel, *Pentagon Papers*, v. 2, pp. 717–725.
11. Herring, *America's Longest War*, p. 94.
12. O'Donnell and Powers, *"Johnny,"* p. 16.
13. Herring, *America's Longest War*, p. 96.
14. Warren I. Cohen, *Dean Rusk* (Totowa, NJ, 1980), p. 189.
15. Robert F. Kennedy, JFKL-OH (John Bartlow Martin interview).
16. Geoffrey Warner, "The United States and the Fall of Diem," *Australian Outlook*, 28 (December 1974), p. 247.
17. Henry Cabot Lodge, Jr., JFKL-OH (Charles Bartlett interview).
18. Herring, *America's Longest War*, p. 97.
19. Ibid., p. 103; Robert E Kennedy, JFKL-OH (John Bartlow Martin interview).
20. Warner, "Fall of Diem," pp. 249–250.
21. Gravel, *Pentagon Papers*, v. 2, pp. 734–735.
22. Roswell Gilpatric, JFKL-OH (Dennis J. O'Brien interview).
23. Maxwell Taylor, *Swords and Plowshares* (New York, 1972), p. 293.
24. Michael Forrestal, interview, February 17, 1981.
25. Roger Hilsman, *To Move a Nation: The Politics of Foreign Policy in the Administration of John F. Kennedy* (Garden City, NY, 1967), p. 489.
26. Warner, "Fall of Diem," p. 252.
27. Robert F. Kennedy, JFKL-OH (John Bartlow Martin interview).
28. Taylor, *Swords*, p. 293.
29. David Halberstam, *The Best and the Brightest* (New York, 1972), p. 264; Gravel, *Pentagon Papers*, v. 2, pp. 728–739.
30. Warner, "Fall of Diem," p. 255.
31. Kennedy, *Public Papers . . . 1963*, p. 652.
32. Hilsman, *To Move a Nation*, p. 500.
33. Gravel, *Pentagon Papers*, v. 2, pp. 245–246.
34. *Washington Post*, September 18, 1963.

35. Gravel, *Pentagon Papers*, v. 2, pp. 750–751, 752–753.
36. Roswell Gilpatric, JFKL-OH (Dennis J. O'Brien interview); Theodore C. Sorensen, *Kennedy* (London, 1965), p. 659.
37. Geoffrey Warner, "The Death of Diem," *Australian Outlook* (April 1975), pp. 12–13; Roger Hilsman, JFKL-OH (Dennis J. O'Brien interview).
38. CIA Chronological Report, October 23, 1963, DDRS (78) 142A.
39. Henry Cabot Lodge, Jr., JFKL-OH (Charles Bartlett interview).
40. Warner, "Death of Diem," p. 14.
41. Gravel, *Pentagon Papers*, v. 2, p. 789.
42. Warner, "Death of Diem," pp. 15–16.
43. Taylor, *Swords*, p. 301.
44. George Smathers, JFKL-OH (Don Wilson interview).
45. Michael Forrestal, interview, February 17, 1981.
46. Blair Clark, interview, July 20, 1977.
47. Michael Forrestal, interview, February 15, 1981.
48. Torbert Macdonald, Jr., interview, August 6, 1979.
49. Phyllis Macdonald, interview, August 9, 1979.
50. Confidential interview, July 25, 1977.
51. Ibid.
52. O'Donnell and Powers, *"Johnny,"* p. 382.
53. Chester V. Clifton, interview, October 1, 1981.
54. Theodore C. Sorensen, JFKL-OH (Carl Kaysen interview).
55. Kennedy, *Public Papers . . . 1963*, p. 892.
56. Dean Rusk, interview, April 27, 1981.
57. Kenneth P. O'Donnell, interview, December 4, 1976.
58. Robert F. Kennedy, JFKL-OH (John Bartlow Martin interview).

7
The Tonkin Gulf Resolution
ROBERT McNAMARA

The closest the United States came to a declaration of war in Vietnam was the Tonkin Gulf Resolution of August 1964. The events surrounding the resolution generated intense controversy that continues to this day.

Before August 1964, the American people had followed developments in Vietnam sporadically and with limited concern. The war seemed far off. Tonkin Gulf changed that. In the short run, attacks on U.S. warships in the gulf and the congressional resolution that followed brought home the possibility of U.S. involvement in the war as never before. More important, in the long run, the Johnson administration invoked the resolution to justify the constitutionality of the military actions it took in Vietnam from 1965 on.

Congress recognized the vast power the resolution granted to President Johnson, but it did not conceive of it as a declaration of war and did not intend it to be used, as it was, as authorization for an enormous expansion of U.S. forces in Vietnam—from 16,000 military advisers to 550,000 combat troops. Securing a declaration of war and specific authorization for the introduction of combat forces in subsequent years might well have been impossible; not seeking it was certainly wrong.

Many people look upon the nine days from July 30 to August 7, 1964, as the most controversial period of the "Twenty-five-year War." No wonder. For three decades, intense debate has swirled around what happened in the gulf; how we reported what happened to the Congress and the public; the authority we sought from Congress in reaction to events; and how the executive branch under two presidents used that authority over the years that followed.

The key questions and my answers are these:

- Attacks by North Vietnamese patrol boats against U.S. destroyers reportedly occurred on two separate occasions—August 2 and August 4, 1964. Did the attacks actually occur?
  Answer: The evidence of the first attack is indisputable. The second attack appears probable but not certain.
- At the time—and still more so in later years—some elements of Congress and the public believed the Johnson administration deliberately provoked the attacks in order to justify an escalation of the war and to obtain, under a subterfuge, congressional authority for that escalation. Does this view have any merit?
  Answer: None at all.
- In response to the attacks, the president ordered a strike by U.S. naval aircraft against four North Vietnamese patrol boat bases and an oil depot. Was the strike justified?
  Answer: Probably.
- Would the congressional resolution have been submitted if the action in the Tonkin Gulf had not occurred and, without that action, would it have passed?
  Answer: Almost certainly a resolution would have been submitted to Congress within a matter of weeks, and very likely it would have passed. But the resolution would have faced far more extensive debate, and there would have been attempts to limit the president's authority.

- Was the Johnson administration justified in basing its subsequent military actions in Vietnam—including an enormous expansion of force levels—on the Tonkin Gulf Resolution?
  Answer: Absolutely not. Although the resolution granted sufficiently broad authority to support the escalation that followed, as I have said, Congress never intended it to be used as a basis for such action, and still less did the country see it so.

The events in the Tonkin Gulf involved two separate U.S. operations: the Plan 34A activities and what were known as DESOTO patrols.

As I have said, in January 1964 the National Security Council had approved CIA support for South Vietnamese covert operations against North Vietnam, code-named Plan 34A. Plan 34A comprised two types of operations: in one, boats and aircraft dropped South Vietnamese agents equipped with radios into North Vietnam to conduct sabotage and to gather intelligence; in the other, high-speed patrol boats manned by South Vietnamese or foreign mercenary crews launched hit-and-run attacks against North Vietnamese shore and island installations. The CIA supported the South Vietnamese 34A operations, and MACV maintained close contact with them, as did General [Victor] Krulak of the Joint Staff in Washington.

The 303 Committee—so named because it originally met in Room 303 of the Old Executive Office Building—reviewed the schedules of the clandestine operations. All of the CIA's covert operations worldwide required clearance by the 303 Committee. The president's national security adviser (Mac [McGeorge] Bundy) chaired the group, whose other members at that time included the undersecretary of state (George Ball), the deputy secretary of defense (Cyrus R. Vance, who had succeeded Ros Gilpatric in early 1964), and the CIA's deputy director for plans (Richard Helms).

The CIA has often been called a "rogue elephant" by its critics, but I consider that a mischaracterization. During my seven years in the Defense Department (and I believe throughout the preceding and following administrations), all CIA "covert operations" (excluding spying operations) were subject to approval by the president and the secretaries of state and defense, or their representatives. The CIA had no authority to act without that approval. So far as I know, it never did.

DESOTO patrols differed substantially in purpose and procedure from 34A operations. They were part of a system of global electronic reconnaissance carried out by specially equipped U.S. naval vessels. Operating in international waters, these vessels collected radio and radar signals emanating from shore-based stations on the periphery of Communist countries such as the Soviet Union, China, North Korea, and, more to the point here, North Vietnam.*[1] These patrols resembled those of Soviet trawlers off our coasts. The information collected could be used in the event U.S. military operations ever became necessary against these countries. Fleet naval commanders—in this case, Pacific Fleet Commander Adm. Thomas Moorer—determined the frequency and course of DESOTO patrols and reviewed them with the Joint Staff in Washington.

Although some individuals knew of both 34A operations and DESOTO patrols, the approval process for each was compartmentalized, and few, if any, senior officials either planned or followed in detail the operational schedules of both. We should have.

*The closest approach to North Vietnam was set at eight miles to the mainland and four miles to the offshore islands. Because the United States had no record of a North Vietnamese assertion regarding its territorial waters, Washington concluded that international waters extended to three miles offshore—the limit established by France when it controlled Indochina. Only *after* the Tonkin Gulf incidents did Hanoi claim a twelve-mile limit. At no time during August 1964 did U.S. ships approach closer than five miles to the offshore islands.

Long before the August events in the Tonkin Gulf, many of us who knew about the 34A operations had concluded they were essentially worthless. Most of the South Vietnamese agents sent into North Vietnam were either captured or killed, and the seaborne attacks amounted to little more than pinpricks. One might well ask, "If so, then why were the operations continued?" The answer is that the South Vietnamese government saw them as a relatively low-cost means of harassing North Vietnam in retaliation for Hanoi's support of the Vietcong.

On the night of July 30, 1964, a 34A mission carried out by South Vietnamese patrol boats attacked two North Vietnamese islands in the Tonkin Gulf thought to support infiltration operations against the South. The next morning, the U.S. destroyer *Maddox* on a DESOTO patrol steamed into the gulf well away from the islands. Two and a half days later, at 3:40 P.M. (3:40 A.M. Washington time) on August 2, the *Maddox* reported it was being approached by high-speed boats. Within a few minutes it was attacked by torpedoes and automatic weapons fire. The *Maddox* reported no injuries or damage. No doubt existed that the vessel had been fired upon: crew members retrieved a North Vietnamese shell fragment from the deck, which I insisted be sent to my office to verify the attack; furthermore, North Vietnam, in its official history of the war, confirmed that it ordered the *Maddox* attacked. At the time of the incident, the *Maddox* lay in international waters, more than twenty-five miles off the North Vietnamese coast.[2]

At 11:30 A.M. on August 2, the president met with his senior advisers to study the latest reports and consider a U.S. response. Cy Vance represented my office. The group believed it was possible that a local North Vietnamese commander—rather than a senior official—had taken the initiative, and the president therefore decided not to retaliate. He agreed instead to send a stiff protest note to Hanoi and to continue the patrol, adding another destroyer, the *C. Turner Joy*.[3]

Max [Maxwell] Taylor, by then ambassador in South Vietnam, opposed the decision not to retaliate. In a cable to the State Department late in the night of August 2, he said that our failure to respond to an unprovoked attack on a U.S. destroyer in international waters would be construed as an "indication that the U.S. flinches from direct confrontation with the North Vietnamese."[4]

At 3:00 P.M. the next day, Dean Rusk and I briefed members of the Senate Foreign Relations and Armed Services committees in closed session on the events of July 30 and August 2. We described the 34A operations, the attack on the DESOTO patrol, and why the president had decided not to retaliate. Although I have been unable to locate any record of the meeting, I believe we also stressed that we had no intention of provoking a North Vietnamese attack on the DESOTO patrol. We informed the senators that the DESOTO patrols, as well as the 34A operations, would continue, and in fact another 34A raid occurred about this time against the coast of North Vietnam (it was then early morning August 4 Saigon time).

At 7:40 A.M. Washington time (7:40 P.M. Saigon time) on August 4, the *Maddox* radioed that an attack from unidentified vessels appeared imminent. *Maddox*'s information came from highly classified reports from the National Security Agency, which had intercepted North Vietnamese instructions. An hour later the *Maddox* radioed that it had established radar contact with three unidentified vessels. A nearby U.S. aircraft carrier, the *Ticonderoga*, launched fighter aircraft to the *Maddox*'s and the *Turner Joy*'s assistance.

Low clouds and thunderstorms on this moonless night made visibility extremely difficult. During the next several hours, confusion reigned in the gulf. The *Maddox* and the *Turner Joy* reported more than twenty torpedo attacks, sighting of torpedo wakes, enemy cockpit lights, searchlight illumination, automatic weapons fire, and radar and sonar contacts.

As the situation intensified, Cy and I met with members of the Joint Staff to consider how to react. We agreed that, assuming the reports were correct, a response to this second unprovoked attack was absolutely necessary. While we had not accepted Max Taylor's view that the August 2 attack required retaliation, a second, and in our minds, unprovoked attack against U.S. vessels operating in international waters surely did. Therefore, we quickly developed a plan for carrier aircraft to strike four North Vietnamese patrol boat bases and two oil depots that supplied them.

At 11:40 A.M., I met with Dean, Mac, and the chiefs to review our options. We continued our discussion at an NSC meeting, and then at lunch with the president, Cy, and John McCone.

North Vietnamese attacks on U.S. destroyers on the high seas appeared to be so irrational (in that they were bound to escalate the conflict) that we speculated about Hanoi's motives. Some believed the 34A operations had played a role in triggering North Vietnam's actions against the DESOTO patrols, but others, pointing at 34A's ineffectiveness, found that explanation hard to accept. In any event, the president agreed that a second attack, if confirmed, required a swift and firm retaliatory strike.

The question then became: Did a second attack actually occur?

As I have said, visibility in the area at the time of the alleged attack was very limited. Because of that and because sonar soundings—which are often unreliable—accounted for most reports of the second attack, uncertainty remained about whether it had occurred. I therefore made strenuous efforts to determine what, indeed, had happened. At my request, Air Force Lt. Gen. David A. Burchinal, director of the Joint Staff, called Admiral [U.S. Grant] Sharp in Honolulu several times to obtain details of the incident.

At 1:27 P.M. Washington time, Cap. John J. Herrick, DESOTO patrol commander aboard the *Maddox*, sent this "flash" message to Honolulu and Washington:

> Review of action makes many reported contacts and torpedoes fired appear doubtful. Freak weather effects on radar and overeager sonar men may have accounted for many reports. No actual visual sightings by *Maddox*. Suggest complete evaluation before any further action taken.[5]

Forty-one minutes later, Sharp telephoned Burchinal and told him that, despite Herrick's message, there was "no doubt" in his mind a second attack had occurred. Captain Herrick sent another message at 2:48 P.M. Washington time, which read: "Certain that original ambush was bona-fide."[6]

I placed several calls myself to obtain as much information as possible. Because the facts remain in dispute even now, thirty years later, I wish to relate some of my conversations (recorded at the time) in detail. At 4:08 P.M., I called Admiral Sharp by secure phone and said, "What's the latest information on the action?"

"The latest dope we have, sir," replied Sharp, "indicates a little doubt on just exactly what went on. . . . Apparently the thing started by a sort of ambush attempt by the PTs." He added, "The initial ambush attempt was definite." However, he mentioned "freak radar echoes" and "young fellows" manning the sonars, who "are apt to say any noise is a torpedo, so that, undoubtedly, there were not as many torpedoes" as earlier reported. Sharp said the *Turner Joy* claimed three PT boats hit and one sunk, while the *Maddox* claimed one or two sunk.

"There isn't any possibility there was no attack, is there?" I asked Sharp. He replied, "Yes, I would say that there is a slight possibility."

I said, "We obviously don't want to do it [launch the retaliatory strike] until we are damn sure what happened."

Sharp agreed and said he thought he could have more information in a couple of hours.[7]

At 4:47 P.M., Cy and I met with the chiefs to review the evidence relating to the alleged second attack. Five factors in particular persuaded us it had occurred: the *Turner Joy* had been illuminated when fired on by automatic weapons; one of the destroyers had observed PT boat cockpit lights; antiaircraft batteries had fired on two U.S. aircraft overflying the area; we had intercepted and decoded a North Vietnamese message apparently indicating two of its boats had been sunk; and Admiral Sharp had determined there had probably been an attack. At 5:23 P.M., Sharp called Burchinal and said no doubt now existed that an attack on the destroyers had been carried out.[8]

At 6:15 P.M., the National Security Council met at the White House. I outlined the evidence supporting our conclusion and presented our proposed response. All NSC members concurred in the action, and the president authorized the launch of our naval aircraft.[9]

At 6:45 P.M., the president, Dean Rusk, the new Joint Chiefs chairman, Gen. Earle G. "Bus" Wheeler, and I met with congressional leaders to brief them on the day's events and our planned response. Explaining the basis for our retaliation, Dean told the leaders that North Vietnam had made a serious decision to attack our vessels on the high seas, that we should not interpret their action as accidental, that we must demonstrate U.S. resolve in Southeast Asia, and that our limited response would show we did not want a war with the North. The president informed the group that he planned to submit a resolution requesting Congress's support for U.S. combat operations in Southeast Asia should they prove necessary. Several of the senators and representatives said they would support this request.[10]

At 7:22 P.M., the *Ticonderoga* received the president's strike authorization message, as did a second carrier, the *Constellation*, a few minutes later. The first planes took off from the carriers at 10:43 P.M., Washington time. In all, U.S. naval aircraft flew sixty-four sorties against the patrol boat bases and a supporting oil complex. It was considered a successful mission—a limited, but we thought appropriate, reply to at least one and very probably two attacks on U.S. vessels.

It did not take long for controversy to attach itself to the incident. On August 6, several senators disputed our report of what had occurred. The dispute was not resolved, and several years later (in February 1968), a Senate hearing was convened to reexamine the evidence. It also challenged the administration's reporting. In 1972, Louis Tordella, then deputy director of the National Security Agency, concluded that the intercepted North Vietnamese message, which had been interpreted as ordering the August 4 attack, had in fact referred to the August 2 action. Ray S. Cline, the CIA's deputy director for intelligence in 1964, echoed this judgment in a 1984 interview. And James B. Stockdale—a *Ticonderoga* pilot in 1964, who later spent eight years in a Hanoi prison and subsequently received the Congressional Medal of Honor—stated in his memoirs that he had seen no North Vietnamese boats while flying over the two destroyers on August 4, and he believed no attack had occurred.[11] The controversy has persisted until this day.

At 9:00 A.M. on August 6, 1964, Dean, Bus, and I entered the Senate Caucus Room and took our seats before a joint executive session of the Senate Foreign Relations and

Armed Services committees to testify on the August 2 and 4 events in the Tonkin Gulf and in support of the joint congressional resolution then before both houses.

Dean began his prepared statement by stressing that "the immediate occasion for this resolution is, of course, the North Vietnamese attacks on our naval vessels, operating in international waters in the Gulf of Tonkin, on August 2nd and August 4th." He continued: "The present attacks . . . are no isolated event. They are part and parcel of a continuing Communist drive to conquer Sough Vietnam . . . and eventually dominate and conquer other free nations of Southeast Asia." I then described the two attacks in detail, and Bus stated the Joint Chiefs' unanimous endorsement of the U.S. retaliatory action, which they considered appropriate under the circumstances.

The committees' questioning centered on two separate issues: What had happened in the gulf? And was the resolution a proper delegation of power to the president to apply military force in the area?

Senator Wayne Morse vehemently challenged our description of events in the gulf, our military response, and the resolution itself:

> I am unalterably opposed to this course of action which, in my judgment, is an aggressive course of action on the part of the United States. I think we are kidding the world if you try to give the impression that when the South Vietnamese naval boats bombarded two islands a short distance off the coast of North Vietnam we were not implicated.
>
> I think our whole course of action of aid to South Vietnam satisfies the world that those boats didn't act in a vacuum as far as the United States was concerned. We knew those boats were going up there, and that naval action was a clear act of aggression against the territory of North Vietnam, and our ships were in Tonkin Bay, in international waters, but nevertheless they were in Tonkin Bay to be interpreted as standing as a cover for naval operations of South Vietnam.
>
> I think what happened is that [Nguyen] Khanh got us to backstop him in open aggression against the territorial integrity of North Vietnam. I have listened to briefing after briefing and there isn't a scintilla of evidence in any briefing yet that North Vietnam engaged in any military aggression against South Vietnam either with its ground troops or its navy.

This last comment went contrary to voluminous, and ever-growing, evidence of North Vietnam's support for the Vietcong—by land and sea, with men and military equipment. The senator concluded his statement by asserting, "American naval vessels [were] conveniently standing by as a backstop" for South Vietnamese 34A operations.

In reply I said, "Our Navy played absolutely no part in, was not associated with, [and] was not aware of any South Vietnamese actions." As I have explained, the U.S. Navy did not administer 34A operations, and the DESOTO patrols had neither been a "cover" for nor stood by as a "backstop" for 34A vessels. Senator Morse knew these facts, for he had been present on August 3 when Dean, Bus, and I briefed senators on 34A and the DESOTO patrols. That portion of my reply was correct. However, I went on to say the *Maddox* "was not informed of, was not aware [of], had no evidence of, and so far as I know today had no knowledge of any possible South Vietnamese actions in connection with the two islands that Senator Morse referred to." That portion of my reply, I later learned, was totally incorrect; DESOTO patrol commander Captain Herrick had indeed known of 34A. My statement was honest but wrong.

The hearing then turned to a discussion of the resolution. Its key passages stated:

> Whereas naval units of [North Vietnam] . . . in violation of . . . international law, have deliberately and repeatedly attacked United States naval vessels lawfully present in

international waters . . . and Whereas these attacks are part of a deliberate and systematic campaign of aggression . . . against its neighbors, . . . the United States is, therefore, prepared, as the President determines, to take all necessary steps, including the use of armed force, to assist any member or protocol state of the Southeast Asia Collective Defense Treaty requesting assistance in defense of its freedom.

Discussing the proposed language, Dean stressed it granted authority similar to that approved by Congress in the 1955 Formosa Resolution, the 1947 Middle East Resolution, and the 1962 Cuba Resolution. His prepared statement noted that "we cannot tell what steps may in the future be required," and he added: "As the Southeast Asia situation develops, and *if it develops in ways we cannot now anticipate, of course there will be close and continuous consultation between the President and the Congress* [emphasis added]."

Senate Foreign Relations committee Chairman William Fulbright—who presided over the hearing, managed the resolution on the Senate floor, and later severely criticized the Johnson administration's handling of the Tonkin Gulf events—offered complimentary remarks that day: "The promptness and decision . . . which all of you exhibited on this occasion was commendable," he said.

Others present endorsed the resolution's extensive delegation of power to the president. Sen. Clifford P. Case (R-N.J.), for example, asked if three resolutions previously referred to contained the broad language "as the President determines." "They have had language equivalent to that," responded Senator Fulbright. Senator Case declared his hearty support. The two committees favorably reported the resolution to the full Senate by a vote of 31–1, with Morse dissenting.[12]

During floor debate that afternoon, Sen. John Sherman Cooper (R-Ky.) had the following exchange with Senator Fulbright:

> COOPER: Are we now giving the President advance authority to take whatever action he may deem necessary respecting South Vietnam and its defense, or with respect to the defense of any other country included in the [SEATO] treaty?
>
> FULBRIGHT: I think that is correct.
>
> COOPER: Then, looking ahead, if the President decided that it was necessary to use such force as could lead into war, we will give that authority by this resolution?
>
> FULBRIGHT: That is the way I would interpret it.[13]

There is no doubt in my mind that Congress understood the resolution's vast grant of power to the president. But there is also no doubt in my mind that Congress understood the president would not use the vast grant without consulting it carefully and completely.

The Senate and House voted on the resolution the next day, August 7. The Senate passed it by a vote of 88–2, Morse and Ernest W. Gruening (D-Alaska) voting nay; the House approved it unanimously, 416–0.

Critics have long asserted that a cloak of deception surrounded the entire Tonkin Gulf affair. They charge that the administration coveted congressional support for war in Indochina, drafted a resolution authorizing it, provoked an incident to justify support for it, and presented false statements to enlist such support. The charges are unfounded.

The resolution grew out of the president's belief that should circumstances ever necessitate the introduction of U.S. combat forces into Indochina—as some of the

Joint Chiefs had been suggesting since January 1964—such deployments should be preceded by congressional endorsement. For that purpose, the State Department had drafted a resolution in late May. However, because Max Taylor, as chairman of the Joint Chiefs, had recommended against initiating U.S. military operations at least until the fall—a recommendation that the president, Dean, Mac, and I concurred in—it had been decided to defer presenting the resolution to Congress until after the Civil Rights Bill cleared the Senate in September.

We had this schedule in mind until the North Vietnamese attacks on U.S. vessels led us to believe the war was heating up and to wonder what might happen next. This, in turn, led to our belief that a resolution might well be needed earlier than we had previously anticipated. The president may also have been influenced by what he saw as an opportunity to tie the resolution to a hostile action by Hanoi, and to do so in a way that made him appear firm but moderate, in contrast to Republican presidential candidate Barry Goldwater's hawkish rhetoric.

The charge of deliberate provocation has endured, in part, because some former government officials endorsed it. George Ball, in a 1977 BBC radio interview stated: "Many of the people who were associated with the war . . . were looking for any excuse to initiate bombing. . . . The DESOTO patrol was primarily for provocation. . . . There was a feeling that if the destroyer got into some trouble, that would provide the provocation we needed."[14]

In contrast, Bill [William] Bundy told the same radio audience that the United States did not intend to create a crisis and had not "engineered" the incidents as an excuse for military action. In fact, he said, "it didn't fit in with our plans at all, to be perfectly blunt about it. We didn't think the situation had deteriorated to the point where we had to consider stronger action on the way things lay in South Vietnam." Elsewhere he wrote, "The case on any Administration intent to provoke the incidents is not simply weak, it is nonexistent."[15]

He went on to make a different but no less crucial point:

> Miscalculation by both the U.S. and North Vietnam is, in the end, at the root of the best hindsight hypothesis of Hanoi's behavior. In simple terms, it was a mistake for an Administration sincerely resolved to keep its risks low, to have the 34A operations and the destroyer patrol take place even in the same time period. Rational minds could not readily have foreseen that Hanoi might confuse them . . . but rational calculations should have taken account of the irrational. . . . Washington did not want an incident, and it seems doubtful that Hanoi did either. Yet each misread the other, and the incidents happened.[16]

I agree with both of these comments. And I believe Dean, Mac, and Max would agree as well.

Of course, if the Tonkin Gulf Resolution had not led to much more serious military involvement in Vietnam, it likely would not remain so controversial. But it did serve to open the floodgates. Nevertheless, the idea that the Johnson administration deliberately deceived Congress is false. The problem was not that Congress did not grasp the resolution's potential but that it did not grasp the war's potential and how the administration would respond in the face of it. As a 1967 Senate Foreign Relations Committee report concluded, in adopting a resolution with such sweeping language, "Congress committed the error of making a *personal* judgment as to how President Johnson would implement the resolution when it had a responsibility to make an *institutional* judgment, first, as to what *any* President would do with so great an acknowledgement of power, and, second, as to whether, under the Constitution, Congress had the right to grant or concede the authority in question [emphases in original]." I agree with both points.[17]

Senator Fulbright, in time, came to feel that he had been misled—and indeed he had. He had received definite assurances from Dean at the August 6, 1964, hearing (and I believe privately from LBJ as well) that the president would not use the vast power granted him without full congressional consultation. But at the February 20, 1968, hearing called to reexamine the affair, Senator Fulbright graciously absolved me of the charge of intentionally misleading Congress. "I never meant to leave the impression that I thought you were deliberating trying to deceive us," he said. Senators Mike Mansfield, Claiborne Pell, and Stuart Symington made similar statements.[18]

The fundamental issue of Tonkin Gulf involved not deception but, rather, misuse of power bestowed by the resolution. The language of the resolution plainly granted the powers the president subsequently used, and Congress understood the breadth of those powers when it overwhelmingly approved the resolution on August 7, 1964. But no doubt exists that Congress did *not* intend to authorize without further, full consultation the expansion of U.S. forces in Vietnam from 16,000 to 550,000 men, initiating large-scale combat operations with the risk of an expanded war with China and the Soviet Union, and extending U.S. involvement in Vietnam for many years to come.

The question of congressional versus presidential authority over the conduct of U.S. military operations remains hotly contested to this day. The root of this struggle lies in the ambiguous language of the Constitution, which established the president as commander in chief but gave Congress the power to declare war.

In December 1990, just before the Persian Gulf War, I testified before the Senate Foreign Relations Committee on the possible use of U.S. forces there. A few days earlier, Secretary of Defense Richard B. Cheney had asserted that President Bush possessed the power to commit large-scale U.S. forces to combat in the gulf (ultimately we had 500,000 men and women there) under his authority as commander in chief. Senator Paul S. Sarbanes (D-Md.) asked my opinion of Cheney's assertion. I replied that I was not a constitutional lawyer and therefore declined to answer. Certain that I would repudiate Cheney's statement, Senator Sarbanes pressed me very hard for a reply.

Finally, I told the senator that he had asked the wrong question. The issue did not come down to legalities. It involved at its most basic level a question of politics: should a president take our nation to war (other than immediately to repel an attack on our shores) without popular consent as voiced by Congress? I said no president should, and I believed President Bush would not. He did not. Before President Bush began combat operations against Iraq, he sought—and obtained—Congress's support (as well as that of the U.N. Security Council).

President Bush was right. President Johnson, and those of us who served with him, were wrong.

Notes

1. See Edward J. Marolda and Oscar P. Fitzgerald, *The United States Navy and the Vietnam Conflict*, vol. 2, *From Military Assistance to Combat, 1959–1965* (Washington: Naval Historical Center, 1986), pp. 396 and 411.
2. See Socialist Republic of Vietnam, *Vietnam: The Anti-U.S. Resistance War*, p. 60; and Marolda and Fitzgerald, *U.S. Navy and the Vietnam Conflict*, p. 415.

3. See William Conrad Gibbons, *The U.S. Government and the Vietnam War: Executive and Legislative Roles and Relationships*, pt. 3, January–July 1965 (Princeton: Princeton University Press, 1989), p. 10.

4. Embtel 282, Taylor to Rusk, August 3, 1964, *Foreign Relations of the United States* (hereafter cited as *FRUS)*, 1964–1968, vol. 1, *Vietnam*, pp. 593–594.

5. 041727Z, Department of State, Central Files, POL 27 VIET S., cited in ibid., p. 609.

6. A Recording—Admiral Sharp to General Burchinal at 2:08 P.M. EDT, August 4, Transcript of Telephone Conversations, August 4–5, p. 31; and 041848Z, both in "Gulf of Tonkin (Miscellaneous)," Country File, Vietnam, Box 228, National Security Files, Lyndon Baines Johnson Library.

7. 4:08 P.M. Telephone Conversation between Secretary McNamara and Admiral Sharp, ibid.

8. A Recording—Admiral Sharp to General Burchinal at 5:23 P.M. EDT, August 4, ibid.

9. See Summary Notes of the 538th Meeting of the National Security Council, August 4, 1964, *FRUS*, 1964–1968, vol. 1, pp. 611–612.

10. See Notes of the Leadership Meeting, August 4, 1964, ibid., pp. 615–621.

11. See *U.S. News & World Report*, July 23, 1984, pp. 63–64; and James Bond Stockdale and Sybil B. Stockdale, *In Love and War* (New York: Harper & Row, 1984), pp. 21, 23.

12. *Joint Hearing on Southeast Asia Resolution before the Senate Foreign Relations and Armed Services Committees*, 88th Cong., 2d sess., August 6, 1964 (Washington: U.S. Government Printing Office, 1966); and *Executive Sessions of the Senate Foreign Relations and Armed Services Committees (Historical Series)*, 88th Cong., 2d sess., 1964 (Washington: U.S. Government Printing Office, 1988), pp. 291–299.

13. Senate debate is in Congressional Record, vol. 110, pp. 18399–471.

14. Michael Charlton and Anthony Moncrieff, *Many Reasons Why: The American Involvement in Vietnam* (New York: Hill & Wang, 1978), p. 108.

15. Ibid., p. 117; and William Bundy, Vietnam Manuscript (hereafter cited as WB, VNMS), Lyndon Baines Johnson Library, p. 14A-36.

16. WB, VNMS, pp. 14A–38, 14A-40.

17. Senate Report 90-797 (1967), pp. 21–22.

18. Senate Foreign Relations Committee, *The Gulf of Tonkin, The 1964 Incidents*, Hearing on February 20, 1968, 90th Cong., 2d sess. (Washington: U.S. Government Printing Office, 1968), pp. 82–87 and 106.

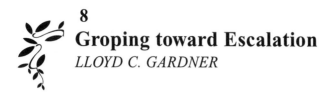

8
Groping toward Escalation
LLOYD C. GARDNER

Near the end of his [1964] Thanksgiving holiday, President Johnson held a press conference at his Texas ranch. No longer a successor, elected in his own right, LBJ felt ready to play a new role. And the ranch was the perfect place to start. He knew he could never banter with reporters like Jack Kennedy or tease them with clever evasions à la FDR. So he would try something else. Johnson constantly groused about "leaks," but in fact he needed the press in order to establish himself as the unmoved mover. He relished opportunities to make it appear the newsmen had "guessed" wrong. From the outset there was a truculent edge to these performances that only grew sharper and cut deeper as Johnson's worst fears about the Vietnam War and racial conflict became nightmarish reality.

But here, in this first postelection news conference, he displayed an appropriately benign demeanor. "I have just been sitting here in this serene atmosphere of the Pedernales for the last few days reading about the wars that you have involved us in and the additional undertakings that I have made decisions on or that General [Maxwell] Taylor has recommended or that Mr. [Robert] McNamara plans or Secretary [Dean] Rusk envisages." Then the edge showed, just a bit. All this speculation was premature. "When you crawl out on a limb," the president lectured the reporters, "you always have to find another one to crawl back on."

Without realizing it, perhaps, LBJ was describing his own predicament. The "working group" Johnson had assigned the task of reformulating Vietnam alternatives had spent the month of November developing options. They all looked like pretty shaky limbs. At the outset the chair, Assistant Secretary of State William Bundy, and John McNaughton, the Pentagon's chief civilian representative, thought about including an option they called "fallback objectives." If the South Vietnamese government simply collapsed and in some fashion made peace, they suggested, it was essential to manage the situation "so that we emerge from it, even in the worst case, with our standing as the principal helper against Communist expansion as little impaired as possible."

That "option" went undiscussed. Instead, Ambassador Maxwell Taylor took over the worst-case scenario. It made no difference, he cabled, whether there was an effective government in Saigon. "If the government falters and gives good reason to believe that it will never attain the desired level of performance," Kennedy's former chief of staff declared dramatically, "I would favor going against the north anyway. The purpose of such an attack would be to give pulmotor treatment for a government in extremis and to make sure that the DRV [North Vietnam] does not get off unscathed in any final settlement."

A defeat sometime in the future was *possible*, Taylor allowed, but not until all that could be done had been done. The "pulmotor treatment" became a favorite image for policy planners. It substituted action for thinking, and it implied that the American obligation was to the Vietnamese people, whether or not they were able to decide on a government to represent them, and whether or not they wished to continue the war. So it was not beyond the realm of the possible, in Taylor's vision, to continue a war against the north even after Saigon fell to the National Liberation Front. An absurdity? Put that way, yes, but not far short of such thinking were arguments already being made for a bombing campaign against North Vietnam to bolster Saigon's sagging morale. Johnson, in fact, constantly worried about something like that. All the Joint Chiefs did every morning, he complained to a White House visitor, was come in and tell him, "Bomb, bomb, bomb"—and come back in the afternoons and repeat, "Bomb, bomb, bomb."

Meanwhile, Taylor had been ordered home to take part in final deliberations on the working group's report. Withdrawal under any guise had been ruled out. And with everyone agreeing that Option A—continuing at roughly the current level of American assistance—was slow defeat, the logical remaining choices came down to rapid or gradual expansion of American intervention, and whether or not to send in combat forces to go with a bombing campaign. The military argued strongly for Option B— heavy bombing of North Vietnamese military bases with a possible ground invasion to follow. Civilian planners hovered uneasily around Option C—a more moderate military escalation accompanied by hints of negotiations to save face for Hanoi.

While the president remained at his ranch in Texas for a few days after Thanksgiving, his senior advisers met to reshape the final version of the report. Taylor dominated these discussions. The situation in Vietnam did not permit a delay in initiating action against the north, the ambassador contended. Perhaps this would help to unify the south, perhaps not, but at the very least such measures would buy time, "possibly measured in years." The debate over Options B and C was simply bypassed in favor of new formulation that incorporated both into a two-phase program of gradually escalating bombing attacks. During Phase I, expected to last for thirty days, the United States would intensify its activities along North Vietnam's borders and launch retaliatory strikes for any "spectacular Viet Cong action in the south," thereby "foreshadowing still greater pressures to come." Phase II would see a steady increase in American bombing raids, a marching forward with air power farther and farther into North Vietnam and ever closer to Hanoi. Meanwhile, Washington would listen carefully for any signs North Vietnam was ready to yield. But Max Taylor's fateful imagery had found its way into the final list of policy recommendations. A moribund government in Saigon could not be allowed to do damage to the image or substance of the American Century. "The US would seek to control any negotiations," read the report, "and would oppose any independent South Vietnamese efforts to negotiate."

Billy Bundy was an easy convert to the Taylor view. Much later he wrote that such attitudes could be "caricatured as simple Occidental 'face' "—but early in January 1965 he had come to the conclusion that the great danger in the immediate future was that "key groups" in South Vietnam might start negotiating with the NLF or Hanoi behind American backs:

> The situation in Vietnam is now likely to come apart more rapidly than we had anticipated in November . . . the most likely form of coming apart would be a government of key groups starting to negotiate covertly with the Liberation Front or Hanoi, perhaps not asking in the first instance that we get out, but with that necessarily following at a fairly early stage. In one sense, this would be a "Vietnam solution," with some hope that it would produce a Communist Vietnam that would assert its own degree of independence from Peiping and that would produce a pause in Communist pressure in Southeast Asia. . . .[But] the outcome would be regarded in Asia, and particularly among our friends, as just as humiliating a defeat as any other.

Johnson had returned to Washington in early December. It was expected he would set in motion the policy of graduated escalation. Instead the president let his advisers know he was unhappy about almost everything. Above all, he declared at the outset, he was not going to send Johnson City boys out to die if the South Vietnamese kept on acting the way they were. All through the "discussion" he jabbed at the planners' conclusions, poking holes in their assumptions. Where were all the other nations that were supposed to be America's allies in these things? They had to do more than send chaplains and nurses. And why was it the South Vietnamese army of 200,000 could not whip 34,000 guerrillas? A day of reckoning was coming, he warned. It could start with a DRV strike at Saigon. When it did, they would be off to the races, and he did not want to have to send a "widow woman to slap Jack Dempsey," If it came because the United States hit Hanoi first, were we really ready? "When I send a man to sock another man—I've got to be ready for them to strike back." Aroused by Johnson's challenge, Ambassador Taylor responded that he did not think the DRV would be very eager to strike back. Johnson had been waiting for that answer: "Didn't [Douglas] MacArthur say the same?"

Before Phase I could begin, Johnson lectured his advisers, Ambassador Taylor was to put some home truths to the South Vietnamese. Nothing could be done without progress toward unity. Indeed, said Johnson, this was the last chance he would give the South Vietnamese. Stop fighting one another, Taylor was to tell the generals, and get on with the war. "If more of the same, then I'll be talking to you, General." This last was probably a more friendly admonition than it sounds from notes of the meeting. But Taylor's instructions commanded the ambassador to say that it was a matter of the utmost difficulty to talk about requiring "great sacrifices of American citizens when reports from Saigon repeatedly give evidence of heedless self interest and short sightedness among all major groups in South Vietnam."

Before he returned to Saigon, Taylor met with the Senate Foreign Relations Committee in executive session. There he reasserted the case for bombing attacks against the north:

> I cannot believe they will sacrifice their economy, that they will sacrifice the society they have constructed at great pains over the last 10 years. It just shouldn't be worth it to them. If we can get that message across and organize that scenario, I would have hopes we can come out of it.

Should the present government fall, Taylor asserted, a "military dictatorship" could provide the necessary stability the U.S. needed as a precondition for the attacks. Peering over his eyeglasses at Taylor, Senator [William] Fulbright expressed deep concern about a decision to send in American troops. "MacArthur said never get into a land war in Asia," Fulbright reminded the general, echoing the president's concern without knowing about the earlier exchange. "I don't care whether it all goes Communist. . . . I don't give a damn what the provocation is. I am not going to vote to send a hundred thousand men, or it would probably be 300,000 or 400,000. The French had 500,000." Yes, the French had tried and failed. But we were not the French, Taylor said. Besides, he was not for sending troops either, he assured Fulbright. "We should respond with our air, punish them appropriately, and let it go at that." The senator worried that if air attacks failed, "they will just go all out." Taylor assured the chairman that the world was too dangerous a place for uncontrolled actions. "I think we have more maturity now."

Despite the doubts he had found in Washington, Taylor returned to Saigon in a sanguine mood about his ability to persuade the Vietnamese to pull together. How could they turn down what the United States had to offer for cooperation—not only the benefits promised from a bombing campaign but a pledge to pay for increasing the South Vietnamese army by 100,000 men, with new opportunities for promotion and patronage? Yet none of Taylor's' inducements produced results. Worse, the Buddhists seemed determined to oust the latest Saigon government, while the Young Turks in the military seemed determined to do their best to demonstrate that no matter how outrageous their behavior, Washington had no choice but to support them or face defeat.

Johnson had also demanded an all-out effort to secure more support from NATO and SEATO allies. But Secretary of State Dean Rusk's attempt to coax aid from them drew a blank. As expected, France's [Charles] de Gaulle, while remaining affable and friendly throughout a long discussion of Vietnam, insisted that the United States could never build a position of strength in that country. "Everything was different there, even Communism." France preferred peace. Whatever the consequences of that choice, he told Rusk, they would be better than war. Should we forget about our great sacrifices in the Pacific in World War II, retorted the secretary of state, and our even greater security interests now? The United States could never accept such reasoning. De Gaulle only shrugged. Of course, he said at length, it was within the power of the United States to keep things going for quite a long time. It could supply arms and technical support. It could wage war against the north, or attack China. Or even go to world war. But what would the final outcome be?

Rusk refused to go down that path with the French leader. Instead he concentrated on what de Gaulle had said earlier about America having inherited French responsibilities in Southeast Asia, without acknowledging the intended irony. The problem would be with us for some time to come, he agreed, given the announced doctrine of Hanoi and Beijing. What the West faced were precisely the same pressures the Communists had exerted against Western Europe earlier in the Cold War. "We believed that if the edges of the Free World were eaten away then we at the center would sooner or later feel these pressures on ourselves."

De Gaulle was hopeless. That had been clear for some time. But Rusk's conversations with the Italian foreign minister suggested that even the least independent-thinking of the NATO allies had serious qualms about a policy that seemed to them to be pushing China back toward Russia, instead of exploiting differences. Certainly, Rusk's language in the interview suggested a consequences-be-damned determination to "win" in Vietnam. Beijing must change its policy, he began. "We are on a collision course. China must not feel she is reaping a harvest from her present behavior. The American people have the impression that our Atlantic allies are just standing by and watching developments in the Far East."

Frenchmen or Italians fighting in Vietnam was not the issue here. But strong evidence of allied support for the United States might convince the Russians that the American government had moral backing for its actions and therefore enough staying power to outlast the NLF *and* the troubled situation in Saigon. Johnson did not wish to go it alone in Vietnam for another reason: domestic opinion. A decision to escalate was sure to produce a potentially divisive public debate. Longtime political adviser Horace Busby had drafted a memorandum about the "image" problem, the first of several cautionary memos on the implications of the election. He and other staff aids, noted Busby, believed that a "watershed" had been crossed in the Lyndon Johnson image. All the old questions about LBJ had centered on the man himself; now the interest of the media and the public centered on what the man stood for. "For all of us, this is a profound change."

Two weeks later Busby submitted a "background" memorandum for the president to use in developing his remarks to a meeting of leading businessmen. It was essential to keep both feet on the ground. "Because we [have] peace, because we have friends and allies in every part of the world, because we are a nation whose use of its strength is trusted, we are in a climate now which permits us to think ahead, plan ahead, act for the future. Given the blessings that are ours in the world, we must conserve and utilize our potential at home by maintaining a spirit of unity in this country—rather than allowing a spirit of division to grow between labor and management, between white and black, between liberal and conservative, etc."

Douglass Cater submitted a similar memorandum on themes for the State of the Union message Johnson would deliver in January 1965. "There is no longer a neat dividing line between domestic and foreign policy," it read.

> What we do to safeguard the civil rights of all our citizens has a fundamental effect on what we try to do abroad. How well we support freedom's cause in the far corners of the world plays a basic part in how we maintain our well-being in the city and on the farm. Neither the President nor Congress can any longer judge a policy or a program in the abstract.

Cater had also forwarded excerpts from a memorandum by NSC staffer Mike Forrestal. "It represents the feeling of frustration by some of those working on the Vietnamese crisis," wrote Cater, "that we are increasingly becoming trapped by the military problem there." Forrestal had suggested to Rusk that the president deliver a speech about regional economic development, "just about the time that military activities in the area are stepped up." Forrestal wanted to see if somehow it was not possible to "convey to our own people and to the rest of the world more of a sense that the U.S. is thinking in constructive political and economic terms with respect to Southeast Asia."

> We are now on the verge of decisions which will tend to heighten rather than moderate this military image of ourselves. There is no doubt that such decisions have been made necessary and we are right in facing up to them. But it seems to me that their adverse political effects can be moderated if, at the same time that we take new military actions, we can announce our readiness to embark upon an international effort to make rapid and dramatic contributions to the economy of Southeast Asia as a whole (including North Vietnam).

Johnson, meanwhile, was confiding his troubles to various persons and friends outside the official policymaking group. On December 5, *New York Times* editor Turner Catledge received a summons to the White House. "We are in bad shape in South Vietnam," Johnson told him. "We must find some way to bring the job off even if we have to set it up so that a withdrawal would have a better face." But there was no intention of withdrawing—not now at least. It was crucial to broaden the base of participation. He wanted moral support all the way from West Germany to India. He had just told Ambassador Chester Bowles to go back to New Delhi and say to Prime Minister Shastri that "he'd better get off his can, and indicate at least some moral judgments in favor of our position.... It won't cost 'em anything, but they'll be in better shape to call on the United States if they should happen to get in more trouble with Red China."

On another occasion Johnson met for three hours with a small group of three reporters. He likened his situation to a man standing on a copy of a newspaper in the middle of the Atlantic Ocean, one of them recalled. " 'If I go this way,' he said, tilting his hand to the right, 'I'll topple over, and if I go this way'—he tilted his hand to the left—'I'll topple over, and if I stay where I am, the paper will be soaked up and I'll sink slowly to the bottom of the sea.' As he said this, he lowered his hand slowly toward the floor."

"If we get into this war," he told still other visitors, "I know what's going to happen. Those damn conservatives are going to sit in Congress and they're going to use this war as a way of opposing my Great Society legislation. People like [John] Stennis and [Harold] Gross. They hate this stuff, they don't want to help the poor and the Negroes but they're afraid to be against it at a time like this when there's been all this prosperity. But the war, oh, they'll like the war. They'll take the war as their weapon. They'll be against my programs because of the war. I know what they'll say, they'll say they're not against it, not against the poor, but we have this job to do, beating Communists. We beat the Communists first, then we can look around and maybe give something to the poor." One of Johnson's listeners said it was eerie listening to the president—like being with a man who has had a premonition of his own death.

LBJ was behaving as he had in the campaign, dropping hints to the press and other White House visitors that he was being forced against his will into an ever tighter corner. The president had many reasons for playing this game. He had tried to make sure that Vietnam did not hurt his chances for an overwhelming mandate in the election. Now he wanted to make sure it did not deprive him of votes in the new Congress for Great Society programs. But Lyndon Johnson's continuing crablike approach to Vietnam also tells us about American history and the ambiguous (if not contradictory) urges in twentieth-century reformism. LBJ's whole sense of himself, his understanding of the Cold War, the convictions he shared with key advisers, were now tightly wrapped around Vietnam.

America found itself in Vietnam *in medias res*, as it were. The nation's supposed manifest destiny took it beyond the narrow imperialist policies of the European era to establish what LBJ called the Great Society and George Bush would later call the New World Order. Like Wilson and Roosevelt before him, each step Johnson took to preserve his opinions actually narrowed future choices. And, more than his predecessors, Johnson feared the outcome. Conspiracy theorists see only deception by the president. There *was* deception involved, and probably more self-deception; but Johnson and his advisers played out their roles convinced that the stern voices that spoke to them from the nation's past permitted no other course. What was most remarkable about the Vietnam War was that with the exception of Charles de Gaulle, George Ball, and a handful of others, so few challenged the fundamental assumptions of the American vision. In part this was true precisely because Johnson felt his way ever so cautiously. Later military critiques of the war faulted the strategy of gradual escalation as a sure way to lose a war. Hawkish analysts complained that it gave the enemy a chance to prepare for each new American step. But Johnson knew he would never have gotten away with an all-out bombing campaign, much less an invasion, without first protecting the moral authority of the United States. He could not fool all the people all the time, but he could force doubters to support him out of fear their dissent would weaken American positions elsewhere in the world. After all, Vietnam would be over some day, wouldn't it? Meanwhile, no one wished to contribute to a perception that the nation had lost its way, morally as well as militarily. What strikes post-Vietnam observers as an amazing failure of nerve, or simple stubbornness or stupidity, was not so clear in the event. It became a case of trying not to allow Vietnam to undermine policy in the rest of the world.

Ambassador Taylor, meanwhile, had to deal with a fresh crisis. Young Turks in the Vietnamese military aligned with General [Nguyen] Khanh had decided to depose the civilian government of Tran Van Huong, a sixty-one-year-old schoolmaster. Huong and a new body, the High National Council, had been attempting to write a constitution and schedule elections. Americans in Saigon prayed Huong would be allowed to succeed and that his efforts would put a solid foundation under civilian rule. The leader of the Young Turks, Nguyen Cao Ky, branded Huong a disaster. "He had no drive, no foresight," Ky wrote in his memoirs, "and, worst of all, no guts when dealing with the thousands of rioters fighting in the Saigon streets against his weak and ineffectual government." The High National Council simply multiplied Huong's weaknesses. "The council was so senile that it was called the High National Museum in the bars of Saigon."

Prodded by General Khanh, the Young Turks soon worked themselves into a wrath over the supposed determination of the HNC to return General Duong Van Minh to power. "Big" Minh had been overthrown several months earlier by Khanh, it will be recalled, ostensibly because he had been plotting with French agents to hold negotiations with the NLF and Hanoi. When Khanh met with the Young Turks and revealed this new "plot," one of the latter cried out, "Who the hell do they think they are?" A quick vote was taken to arrest the members of the HNC to put an end to the chicanery. "It's getting late," said one of Ky's lieutenants as dusk fell. "It's time to round up the chickens and put them in the coop."

Ky commanded the air force, so it was easy for him to have Minh and several others arrested and spirited off to Pleiku in the highlands early Sunday morning, December 20. Ky had scarcely issued the orders to fly the "prisoners" north, however, when the telephone rang at general staff headquarters. It was Ambassador Taylor. Khanh listened to the ambassador for some time, occasionally saying "yes" or "no." When he put down the phone, he turned to the others present. "Taylor wants to see us all at the American Embassy right away." Khanh refused to go. But he wanted someone to represent him. No one volunteered. "Come on Ky," he urged, "you are the leader of the Young Turks, you had better go."

Taylor was himself in a bit of a quandary about what to say or do. He had told the Senate Foreign Relations Committee that, if it came to that, Washington might eventually have to accept a military dictatorship to hold things together, or even to carry out the "pulmotor treatment." But not this way, or at this time. When the Vietnamese arrived at the embassy, Taylor dressed them down like West Point plebes who had gotten into trouble in New York City. "I told you all clearly," he began in English, "we Americans are tired of coups. Apparently I wasted my words. Maybe this is because something is wrong with my French because you evidently didn't understand. . . . Now you have made a real mess. We cannot carry you forever if you do things like this."

Ky claimed they had simply forced the civilian government to clean house. "If we have achieved it, fine. We are now ready to go back to our units." Exasperated by such naïveté, Taylor shot back, "You cannot go back to your units, General Ky. . . . You are up to your necks in politics." After some discussion about how to get things back on track, Taylor started thinking out loud about things Johnson had said back in Washington and where matters stood: "I have real troubles on the U.S. side. I don't know whether we will continue to support you after this. . . . You people have broken a lot of dishes and now we have to see how we can straighten this out."

Khanh was the main obstacle, the ambassador had decided. One way or another he must be gotten out of the way. It was obviously getting easier and easier, even for Taylor who had opposed overthrowing Diem, to think about removing such obstacles to the American mission. Over the next several days Taylor and the Vietnamese general carried on a debate waged both in private and in the newspapers. Taylor declared that Khanh had outlived his usefulness. Khanh retorted that Taylor had interfered in Vietnamese affairs "beyond imagination" for an ambassador. "We make sacrifices for the country's independence and the Vietnamese people's liberty, not to carry out the policy of any foreign country."

General Khanh may have made a most unconvincing "nationalist" figure to be prating on about American intervention in Vietnamese affairs, but each of his predecessors—and his successors as well—ultimately took refuge in that stance. In truth they needed protection against the Americans as well as against the NLF if there was to be anything substantive to the Saigon regime. Khanh's *cri de coeur* rang hollow, but that was because he had put himself in Washington's service since the overthrow of Diem. Now he was being discarded. The new American military commander, General William Westmoreland, watched the melodrama unfold at close quarters. "Khanh was obviously trying to demonstrate how well he could resist the role of puppet, thereby hoping to regain control over the generals; but in the process he inevitably revealed that the American mantle was slipping from his shoulders. Men as astute as [Nguyen Van] Thieu and Ky could hardly have missed noting that."

For a time matters remained in flux. Khanh did not dare go as far as to declare Taylor persona non grata; and neither the ambassador nor Washington dared to suspend American military actions against the NLF. On Christmas Eve an NLF sapper unit placed explosives in the American officers' billet in the heart of Saigon. When the bomb went off, two Americans were killed and thirty-eight injured. Taylor recommended an air strike against North Vietnam. This was the very sort of "spectacular" demanding retaliation that had been envisioned when the advisers drew up the Phrase I plan earlier in the month. Johnson rejected the appeal. The plain fact was that the situation in Saigon was so bad that reprisal bombing would be certain to produce a "strong reaction in US opinion and internationally" that the administration was "trying to shoot its way out of an internal [Saigonese] political crisis."

He had no intention of being drawn into a war against North Vietnam because "our own people are careless or imprudent," the president declared. "I have not yet been told in any convincing way why aircraft cannot be protected from mortar attacks and officers quarters from large bombs." This was a curious way of putting his doubts. Ever since the second series of Gulf of Tonkin "incidents" the previous September, the president had expressed skepticism about American intelligence and security efforts. Here he came close to implying that someone was in fact plotting an incident. In a scorching rebuke to Taylor, the president said, "If we ourselves were uncertain for several days about the source of the Brink's [i.e., the officers' billet] bombing, we cannot expect the world to be less uncertain." But then he startled the ambassador by seeming to call for a land war in Asia:

> Every time I get a military recommendation it seems to me that it calls for large-scale bombing. I have never felt this war will be won from the air, and it seems to me that what is much more needed and would be more effective is a larger and stronger use of Rangers and Special Forces and Marines, or other appropriate military strength on the ground and on the scene. I am ready to look with great favor on that kind of increased American effort, directed at the guerrillas and aimed to stiffen the aggressiveness of Vietnamese military units up and down the line. Any recommendation that you or General Westmoreland make in this sense will have immediate attention from me, although I know that it may involve the acceptance of larger American sacrifice. We have been building our strength to fight this kind of war ever since 1961, and I myself am ready to substantially increase the number of Americans in Vietnam if it is necessary to provide this kind of fighting force against the Viet Cong.

Johnson's message alarmed Taylor. He replied with a sharp warning against any plan to introduce U.S. combat forces. Here began a "debate" that raged throughout the Vietnam War and continues to figure largely in memoirs and studies of American strategy. On one level the argument concerns the wisdom of gradual escalation versus a relatively quick passage to whatever was needed to "win." Military critics of the Johnson administration have argued that the pace of American escalation, and the micro-management of the war from Washington, practically assured what Admiral Ulysses S. Grant Sharp called *Strategy for Defeat*. At a second level, however, the Johnson/Taylor disagreement was about the "lessons" of the Cuban missile crisis, and which varia-tions should be tried in Vietnam. This was a particularly tricky business because, as LBJ said, the Kennedy administration had inaugurated a program of counterinsurgency training to deal with situations like Vietnam. Yet the Cuban missile crisis suggested to others that the most effective signals—the best deterrents—were those that demon-strated American capacity and will to use its technological superiority, if necessary, to destroy, as Taylor had put it to the Senate Foreign Relations Committee, "the society they have constructed at great pains over the last 10 years. It just shouldn't be worth it to them."

Although the Taylor position later became the basis for bombing advocates, the general had in mind a variation on "crisis management" techniques. Taylor tried to elaborate on this point at some length in his January 6, 1965, reply to the president's objections to reprisal bombing. He agreed, he said, with Johnson's feeling that a war against guerillas could not be won—"if we are thinking in terms of the physical de-struction of the enemy."

> The Phase II program is not a resort to use bombing to win [per] Douhet theory (which I have spent considerable past effort in exposing) but is the use of the most flexible weapon in our arsenal of military superiority to bring pressure on the will of the chiefs of the DRV. As practical men, they cannot wish to see the fruits of ten years labor destroyed by slowly escalating air attacks (which they cannot prevent) without trying to find some accommodation which will exercise [sic] the threat. It would be to our interest to regulate our attacks not for the purpose of doing maximum physical de-struction but for producing maximum stresses in Hanoi minds.

Taylor's logic suited the thinking used in the Kennedy administration when it de-vised its flexible response strategy. And it suffered from all the flaws in that logic concealed by the praise (and *self*-praise) heaped on Kennedy and his "crisis manag-ers" in the aftermath of the Cuban missile crisis. Taylor now declared once again (as if to convince himself) that as "practical men," Hanoi's leaders would not wish to see the fruits of their "ten years labor destroyed by slowly escalating air attacks." But Secre-tary Rusk, at the time of the Gulf of Tonkin crisis, had argued that he could only explain the DRV's action as the aberrant behavior of people who thought about things quite differently from the men who manned strategy centers in the basement rooms of the White House or the Pentagon. Rusk's pejorative labeling of the North Vietnamese as semirational creatures aside, the secretary's comment went to the heart of the prob-lem: American bombs could destroy buildings, but they could not "take out" the adversary's nonmaterial foundations.

However selectively and precisely Taylor wanted to increase the "maximum stresses in Hanoi minds," if the bombing technique proved to be futile and costly, pressure to go straight for saturation bombing was likely to prove irresistible. Taylor's messages were composed as if from some European capital, not Saigon. For all the supposed sophistication of his argument, the former army general, like his compatriots still in the Pentagon, had either not absorbed or not accepted much of the counterinsurgency thinking that the Kennedy planners had gone to such pains to develop. The army "con-cept" for fighting the Vietnam War was to treat it as a mid-level contest, of the sort that had been expected to break out some day in Europe. Taylor differed with this concept in believing that the bombings could substitute for American soldiers. If the DRV could be dissuaded from helping the insurgents in the south, enough time could be bought to enable Saigon to get on its feet and win the war.

Taylor also opposed the president's desire to withdraw American dependents from South Vietnam. It was a matter of timing. The situation was so bad, he feared, that to withdraw American dependents would indicate that the United States was abandoning the fight, getting ready to clear out altogether. It would cause panic in South Vietnam and adversely affect "our ability to obtain third country assistance from our *less sturdy friends.*" But if other action—the bombing, he meant—were taken first, such a decision to withdraw dependents could "reinforce the tonic effects" of such action. "I have, for example, in mind the successful way in which we used the evacuation of our dependents from Guantanamo during the Cuban crisis to reinforce the signals that we were seeking to communicate to both Havana and Moscow."

As for Johnson's complaint that lax security could not be a reason for going to war, Taylor found a way to turn the argument. He had consulted with General Westmoreland, Taylor said, and found the "startling" news that complete protection would require at least 75,000 American troops. These troops sitting in static positions would hardly speed up the conclusion of the war. Still worse, they would represent an occupying force. If the advisory effort had failed to instill the South Vietnamese with the proper motivation to carry on the fight, there was little reason to believe the situation could be rescued with American troops. Instead, as the Americans took on the burden of the fighting, said the ambassador, the likelihood was that the majority of Vietnamese would "actively turn against us . . . until, like the French, we would be occupying an essentially hostile country."

None of the challenges Johnson had put to his advisers in December, nor indeed any he would put later in the war, ever received adequate answers, not in Taylor's cables and not in anything he heard elsewhere. Yet how long could matters go on as they were? The president might rail at columnist Joseph Alsop for his attempts to force his hand—and suspect that the Bundys were feeding their friend information about high-level deliberations—but he accepted Alsop's estimate of the stakes:

> For Lyndon Johnson, Vietnam is what the second Cuban crisis was for John F. Kennedy. If Mr. Johnson ducks the challenge we shall learn by experience about what it would have been like if Kennedy had ducked the challenge in October, 1962.

Oddly enough, General Westmoreland was one of the few who believed that domestic and foreign opinion would have understood a decision to leave Vietnam to its fate. He later wrote of the situation in early 1965:

> Whether the United would, in fact, have pulled out of Vietnam in 1965 if the political instability showed no signs of abating is problematical. I think it likely that Washington was already too deeply committed in word and deed to do other than more of the same. Yet so obvious was the bickering, the machination, the inefficiency, the divisiveness among the Vietnamese that I suspect few in the world would have faulted us at that point had we thrown up our hands in despair. When we failed to renege on our commitment under such blatantly exigent conditions, the time when we could have withdrawn with some grace and honor had passed.

The more perilous the situation inside Saigon, the harder Johnson tried to make it appear that South Vietnam had powerful friends around the world. German Chancellor Ludwig Erhard and the Japanese prime minister were persuaded, for example, to close their visits to Washington with strong public endorsements of American policy in Vietnam from the portico of the White House. Erhard was said to have impressed on Johnson during their talks "the importance of mutual solidarity in dealing with communist aggression," while the Japanese prime minister supposedly "agreed that continued perseverance would be necessary for freedom and independence in South Vietnam."

LBJ was steadily building up arguments that he would find it impossible to ignore; still he hedged about a bombing campaign against the DRV. Down deep he may have understood the biggest flaw of all in Taylor's argument; bombing North Vietnam could never win the war in the south. In any event, the ambassador was instructed to allow it to become known that the United States had decided to adopt a reprisal policy. It was left to Taylor to handle this without making it seem a definitive change. "We would prefer that this indication be given by inconspicuous background briefings rather than formal public statement. . . ." Targets selected for reprisal bombings should be in the southern section of the DRV. All air attacks were subject to the president's review before the execute order could be given. Meanwhile, the ambassador and General Westmoreland were urged yet again to seek better cooperation from the South Vietnamese in planning and executing military actions inside South Vietnam. "A few solid military victories achieved by use of U.S. military command judgment and energy would be worth all the rest of this program put together."

Washington's latest instructions puzzled the ambassador. They seemed to add new conditions, not remove obstacles to a clear-cut policy. They could even be regarded as a step backward. Could he not say to the Vietnamese, plain and simple, Taylor cabled, that a firm decision had been made to go ahead with Phase II, with the understanding that no commitments had been made as to timing or scale? The message produced no clarification. The president would go no further. And there matters stood.

While Taylor fretted about Washington's dillydallying, rumors of an impending change had reached Congress. Questioned closely by Senator Fulbright in executive session, Secretary Rusk coyly refused to say if the Foreign Relations committee would be consulted. "I myself feel that strikes against the North are a part of the problem on which the leadership and President would be in consultation, because this would be a significant development of the situation."

Taylor had convinced McGeorge Bundy and Robert McNamara, however, and they were determined to move the president into Phase II of Operation Vietnam—a steady escalation of bombing—before things finally fell apart. In Saigon, General Khanh was once again scheming to gain power. The worse aspect of his maneuvering was his surprise "alliance" with Buddhist factions. At least the Young Turks were anxious to continue the war. Even if Khanh thought he would be able to use the Buddhists, there was always the chance he would be the one to be used. "I'm convinced," Vice-President Hubert Humphrey was heard to say, "that we don't have to worry about this [whether to escalate] because, before this bombing can be undertaken, there will be a neutralist government in Saigon and we will be invited out."

Alerted to the possibility that Khanh was about to seize power, Mac Bundy asked for a meeting with Johnson to discuss whether "this back-and-forth in the government in Saigon is a symptom, not a root cause of our problem." Even to phrase the issue in this fashion helped to predetermine the answer to the question. Meanwhile, Bundy promised, he would prepare a paper explaining the president's options. On the morning of January 27, 1965, Bundy and McNamara met with the president to receive his decision. General Khanh had staged his expected coup during the interim. But Bundy had successfully reversed, as he hoped to do, symptoms and root causes. Khanh's coup was no reason to think about getting out. "Both of us are now pretty well convinced that our current policy can lead only to disastrous defeat," the national security adviser began, referring to McNamara and himself. The continuing difficulties in Saigon arose, he went on, from the spreading conviction that "the future is without hope for anti-Communists." "More and more the good men are covering their flanks and avoiding executive responsibility for firm anti-Communist policy." Such a novel reading of Vietnamese politics obscured practically all the major forces at work in favor of an imposed history constructed according to cold war exigencies, but Bundy had little patience with those unable to perceive the higher truth. "Our best friends"—not presumably the Vietnamese living in the countryside where the war was going on—"have been somewhat discouraged by our own inactivity in the face of major attacks on our own installations."

> The Vietnamese know just as well as we do that the Viet Cong are gaining in the countryside. Meanwhile, they see the enormous power of the United States withheld, and they get little sense of firm and active U.S. policy. They feel we are unwilling to take serious risks. In one sense, all of this is outrageous, in the light of all that we have done and all that we are ready to do if they will only pull up their socks. But it is a fact—or at least so McNamara and I now think.

Given the determination he and other policymakers had exhibited in denying [Ngo Dinh] Diem or [Duong Van] Minh and now Khanh any opportunity to follow a policy except in accordance with the war aims of the United States, Bundy's ability to speak about what frightened the Vietnamese people, and what would bolster their spirits, seems suspect. But there was more. This time around, he and McNamara had determined, there would be no other choice for Johnson but "honest" commitment.

This uncertainty that "pervades" the Vietnamese people, stated the national security adviser, was increasingly visible "among our own people, even the most loyal and determined." Again, a curious phraseology, why "even the most loyal and determined"? It could mean several things, all of which presumably spelled trouble for Lyndon Johnson's ability to hold his administration together if he did not decide to go forward. The ground raked smooth, all the clumps of doubt broke up, Bundy set out the two alternatives: "The first is to use our military power in the Far East and to force a change of Communist policy. The second is to deploy all our resources along a track of negotiation, aimed at salvaging what little can be preserved with no major addition to our present military risks."

"Bob and I," he said, "*tend* to favor the first course, but we believe that both should be carefully studied and that alternative programs should be argued out before you." Rusk did not agree with their recommendation, Bundy noted, because he feared the consequences of veering off in either direction. He felt the present policy had to be made to work. "This would be good if it was possible. Bob and I do not think it is."

"A topic of this magnitude," Bundy's memorandum read, "can only be opened for initial discussion this morning, but McNamara and I have reached the point where our obligations to you simply do not permit us to administer our present directives in silence and let you think we see real hope in them." Was there the slightest hint here that they could not administer their present directives in silence—period? Did this sentence go with the phrase about doubts among "even the most loyal"? A president a good deal less sensitive concerning his origins, or a good deal more secure in his grasp of foreign policy questions, would have paid more than casual attention to the wording of this memorandum. Johnson was neither. Summed up in a few sentences, the memo read: We are losing the war. The Vietnamese are now incidental to the outcome. But you need Vietnam to save your administration. If we lose because we have withheld our military power, you will be blamed and nothing can undo the damage.

By the time Johnson finished reading Bundy's memorandum he hardly cared any more about the ups and downs of South Vietnamese politics: the implicit warnings in the second half of Bundy's memorandum—backed by McNamara's presence at the meeting on the morning of the 27th—were enough. "Stable government or no stable government," Johnson declared, "we'll do what we have to do—we will move strongly. I'm prepared to do that." That same evening the president cabled Ambassador Taylor: "Once we get the dependents out of there, I am determined to make it clear to all the world that the U.S. will spare no effort and no sacrifice in doing its full part to turn back the Communists in Vietnam."

Bundy himself cabled the next day that even on the question of getting the dependents "out of there" the president had relented. Now he only demanded a "decision" to remove the dependents. The timing and method could be worked out when the national security adviser arrived in Saigon to talk about the general political situation. Taylor had asked earlier for a Bundy visit, but now it took on special meaning because the ambassador was having his own quarrel to settle with General Khanh. If Taylor had his way, Khanh would be sent packing to some place close to the North Pole. But the national security adviser had little desire to carry on a time-wasting vendetta against the errant general with the odd-looking goatee. See him, Bundy instructed Taylor. Find out if he was willing to carry on the war. If he indicated he was—as Washington expected—then "we think you should certainly respond that U.S. is equally determined to go on supporting Vietnamese government and people." As proof of American determination, Taylor was to tell Khanh that the DESOTO patrols in the Gulf of Tonkin would be resumed the following week. "Object of meeting should be to establish firmness of both sides and create atmosphere that would begin to bury past problems."

Bundy's cables left no doubts about the new firmness in Washington's attitude, nor about *his* new role. Deputized by LBJ to act on his behalf, Bundy was coming to Vietnam to see that things got done. No more shilly-shallying. "Intense, abrupt, at moments a bit arrogant," General Westmoreland noted his impressions of Bundy, "like numbers of civilians in positions of some government authority, once he smelled a little gunpowder he developed a field marshal psychosis."

Bundy's first impression of the political situation in Saigon could scarcely have encouraged the president to believe he had made the right decision. "The current situation among non-communist forces gives all the appearance of a civil war within a civil war." The main stumbling block was the Buddhist leadership. There was "no present prospect of a government acceptable to us which would also be acceptable to the leaders of the Buddhist institute," Bundy reported. But that gave him no pause. "In this situation, the construction of a government of national unity may well require sharp confrontation with Buddhists before, during, or after the construction job."

Given the current success of the NLF on the battlefield, the prospect of a "sharp confrontation" with another faction in the tangled world of Vietnamese politics was not something Lyndon Johnson cared to think about. The next news out of Vietnam was something altogether different. At 2 A.M. on February 7, Viet Cong soldiers launched an attack against a U.S. helicopter base and barracks at Pleiku in the Central Highlands. Eight Americans were killed and 126 wounded; ten planes were destroyed and many other damaged. Other South Vietnamese installations were attacked that day, ten in all, but Pleiku was the only place where Americans were involved. Two Americans had been killed in late December by the bombs placed in the Brinks barracks in Saigon. Johnson had stayed his hand on that occasion, but not now—not when he had been told it might be his last chance to send what he hoped would be an unmistakable signal to Hanoi—and Saigon.

There was only one difficulty. Soviet Premier Alexei Kosygin was in Hanoi at the head of "an unusually strong delegation." To bomb North Vietnam while Kosygin was meeting with Ho [Chi Minh] and his lieutenants risked forcing the Russians to play a deeper role in the conflict. On the other hand, not to retaliate risked giving the impression that the United States was a paper tiger. "We cannot put ourself in the position of giving the Russians control over our actions," declared the unabashed Mac Bundy, "by their moving Soviet diplomats from one place to another." That Alexei Kosygin ranked somewhat above a diplomat apparently made no difference.

Johnson wrote in his memoirs that CIA Director John McCone told him the Kosygin visit to Hanoi "promised only more trouble." The new Soviet leaders had decided to reverse Khrushchev's policy of relative inaction, Johnson recorded McCone's opinion. They had concluded Hanoi was about to win and desired to "move in to share credit for the anticipated victory." As Communist leaders toasted one another in Hanoi, preparing to celebrate the fall of yet another nation on the border of the Free World, the president of the United States—in this accounting—had to act or face humiliation.

Johnson did act. While members of the National Security Council listened, the president read a list of proposed targets. Pentagon estimates indicated that if four barracks complexes were hit, as proposed, casualties could run as high as 4,500. No one dissented. "We are all in accord that action must be taken," began Under Secretary of State George Ball, sitting in for Rusk, even though he could not have been happy contemplating what it meant to send 132 carrier-based jets over North Vietnam. Only Senate Majority Leader Mike Mansfield objected, and then only obliquely. "The North Vietnamese attack has opened many eyes," he said. "We are not now in a penny ante game. It appears that the local populace in South Vietnam is not behind us, else the Viet Cong could not have carried out their surprise attack."

In the event, bad weather prevented the American planes from hitting more than one of their selected targets. This gave Johnson the opportunity to put off for a few more days a decision to do more than launch reprisal raids. "We all felt," Johnson wrote, "that a second-day strike by U.S. planes might give Hanoi the impression that we had begun a sustained air offensive. That decision had not been made." At a briefing for congressional leaders, however, the president declared that the Gulf of Tonkin Resolution "plus the legal power of the Presidency made it possible for him to carry out at a manageable level an effort to deter, destroy and diminish the strength of the North Vietnamese aggressors and to try to convince them to leave South Vietnam alone." As the meeting ended, Johnson repeated that "our actions will be kept at a manageable level." No one challenged his interpretation of the Gulf of Tonkin Resolution. And why should they? He had promised to keep things under control. Yet in conversations outside the formal setting of an NSC meeting, Johnson portrayed himself as under enormous pressure from the military. "Just between you and me," he told Carl Rowan, "all I want to do is bloody their noses a little bit and maybe they'll leave their neighbors alone." He had to approve the bombing "because that damn cigar-smoking [Air Force General] Curtis LeMay is pushing me, and I gotta let him know that I'm as tough as he is."

So Johnson launched what soon became Operation Rolling Thunder to show that he was just as tough as Ho Chi Minh, Alexei Kosygin, General Curtis LeMay, and, equally if not more important, former Kennedy advisers Robert McNamara and McGeorge Bundy. It was launched, even more fatefully, in a confused atmosphere of what the bombing was supposed to accomplish. Since the December meetings in Washington, Ambassador Taylor and other advocates of the "pulmotor treatment" had been arguing for bombing the north to pull the south together, and to punish Hanoi. Bundy and McNamara had likewise claimed that the U.S. was headed for defeat because the South Vietnamese lacked any feeling of confidence about American willingness to use its power against the enemy. Now the McNamara/Bundy position began to shade off into a dangerous self-delusion that air power could "win" the war, ultimately the most dangerous policy quagmire Vietnam presented.

Thus, where Taylor's unstated premise had been that America held Vietnamese national self-determination in trust for some future Saigon government, Bundy's report on his return from Saigon stressed that American policy must do something immediately to fulfill that responsibility, that Washington had yet to provide an adequate response to the yearning and groping for a genuine revolution. "This is the overriding reason for our present recommendation of a policy of sustained reprisal. Once such a policy is put in force, we shall be able to speak in Vietnam on many topics and in many ways, with growing force and effectiveness."

Bundy once quipped, "Pleikus are like streetcars." One came along every ten minutes or so. Yet the timing of the Pleiku raid was highly important in providing a receptive audience for the report he presented upon his return from Saigon. As pressure built from December onward for a bombing campaign, other pressures were also mounting for a new diplomatic initiative. Public opinion divided, as might be expected, expressing a desire for negotiations but not wanting a defeat. State Department aides discounted serious public opinion difficulties over Vietnam, because they imagined that the president's huge approval ratings in general would carry the nation along whatever course he chose. Yet the mood was shifting in many places, noted William Bundy, nationally and internationally, that pointed "quite markedly in the direction of seeking a negotiated outcome."

Public opinion against the bombing might also bring pressure on Hanoi by focusing world attention on the war. Johnson had declared at the congressional briefing on the retaliatory attack that he would not allow the views of a "few senators" to control his actions. The next day, however, he received a memorandum from Mike Mansfield urging him to see if the cochairs of the 1954 Geneva Conference, Russia and Great Britain, could not reconvene that forum—or some other group—to seek some way to end the fighting. But the attack at Pleiku and the retaliatory raid had made it difficult for Mansfield, let alone lesser figures, to argue for a conference that could only end either with a concession to the political legitimacy of the NLF, or a walkout and the likelihood of rapid escalation with the danger of war with China. Even Mansfield ended his letter with a pledge that regardless of his "individual" views he would do whatever he could to support the president "in the exercise of your grave responsibility."

American officials had rightly concluded that *any* negotiations would mean the failure of the rescue mission they had set for themselves. Confident that Hanoi was ready to deliver the death blow to Saigon, Moscow and Beijing were both jockeying for position. Thus, China had launched a psychological warfare campaign against Thailand while Russia sent Kosygin to North Vietnam to promise greater support from Moscow. Certain Asian leaders had chosen sides already. Cambodia's Prince Sihanouk had made a trip to Beijing and had then refused to accept a new American ambassador. Indonesia's Sukarno menaced Malaysia and indicated his preference for Mao over any Western leaders. If this nightmare scenario played out as indicated, the loss of Vietnam would reduce the American role to observer while the Communist rivals vied for supremacy across Asia.

From Laos, Ambassador William H. Sullivan cabled a warning against negotiations on the basis of the 1954 Geneva Agreement. Washington's public position, albeit stated ambiguously most of the time, was that all the Communists had to do was to return to the 1954 agreements. The DRV (and now the French) had been insisting for some time that those agreements had been violated when "free general elections" were not held in 1956, as stipulated in paragraph seven of the final declaration. Sullivan admitted as much. "This, of course, would merely be non-violent means of achieving subversion," the ambassador said, "which DRV would have been unable [to] carry out by force of arms." What was needed was a "codicil" to the 1954 agreement, providing for the "indefinite existence of two separate entities north and south, postponing elections sine die and perhaps including certain economic clauses tempting to [the] DRV."

Sullivan's candor was unusual, even in cable traffic between Washington and diplomatic posts abroad. The United States had supported Diem's rejection of Hanoi's efforts to hold all-Vietnamese elections in 1956, a clear violation of the Geneva accords, but not one American official talked about it, even in private. There were no indications, however, that the North Vietnamese wanted anything so chancy as a return to the 1954 accords. What did seem to be emerging was a possible North Vietnamese ploy, as related by French sources, to allow South Vietnam to remain nominally independent and "neutral" but controlled by the NLF, as part of a two-stage process leading to eventual reunification. All this supposedly would be worked out at a new conference convened by the Soviet Union and Great Britain.

This explanation might account for the Hanoi-Moscow rapprochement of recent weeks, both in terms of Soviet promises and Russian concern that the North Vietnamese not do anything to force the United States into an irrevocable escalation of its role in the war. In that case, the Pleiku attack had been a mistake, or possibly a miscalculation. More likely, however, the North Vietnamese were showing their independence of *any* foreign control (so as not to alienate China) as well as a lot of self-confidence. Thus, even if the French sources were correct, all the Americans were being offered was an opportunity through "negotiations" to make a graceful exit.

If American policymakers hoped that the retaliatory bombing of North Vietnam, and a second strike a few days later in response to a similar attack at Qui Nhon that killed twenty-three American enlisted men, would quiet calls for an international conference or bilateral negotiations, such expectations went unrealized. In the United States there was a rally-round-the-flag response to events in Vietnam, but the bombing raids intensified international effort to bring about peace talks.

UN Secretary General U Thant tried to prod Washington toward peace talks with Hanoi, and, when rebuffed by Secretary Rusk, disclosed the background of his effort at a news conference. "I am sure," he said to startled reporters, "that the great American people, if only they knew the true facts and the background to the developments in South Vietnam, will agree with me that further bloodshed is unnecessary." U Thant's "meddling" was especially hard to take, based as it was on an accusation that the American government was not telling its people the truth. Upon his return to Moscow, Alexei Kosygin issued an appeal for peace in Vietnam. He denounced the American attacks as a "personal insult" and again promised greater aid to North Vietnam; but he was also quick to support both U Thant's initiative and to second Charles de Gaulle's call for reconvening the Geneva Conference.

In London, Prime Minister Harold Wilson faced a sharp reaction to the bombings from Labour back-benchers, many of whom did not usually join in left-wing America bashing. Wilson proposed to take the heat off himself by going to Washington for a talk with LBJ, just as Clement Attlee had flown over to reassure his back-benchers that Harry Truman was not going to start throwing atomic bombs during the Korean War. Johnson was furious at the idea. "I won't tell you how to run Malaysia," the president fairly shouted into the telephone, "and you don't tell us how to run Vietnam. . . . If you want to help us some in Vietnam send us some men and send us some folks to deal with these guerrillas. And announce to the press that you are going to help us."

Wilson's efforts to get cooperation from the Russians in calling for a reconvening of the Geneva Conference did not bring an immediate response. By the time Moscow finally replied to the British effort, the tit-for-tat bombing had become Operation Rolling Thunder, the Phase II plan for bringing steadily increasing pressure on North Vietnam. And Hanoi's response had become what it would remain over the next three years: the bombing must stop before there could be any talk of negotiations.

Dean Rusk put the administration's position on negotiations very succinctly to congressional leaders:

> If Hanoi and Peking bring themselves to a point where they are prepared to leave these people alone, there are a dozen channels which could register that very quickly, and this whole situation could move very fast. But thus far there has been no indication that that is their purpose, and therefore, there arises the great issue as to what a negotiation would be about, and against the background that a negotiation . . . failed, [that] could add immeasurably to the danger.

The "negotiations" problem was vastly more complicated than simply inviting the other side to talk about the terms of its surrender, however, as Rusk understood only too well. The secretary had built his case for American intervention in Vietnam on recitations of Communist perfidy in breaking solemn agreements. This was a Cold War staple, going back to Harry Truman's day. President Johnson had stated many times that he would be only too happy to withdraw American forces from Vietnam as a result of a peace settlement. And what then? There had been nine changes of government since Diem's death, as Rusk himself told the congressional leaders. Now fully confident that he had Johnson with him all the way, Mac Bundy pointed out to French Foreign Minister Couve de Murville that aside from de Gaulle's assessment of Chinese motives, there was another difference between Paris and Washington. "France seems to think that there can be no solution to the problem of stable government in South Vietnam while the United States remains there, while we think that there can be no solution if we leave."

Dean Rusk liked to invoke the Greek civil war of the late 1940s when he discussed negotiations. There were no negotiations in that case, just disengagement when the Communist guerrillas realized that the United States would not be driven out of the Mediterranean. Bundy preferred the situation in Berlin as his model. American policymakers from Truman to Johnson had refused to "negotiate" a change in Berlin's status as a divided city. "I saw a message the other day from President [James] Conant of Harvard," Bundy told congressional leaders, reminding them that Conant had been the American high commissioner in Germany at the height of early Cold War tensions in Europe. Conant was not a belligerent man, the national security adviser continued, but "the burden of his message was that the defense of Berlin, right now, is in Vietnam."

> And I believe this to be true, gentlemen. This is a test of our ability to take and deal with the most difficult and dangerous challenges, proudly stated by the Communists in their doctrine of wars of national liberation. The frustrations which you gentlemen feel are frustrations which we all feel. The point is that we have to get beyond them and have the courage to stay with the task.

And to Johnson in a private memorandum, Bundy added the logical conclusion of all he had been saying since returning from Saigon:

The pressure for negotiations is coming mostly from people who simply do not understand what the word means in Asian ears right now. If the U.S. proposes negotiations or even indicates a desire for them, the word in Saigon will be that we are getting out. And the consequences of that rumor would be very severe for our whole position.

Former President Dwight D. Eisenhower was equally opposed to the idea of negotiations. His analogy was the American Civil War. Seeking bipartisan support to ward off expected criticism once Rolling Thunder began, Johnson had invited Eisenhower to a well-publicized meeting in the White House. Eisenhower held practically the same views as Johnson's key advisers: bombing the north was essential to the morale of South Vietnam and to the weakening of morale in North Vietnam. He would put the importance of morale, the old soldier-politician said, even higher than Napoleon had rated it at 3 to 1 over the material element. When Johnson said that some of his advisers were pushing for negotiations, Eisenhower answered with a rumination about Lincoln and the Emancipation Proclamation. Lincoln had had the proclamation ready for a long time, he began, and he yearned to put it out. But he had to wait through long, dreary months of military reverses before he could seize upon a Confederate defeat as the occasion to issue it. Negotiations from weakness could only be disastrous. His answer to all those who wanted negotiations would be, "Not now, boys."

The Greek civil war, Berlin, the American Civil War—Johnson found himself surrounded by analogies that all but walled off the reality of the situation in Saigon and the countryside. A disturbing fragment of that reality, nevertheless, provided yet another complication to the negotiations conundrum. At a press conference on February 4, 1965, the president was asked about rumors that the north and south were negotiating behind the scenes. Would the United States leave if asked by South Vietnam? "I would not anticipate that we would receive such an invitation," Johnson shot back. He would cross that bridge *if* he ever got to it, but he did not expect to get to it. What about the suggestions of certain senators that Washington should explore the negotiations path? "You will find from time to time that Senators from both . . . parties will have different viewpoints, to which they are entitled, and they will express them, as I have expressed mine."

Johnson's testiness, it can be argued, stemmed from a concern that while the bombing might be "manageable," as he kept telling congressional leaders, the pressure for negotiations might easily get out of hand. In the aftermath of the first bombing raid on North Vietnam, a Committee to Defend the Peace was established in Saigon. A petition campaign gathered thousands of signatures denouncing the attacks on the north and calling for negotiations. The leader of the group was arrested, but it managed to stage a press conference anyway. More arrests followed. Those detained constituted a substantial proportion of Saigon's professional and business classes. The police station, quipped one of the committee members, suddenly looked as if "the city's elite had somehow mistaken the address of an upper-crust social gathering."

It was terribly important, Johnson told the National Security Council, that the government in Saigon not get the impression that the United States was seeking negotiations prematurely. "Under these circumstances Saigon might begin its own negotiations quickly and without our knowledge or participation." Despite his abrupt dismissal of unverified reports from Paris about General Khanh's contacts with Hanoi and the NLF, the president and his advisers had in fact been alerted by the CIA to the general's ambition to "make himself the 'Prince Sihanouk' of Vietnam by negotiating a deal with the Viet Cong's National Liberation front to neutralize South Vietnam." Johnson told French Foreign Minister Couve de Murville that "we might have to leave South

Vietnam for some reason but we hoped not." One wonders what the Frenchman made of the president's next statement:

> We have no ambitions, but if we were to abandon Vietnam, we would be forced to give up Laos, Thailand, Burma, and would be back to Hawaii and San Francisco.

Perhaps he was reminded of former Secretary of State Dean Acheson's statement that American policy was to enable peoples who thought the way Americans did, to live the way they wanted to. In any event, the president committed himself in principle to a sustained bombing campaign against North Vietnam on February 13, 1965. He reserved for a final decision the timing and implementation of the campaign. As each day passed, Bundy and McNamara grew more restless. "We have waited many months to put it into effect," the national security adviser wrote in as near exasperation as one dared to use with LBJ. "There is a deep-seated need for assurance that the decision has in fact been taken."

> When you were out of the room yesterday, Bob McNamara repeatedly stated that he simply has to know what the policy is so that he can make his military plans and give his military orders. This certainty is equally essential if we are to get the necessary political effects in Saigon.

Ambassador Taylor and General Westmoreland, meanwhile, had been wrestling with the problem of getting rid of Khanh, whose maneuvering between the Young Turks and the Buddhists had kept alive fears that America would be "invited" to leave. After a complicated set of countermaneuvers, U.S. officials managed to secure a "vote" in the Vietnamese Armed Forces Council in late February dismissing Khanh from all power and authority and leaving him with an empty title, "roving ambassador." When his plane took off from Saigon, the final obstacle to Rolling Thunder had been removed.

The nominal prime minister under Khanh, Pham Huy Quat, remained nominal under the new regime, closely controlled by the Armed Forces Council. On March 1, 1965, Air Marshal Ky, speaking for the council, declared that it would replace any government that in its judgment "threatened to betray the country." The next day American planes began the sustained bombing of North Vietnam.

"The policy of gradual but steady reprisal against North Vietnam for its continuing aggression in the South had been put into action," Johnson wrote in his memoirs. "The decision was made because it had become clear, gradually but unmistakably, that Hanoi was moving in for the kill." A few days after the bombing began, however, Johnson was in a dark mood. Outside the White House, blacks were marching for the right to vote. Preoccupied with his many problems, Johnson mused about his predicament. He was not optimistic the bombing would prove the answer. "I can't get out. I can't finish it with what I have got. So what the Hell can I do?" His advisers were urging him to announce a Johnson Doctrine, a promise to undertake the "other" war in Vietnam, to bring the Great Society to Southeast Asia.

9
The Tet Offensive
LARRY BERMAN

War is an ugly thing, but not the ugliest: the decayed and degraded state of moral and patriotic feeling which thinks nothing worth a war is worse. . . . A man who has nothing which he cares about more than his personal safety is a miserable creature who has no chance of being free, unless made and kept so by the exertions of better men than himself.

—On February 8, 1968, President Johnson sent this quotation from John Stuart Mill to Dean Rusk, Robert McNamara, Clark Clifford, and the Joint Chiefs.

I just don't understand it. Am I that far off? Am I wrong? Has something happened to me? My wife said, I think so. But she said you don't know what year you are living in. This is '68.

—Remarks by President Lyndon Johnson to a Congressional delegation in the White House, January 30, 1968.

Khe Sanh

On January 11, 1968, U.S. intelligence detected a buildup of forces in the Laotian panhandle west of the demilitarized zone, threatening the Marine base at Khe Sanh in western Quang Tri province of South Vietnam. Khe Sanh was located eight miles east of Laos and eighteen miles south of the DMZ. The base occupied a strategically important location for the purposes of hindering enemy infiltration down the Ho Chi Minh Trail as well as providing a staging post for possible operations into Laos.

The enemy force buildup of two additional North Vietnamese divisions was incontrovertible; but Hanoi's motives were wildly disputed. Prisoner reports and captured documents revealed that a massive winter-spring offensive was being planned. Truck traffic down the Ho Chi Minh Trail had reached massive proportions and major North Vietnamese troop reinforcements were in the border areas. Was Hanoi merely setting the stage for negotiations or was the offensive intended to topple the government of South Vietnam? What was the enemy up to? General [William] Westmoreland believed a maximum military effort was under way, possibly to improve chances of achieving an end to the war through negotiations that would lead to a coalition government involving the NLF. A major offensive by Hanoi might also be aimed at achieving one major psychological victory in the United States prior to the start of the presidential campaign.

The enemy was finally coming to Westmoreland for battle. This would not be search and destroy in the jungle. Years of waiting for the enemy were almost over, and even though U.S. forces were significantly outnumbered, Westmoreland cabled [Earle] Wheeler on January 12 that a withdrawal from Khe Sanh was unthinkable. "I consider this area critical to us from a tactical standpoint as a launch base for Special Operations Group teams and as flank security for the strong point obstacle system; it is even more critical from a psychological viewpoint. To relinquish this area would be a major propaganda victory for the enemy. Its loss would seriously affect Vietnamese and US morale. In short, withdrawal would be a tremendous step backwards."

With 15–20,000 North Vietnamese reinforcements circling Khe Sanh, Westmoreland bit the lure by ordering the 6,000 Marine troops to defend the garrison. General Westmoreland also set in motion plans for implementing Operation Niagara (evoking an image of cascading bombs and shells), which became the most intense and successful application of aerial firepower yet seen in the war.

During the predawn hours of January 21, 1968, Khe Sanh came under constant rocket and mortar fire from the North Vietnamese. The battle was on, and it appeared to President Johnson and his principal advisors that the North Vietnamese envisioned Khe Sanh as a potential Dien Bien Phu. During a January 23 White House meeting with members of the Democratic leadership, the president reported that "intelligence reports show a great similarity between what is happening at Khe Sanh and what happened at Dien Bien Phu." Johnson became preoccupied with the analogy and had a table model made of sand of the Khe Sanh plateau constructed in the bunker-like Situation Room of the White House. He feared that Khe Sanh would be his "Dinbinphoo," as LBJ was prone to pronounce it.

The Khe Sanh–Dien Bien Phu analogy was fraught with historical misapplication. The actual siege by the Viet Minh of Dien Bien Phu in 1954 had lasted 56 days. The French forces included Montagnards, North Africans, Vietnamese, and Foreign Legionnaires. The total force was about 13,000 and casualties amounted to 1,100 killed, 1,600 missing, and 4,400 wounded. The Vietminh totaled 49,500 combat troops plus 55,000 support troops. At Khe Sanh, U.S. forces numbered 6,000 against an enemy strength of about 20,000. The enemy's advantage was less than 4 to 1 rather than 8 to 1 (including support troops) as it had been at Dien Bien Phu. Moreover, usable supplies parachuted into Dien Bien Phu had averaged about 100 tons per day; General Westmoreland had a capability of 600 tons per day. The French had possessed 75 combat aircraft and 100 supply and reconnaissance aircraft. By comparison, the United States had more than 2,000 aircraft and 3,300 helicopters.

Uncertainty about the military situation at Khe Sanh led LBJ to question the Joint Chiefs. At a meeting on January 29, the president requested that each member submit "his views concerning the validity of the strategy now pursued in South Vietnam by the Free World Forces." The declassified meeting notes show that LBJ had asked the chiefs "if they were completely in agreement that everything has been done to assure that General Westmoreland can take care of the expected enemy offensive against Khesanh." General Wheeler and the Joint Chiefs "agreed that everything which had been asked for had been granted and that they were confident that General Westmoreland and the troops were prepared to cope with any contingency."

It was during this period that Johnson, finding it difficult to sleep, would walk the halls of the White House or call down to the Situation Room for a report on Khe Sanh. Secretary of State Dean Rusk recalled that, "We couldn't break him of the habit, even for health reasons, of getting up at 4:30 or 5:00 every morning to go down to the operations room and check on the casualties from Vietnam, each one of which took a little piece out of him."[1]

NSC staff assistant, Colonel Robert Ginsburgh, frequently found himself on night watch at the Situation Room in the basement of the White House. The Situation Room was actually two rooms—one a windowless room with a long table for private meetings; the other an active hub of communications with AP, UPI, and Reuter teletypes. Four clocks were mounted on the wall—Washington, GMT, Saigon, and the official presidential time which was set to follow LBJ's travels. The room also contained three television sets and other forms of technology befitting a White House communications center—especially a telephone. Ginsburgh recalled that during the battle for Khe

Sanh, "I had the night-time watch. And so, every two hours I was either in touch with the President on the phone, that is, he would call me or I would have sent him a message, a little memo to try and preclude his calling. He wanted to know, 'How is it going, what is happening?' "[2]

Johnson wanted to know how things were going because he was running out of trust for those who had brought him to this point. Johnson later denied pressuring the chiefs, but the declassified record contradicts his position. Meeting on February 2 with White House correspondents, the president discussed the JCS [Joint Chiefs of Staff] assurances about Khe Sanh. In the meeting notes he is recorded as saying, "I asked the JCS to give me a letter saying that they were ready for the offensive at Khesanh." Yet, when reporters wrote that Johnson had obtained these letters from the chiefs, the president vehemently denied the claim.

The president then asked his assistant Tom Johnson to review all meeting notes to see whether there was any proof to the press reports. Tom Johnson wrote the president, "I have reviewed all of the notes of meetings held during the past two weeks. In addition, I have searched my memory thoroughly . . . At no time do my notes show, or my memory recall, an incident when the President said: 'I do not want any Damn Dien Bien Phu.' The President said we wanted to make sure we had done everything here and the JCS had done everything to make certain there is not another Dien Bien Phu. The word 'damn' was not used in any meeting I attended in this context. Never did the President say he had 'made each chief sign a paper stating that he believed Khe Sanh could be defended.' " LBJ could thus claim that he had not said either "damn" or "each chief"; but he had made the Dien Bien Phu analogy and he had at least told members of Congress that the chiefs had signed a paper.[3]

During a particularly contentious morning meeting on January 30 with the Democratic congressional leaders, Senator Robert Byrd remarked, "I am very concerned about the buildup at Khesanh. I have been told that we have 5,000 troops there compared with 40,000 enemy troops. Are we prepared for this attack?" The president responded, "This has been a matter of great concern to me. I met with the Joint Chiefs yesterday. I went around the table and got their answer to these questions. In addition, I have it in writing that they are prepared. I asked, 'Have we done all we should do?' They said yes. I asked, 'Are we convinced our forces are adequate?' They said yes. I asked, 'Should we withdraw [troops to be used in Vietnam] from Korea?' They said no, that Khesanh is important to us militarily and psychologically."

General Wheeler, who was also at the meeting, sought to provide clarification for Byrd's queries: "On the matter of your question, Senator Byrd, about 5,000 U.S. troops versus 40,000 enemy troops. Khesanh is in very rugged areas. There are 5,900 U.S. troops in the Khesanh Garrison. There are support troops including 26th Marines and a battalion of the ARVN. . . . There are 39,968 friendly forces versus 38,590 enemy forces. Roughly, there are 40,000 allied troops to match the 40,000 enemy. We think we are ready to take on any contingency. In addition, there are 40 B-52 sorties and 500 tactical air sorties in the area Niagara each day hitting the enemy. . . . General Westmoreland is confident he can hold the position. To abandon it would be to step backward. The Joint Chiefs agree with General Westmoreland. The Joint Chiefs believe that he can hold and that he should hold. General Westmoreland considers it an opportunity to inflict heavy casualties on North Vietnam. We have 6,000 men there, and 34,000 available. It is 40,000 versus 40,000."

A week later during a White House meeting of the principals the president again asked Wheeler, "Are you as confident today as you were yesterday that we can handle the situation at Khesanh?" General Wheeler answered, "I do not think the enemy is capable of doing what they have set out to do. General Westmoreland has strengthened his position. He has contingency plans and can meet any contingency. There is nothing he has asked for that he has not been given. Khesanh is important to us militarily and psychologically. It is the anchor of our defensive situation along the DMZ." Johnson again asked General Wheeler, "Are you sure that you have everything that is needed to take care of the situation in Khesanh?" Wheeler responded, "Yes, we are. General Westmoreland has been given everything he has requested."

Prometheus Bound

The enemy buildup at Khe Sanh was followed on January 23, 1968, by North Korea's capture of the U.S. Navy Intelligence ship *Pueblo* on grounds of espionage. Seized in international waters some 26 miles off the coast of Japan, the 906-ton USS *Pueblo* was on its first electronic surveillance mission. The crew of 83, captained by Lloyd Bucher, was forced into the North Korean port at Wonsan, the first U.S. naval vessel captured since the USS *Chesapeake* in 1807—during the Napoleonic Wars.

Had the seizure been a pre-planned effort to provoke a U.S. response and to exert pressure on the United States in Vietnam? Were the North Koreans supporting their Communist allies in North Vietnam and trying to create fear in South Korea? "Prometheus Bound," proclaimed a *Newsweek* article in describing how "a tenth-rate country" had "abruptly confronted Lyndon B. Johnson with one of the most delicate and intractable emergencies of his crisis-wracked Administration."[4] Secretary of State Dean Rusk declared publicly, "I would not object to designating this an act of war in terms of the category of actions to be so construed. My strong advice to North Korea is to cool it." But North Korea had no intention of cooling it; instead, it released a confession signed by the *Pueblo*'s skipper, Commander Bucher, obviously obtained under duress, which contained alleged admissions of CIA contacts and proposed aggression against Korea.

Ironically, the seizure allowed Johnson to mobilize 15,000 Air Force and Navy Reservists as well as 370 inactive aircraft. Johnson also convened a "crisis" meeting of an informal planning committee which included all of the principal advisors to the president, somewhat like President Kennedy's Executive Committee (ExComm) during the Cuban Missile Crisis of 1962. The president was determined not to act hastily and to do everything possible diplomatically to get the crew returned safely. (Which succeeded only after a protracted period of eleven months.)

The seizure raised difficult problems for Johnson's political leadership. The president could hardly afford a second war front in Asia, yet he was being pressured at home to retaliate against what Massachusetts congressman William Bates, senior Republican on the House Armed Services Committee, called "a dastardly act of piracy." Hawks were not the only ones pressuring Johnson. Democratic senator Frank Church of Idaho, one of the Senate's most outspoken doves on Vietnam, derided the *Pueblo*'s seizure as "an act of war," in which the honor of the United States was at stake.

Tet: Move Forward to Achieve Final Victory

During the early morning hours of January 31 (the Vietnamese New Year, Tet) approximately 80,000 North Vietnamese regulars and guerrillas attacked over 100 cities throughout South Vietnam. Tet involved enemy attacks on 35 of 44 province capitals,

36 district towns and many villages and hamlets. For weeks prior to the offensive, enemy forces had been infiltrating into Saigon in civilian clothes in preparation for a well-planned campaign of terror. The goal was to achieve a popular uprising against the GVN and to show the American public that the very notion of security in the South was null and void.

Communist forces had been given the general order "Move forward to achieve final victory." Combat orders had urged the assaulters to do everything possible to completely liberate the people of South Vietnam. The orders found on captured guerrillas described the Tet strategy as one that would be "the greatest battle ever fought throughout the history of our country." The infiltrators were exhorted to "move forward aggressively to carry out decisive and repeated attacks in order to annihilate as many American, Satellite and Puppet troops as possible in conjunction with political struggles and military proselyting activities. . . . Display to the utmost your revolutionary heroism by surmounting all hardships and difficulties and making sacrifices as to be able to fight continually and aggressively. Be prepared to smash all enemy counter attacks and maintain your revolutionary standpoint under all circumstances. Be resolute in achieving continuous victories and secure the final victory at all costs."

While the attack itself did not surprise the principals, its timing during the Tet holiday phase-down did. In Washington, Walt Rostow was called away from a foreign-affairs advisors' luncheon to receive news of the offensive. Rostow quickly returned to report, "We have just been informed we are being heavily mortared in Saigon. The Presidential Palace, . . . the Embassy and the city itself have been hit." General Wheeler did not seem very alarmed: "It was the same type of thing before. You will remember that during the inauguration that the MACV [Military Assistance Command, Vietnam] headquarters was hit. In a city like Saigon people can infiltrate easily. They carry in rounds of ammunition and mortars. They fire and run. It is impossible to stop this in its entirety. This is about as tough to stop as it is to protect against an individual mugging in Washington, D.C. We have got to pacify all of this area and get rid of the Viet Cong infrastructure. They are making a major effort to mount a series of these actions to make a big splurge at TET."[5]

But General Westmoreland quickly cabled Admiral [U. S. Grant] Sharp that the enemy attacks constituted more than a D.C. mugging. The enemy "appears to be [using] desperation tactics, using NVA troops to terrorize populated areas. He attempted to achieve surprise by attacking during the truce period. The reaction of Vietnamese, US and Free World Forces to the situation has been generally good. Since the enemy has exposed himself, he has suffered many casualties. As of now, they add up to almost 700. When the dust settles, there will probably be more. All my subordinate commanders report the situation well in hand."

From a military assessment, the VC suffered a major defeat at Tet. Over half of their committed force was lost and perhaps a quarter of their whole regular force. Moreover, the Communists failed to bring about the diversion of U.S. forces from Khe Sanh or elsewhere. Nevertheless, the psychological impact of Tet was demoralizing to the American public. The enemy had demonstrated a capability to enter and attack cities and towns and had employed terrorism for doing vast damage. [Ellsworth] Bunker cabled Johnson on February 8, "Hanoi may well have reasoned that in the event that the TET attacks did not bring the outright victory they hoped for, they could still hope for political and psychological gains of such dimensions that they could come to the negotiating table with a greatly strengthened hand. They may have very well estimated that the impact of the TET attacks would at the very least greatly discourage the

United States and cause other countries to put more pressure on us to negotiate on Hanoi's terms."

The impact on the American public was indeed great. A front-page photograph on the *New York Times* February 1 edition showed three military policemen, rifles in hand, seeking protection behind a wall outside the consular section of the U.S. Embassy in Saigon. The bodies of two American soldiers slain by guerrillas who had raided the compound, lay nearby. All 19 guerrillas had been killed, but not until they had blasted their way into the embassy and had held part of the grounds for six hours. Four MPs, a Marine guard, and a South Vietnamese employee were killed in the attack. President [Nguyen Van] Thieu declared a state of martial law, yet during a news conference from the Cabinet room, President Johnson likened Tet to the Detroit riots, asserting "a few bandits can do that in any city."

Meeting with key congressional leaders in the evening of January 31, LBJ reviewed the events preceding Tet as well as Khe Sanh. "The Joint Chiefs, and all the Joint Chiefs, met with me the day before yesterday and assured me that they had reviewed the plans and they thought they were adequate. I told them I thought I almost had to have them sign up in blood because if my poll goes where it has gone, with all the victories, I imagine what it would do if we had a good major defeat. So General Westmoreland and the Joint Chiefs of Staff are sure that we are not anticipating some major activity there that we have not heard about."

General Wheeler then explained that Hanoi's military purpose in the Tet offensive had been to draw forces away from the Khe Sanh area. The second objective seemed to have been more political, to demonstrate to the South Vietnamese people and the world, that the Communists still possessed a considerable strength in the country and thereby shake the confidence of the Vietnamese people in the ability of their government to provide them security, even when they were within areas held by government and U.S. troops. "A significant thing about this attack," Wheeler said, "is that in many areas, particularly in Saigon, and at Bien Hoa, the attackers were dressed in one of three [*sic*] types of clothing: Civilian clothes, military, ARVN military police uniforms, or national police uniforms. Apparently, they gave no attention at all to whether or not they killed civilians. This is a sort of an unusual action for them because they have posed as the protectors of the civilian populace. Apparently this is the effort to reestablish by terror a degree of control over the population."

The meeting of congressional leaders was followed by a Cabinet meeting which Johnson opened by acknowledging, "There is a lot of stress and plenty of overtime for us all." President Johnson then engaged in a series of free-flowing remarks in which he came close to blaming the pope for Tet:

> I think I admired President Kennedy most during the Bay of Pigs when he said 'no one is to blame but me.' I know that wasn't true. . . . We went into Rome at night and we could have been faced with two million Red demonstrators. The Pope appealed to me. We had no differences, no quarrels. He said 'I want to do something, anything for peace—can't you give us one extra day of the holiday truce?' General Westmoreland told me how many American lives it would cost, but we did give the Pope his extra day. Now it's hard not to regret the number of boys who were killed. It is now so much worse after the Tet truce. Westmoreland cancelled the Tet truce because the house was on fire. So you look at *Pueblo*, Khe Sanh, Saigon and you see them all as part of the Communist effort to defeat us out there. We can dodge it by being weak-kneed if we want to. I said at San Antonio that we have gone as far as we could—farther, I might add, than the military wanted. We made it clear how much we want to talk and not bomb, just so long as there is some prompt and productive response. But if you sneak

in the night and hit us, we can't stop bombing. Now we have their answer with this new offensive. It just should satisfy every dove who loves peace as much as any mother does.

The president then read excerpts from a memorandum received from Ambassador Bunker, calling particular attention to a passage recalling Thomas Paine's remark, "These are the times that try men's souls. . . . What we attain too cheaply, we esteem too lightly."

Attending the annual presidential prayer breakfast at the Shoreham Hotel, the president sounded weary and burdened by events. "The nights are very long. The winds are very chill. Our spirits grow weary and restive as the springtime of man seems farther and farther away. I can, and I do, tell you that in these long nights your President prays." Indeed, as these personal pressures grew, LBJ sought private solace in late-night prayer at St. Dominic's Church, in southwest Washington. Accompanied only by the secret service, the president and his "little monks" would read scriptures, psalms, and sing hymns.[6]

On February 1, Wheeler cabled Sharp and Westmoreland raising the possibility of "whether tactical nuclear weapons should be used if the situation in Khe Sanh should become that desperate." While Wheeler considered that eventuality unlikely, he requested a list of susceptible targets in the areas "which lend themselves to nuclear strikes, whether some contingency nuclear planning would be in order, and what you would consider to be some of the more significant pros and cons of using tac [tactical] nukes in such a contingency."

Westmoreland responded, "The use of tactical nuclear weapons should not be required in the present situation." However, should the situation change, "I visualize that either tactical nuclear weapons or chemical agents would be active candidates for employment." During an emotional February 16 news conference, Johnson vehemently denied that nuclear weapons had ever been considered, adding even more fuel to the credibility gap fire. LBJ stated that it was "against the national interest to carry on discussions about the employment of nuclear weapons with respect to Khesanh."

While Wheeler and Westmoreland privately discussed tactical nukes, Walt Rostow privately drew charts for his wife Elspeth. "Responding to a question from Elspeth last night," Rostow wrote Johnson, "I explained events in Vietnam as follows. The war had been proceeding in 1967 on an attritional basis with our side gradually improving its position, the Communists gradually running down. . . .

But administration critics weren't convinced. Satirist Art Buchwald likened administration optimism to another historical event: " 'We have the enemy on the run,' says General Custer at Big Horn. 'It's a desperation move on the part of Sitting Bull and his last death rattle.' " Senator George Aiken wryly remarked, "If this is a failure, I hope the Viet Cong never have a major success." Yet Rostow again wrote Johnson that the degree of Communist terrorism during the Tet period would actually strengthen the South Vietnamese resolve to get even with these terrorists. "There is a chance that South Viet Nam will emerge in the weeks and months ahead with stronger political institutions and a greater sense of nationhood and common destiny than before."

More Troops

General Wheeler understood the severity of Westmoreland's military position. Allied forces were stretched to their maximum extent and effectiveness. On February 3, Wheeler cabled Westmoreland, "The President asks me if there is any reinforcement or help that we can give you?" Receiving no answer, Wheeler tried again on February 8: "Query: Do you need reinforcements? Our capabilities are limited. . . . However, if you consider reinforcements imperative, you should not be bound by earlier agreements. . . . United States government is not prepared to accept defeat in Vietnam. In summary, if you need more troops, ask for them."

Westmoreland now cabled Wheeler that there was cause for alarm. "From a realistic point of view we must accept the fact that the enemy has dealt the GVN a severe blow. He has brought the war to the towns and the cities and has inflicted damage and casualties on the population. Homes have been destroyed, distribution of the necessities of life has been interrupted. Damage has been inflicted to the LOC's [lines of communication] and the economy has been decimated. Martial law has been invoked, with stringent curfews in the cities. The people have felt directly the impact of the war."

While U.S. forces had repelled the Communist onslaught and inflicted major losses on the enemy manpower pool, Tet revealed the enemy's great skill in planning, coordination, and courage. The enemy had infiltrated previously secure population centers and exploited the GVN claim of security from attack. But there had been no general uprising, and the enemy did not hold a single city, although enemy units had waged a fierce three-week battle at the ancient city of Hué where they had occupied the Citadel —a nineteenth century fortress which shielded the nation's historic imperial palace. Hué, a city of 100,000, was also the traditional center of religious and intellectual life in Vietnam. After weeks of fighting, U.S. and ARVN forces secured Hué, but not until some of the worst carnage of the war had been unleashed on its civilian inhabitants.

Westmoreland cabled Wheeler that enemy activity at Hué and elsewhere had helped Hanoi to score "a psychological blow, possibly greater in Washington than in South Vietnam, since there are tentative signs that the populace is turning against the Viet Cong as a result of these attacks." The enemy had also succeeded in temporarily disrupting South Vietnam's economy, and Westmoreland believed the enemy would continue to strain the will of the people by maintaining pressure on the populated areas with his forces already committed. The general also expected another major offensive in the Saigon area, commencing in mid-February.

Meeting with the Democratic congressional leadership at breakfast on February 6, 1968, the president once again faced tough questions from Senator Robert Byrd. "I am concerned about: 1. That we had poor intelligence; 2. That we were not prepared for these attacks; 3. We underestimated the morale and vitality of the Viet Cong; 4. We over-estimated the support of the South Vietnamese government and its people." Johnson shot back at Byrd: "I don't agree with any of that. We knew that they planned a general uprising around TET. Our intelligence showed there was a winter-spring offensive planned. We did not know the precise places that were going to be hit. General [Creighton] Abrams said the Vietnamese are doing their best. There was no military victory for the Communists. Just look at the casualties and the killed in action."

The discussion then moved to a more general level of political analysis:

SENATOR BYRD: I have never caused you any trouble in this matter on the Hill. But I do have very serious concerns about Vietnam. I think this is the place to raise these questions, here in the family.

CONGRESSMAN HALE BOGGS: What about Bob Byrd's charge that we are under-estimating the strength of the VC? I personally do not agree with that.

THE PRESIDENT: I have never under-estimated the Viet Cong. They are not push-overs. I do not think we have bad intelligence or have under-estimated the Viet Cong morale.

SENATOR BYRD: Something is wrong over there.

THE PRESIDENT: The intelligence wasn't bad.

SENATOR BYRD: That does not mean the Viet Cong did not succeed in their efforts. Their objective was to show that they could attack all over the country and they did.

THE PRESIDENT: That was not their objective at all.

SENATOR BYRD: You have been saying the situation with the Viet Cong was one of diminishing morale. When I say you, I mean the Administration.

THE PRESIDENT: I personally never said anything of the sort. I am not aware that anyone else has been saying that. What do you think the American people would have done if we had sent in troops and had lost 21,000 of them as the enemy has?

SENATOR RUSSELL LONG: If we had planned to have an up-rising in Cuba and you had caused 21,000 men to be lost as the Viet Cong did, I am sure you would have been impeached.

THE PRESIDENT: I am of the opinion that criticism is not worth much. I look at all these speeches that are in the [Congressional] Record. I look at all the people who are going around the country saying our policy is wrong. Where do they get us? Nowhere. The popular thing now is to stress the mis-management to Vietnam. I think there has been very little. I wish Mike [Senator Mansfield] would make a speech on Ho Chi Minh. Nothing is as dirty as to violate a truce during the holidays. But nobody says anything bad about Ho. They call me a murderer. But Ho has a great image.

SENATOR BYRD: I don't want the President to think that I oppose you. I am just raising these matters.

THE PRESIDENT: I don't agree with what you say.

SENATOR LONG: I am happy you raised the point, Bob.

THE PRESIDENT: Everybody should say and do what they want to. But we have put our very best men that we have out there. I believe that our military and diplomatic men in the field know more than many of our Congressmen and Senators back here. Anybody can kick a barn down. It takes a good carpenter to build one. I just wish all of you would expose the Viet Cong and Ho. We have got some very crucial decisions coming up. Personally, I think they suffered a severe defeat. But we knew there would be a general uprising, and they did not win any victory. It seems to be an American trait to ask why. I just hope that we don't divert our energies and our talents by criticizing unnecessarily. We've got all we can of this "what's wrong with our country?" [William] Fulbright, [Stephen] Young and [Ernest] Gruening haven't helped one bit.

SENATOR BYRD: I do not want to argue with the President. But I am going to stick by my convictions.

Notes

For a complete list of documents used in this article consult the National Security Council History, "The March 31st Speech" at the LBJ Library. The project traces the events between the 1968 Tet attacks and the president's speech on March 31st in which he announced the partial cessation of the bombing and his decision not to seek reelection.

1. Quoted in Kenneth Thompson, ed., *The Johnson Presidency* (Lanham, MD: University Press of America, 1987), pp. 89–90, 258.
2. Robert Ginsburgh, deposition for CBS-Westmoreland trial in author's possession.
3. See Tom Johnson's meeting notes, Lyndon Baines Johnson Library.
4. See *Newsweek*, February 2, 1968.
5. See Tom Johnson's meeting notes.
6. See Doris Kearns, *Lyndon Johnson and the American Dream* (New York: Harper & Row, 1976), pp. 360–1.

10
A Dissenter in the Government
GEORGE W. BALL

The Critical Decision

The war continued to go badly. When my colleagues and I assembled at the White House on the morning of July 21,1965, we were given a memorandum from the Joint Chiefs of Staff. Only the prompt deployment of large bodies of American troops could, it argued, save the situation. That meant committing thousands of our young men not merely to passive defense missions but to aggressive combat roles. The war would then become unequivocally our own. There would be no turning back for months, perhaps years—not until we had suffered horrible casualties, killed thousands of Vietnamese, and raised the level of national anxiety and frustration above the threshold of hysteria.

Because of the importance of the July 21 meeting it may be useful to outline the colloquy which suggests the substance and flavor of our many long discussions.[1] It also provides some sense of the President's agonizing reluctance to go forward, his desire to explore every possible alternative, and, finally, his inability to reconcile his vaunted Texas "can-do" spirit with the shocking reality that America had painted itself into a corner with no way out except at substantial costs in terms of pride and prestige.

The President began with searching questions. Could we get more soldiers from our allies? What had altered the situation to the present point of urgency? McNamara produced a map. The Viet Cong, it showed, controlled about 25 percent of the South. United States forces would not be committed in those areas; they would be deployed "with their backs to the sea, for protection." They would conduct search and destroy operations against large-scale units.

"Why," I asked, "does anyone think that the Viet Cong will be so considerate as to confront us directly? They certainly didn't do that for the French." General Wheeler, the chairman of the Joint Chiefs of Staff, replied, "We can force them to fight by harassment."

After the others had expressed support for the proposed new escalation, the President asked whether any of us opposed it, looking directly at me. I made my usual speech, pointing out that we would be embarking on "a perilous voyage" and could not win. But, he asked, what other courses were available? We must, I replied, stop deceiving ourselves, face reality, and cut our losses. "If we get bogged down, the costs will be far greater than a planned withdrawal, while the pressures to create a larger war could become irresistible. We must stop propping up that absurd travesty of a government in Saigon. Let's let it fall apart and negotiate a withdrawal, recognizing that the country will face a probable take-over by the Communists."

The President replied, "You've pointed out the dangers but you've not really proposed an alternative."

After others had expressed similar sentiments, the President once more turned to me. "George," he asked, "do you think we have another course?" I answered, "I certainly don't agree with the course Bob McNamara's recommending." "All right," said the President, "we'll hear you out; then I can determine if any of your suggestions are sound and can be followed. I'm prepared to do that if convinced."

I could, I said, present to him only "the least bad of two courses." The course I could recommend was costly, but we could at least limit the cost to the short-term. At that point—just as I was beginning to speak—the President interrupted. "We'll have another meeting this afternoon where you can express your views in detail." Meanwhile, he wanted a further justification for the introduction of one-hundred-thousand more troops. In response to the President's concern about increased losses, General Taylor directly contradicted a view expressed earlier by Secretary McNamara that our losses in Vietnam would be proportional to the number of our men in that country. "The more men we have," the General now declared, "the greater the likelihood of smaller losses."

When we reconvened at 2:30 that afternoon, the President asked me to explain my position. I outlined why, in my view, we could not win. Even after a protracted conflict the most we could hope to achieve was "a messy conclusion" with a serious danger of intervention by the Chinese.[2] In a long war, I said, the President would lose the support of the country. I showed him a chart I had prepared showing the correlation between Korean casualties and public opinion. As our casualties during the Korean War had increased from 11,000 to 40,000, the percentage of those Americans who thought that we had been right to intervene had diminished from 56 percent in 1950 to a little more than 30 percent in 1952. Moreover, as our losses mounted, many frustrated Americans would demand that we strike at the "very jugular of North Vietnam" with all the dangers that entailed. Were it possible for us to win decisively in a year's time, friendly nations might continue to support us. But that was not in the cards.

"No great captain in history ever hesitated to make a tactical withdrawal if conditions were unfavorable to him," I argued. "We can't even find the enemy in Vietnam. We can't see him and we can't find him. He's indigenous to the country, and he always has access to much better intelligence. He knows what we're going to do but we haven't the vaguest clue as to his intentions. I have grave doubts that any Western army can successfully fight Orientals in an Asian jungle."

"That's the key question," the President remarked. "Can Westerners, deprived of accurate intelligence, successfully fight Asians in the jungles and rice paddies?"

We had, I continued, underestimated the critical conditions in South Vietnam. "What we are doing is giving cobalt treatment to a terminal cancer case. A long, protracted war will disclose our weakness, not our strength."

Since our main concern was to avoid undermining our credibility, we should shift the burden to the South Vietnamese government. We should insist on reforms that it would never undertake, which would impel it to move toward a neutralist position and ask us to leave. "I have no illusions," I said, "that after we were asked to leave South Vietnam, that country would soon come under Hanoi's control. That's implicit in our predicament." I then discussed the effect on other nations in the area.

The President then asked the question most troubling him, "Wouldn't we lose all credibility by breaking the word of three Presidents?" I replied, "We'll suffer the worst blow to our credibility when it is shown that the mightiest power on earth can't defeat a handful of miserable guerrillas."

Then, asked the President, "aren't you basically troubled by what the world would say about our pulling out?"

"If we were helping a country with a stable, viable government, it would be a vastly different story. But we're dealing with a revolving junta. How much support," I asked rhetorically, "do we really have in South Vietnam?"

The President then mentioned two of my points that particularly troubled him. One was that Westerners could never win a war in Asia; the other was that we could not successfully support a people whose government changed every month. He then asked, "What about the reaction of the Europeans? Wouldn't they be shaken in their reliance on us if we pulled out of Vietnam?"

"That idea's based on a complete misunderstanding of the way the Europeans are thinking," I said. "They don't regard what we are doing in Vietnam as in any way comparable to our involvement in Europe. Since the French pulled out of Vietnam, they can hardly blame us for doing the same thing; they cut their losses, and de Gaulle is urging us to follow suit. Having retired from their empire, the British recognize an established fact when they see one. They're not going to blame us for doing the same thing, although they might get a little mischievous pleasure from it—what the Germans call *schadenfreude*. But basically they only care about one thing. They're concerned about their own security. Troops in Berlin have real meaning; troops in Vietnam have none."

I then summarized the alternatives. "We can continue a dragged out, bitterly costly, and increasingly dangerous war, with the North Vietnamese digging in for a long term since that's their life and driving force." Or "we can face the short-term losses of pulling out. It's distasteful either way; but life's full of hard choices."

McGeorge Bundy then intervened to suggest that, while I had raised truly important questions, the course I recommended would be a "radical switch in policy without visible evidence that it should be done." "George's analysis," he said, "gives no weight to losses suffered by the other side. The world, the country, and the Vietnamese people would have alarming reactions if we got out." Dean Rusk then stated that, if the Communist world found out that we would not pursue our commitment to the end, there was no telling where they would stop their expansionism. He rejected my assessment of the situation. The Viet Cong had not established much of a position among the Vietnamese people, and he did not foresee large casualties unless the Chinese should come in. Ambassador Lodge agreed. There would, he said, be a greater threat of starting World War III if we did not go in with our forces. There were great seaports in Vietnam, and we did not have to fight on the roads.

After more talk along the same lines the meeting was adjourned.

Support from an Unexpected Quarter

The next day we met once more to hear the President's report of what the generals had told him. That meeting stands out in my memory not for anything I said—I had, after all, exhausted my persuasive arsenal—but rather because, for the first time, I found support from an unexpected quarter.

The President had asked his old friend Clark Clifford to attend and called on him to express his views. Presenting his argument with elegant precision and structure as though arguing a case before the Supreme Court, Clifford voiced strong opposition to the commitment of combat forces. He put forward the same arguments I had made the day before; in addition, he gave the President a more authoritative assessment of the probable domestic consequences. Whether or not President Johnson knew in advance of the position Clifford would take I cannot say; sometimes I suspected that he staged meetings for the benefit of the rest of us. But, whatever the answer to that question, Clifford emerged as a formidable comrade on my side of the barricades.

When the meeting was over, I asked Clifford to join me in the Fish Room. I told him that ever since the fall of 1961 I had been making the same arguments he now made so eloquently, and I gave him copies of the memoranda I had submitted to the

President. The next day Clifford told me that he had spent the previous evening until two in the morning carefully studying my memoranda. They were, he said, "impressive and persuasive." Throughout the last year he had come more and more to my opinion as he continued to receive reports of our deteriorating situation.

I told Clark that judging from the meeting we had just had that day with the President, his intervention had had a salutary effect. Clifford replied that he had been told through "another source" that there would have to be a great effort made if we were to block this critical escalatory step that would change the character of the war. Though he hoped that through our combined exertions we could make progress, he was not optimistic. Unfortunately, "individuals sometimes become so bound up in a certain course it is diffficult to know where objectivity stops and personal involvement begins." In any event, he had tried to impress on the President that we should down-play the talk that "this was the Armageddon between Communism and the Free World."

Clark Clifford had been close to the President for many years. Perhaps his opposition might turn the balance. We had one other powerful supporter, Senate Majority Leader Mike Mansfield, who, at the President's meeting with the Congressional leadership, had weighed in along the same line we were taking. There was, he had argued, no legitimate government in South Vietnam and we owed nothing to the current cabal. We were being pushed progressively deeper into the war, and even total victory would be enormously costly. Our best hope was for a quick stalemate and negotiation; the American people would never support a war that might last three to five years. We were about to get into an anti-Communist crusade. "Remember," he had concluded prophetically, "escalation begets escalation." Finally. there was my friend Senator J. William Fulbright, who had arrived at a position similar to mine, but the President had already written him off and rejected his view of the war.

As the whole world now knows, we did not carry the day—neither Mansfield, Clifford, Fulbright, nor I—and the balloon went up farther and farther.

As the war became progressively larger and bloodier, some of my colleagues talked with increasing wistfulness of a negotiated solution, which, in their vocabulary, meant Hanoi's capitulation. That was, I thought, quite unrealistic; the North Vietnamese would never stop fighting until they had obtained terms that would assure their takeover of the entire country. I had, therefore, only a marginal interest in efforts to open channels: they were not the answer. I did not see us achieving peace by the two techniques then being strongly urged: bombing pauses and the establishment of a multiplicity of diplomatic contacts. The battle-hardened leaders in Hanoi had no interest in mechanisms that would facilitate their crying "Uncle" in a low voice and with minimal loss of face: their interest was in forcing us to go home.

Bombing Pauses

A bombing pause, unaccompanied by significant concessions was merely pulling up a plant to see how well its roots were growing. From the middle of 1964 until the end of September 1966, when I left the State Department, there were two pauses. I supported both, not because I expected anything to come of them, but because I hoped they would break the rhythm of escalation. The first pause, which began on May 13,1965, and lasted only until May 18, was, as I pointed out to my staff, not so much a pause as a hiccup. We told the Soviets in advance and tried to pass word to Hanoi (which rejected the receipt of our message) but we neglected to tell the American people or even the American military. The foreign minister of Hanoi denounced the pause as a "deceitful maneuver to pave the way for American escalation"—which I thought a perceptive appraisal. Peking called it a "fraud."

In spite of the failure of the first pause, Secretary McNamara continued to advocate "low-key diplomacy" to lay the groundwork for a settlement, stating that "We could, as part of a diplomatic initiative, consider introducing a 6–8 week pause in the program of bombing the North."[3] He repeated that recommendation in a memorandum to the President on November 3. On November 30, 1965, he sought to justify it as primarily a ritual gesture "before we either greatly increase our troop deployments to Vietnam or intensify our strikes against the North." It would, he argued, "lay a foundation in the mind of the American public and in world opinion for such an enlarged phase of the war, and"—he added, I thought, with no conviction—"it should give North Vietnam a face-saving chance to stop the aggression."[4] Secretary Rusk was not convinced; a pause was a serious diplomatic instrument; it could be used only once, and this was not the time to use it. President Johnson had a different concern; a pause that evoked no response would, he feared, provoke a demand for much stronger action from the American right wing—and they, he warned me, were "the Great Beast to be feared."

For several weeks the debate continued. On December 23, I left to spend Christmas at our family house in Florida. On the evening of Monday, December 28, the President telephoned me to say, "George, you wanted a pause and I'm giving you one. Now I need you to get it going. I'm sending a plane for you in the morning."

The President called me home to help plan a diplomatic extravaganza. He would send Administration personalities flying all over the world; they would tell heads of state and chiefs of government about the pause and enlist their help to bring Hanoi to the negotiating table. Averall Harriman would visit Poland and Yugoslavia, McGeorge Bundy Canada, Ambassador Foy Kohler would speak with Soviet officials, while Arthur Goldberg would call on General de Gaulle, Prime Minister Wilson, the Pope, and the Italian government.[5] My own travel assignments were modest. I was to fly to Puerto Rico to meet Senator Fulbright fresh off the eighteenth green and then to Florida to see Senators Dirksen and Mansfield.

Although President Johnson obviously enjoyed this frenetic to-ing and fro-ing (he delighted in his ability to send well-known people flying all over the world), I thought the spectacle futile and unbecoming. Still, as I was to reflect later, better a Christmas peace extravaganza than the Christmas bombing Nixon ordered in 1974 [1972]. If that was part of the price we paid for a bombing pause, so be it; we at least broke the momentum of escalation, even though we would be under grave pressure to increase the pace of the war once the pause was completed.

Negotiating Gestures

The Administration constantly scanned the sky for smoke signals from Hanoi. It used disavowable envoys to try to provoke indications of willingness to talk and carried on probing operations with Iron Curtain diplomats.[6] Meanwhile, more and more of our young men were being sent to South Vietnam and casualties were rising. To borrow a phrase I had once heard Walter Lippmann use to describe his own frustrations, I felt I was "trying to swim up Niagara Falls." Not that I was idle; the President constantly pressed me for new negotiating ideas—though he really meant merely new channels and procedures. We were, as I told my colleagues, "following the traditional pattern for negotiating with a mule: just keep hitting him on the head with a two-by-four until he does what you want him to do." But that was useless with Hanoi; the mule's head was harder than the two-by-four.

On January 5, 1966, I sent the President two memoranda. One called for him to approach the heads of governments of the United Kingdom, Soviet Union, China, North Vietnam, and South Vietnam to request a secret meeting of the foreign ministers of those five countries with the United States to be held in Vienna beginning January 17, for preliminary discussions of the problem of Vietnam. The timing seemed propitious since a key member of the Soviet politburo, Alexander Shelepin, would shortly be visiting Hanoi, and we might thus arm him with specific proposals to press on the North Vietnamese. The second memorandum discussed possible ways and means of involving the United Nations in a peace effort, using either the Security Council or a special session of the General Assembly. Though I had little faith the United Nations could be useful, I still included a draft Security Council resolution.

As expected, the bombing pause evoked no response: by January, pressures were mounting to resume bombing and escalate the war. On January 20, I sent a memorandum to the President arguing that "the resumption of bombing may well frustrate the very political objectives we have in mind. There is no evidence that bombing has so far had any appreciable effect in weakening the determination of Ho Chi Minh and his colleagues. Whatever evidence there is points in the opposite direction." I recalled my experience on the Strategic Bombing Survey, pointing out that in both Europe and Japan the Survey found that "one does not break the will of the population of a police state by heavy bombing."

I followed my memorandum against bombing with a long analytical memorandum to the President. Prepared with the advice of recognized China experts Professors Allen Whiting and Fred Green, it pointed out why and how our bombing posed grave dangers of war with China. Today— with the wisdom of hindsight—it is clear that I overestimated the prospect of Chinese intervention. But President Johnson was deeply preoccupied with the China menace and the more I emphasized it, the stronger was my case for cutting our losses.

McNamara's Views

I had a distaste for ex parte Presidential approaches and whenever I wrote a memorandum to the President calling for our extrication, I showed it first to Rusk, McNamara, and Mac Bundy. Secretary McNamara and John McNaughton almost always responded by a prompt and courteous visit. Two or three times they showed me memoranda prepared by McNaughton commenting on what I had written, sometimes expressing views along the same general line while avoiding my hard conclusions. Though momentarily exhilarated by this prospect of support, I found McNamara unwilling to express those same realistic, if discouraging, views in meetings called by the President to discuss my various memoranda. Whether he privately discussed them with the President I do not know.

By May 1967, seven months after I had left the government, a draft memorandum by John McNaughton finally accepted the analysis I had been urging for the three previous years: "it now appears that no combination of actions against the North short of destruction of the regime or occupation of North Vietnamese territory will physically reduce the flow of men and materiel below the relatively small amount needed by enemy forces to continue the war in the South."[7]

First Meeting of "The Usual Suspects"

Even after my resignation in September 1966, I could not free myself from the oppressive burden of the war. It was a blight on all America—the continued killing, the dark apprehensions as we ventured more and more onto bottomless quicksand, and the hysteria in the universities that was taking an increasingly nasty turn. On November 1, 1967, at President Johnson's request, I attended a meeting at the State Department as a member of the so-called Senior Advisory Group—or, as the press called us, "the wise old men," the "elder statesmen" or, more derisively, "the usual suspects." We had dinner with Secretary Rusk and then met the following morning with the President. I made my usual plea for extrication to the usual deaf ears; the war, said the other members of the group, must be vigorously pursued. The major problem, they superciliously asserted, was how to educate American opinion. As I came out of the Cabinet Room, I said to Dean Acheson, John J. McCloy, and—if I recall properly—John Cowles of Minneapolis, "I've been watching across the table. You're like a flock of old buzzards sitting on a fence, sending the young men off to be killed. You ought to be ashamed of yourselves." I was as surprised as they—and a little embarrassed—by the intensity of my outburst.

The year 1968 caught Washington off guard with the shattering Tet offensive, which lasted for twenty-five days, from dawn on January 31 until February 24. In February, the President commissioned Dean Acheson to make an independent study of the war. Much to the President's dismay, Acheson concluded that we could not win without an unlimited commitment of forces—and that even then it might take five years. The country, Acheson told Johnson, was no longer behind the Administration, nor did Americans any longer believe what the President was telling them. Then, during the next few months, Clark Clifford, the newly appointed Secretary of Defense, accumulated mounting evidence that the war could not be won.[8] Outnumbered eight to one within the circle of advisers closest to the President, and now faced with a request from General Westmoreland for the deployment of 206,000 additional men, Clifford looked about, as I had done earlier, for outside help. The President should, he proposed, meet once again with members of the Senior Advisory Group, who would be briefed on the war and asked to express their views.

Second "Senior Advisory Group" Meeting

At 7:30 P.M. on Monday, March 25, 1968, five months after our earlier meeting, we met in the office of Secretary of State Dean Rusk: Dean Acheson, Omar Bradley, McGeorge Bundy, Arthur Dean, Douglas Dillon, Abe Fortas, Robert Murphy, General Matthew Ridgway, Cyrus Vance, and I. After dinner we heard briefings from three government officials: Deputy Assistant Secretary of State Philip Habib, who reviewed the political situation, Major General William DePuy, who spoke of our military posture, and George Carver of the CIA, who talked about pacification and the condition of the enemy. If the North Vietnamese were to be expelled from the South and the country pacified, it would—so our briefers estimated—take at least five to ten more years. The following morning, we talked with the senior officials of the government: Dean Rusk, Clark Clifford, and others. Secretary Clifford spoke bluntly about the choices our country faced. We could either expand the war and muddle along or pursue a "reduced strategy"— cutting back on the bombing and using American troops only to defend certain populated areas.

Dean Acheson was the first of our group to acknowledge that he had changed his mind; we could not, he said, achieve our objective through military means.[9] Views were expressed around the table, and I thought to myself, "there's been a mistake in the invitation list; these can't be the same men I saw here last November." Toward noon, we went to the White House to lunch with the President in the family dining room. During lunch, General Creighton Abrams, just back from Vietnam, told us how he was training the South Vietnamese army with the object of "Vietnamizing" the war.

The President then dismissed all members of the government so as to meet alone with our group of outsiders. When we had gathered in the Cabinet Room, he asked McGeorge Bundy to summarize our collective views. Bundy mentioned particularly Dean Acheson's current opinion that we could not achieve our objectives within the limits of time and resources available. We would therefore have to change our policy drastically. Though that reflected the general view of the group he noted that Abe Fortas and Bob Murphy had dissented. Bundy then made a remark that deeply impressed me not merely for its import but its generosity: "I must tell you what I thought I would never say—that I now agree with George Ball." Bombing in the North, which Bundy had earlier favored as the way of raising the price of insurgencies around the world, staving off defeat in the South, and providing an ultimate bargaining chip was, he had now decided, doing more to erode the support of the war on the homefront than harming the North Vietnamese.

Dean Acheson announced his position in his clear, lawyerlike way. We could not stop the "belligerency" in Vietnam by any acceptable means within the time allowed to us. In view of our other problems and interests, including the dollar crisis, we should seek to disengage by midsummer. There was little support for the war in South Vietnam or in the United States. Acheson did not think the American people would permit the war to go on for more than another year. Douglas Dillon spoke against sending additional troops and advocated stopping the bombing in an effort to move toward a negotiated settlement. He had been deeply impressed by the comments he had heard the night before that it would take five to ten years to conclude the war. General Ridgway, who had, from the first, opposed our intervention, also recommended the withdrawal of American forces, while Cyrus Vance, who, when Deputy Secretary of Defense, had always appeared to support our Vietnamese efforts, now insisted that since the war was bitterly dividing the country, it was time to seek a negotiated settlement.

I made my usual speech against the war. We could not hope to negotiate a sensible withdrawal until we stopped bombing North Vietnam. I emphasized, as I had done many times before, that the war was demoralizing our country and creating grave political divisions and that we had to get out.

There is no doubt that the unexpected negative conclusions of the "elder statesmen" profoundly shook the President. Later he grumbled to me, "Your whole group must have been brainwashed and I'm going to find out what Habib and the others told you."

No one will ever know the extent to which our advice contributed to President Johnson's decision—announced to the American people in a television speech six days after our meeting—that he would not run for President in 1968. He had, he announced, "unilaterally" ordered a halt to the air and naval bombardment of most of North Vietnam. Even that "very limited bombing of the North could come to an early end if our restraint is matched by restraint in Hanoi." Only at the end of his address did he announce his decision to withdraw from the Presidential race.

Though I knew President Johnson desperately wanted to get us out of Vietnam, he was incapable of it. His Administration had accumulated too much baggage of past statements and actions, too many fixed ideas, and too many positions it could not easily reverse. But by taking himself out of the Presidential race, Lyndon Johnson had paved the way for America's extrication, and I hoped our Vietnamese nightmare might soon be over. In spite of Hubert Humphrey's loyal and excessively exuberant support for President Johnson, I knew that he was personally revolted by the war. Once a Humphrey Administration were in place, we might then move promptly toward extrication.

Notes

1. Based on Jack Valenti, *A Very Human President* (New York: W. W. Norton, 1975), pp. 319–40, supplemented and modified by the information from my own notes and recollections.
2. Though in the light of subsequent knowledge, I may have overstated the dangers of a possible Chinese intervention, we then knew almost nothing about what was going on in Chinese foreign policy. Governmental and party announcements repeatedly emphasized that an historic moment had arrived for the world revolution under Communist leadership, and the United States was ritualistically denounced as the major impediment. In September 1965, Marshal Lin Piao, Minister of Defense and the Deputy Premier, was to startle the Administration—and particularly upset Secretary of Defense McNamara—by publishing a long harangue announcing China's support for "wars of national liberation." That emphasized the people's struggle against United States imperialism in Vietnam and elsewhere, including areas of Asia, Africa, and Latin America. In that climate, it was normal to feel concerned at the prospects of such a move. After all, my memorandum was written only fourteen years after we had precipitated a Chinese intervention in Korea by getting too near the Chinese border, and no American could say with assurance that we might not bring down Chinese mass armies on our troops.
3. *The Pentagon Papers*, as published by the *New York Times* (New York: Bantam Books, Inc., 1971), p. 470.
4. *The Pentagon Papers*, the Senator Gravel Edition, *The Defense Department History of the United States Decisionmaking on Vietnam* (Boston: Beacon Press, n.d.), vol. 4, p. 623.
5. Betraying his prime interest in influencing American opinion, President Johnson told me with some pride: "That's the right touch. Send a Jew to see the Pope."
6. Janos Radvanyi, *Delusion and Reality: Gambits, Hoaxes & Diplomatic One-Upmanship in Vietnam* (South Bend, Indiana: Gateway Editions, Ltd., 1978).
7. *The Pentagon Papers*, New York Times, *op. cit.*, pp. 579–80.
8. Before his appointment to the Pentagon, Clifford had, as chairman of the President's Foreign Intelligence Advisory Board, toured the Pacific with General Maxwell Taylor to solicit Asian governments to send troops to assist in Vietnam. He was, he told me later, profoundly shaken by the refusal of Asian nations to offer anything more than advice and encouragement. If Vietnam's neighbors did not take the war seriously enough to help the United States, why should we carry on alone at such great cost?
9. He was later sufficiently generous to observe in my presence and that of a number of other people that "George Ball was the only one who was right all along and we made a great mistake not to follow him."

New York. National Security Adviser Henry A. Kissinger gestures as he talks with President Nixon on November 25, 1972, at the Waldorf-Astoria Hotel. UPI/CORBIS-BETTMANN NEWSPHOTOS

CHAPTER 4

Getting Out
1968–1975

In the aftermath of the Tet offensive, many Americans grew tired of the war and responded to politicians who promised a way out of Vietnam. During the 1968 presidential campaign the Democratic candidate, Vice President Hubert Humphrey, was unwilling to challenge publicly the policies of President Johnson, whereas Republican candidate Richard Nixon was elected in good part because he made himself credible as a man of peace. How to extricate the United States from the conflict was the real challenge for President Nixon and his national security adviser (later secretary of state), Henry Kissinger. Stephen Ambrose, one of Nixon's most perceptive biographers, depicts here the president's struggle to balance the imperatives of détente—roughly, accommodation with the Soviet Union and China—and the felt need to stay the course in Vietnam. The North Vietnamese spring offensive in 1972 exposed the tensions of Nixon's two-track policy. Historian Gareth Porter looks closely at the 1972 Christmas bombings of North Vietnam by the United States and the period following the signing of the Paris peace agreement in January 1973. He concludes with a sharply critical assessment of American policy.

The author of the last selection in the chapter is William Colby, a longtime master spy who joined the OSS during the Second World War and came to Vietnam in 1959 as deputy chief of the CIA station in Saigon. By 1971, the year in which this account opens, Colby was head of pacification for all of Vietnam. He was most strongly associated with the Phoenix program, which was designed to "neutralize" National Liberation Front agents operating in southern villages. In its own terms the program was successful, but it was denounced by antiwar Americans as indiscriminate and immoral, and Colby's picture appeared on "Wanted" posters on college campuses everywhere. In this excerpt from his autobiography, Colby lashes back at his critics.

11
Bombing Hanoi, Mining Haiphong, and the Moscow Summit
STEPHEN E. AMBROSE

With the opening to China behind him, Nixon's next move in establishing triangular diplomacy was his upcoming journey to Moscow. The summit, scheduled for the third week in May [1972], would be the culmination of his diplomacy, marking the completion of his creation of a new era of world power politics. The trip to Peking had been more symbol than reality, the meeting marked by flowery speeches and generalizations rather than direct, specific deals. The trip to Moscow would be just the opposite. And it would be more important, for the simple reason that the U.S.S.R. was incomparably more powerful than the P.R.C. China could be an irritant to the United States in various parts of Asia; the U.S.S.R. could destroy the United States in a flash.

Since 1969, Nixon had moved carefully, cautiously, but steadily toward an arms-control agreement. The obstacles were great: ingrained suspicions of the Soviets, the clamor of the hawks, the economic needs of the military-industrial complex, the war in Vietnam, tension in the Middle East and South Asia, and so forth. But Nixon had persevered, and by the spring of 1972 he was on the verge of prevailing.

He had not created the possibilities all by himself. [Henry] Kissinger's academic brilliance and Metternich-like conceptions had certainly played some role, but more important was the confluence of events and needs. The first of these was the necessity felt by both superpowers to reduce the cost and dangers of the arms race. More specifically, the Soviets had some critical interests at stake. They needed to offset Nixon's Peking trip, for fear of a Sino-American alliance (the beauty of Nixon's triangular diplomacy was that only he could talk to the other two sides of the triangle). Further, the Soviets wanted to promote détente in Europe, which, while progressing, was still in a delicate formative stage. They also wanted expanded trade relations with the United States; indeed they were almost desperate for American grain. In addition, they had long sought a recognition of parity and a compact of equality with the United States.

Nixon was eager to sell the grain and willing to accept détente in Europe. Already playing off the Chinese against the Russians, he now wanted to play off the Russians against the Chinese. But most of all, what he wanted from the summit was credit for an arms-control agreement and progress toward peace in Vietnam. He had already warned Chou [En-lai] that if the North Vietnamese launched a spring offensive, he would react with the full fury of the mad bomber. Now he wanted to let [Leonid] Brezhnev and his pals know that the price for détente was help in ending the war in Vietnam.

For all Nixon's acceptance of the new realities of the world balance of power, however, other more personal things mattered more to him.

As to SALT [Strategic Arms Limitation Talks], Nixon's own words made it clear that he was more concerned with getting credit for an arms-control agreement than he was in reaching an arms-control agreement. He wanted both, of course, but if he had to choose, credit came before reality.

In early March 1972, it appeared that Gerard Smith and the American negotiating team in Vienna were on the verge of completing the SALT treaty, so that when Nixon went to Moscow it would be not to negotiate anything but simply to indulge in a ceremonial signing. Nixon responded with a March 11 memorandum to [H. R.] Haldeman.

"What I am concerned about," he began, "is not that we will fail to achieve the various goals . . . but that when we do make the formal agreements there will be no real news value to them." Nixon insisted that it was "vitally important that no final agreements be entered into until we arrive in Moscow." He instructed Haldeman to "begin a line of pessimism" about progress on SALT, and explained that otherwise "our critics will make it appear that all of this could have been achieved without any summit whatever, and that all we did was to go to Moscow for a grandstand play to put the final signature on an agreement that was worked out by Gerry Smith, State, etc."

As to the policy of détente in general, Nixon was ready to sacrifice it if necessary to avoid what he regarded as humiliation in Vietnam, as his actions in April and May showed, when he came exceedingly close to doing just that in response to a North Vietnamese challenge.

On March 30, the NVA launched the first phase of an offensive against South Vietnam. Using tanks and artillery in numbers never before seen in the war, the Communist forces crossed the DMZ and headed toward Quang Tri. The area had once been defended by U.S. Marines; now it was held by ARVN units that, after some initial resistance, cracked.

On his News Summary for April 3, Nixon underscored the lines that hurt the most: " 'Rout,' 'disarray,' 'crushing,' are terms used to describe ARVN retreat in first test of Vietnamization." "GIs quoted by UPI see little chance of ARVN holding at Quang Tri. And several voice strong opposition to the war itself." (The second sentence got a double underscoring plus a marginal order: "K—note!") "CBS and NBC film of thousands of refugees fleeing as enemy uses artillery more intensively than at any time in war. . . . DOD [Department of Defense] feels ARVN was taken by surprise. Situation is expected to get worse."

A catastrophe loomed. It did no good to say that the offensive, after the two-year lull in the fighting in South Vietnam, had long since been anticipated. Nixon had to react. Any hesitation, and he might well face personal as well as national disaster. If the North Vietnamese won the war through force of arms, Nixon's three-year-old policy of Vietnamization would be exposed as a fraud, he would be humiliated and lose the election, and the United States would be disgraced.

Nixon did react, instinctively and immediately. Brushing aside bureaucratic opposition and counsels of moderation, he ordered an all-out counterattack by sea and air power. He sent in B-52s, more fighter-bombers, more aircraft carriers, more cruisers; he took off all budgetary restraints on air sorties; he ordered tactical air strikes up to the eighteenth parallel in North Vietnam; he ordered naval attacks twenty-five miles up the coast of North Vietnam.

In short, he counterattacked with almost everything he had available. What he did not do was launch a counteroffensive. He did not send in troops; he did not even slow the pace of ground forces withdrawal; he did not invade North Vietnam; he did not bomb Hanoi or Haiphong. His relative restraint was all the more remarkable because his anger was boundless. He thought the Communists had played with him for years, using negotiations as a smoke screen to prepare for a massive invasion. He was furious with the Soviets, whose tanks and artillery made the offensive possible. He felt that everything he had worked to achieve was threatened.

But his anger was more understandable than it was justified. In 1970 and 1971 he had been the one to launch offensives in Cambodia and in Laos. Even after they failed, his negotiating stance remained: give back the POWs, pull back your forces to North Vietnam, abandon your gains in Cambodia and Laos, and some months later the United States will complete its withdrawal (although he was never explicit on whether this withdrawal would include American air and sea power). Meanwhile, [Nguyen Van] Thieu would still be in power in Saigon (the promise that he would step down one month before elections was meaningless, as all his appointees would remain in charge and would be the ones to conduct the election).

Nixon, in other words, was demanding that Hanoi surrender its war aims, even as he withdrew American ground forces. How could he have expected the NVA not to attack when its leaders judged the moment to be right?

With regard to the Soviets, Nixon's complaints that they made the offensive possible were certainly true, but he ignored other relevant points. The United States was supplying more material to Saigon than the Soviets were to Hanoi. Soviet control of the actions of the men in Hanoi was never as complete as Nixon assumed it was. The Soviets had not sped the shipment of arms in the winter of '71–'72, nor had they ordered the offensive. The NVA had accumulated the arsenal thanks to the two-year lull on the battlefield, and decided on its own when and how to strike.

Nor did Nixon pay sufficient attention to what the Soviets did *not* do. While they gave Hanoi MiGs and SAMs to defend their airspace, they did not give the NVA fighter-bombers with which to attack the American air bases in Thailand, nor submarines with which to attack the American aircraft carriers in the Gulf of Tonkin. Like Nixon, they exercised some degree of restraint.

Nixon nevertheless had Kissinger tell [Anatoly] Dobrynin on April 3 that Soviet complicity in Hanoi's attack was jeopardizing the summit.

Kissinger was not happy with the assignment. He knew that "Nixon was determined on a showdown," that "he saw no point in further diplomacy until a military decision had been reached." Kissinger, encouraged by Dobrynin to believe that the North Vietnamese would be forthcoming in a scheduled secret meeting between Kissinger and Le Duc Tho on April 24, was not so ready to abandon diplomacy, although he was as one with his boss on the need for an all-out counterattack.

To Nixon's extreme frustration, that attack was slow to get going. According to the Pentagon, bad weather was the cause. Nixon had his doubts. At an afternoon meeting on April 4 with [John] Mitchell and Haldeman, the President said, "Damn it, if you know any prayers say them. . . . Let's get that weather cleared up. The bastards have never been bombed like they're going to be bombed this time, but you've got to have weather."

"Is the weather still bad?" Mitchell inquired.

"Huh!" Nixon answered. "It isn't bad. The Air Force isn't worth a—I mean, they won't fly." He wished he had George Patton.

On April 7, the NVA moved into the second phase of its offensive, attacking from Cambodia to the northwest of Saigon, toward Tay Ninh and An Loc. By then, the American counterattack was under way, as B-52s struck 145 miles north of the DMZ (the first use of B-52s in North Vietnam since early 1968), inflicting heavy casualties. Still the NVA came on; still ARVN failed to do its duty. Nixon had Kissinger's assistant, Al Haig, prepare a contingency plan; if all else failed, it called for bombing all military targets throughout North Vietnam and the mining of North Vietnamese ports.

For all his bellicosity, Nixon was downcast by events. Kissinger told him that even if the worst happened and the remaining American troops pulled out as the NVA won the war, he would still be able to claim credit for ending the war. Nixon said that prospect was "too bleak even to contemplate." He told Kissinger defeat was "simply not an option." But it was certainly a possibility. He expressed his depression in his diary: "If we fail it will be because the American way simply isn't as effective as the Communist way. . . . I have an uneasy feeling that this may be the case. We give them the most modern arms, we emphasize the material to the exclusion of the spiritual and the Spartan life, and it may be that we soften them up rather than harden them up for the battle."

Nixon was also unhappy with Kissinger: "Henry, with all of his many virtues, does seem too often to be concerned about preparing the way for negotiations with the Soviets. . . . Both Haldeman and Henry seem to have an idea—which I think is mistaken—that even if we fail in Vietnam we can still survive politically. I have no illusions whatever on that score, however. The U.S. will not have a credible foreign policy if we fail, and I will have to assume the responsibility for that development."

On April 10, Nixon increased the pressure on the Soviets. Speaking at a State Department ceremony for the signing of an international convention for the banning of biological warfare, with Dobrynin in the audience, he said that every "great power" must follow the principle that it should not encourage "directly or indirectly, other nations to use force or armed aggression against its neighbors."

On the battlefield, meanwhile, the B-52s were dropping hundreds of tons of bombs on the enemy around An Loc, but still ARVN was unable to push back the NVA. Nixon railed at the Pentagon. Why couldn't more be done? He wanted more B-52s sent north, to hit targets that were strategic and diplomatic, as well as tactical targets in the south.

[Melvin] Laird dissented. He feared that the relatively slow and not very maneuverable eight-jet bombers would be easy targets for Hanoi's SAMs. He also feared the congressional uproar that would follow. [William P.] Rogers feared that such an escalation would endanger the summit.

Nixon insisted. He ordered B-52 raids against the oil depots around Hanoi and Haiphong; he even announced them in advance. On April 14, the President said that 150 B-52s, each one carrying thirty tons of bombs (ten times the capacity of the F-4 Phantom fighter-bombers), would hit North Vietnam the following day. It was obvious that such raids would have no effect on the battles around An Loc and Quang Tri; a Pentagon spokesman explained that the purposes were to slow the flow of supplies south, to demonstrate to President Thieu that he could count on Nixon, and to create a bargaining chip.

The next day, April 15, the bombers moved in. They struck inside and outside Hanoi and Haiphong. They caused extensive damage, but the NVA claimed that eleven American planes had been shot down. Still, Nixon was pleased. He told Haldeman, "Well, we really left them our calling card this weekend."

But that same day the North Vietnamese canceled the Paris meeting scheduled for April 24; as this was the meeting at which Dobrynin had hinted the enemy would be forthcoming, the cancellation was a blow. "Henry obviously considered this a crisis of the first magnitude." Nixon wrote in his diary. "I laid down the law hard to him that under these circumstances he could not go to Moscow." Kissinger had been slated to make a secret presummit trip to Moscow to prepare the way for Nixon. The President felt that the Soviets wanted Kissinger to come to discuss SALT, trade arrangements, and the like, when what needed to be discussed was Vietnam.

Nixon realized that his decision to keep Kissinger home "shook him because he desperately wants to get to Moscow one way or the other." But Nixon did not want to discuss SALT; he wanted to "consider our option with regard to imposing a blockade."

On the afternoon of April 15, Nixon had "a pretty candid talk with Henry." The President was depressed. He told Kissinger that if he had to cancel the summit and impose a blockade, "I had an obligation to look for a successor." Nixon speculated on who might replace him; he mentioned [Nelson] Rockefeller, [Warren] Burger, [Ronald] Reagan, and [John] Connally.

Kissinger threw up his hands. He said that "none of them would do," and added that any Democrat was out of the question.

Nixon mused that if Kissinger would stay on, "we could get continuity in foreign policy." Kissinger, not averse to a little flattery himself, "became very emotional." He said Nixon "shouldn't be thinking this way or talking this way. . . . He made his pitch that the North Vietnamese should not be allowed to destroy two Presidents."

Later that evening, Kissinger called Nixon to inform him that Dobrynin was "desperate" to have him come to Moscow, and had promised that Vietnam would be the first item on the agenda. Nixon then reconsidered. He said Kissinger could go to Moscow.

The following day, American bombers hit four Soviet merchant ships at anchor in Haiphong harbor. The Soviets protested, but in a relatively low-key manner, indicating their desire to go ahead with the summit.

Still Nixon had third and fourth thoughts about the wisdom of the Kissinger trip. Kissinger reassured him and Nixon again agreed to let him go. That left the problem of how to inform the Secretary of State. A month earlier Rogers had sent a memo to Nixon saying that he intended to "take personal charge" of the Moscow summit preparations. That was not Nixon's plan at all. He had Haldeman tell Rogers that all communications with the Soviets by the State Department had to be cleared in advance by the White House.

Nixon decided to use a bit of subterfuge in informing Rogers. After Kissinger left for Moscow, Nixon would call Rogers to Camp David to tell him that Kissinger had received a sudden and unexpected summons from Brezhnev to discuss Vietnam. Nixon would assure Rogers that the only subject of discussion would be Vietnam (in the event, when Rogers learned that Kissinger talked about the full range of summit issues, he was "highly indignant." To complete the exclusion of the State Department from this most fundamental of all foreign-policy issues, Kissinger slipped into and out of Moscow without the American ambassador even knowing that he was there. Never before had an American President so personalized basic diplomacy, or so insulted the Department of State).

It was not entirely Nixon's fault. He gave clear oral instructions to Kissinger: Vietnam was to be the first item discussed, and if the Soviets proved "recalcitrant on this point, he should just pack up and come home."

Nixon told Kissinger that while the summit had the potential of being the most important diplomatic encounter "of this century." It was "indispensable" to have "progress" on Vietnam" "*by the time of the summit*." The President instructed his National Security Adviser to insist on a withdrawal of the NVA across the DMZ; he said that action was a "precondition of our ending the bombing of North Vietnam."

Nixon also told Kissinger how to describe the President to Brezhnev: "direct, honest, strong . . . fatalistic—to him election [is] not key. Will not be affected one iota by public opinion. No other President could make SALT agreement while war is still going on."

Kissinger got around this set of orders by the simple expedient of ignoring them. While Kissinger was in Moscow (April 21–24). Nixon was at Camp David with [his friend Bebe] Rebozo ("a conjunction that did not usually make for the calmest reflection," Kissinger noted). Haig was also at Camp David. Nixon bombarded Kissinger with instructions to hang tough, to keep Vietnam up front, and so on. Kissinger in fact brushed past Vietnam, rightly expecting no progress, and plunged into the summit issues. It was the Soviets who insisted on some progress on Vietnam, and Kissinger gave it to them with hints that the United States, for the first time, might be willing to discuss a coalition government, and would not insist on the withdrawal of the NVA from South Vietnam.

Nixon, rightly suspecting that Kissinger was making unauthorized deals, demanded explanations. Kissinger sent a wire: "Brezhnev wants a summit at almost any cost." He told Haig to tell the President, "He must trust me. I have not exactly let him down on other missions." But Nixon feared Brezhnev would cancel the summit, which would be embarrassing: if it was going to be canceled, he wanted to be the one to do it. Further, Haig informed Kissinger, Nixon was in a "starchy mood" because polls indicated his popularity had risen thanks to the bombing campaign. Haig, who to Kissinger's discomfort was becoming one of the Nixon insiders, told Kissinger that the President had telephoned him and said "he views Soviet positions on South Vietnam as frenzied and frivolous and, therefore, is determined to go forward with additional strikes on Hanoi and Haiphong."

In a message of his own to Kissinger, Nixon asserted that SALT was of concern only to "a few sophisticates." The main issue was Vietnam. The President wanted to go all out against the North Vietnamese and was willing to cancel the summit rather than forgo that option. Then, despite the way in which Kissinger had changed the basis of American foreign policy making, from a two-man team to a one-man show, in direct contradiction of clear orders, Nixon praised Kissinger for his "skill, resourcefulness, and determination," and concluded his message, "However it all comes out, just remember we all know we couldn't have a better man in Moscow at this time than Kissinger. Rebozo joins us in sending our regards."

Kissinger speculated that a lot of drinking was going on that weekend at Camp David. Whatever the cause, the result was a set of contradictory presidential messages and orders. Apparently the chief executive of the United States did not know what he wanted, and left it to the National Security Adviser to sort out.

Kissinger returned on April 24. He justified his actions in a long memorandum; in his oral report he made the clinching argument: "If the summit meeting takes place, you will be able to sign the most important arms control agreement ever concluded." Nixon decided not to hold Kissinger to account, perhaps a reflection of the independent power base Kissinger had managed to build, thanks in no small part to the enormously favorable publicity he had received in the past six months. Nixon now needed Kissinger almost as much as Kissinger needed him.

While Kissinger was in Moscow, the North Vietnamese launched the third phase of their offensive, attacking out of Laos and Cambodia into the Central Highlands, toward Kontum and Pleiku. Nixon responded with a televised speech in which he described the NVA attacks as "a clear case of naked and unprovoked aggression across an international border. There is only one word for it—invasion." He "flatly rejected" proposals from dovish senators that he stop the bombing in order to get the enemy back to the negotiating table. "They sold that package to the United States once before, in 1968, and we are not going to buy it again in 1972." He concluded with a bit of Nixonian hyperbole: "If the United States betrays the millions of people who have relied on us in Vietnam . . . it would amount to a renunciation of our morality, an abdication of our leadership among nations, and an invitation for the mighty to prey upon the weak all around the world."

He balanced his bellicosity with some encouraging words. Although Kontum and Quang Tri were surrounded, he asserted that the ARVN was doing well, so well that he could announce a further withdrawal of twenty thousand troops. And he held out hope for negotiations; despite what he said about the bombing, he announced that the canceled April 24 meeting with the North Vietnamese would be held on May 2. There was a further conflicting signal; he greeted a Chinese Ping-Pong team in the Rose Garden.

On the morning of April 30, he called Kissinger on the telephone. He warned again that he intended to cancel the summit "unless the situation militarily and diplomatically substantially improves by May 15. . . . We have crossed the Rubicon and now we must win." He said Hanoi could not be trusted, "they will break every understanding." When Kissinger talked to the North Vietnamese in Paris, he should be "brutally frank from the beginning—particularly in tone." Tell them, he said, "the President has had enough and now you have only one message to give them—Settle or else!"

Later that morning, Nixon flew down to Floresville, Texas, for a barbecue hosted by John Connally on his ranch, and attended by some two hundred Texas moneymen. George Brown, head of the state's largest construction company, Brown & Root, and LBJ's original backer, was there, as were John Murchison, Dallas oilman, and former Democratic governor Allan Shivers, along with the other key supporters of LBJ throughout his career. These were the same men, Democrats all, who had backed Lloyd Bentsen in his winning senatorial race against George Bush in 1970, and had made Connally governor.

Nixon, delighted to be the guest of honor in a gathering of his old political foes (these were the men who, some thought, had stolen Texas from Nixon for Kennedy in 1960), bubbled over. "I think that I have learned more about Texas on this brief visit than at any other time," he declared. Connally commented. "I have never learned much in politics, but I have learned that you have to fish with live bait. And we are not without some in this gathering this evening."

After the drinks, the beef tenderloin, and the corn on the cob, Nixon answered questions. The Texans wanted to know if he had thought about bombing the dikes in North Vietnam. He said he had, but pointed out that it would cause heavy civilian casualties. Then he added, "We are prepared to use our military and naval strength against military targets throughout North Vietnam, and we believe that the North Vietnamese are taking a very great risk if they continue their offensive in the South." To do less, he said, would insure a "Communist take-over," which would weaken the office of the Presidency, damage respect for the United States around the world, "destroy the confidence of the American people," and lead to further Communist adventures elsewhere.

Those words, in that setting, gave reporters present a sense of *déjà vu*. They had heard it all before, from another President, on another Texas ranch, but before the same audience, between 1965 and 1968. The similarities between LBJ in '68 and Nixon in '72 were growing in size and in number.

Back in Washington, the sense of *déjà vu* increased. Headlines proclaimed that Quang Tri had fallen to the enemy. Nixon had a report on his desk from General [Creighton] Abrams saying that ARVN had evidently lost its will to fight. Adding to Nixon's woes, the newspapers proclaimed that the *New York Times* had won the Pulitzer Prize for the Pentagon Papers.

Kissinger was in the Oval Office on the afternoon of May 1, for last-minute instructions before flying to Paris to meet Le Duc Tho. Don't give an inch, Nixon told him. "No nonsense. No niceness. No accommodations." He also wanted Kissinger to let Dobrynin know that "under no circumstances will I go to the summit if we're still in trouble in Vietnam."

Kissinger flew to Paris, where he found Le Duc Tho "icy and snide." After three fruitless hours, he broke off the talks and headed home.

Nixon was not surprised. He wrote in his diary that Kissinger was so "obsessed with the idea that there *should* be a negotiated settlement" that he failed to see "there really isn't enough in it for the enemy to negotiate at this time."

Nixon recorded that he had a long talk with Haig, who like Kissinger knew that the way to the President's heart was to talk tough. On this occasion, Haig urged Nixon to take stronger action than Kissinger recommended. Nixon further steeled himself in his diary entry: "I must make whatever hard choices have to be made, and take whatever risks need to be taken."

Haig presented the President with an irresistible argument: he "emphasized that even more important than how Vietnam comes out is for us to handle these matters in a way that I can survive in office." That was putting first things first, and moved Haig up even higher in Nixon's esteem. So high, in fact, that the President told [Charles] Colson later that day that Haig and Connally "are the only two men around here qualified to fill this job when I step down."

Haig was as good as Kissinger himself at telling one man one thing, another man another, at backbiting, and at manipulating Nixon. He told Admiral Elmo Zumwalt (Chief of Naval Operations), for example, "that he [Haig] had to exercise considerable dexterity to stiffen the President's backbone when the President was in a bug-out mood, and that he lived in dread that some day the President would be with Henry instead of him when the bug-out mood came on and Henry would be unable to handle it."

Kissinger returned to Washington the evening of May 2. Nixon had a helicopter waiting for him, to bring him to the Washington Navy Yard for a cruise on the *Sequoia*. Haig was also along.

Nixon wanted to launch B-52 strikes against Hanoi and Haiphong on May 5. Kissinger urged caution. He reminded the President that General Abrams wanted to use B-52s inside South Vietnam, to break up the enemy attacks at the point of contact, not hundreds of miles behind the lines, where the effect of the raids would not be felt on the battlefield for months. And he warned Nixon that he could not bomb and have the summit too, that the Soviets would have to cancel, blaming Nixon and the bombing. Then Nixon would really catch it from the doves, who would go after him over the bombing and over the cancellation of the summit.

Nixon acknowledged that "it was hard to see how I could go to the summit and be clinking glasses with Brezhnev while Soviet tanks were rumbling through [South Vietnam]," But he wanted to bomb so badly. But he wanted to go to Moscow so badly. He was in an agony of indecision.

He decided to postpone a decision on Hanoi-Haiphong and the summit until the following week. Meanwhile he ordered plans prepared and told Kissinger to get ready to cancel the summit. If he decided on all-out action, he wanted to preempt the Soviets by canceling first.

Whatever he decided about Hanoi-Haiphong, he was determined to escalate the air war to teach the enemy a lesson. On May 4 he ordered fifty additional fighter-bombers to Southeast Asia, and ordered the fleet brought up to six aircraft carriers on active-duty station. This meant that in the past month he had increased the B-52 force in the war from 80 to 140, the number of fighter-bombers from 400 to 900, the number of carriers from three to six, and the air-navy personnel from 47,000 to 77,000. Meanwhile, he had reduced the number of ground troops from 95,000 to 68,100. None of those figures include the ARVN air force, by 1972 the fourth-largest in the world.

But the enemy could escalate too. On the day Nixon sent in the carriers and the fifty fighter-bombers, the Vietcong announced the establishment of a "provisional revolutionary administration" in Quang Tri City. It was the first time in the war the

Communists had succeeded in setting up a government on a provincial level in South Vietnam.

"What will he do, they ask," Max Frankel wrote in the *New York Times*. "What will he do if the North Vietnamese keep coming, the South Vietnamese keep crumbling, the Russians keep stalling and the political risks keep mounting?" Noting Nixon's "propensity for psychic rage and for diplomacy by thunderclap," Frankel reviewed the options. Nixon could hardly increase the air counterattack in the South, as he had already put almost everything available into the battle. He might bomb the dikes, or use nuclear weapons, or invade North Vietnam with marines, but none of that seemed likely. He could pressure the Russians by bombing or mining Haiphong harbor, at a risk to the summit. Or he might make some concessions to the enemy in the hope of achieving a negotiated settlement. But, Frankel concluded lamely, "no one really does know what he might do."

Not even Nixon knew. He continued to waver. He badly wanted and desperately needed advice, not from Kissinger or Haig (he knew their views), not from the Joint Chiefs or the State Department (he saw them as tools, not advisers), but from someone he trusted and respected (and there was almost no one he did).

He decided to turn to John Connally. Connally had once had some military experience; he had served for a few months as Kennedy's Secretary of the Navy. Nixon respected him; he constantly indulged himself in the fantasy that Connally could follow him into the White House. Kissinger acknowledged that Connally had "the best political brain in the Administration." Nixon ordered Haldeman and Kissinger to go to Connally to find out what to do.

Big Jawn did not duck or shirk the responsibility. He was decisive. Haldeman reported to the President that Connally emphatically said, "Most important—the President must not lose the war! And he should not cancel the summit. He's got to show his guts and leadership on this one. Caution be damned—if they cancel, and I don't think they will, we'll ram it right down their throats."

That was what Nixon wanted to hear. Once he knew Connally's views, he asked Connally to join him, Haig, Haldeman, and Kissinger in his EOB office for a council of war.

They reviewed the options, including the possibility of declaring a blockade. They decided a blockade would be too risky, as it carried the danger of having to confront the Soviet Navy. Mining was better.

Nixon pumped himself up. "As far as I'm concerned," he declared, "the only real mistakes I've made were the times when I didn't follow my own instincts." He wished he had bombed North Korea in 1969 after the EC-121 was shot down. He wished he had bombed the hell out of North Vietnam in 1970, when he went into Cambodia. "If we'd done that then, the damned war would be over now. . . . The summit isn't worth a damn if the price for it is losing in Vietnam. My instinct tells me that the country can take losing the summit, but it can't take losing the war."

Kissinger described the commander in chief at this critical moment: "The only symptom of his excitement was that instead of slouching in an easy chair with his feet on a settee as usual, he was pacing up and down, gesticulating with a pipe on which he was occasionally puffing . . . he was playing [General Douglas] MacArthur. . . .

"Nixon then and there decided upon the mining," Kissinger wrote. "It was one of the finest hours of Nixon's Presidency."

Still he needed reassurance. He went up to Camp David for the weekend. Ed and Tricia Cox joined him, as did Julie Eisenhower. He told his daughters of his decision. Julie was worried: would it work? Nixon told her that if he did not do it, "the United

States would cease to be a respected great power." She assured him that David would "totally agree." Tricia, Nixon wrote in his diary, "was immediately positive because she felt we had to do something, and frankly didn't know what else we could do to avoid a continued deterioration in the battle areas."

Nixon called John Mitchell. He thoroughly approved.

That left the congressional leadership, the JCS, the DOD, the State Department, and the NSC. None had been consulted, all had to be informed. On Monday morning, May 8, Nixon told the NSC. The meeting lasted more than three hours and the President found it "pretty tough." Laird opposed the decision, Rogers was hesitant, [Senator Jesse] Helms warned that mining Haiphong would not be decisive because the enemy had alternate supply routes available, and the professional military were more interested in fighting the battle in South Vietnam than engaging in strategic projects of dubious immediate benefit in North Vietnam.

Nixon defended his decision. "The real question is whether the Americans give a damn anymore," he said. He warned that if he followed the lead of *Time* magazine, the Washington *Post*, the *New York Times*, and the networks and just pulled out, "The U.S. would cease to be a military and diplomatic power. If that happened, then the U.S. would look inward towards itself and would remove itself from the world." But if the United States stayed strong and willing to act, "then the world will remain half-Communist rather than becoming entirely Communist."

With nearly ten thousand atomic weapons, plus all its additional firepower, plus its unrivaled economic strength, it is difficult to see how the United States would have ceased to be a great power if it failed to mine Haiphong harbor, but evidently no one at the NSC protested against Nixon's statement.

The President himself, however, appeared to backtrack later that day. In an afternoon meeting in the EOB with Haldeman and Kissinger, he told Kissinger that Haldeman had raised new questions. Haldeman then described the dire impact that mining Haiphong would have on public opinion; it might lead to Nixon's defeat in November. Kissinger "passionately defended the decision."

Nixon excused himself to go to the bathroom. Kissinger whirled on Haldeman and castigated him for interfering at such a moment. Haldeman, Kissinger later wrote, "grinned shamefacedly, making clear by his bearing that Nixon had put him up to his little speech." When Nixon returned from the bathroom, he signed the order without another word.

Kissinger confessed that he was unable to comprehend why Nixon had played this little game, until a year later when he learned of the taping system. "[This] suggested a possible motive: Nixon wanted me unambiguously on record as supporting the operation." (According to Haldeman, Nixon's motive was to test Kissinger's degree of conviction.)

At 8 P.M., May 8, Nixon met with the joint congressional leadership. He knew what the politicians' advice would be—don't risk the summit, don't escalate—so he did not ask for it. Instead, he told them what he was going to do, and then concluded, "If you can give me your support, I would appreciate it. If you cannot, I will understand." He then walked out of the room.

At 9 P.M., he went on nationwide radio and television. He opened with a review of the military situation. "There is only one way to stop the killing," he said. "That is to keep the weapons of war out of the hands of the international outlaws of North Vietnam." To that end, "all entrances to North Vietnamese ports will be mined. . . . Rail and all other communications will be cut off to the maximum extent possible. Air and naval strikes against military targets in North Vietnam will continue."

He held out one carrot to the North Vietnamese. He would stop the bombing and remove the mines when the POWs were released and there was a cease-fire throughout Indochina. "At that time we will proceed with a complete withdrawal of all American forces from Vietnam within 4 months." Although it was ambiguous, the promise seemed to indicate that (1) "all" included air and naval forces, and (2) by implication, the NVA could hold on to its recent gains and would not be required to simultaneously withdraw from South Vietnam. If that was what he meant, it represented a significant concession on Nixon's part.

To the Soviets, Nixon directed some carefully worded paragraphs: "We respect the Soviet Union as a great power. We recognize the right of the Soviet Union to defend its interests when they are threatened. The Soviet Union in turn must recognize our right to defend our interests.

"No Soviet soldiers are threatened in Vietnam. Sixty thousand Americans are threatened. We expect you to help your allies, and you cannot expect us to do other than to continue to help our allies but let us, and let all great powers, help our allies only for the purpose of their defense, not for the purpose of launching invasions against their neighbors."

He noted the progress that had been made on arms limitation, trade, and other issues. "Let us not slide back toward the dark shadows of a previous age." He said the United States and the Soviet Union were on the threshold of a new relationship. "We are prepared to continue to build this relationship. The responsibility is yours if we fail to do so."

The following morning Nixon, quite full of himself, went after the Pentagon. He regarded the additional bombing proposals the military had put forward as "timid" at best. He sent a memorandum to Kissinger (who had somehow become his executive officer for implementing military decisions). He told Kissinger he was determined to "go for broke. . . . Our greatest failure now would be to do too little too late. . . . I intend to stop at nothing to bring the enemy to his knees. . . . I want the military to get off its backside. . . . We have the power to destroy [the enemy's] war-making capacity. The only question is whether we have the *will* to use that power. What distinguishes me from Johnson is that I have the *will* in spades. . . . For once, I want the military . . . to come up with some ideas on their own which will recommend *action* which is very *strong, threatening,* and *effective.*"

He never meant any of that; he was just puffing himself up. He had already ruled out any truly decisive action, such as reintroducing American ground troops, or invading North Vietnam, or bombing the dikes, or using nuclear weapons. He was making war by temper tantrum, his rage had no sustaining power to it. Mining Haiphong and bombing Hanoi were not decisive acts; they were irritants, major irritants to be sure, but hardly enough to turn back an enemy so determined as the North Vietnamese.

What Nixon had done was demonstrate his determination not to be humiliated. He was hurting Hanoi, not destroying it; he had, in effect, conceded Hanoi's right to keep troops in South Vietnam; what he had not done was agree to abandon Thieu, and made it clear he never would do that. He would even risk the summit, détente, his whole new era of peace, to preserve the government of South Vietnam. He had given Hanoi and Moscow much to think about; he had not changed the course of the War.

The political reaction was predictable. Representative [Gerald] Ford was in full support, as were most Republicans. Senator [George] McGovern called the action "reckless, unnecessary and unworkable, a flirtation with World War III. The only purpose of this dangerous new course is to keep General Thieu in power a little longer, and perhaps to save Mr. Nixon's face a little longer."

Senator [Edward] Kennedy called the mining of Haiphong "a futile military gesture that demonstrates the desperation of the President's Indochina policy. I think his decision is ominous and I think it is folly."

Nixon ignored them. The reaction that mattered was Moscow's. It came quickly enough. The Soviets protested, they demanded, they made accusations—but they never mentioned the summit. Kissinger saw Dobrynin. He wondered why there was no mention of the summit.

"We have not been asked any questions about the summit," Dobrynin replied, "and therefore my government sees no need to make a new decision."

"I think we have passed the crisis," Kissinger reported to Nixon exuberantly. "I think we are going to be able to have our mining and bombing and have our summit too."

Nixon had pulled off one of his great triumphs. Now, if only ARVN could hold on the battlefield, everything had fallen into place, at a perfect time to sustain his re-election bid.

12
The Failure of Force
GARETH PORTER

The Battle of Hanoi

Since the beginning of 1969 Richard Nixon had used the threat of unprecedented dev-astation of North Vietnam for a variety of diplomatic purposes: to prod the DRV into moving toward terms acceptable to the United States, to deter any move to upset his Vietnamization policy, to warn Hanoi to call off its offensive and finally to accept American terms for a revised settlement. The December [1972] bombing was the logi-cal culmination of his heavy reliance on this ultimate sanction to gain leverage over the Vietnamese revolutionaries.

The retribution which Nixon and Kissinger had so often threatened was to be swift, sudden, and brutal, unlike the Johnson administration's cautious and gradual escala-tion. Nixon was hoping that intensive attacks on the only two remaining urban ag-glomerations in North Vietnam would force Hanoi to accept his terms for an agreement. And if the suddenness and indiscriminateness of the bombing of those cities fright-ened the rest of the world, Nixon told columnist Richard Wilson on December 18, so much the better. "The Russians and Chinese might think they were dealing with a madman and so had better force North Vietnam into a settlement before the world was consumed by a larger war."[1]

All 200 B-52s in Southeast Asia—one-half of the entire B-52 fleet—were involved in the effort.[2] And three-fourths of all the Strategic Air Command's combat crews were mobilized to participate in the campaign.[3] There were also F-111s and F-4s carrying out strikes in the area, but Linebacker II was an operation planned around the B-52.

American officials acknowledged that the attacks were "aimed at crippling the daily life of Hanoi and Haiphong and destroying North Vietnam's ability to support forces in South Vietnam."[4] The target list was not limited to military objectives but included political, social, and economic targets as well, including the water infiltra-tion plant for Hanoi and factories manufacturing textiles and noodles.[5] It was accepted by the planners that populated areas of Hanoi and Haiphong located next to the targets would simply be wiped out. The B-52 was, of course, a weapon for destroying a large area, not for hitting a specific building or other target. The *Baltimore Sun* pointed out that the usual three-plane mission would drop 276 500- or 750-pound bombs in a rect-angular area a mile and a half long and a half mile wide. The result was that little remained within the target area except rubble.[6]

Nixon clamped an unprecedented complete blackout on the targets and the actual destruction done by the B-52s in Hanoi and Haiphong.[7] But foreign journalists saw the remains of an entire residential neighborhood in Hanoi razed by B-52s on the night of December 26–27. Kham Thien district in the heart of Hanoi had been home for 28,198 people. Most of them had fortunately been evacuated to the countryside already. What remained was a swath of destruction about a mile and a half long and a half mile wide, within which only a few houses without roofs or windows remained standing.[8] The main train station, which was located in Kham Thien, had already been demolished one week earlier, along with the bus station.[9]

Although Kham Thien was apparently the most heavily destroyed residential area, it was not the only one. Telford Taylor, chief prosecutor at the Nuremberg war crimes trials, who saw the ruins of a housing project in the An Duong district, wrote, "Some 30 multiple dwelling units covering several acres had suffered 20 or more hits leaving fresh bomb craters 50 feet in diameter and virtually total destruction of the homes."[10]

The most famous target of Linebacker II, however, was the Bach Mai hospital on the southwest edge of Hanoi. The 900-bed hospital, composed of many buildings spread over five acres, was the country's most complete, modern health facility, with 250 doctors and 800 medical students.[11] According to Telford Taylor the hospital was "completely destroyed."[12] A French doctor who was visiting instructor in genetics at the hospital had photographs of the damage showing the destruction of many buildings. According to hospital officials, Bach Mai was hit by three bombs on December 19 and more than 100 bombs at 4:00 A.M., December 22.*

After nine days of heavy bombing, French correspondents reported seeing "craters and uprooted trees" in the main streets of Hanoi, which were delaying the movement of ambulances and rescue teams. More and more of the remaining families were moving into the diplomatic section of the city in the hope that they would be safer from B-52 attacks.[13] The pattern of bombing in and around Hanoi suggested to the North Vietnamese that the purpose was to paralyze the city and isolate it from the rest of the world (Gia Lam, North Vetnam's only international airport, was destroyed by the bombing, but planes continued to take off and land). The bombing appeared to be aimed at leaving Hanoi, in the words of one DRV official, "without any electricity, traffic or relations abroad, and its voice shut—a complete blockade by air."[14]

If that was the strategy of Linebacker II, it was a failure. Despite the fact that the Radio Hanoi transmitters were struck four times in three days, the station was only off the air for nine minutes before resuming with a standby transmitter. Similarly, although 80 percent of the city's electrical power was wiped out, Hanoi had many small power generators with which it could replace power facilities destroyed by the bombing in order to carry out essential services.[15] DRV authorities claimed that, because of previous evacuation of the city and Hanoi's effective system of air raid shelters, only 2,200 people were killed in the capital—far fewer than the 5,000 to 10,000 deaths estimated by US intelligence.[16]

In fact, the idea of coercing the DRV by destroying or paralyzing its urban centers was illusory. For it failed to take account of either the psychology of the North Vietnamese or their capacity to adapt successfully to an all-out war of destruction.

The North Vietnamese had from the beginning of the war expected that their cities would be destroyed, and had made plans to deal with that contingency. In 1966 Jacques Decornoy told of being startled to hear the Vietnamese sitting with him in a Hanoi hotel lobby say, "This lobby in which you are now sitting—we already consider it destroyed. We are ready. We are accepting it all beforehand."[17] And in 1972, at the height of the offensive in the South, DRV officials were certain that the United States would still destroy Hanoi and Haiphong in a last spasm of violence before the end of the war. American visitors were reminded that Ho Chi Minh wrote before he

---

*Pentagon spokesman Jerry Friedheim, asked about the reports of the destruction of Bach Mai, replied on December 28 that the Department had "no information" that indicated any attack on "any large 1,000 bed civilian hospital." On January 2, he admitted that there had been limited damage to the hospital. Only ten months later, after considerable prodding by the Senate Subcommittee on Refugees, did the Pentagon admit that the hospital was indeed virtually destroyed in the December bombing. (Boston *Globe*, December 28, 1972 and September 2, 1973.)

died that the two cities would be destroyed just when they were closest to victory.[18] Factories, schools, universities—everything but the skeleton of the urban centers— had already been moved to the countryside. In fact, the government itself had moved its decision-making headquarters out of the city into areas which were safe from American bombs, and high officials traveled back to the city only to receive foreign dignitaries.[19]

More important than the failure of the bombing to disrupt the functioning of government in North Vietnam, however, was the damage which the North Vietnamese were able to inflict on the US air armada, which had only lost one B-52 in the war before Linebacker II. During 1972 the DRV had been secretly making radical improvements in the capability of its radar system for tracking US planes, increasing its coverage from an extremely low percentage of the incoming planes to a very high percentage. North Vietnamese scientists had made the improvements without the help—or the knowledge—of the Soviet Union, according to DRV officials.

Armed with this new capability for foiling the electronic countermeasures used by US bombers to evade the antiaircraft missiles around Hanoi, the North Vietnamese prepared their defense of the capital meticulously. The respite between October 25 and December 18 was used to build up the supply of antiaircraft missiles, and by the time the bombing began the capital was ringed by an estimated 850 SAM missile launchers.[20]

The result of Hanoi's strategic surprise was a toll of B-52s which shocked US strategists. In the twelve days of bombing, the DRV claimed to have brought down thirty-four B-52s.[21] The US claimed only fifteen were lost and that this was less than had been expected.[22] But it was unofficially leaked to the press by Pentagon officials who were obviously unsympathetic to the use of the strategic bomber fleet over Hanoi and Haiphong that this figure did not include planes which had gone down at sea or planes which managed to get back to their bases but were actually put out of action. A high administration source was quoted as saying that the actual number of B-52s damaged seriously was "nearer to what Hanoi says than what we have been saying."[23]

Pentagon officials, who had expected to lose few if any B-52s, conceded privately that they could not accept losses at this rate much longer.[24] Although Admiral Moorer would later call Linebacker II "the greatest devastation of the war" to North Vietnam,[25] it was actually the US Air Force which suffered the most serious loss, since the B-52s were no longer in production and could not be replaced.* Within a few days, the mounting air losses were bringing strong pressure on Nixon from the military to end the bombing soon.[26]

Meanwhile, the bombing brought opposition of unprecedented intensity in countries normally friendly to the United States. Not only the government of Sweden, which had long been openly critical of US policy in Vietnam, but the governments of Den-

---

*The feelings of shock and bewilderment at the heavy losses which the DRV inflicted on the US strategic bomber fleet were apparent in the statement of Congressman Daniel Flood of the House Defense Appropriations Committee in a hearing with Admiral Moorer just ten days after the bombing was halted: "My, my, my . . . that the . . Department of Defense, the Pentagon, that they were going to be handcuffed by some little country called North Vietnam and completely knocked off balance, good gravy . . . here this little backward, these gooks . . . are knocking down your B-52s like clay pigeons, with all the sophisticated hardware which was beyond our own ken, being run by 'gooks.' This is some kind of lesson." (*Department of Defense Appropriations*, Hearings before a Subcommittee of the Committee on Appropriations, House of Representatives, 93rd Congress, 1st Session, 1973, p. 30.)

mark, Finland, Belgium, Italy, Canada, Australia, New Zealand, and Japan openly expressed varying degrees of hostility or dismay toward the bombing, and the governments of Britain and West Germany were under strong pressure to express their opposition as well.[27] Even Pope Paul, who had been previously reluctant to criticize the United States in Vietnam, deplored the "sudden resumption of harsh and massive war actions" in Vietnam.[28]

Perhaps even more important, there was evidence that the bombing was threatening Nixon's détente with the Soviet Union and China. Immediately after the battle of Hanoi began, the United States was in contact with both governments, seeking their help in bringing Hanoi back to the negotiating table in a more cooperative mood.[29]

But in contrast to their reactions to the events of April, both the Soviet Union and China now not only strongly reaffirmed their support for the Vietnamese negotiating position but also suggested that they would put opposition to American policy in Vietnam ahead of their desire for improvement in relations with the United States. On December 21, with Truong Chinh in the audience, Brezhnev devoted a substantial portion of a three and a half hour speech to the Vietnam issue, in which he "emphatically stressed" that the future of Soviet-American relations depended on "the question of ending the war in Vietnam."[30] In early January *Pravda* revealed that the Soviets had stepped up deliveries of antiaircraft sales and jet fighter planes to the DRV during the December bombing, thus confirming US intelligence of such an increase in military assistance.[31]

Peking was even more disturbed by the US *volte-face* of October and November. The Chinese made it clear, both in public and in private communications, that they were not interested in any further negotiations with the United States as long as the bombing continued.[32] The state of Sino-American relations was described by one US official in January as "frozen as hard as before the President went to China."[33]

On December 29 the first anti-United States mass rally in more than a year was held in China to condemn the bombing.[34] Hanoi thus achieved a diplomatic united front with its socialist allies at a time when the United States faced the open opposition of many countries that were friendly or militarily allied with it.

The December bombing further seriously eroded the Nixon administration's already shrinking political support at home for continuing the war. There was a wide consensus among political figures, editorialists, and other opinion-makers that the bombing was an outrage. Typical of the reaction was a *Los Angeles Times* editorial which said that "of all the willful uses of arbitrary power, this is one of the most shocking because the means used are so grossly disproportionate to the ends sought."[35]

There were clear signs that Congress did not support the resumption of the bombing north of the 20th parallel and would move quickly to end the war through legislation. Senators' polls by *Congressional Quarterly* on December 21 opposed the renewed bombing by 45 to 19, with 9 expressing no opinion, and favored legislation to end US involvement in the war by a similar 45 to 25 margin.[36] Republican Senators Charles Mathias and Clifford Case issued statements condemning the bombing and warning that they would urge the Senate to end the war through legislation.[37] Chairman of the House Ways and Means Committee Wilbur Mills predicted that in 1973 Congress would approve legislation forcing the United States to withdraw its forces from Indochina.[38]

Nixon thus found himself under pressure not only from foreign allies and adversaries, but from Congress and even his own military leaders, to end the bombing and go back to negotiations once more. He had insisted when the bombing began that it would go on "until a settlement is arrived at," apparently assuming that the North Vietnamese could be forced to negotiate while their capital was being bombed.[39] But after five days of bombing he altered that position to insist on some indication from Hanoi that it would negotiate "in a spirit of good will and in a constructive attitude."[40] This was formula which would permit Nixon to end the bombing at any time without loss of face, should he decide that it was necessary.

On December 30, after domestic and foreign pressures had continued to build for several more days, Nixon gave in. The White House press spokesman avoided any mention of the bombing when he said on December 30: "The President has asked me to announce this morning that negotiations between presidential adviser Dr. Kissinger and special adviser Le Duc Tho and Minister Xuan Thuy will be resumed in Paris on January 8. Technical talks will be resumed on January 2. That is the extent of the announcement."[41]

It was only under questioning that the spokesman said, "The President has ordered that all bombing will be discontinued above the 20th parallel as long as serious negotiations are under way." Despite the implied threat of a renewal of bombing if the North Vietnamese did not agree to the US demands, it would have been difficult for Nixon to repeat the December bombing.

The White House was silent on the reason for the reversal of Nixon's earlier threat to continue the bombing "until a settlement is arrived at." But the White House plan for forcing the acceptance of its demands for a revised agreement had clearly been foiled by the unexpected military reverses over Hanoi and the surprisingly strong political reaction at home and abroad. According to Lao Dong Party Central Committee spokesman Hoang Tung, the crucial factor in defeating Nixon's effort to rewrite the agreement was the strategic surprise which Hanoi's antiaircraft units had in store for the US bomber fleet. "If we had not been able to bring down the B-52's," he said, "the situation might have been different. Their side would have made other steps forward to impose their conditions."[42]

As Kissinger and Le Duc Tho prepared to return to the negotiating table in Paris, Nixon's bargaining hand had been greatly weakened. His last major bargaining chip had been used to no avail, and now his administration was under even more intense pressure than before to reach agreement without much delay. Far more than in the October or November-December rounds, the DRV was in a position to reject American demands.

Later the administration would do its best to persuade the US public that the bombing had made the North Vietnamese more cooperative at the peace table.* A Gallup poll taken some weeks later showed that 57 percent of those polled believed that the Christmas bombing had contributed to the peace settlement.[43] In an ironic way, it was true: by its political and military failure, the bombing of Hanoi and Haiphong made the Paris Agreement possible. For it forced Nixon and Kissinger to accept the very terms which they had rejected in October, November, and December. While the threat of massive bombing had seemed to give Nixon leverage over the North Vietnamese,

---

*In an interview with CBS News, Kissinger was asked whether he wasn't leaving the public with the "assumption . . . that without that kind of heavy bombing the North Vietnamese would not have become serious—your term—and that therefore one could conclude that it was the bombing that brought the North Vietnamese into a serious frame of mind?" Kissinger replied carefully that the bombing "came at the end of a long process in which they too had suffered a great deal." He added that, on the eve of his own trip to Hanoi, it would "not serve any useful purpose for me . . . to speculate about what caused them to make this decision." (Transcript of "A Conversation with Henry Kissinger," CBS News Special Report, February 1, 1973, p. 7.)

the battle of Hanoi showed how that apparent strength could be transformed into diplomatic weakness. . . .

Only a few weeks after this manuscript was originally completed in February [1975], the end of the Vietnam war came with stunning swiftness and finality. Both sides had been prepared for a struggle which would continue for many more months. But military pressure by the PLAF against a military and administrative structure which was far more fragile than American officials had ever acknowledged publicly produced a process of unraveling so rapid that the Communist forces could scarcely keep pace.

This process of disintegration, which took place over a period of six weeks, overtook the formula for a political solution which had been outlined in the Paris Agreement and offered by the PRG. Although the shifting balance of military and political forces made it clearer than ever that a tripartite National Council of National Reconciliation and Concord would be dominated by the PRG, this body still offered a way of ending the war by a peaceful transition rather than a military victory for the Communists. But the United States made no diplomatic effort to achieve a political settlement by replacing Thieu until the very last minute, and then only to gain time to evacuate the Vietnamese it had already promised to get out of the country.

By the time a leader was finally brought in who *could have* negotiated a settlement earlier, there was nothing left to negotiate, and the higher echelons of the Saigon administration and army were already in the process of fleeing. Thus, Washington chose, in effect, to have the end come through a military victory for the Communist forces rather than a face-saving arrangement such as it had vainly sought in Cambodia. It appeared, in fact, that Kissinger wished to be able to argue that the Communists had never really been interested in a nonmilitary solution, and that the United States had no alternative but to support Saigon's war effort to the end.

The Communist's 1975 dry season campaign, as originally envisioned by PLAF military planners, was aimed at creating stronger pressures for Thieu's removal by further eroding Saigon's control and destroying part of his army. Although it was to include the capture of several objectives with great psychological impact, it was not expected to end the war immediately but rather to lay the groundwork for a war-ending offensive the following year.[44] Nevertheless, it set in motion a dynamic which went far beyond that. For it turned an army which had appeared to be a formidable fighting force into a mob of frightened and demoralized men who made the unspoken decision that the war was over for them.

Despite its massive size and modern armaments, the Saigon army's morale had long since declined to a point where disintegration was an ever-present danger. ARVN was not held together by any commonly held aspirations or cause, nor by any personal bonds of respect and affection between officers and men. It had been able to survive until the Paris Agreement under the umbrella of American power, on which ARVN troops had come to depend. The absence of US air support after the agreement and the growing military potential of the PLAF had created profound doubts that the ARVN could resist a determined offensive effort by the Communists, while PRG propaganda on the Paris Agreement and reconciliation policy had further reduced the willingness of ARVN soldiers to continue fighting. An American consular official in Quang Ngai province, Paul Daley, told a journalist in early March 1975 that he had visited an ARVN unit on the front line and had seen some soldiers taking off on Hondas. When he asked the battalion commander why he let them go, Daley said, the reply was, "What can you do?" The problem was, Daley continued, "These guys think that peace should have come twenty-four hours after the agreement was signed."[45]

Finally, due to soaring inflation, ARVN troops had been reduced more and more to robbery and pillage for their daily economic survival. By mid-1974, 92 percent of the soldiers surveyed by the US Defense Attaché's Office said their pay and allowances were not adequate to provide food, clothing, and shelter for their families. The DAO concluded that the economic crisis had caused a "deterioration of performance, which cannot be permitted to continue, if [the ARVN is] to be considered a viable military force."[46]

Accommodation and outright desertion or defection to the PLAF were rampant in 1974. One ARVN outpost, originally carrying 129 men on its rolls, lost all but twenty-three of them in desertions and defections before it was finally abandoned. When ARVN tried in 1974 to assign local militiamen to the regional forces, which were expected to fight farther away from home within the same province, the result was mass desertion. In one newly formed battalion of six hundred men drawn from the local forces, only three soldiers were left after a few weeks away from their home villages.[47]

The dry season campaign began with a move calculated to have a particularly devastating effect on Saigon's morale: an attack on Ban Me Thuot by troops of the Montagnard autonomy movement, FULRO, which had pledged its allegiance to the government in January 1969 but had drawn closer to the PRG because of Saigon's exploitative policies toward the tribal minorities. On March 10, FULRO troops fought their way into the central highlands capital and on the following day, they gained uncontested control of the city.[48]

Suddenly realizing that the central highlands were indefensible, Thieu ordered an unexpected strategic withdrawal from the remaining highlands provinces, Pleiku and Kontum. But the withdrawal quickly turned into a rout, as the 23rd Division was outflanked and essentially destroyed before it reached the coast. At the same time, Thieu decided to give up the provinces of Quang Tri and Thua Thien in order to establish a new defense line at Danang. He later changed his mind, fearing the political impact of the withdrawal from Hué, and ordered his troops once more to stand and fight for Hué. Although the Marines turned back toward Hué, the 1st Division troops refused the orders and ARVN began to fall apart as they streamed into Danang in complete disorder. Meanwhile, resistance to the PLAF melted away all along the central coast, as Quang Nam, Quang Tin, and Quang Ngai quickly fell without a fight, having been abandoned by their defenders.[49]

The demoralized Saigon soldiers who fled to Danang from other provinces brought social chaos and panic in their wake, just as they had in Hué in 1972. Their despair signaled to the population of Danang that the city was already lost, and the exodus began almost immediately. Within two days after the fall of Hué to the Communists, most government officials, including nearly all the policemen, had already disappeared from their posts in Danang, and order inevitably broke down.[50] Danang was ruled by horror for three days, as hysterical troops began to shoot civilians indiscriminately in the streets. The worst disorders occurred when Americans attempted to evacuate refugees from the airport and then from the port of Danang. Soldiers shot and killed hundreds of civilians in order to get themselves and their families on to evacuation aircraft. On board an American refugee ship, they beat and raped refugees and killed those who protested.[51] On March 30, Liberation Army troops moved into Danang without resistance and established order within less than an hour, according to eyewitness reports.[52]

The rout continued southward down the coast. In only three days Qui Nhon, Tuy Hoa, Nha Trang, Cam Ranh, and Dalat went through the same sequence of developments: officers and civilian officials pulled out, soldiers began looting, and finally Liberation Army forces arrived to restore order.[53]

By April 2, the PRG found itself master of two-thirds of the country, with its foes in a state of shock. Saigon appeared for the first time to be virtually indefensible with its dwindling and demoralized forces. Six Saigon divisions had been eliminated from the battlefield, including the most reliable combat units, and half of its air force was gone. The PLAF, which had overwhelmingly superior forces around Saigon, was now in a position to force a quick end to the war.

Assessing the new situation, the Party leadership quickly revised its strategy to take advantage of the Saigon government's collapse, in two-thirds of the country. On April 4, the PLAF sent out orders to its units to prepare for an attack on Saigon itself.[54] While making plans for a military take-over, however, PRG officials did not rule out a return to the Paris formula, provided that the United States would replace Thieu with a government which would renounce the violently anti-Communist policies of the past. On April 1, and again on April 2, the PRG offered to negotiate with such a government on the basis of the Paris Agreement.[55] In the latter statement PRG Foreign Minister Nguyen Thi Binh suggested for the first time that General Duong Van Minh would be a logical replacement for Thieu: "We understand that General Minh is ready to negotiate peace, and we are ready to talk with him," she said. On April 9, in a press conference, she again demanded a government which would "insure strict application of the Paris Agreement," offering once again to arrive at a political settlement with such a regime.[56]

But the offer to return to the Paris Agreement's political formula was ignored by Washington and the US Embassy in Saigon. State Department officials had gone out of their way in late March to make it clear to the press that the Peace Agreement was, in their view, "inoperable," and that there was no possibility of a negotiated settlement.[57] In mid-April, Ambassador Graham Martin said in an interview, "There has been no advice from Washington for Thieu to step down."[58] At the same time, Martin was actively discouraging a military coup against Thieu, assuring former Vice-President Ky that Thieu would soon step down.[59] This attitude of determined disinterest in a political solution was consistent with earlier reports from State Department sources familiar with Kissinger's thinking emphasizing that a North Vietnamese military victory was already considered inevitable and that Kissinger's only concern was to appear to be a "good ally" to the very end.

Instead of trying to end the killing as soon as possible by pressing for a change of regime in Saigon, therefore, the Ford administration went through the motions of asking for an additional $722 million in military aid on April 11. Kissinger, in a background briefing for the press, suggested that the administration understood that the war was already lost, and hinted that the posture of all-out support for the Thieu regime was necessary in order to have its cooperation in the evacuation of Americans from Saigon. Kissinger spoke of trying to establish a perimeter around Saigon in the hope of negotiating a cease-fire and evacuating large numbers of Vietnamese from the city. But he did not indicate any intention to work for a political solution by replacing Thieu.[60]

On April 19, with the Liberation Army poised to begin its final drive on the capital, the PRG spokesman at Tansonnhut, Colonel Vo Dong Giang, publicly warned that there would be a military takeover if negotiations were not begun soon by a new government without the "Thieu clique."[61] At the same time, according to US sources, an ultimatum was passed on to the United States through the Hungarian and Polish ICCS delegations demanding that Thieu resign within forty-eight hours and that a new government be established within a few days with which the PRG could negotiate a political settlement. The note gave assurances that during those few days, there would be no military interference with the American evacuation of its personnel.[62]

The ultimatum finally mobilized the Embassy to action. It needed more than forty-eight hours to evacuate the Americans and South Vietnamese who had been promised evacuation. The Embassy immediately put intense pressure on Thieu to step down. As a high Embassy official put it, "The old man had to lean on him substantially."[63] On the evening of April 21, Thieu announced his resignation and was soon on a US military plane bound for Taiwan. The PLAF, which was conceded to be in a position to attack the city at will, then reduced its military activities to a minimum.

For the next six days, as the military lull and the stepped-up US evacuation continued, Thieu's successor, the ailing, seventy-one-year-old Tran Van Huong, who had been closely identified with Thieu's rule for many years, seemed unable or unwilling to turn the government over to General Duong Van Minh, who could have negotiated peace. Not until April 27 did the National Assembly finally vote unanimously to turn the Presidency over to Minh. But by that time the lull had ended and with it any chance for a negotiated settlement.[64] As the PRG began its "Ho Chi Minh" campaign to take the city, the PRG delegation in Paris raised the new demand that the Saigon army and administration be dissolved.[65] And even as Minh was being inaugurated, virtually the entire military and civilian leadership of the Saigon government was fleeing the country in the US airlift.[66]

After futile attempts to get the PRG representatives at Tansonnhut to negotiate with him, Minh ordered his troops to surrender on April 29. Liberation Army troops entered Saigon shortly thereafter to find that the Saigon Army in and around the city had vanished into history, leaving tens of thousands of boots, helmets, and uniforms lying in the streets and sidewalks.[67] Within hours of the departure of the last American, the military and administrative apparatus which the United States had spent more than twenty years and billions of dollars building up and protecting had ceased to exist. The quarter-century effort by the United States to prevent the completion of the Vietnamese revolution was ending in complete victory for the revolutionaries. When the revolutionary troops entered the presidential palace, General Minh told them that he was ready to meet with them to "hand over the administration." But the PLAF officer responded, "One cannot hand over what one does not control."[68]

Now that the whole experience of the Vietnam intervention is behind us, it should be possible to view the policies of the parties to the struggle with greater detachment and to discern certain historical realities which were more or less obscure at the time. Inevitably, the relentless researching of the history of this war will show that the claims of successive administrations about their own policies and those of their adversaries were false or misleading. For it was the kind of war in which dishonorable and ultimately futile deeds were always clothed in the rhetoric of peace.

This study was intended as a contribution to the process of clarifying the record of the Vietnam war, so that the right lessons might be learned from a tragic and ignoble chapter in American history. Some of the major conclusions which emerged from the foregoing narrative and analysis are worth repeating for emphasis:

1. *The US executive's definition of America's interests in Vietnam required that it deny peace to that country from the beginning of its involvement to the very end.* American geopolitical interests were invariably held to be absolute ones which took priority over any consideration of the interests and aspirations of the Vietnamese people them-

selves. Permitting a political solution at any time which would have given up the right of American intervention would have meant jeopardizing the client regime's chances for survival. Despite many opportunities to resolve the conflict by diplomatic formulas which, in other contexts, would have been regarded as fair and acceptable, the United States invariably chose to rely on force to try to consolidate the power of the anti-Communist regime.

2. *The Christmas bombing of 1972 was probably the most important defeat suffered by the US executive in the entire war.* Although there was no single decisive battle in the fifteen years of war in Vietnam, there were campaigns which opened up a new phase of the conflict, representing a strategic setback for the United States and a gain for the revolutionaries. The bombing of Hanoi and Haiphong in December 1972 appears to have been the most important such campaign. Intended to facilitate a more favorable agreement and to suggest that the United States could reintervene if necessary, it made such reintervention far less likely. It aroused strong public opposition and provoked Congressional moves to cut off funds for any further bombing. It not only failed to force North Vietnam to rewrite the Paris Agreement in order to make it easier for Saigon to accuse its foes of violations; it also prepared the way for the mid-1973 legislative prohibition against any further military action in Indochina without prior Congressional approval.

3. *The Paris Agreement could not end the war, because Thieu had been assured by the Nixon Administration that he would get full US backing for a policy of avoiding political accommodation and continuing the military offensive.* Thieu had a strong incentive, moreover, to provoke a military confrontation with the Communists while he still had the strong support of the White House. The Nixon administration's backing for Thieu—and especially its pledge to resume bombing in the event of any "violation"—thus had the effect of nullifying the terms of the accord, which depended upon Thieu's having an incentive to make political compromises which he had been adamantly resisting for years. The United States thus rejected an opportunity to bring about a cease-fire and political settlement, to which the Communist leaders were willing to agree for their own reasons in 1973.

4. *The conflict ended in complete military victory for the PRG rather than in a negotiated political solution, because the United States refused to adjust its policy to the new balance of forces reflecting the fact that the United States clearly would not again intervene with air power in Vietnam.* Kissinger and Nixon refused to use their power to force a political change because they found it more compatible with both domestic political needs and foreign policy objectives to lose militarily while playing the "good ally" than to actively seek a political solution to bring an end to the war. The Paris Agreement's formula depended on a US interest in finding a way to end the war short of total defeat; in the absence of such an interest, a Saigon regime whose *raison d'être* had been to repress the revolutionaries had to be replaced by a regime established by those very revolutionaries.

Notes

1. Quoted in Thomas L. Hughes, "Foreign Policy: Men or Measures?" *Atlantic*, October 1974, p. 56.
2. *Washington Star-News*, December 20, 1972.
3. *Los Angeles Times*, July 22, 1973.
4. Associated Press dispatch, *Baltimore Sun*, December 30, 1972.

5. "Bach Mai Witness: Dr. Yvonne Capdeville," Paris Chapter, Committee of Concerned Asian Scholars, Information Packet No. 9 (January 1973), p. 2; *Washington Post*, December 30, 1972.

6. *Baltimore Sun*, December 28, 1972.

7. *New York Times*, December 22, 1972.

8. Agence France-Presse dispatch, *Le Monde*, December 30, 1972.

9. Marder, *Washington Post*, February 4, 1973.

10. *New York Times*, December 31, 1972.

11. "Bach Mai Witness," p. 1.

12. *Baltimore Sun*, December 28, 1972.

13. *Washington Post*, December 30, 1972.

14. Marder, *Washington Post*, February 4, 1973.

15. Ibid.

16. *U.S. News & World Report*, February 5, 1973, p. 18.

17. *Le Monde*, November 25, 1966.

18. Interview with Marge Tabankin, former president of the US National Student Association, on a visit to the DRV in June 1972, in *Off Our Backs*, September 1972, p. 26.

19. Marder, *Washington Post*, February 4, 1973.

20. Hanson Baldwin, *Boston Globe*, January 22, 1974.

21. Marder, *Washington Post*, February 4, 1973.

22. *Department of Defense Appropriations*, Hearings before Subcommittee of the Committee on Appropriations, House of Representatives, 93rd Congress, 1st Session, 1973, p. 18.

23. *Manchester Guardian Weekly*, January 6, 1973, p. 10; also Jack Anderson, *Washington Post*, January 3, 1973.

24. *U.S. News and World Report*, January 8, 1973, p. 17; ABC Evening News, December 22, 1972.

25. *Department of Defense Appropriations*, p. 14.

26. *Manchester Guardian Weekly*, January 6, 1973, p. 10.

27. *Washington Post*, December 21, 30, 1972; *New York Times*, December 21, 24, 1972; on Japan's reaction, see *Christian Science Monitor*, December 26, 1972. Reactions from foreign governments were reported to be far worse than anticipated. See Jack Anderson, *Syracuse Post-Standard*, January 9, 1973.

28. *Washington Post*, December 21, 1972.

29. *New York Times*, December 19, 1972.

30. *Washington Post*, December 22, 1972; also see *Baltimore Sun*, December 30, 1972.

31. *Baltimore Sun*, January 29, 1973.

32. *Baltimore Sun*, December 21, 1972; *U.S. News & World Report*, January 22, 1973, p. 8.

33. *U.S. News & World Report*, January 22, 1973, p. 8.

34. *Baltimore Sun*, December 30, 1972.

35. Quoted in *Time*, January 8, 1973, p. 14.

36. "The Vietnam Bombing: Senate Opposition Grows," *Congressional Quarterly Weekly Reports*, December 23, 1972, p. 3171.

37. *Baltimore Sun*, December 30, 1972.

38. *Washington Post*, December 30, 1972.

39. White House press secretary Ron Ziegler, quoted in *New York Times*, December 19, 1972.

40. *New York Times*, December 23, 1972.

41. *Boston Globe*, December 31, 1972.

42. Interview with Hoang Tung, Hanoi, January 7, 1975.

43. Richard Dudman, "The Lesson of Vietnam," *Congressional Record*, February 26, 1973, p. S3275.

44. *Time*, March 24, 1975, p. 20.

45. William Goodfellow, Pacific News Service dispatch from Quang Ngai, March 3, 1975.

46. *Christian Science Monitor*, April 1, 1975.

47. Don Oberdorfer, *Washington Post*, April 7, 1975.

48. The report of FULRO troops leading the operation on Ban Me Thuot was reported by Agence France-Presse correspondent Paul Leandri in *Le Monde*, March 14, 1975. Leandri was summoned to the National Police station for questioning about his dispatch and was shot by police as he tried to leave his compound in his car. *New York Times*, March 16, 1975. Leandri's story was confirmed by Catholic leader Father Tran Huu Thanh on the basis of conversations with refugees and priests from Ban Me Thuot. *Le Figaro*, March 19, 1975.

49. Oberdorfer, *Washington Post*, April 7, 1975.

50. Ibid.

51. Agence France-Presse dispatch by George Herbouze, *Los Angeles Times*, March 31, 1975 (Herbouze interviewed a French schoolteacher who was in Danang when the PRG took over); Associated Press dispatch from aboard the freighter *Pioneer Contender, Washington Star*, March 31, 1975.

52. Agence France-Presse dispatch, *New York Times*, April 24, 1975.

53. *Christian Science Monitor*, April 3, 1975.

54. In his news conference of April 19, PRG spokesman Vo Dong Giang announced that the general order for the assault on Saigon had gone out on April 4. *Washington Post*, April 20, 1975.

55. *New York Times*, April 2 and 3, 1975.

56. *Washington Post*, April 10, 1975. In an interview with a group of Americans, including the author, on April 7, 1975, the PRG ambassador to the Political Talks in Paris, Dinh Ba Thi, went considerably further in indicating his government's willingness to return to the political formula of the Paris Agreement. "We aimed at a higher goal during the negotiations," he said, "but Kissinger wouldn't accept it, so the power of the National Council was very limited. But since the agreement talked about the National Council we must implement that." He further confirmed that the PRG was still prepared to accept the existence of two administrations through the electoral process outlined in the agreement, and that they were ready to reconstitute the Joint Military Commission by negotiations with a new Saigon government.

57. *Los Angeles Times*, March 22, 1975.

58. *Time*, April 21, 1975, p. 19.

59. See the interview with Ky's personal assistant, Deputy Nguyen Van Cu, *Chicago Tribune*, April 24, 1975.

60. Kissinger's background briefing, including substantial quotations, is covered, without naming Kissinger, in the *Los Angeles Times*, April 12, 1975.

61. *Washington Post*, April 20, 1975.

62. *Washington Post*, April 26, 1975, and May 5, 1975.

63. *Time*, May 5, 1975.

64. A Liberation Radio broadcast on April 30 said the final drive on the city began at 5 P.M. April 26. The highways leading out of Saigon were immediately cut and the airport was rocketed by the following night. *Washington Post*, April 26, 1975.

65. *Washington Post*, April 18, 1975.

66. *Time*, May 12, 1975; *Washington Star*, April 29, 1975; *Chicago Tribune*, April 29, 1975.

67. For an eyewitness account of the Saigon army's surrender, see James Fenton, "How War's End Came to Saigon," *Washington Post*, May 11, 1975.

68. Interview with Hoang Tung by an American delegation in Hanoi, May 6, 1975 (*Indochina Peace Campaign Newsletter*, May 18, 1975).

13
Stabbed in the Back
WILLIAM COLBY

In the spring of 1971, I began to appreciate a new factor in the war—the virulence of the antiwar movement in the United States. It had erupted earlier, of course, over our incursion into Cambodia in 1970, but that seemed only a faraway and misguided protest against what on the ground was a clearly justified effort to clean out the Communist base areas along the frontier with South Vietnam. The scale of the Khmer Rouge atrocities in Cambodia that were to follow on the Communist victories was a shock to the world when the news finally leaked out of that unhappy land, but this prospect was unperceived in the early 1970s by the antiwar activists, who saw only American and South Vietnamese faults in Indochina.

We in Vietnam were, of course, focused on the situation we saw before us. The Americans were leaving, the pacification program was doing very well, the Vietnamese Army was being strengthened to take over the military defense of South Vietnam, and it finally seemed that a positive outcome from the years (and blood) committed by our Vietnamese friends and by the Americans to the cause of a free South Vietnam was possible. Such incidents in the United States as the killing of four students at Kent State University in Ohio by a National Guard unit in May 1970 certainly demonstrated that there was a major protest at home about the war. We mourned those deaths, as we did so many during those years, and they pressed upon us the fact that the time available to complete our Vietnamization and pacification tasks was, as we knew, short.

Problems related to antiwar sentiment arose in Vietnam itself, giving us concern. One was the rising use of drugs by American troops. Another was the increasing number of incidents of "fragging"—troops surreptitiously attacking their own officers by rolling fragmentation grenades at them. The erosion of national will at home was being reflected in an erosion of discipline and morale among the remaining American troops in Vietnam.

I had a curious personal encounter with the degree to which antiwar sentiments had penetrated even our military in Vietnam. I chatted at dusk one evening with an American soldier standing guard at the rampart around a rural team site I was visiting on one of my nights in the country. He mused that he really didn't understand why we, and he, were in Vietnam. I replied from my World War II perspective that we were protecting our country and our allies against the spread of a Communist threat, and doing it far from home rather than finally at home. He responded that he did not agree with that, and that we should fight only if we were directly engaged. I then asked whether he thought we should fight in Europe or Canada and in each case evoked a "No." Somewhat startled, I asked whether he (from New Jersey) would fight in Maine and got another "No." I gave up at that point, wishing him well as he stood guard over us in that faraway place. I was confident that he would do his duty to protect us while we slept, but I could not help but marvel at the far reach of his negatives.

But my own direct experience of the intensity of the antiwar ferment at home began when I was asked to return to Washington in April 1971 to testify about our assistance to refugees before Senator Edward Kennedy's Subcommittee on Refugees of the Senate Judiciary Committee. In Washington, jurisdiction over refugee programs rested with the Administration for International Development in the Executive Branch and, in the Senate, with the Judiciary Committee, which would presumably control American immigration policy. In Vietnam, the program had been integrated into CORDS [Civil Operations and Revolutionary Development Support] to ensure that it would work in close coordination with the pacification program and the military, with a separate Ministry of the Vietnamese Government managing the refugee centers and dispensing the necessary benefits to the refugees. I was thus the appropriate spokesman to present the situation to the Senate Committee when it wanted to be brought up to date on what was being done for the refugees in Vietnam with American support. In preparation, I had spent several days just before the trip home visiting each of the refugee centers that I knew the Committee's staff had focused on so that I could testify about them from personal knowledge.

As I testified, in the rear of the hearing room a group of antiwar veterans in beards and camouflage uniforms hooted denunciations of me as lying or supporting an American policy of genocide. This did not particularly bother me, especially as Kennedy made it clear that he insisted on order at his hearing.

What was unnerving was the surreal atmosphere of discussing American and South Vietnamese actions as though there were no enemy at all in Vietnam. Kennedy repeatedly tried to make the point that refugees were generated by U.S. military action. When I made it clear that most of the cases he referred to involved South Vietnamese military action in response to Communist attacks (many American forces having gone home by then), he turned to using the term "U.S.-supported actions," to which I replied "Vietnamese action primarily." He referred to one incident as "in the area of My Lai" (the site of the 1968 murder of Vietnamese civilians by an American unit), and I had to point out that the incident was some thirty or forty kilometers from My Lai, which made the reference irrelevant, however dramatic. I also had to point out the elemental fact that the greatest surge in refugees came at the time of the Tet attacks in 1968.

When I tried to stress that millions of refugees had been cared for at least to some degree by the Vietnamese Government's programs over the past several years and that the program had been expanded to cover "war victims" (people who had been hurt but were still in their own homes) rather than only refugees, Kennedy turned to the small scope of South Vietnam's civilian social welfare program, which we had been able to broaden in the preceding year but which could hardly match that of Massachusetts.

At one moment, I had to ride over his question to insist on the full story:

Mr. Colby: In June 1970, Senator, in Quang Tri Province, what that stemmed from was an effort by about three companies of North Vietnamese to sally down into the lowlands.

Senator Kennedy: Doesn't it appear that those are the ones . . .

Mr. Colby: When they got there the friendly forces, including the local self-defense and local territorial forces, held them and fought with them and the ARVN [South Vietnamese Army] came and chased them out and destroyed them. In the course of that kind of fight you do get that kind of damage to the houses, because there was a lot of shooting going on and a lot of shooting done by our forces and the Vietnamese forces. I don't think there were any American forces involved in that one. But I think that is the origin of that particular incident in Quang Tri Province.

We then got into a theological [*sic*] discussion of whether populations should ever be relocated so that their isolated settlements would not be involved in our battles with North Vietnamese forces. When I tried to stress President [Nguyen Van] Thieu's policy of moving security to the people rather than the people to security wherever possible, and his requirement that relocation be conducted only with high-level approval and with proper preparation, a few cases of inadequate handling (which our officers had reported and which we were trying to correct) were adduced as evidence sufficient to denounce the entire effort. My reference to the fact that many nations had relocated populations in wartime situations (e.g., the Japanese-Americans from California in 1942) was set aside as not justifying the action in a more enlightened today.

I had brought along a Chinese 82-millimeter mortar fin I had picked up in one refugee camp in the highlands to illustrate the Communist practice of attacking refugees in order to drive them back into Communist areas to serve as porters and food growers. But I decided that displaying it would just be contentious, have no effect on the overall atmosphere, and detract from, rather than strengthen, the impression I was trying to project that the situation was by no means perfect, but that the Vietnamese and the Americans on the spot were working on it and fully understood its moral dimensions. My approach seemed to pay off to a degree when Kennedy summed up saying that I had done "an excellent job in attempting to defend an indefensible policy." But the gulf between the reality of making progress in the myriad problems in Vietnam and the American insistence on immediate perfection still persisted; everything bad was blamed on American and South Vietnamese actions.

On June 13, 1971, more fuel was added to the fire directed against our efforts in Vietnam by the start of publication of the so-called Pentagon Papers, followed by the Supreme Court decision, over the Nixon Administration's objections, allowing their publication in full. I had no real problem with their accuracy, but I did with their scope, their coverage ending in May 1968, just when CORDS had begun its work. They thus focused on the [Ngo Dinh] Diem period and his overthrow, the revolving-door governments that followed him, the major American military buildup, and the dramatic Communist Tet 1968 offensive. Their description of the formation of CORDS ended on the hopeful note that "at least the Mission was better run and better organized than it ever had been before, and this fact may in time lead to a more efficient and successful effort" (Gravel edition II, 622). The years that followed certainly showed this to be an accurate statement. But the main effect of the publication of the Papers was once again to call attention to the confused and ineffective conduct of the war prior to the period of success that followed 1968, and to reinforce the feeling of futility about Vietnam, which by then had become fixed.

At the end of June 1971, I returned from Vietnam to Washington for the last time. My daughter Catherine was extremely sick. Some critics have alleged that her sickness and later death in 1973 was a protest against my work in Vietnam and particularly my direction of the Phoenix program. I know this to be false, as she was invariably supportive of my efforts on behalf of Vietnam, where she was perhaps happiest during her childhood. After my return she had a series of good and bad periods, but her epilepsy and her depression gradually slipped into anorexia, which finally took her life in 1973 despite the efforts of the medical experts in Washington and at Johns Hopkins in Baltimore.

When I left Vietnam, I turned CORDS over to my most helpful Deputy, George Jacobson, who had begun his service in Vietnam as a military officer, had left, returned in the early 1960s, and had been there since. George enjoyed some fame for leaning out of an upstairs window next door to the Embassy during the 1968 Tet attack to ask that a friend throw him a pistol, with which he then disposed of an attacker heading up the stairs toward him—the incident making great television drama. He was to lead CORDS until its dissolution at the time of the 1973 Peace Treaty, but he stayed thereafter until the last days in 1975.

My return in 1971 fully opened my eyes to the intensity of the antiwar movement. In July the Subcommittee on Foreign Operations and Government Information of the House of Representatives Committee on Government Operations decided to hold hearings on our assistance program in Vietnam, and I took the full impact of the new atmosphere. The Committee began on the somewhat mundane subject of accounting for the budgets devoted to the CORDS effort. A General Accounting Office team had recently visited Vietnam to examine the subject and had been startled at my statement that I did not know in dollar terms what my program cost. Being an intelligent team, they soon understood that I did know about the funds we actually managed in the field but that the full cost of our programs frequently included the costs of weapons or other equipment that were written off when shipped from the United States and delivered to the Vietnamese Government. Also, some assistance programs were handled by different agencies in the United States and in Saigon, but by CORDS at the rural level. The GAO examiners even accepted my statement that we had been putting our efforts into fighting the war rather than into accounting, extracting in return my concession that things were in fact now going well enough that it was appropriate for us to devote some attention to better accounting and financial controls.

The House Subcommittee huffed and puffed a bit about this problem and then repeated much of Senator Kennedy's concern over refugees and the civilian victims of the war. Two congressmen bored in, however, on Phoenix. One, Paul McCloskey of California, had been to Vietnam, where he was escorted around by one of the best of the CORDS officers, Frank Scotton, on detail to CORDS from the USIA [United States Information Agency]. Scotton spoke Vietnamese fluently and operated under my instruction to let the Congressman see anything he wanted to, to tell him the truth even if it hurt, but to try to give him some sense of proportion and of the wartime reality in which we carried on our work. McCloskey was having little of that, however, and focused on nuggets he could use to denounce the program.

The other Congressman, Ogden Reid of New York, concentrated on whether Phoenix met the standards of American Constitutional due process, with right to counsel, court procedures, etc. Since my Constitutional law studies were as good as his (we both graduated from Columbia University Law School), I frankly said that they did not, but that we were doing all we could to improve the procedures under which this necessary program of the war would be carried out. My defense that a war clearly involves an attempt to achieve the capture, the surrender, or the death of the enemy cut little ice with my critics, whose simplistic position was that a war should not be going on in Vietnam and would not be if the Americans were not there.

While I had opened my description of Phoenix with the fact that the Viet Cong terrorism that it was designed to combat had killed some 6,000 South Vietnamese local leaders and ordinary citizens during the past year, the statistics that caught the attention of the press in its accounts of my testimony were those of the effects of Phoenix on the enemy. I recounted that during the years since it began in 1968, the Phoenix program had brought about the capture of some 28,978 Communist leaders in the Viet Cong Infrastructure [VCI], that some 17,717 had taken advantage of the amnesty program, and that some 20,587 had been reported as killed. I made it quite clear that those killings occurred "mostly in combat situations" and supported that statement with the further details that some 87.6 percent of those killed were killed by regular or paramilitary forces, and only 12.4 percent by police or irregular forces.

Mr. Reid then asked, "Can you state categorically that Phoenix has never perpetrated the premeditated killing of a civilian in a noncombat situation?"

"No," I replied, "I could not say that, but I do not think it happens often. I certainly would not say never," adding, "Phoenix, as a program, I say, has not done that. Individual members of it, subordinate people in it, may have done it. But as a program, it is not designed to do that." Reid then tried to get me to make an admission in specific numbers of people who may have been inaccurately identified as members of the VCI, which I successfully resisted. I did not know the answer, and I understood that he was seeking a good headline.

We then had a direct debate over Mr. Reid's contention that the United States should cut off its assistance to the program. I countered this by stating that if we did not approve, we should go further—we should use our influence to have the program stopped. But I said that the program was designed to eliminate the problems he was concerned about and should be continued. Then I said:

> Mr. Congressman, I have said on several occasions that unfortunately the Vietnamese are not going to live happily ever after. They are going to face a security threat from North Vietnam and from the Viet Cong over a number of years. They are going to lose a few and they are going to win a few. But I believe that the probabilities are very clear that they will be able to sustain themselves in the future without the U.S. presence there that there has been in the past.

My testimony was followed a day or so later by an account by a former American soldier who presented the most sensational and bloody picture of his "role as it was peripheral to the Phoenix program" and "associated with both military intelligence and the CIA." Mr. K. Barton Osborn never did say precisely with which unit he had served, but he claimed he had worked with the U.S. Marines and Army and that he did not "work with the Vietnamese in any capacity"—a clear indication that he could not in reality have worked with Phoenix, which was by definition a Vietnamese program with our U.S. military Phoenix advisers in a support capacity. Mr. Osborn also indicated that he left Vietnam in 1968, when the Phoenix program had just begun to work as part of the Accelerated Pacification Program, again indicating that whatever he may have done had nothing to do with Phoenix. But his lurid testimony of throwing Communist captives and suspects from helicopters and my report of the numbers affected by this struggle cast in concrete one of the most repulsive, and flatly wrong, images of the Vietnam war, namely, that the Phoenix program under my control had murdered some 20,000 Vietnamese.

This was despite my emphasis that the deaths involved were mostly during military actions and had been identified on the battlefield after the fight as known members of the Communist apparatus. My problem was that I could not and would not say that no wrongful death had ever occurred, so that the sensational item for the press was my admission that some had happened. The Congressmen also did not pick up the key facts about their witnesses, which any attorney would have caught as affecting their credibility, but instead wallowed in the accounts of bloody misdeeds, with the media recording it all. A small solace was that the next day's report in the *New York Times*, while repeating my statistics, gave a straightforward account of the hearing, headlining that I had defended the program "despite killings of civilians" and stating that with "quiet persistence" I had argued that "the program was designed to protect the Vietnamese people from terrorism."

But the fact that Phoenix was reducing the arbitrary way in which the war had been fought was lost in the impression of wrongful death. The fact that the figures were only supplemental to those I had reported during my testimony to Senator [William] Fulbright in early 1970, and not different in proportion, was more a mark of the different atmosphere that had grown up around the question of Vietnam than of the figures themselves. I was moved to consider the words of the moralist that if one is not concerned with the death of each person, one is not concerned with the death of any, and thought my critics were concerned primarily with the political capital that could be made of the statistics.

Over a year after this dramatic testimony, the Subcommittee submitted its report on the hearings, which was more significant for what it did not say than for what it did, so it received practically no media coverage. The sole recommendation dealing with the Phoenix testimony was that the Secretary of Defense investigate the allegations of crimes committed by U.S. military personnel against civilians. The Subcommittee also recorded its concern over the problems of the Phoenix program about which I had testified and that our advisory terms were working to overcome. But no recommendation issued from the Subcommittee that the program or its American support be halted.

The Subcommittee and its staff apparently concluded, on a conscientious review of the full record, that the sensational allegations of the witness did not really stand up as an indictment of the Phoenix program, although some of the incidents may have happened and should be prosecuted. But this is a rather subtle conclusion to be drawn from the report, and it drew no attention from the media or the antiwar movement, both of which continued to repeat the sweeping charges of the witness and to apply them to Phoenix as a whole. It was clear from the experience surrounding the testimony that many Americans, including my two Congressional interrogators, were totally opposed to what we were trying to accomplish in Vietnam. They wanted, in the slogan used by the antiwar movement, "America Out of Vietnam!"—without condition and without consideration of what the Vietnamese might want.

In this account of the Vietnam War, I have omitted any discussion of the various diplomatic efforts that were made to settle it. This was not from inadvertence, nor was it from the fact that the subject never really fell within my responsibilities either in Vietnam or in Washington. Rather, it reflects my belief, then and now, that the process was largely irrelevant to the struggle in the countryside. I was convinced that the North Vietnamese Communist leadership was determined to conquer South Vietnam and would accept nothing less than victory in any negotiations that might take place. They had certainly given full evidence of their determination to prosecute the war, whatever their casualties on the battlefield: I was certain they would not be turned from their objectives by diplomatic persuasion or bargaining.

At various stages, the political leadership of the United States—President Johnson, President Nixon, Henry Kissinger, their aides and diplomats—thought that approaches to the Soviet Union could produce pressures on the North Vietnamese to get them to accept some compromise solution. My own view was that this did not give sufficient weight to North Vietnamese determination and that it missed the most interesting of the balancing acts that occurred during the Vietnam conflict—the exquisite skill of the North Vietnamese in manipulating their Soviet and Chinese sources of supply to extract the maximum from each. Locked as the two Communist giants were in rivalry between Mao's [Mao Tse-tung] Cultural Revolution and Moscow's revisionism for leadership of the Communist cause worldwide, the North Vietnamese involved them in a competition in which each sought to demonstrate superior credentials as fellow Communists—the gauge being support of Hanoi.

Some of the CIA's counterintelligence personnel considered this Sino-Soviet ideological dispute a charade to confuse the West and advance the cause of Communism, but I accepted it at face value as reflective of an internal theological dispute, and of the national antagonisms that had characterized Russian and Chinese relations for centuries. The North Vietnamese correctly saw in the dispute a chance to play each supporter off against the other and to derive a rich reward in military hardware therefrom. The one thing that seemed obvious to me was that in this situation the Soviets did not have enough influence over the North Vietnamese to halt their operations against South Vietnam. With the frustrations Americans suffered trying to make the South Vietnamese conform to American ideas of what was good for them, I saw little chance that the Soviets could control their far more tough-minded and determined cousins in the North.

I accordingly paid slight attention to the various secret probes and intermediaries or to the direct approaches to Moscow that diverted high-level concentration from the war in the South during the mid-1960s. Even when formal negotiations began in Paris in 1968, it was plain to me that no compromise solution was possible through diplomatic channels. The North Vietnamese had the French model to sustain them. Their steely determination had finally worn down French willingness to continue the war effort in 1954, leading to concessions from Paris far beyond what the Communists had actually won at Dien Bien Phu. And in that performance lay at least one of the factors that kept the North Vietnamese to a hard line in the 1960s and 1970s. It was that they had actually compromised in Geneva in 1954 under the pressure of the Soviets and China, only to see their hope for subsequent "inevitable" total victory frustrated by the unexpected ability of Ngo Dinh Diem, with American support, to revive South Vietnam.

The principal North Vietnamese negotiators in the 1968–1973 period often were quite frank in their references to the strength of the American antiwar movement as a principal factor that would force the United States to withdraw from the war in South Vietnam and cease its support of the Thieu Government. This was put directly to Kissinger by senior North Vietnamese negotiator Le Duc Tho. Despite Kissinger's sharp replies that Tho had no idea of how to deal with an opposition and that Kissinger would not discuss American public opinion with him, the many contacts of the North Vietnamese with Americans in Europe and visiting North Vietnam convinced them that they had only to be intransigent and the Americans would give in. The North Vietnamese attitude was perhaps best expressed by their suggestion at one point that the principal obstacle to a "solution" to the impasse that persisted between the parties could be removed by the simple act of assassinating President Thieu—perhaps in their view a fair comment on how the Americans had treated his predecessor, President Diem, when he failed to follow American direction.

We in Vietnam were well aware of this firm attitude by our enemies across the battle lines and were fearful that the North Vietnamese were correct, so the only hope was to build up the South sufficiently rapidly so that it could sustain itself against the North without American participation. But we knew it would need American logistics and air support, as we had provided in 1972.

The invisible participant at the negotiating table, on which the North Vietnamese depended to split the American delegation from its South Vietnamese negotiating partner was the American antiwar movement. The North Vietnamese assiduously courted its members through contacts in Europe, visits to Hanoi, and appeals to liberal sympathy with anticolonialism. This was immensely assisted by the American media's full access to South Vietnam and their inability to penetrate North Vietnam's tight security screen, thus providing the American public with a rich diet of stories of the failures and imperfections of the South Vietnamese regime and little or nothing about North Vietnam beyond the image Hanoi wished others to see. What the American public saw, read, and heard was, on balance, another element in the pressures the North counted on the antiwar movement to put on the American Government to ultimately withdraw from Vietnam and, as the French Government did in 1954, leave South Vietnam to its fate.

The most difficult aspect of the antiwar sentiment for us in Vietnam to understand was the fact that when public interest in Vietnam declined with the withdrawal of American troops and the consequent reduction of American casualties, prevailing liberal and antiwar opinion shifted its emphasis from halting American military action to stopping the Vietnam war entirely—at the cost of North Vietnamese victory if need be. Indeed, many antiwar leaders actually believed that a North Vietnamese victory would be the best possible outcome.

These pressures weighed especially heavily on President Richard Nixon and his National Security Assistant, Henry Kissinger. Nixon faced the election campaign in 1972 opposed by George McGovern's flat call for an end to all American involvement in South Vietnam. Kissinger realized that the only possible answer to that challenge was to bring about a peace agreement, and he searched insistently for a formula that would satisfy the North Vietnamese, yet allow President Nixon to assert that the United States had achieved an honorable settlement.

The North Vietnamese had an additional card to play in the persons of the American military captives held in North Vietnam, mostly Air Force and Navy airmen shot down there. Their captors cynically exploited them at the same time they abused them, parading them before antiwar activists like Jane Fonda in order to add this public pressure on President Nixon to yield to their demands. Their own spectacular courage and discipline under pressure (one blinking out the Morse Code letters T-O-R-T-U-R-E with his eyelids before the television cameras recording such a meeting; a group giving a rude hand signal to the still photographers, which *Life* magazine had the bad taste to publish, thus ensuring punishment for the captives) were hardly recognized by a nation that had decided that what they had done in the service of their country was flawed, and that they should be repatriated out of charity, not pride. The effect of this cynical manipulation of these prisoners was summed up in a remark Kissinger later made to me (I had no role in the negotiation from my administrative post in the CIA) when I commented that I could never understand how anyone could have believed that the North Vietnamese would comply with the "Peace" Agreement they finally signed: "You have no idea of the pressure we were under to get the POWs out."

The fundamental issue in the negotiations came down to whether Hanoi could maintain the presence in South Vietnam that they had lost to Thieu's pacification campaigns. Thieu saw this as an impossible outcome, as he fully realized that a peace agreement would mean only one thing—that the United States would end its involvement and support of South Vietnam while the North Vietnamese would return to the attack as soon as the situation seemed propitious. North Vietnam's assistance from its Soviet and Chinese allies would certainly continue, but America's to South Vietnam would as certainly dry up. Thieu thus resolutely refused to accept continued North Vietnamese presence in the South, which would give the North a clear advantage for the succeeding, and inevitable, attack.

Kissinger's accomplishment in the negotiations of finally obtaining North Vietnam's acceptance of the authority of the Thieu Government as an equal to the Communist "Provisional Government" in South Vietnam was of no value to Thieu, who knew that the war would resume as soon as the Americans were removed from the scene, and that the balance of forces without the Americans would certainly favor the Communists and their allies. Kissinger was seeking the best possible compromise with the Communists, trading agreement for their continued presence in South Vietnam, albeit with a promise that they would stop further infiltration, for acceptance of a continued role for the Thieu government. He asserts in his *White House Years* that he assumed that the South Vietnamese Army, with American support, could handle minor violations of the agreement and that the United States would return to aid against major ones in the way it had done in the spring of 1972. He did not contemplate only a "decent interval" between an American departure and a South Vietnamese defeat.

Thieu was both suspicious and resentful during his dealings with Kissinger. In later interviews for Nguyen Tien Hung and Jerrold L. Schecter's *The Palace File*, a book based on the many assurances he received of American support if he would agree to the "peace" conditions Kissinger had arranged with the North Vietnamese, Thieu recounted the various and sometimes petty and denigrating ways in which Nixon and Kissinger handled him very much as a colonial dependent, meeting him in Midway rather than Honolulu and giving him a smaller chair than Nixon (which Thieu changed), keeping from him some of the critical negotiations with the North Vietnamese, and even presenting only an English text of an agreement they had negotiated when the crucial question was the meaning of some of its key phrases in Vietnamese. The pressures to which Thieu was subjected understandably raised in his mind the image of the two Ngo brothers [Ngo Dinh Diem and Ngo Dinh Nhu] as the victims of an American-encouraged coup, lying finally in their own blood in a Vietnamese Army vehicle.

Kissinger recounts his version of the final negotiations in great detail. He had to overcome Thieu's resistance to allowing the North Vietnamese to remain in the South (which Kissinger had already conceded to the Communists), and his first try was to assert to Thieu that later elections to be arranged by the two Vietnamese parties could gauge the balance between the rival authorities. Kissinger's problem was that the conditions he had obtained in his secret bargaining with the North Vietnamese were better from the viewpoint of the South than the ones Thieu had previously authorized him to offer, so that Kissinger knew that the political consequences in the Untited States, particularly from the antiwar movement, would be severe if he did not now secure Thieu's agreement to the settlement. Thieu's problem was that he had indeed given Kissinger such authorization but had done it when the prospects of a favorable outcome of the negotiations through Hanoi's acceptance of any future whatsoever for Thieu's government seemed remote. Now that an agreement appeared logically imminent because of the concessions Kissinger had extracted from the North, it was clear to Thieu, as it was to the North, that any agreement that left the North in the South would only mean a resumption of the war without American support, with defeat almost a certainty. Thieu thus dug in his heels and used every stratagem possible to avoid agreement with Kissinger's program.

While President Nixon made it clear that Kissinger's negotiations should not be affected by the forthcoming American Presidential election, both of them were in fact pressed by the manifest evaporation of American public and Congressional support for Vietnam, and were anxious to extract a peace agreement to forestall a unilateral suspension of American assistance. The North Vietnamese were equally anxious for an agreement to fix an American withdrawal, which they correctly foresaw would bar any return, and made a series of concessions, such as agreeing to withdraw from Laos and Cambodia, to obtain it.

Thus, the two actual negotiators had come to an agreement, but were unable to complete it because Thieu was resisting. Even the promise of a pretruce massive infusion of military supplies to South Vietnam, which could thereafter under the agreement be replaced on a one-for-one basis, did not overcome Thieu's resistance. He judged that the key question was continued American will and involvement, which he correctly thought would melt away, rather than the words on the paper of the agreement. Thus, he reacted with a combination of hysterical tears, fears that the United States was planning a coup to overthrow him, rudeness to the American envoys, and intransigent rejection of the carefully constructed agreement, despite President Nixon's strongly worded expressions that American support would be forthcoming if the agreement were violated but that he would be unable to maintain American support if the agreement were not signed. The impasse with Thieu became obvious to the North Vietnamese, who then decided they would hold up the agreement to get better terms than those they had already agreed to.

The situation was opened up only by a forceful thrust against both Vietnamese parties. The North Vietnamese were subjected to a powerful bombing attack at Christmas 1972 at President Nixon's express order to make clear to them that this attack was different from the delicately applied, gradual bombing campaigns that had characterized the 1960s. Its force, despite the hysterical opposition aroused among the antiwar factions in the United States, was both precise and effective. The North Vietnamese massively publicized the destruction of a hospital in Hanoi but omitted reporting that it was across the street from the railway yards. They made a mistake in announcing the death toll as 1,300 to 1,600, which to anyone familiar with World War II bombing casualties in urban communities indicated clearly that the attack had been no "carpet bombing."

And it worked. The North Vietnamese quickly requested a resumption of the negotiations they had stalled, with a view to coming to a final peace agreement along the lines of the concession they had made. Nixon has since stated that he regretted not having hit the North Vietnamese as hard in 1969 as he did in 1972. He is right.

President Nixon's forcefulness was equally effective with President Thieu and the South Vietnamese. To convince him that the Christmas bombing did not reflect any change in the U.S. determination to make an agreement with the North Vietnamese along the lines that had been negotiated, Nixon advised Thieu that "you must decide now whether you desire to continue our alliance or whether you want me to seek a settlement with the enemy which serves U.S. interests alone." Thieu gave a response that withdrew some of his objections but said that he could not "accept" the continued presence of North Vietnamese troops in the South. He thought this formulation would not stop the Americans from the negotiations but would have kept his conscience clear that he had not acquiesced in a provision that he accurately foresaw could lead to the defeat of his country. Nixon then supplemented his forceful letter to Thieu with another that offered his "assurance of continued assistance in the post-settlement period and that we [the U.S.] will respond with full force should the settlement be violated by North Vietnam." And Kissinger returned to Paris to wrap up the arrangement with the North Vietnamese.

When the final Agreement had been settled in Paris and was taken to Saigon for Thieu's acceptance, it was accompanied by a Nixon letter saying that he would sign the Agreement "if necessary, alone. In that case I shall have to explain publicly that your Government obstructs peace. The result will be an inevitable and immediate termination of U.S. economic and military assistance." Despite a flurry of last-minute attempts to salvage something for his country, Thieu accepted the American decision. The die was cast for "peace" in Vietnam. The Peace Agreement was initialed in Paris on January 23, 1973, and finally signed on January 27. The day was marked by the announcement that the American draft was ended, perhaps a more important concession to antiwar movement adherents than the Peace Agreement itself. An emotional television bath followed the return of the POWs from Hanoi, giving them the honor they were due, but clearly putting the final stamp on the fact that America's war, and interest, in Vietnam was over.

It was plain that the Peace Agreement was not a formal treaty, which could have engaged the United States Senate in a ratification vote, with presumably some responsibility for ensuring compliance. To the North Vietnamese, the Agreement was no different from the others they had signed, as was their violation of it in a matter of days after the signing by shipping further military forces and supplies south. The American military had flooded South Vietnam with as much military equipment as it could before the ban of the Peace Agreement was effective so that it could be legally replaced one-for-one while the Agreement was in effect. The North Vietnamese were less concerned with such legalities, for their supplies were to continue in defiance of the Agreement.

TWO

IN COUNTRY

July 29, 1966. U.S. Marines look on as a South Vietnamese officer interrogates a suspected Vietcong guerrilla. OFFICIAL U.S. MARINE CORPS PHOTO

CHAPTER 5

The American Enemy

Through one of his characters, Pogo, the cartoonist Walt Kelly once made the memorable comment: "We has met the enemy, and it is us." Although this phrase applied to some extent to U.S. intervention in Vietnam, the war there was finally won by the Vietnamese, who fought with patience, skill, and ferocity. The readings in this chapter concern some of the principles and methods of the Communists and their allies as they struggled against the Americans, whom they regarded as the latest in a long line of imperialists. Like many revolutionary Vietnamese, Truong Nhu Tang received a political education in Paris, where he had gone to study pharmacy in 1946. He returned to Saigon and helped to found the National Liberation Front (NLF), called the Vietcong by the South Vietnamese government. (In a split foreshadowed in this selection, Tang later left the NLF when it became, in his judgment, a tool of rigid ideologues from the north.)

At the height of the American war in 1966 and 1967, analyst Konrad Kellen interviewed captured and deserting NLF and North Vietnamese fighters. The evidence presented here suggests that the Communists and their allies were able to persuade people in the countryside that their battle against the Americans was both necessary and virtuous. Historian William Duiker summarizes reasons why the Communists won the war; and he looks briefly at Vietnamese efforts to reconstruct their country after 1975, as they worked to overcome problems that were both external and self-inflicted. The last excerpt, by Tom Mangold and John Penycate, is an imaginative and compelling story of an NLF soldier who combats the Americans within the vast system of underground tunnels that his comrades had constructed in the south. This passage vividly contrasts the stealthy confidence of the NLF and the technocratic blunderings of the American troops. Partly on the basis of accounts like these four, many scholars have argued that the United States could not have won the war. The NLF drew on a long tradition of struggle against foreign invaders, knew how to take strength from the people and the land, and understood that it had to mobilize the people politically before it could expect their military assistance—something that three American presidents proved unable to do.

14
The Birth of the National Liberation Front
TRUONG NHU TANG, WITH DAVID CHANOFF
AND DOAN VAN TOAI

By the time 1957 merged into 1958, Ngo Dinh Diem had exhausted the patient hope-fulness that had initially greeted his presidency. From the first he had moved ruth-lessly to consolidate his personal power, crushing the private army of the Binh Xuyen,* then subduing the armed religious sects. From there he attacked those suspected of Communist sympathies in what was called the To Cong ("Denounce the Communists") campaign, jailing and executing thousands who had fought against the French. Each of these moves was carried out with surprising energy, and in their own terms they suc-ceeded. As he surveyed the political landscape three years after assuming power, Diem could see no well-organized centers of opposition to his rule. The National Assembly was wholly dominated by his brother's National Revolutionary Movement, the trouble-some private armies had been severely handled, the Communist-dominated resistance veterans were cowed and in disarray.

But Diem's successes had all been of a negative sort. Though he had asserted his authority and gained time, he had done nothing about establishing positive programs to meet the nation's economic and social needs. He had not used the time he had gained. After three years it was apparent that the new president was a powermonger, not a builder. For those who could see, the fatal narrowness of his political understanding was already evident.

In the first place, Diem's armed enemies had for the most part only been mauled, not destroyed. Elements of the defeated sect armies went underground, licking their wounds and looking for allies. Gradually they began to link up with groups of former Vietminh fighters fleeing from the To Cong suppression. The core of a guerrilla army was already in the making.

Even as old enemies regrouped, Diem was busy adding new ones. In the country-side he destroyed at a blow the dignity and livelihood of several hundred thousand peasants by canceling the land-redistribution arrangements instituted by the Vietminh in areas they had controlled prior to 1954. He might have attempted to use American aid to compensate owners and capitalize on peasant goodwill; instead he courted the large landholders. Farmers who had been working land they considered theirs, often for years, now faced demands for back rent and exorbitant new rates. It was an eco-nomic disaster for them.

In 1957 Diem promulgated his own version of land reform, ostensibly making acreage available, though only to peasants who could pay for it. But even this reform was carried out primarily on paper. In the provinces it was sabotaged everywhere by landowners acting with official connivance. The result of all this was a frustrated and indignant peasantry, fertile ground for anti-Diem agitation.

Meanwhile, the city poor were tasting their own ration of misery. In Saigon the government pursued "urban redevelopment" with a vengeance, dispossessing whole

---

*A tightly run organized crime syndicate that controlled underworld activities in Saigon and Cholon and was not averse to injecting itself into politics.

neighborhoods in favor of modern commercial buildings and expensive apartments, which could only be utilized by Americans and the native upper classes. Not a few times, poorer quarters were completely razed by uncontrollable fires (Khanh Hoi and Phu Nuan were particularly calamitous examples). Few thought these fires were accidental; they were too closely followed by massive new construction. The displaced moved onto sampans on the river or to poorer, even more distant districts. In the slums and shanty villages resentment against the Americans mixed with a simmering anger toward the regime.

In the highland regions of the Montagnards too, Diem's policies were cold-blooded and destructive. Attempting to make the tribes-people more accessible to government control, troops and cadres forced village populations down out of the mountains and into the valleys—separating them from their ancestral lands and graves. In Ban Me Thuot and other areas, the ingrained routines of social life were profoundly disrupted by these forced relocations, which seemed to the tribespeople nothing more than inexplicable cruelty.

By the end of 1958, Diem had succeeded brilliantly in routing his enemies and arrogating power. But he had also alienated large segments of the South Vietnamese population, creating a swell of animosity throughout the country. Almost unknown at first, in a few short years he had made himself widely detested, a dictator who could look for support only to the Northern Catholic refugees and to those who made money from his schemes. Most damning of all, he had murdered many patriots who had fought in the struggle against France and had tied his existence to the patronage of the United States, France's successor. To many nationalist-minded Vietnamese, whose emotions were those of people just emerging from a hundred years of subjection to foreigners, Diem had forfeited all claims to loyalty.

In light of Diem's conduct of the presidency, two facts were clear: First, the country had settled into an all too familiar pattern of oligarchic rule and utter disregard for the welfare of the people. Second, subservience to foreigners was still the order of the day. We had a ruler whose overriding interest was power and who would use the Americans to prop himself up—even while the Americans were using him for their own strategic purposes.

As far as I was concerned, this situation was intolerable. Replacing the French despots with a Vietnamese one was not a significant advance. It would never lead to either the broad economic progress or the national dignity which I (along with many others) had been brooding about for years. Among my circle of friends there was anger and profound disappointment over this turn of events. We were living, we felt, in historic times. A shameful, century-long era had just been violently closed out, and a new nation was taking shape before our eyes. Many of us agreed that we could not acquiesce in the shape it was taking. If we were not to be allowed a say about it from within the government, we would have to speak from without.

By the end of 1958, those of us who felt this way decided to form an extralegal political organization, complete with a program and plan of action. We had not moved toward this decision quickly; it was an undertaking of immense magnitude, which would require years of effort before giving us the strength to challenge Diem's monopoly on power. To some, that prospect seemed quixotic at best. But most of us felt we had little choice.

From casual discussions, we began to meet in slightly more formal groups, sometimes only a few of us, sometimes eight or ten together. Two doctors, Duong Quynh Hoa and Phung Van Cung, took active roles, as did Nguyen Huu Khuong, a factory owner, Trinh Dinh Thao, a lawyer, and the architect Huynh Tran Phat. We were joined by Nguyen Van Hieu and Ung Ngoc Ky, who were lycée teachers, and other friends such as Nguyen Long and Tran Buu Kiem. Our first order of business was to identify and make contact with potential allies for what we knew would be a long and bitter struggle.

To do this we formed what we called the mobilization committee, whose members were myself, Hieu, Kiem, Ky, Long, Cung, and architect Phat. Through friends, relatives, business and political contacts we began to establish a network of people who felt as we did about Diem and his policies. Phat and a few of the others were old resisters and had kept their ties with fellow veterans of the French war, many of whom were hiding with friends and family from the To Cong hunters. They too were beginning to organize, and they had colleagues and sympathizers in every social stratum throughout the country. They were natural allies.

Among us we also had people with close ties to the sects, the legal political parties, the Buddhists. In each group we made overtures, and everywhere we discovered sympathy and backing. Sometimes individuals would indicate their desire to participate actively. More often we would receive assurances of quiet solidarity. At the same time, we sent Nguyen Van Hieu to Hanoi to begin working out a channel of support from our Northern compatriots.

At each stage we discussed carefully the ongoing search for allies, wary about how to gather support and still retain our own direction and freedom of action. It was a delicate and crucial problem, of the utmost complexity. The overwhelming strength of our enemy urged us to acquire whatever assistance we could, from whatever source. In addition, the anticolonial war had not simply ended in 1954; a residual Vietminh infrastructure was still in place and was beginning to come alive again. For better or worse, our endeavor was meshed into an ongoing historical movement for independence that had already developed its own philosophy and means of action. Of this movement, Ho Chi Minh was the spiritual father, in the South as well as the North, and we looked naturally to him and to his government for guidance and aid. . . . And yet, this struggle was also our own. Had Ngo Dinh Diem proved a man of breadth and vision, the core of people who filled the NLF and its sister organizations would have rallied to him. As it was, the South Vietnamese nationalists were driven to action by his contempt for the principles of independence and social progress in which they believed. In this sense, the Southern revolution was generated of itself, out of the emotions, conscience, and aspirations of the Southern people.

The complexity of the struggle was mirrored in the makeup of our group. Most were not Lao Dong ("Workers' Party"—the official name of the Vietnamese Communist Party) members; many scarcely thought of themselves as political, at least in any ideological way. Our allies among the resistance veterans were also largely nationalist rather than political (though they had certainly been led and monitored by the Party). But we also had Party activists among us, some open, some surreptitious. Tran Buu Kiem, the architect Phat, and the teachers Hieu and Ky I knew as politically-minded individuals, who had been leaders of the New Democratic Party during their student years at Hanoi University in the early forties. This militant student union had been absorbed by the Lao Dong in 1951, some of its members enrolling in the Party, some defecting altogether, some simply accepting the change in leadership without themselves becoming Communists. What I didn't know was that Phat had been a secret Party member since 1940 while Hieu, Ky, and Kiem had rallied to the Party in 1951.

But I was not overly concerned at the point about potential conflicts between the Southern nationalists and the ideologues. We were allies in this fight, or so I believed. We needed each other, and the closest ties of background, family, and patriotism united us in respect for each other's purposes. This was my reading of the situation in 1959 as the yet-to-be-named National Liberation Front gathered momentum. I was not alone in drawing this conclusion. And I was not the only one whom time would disabuse.

In addition to making contacts and setting up working relationships with supporters, we also began searching for a leader. Our requirements were clear: someone who was well known and who had a reputation for integrity, someone associated with neither the French nor the Communists. This person had to strike a note of moderation and goodwill, attracting support from all sides and alienating no one. Several names kept surfacing in our discussions about this, and finally we drew up a list of four candidates.

Our first choice was Tran Kim Quan, a pharmacist who had been president of the South Vietnamese Student Association at Hanoi University and chairman of the Peace Movement in 1954. Quan met all the criteria; he had an established reputation as a patriot and was widely respected as a man of principle. Kiem was delegated to approach him for us. But though Quan turned out to be sympathetic to our goals, he was unwilling to accept our offer. Perhaps he had a premonition of the tortuous course this struggle would take.

There were two second choices, Trinh Dinh Thao, already one of our colleagues, and Michael Van Vi. Thao was a high official of the Cao Dai sect and had been a minister in the old imperial cabinet. Accordingly, he was conspicuously free from any Communist taint. Van Vi, director of the Franco-Chinese Bank, was likewise distant from leftist ideology. His nonprofessional interests ran largely to culture; he chaired the Society for the Propagation of the Vietnamese Language. I was appointed to sound out Thao and Van Vi but my luck was no better than Kiem's had been. They were willing to play a supporting role, but would not assume the leadership.

By elimination our list now was narrowed to Nguyen Huu Tho, a lawyer who, with Quan, had been cochairman of the Peace Movement, a vaguely leftist group of Saigon intellectuals who had tried to encourage Diem to hold reunification elections as stipulated by the Geneva Accords. But talking to Tho would be a complicated matter. His peace activities had landed him under house arrest in Tuy Hoa, a town in the center of Vietnam. Phat, who had contacts with the resistance veterans in the area, was assigned the job of stealing Tho away from his guards.

As Phat was making his plans, we began to refine our working procedures. Up to this point we had not been terribly afraid of the police. Ours could easily be construed as just another circle of talkative Saigon intellectuals engaged in the national sport of arguing about politics. There was nothing we had actually done. But by the fall of 1959 our organization had grown considerably. As we began working toward a first large-scale general meeting, the time had come to shift over to more formal, security-conscious methods.

Now we divided up our more numerous membership into many small working groups of three, four, or five people, no single group knowing who belonged to the other groups. This cell structure is sometimes thought of as a Communist innovation, but for the Vietnamese, with their long history of secret societies, it is practically second nature. Each cell included people from different classes and backgrounds to insure a wide range of thinking. I found myself working with three others: Sau Cang, a small businessman; Le Van Phong, a resistance veteran; and Truong Cao Phouc, a schoolfellow of mine who had also fought with the Vietminh and whose family owned a large rubber plantation.

The mobilization committee also appointed a leadership group made up of Phat, Hieu, and Kiem—responsible for overseeing the details of organization and bringing together input from the different working groups. After two months or so of intense activity throughout the organization, the leadership was ready to circulate a consensus of the ideas that had been generated. General agreement had been reached on the following objectives:

1. Bring a sense of unity to the different classes of people in the South, regardless of their position in society or their political or religious views.
2. Overthrow the Diem regime.
3. Achieve the withdrawal of American advisers and an end to American interference in the self-determination of the South Vietnamese people.
4. Defend and protect the rights of Vietnamese citizens, including democratic freedoms and respect for private property rights.
5. Carry out a "land to the tiller" policy.
6. Build an independent economy.
7. Establish an educational system that will protect Vietnamese traditions and culture.
8. Establish a pluralistic national government, nonaligned and neutral.
9. Unify the North and the South on the basis of mutual interest through negotiations, without war.

As we finished shaping our broad objectives and began grappling with their ramifications, we also set a tentative date for the first general meeting: December 19 and 20 of the following year. We decided too on a name for our movement: the National Liberation Front of South Vietnam. We devised a flag (later to become famous as the flag of the Vietcong) and an anthem, "Liberate the South." At the same time, Hieu was sent North again, this time for guidance from Uncle Ho on the platform we had enunciated. By the end of 1959, work was complete on transforming these general principles into a manifesto and a formal political program.

Reading through the finished documents, I was impressed by the analysis they presented of the South's political situation and the balance of forces within the country as well as in Southeast Asia and throughout the world. It was clear that these works had been finely crafted to appeal to the broadest spectrum of people in the South and to marshal the anticolonial emotions that animated almost everyone. At the same time, the manifesto and program responded forcefully and specifically to the interests of the various elements of South Vietnamese society—the intellectuals, students, middle class, peasants, and workers.

As I read, I had the distinct sense that these historical documents could not have been the work of just the leadership group. They had too much depth, they showed too expert a grasp of politics, psychology, and language. I suspected I was seeing in them the delicate fingerprints of Ho Chi Minh. There seemed nothing strange about this. Ho's experience with revolutionary struggle was not something alien, to arouse suspicion and anxiety. It was part and parcel of our own background.

We were now, in the winter of 1959–1960, ready to move into the next phase of the struggle. In early March as internal tension grew, the Resistance Veterans' Association suddenly launched an appeal to the people of the South. Spread through leaflets and posters, broadcast by Hanoi Radio, it called for an armed struggle to begin. It was a signal that the political action, which had been our focus for the past two years, would now acquire a coordinated military dimension. With this step, the Northern government had reinforced the Front's credibility and had flashed its own readiness for a wider conflict.

I felt a hint of trepidation at this. For several years there had been violence in the countryside; indeed, violent conflict had been a fact of life since Diem's suppression of the sects and the former Vietminh fighters. But the struggle we were now embarked on would involve military confrontation on a different scale altogether. My colleagues and I had known from the start that moving Diem into any serious negotiations regarding political participation would require the sustained use of force. Regardless of our personal predilections, there was no choice in this. But our priorities had always been distinctly political. We envisioned as our goal a political settlement that could be brought about largely by political means. Military victory was seen neither by us nor by anyone else as a serious possibility. Diem's own army was vastly superior to any forces we might deploy—and behind Diem were the Americans. A high level of warfare would bring with it the grave danger of direct American intervention, which we wished at all costs to avoid. What all this meant was that violence was called for, but a carefully controlled violence that would serve political ends. In addition, I believed that the core group of the NLF, men who felt much as I did, would act as an effective brake against those who might be tempted to look for a military solution. Nevertheless, now that the engagement was opened, there was occasion for a surge of doubt.

But events quickly pushed trepidation aside. The signal given by the Resistance Veterans' Association was loudly confirmed by the Third National Congress of the Workers' Party, which met in Hanoi during the second week of September. Proclaiming the liberation of the South as a major priority, the Northern government was formally announcing its readiness in the most unambiguous fashion. The stage was now fully set.

Meanwhile Huynh Tan Phat had organized a raid to liberate President-designate Tho from his detention in Tuy Hoa. The region around this town had been a center of Vietminh activity in the French war and was crawling with former guerrillas. From these Phat had put together a commando unit whose job was to grab Tho and spirit him away to a safe area on the Laos/Cambodia/Vietnam border. Here he could hide until preparations were completed for the general meeting scheduled for December 19. Phat's deadline was approaching fast.

Along with a number of other peace activists, Tho was being held in a loosely guarded house, looked after by local soldiers. Neither he nor his fellow detainees were considered high security risks, their crimes having consisted of some relatively innocuous agitation for elections several years earlier. No one, neither Tho nor his wardens, suspected that he was about to become a prime object of guerrilla attention. Taking advantage of the relaxed atmosphere, Phat's commandos were able to lure the guards away by having relatives call them with various family emergencies that required their immediate presence. With the guards out of the way, the kidnappers simply walked into the house. Unfortunately, so unaware was Tho that anything was brewing that he had requested (and had received) permission for a private visit with his family. At the moment his would-be rescuers began looking through the house, the object of their search was in a government compound on the other side of town, enjoying a reunion with his wife and children.

In a series of comic-opera mistakes, none of the commandos—all of whom were from the Tuy Hoa area—had ever actually seen Tho, though they had been provided with a picture of him as an aid to identification. Now they paraded through the house asking questions and trying to match up the various prisoners with the face in the photo. Unsure as to who was who and skeptical of the story about Tho's outing, they decided to take along the two candidates who most nearly resembled their quarry.

These two quickly found themselves transported to the border hideout, where their protestations of mistaken identity were finally confirmed, much to the discomfiture of the commandos.*

Having liberated the wrong men, the commandos were now forced to launch a second operation, organized a little more carefully this time, and including someone who could recognize Tho by sight. But because of the first mix-up, we were still without a president as the December 19 meeting came on.

Early on the morning of December 17, 1960, I left my house for the Saigon bus station, where Le Van Phong, one of my work-group colleagues, was waiting for me. After a few minutes we were approached by a woman whom Phong introduced as Ba Xuyen ("Woman Number Three"). "Ba Xuyen," he told me, "will take you where you have to go." My guide and I bought tickets for Tay Ninh, about seventy miles from Saigon and the home province of the Cao Dai sect, a place I knew intimately from my childhood visits to the sect's "Vatican." On the bus, Ba Xuyen gave me explicit instructions. "If any security people stop us," she said "let me do the talking. If you have to answer, say that we are going to Can Dang to visit our Uncle Kiem."

The trip was uneventful though, and at Tay Ninh we switched to a Lambretta three-wheel carrier headed for Can Dang, a government outpost village about ten miles from the Cambodian border. At the outpost we stopped for a minute while Ba Xuyen passed a few words with the soldier on duty, slipping something into his breast pocket as she talked. Back on the Lambretta, she directed the driver to follow a dirt path into the jungle. About a mile and a half along this track we arrived at a tiny hamlet, the home, it turned out, of the "uncle" we were visiting. Here we got off, and my guide led me into one of the houses, where old Kiem himself was waiting. As Ba Xuyen slipped out the front door, Kiem showed me to a little outbuilding behind the house, where I would wait my escort for the next stage of the journey.

Here we had lunch, and I dozed off on a cot next to the wall. Sometime later I was awakened to find Kiem gently shaking me, a set of black pajamas in his hand, which he indicated I was to change into. Darkness had fallen. As I put on the pajamas, I became aware that someone was standing in the doorway, a young man also dressed in black. He had come on a bicycle to chauffeur me to the next rendezvous. Sitting on a makeshift seat attached over the rear wheel of his bike, I rode with him through fields of sugarcane and manioc that were barely visible in the last of the twilight. About an hour later we arrived at a small cottage deep in the jungle. Inside, sitting around a table dimly lit by a smoking oil lamp, sat three local guerrillas, drinking tea.

They offered me a cup, and I sat down with them for a few minutes, happy for the rest. Before long, however, another bicycle driver appeared for the next leg. This was turning out to be quite an adventure—and, I realized, quite a meticulously organized one. My new driver pedaled into the heart of the blackened jungle, the invisible trail sloping upward as we came into the foothills of the border region. We drove until well past midnight, stopping every hour or so at a guerrilla cottage for a cup of tea and a brief rest. Sometime in the early hours of the morning we found ourselves among a cluster of small buildings—we had arrived at the meeting site.† I was sore and exhausted from sitting on the back seat for so long, and I marveled at the endurance of

---

*As a footnote to these goings-on, in 1968 I met these two men, both of whom had chosen to stay with the resistance. They had been nicknamed Ba Hoa Binh and Muoi Hoa Binh, that is, Number Three Peaceful and Number Ten Peaceful, referring to their place in family and the fact that they came to the Front through the Peace Movement.

†When I returned to the jungle in 1968, I learned that this original meeting had been held at Xom Giua ("Middle Hamlet"), along the Vam Co River near the Cambodian border.

my driver. In a minute though, I had been escorted to one of the cottages, and whatever thoughts I was having about this remarkable journey were blotted out in a dreamless sleep.

I awoke refreshed on the morning of the eighteenth, alone in the cottage. As I got up to look around, however, a black-pajamaed guerrilla appeared in the doorway, introducing himself as my escort for the next two days. He told me that, like the other secret delegates, I would be staying alone, and that he would take care of my needs. He also described the security precautions. I would be shielded from contact with others and was to use only the code name "Ba Cham" when I talked with anybody. Soon Huynh Tan Phat came by with another man whom he introduced as Hai Xe Ngua ("Brother Two Horse Car"). Brother Two Horse Car was about fifty years old and especially large for a Vietnamese, though trim and muscular. He was, Phat said, in charge of finances for the Front. (I later found out that this personage was Nguyen Van So, a Central Committee member of the Workers' Party.) We exchanged pleasantries, and Brother Two Horse gave me a sheaf of papers. If I had any suggestions or comments, I was to write them out, and they would be taken into account at the meeting.

I spent the day poring over these documents, breaking for a light lunch and dinner prepared by my helpful attendant. That evening, I was given a large checkered scarf to muffle my face, and shepherded to a hall with a low stage on one end and a row of curtained boxes along the left side—into one of which I was ushered. Slowly the benches in the middle of the hall filled, and I heard the shuffle of people being shown to the boxes alongside mine. When everybody had arrived, a troupe of entertainers took the stage, a unit of resistance veterans there to put on a rousing variety show. Singers, mimes, and comic acts followed each other, with a heavy emphasis on political satire, which the audience enjoyed hugely. When it was over, my escort led me back to the cottage, taking pains to avoid other members of the audience, some of whom were, like me, carefully attended.

The next morning, December 19, I was again taken to the hall, which now had acquired a different set of trappings. Over the entrance hung a red-and-white banner proclaiming "Welcome General Congress for the Foundation of the National Liberation Front for South Vietnam." Flanking this banner were two flags, red and blue with a yellow star in the center, the flag we had devised during our working meetings the previous year. Inside, last night's stage had become a dais, above which the same banner was draped. On the dais sat Phat, Hieu, and Kiem, our leadership group, together with Ung Ngoc Ky, Dr. Cung, and several others I didn't recognize. These others turned out to be representatives of various groups, youth, peasants, workers, and women— Pham Xuan Thai, Nguyen Huu The, Nguyen Co Tam, and Nguyen Thi Dinh respectively. Again I was shown into one of the curtained boxes along the side, hidden from the public delegates, who were seating themselves on the middle benches and from the other secret members occupying the adjoining boxes.* There were perhaps sixty participants in all, including twenty or so behind the curtains. Over all of us a sense of expectancy began to build, as a spokesman got up to announce the agenda.

After the agenda was read, a security force representative described the safety measures that had been taken and gave instructions about what to do should there be an alarm or an attack by air or land forces. Then Dr. Cung arose for a short inaugural statement, declaring the congress in session and wishing us success in our great

---

*The "public" delegates were people who were living in the jungle as full-time revolutionaries. "Secret" delegates were those who, like me, led open lives in government-controlled areas and whose Front identities had to be closely guarded.

undertaking. He was followed by Kiem, who read a report on the political situation in South Vietnam, and Hieu, who presented the manifesto and political program.

The hortatory language of these documents seemed to heighten the drama of what was happening; each individual in the hall was aware that he was participating in a historic event. Sensing the excitement, Hieu went on to explain that the name "National Liberation Front for South Vietnam" symbolized the unity of the Southern people in their struggle to free the country from *My Diem* ("America/Diem"). The flag, he said, red and blue, signified the two halves of the nation, united under the star—in a single purpose. The anthem, "Liberate the South," echoed the appeal with simple clarity.

At midday when the meeting broke for lunch, the delegates were visibly moved by feelings of brotherhood and resolution. For me, though, these feelings were to remain private as, muffled in my scarf, I was led back to the cottage to eat in solitude.

After lunch, the meeting reconvened to hear statements from representatives of various social elements—the sects, the intellectuals, students, peasants—each speaking of the aspirations of his group. When these had been given, we recessed for a dinner of soup, vegetables, and rice, returning to hear statements and suggestions from those who had submitted them in writing the previous day. Near midnight we voted to accept the manifesto, program, flag, everything that was before us. There were no dissenters.

Finally, Huynh Tan Phat moved that we adopt a suggested list of names as a Provisional Committee to carry the movement forward until the next general congress could be held. Specifically, the Provisional Committee would proclaim the creation of the NLF and publicize its manifesto and program not only throughout Vietnam but internationally as well. (The diplomatic front was to open immediately.) The committee would also intensify our proselytizing efforts and make preparations for the next congress, at which a regular Central Committee and organizational hierarchy would be established. It would, in addition, continue to develop our infrastructure throughout the South, with special attention to the Saigon/Cholon/Giadinh zone.

Phat's proposal was passed, again unanimously, and Dr. Cung was elected chairman of the Provisional Committee, with Hieu to serve as secretary general. In the early hours of December 20, we adjourned.

Once finished with our business, the delegates dispersed as quickly as they could, knowing that each moment the danger of discovery increased. I left immediately by bicycle, retracing the arduous trail back to old Kiem's house, where I arrived dead with fatigue but spiritually exalted. In the little outbuilding I changed out of the pajamas into my own clothes and boarded the Lambretta for Tay Ninh. There a bus was waiting to take me back to Saigon. This time I had no need of a guide.

By the following morning I had fully recovered from the lost night's sleep, though my body still ached. From Hanoi that morning a special broadcast reached every corner of the South, announcing the formation of the NLF and offering congratulations from the Workers' Party and the Northern government. It was a time for nourishing the most sublime hopes.

15
The People and the Americans
KONRAD KELLEN

The Fish and Its Water Reserves

Even though Mao's famous quotation about the fish and the water ["the people are like water and the army is like fish"] may no longer fully apply to the situation in Vietnam,* his comparison continues to reflect the vital needs of the "fish": For the VC, their relationship with the people in the countryside is of great importance, both physically and psychologically. To some extent, their food, shelter, security, intelligence, mobility, and sense of mission depend on that relationship.

In the early days of the insurgency, the villagers were apparently much attracted to the VC. "When they first came to the village," reports a hamlet guerrilla who defected in mid-1966, "they made propaganda. They said beautiful things. They told the villagers of the liberation of the South and the unification of the country. What they told us appealed to us. Later," said the guerrilla, "some villagers became 'distrustful' of the VC, when 'nothing the VC had promised actually materialized.' " Still, according to the respondent, "the villagers mostly [continued to] like the Front cadres because the latter knew how to appeal to the people's emotions. They talked about beautiful things, and what they said was so pleasant to hear." This deposition, it should be noted, was made at a time when people in the hamlets might have had ample opportunity to become sufficiently disillusioned no longer to "like the Front cadres." Yet, at least according to this source, they continued to do so, which may indicate, among other things, that even a certain amount of "distrust" or disappointment does not automatically produce dislike or actual hostility.

A captured Main Force lieutenant, a regroupee from the North, put his claim to the people's devotion in sterner terms: "We are the people's sons. We and the people are one. We and the people are like body and shadow. Therefore we get cover and protection from the people. They do not drive us away when we come to them. Instead, they give us food and shelter. Our relationship with the people is very close, now as in the Resistance days."

To attain and maintain satisfactory working relations with the village population, the VC not only resort to propaganda, but exhort their men to treat the people well. An NVA corporal, when asked what he had been told his behavior toward the people must be, couched his reply in Mao's dictum: "Towards the people: no stealing, not even a needle or a piece of thread." As a result, according to some of the interviews, harmony reigns between the VC and the people, despite the pressures the war is exerting on

---

*Mao speaks of guerrillas existing in the enemy's rear who "cannot alienate the people as long as they are disciplined." (*On Guerrilla Warfare*, translated by S. Griffith, New York, 1956). Mao did not foresee—at least not in this passage—that in a protracted war guerrilla forces may be forced, whether they are disciplined or not, to resort to measures such as heavy taxation, forced draft and so on that strain their relationship with the people.

173

both.* To the question as to whether the villagers were happy to "have you camp in their homes," one captive, a corporal, replied: "The people in Nhan Thinh [Binh Dinh Province] were very happy to have us stay in their homes; some even lent us their cooking implements, others cooked for us. The people liked the soldiers very much and treated them like their relatives." Or another prisoner, a platoon leader: "In my area of operations [the Highlands] the villagers were friendly toward us. We were given food. From time to time, the villagers gave us money, too." And a Local Force private had this to say: "My company never had to buy rice. All the rice we ate was the people's contribution to the Front. . . . Some people refused us salt, but they were very few."

One guerrilla speaks of a different experience: "Once we were short of rice when our supplies were delayed, and so we went to several villagers to ask for a few cans of rice, but each of them refused." However, perhaps significantly, the soldier had no hard feelings: "I think the villagers were right. They were poor themselves. How could we expect to receive help from them?" The answer seems to indicate that the VC—if they so elect—can be as forbearing with the villagers as the villagers can be with them, a forbearance likely to bring flexibility into the relationship.

A guerrilla platoon leader made this estimate: "About one-third of the people liked us because they were VC sympathizers. The rest of the people didn't." In terms of percentages, a third may not be very much. But, considering the fact that in revolutionary situations the activists, though generally in the minority, are the ones that count, even this figure—if accurate—would be quite impressive. As to "the rest" the VC continued the struggle for their "hearts and minds," VC-style: "The people had to put up with us. They were told to help the Revolution. They had no choice. If they had shown dissatisfaction, they would have been sent to reeducation sessions. They had to please us in order to avoid trouble." One respondent stated that the villagers supported the VC not just with food and shelter, but also with care of the disabled: "The sick and severely wounded were entrusted to the care of the villagers' families. The amputees, too, were sent to the various villagers where families belonging to various Front organizations took care of them."

Were the villagers not worried about the VC presence? According to a captured platoon leader, "The villagers seemed to be afraid that our presence might cause the village to be bombarded by GVN artillery or aircraft, but they never asked us to leave." The same topic received the following treatment in a captured VC document: "People's attitudes: no longer afraid of troops in the area. The people also stopped reporting our arrival to the enemy. Instead, when our troops come to the village, the people buy rice for them, cook for them and protect them." One captured fighter, when asked how the villagers had reacted to his unit being stationed in their village, presented this idyllic picture: "The people were very happy about it, because life in the village became much gayer. At night we gathered all the children and sang. It was fun and the villagers liked it a lot." But were they not scared their village might be bombed? "A number of villag-

---

*It is this analyst's impression that rejection of VC troops by villagers, where it occurs, is of a different nature from rejection of GVN soldiers. Negative villagers' feeling to the VC seems to be the result of actual damage incurred by bombings in response to VC presence, taxation, draft, and, occasionally, disappointment with a lack of VC victory, whereas negative villager feeling toward the GVN seems to be a more basic hostility resulting from GVN aims and behavior. . . . In fact, it is one of [our] tentative findings . . . that negative feelings toward the VC, where they occur, differ substantially from those toward the GVN. Villagers apparently reject the VC "in sorrow rather than in anger," but reject the GVN, where they reject it, "in anger rather than in sorrow." It is clear that, should this hypothesis stand up to further analysis, it would have some bearing on any struggle "for the hearts and minds" of the villagers.

ers were afraid of this, but these people were in the minority. Most villagers said the Americans bombed anywhere and any way, and didn't bomb troops only. So, they said, if the Americans wanted to bomb the village they would do so whether the troops were there or not."

Still, the soldiers's unit eventually moved into the forest. Why did they move? "Because we would have more security living in the forest than in the village. If we were detected and bombed, the people would be caught in the bombing." This response suggests that the VC were in some instances not merely concerned with their own security, but also with the lives of the villagers. Whether this was due to their chivalrous concern, or whether the statement was merely propagandistic embroidery around a military necessity, the cadre reported it as part of the VC's motivation to take the additional hardships of jungle life upon themselves in order to save the population unnecessary exposure to bombs. The people might well have been grateful for such consideration.

Some villagers, in turn, apparently responded on occasion in ways that would reflect true sympathy and encouragement for the VC: "I myself have seen dead revolutionaries receive honors from the people. I participated in the attack on Tanh Binh Thay Post, near My Tho. It wasn't a successful attack, and four bodies of my comrades were left behind. The local people around there took up a collection, bought four nice coffins and then asked the authorities in the post for permission to let them bury the four bodies. I saw the four graves side by side in the cemetery. This was done by people who were not related to the dead fighters. The people mourned their deaths." The respondent in this case is an assistant company commander.

In a rallier's account of a dramatic moment of high excitement, the villagers seemed to have actively and spontaneously sided with the VC: "At Son Chau I witnessed a would-be deserter get caught . . . he was one of four soldiers coming into the village. Suddenly he began running toward the GVN military post at Hui Tron. . . . The three other soldiers opened fire, and the people started running after the man with machetes and sticks. They caught up with him, and he had to surrender. . . ." Another soldier, a captured fighter, reports a general reaction—shared by himself—that attests to the hold of VC propaganda on villagers in certain instances of stress and confusion: "Once every two months the ARVN came [to a village formerly under GVN control] and all the village youth would run away."—"Why were the villagers so afraid of the GVN?"—"I don't understand why, but after listening to VC propaganda I got frightened too. I had lived happily under the GVN; I had been able to go to school there, and never heard my mother complain about high taxes there. Yet, the VC had a way of scaring the wits out of us."

Few, if any, of the villagers are reported in the interviews as having behaved in an actively hostile fashion to the VC soldiers, let alone voiced hostility to the VC cause. This finding concerning the villagers' attitudes and actions is thrown into clearer relief if viewed in the light of the striking absence, in the interviews, of evidence that the villagers liked the GVN or favored their victory, or actually helped them. While some allegiance for the GVN in GVN areas is reported by some respondents, none report hidden sympathies for the GVN in VC-controlled hamlets. Thus, as suggested by the foregoing, what began as a romance between the villagers and the VC may have lost some of its luster; but there is some evidence that instead of evanescing, the romance has rather turned into a workable marriage of convenience, and there is nothing to indicate that the two hard-pressed partners are considering an early divorce. The analogy, of course, limps, as the VC would not seek a divorce from the people in any event. But—from the interviews examined here—the people do not give any evidence of seeking it either, least of all because of blandishment from the Saigon suitor. This is of crucial importance for the VC who, in the words of one prisoner, "couldn't exist for a month without the people's help." Thus, continued and apparently often voluntary support by the villagers emerges as one of the elements of support which the VC need to maintain cohesion and give battle.

The Evil Americans

If strong hostility to the enemy and all he stands for is one token of an army's cohesion and resolve, the VC leadership can be pleased with the attitudes prevailing in its forces on this score. Even though a captive or rallier who is careful and pragmatic—and many Vietnamese apparently are— might think twice before telling his interrogator that he hated Americans, the underlying materials collected during 1966–1967 contain so many examples of strong VC hostility to Americans on so many different grounds that it is hard to select the most telling examples.

Some respondents, of course, attribute imperialist designs to the Americans. One captured Main Force corporal, when asked what his cadres had said about the Americans, reported: "The cadres explained that the Americans do not think the GVN capable of defeating the Front. . . . The Americans, they said, had come to help the GVN, but in reality they had come to take over South Vietnam. The cadres also said that . . . after having taken over the South, the Americans would take over North Vietnam, and then attack Red China." Did the men in his unit believe what they were told? "Yes, everyone of us did." The corporal added: "Thus, to liberate the South would also serve the purpose of defending the North." It must be conceded to the VC that this is a rather clever—and in this instance apparently effective—line to take with an NVA soldier (as this man was); should the NVA soldiers become weary of "liberating the South," they are to remember that they are not fighting in the South for altruistic reasons only, but to protect their homeland which the Americans would otherwise take.*

The same corporal was even willing to give American soldiers the benefit of the doubt: "If asked, any American G.I. would say in all sincerity that he believes the Americans have indeed come to help the GVN." But the respondent said he knew better: "I personally think this war has cost the United States a lot, and if the United States should win, South Vietnam would have nothing to pay them back. When that time comes, whether anybody wants it or not, the United States will have to rule over South Vietnam. The Americans are good people, but they will be forced to do this to compensate themselves for what they have put into Vietnam. In short, South Vietnam would take over sooner or later."

The same doctrinal view, to the effect that there is a split between the Americans and their leaders, recurred in this sergeant's statement: "The cadre said that only the American imperialists were bad men, and that the American people were very nice. Some Americans told their sons not to go to Vietnam to shoot at the Vietnamese people. They said some elements in the United States had staged antiwar demonstrations." This interviewee added a note which appears frequently also in other interviews: "The cadres said the war could only end if the Americans withdrew. . . . " On the subject of

---

*Of course, NVA soldiers tend to insist on the "one country" view with regard to South and North Vietnam, so that by definition they cannot consider themselves aggressors while fighting in the South. Thus, their minds may be regarded as free of the corroding thought that their mission is not legitimate.

imperialist intent, a captured Main Force private presented this rather original version: "The cadres said the American imperialists were kind to the GVN now . . . so that when the South was pacified, they could start exploiting the people in the South just as in the old times when the emperors forced the people to dive for pearls, or hunt for elephant tusks in the forests. . . ." The respondent gave no indication whether he believed this.

In most instances the response to the Americans is less abstract. One Labor Youth Group member made this entry in his diary: ". . . in my first engagement I recieved two wounds on my body that left, I think, permanent marks. Every time I looked at them, my hatred against the imperialists and capitalists, particularly the Americans, welled up." Almost equally personal and direct is an account by a captured corporal: "The cadre said to us . . . as you can see, the Americans never let our people live in peace. They are bombing the North. . . . Peace-loving people, children and students are killed in the North. Market places are attacked. What do you think, comrades? Should we let them do all that?" And the corporal who reported this speech by his cadre, added in conclusion: "Frankly, we hated the Americans."

A rallier presented a racial version, which he seemed to have accepted: "I was told the Americans hired the GVN to wage war on their behalf. This would kill many Vietnamese young people and leave the Americans free to take all the Vietnamese girls. I was told it was our duty to help the Front save our race." A captured regroupee lieutenant, when asked what he had been told about the American forces while in the Front, simply stated: "I heard that the Americans had come to kill the Vietnamese people"—an explanation he apparently believed. Similarly negative was this reported response of the villagers: "They said that [because of the spraying] they could not live with the invaders." When asked what the villagers would have meant by the "invaders," the respondent (a captured fighter) replied: "By the invaders they meant the Americans." A hamlet guerrilla reported the negative attitude of the population in the following interchange: "Did the people in your village want the Americans to leave the South?"— "Will any harm come to me if I tell you the truth?"—"No."—"Well, I can tell you this: the majority of the people in the village would prefer the Americans to leave the South."

A more drastic response by villagers to the Americans was reported by this assistant company commander in the Local Forces, who added that he shared that response: "They [the people] hated the Americans. This is the truth. Take me, for example. I consider the Americans my enemy. The people blamed the Americans for the attacks [on the villages] . . . The Vietnamese couldn't have done that. People of the same race, the same country, wouldn't kill each other. Only the Americans would kill so senselessly . . ." The speaker, a Party member in addition to his rank in the Local Forces, was here expressing a view contrary to demonstrable reality: after all, Vietnamese have found it quite easy in this war to kill each other. But he sounds convinced and, to his men, probably quite convincing.

Some respondents give evasive answers when asked, "What do you think about the Americans?": "I only see that the people are suffering hardships. Now, I only want to know what can be done to make the Americans go back to their country so that both (Vietnamese) governments can come to an agreement to relieve the people's suffering." Others express perplexity as to the American presence and purpose; such as this fighter, a captive: "Certainly, to come here like this, they (the Americans) must want something, but what it is I cannot understand." Or: "From the newspapers I know that America is a rich country. It helps the GVN fight the Communist government. I don't know what America wants in Vietnam." A more definite view of the American presence was expressed by a Local Force platoon leader: "It is my opinion that if the

Americans hadn't come to South Vietnam, the differences between North and South Vietnam could have been settled by different and more peaceful means." And the same captive, also a Party member and guerrilla instructor, added: "The Nationalist government claims that the North wanted to take over the South, and that it therefore needed assistance from the Americans. This was the cause of all the fighting."

Some men—in this case a fighter—have no opinions of their own about the American presence: "I have no particular thoughts about the Americans. We were told the Americans were aggressors, and we just took them as such." A captured senior lieutenant, on the other hand, regarded Americans as inherently evil: "Why do you think the Americans are bombing North Vietnam?"—"You should know that better than I do."—"I want your opinion."—"The Americans are a warlike people. They bomb North Vietnam because they like to."

But, perhaps surprisingly, some VC respondents who showed strong hostility to the Americans and deplored their presence in Vietnam—aside from seeing in that presence the "cause for all the fighting" and *the* obstacle to peace—did not seem to consider the American presence a reason to expect a quick defeat for their cause. As one private put it: "You see, when you look at the facts, and when you see that today American troops in Vietnam exceed 300,000, and that more and more Americans directly participate in the war, how can peace come, how can anyone hope for the end of the war to come?" In other words, this respondent did not conclude that such a large American force could terminate the war quickly in its favor. Similarly, a corporal, when asked whether the influx of American troops had had any effect on his men's morale replied: "Yes. They thought it would be harder for them to end the war and liberate the South, because the more ARVN soldiers they killed, the more Americans would arrive to take their place." Harder—not hopeless. Another corporal, on the same subject: "In my view the war will last longer because we now have to fight the Americans, too. As to the effects of the American presence on the outcome of the war, I don't know."

Hand in hand with the conviction, held by some VC soldiers, that American assistance to the GVN will not lead to a VC defeat (although, on the whole they do not hold positive expectations of victory either) is the feeling encountered in some interviews that with some effort, the Americans can be coped with on the field of battle. At least one NVA squad leader gave evidence that such efforts to put Americans in their place had worked, as shown by this cool appraisal: "I have had contact with American soldiers. Generally speaking, they have their strong points: They are very brave and their marksmanship is good. Their weak points are, they are too much used to modern battlefields, and to apply the same tactics to this battlefield is not advisable. Take this example: When they move toward a certain position, they all move forward at once. Meanwhile, the other side uses guerrilla tactics—a few fighters hide here, fire a few rounds, and run to another place. When the Americans move in where the shots have come from, they find nothing. Meanwhile the same few fighters fire a few more shots from their new hideouts. These shots cause the Americans casualties, dead or wounded." The man sounds rather confident.

As to American aims, do individual VC captives or ralliers ever say anything positive, or do they ever report anything positive about such aims being said by their comrades?* Not according to the available data. Thus, if being "soft on Americans" could be regarded as a factor gnawing away at cohesion, that factor seems absent. True, some VC prisoners and ralliers occasionally make positive statements about American aims

---

*As, for example, many *Wehrmacht* soldiers did among themselves prior to capture in World War II.

and behavior, but they invariably add that they came to hold such positive views only after capture or surrender, and not while they still served in the VC. There is, then, much reason to assume that the VC machine derives considerable strength and cohesion from a genuinely felt rather than merely propagandistically spread or superficially accepted hostility to Americans. This may be regarded as reinforced by their vague, yet presumably quite sustaining, feelings that the Americans can be coped with in one way or another.

16
Why the Communists Won
WILLIAM DUIKER

The most significant fact about [the Vietnam] conflict is not that the United States lost but that the Communists won. Since the end of the war in 1975, one of the main issues raised in the long debate over the "lessons of Vietnam" has been whether that war could have been won at an acceptable risk and cost. Although few would deny that U.S. policymakers made a number of mistakes in the course of the country's long involvement in Vietnam, the view presented here is that it was not those errors but the actions taken by Washington's adversaries in Hanoi that were decisive in determining the outcome.

Over the years, a variety of factors have been advanced to explain the Communist victory in the Vietnam War. It has been popular to search for single causes. Some have ascribed it primarily to the party's superior organizational ability or to its selective use of terror to intimidate or eliminate opponents. Others have referred to the aura of legitimacy that the Communist Party acquired among the Vietnamese people by virtue of its generation of struggle against the French. Others still point to the extraordinary personality and capability of Ho Chi Minh and contend that, had France or the United States responded to his appeal for support in 1945, the outcome of the revolution might have been far different.[1]

An analysis of the record shows that all of these factors played a role in the final outcome. The emphasis here, however, is placed primarily on the Communist Party's program and strategy. The genius of that program was that it was able to combine patriotic and economic themes in an artful way to win the allegiance of a broad spectrum of the Vietnamese population in the party's struggle against its adversaries. The political program of the Vietminh Front in 1941 linked the ICP [Indochinese Communist Party] with the most dynamic forces in Vietnamese society under French colonial rule, the desire for economic and social justice as well as the drive for the restoration of national independence. The alliance between those two forces enabled the Vietminh to mobilize a solid popular base for their struggle against the French. That alliance was revived during the war against the United States, when the NLF won widespread support from the rural and urban poor by its promises of social reform and national self-determination while at the same time allaying the fears of urban moderates and foreign observers alike that it would embark on a program of radical social change after the seizure of power in Saigon.

By contrast, rival nationalist parties were consistently unable to formulate a program that could appeal widely to the mass of the Vietnamese population. The ineffectiveness of the nationalist movement forced its political leaders from Bao Dai to Ngo Dinh Diem and Nguyen Van Thieu to rely on outside support for their survival. From the beginning, such individuals and their organizations were compromised in the minds of many Vietnamese by their lack of a coherent program for nation building and by their willingness to collaborate with the French or, later, with the United States. It is not too much to say that the ICP had won the political battle with its rivals by the mid-1940s and, despite massive efforts by the French and the Americans, was able to retain that advantage for the next generation.

A second major factor in Communist success lay in the domain of revolutionary strategy. Here the genius of the party's approach lay in its ability to make optimum use of a combination of political and military struggle. Those who claim that Hanoi's victory was primarily a military one miss the mark. The evidence shows that in the absence of foreign intervention, the party would have easily bested its nationalist rivals in the political arena. That had been the lesson of the August Revolution, and it was reaffirmed during the later struggles against the French and the United States. It was the political superiority of the Communists over their nationalist rivals that forced Paris, and then Washington, to turn to the military option and thus transform a civil conflict into a revolutionary war.[2]

It was the introduction of outside armed force that compelled the Communists themselves to adopt a strategy of revolutionary violence. At first they seized on the Maoist model of people's war, which had worked so well in China. But they soon discovered that moving to the Maoist third stage of general offensive was not as easy against a powerful Western adversary as it had been for the CCP [Chinese Communist Party] against Chiang Kai-shek. The result was the gradual adoption of a more flexible strategy that relied on a combination of political and military techniques in both urban and rural areas with a diplomatic and psychological offensive that undermined public support for the party's rivals, in France and the United States as well as in Vietnam itself. Once the conflict had escalated into a military conflict, Hanoi's ultimate strategic objective was not to win a total victory on the battlefield, but to bring about a psychological triumph over its adversaries, leading to a negotiated settlement under terms favorable to the revolution. Although, as many have pointed out, the final 1975 campaign was a conventional military assault by regular units of the North Vietnamese army, it was the strategy of combined political and military struggle, supplemented by diplomatic and psychological tactics to undermine the strength of the enemy, that had brought the war to that point and enabled the offensive to realize total success.

Because of his ability to grasp the underlying nature of the dynamic forces at work in modern Vietnam and to formulate a program and strategy appropriate to the circumstances, Ho Chi Minh is the central figure in the Vietnamese revolution. Although his compelling personality and his talent for reconciliation were trump cards in his contest with his adversaries, the ace in the hole lay in his ability to conceptualize the fundamental issues at stake in the Vietnamese revolution, and thus to give his movement an aura of legitimacy that was the underlying factor in its victory.

All of the above theories help to explain the Communist victory in Vietnam, but none of them gets to the heart of the matter. Why were the nationalist parties not as well organized, motivated, and effectively directed as their rivals? Why was it the Communist Party which most effectively donned the mantle of legitimacy in the Vietnamese struggle for national independence, and why did Ho Chi Minh, who was clearly the most talented political figure of his generation in Vietnam, choose Leninism for his model instead of the U.S. Declaration of Independence or the French Declaration of the Rights of Man?

The answer, of course, might simply be a historical accident. But some observers have ascribed the Communist victory to deep-seated historical factors at work in Vietnamese society. It has been argued, for example, that French efforts to eliminate all forms of nationalist opposition in colonial Vietnam discredited the moderate approach to national liberation and inadvertently provided an advantage to clandestine organizations like the ICP. Others have pointed to alleged similarities between Confucianism and Marxist doctrine, characteristics which made it easier for talented and dedicated Vietnamese intellectuals like Ho Chi Minh, Vo Nguyen Giap, and Truong Chinh to embrace the Leninist vision of social revolution than the individualist doctrines of Western capitalism.[3]

One of the more interesting recent hypotheses has been presented by the historian Gabriel Kolko. In a provocative study entitled *Anatomy of a War*, Kolko explains the Communist victory as a consequence of the weakness of the Vietnamese bourgeoisie under the domination of the French colonial system. In his analysis, that weakness prevented the Vietnamese middle class from taking the lead in waging a capitalist revolution, thus leaving a historical vacuum that was ultimately filled by the small but articulate working class led by its vanguard organization, the Communist Party.[4]

Kolko's argument is persuasive in pointing out that the weakness of the Saigon regime had deep historical roots that transcended the personalities and actions of individual leaders. As he has noted, one of the factors responsible for that weakness lay in the failure of the French to encourage the emergence of a strong and vibrant middle class capable of providing leadership and purpose after the realization of national independence. That fact was never totally grasped by U.S. policymakers, who, while recognizing the endemic weakness of the nationalist forces in Vietnamese society, constantly deluded themselves into believing that the key to a stable South Vietnam was just around the corner.

But Kolko does not adequately explain why similar results did not then occur in other colonial societies in Southeast Asia, where the local middle class faced comparable obstacles from colonial regimes. As Indian and Indonesian nationalist leaders would be quick to point out, the performance of the British and the Dutch was little better than the French in that regard. Nor does he explain why the Vietnamese Communist movement was able not only to fill the consequent vacuum but then to surmount enormous challenges to triumph over the concentrated power first of France and later of the United States.

Perhaps a more persuasive answer for the weakness of the middle class in modern Vietnam was the historic weakness of the commercial sector during the traditional period. Like China, Vietnam had been a predominantly agricultural society, and trade and manufacturing had never realized the influential position that they acquired in Europe or in several other countries of Asia. Confucian official doctrine displayed a distaste for the crass pursuit of wealth allegedly represented by the merchant class and expressed a clear preference for the honest labor of the rice farmer, whose fields produced the food necessary for sustenance of the entire population. Such prejudices undoubtedly affected attitudes and behavioral patterns in colonial Indochina and contributed to the distaste for Western capitalism on the part of many Vietnamese intellectuals.

Historical factors may also help to explain the surprising strength of the Communist movement in Vietnam. As the contemporary Marxist intellectual Nguyen Khac Vien has pointed out, some of the key characteristics of Confucian doctrine predisposed Vietnamese intellectuals to the Marxist, rather than the capitalist, vision of the contemporary world. While in many respects Marxism and Confucianism are strikingly different, key similarities between the two doctrines may have facilitated the appeal of Marxist ideology to traditional elites in Vietnam: a common emphasis on collective responsibility versus individual rights; the concept of an educated elite with unique access to a single truth as embodied in classical doctrine; and the stress in both ideologies on personal ethics and service to society. As Nguyen Khac Vien has noted, for centuries Vietnamese Confucianism was closely identified with the concept of selfless devotion to the cause of the fatherland, a tradition that Ho Chi Minh and his colleagues never tired of pointing out. The great Confucian statesman and strategist Nguyen Trai, who assisted Le Loi in driving out Chinese invaders in the fifteenth century, was cited as one of the nation's historic leaders in DRV literature during the Vietnam War. It was probably no accident that a high percentage of the founding members of the Indochinese Communist Party came from families connected with the Confucian ruling elite.[5]

The ideological preferences of intellectuals in colonial Indochina were hardly the decisive factor in the outcome of the Vietnam War, of course. Certainly few U.S. policymakers would have accepted the assumption that such factors decreed the defeat of capitalist forces in Vietnam. Still, the appeal of Marxist ideas among intellectuals and the historical weakness of the entrepreneurial tradition were undoubtedly significant explanations for the unusual popularity and effectiveness of communism in modern Vietnam. While they were probably not conscious of such factors, U.S. officials were well aware of that popularity, but they nonetheless resolved to press on. To some, the stakes were too high to accept a defeat. For others, the prospects of victory were uncertain, but a failed effort was considered better than no effort at all.

If these judgments are valid, it must be asked whether and how the United States could have won the Vietnam War. To some, the answer is obvious. With a massive application of firepower, it could have destroyed the war-making capacity of the DRV and reduced, if not entirely eliminated, the insurgent movement in the south. Such, at any rate, are the views of some recent critics, who maintain that the U.S. defeat in Vietnam was above all the result of a failure of will or strategic thinking in Washington.[6]

Few would deny that the United States had the capacity to bring about the massive, if not total, destruction of the North Vietnamese regime. But there were serious risks in undertaking such an approach. In the first place, any U.S. military action that threatened the survival of the DRV raised the very real possibility of direct Chinese, if not Soviet, intervention. While Chinese leaders were obviously anxious to avoid a direct military confrontation with the United States, debate over how to deal with the growing U.S. role in the war was intense in Beijing, and a massive intervention by Chinese forces along the lines of the "volunteers" in the Korean War could not be ruled out.

Even if China had not intervened, it seems clear that, short of the total destruction of North Vietnam, any direct U.S. attack on the north would have been a lengthy and exceedingly costly operation. Communist leaders had undoubtedly anticipated the possibility of a massive U.S. invasion of the north and prepared accordingly. While such a strategy might have relieved the immediate threat of a Communist takeover of the south, it would have embarked U.S. forces on a much more difficult conflict with few prospects of quick success. From the evidence presented here, it is clear that North Vietnamese resistance would have been stubborn and protracted in nature. It is hard to imagine the American people according their firm public support for such an enterprise unless the danger to U.S. national security was a clear and present one.

The question then arises: Was the avoidance of a Communist victory in Indochina sufficiently important to justify such risks? For all the rhetoric about falling dominoes in Washington, several U.S. presidents from Truman to Kennedy had tacitly answered that question by refusing to embark on the road to a direct military role in the conflict. Eisenhower and Kennedy had come perilously close, but both had ultimately concluded that it was a Vietnamese war to win or lose. Even Lyndon Johnson, who transformed the Vietnamese civil conflict into an American war, tacitly conceded in his final months in office that there were limits to how far the United States could go in guaranteeing the survival of an independent South Vietnam. Presidents Nixon and Ford put on the final touches by first accepting a compromise settlement and then refusing to take military action to prevent a Communist victory in the spring of 1975. In extremis, a generation of U.S. presidents, by their actions if not by their words, had recognized that Vietnam was not vital to U.S. national security. . . .

History teaches that the most difficult stage of a revolution often takes place after the seizure of power, when new leaders must seek to harvest the fruits of the revolution. Such was certainly the case in Vietnam. In a comment to journalist Stanley Karnow, Pham Van Dong more or less conceded the point. "Waging a war is simple," he noted, "but running a country is very difficult."[7] Today, [over] two decades after the fall of Saigon, Pham Van Dong's comment remains apt. Vietnam is one of the poorest countries in Asia. Until recently, it has been a virtual pariah in foreign affairs and its leaders still feel surrounded by enemies. By its own actions, the ruling Communist Party has lost the support of a large proportion of the Vietnamese people and seems uncertain about the future of the revolution.

Why were leaders who were so adept at making war so unsuccessful at winning the peace? Part of the answer undoubtedly stems from the difficulties encountered in recovering from the physical damage and psychological bitterness caused by the war and making the transition to a peaceful society. Ironically, however, an additional answer to the question may be that in the case of the North Vietnamese, their very success in the war deluded them into underestimating the challenges they faced in the postwar era. Seduced by their own propaganda, which had portrayed the final victory over Saigon as confirmation of their self-image as the legitimate representatives of the Vietnamese people and the vanguard of the Vietnamese revolution, they embarked on an overly ambitious course of action which has led their nation into severe difficulties, both at home and abroad.

Perhaps the primary source of their problem was the assumption by party leaders that at war's end, the vast majority of the Vietnamese people, from north to south, were ready to advance rapidly toward the creation of a unified and fully socialist society throughout the entire country. That, of course, had not been the original plan. The program of the NLF had indicated that after the victory of the revolution in the south, the political and economic reunification of the two zones would take place gradually and by peaceful means. That policy had been based on the assumption that the initial victory in the south would be a partial one and would be followed by a negotiated withdrawal of U.S. forces and the formation of a coalition government dominated by the Communists. At some unspecified date, that government would hold negotiations with the DRV on the final reunification of the entire country.

Hanoi's primary reason for adopting such a gradual approach was undoubtedly to keep the United States from reentering the war. But a second factor was probably the assumption that it would take time to reassure southerners and induce them to support the policies to be adopted by the new revolutionary government. One way to provide that reassurance was to adopt a moderate program that delayed reunification and postponed the transition of the south from a capitalist to a fully socialist society.

As it turned out, the war ended in quite a different manner from what party leaders had expected. There were no negotiations, no deals with Washington, and no coalition government. Over 100,000 supporters of the Saigon regime fled from the country in the final weeks of the war, and Hanoi was able to put in place a provisional revolutionary regime with virtually no open resistance from the local populace.

Faced with such unanticipated circumstances, Hanoi abandoned its original plan and decided instead to embark on a program of rapid unification and socialist transformation. In July 1976, a unified Socialist Republic of Vietnam (SRV) was formally inaugurated. The capital remained at Hanoi and the wartime government, seeded with a few additions selected from leading figures in the southern movement, remained in charge of the country. The NLF itself was merged into the Fatherland Front, while the Vietnam Workers' Party, now merged with its southern subsidiary, the People's Revolutionary Party, was renamed the Vietnamese Communist Party, or VCP. At least on paper, Vietnam was now one government, one party, one people.

The decision to dismantle the capitalist system in the south was made almost as quickly. After the occupation of Saigon at the end of April 1975, the regime had assured the local population that their property and their profits were secure. But in March 1978, Hanoi suddenly announced the nationalization of all industry and commerce above the family level, while in the countryside, farmers were herded into hastily constructed low-level cooperative organizations.[8]

Whatever the rationale for the decision, it was a disaster. Although there had been little open resistance in the south to the unification of the country in 1976, under the surface, resentment among southerners at the arrogance of soldiers and bureaucrats from the north was growing, even among former members of the NLF. Although no open bloodbath of supporters of the Saigon regime had taken place, several hundred thousand southerners were sent for varying periods of time to so-called reeducation camps, while countless others were under constant surveillance and prohibited from taking meaningful employment because of their background. In some cases following the takeover of Saigon, local youths were dragged off buses by puritanical northern cadres who clipped off their long hair and stripped them of their Western-style clothes. Many southerners felt betrayed by the revolution and saw themselves as strangers in their own country.[9]

The sudden and brutal decision to eliminate the private economy in early 1978 added fuel to that resentment. A surge of refugees, an estimated two-thirds of them ethnic Chinese, fled the country on foot or by boat during the next few months, and widespread unhappiness and alienation prevailed among many of those who remained. There were widespread reports of revolts among mountain minority groups, and the arrest and trial of dissident elements among Catholics and Buddhist religious associations. Industrial production dropped and a severe grain shortage forced the government to introduce food rationing amidst fears of widespread starvation. Even official sources began to concede that many Vietnamese now doubted the party's ability to lead the country effectively, while the noted Marxist intellectual Nguyen Khac Vien called on the party to listen to the needs of the people. Clearly, the regime had tried to accomplish too much, too soon.

To compound its problems, Hanoi had also badly misjudged the situation in foreign affairs. Its victory over the powerful forces of the United States had undoubtedly been a heady experience and may have lulled senior party figures into the conviction that imperialism was on the decline, not only in Southeast Asia but all around the world. In a major policy address before the new SRV National Assembly in the summer of 1976, party First Secretary Le Duan declared that the regime's postwar foreign policy objectives could be summed up in three general propositions: to guarantee national security, to play an active and independent role in regional and global affairs, and to maintain good relations with other countries in the socialist camp. The "foundation stones" of Vietnamese foreign policy would be a close relationship with the USSR and the establishment of intimate ties with neighboring Laos and Cambodia, which had just come under the rule of the Pathet Lao and the Khmer Rouge, respectively. The latter arrangement was to be labeled a "special relationship," a somewhat less precise version of the old Indochinese Federation, which had been discarded in the early 1950s.

There was nothing inherently unreasonable in the regime's desire to maintain a close relationship with Moscow and carry out an independent policy in world affairs. But the "special relationship" with Cambodia and Laos presented problems because it clashed with the intentions of the highly xenophobic Pol Pot government (formally called Democratic Kampuchea), which had just come to power in Phnom Penh. Also such an assertion of Hanoi's hegemony in mainland Southeast Asia surely aroused discomfort not only in other Southeast Asian capitals but also in Beijing.

The most violent response came from Phnom Penh, where the new Khmer Rouge regime interpreted Hanoi's call for a "special relationship" as a disguised effort to reassert Vietnamese domination over the Khmer people, a domination that dated back to the Vietnamese conquest of the Mekong River delta in the seventeenth century. The new Cambodian government punctuated its refusal to discuss the issue by launching military attacks along the common border with the aim of regaining control over territories lost to the Vietnamese in past centuries. The reaction from China was more subdued, but it was clear that Beijing had no desire to see Hanoi establish a dominant position over all the states of the old French Indochina.

At first the Vietnamese had tried to use a carrot-and-stick approach with the Pol Pot regime, but when Phnom Penh continued to refuse Hanoi's offer of alliance and brutally purged party members suspected of collaboration with the enemy, Vietnamese leaders gradually lost patience. Their concern was heightened when it became clear that Beijing was backing Pol Pot in his rejection of Hanoi's overtures. In December 1978, having attempted to protect itself by signing a defense treaty with Moscow, Hanoi ordered Vietnamese troops into Cambodia to overthrow the Pol Pot regime and install a new government in Phnom Penh sympathetic to the idea of a special relationship. Declaring that the "Moscow's puppet" must be punished, Beijing reacted by launching a brief but bloody punitive attack across the Sino-Vietnamese border.

The Vietnamese invasion of Democratic Kampuchea was undoubtedly welcomed by many Cambodians. With a ferocity unparalleled since the days of Adolf Hitler, in his first days in power Pol Pot had attempted to eliminate all elements in the country considered unsympathetic to the goals of the new order. The city of Phnom Penh was emptied of all its residents, and thousands were put to work in slave-labor camps in the countryside. Thousands more were tortured and killed, and their remains dumped in mass graves around the country. Pol Pot's new order was the sign of a revolution gone mad. To the relief of many Cambodians, the new pro-Hanoi government installed in Phnom Penh adopted moderate policies to win the trust of the people.

But Hanoi's invasion of its neighbor also provoked suspicion of Vietnamese intentions in the capitals of nearby countries in Southeast Asia, as well as in the West, reviving fears of the domino theory reminiscent of the height of the Cold War. During the 1980s, an unlikely alliance of China, the noncommunist states of Southeast Asia (recently united in a multilateral alliance known as the Association of the Southeast Asian Nations, or ASEAN), and a number of Western nations including the United States, patched together a coalition of anti-Hanoi Cambodian groups to wage a guerrilla resistance struggle against the new government in Phnom Penh. To the discomfort of many outside observers, the dominant military force in that coalition was the Khmer Rouge, whose brutal behavior while in power had aroused demands that Pol Pot and other key leaders be tried in an international court on charges of genocide.

The dual crisis in domestic and foreign affairs created cruel dilemmas in Hanoi. Should economic or national security concerns be considered paramount? Should the regime adopt a firm approach on Laos and Cambodia at the expense of economic dislocation and improving relations with its neighbors? Should it maintain a rapid pace of socialist transformation at the risk of further antagonizing the already restive population in the south?

These dilemmas badly split the Politburo. Although some party leaders reportedly argued against policies that might create tensions at home while simultaneously antagonizing foreign powers, advocates of a tough position against China were able to assert the primacy of national security concerns and bring about the ejection of a number of reputedly "Maoist" elements from within the ranks of the party leadership. But as the internal crisis deepened, pragmatic elements argued persuasively for reforms in domestic policy, and during the early 1980s the government adopted a number of policies to reduce the pace of socialist transition and stimulate productive efforts in the economy. Conservative elements, however, reportedly resisted such measures and were able to limit their effectiveness. By the middle of the decade, the economic situation remained stagnant, and the popular mood was sour. Complaints appeared ever more frequently that the party's veteran leadership had known how to wage the war, but not how to win the peace. Surely, Ho Chi Minh would not have ignored the material needs of the Vietnamese people![10]

The tension finally began to ease in 1986. In June, Le Duan died of illness at the age of 78. At a national congress of the VCP held six months later, a new leadership was elected which promised to introduce reforms to improve the national economy and hearken to the voice of the people. Veteran party leaders such as Truong Chinh, Pham Van Dong, and Le Duc Tho were dropped from the Politburo, although they retained a measure of influence as the sole members of a newly created Council of Elders.

The new general secretary was the one-time chief of party operations in the south, Nguyen Van Linh. On the face of it, the new lineup in Hanoi appeared to be a signal that the party was ready to move, however cautiously, in the direction of reform. Although Linh was somewhat of an unknown quantity, even to many of his countrymen, he soon displayed a willingness to experiment, calling for renovation (*doi moi*) and glasnost (*cong khai*) in the domestic arena, and even hinting at the need for "new thinking" in foreign affairs. He publicly conceded that the regime had attempted to move too quickly toward socialism during the 1970s and called on the Vietnamese people to speak frankly about past errors committed by their leaders. Foreign observers began to describe Linh as Hanoi's "little Gorbachev."

But like many of his veteran colleagues, Nguyen Van Linh was cautious by nature, and the regime soon indicated its reluctance to launch major economic changes such as those that had been recently adopted by the Deng Xiaoping leadership that had recently come to power after Mao Zedong's death in China. The all-pervasive bureaucracy stifled efforts by enterprising elements to broaden their activities in the private sector, while members of Catholic and Buddhist organizations were convicted of antiregime activities for demanding greater religious freedoms. Writers such as Duong Thu Huong and Nguyen Huy Thiep were muzzled and sometimes arrested for being too outspoken in their demands for more radical change.[11]

Hanoi's reluctance to initiate major reforms was undoubtedly strengthened when the massive popular demonstrations in downtown Beijing in the spring of 1989 underlined the risks to a totalitarian regime when it engaged in political liberalization. The Tiananmen incident, followed shortly thereafter by the collapse of Communist systems in Eastern Europe and the USSR, confirmed to suspicious minds in Hanoi that too much openness was dangerous to the survival of Marxist-Leninist parties.

Henceforth, the regime pursued a delicate line of cautious economic liberalization combined with continued party dominance over political affairs. To this date, the results have been mixed. Sparked by the rise of a small but vibrant private sector, economic conditions in the SRV have improved slightly, but serious structural problems continue to hinder the economy, and the contrast between the bureaucratic north and the more entrepreneurial south is as sharp as ever. It remains to be seen whether the regime's uneasy balance between socialism and capitalism can work.

At the heart of the problem has been Vietnam's continuing isolation in the world. As a result of the bitter dispute with China and the recent collapse of the USSR, Hanoi has lost its two most powerful friends and economic benefactors from the Vietnam War. In the meantime, the Western trade boycott, established to pressure Hanoi to withdraw its forces from Cambodia, continued to cut the SRV off from commercial relations with the capitalist world. Although the defense of the pro-Vietnamese regime in Phnom Penh had cost Vietnam an estimated 50,000 dead and a quarter of a million wounded, in the late 1980s Hanoi finally agreed to abandon its special position in Cambodia and seek a compromise settlement in the country in a patent effort to bring an end to the economic embargo.

At a recent international conference, all sides finally reached a consensus on a peace process calling for UN-supervised free elections to choose a new Cambodian government. Those elections, held early in 1993, were won by a faction loyal to Prince Norodom Sihanouk, but the unwillingness of the Khmer Rouge to cooperate in the settlement casts serious doubt on its potential for success. For the Vietnamese, however, the agreement achieved at least part of its purpose, as restrictions on trade with the SRV have been relaxed by a number of capitalist countries, and international agencies are now actively considering assisting the Vietnamese in putting their economic house in order.

For Hanoi, however, the problem of Cambodia is only a part of its larger dispute with China. After the bitter interlude of the early 1980s, when Beijing and Hanoi argued over territorial issues as well as the latter's ties with Moscow and the "special relationship" in Indochina, in recent years China and Vietnam have moved closer, as conservative elements in both parties share a sense of being among the sole survivors of the now disintegrating socialist community. But Chinese arrogance—manifested today by Beijing's stubborn refusal to compromise on a dispute over the ownership of disputed islands in the South China Sea—arouses old fears of Chinese domination in Hanoi. Although Sino-Vietnamese relations have improved, the fraternal comradeship that marked the early years of the Vietnam War is not likely soon to be renewed.

Notes

1. For the above interpretations, see Douglas Pike, *Viet Cong* (Cambridge: MIT Press, 1967), Paul Mus and John T. McAlister, *The Vietnamese and Their Revolution* (Boston: Harper & Row, 1971), and Archimedes Patti, *Why Vietnam? Prelude to America's Albatross* (Berkeley: University of California Press, 1980).
2. For the argument that the Vietnam War was above all a conventional military contest, see Harry G. Summers, Jr., *On Strategy: A Critical Analysis of the Vietnam War* (Novato, Calif.: Presidio Press, 1982). To be fair, Summers concedes that political factors were dominant before 1963, but he appears to believe that once the war had escalated in the mid-1960s, the solution was primarily military in nature.

3. Two proponents of these respective points of view are Joseph Buttinger, *Vietnam: A Dragon Embattled*, 2 vols. (New York: Praeger, 1967), and Nguyen Khac Vien, "Confucianism and Marxism in Vietnam," in Nguyen Khac Vien, ed., *Tradition and Revolution in Vietnam* (Berkeley, Calif.: Indochina Resource Center, 1974), pp. 15–74.

4. Gabriel Kolko, *Anatomy of a War: Vietnam, the U.S., and the Modern Historical Experience* (New York: Random House, 1985).

5. Nguyen Khac Vien, "Confucianism and Marxism," pp. 34–41. To distinguish the patriotic component of Vietnamese Confucianism from its more feudal nature, Vien made a clear distinction between the Confucianism of the mandarins and the Confucianism of the people.

6. Summers, *On Strategy*, is the best-known example. Also see General Bruce Palmer, Jr., *The 25-Year War: America's Military Role in Vietnam* (Lexington: University of Kentucky Press, 1984), and Norman B. Hannah, *The Key to Failure: Laos and the Vietnam War* (Lanham, Md.: Madison Books, 1987).

7. Cited in Stanley Karnow, *Vietnam: A History* (New York: Viking Press, 1983), p. 9.

8. The reasons for that decision have never been satisfactorily explained. One possible factor may have been growing official fears that the southern capitalist economy, dominated by overseas Chinese interests, could ultimately undermine the socialist system in the north and delay the transition to socialism throughout the country. The official press frequently referred to "poisonous weeds of bourgeois capitalism" in the south that could allegedly have a corrupting effect on the population of the socialist north. Party leaders may have also feared that Chinese economic interests in Saigon could deliberately sabotage the national economy at a time of growing tension in Sino-Vietnamese relations.

9. For the view that a bloodbath did indeed take place, see Jacqueline Desbarats and Karl D. Jackson, "South Vietnam Was a Bloodbath After All," in the *Asian Wall Street Journal*, April 18, 1985. One autobiographical account of a southerner's sense of disillusionment is Nguyen Long, with Harry H. Kendall, *After Saigon Fell: Daily Life under the Vietnamese Communists* (Berkeley: Institute of East Asian Studies, 1981).

10. In fact, in his testament, written shortly before his death in 1969, Ho Chi Minh had appealed to party leaders to cut agricultural taxes in order to reduce the financial burden of the war on the Vietnamese people. Ho's appeal was ignored, and the published version of Ho's testament did not mention the request. For a recent discussion of the issue, see *The Testament of President Ho Chi Minh* (Hanoi: Central Committee of the Vietnamese Communist Party, 1989).

11. Shortly after his election as VCP general secretary, Nguyen Van Linh wrote articles in the party newspaper under the pseudonym NVL, which, he explained to questioners, meant "speak and act" (*noi va lam*). As the regime backed away from its promise to encourage the freedom of speech, bitter Vietnamese reinterpreted the letters as "speak and cheat" (*noi va lua*). For a brief reference to the official persecution of critics, see F. W. Warner, "Writers' Woes," in *Far Eastern Economic Review*, May 7, 1992.

17
The National Liberation Front and the Land
TOM MANGOLD AND JOHN PENYCATE

He heard the tracks of the armored personnel carriers long before the malignant clouds of dust came into view. Nam Thuan lay very still, trying to count the number, but in his eyes and ears was only the fusion of squeaky steel belts and the approaching halo of dirt as the American armor moved busily out of the early morning sun and straight toward him.

As Communist party secretary of Phu My Hung village with its six small hamlets, Nam Thuan was automatically political commissar of the village defense force, a small unit already much depleted by action and promotions to the regional fighting forces. His small platoon that morning comprised a good deputy commander and a couple of village farm boys. His orders had been simple enough: He was to delay any American thrust on Phu My Hung by luring the enemy into engagement. He would destroy them if possible; if not, his diversionary battle would allow ample time for the village to be evacuated and the arms and guerrillas to be hidden.

It was August 1968; the war against the Americans was three years old. The great Tet offensive seemed to have taken many lives, yet South Vietnam had still not been reunited with the North. If anything, Thuan thought, the Americans seemed more confident and more powerful than ever. But at least they were predictable—it was a necessary consolation as the small armored column rattled nearer; the Americans always came when expected, came noisily, and came in strength.

He counted thirteen M-113 carriers. It was a larger force than he had expected. Thuan needed to move quickly if he was to draw the column toward him and toward the tunnels. To fight with he had just two remote-controlled mines which he would detonate, and a boxful of captured American M-26 grenades. In the confusion, he would retreat and escape down the tunnel, but not so quickly that the Americans would not see him.

Things went wrong from the beginning. He detonated the first DH-10 mine prematurely and it exploded harmlessly just ahead of the lead American APC. The second mine failed to go off. The column was still too far away for Thuan to hurl the grenades. He stood up, deliberately breaking cover, and began to run awkwardly toward the tunnel entrance—its position marked by the open trapdoor—hugging the box of grenades. The lead APC spotted him and changed course to follow. Thuan wondered whether the Americans would now fire the turret-mounted machine gun; even if they did, it was improbable that a bumping gun would hit a small running target. Hands reached out of the open tunnel trapdoor to take the box of grenades. Thuan vaulted into a shaft and closed the door above his head. Blinded by the sudden change from sunlight to darkness, Thuan remained still for a few moments, crouching in the three-foot-deep shaft, gathering breath, waiting for images to return to his retinas. At the bottom of the shaft in which he stood and almost at a right angle to it began a sixty-foot communication tunnel. Thuan wriggled easily into its secure embrace. He realized he could no longer hear the noisy tracks of the APCs. Control of the battle had now passed from his hands to those of an American above ground. If the carriers passed overhead it would be impossible to rechallenge them before they reached Phu My Hung. He had been ordered not to allow that to happen.

For a few moments Thuan considered his environment. He had just entered the shaft that connected with the communication tunnel. At the end of the communication tunnel was a second shaft going down another three feet and at the end of that was a second communication tunnel. If he crawled along that, he would eventually reach a similar shaft and tunnel system leading up and out. However, the exit point for *this* system was some 120 feet away from the place where the Americans had seen him. It was crucial to his plan that they never discover the second exit. It was only sparsely camouflaged, but he had his own man hidden there who could tell him with minimum delay what the Americans were doing above ground while Thuan was below.

The tunnel was still cool from the evening air of the night before. Thuan crawled carefully into a small alcove dug some four feet into the first communication tunnel. As he hunched inside, he heard a muffled explosion followed by a blast, and a sudden beam of dust-filled sunlight pierced the shaft. The Americans had hit the tunnel trapdoor, blowing it clean away. It was what he had prayed for. The column was bound to stop while the tunnel system was fully explored and then destroyed by the Americans. As the dust and debris stung his eyes, Thuan squinted through the gloom and picked up his AK-47 automatic rifle, hugged it to his chest, and waited quietly in the alcove.

He waited over an hour. When he heard the first American helicopter he knew there would be no attempt to explode the tunnel without exploration. As the machine clapped and whirred its noisy way to the ground, Thuan assumed that the Americans had flown in their special tunnel soldiers, trained to fight in the honeycomb of underground tunnels and caverns that spread beneath the protective clay of the district of Cu Chi.

Thuan's observer, secreted above ground in the second hidden tunnel exit, had sent a messenger through the tunnels to Thuan in the alcove. The message was wholly predictable. The Americans had indeed brought more men by helicopter. They were small. They were tunnel soldiers.

The first GI did not even approach the open tunnel entrance for another hour. Earlier, Thuan had heard some conversation above his hiding hole, but nothing for about thirty minutes. Whatever happened, only one American could come in at a time. Both the first entrance shaft and the second long communication tunnel were only just wide enough for one thin man. The tunnel soldiers were thin; they fought well, but unlike Nam Thuan and his small village platoon of Communist guerrillas, they had not spent years inside the tunnels of Cu Chi; they had not fought many battles in their dank blackness.

Thuan could not conceive of failure. He had already been awarded one Victory Medal third class and one Victory Medal second class. He was about to earn another. Small even by Vietnamese standards, naturally slender, Thuan had never known peace in his land. His father had fought the French from similar tunnel complexes in Cu Chi when Thuan was still a child. Thuan had been allowed occasional tunnel sorties, playing soldiers with his friends. The enemy had been other village boys, ludicrously made up to look like the French soldiers, with charcoal mustaches and charcoaled arms, in an attempt to ape the perpetual wonder of hirsute Westerners.

As he grew up, it was the Americans who took the place of the French, and their hairy arms and large frames were no joke to the handful of village children who had been selected by the Communist party to receive a full education. He soon hated the Americans. A friend from Hanoi had told him the Americans called the village fighters Viet Cong, to him an insulting and derogatory term. Now, at thirty-three and still unmarried, Thuan was waiting for the call to join the regular soldiers, but the party had deliberately kept him as a village commander of the part-time self-defense force. He had fought a brave war. He was cunning and ruthless and, above all, he was one of the few cadres who knew the geography of all the eight miles of underground tunnels that the villagers had built in the area. Sometimes he was the only man who could guide the soldiers from Hanoi along the tunnels on their secret journeys through Cu Chi; the men from the North marveled at being able to travel safely under the Americans' noses.

A small earth-fall from the exposed tunnel entrance warned Thuan that the first American tunnel soldier was descending. He had purposely ordered that the first shaft be dug just over three feet deep; it meant the American would have to descend feet first and then wriggle awkwardly into the long communication tunnel where Thuan waited, hidden in an alcove. In the past, as a GI's feet had touched the bottom, Thuan had stabbed the soldier in the groin with his bayonet. This time, as the green-and-black jungle boots descended, Thuan leaned out of his alcove and, using the light from the tunnel entrance, shot the soldier twice in the lower body.

Above ground, the Americans were now in trouble. They could not drop grenades down the shaft because their mortally wounded comrade jammed the hole—anyway, he might still be alive. Slumped in the narrow shaft, he prevented other soldiers from making their way down to chase Thuan. He guessed it would take the Americans at least thirty minutes to get the ropes slipped under the dying man's arms and then haul him out. The Americans' concern for their dead and wounded remained a source of bewilderment and relief to the Communist soldiers. Anything that delayed the battle inevitably favored the weaker side and allowed reloading, regrouping and rethinking.

Once the American's body had been removed from the shaft, Thuan anticipated that his comrades would probably drop a grenade or two down the hole, wait for the smoke to clear, then climb into the shaft and crawl quickly into the first communication tunnel, firing ahead with their pistols. They would be smarter this time and they would be angrier. He would not wait where he was.

His next fighting position was the second shaft, some four feet deep, which connected the first communication tunnel with the second lower one. There was a trapdoor at the top of the second shaft, but Thuan had to remove it for his next operation to succeed. He prayed the Americans would not be using gas at this early stage to flush him out. If they did not, and he was very lucky, the Americans would follow him, using flashlights. Thuan hid in the second shaft, its trapdoor off. He crouched low enough to be invisible to the Americans as they groped their way along the communication tunnel toward him. And yes, they were using flashlights. They might as well have been using loudspeakers to announce their intentions.

The tunnel soldiers had not thrown grenades but they had fired their pistols in volleys to clear the tunnel ahead. From his crouching position in the shaft at the end of this tunnel, Thuan could look up and feel sharp splinters of clay falling on his face as the bullets struck the end of the tunnel above the open shaft. The noise of the firing was deafening. Now the tunnel soldiers were slowly advancing. As soon as their flashlights saw an open shaft entrance ahead, they would roll a grenade down it and Thuan would be blown to pieces. The timing was now critical. He waited for a pause in the pistol volleys and then popped his head and shoulders out of the shaft. He saw at least two flashlights; they blinded him. As a foreign voice shouted, he fired the first clip from his AK-47, loaded the second by touch, and fired that, too. The tunnel exploded in a roar of noise, orange light, and screams of the wounded. He ducked back into the shaft, picking up the trapdoor from the bottom and replacing it above his head. He wriggled down the shaft and slipped along the second communication tunnel far enough for safety should the Americans be able to remove the trapdoor and throw grenades down after him. He lay breathless and sweating on the earth.

From his hiding place above ground at the top of the secret shaft, about 120 feet away from the American position, Thuan's observer watched as the Americans slowly brought out their dead and wounded from Thuan's attack. Three helicopters arrived for the victims. Thuan carefully noted all the information the messenger brought him from above ground. It gave him the basic material to make this next plan for below ground. Thuan's deputy was convinced that now, surely, the Americans would dynamite the tunnel. Thuan was not so sure. It was four in the afternoon, and the Americans would want to leave, spend the night in Dong Zu base, next to Cu Chi town, and return by helicopter at first light. They still had not discovered the second secret tunnel entrance; they had lost surprise; they had lost men. They might hope there was a tunnel complex large enough to be worth exploring for documents or Communist military equipment. Thuan still had his box of grenades and a perfect escape route behind him. He gambled on another battle.

That night Thuan developed a mild fever and went to a small sleeping hole inside the tunnel. Just large enough for one man but with the luxury of a specially dug air ventilation hole leading in from the surface three feet above, the hole was also used for the wounded before they could be taken by tunnel on the longer trip to the underground tunnel hospital at Phu My Hung. Indeed, there were still bloodstained bandages in the hole. The guerrillas had been unable to burn them or bury them since the last battle. The incessant heavily armored sweeps mounted by the 25th Division from their huge fortress next to Cu Chi town had kept the Communist defense forces pinned inside their tunnels for weeks on end. Sometimes there had been surprise raids by the tunnel soldiers; sometimes there had been many deaths. As Thuan sweated his way through the night, he assumed the new tunnel soldiers would be more careful and cautious than the last squad. Success would depend on the Americans' not knowing the layout of the system, and anticipating that the Communists had now fled.

This time, he would allow the Americans to crawl forward without any impedance and let them travel much farther than they had gone before. Their journey would take them down the first shaft and along the first communication tunnel, then down the second shaft (scene of the previous day's attack) and along the second, or bottom, communication tunnel. They would then reach a third shaft, one that led *up*. The tunnel soldiers would know what Nam Thuan knew, that this was the most dangerous and critical moment of any tunnel exploration. Thuan would be waiting for them.

He called one of the village boys and ordered him to fill a bag with earth. Then he checked and rechecked his grenades. The American ones were infinitely superior to the homemade ones or even the grenades the Chinese had sent, but tunnels had a way of destroying sensitive mechanisms. In the kind of war that Nam Thuan fought in the tunnels, there were only first chances—never second.

The Americans came, as they always seemed to, shortly after eight in the morning. A team crawled with exaggerated care through the tunnel system that had seen such havoc the day before. They moved by inches, looking for tunnel booby traps, but Thuan had dismantled everything—he wanted the soldiers dead, not saved through their own vigilance. He waited until the first dim hint of light announced they were now on their way along the second, the lower, communication tunnel. The leader would find himself facing the shaft at the end of the tunnel. He would shine his flashlight up. He might even have time to see the grenade that would fall to end his life.

In the five seconds before the grenade exploded in the middle of the Americans—Thuan never knew how many there were—he had time to slam the trapdoor shut and heave the heavy bag of earth on top and himself on top of the bag. The explosion just managed to lift the trapdoor with its extra weight. Afterward there was complete silence.

Before American soldiers later destroyed the tunnel with Bangalore torpedoes— chains of explosives linked by detonating cord—Thuan's men had time to retrieve four working pistols, all .38s, and two broken flashlights left by the Americans. His platoon escaped from the secret exit. In fact, the explosions destroyed only some seventy feet of the tunnel complex, and the system was usable again within a few weeks.

Fourteen months later, Nam Thuan was invited to join the regular forces as an officer. He became fully responsible for the defense of the six hamlets of Phu An village. Three years later, in November 1973, the Americans were gone and the war was being fought only by the South Vietnamese army; Thuan was a member of the district party committee when the guerrilla forces of Cu Chi, strengthened by regular troops from North Vietnam, went on the offensive for the first time in five years. They wiped out forty-seven South Vietnamese military posts in one month alone. Two years later, on 28 March 1975, Thuan was with the forces who raised the flag of the Communist National Liberation Front over the town of Cu Chi. He is now a major in the People's Army of Vietnam.

CHAPTER 6

The Battlefield

Most Americans who went to Vietnam—either to join the battle, report on it, or attempt to repair its ravages—described it as a lushly beautiful place in which it was impossible to fight a civilized war. The heat was incredible. Soldiers who slogged through rice paddies were almost never dry or clean, and they suffered a variety of ailments from trench foot to dysentery to fevers that would not break. They were bitten by insects and snakes and sucked by leeches. The human enemy, often unseen for days, turned up suddenly, firing from a village only recently "pacified" by the Americans. Women and children frequently helped the Vietcong, or indeed were the Vietcong. Trails were booby-trapped with horrific devices, the mere thought of which jangled the nerves of the toughest GIs.

The most powerful writing about the Vietnam War was done by those who experienced or witnessed it firsthand. Philip Caputo was a gung-ho Marine from Chicago who arrived in Vietnam with the first Marine units in March 1965. By the time he led his patrol down Purple Heart Trail, Caputo had changed his thinking, as the excerpt here indicates. The chapter's second piece is the story of 1st Lt. Archie "Joe" Biggers, as told by himself to Wallace Terry. Biggers was a black Marine platoon leader from Texas whose tale is straightforward, but his message is as harrowing as Caputo's. Lynda Van Devanter went to Vietnam in 1969 because she wanted to help people. Like all American nurses there she found more than she bargained for, but what shocked her most was the hostility with which she was greeted by her fellow Americans when she returned to "the real world" the following year. Tim O'Brien also went to Vietnam. The final reading in this chapter is an excerpt from his astonishing novel *Going After Cacciato*, in which the title character decides to run away from the war and head for Paris.

Vietnam. The eyes of Pfc. Kevin J. Campbell display concern. OFFICIAL U.S. MARINE CORPS PHOTO

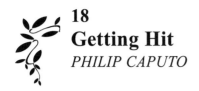

18
Getting Hit
PHILIP CAPUTO

The platoon reached Hill 92 in the midafternoon. The men were worn out by that time, their shoulders aching from the weight of rifles, packs, and flak jackets. They had been under one kind of fire or another for twenty-four hours and were dazed with fatigue. Rigging shelters against the drumming rain, they lay down to rest. Some did not bother to build shelters. They had ceased to care even for themselves. I walked around, checking their feet. A few had serious cases of immersion foot, their shriveled skin covered with red pustules and blisters. It amazed me that they could walk at all. We ate lunch. Our rations were the same as the Viet Cong's: cooked rice rolled into a ball and stuffed with raisins. The riceballs were easier to carry than the heavy C-ration tins and alleviated the diarrhea from which we all suffered. Eating the rice on that desolate hill, it occurred to me that we were becoming more and more like our enemy. We ate what they ate. We could now move through the jungle as stealthily as they. We endured common miseries. In fact, we had more in common with the Viet Cong than we did with that army of clerks and staff officers in the rear.

I was putting on dry socks when Captain Neal called on the radio. A Christmas cease-fire had gone into effect. The operation had been secured. My platoon was to return to friendly lines as quickly as possible. Why not lift us out with helicopters? I asked. No, Neal said, that was out of the question. I passed the word and the troops cheered. "Hey-hey. We're gonna get some slack. Merry fuckin' Christmas."

"No, no. I want to stay out here," said Pfc. Baum. "I just love it out here in the mud and the rain and the shit."

Shouldering our packs, we tramped down to Purple Heart Trail, the quickest route back. The trail forked near Dieu Phuong, a hamlet several hundred yards west of Charley Hill. The right fork led along the river, the left over the foothills toward the outpost. We took the latter because it was shorter and less likely to be mined or ambushed.

Outside the hamlet was a flooded rice paddy with a steep embankment at its far end. A barbed wire fence, anchored at one end to a dead tree, ran along the length of the embankment. The trail climbed through a hole in the fence near the tree. The lead squad, Sergeant Pryor's, Jones, and I crossed the rice paddy. The water was cold and chestdeep in places, and the rain dimpled the water in a way that reminded me of an evening rise on a trout stream. That was how the Ontonogan River looked in the evenings, in the place where it made a slow, wide bend around a wooded bluff upstream from the rocky, white-water narrows at the Burned Dam. There, the river had been deep and smooth where it curved, and the big trout rising made rings in the copper-colored water. Bill, my fishing buddy, and I used to cast for browns in the deep pool at sunset. We never caught many, but we had a fine time, casting and talking about the things we were going to do when we left school, about all that awaited us in the great outside world, which seemed so full of promise. We were boys and thought everything was possible. The memory sent a momentary pang through me: not so much a feeling of homesickness as one of separation—a distancing from the hopeful boy I had been, a longing to be like that again.

Pryor's squad climbed the embankment, the men slipping on the muddy trail, slipping and falling into each other until they were bunched in a knot. The rest of the platoon waded through the rice paddy behind us, holding their rifles in the air. A snake made a series of S's in the black water as it slithered between two men in the column. On dry ground again, Pryor's marines picked up their interval and hiked up the ridgeline that rose above the embankment. The Cordillera loomed in the distance, high and indomitable. The last two squads started to struggle up the bank, bunching up as one man after another slipped and slid into the man behind him.

Standing by the dead tree, I helped pull a few marines up the trail. "Pass it back not to bunch up," I said. To my left, a stream whispered through a brushy ravine. "Don't bunch up," a marine said. "Pass it back." On the other side of the paddy, the rear of the column was filing past a hut at the edge of the hamlet. Smoke started to roll from the hut and a woman ran out yelling.

"Bittner," I called to the platoon sergeant, who was bringing up the rear, "what the hell's going on?"

"Can't hear you, sir."

"The hut. Who the hell set fire to the hut?"

"Somebody said you passed the word to burn the hut, sir."

"What?"

"The word came back to burn the hut, sir."

"Jesus Christ. I said, 'Don't bunch up.' DON'T BUNCH UP. Put that fire out."

"Yes, sir."

I stood by the leafless tree, watching the marines douse the fire with helmets full of water. Fortunately, the thatch had been wet to begin with and did not burn quickly. Turning to walk back toward the point squad, I saw Allen stumbling on the trail.

"Allen, how're you doing?" I asked, extending my arm. Taking hold of it, he hauled himself over the lip of the embankment.

"Hackin' it, lieutenant. I'm hackin' it okay," Allen said, walking beside me. Ahead, I could see Pryor's squad trudging up the ridge and the point man briefly silhouetted on the ridgeline before he went down the other side. "But this here cease-fire's come along at the right time," Allen was saying. "Could use a little slack. This here cease-fire's the first slack. . . ."

There was a roaring and a hot, hard slap of wind and a needle pricking my thigh and something clubbed me in the small of the back. I fell face down into the mud, my ears ringing. Lying on my belly, I heard an automatic carbine rattle for a few seconds, then someone calling "Corpsman! Corpsman!" Because of the ringing in my ears, the shots and voice sounded far away. "Corpsman! Corpsman!" Someone else yelled "Incoming!" I got to my hands and knees, wondering what fool had yelled "incoming." That had not been a shell, but a mine, a big mine. Who the hell had yelled "incoming"? You did, you idiot. It was your voice. Why did you say that? The fence. The barbed wire fence was the last thing you saw as you fell. You had fallen toward the fence, and it was like that time when you were six and walking in the woods with your friend Stanley. Stanley was nine, and he had been frightening you with stories about bears in the woods. Then you had heard a roaring, growling sound in the distance and, thinking it was a bear, you had run to the highway, tried to climb the barbed wire fence at the roadside, and caught your trousers on the barbs. Hanging there, you had cried, "Stanley, it's a bear! A bear, Stanley!" And Stan had come up laughing because the growling noise you had heard was a roadgrader coming up the highway. It had not been a bear, but a machine. And this roaring had not been a shell, but a mine.

I stood, trying to clear my head. I was a little wobbly, but unmarked except for a sliver of shrapnel stuck in one of my trouser legs. I pulled it out. It was still hot, but it had not even broken my skin. Allen was next to me on all fours, mumbling. "What happened? I don't believe it. My God, oh my God." Some thirty to forty feet behind us, there was a patch of scorched, cratered earth, a drifting pall of smoke, and the dead tree, its trunk charred and cracked. Sergeant Wehr was lying near the crater. He rose to his feet, then fell when one leg collapsed beneath him. Wehr stood up again and the leg crumpled again, and, squatting on his good leg, holding the wounded one straight out in front of him, he spun around like a man doing a cossack dance, then fell onto his back, waving one arm back and forth across his chest. "Boom. Boom," he said, the arm flopping back and forth. "Mah fust patrol, an' boom."

Allen got to his feet, his eyes glassy and a dazed grin on his face. He staggered toward me. "What happened, sir?" he asked, toppling against me and sliding down my chest, his hands clutching at my shirt. Before I could get a grip on him, he fell again to all fours, then collapsed onto his stomach. "My God what happened?" he said. "I don't believe it. My head hurts." Then I saw the blood oozing from the wound in the back of his head and neck. "Dear God my head hurts. Oh it hurts. I don't believe it."

Still slightly stunned, I had only a vague idea of what had happened. A mine, yes. It must have been an ambush-detonated mine. All of Pryor's squad had passed by that spot before the mine exploded. I had been standing on that very spot, near the tree, not ten seconds before the blast. If it had been a booby trap or a pressure mine, it would have gone off then. And then the carbine fire. Yes, an electrically detonated mine set off from ambush, a routine occurrence for the rear-echelon boys who looked at the "overall picture," a personal cataclysm for those who experienced it.

Kneeling beside Allen, I reached behind for my first-aid kit and went numb when I felt the big, shredded hole in the back of my flak jacket. I pulled out a couple of pieces of shrapnel. They were cylindrical and about the size of double-O buckshot. A Claymore, probably homemade, judging from the black smoke. They had used black powder. The rotten-egg stink of it was in the air. Well, that shrapnel would have done a fine job on my spine if it had not been for the flak jacket. *My spine.* Oh God—if I had remained on that spot another ten seconds, they would have been picking pieces of me out of the trees. Chance. Pure chance. Allen, right beside me, had been wounded in the head. I had not been hurt. Chance. The one true god of modern war is blind chance.

Taking out a compress, I tried to staunch Allen's bleeding. "My God, it hurts," he said. "My head hurts."

"Listen, Allen. You'll be okay. I don't think it broke any bones. You'll be all right." My hands reeked from his blood. "You're going to get plenty of slack now. Lotsa slack in division med. We'll have you evacked in no time."

"My God it hurts. I don't believe it. It hurts."

"I know, Bill. It hurts. It's good that you can feel it," I said, remembering the sharp sting of that tiny sliver in my thigh. And it had done nothing more than raise a bump the size of a bee sting. Oh yes, I'll bet your wounds hurt, Lance Corporal Bill Allen.

My head had cleared, and the ringing in my ears quieted to a faint buzz. I told Pryor and Aiker to form their squads into a perimeter around the paddy field. Casualty parties started to carry the wounded out of the paddy and up to the level stretch of ground between the embankment and the base of the ridgeline. It was a small space, but it would have to do as a landing zone.

A rifleman and I picked up Sergeant Wehr, each of us taking one of the big man's arms. "Boom. Boom," he said, hobbling with his arms around our necks. "Mah fust patrol, lieutenant, an' boom, ah got hit. Gawd-damn." A corpsman cut Wehr's trouser leg open with a knife and started to dress his wounds. There was a lot of blood. Two marines dragged Sanchez up from the paddy. His face had been so peppered with shrapnel that I hardly recognized him. Except for his eyes. The fragments had somehow missed his eyes. He was unconscious and his eyes were half closed; two white slits in a mass of raspberry red. Sanchez looked as if he had been clawed by some invisible beast. The marines fanned him with their hands.

"He keeps going out, sir," said one of the riflemen. "If he don't get evacced pretty quick, we're afraid he'll go out for good."

"Okay, okay, as soon as we get the others up."

"Rodella, sir. Get Rodella up. Think he's got a sucking chest wound."

I slid down the embankment and splashed over to where the corpsman, Doc Kaiser, was working to save Corporal Rodella. There were gauze and compresses all over his chest and abdomen. One dressing, covering the hole the shrapnel had torn in one of his lungs, was soaked in blood. With each breath he took, pink bubbles of blood formed and burst around the hole. He made a wheezing sound. I tried talking to him, but he could not say anything because his windpipe would fill with blood. Rodella, who had been twice wounded before, was now in danger of drowning in his own blood. It was his eyes that troubled me most. They were the hurt, dumb eyes of a child who has been severely beaten and does not know why. It was his eyes and his silence and the foamy blood and the gurgling, wheezing sound in his chest that aroused in me a sorrow so deep and a rage so strong that I could not distinguish the one emotion from the other.

I helped the corpsman carry Rodella to the landing zone. His comrades were around him, but he was alone. We could see the look of separation in his eyes. He was alone in the world of the badly wounded, isolated by a pain none could share with him and by the terror of the darkness that was threatening to envelop him.

Then we got the last one, Corporal Greeley, a machinegunner whose left arm was hanging by a few strands of muscle; all the rest was a scarlet mush. Greeley was conscious and angry. "Fuck it," he said over and over. "Fuck it. Fuck it. Fuck the cease-fire. Ain't no fuckin' cease-fire, but they can't kill me. Ain't no fuckin' booby trap gonna kill me." Carrying him, I felt my own anger, a very cold, very deep anger that had no specific object. It was just an icy, abiding fury; a hatred for everything in existence except those men. Yes, except those men of mine, any one of whom was better than all the men who had sent them to war.

I radioed for a medevac. The usual complications followed. How many wounded were there? Nine; four walking wounded, five needing evacuation. *Nine?* Nine casualties from a single mine? What kind of mine was it? Electrically detonated, black-powder, a homemade Claymore probably. But what happened? Goddamnit, I'll tell you later. Get me a medevac. I've got at least one, maybe two who'll be DOW if we don't get them out of here. How big was the mine? Four to five pounds of explosive, plenty of shrapnel. It was placed on an embankment and the platoon was down in a rice paddy below it. Most of the shrapnel went over their heads. Otherwise, I'd have several KIAs. Okay? Now get me those birds. "Boom. Boom," said Sergeant Wehr. "Mah fust patrol an' boom, ah get hit." Charley Two, I need the first letter of the last names and the serial numbers of the WIAs needing evac. Now? Yes, now. Rodella and Sanchez had lapsed into unconsciousness. The corpsmen and some marines were fanning them. Doc Kaiser looked at me pleadingly.

"Hang loose, doc," I said. "The birds'll be here, but the assholes in the puzzle-palace have to do their paperwork first. Bittner! Sergeant Bittner, get me the dog tags of the evacs, and hustle."

"Yes, sir," said Bittner, who was one of the walking wounded. A green battle dressing was wrapped around his forehead. One of the walking wounded. We were all walking wounded.

Bittner gave me the dog tags. I tore off the green masking tape that kept the tags from rattling and gave Captain Neal the required information. Then the radio broke down. Jones changed batteries and started giving long test-counts: "Ten-niner-eight-seven. . . ." I heard Neal's voice again. Did I have any serious casualties? For Christ's sake, yes, why do you think I'm asking for a medevac?

"Charley Two," said Neal, "you must have not been supervising your men properly. They must have been awfully bunched up to take nine casualties from one mine."

"Charley Six," I said, my voice cracking with rage. "You get me those birds now. If one of these kids dies because of this petty bullshit I'm going to raise some kinda hell. I want those birds."

There was a long pause. At last the word came: "Birds on the way."

The helicopters swooped in out of the somber sky, landing in the green smoke billowing from the smoke grenade I had thrown to mark the LZ. The crew chiefs pushed stretchers out of the hatches. We laid the casualties on the stretchers and lifted them into the Hueys, the rain falling on us all the time. The aircraft took off, and watching the wounded soaring out of that miserable patch of jungle, we almost envied them.

Just before the platoon resumed its march, someone found a length of electrical detonating cord lying in the grass near the village. The village would have been as likely an ambush site as any: the VC only had to press the detonator and then blend in with the civilians, if indeed there were any true civilians in the village. Or they could have hidden in one of the tunnels under the houses. All right, I thought, tit for tat. No cease-fire for us, none for you, either. I ordered both rocket launcher teams to fire white-phosphorus shells into the hamlet. They fired four altogether. The shells, flashing orange, burst into pure white clouds, the chunks of flaming phosphorus arcing over the trees. About half the village went up in flames. I could hear people yelling, and I saw several figures running through the white smoke. I did not feel a sense of vengeance, any more than I felt remorse or regret. I did not even feel angry. Listening to the shouts and watching the people running out of their burning homes, I did not feel anything at all.

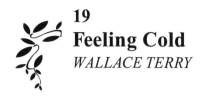

19
Feeling Cold
WALLACE TERRY

The first one I killed really got to me. I guess it was his size. Big guy. Big, broad chest. Stocky legs. He was so big I thought he was Chinese. I still think he was Chinese.

We were on this trail near the Ashau Valley. I saw him and hit the ground and came up swinging like Starsky and Hutch. I shot him with a .45, and I got him pretty good.

He had an AK-47. He was still holding it. He kicked. He kicked a lot. When you get shot, that stuff you see on Hoot Gibson doesn't work. When you're hit, you're hit. You kick. You feel that stuff burning through your flesh. I know how it feels. I've been hit three times.

That's what really got to me—he was so big. I didn't expect that.

They were hard core, too. The enemy would do anything to win. You had to respect that. They believed in a cause. They had the support of the people. That's the key that we Americans don't understand yet. We can't do anything in the military ourselves unless we have the support of the people.

Sometimes we would find the enemy tied to trees. They knew they were going to die. I remember one guy tied up with rope and bamboo. We didn't even see him until he shouted at us and started firing. I don't know whether we killed him or some artillery got him.

One time they had a squad of sappers that hit us. It was like suicide. They ran at us so high on marijuana they didn't know what they were doing. You could smell the marijuana on their clothes. Some of the stuff they did was so crazy that they had to be high on something. In the first place, you don't run through concertina wire like that. Nobody in his right mind does. You get too many cuts. Any time you got a cut over there, it was going to turn to gangrene if it didn't get treated. And they knew we had the place covered.

Another time this guy tried to get our attention. I figured he wanted to give up, because otherwise, I figured he undoubtedly wanted to die. We thought he had started to *chu hoi* [defect]. And we prepared for him to come in. But before he threw his weapon down, he started firing and we had to shoot him.

And, you know, they would walk through our minefields, blow up, and never even bat their heads. Weird shit.

But I really thought they stunk.

Like the time we were heli-lifted from Vandergrift and had to come down in Dong Ha. There was this kid, maybe two or three years old. He hadn't learned to walk too well yet, but he was running down the street. And a Marine walked over to talk to the kid, touched him, and they both blew up. They didn't move. It was not as if they stepped on something. The kid had to have the explosive around him. It was a known tactic that they wrapped stuff around kids. That Marine was part of the security force around Dong Ha, a lance corporal. He was trying to be friendly.

I think it stinks. If those guys were low enough to use kids to bait Americans or anybody to this kind of violent end, well, I think they should be eliminated. And they would have been if we had fought the war in such a manner that we could have won the war. I mean total all-out war. Not nuclear war. We could have done it with land forces.

I would have invaded Hanoi so many times, they would have thought we were walking on water.

The people in Washington setting policy didn't know what transpired over there. They were listening to certain people who didn't really know what we were dealing with. That's why we had all those stupid restrictions. Don't fight across this side of the DMZ, don't fire at women unless they fire at you, don't fire across this area unless you smile first or unless somebody shoots at you. If they attack you and run across this area, you could not go back over there and take them out. If only we could have fought it in a way that we had been taught to fight.

But personally speaking, to me, we made a dent, even though the South did fall. Maybe we did not stop the Communist takeover, but at least I know that I did something to say hey, you bastards, you shouldn't do that. And personally I feel good about it. People like Jane Fonda won't buy that, because they went over there and actually spent time with the people that were killing Americans. That's why I feel that I shouldn't spend $4 to see her at the box offfice. She's a sexy girl and all that other kind of stuff, but she's not the kind of girl that I'd like to admire. She was a psychological setdown, and she definitely should not have been allowed to go to Hanoi.

I learned a lot about people in my platoon. I learned you have to take a person for what he feels, then try to mold the individual into the person you would like to be with. Now my platoon had a lot of Southerners, as well as some Midwesterners. Southerners at the first sign of a black officer being in charge of them were somewhat reluctant. But then, when they found that you know what's going on and you're trying to keep them alive, then they tried to be the best damn soldiers you've got. Some of the black soldiers were the worse I had because they felt that they had to jive on me. They wanted to let me know, Hey, man. Take care of me, buddy. You know I'm your buddy. That's bull.

As long as a black troop knows he's going to take a few knocks like everybody else, he can go as far as anybody in the Corps. Our biggest problem as a race is a tendency to say that the only reason something didn't go the way it was programmed to go is because we are black. It may be that you tipped on somebody's toes. We as blacks have gotten to the place now where we want to depend on somebody else doing something for us. And when we don't measure up to what the expectations are—the first thing we want to holler is racial discrimination. My philosophy is, if you can't do the job—move.

Let's face it. We are part of America. Even though there have been some injustices made, there is no reason for us not to be a part of the American system. I don't feel that because my grandfather or grandmother was a slave that I should not lift arms up to support those things that are stated in the Constitution of the United States. Before I went to Vietnam, I saw the "burn, baby, burn" thing because of Martin Luther King. Why should they burn up Washington, D.C., for something that happened in Memphis? They didn't hurt the white man that was doing business down there on 7th Street. They hurt the black man. They should have let their voices be known that there was injustice. That's the American way.

I still dream about Vietnam.

In one dream, everybody has nine lives. I've walked in front of machine guns that didn't go off. When they pulled the trigger, the trigger jammed. I've seen situations where I got shot at, and the round curved and hit the corner. I'd see that if I had not made that one step, I would not be here. I think about the time where a rocket-propelled grenade hit me in the back, and it didn't go off. We were in a clear area and got hit by an enemy force. The RPG hit me. Didn't go off. Didn't explode. We kept walking, and five of us got hit. I got frays in the lower back and right part of the buttocks. I didn't want to go back to the hospital ship, so I just created the impression that I could handle it. But the stuff wouldn't stop bleeding, and they had to pull the frays out. There was this doctor at Quang Tri, Dr. Mitchell, who was from Boston, a super guy. He painted a smile on my rear end. He cut a straight wound into a curve with stitches across so it looks as if I'm smiling. When I drop my trousers, there's a big smile.

I dream about how the kids in my platoon would come to talk to you and say things about their families. Their families would be upset when they heard I was black. But then some guy would give me a picture of his sister. He would say, "She's white, but you'd still like her. Look her up when you get back to the States." And there would be the ones who did not get a letter that day. Or never got a letter their whole tour. In those cases, I would turn around and write them letters and send them back to Vandergrift.

And you dream about those that you lost. You wonder if there was something you could have done to save them. I only lost two kids. Really.

Cripes was a white guy. I think he was from St. Louis. He was a radio operator. You could tell him. "Tell the battalion commander that everything is doing fine." He would say, "Hey, Big Six. Everything is A-okay. We are ready, Freddie." You know, he had to add something to whatever you said. Otherwise, he was a very quiet guy. But one big problem he had was that he wanted to get into everything. He was trying to prove something to himself. If he saw somebody move, he was going to follow him. No matter what you could do to tell him not to fire, he'd fire. One night, after we got out to Fire Support Base Erskine, we got hit. It was about eleven. Cripes got shot. We don't know if he got hit by our fire or their fire. I just know he crawled out there. He must have seen something. Cripes just had a bad habit of being in the wrong place at the wrong time.

Lance Corporal Oliver was a black kid from Memphis. He carried an automatic rifle. He had been with us maybe three months. He was a very scary kid. He was trying to prove a lot of things to himself and to his family, too. So he was always volunteering to be point. It was very difficult to appoint someone as a point man. A lot of times when you had a feeling you were going to be hit, you asked for volunteers. Oliver always volunteered.

We were on Operation Dewey Canyon. In February of 1969. We had been told the NVA was in there that night. One platoon had went out and got hit. And we got the message to go in next. I got the whole platoon together and said, "Listen. I'm going to walk point for you." My troops said, "No, sir, you don't need to walk. We will arrange for someone to walk point." So the next day the whole platoon got together and said, "Who wants to walk point today?" Oliver stuck up his hand. I said, "I'll be the second man."

Now we had this dog to sniff out VC. Normally he would walk the point with the dog handler. His handler, Corporal Rome from Baltimore, swore Hobo could smell the Vietnamese a mile away. If he smelled one, his hair went straight. You knew something was out there.

One time, when we were walking a trail near Con Thien, this guy was in this tree. At first we thought he was one of the local indigenous personnel, like the ARVN. He turned out to be something else. He had his pajamas on and his army trousers. He wasn't firing. He was just sitting there. Hobo just ran up in that tree, reached back, and tore off his uniform. He was armed with an AK-47. Hobo took that away from him, threw him up in the air, and grabbed him by the neck and started dragging him. We learned a lot from that guy. You put a dog on a guy, and he'll tell you anything you want to know.

Another time at Vandergrift, Hobo started barking in the officers' hootch. We had sandbags between us. And Hobo just barked and barked at the bags. Nobody could figure out what was wrong. Finally I told Hobo to shut up, and I walked over to the sandbags. There was this viper, and I took a shotgun and blew its head off.

We used to dress Hobo up with a straw hat on his head and shades on. All of us had shades. And we used to take pictures of Hobo. And sit him on the chopper. And he'd be in the back of the chopper with his shades on and his hat, and he would smile at us.

We got to the place where we could feed him, and put our hands in his mouth. We would give him Gravy Train or Gainesburgers. If we ran out on patrol, we would give him our C-rations. He really liked beef with spice sauce.

Hobo was so gullible and so lovable that when you had a problem, you ended up talking to him. You could say, "Hobo, what the hell am I doing here?" Or, "Hey, man. We didn't find nothin' today. We walked three miles and couldn't find nothin'. What the hell are you doing walking this way?" And he'd look at you and smile, you know, in his own little manner. And he'd let you know that he should really be here to understand all this shit we're putting down. Or he would do things like growl to let you know he really didn't approve of all this bullshit you're talking. It's hard to explain. But after eight months, Hobo was like one of the guys.

Hobo signaled the ambush, but nobody paid any attention. We walked into the ambush. A machine gun hit them. Oliver got shot dead three times in the head, three times in the chest, and six times in the leg. Rome got hit in the leg. Hobo got shot in the side, but even though he was hit, he got on top of Rome. The only person that Hobo allowed to go over there and touch Rome was me.

It never got better. It seemed like everyday somebody got hurt. Sometimes I would walk point. Everybody was carrying the wounded. We had 15 wounded in my platoon alone. And the water was gone.

Then on the twelfth day, while we were following this trail through the jungle, the point man came running back. He was all heated up. He said, "I think we got a tank up there." I told him, "I don't have time for no games." The enemy had no tanks in the South.

Then the trail started converging into a really well-camouflaged road, about 12 feet wide and better made than anything I had ever seen in Vietnam. Then I saw the muzzle of this gun. It was as big as anything we had. And all hell broke open. It was like the sun was screaming.

I thought, my God, if I stay here, I'm going to get us all wiped out.

In front of us was a reinforced platoon and two artillery pieces all dug into about 30 real serious bunkers. And we were in trouble in the rear, because a squad of snipers had slipped in between us and the rest of Charlie Company. My flanks were open. All the NVA needed to finish us off was to set up mortars on either side.

Someone told me the snipers had just got Joe. He was my platoon sergeant.

That did it. I passed the word to call in napalm at Danger Close, 50 meters off our position. Then I turned to go after the snipers. And I heard this loud crash. I was thrown to the ground. This grenade had exploded, and the shrapnel had torn into my left arm.

The Phantoms were doing a number. It felt like an earthquake was coming. The ground was just a-rumbling. Smoke was everywhere, and then the grass caught fire. The napalm explosions had knocked two of my men down who were at the point, but the NVA were running everywhere. The flames were up around my waist. That's when I yelled, "Charge. Kill the gooks. Kill the motherfuckers."

We kept shooting until everything was empty. Then we picked up the guns they dropped and fired them. I brought three down with my .45. In a matter of minutes, the ridge was ours. We had the bunkers, an earth mover, bunches of documents, tons of food supplies. We counted 70 dead NVA. And those big guns, two of them. Russian-made. Like our 122, they had a range of 12 to 15 miles. They were the first ones captured in South Vietnam.

Well, I ordered a perimeter drawn. And since I never ask my men to do something I don't do, I joined the perimeter. Then this sniper got me. Another RPG. I got it in the back. I could barely raise myself up on one elbow. I felt like shit, but I was trying to give a command. The guys just circled around me like they were waiting for me to tell them something. I got to my knees. And it was funny. They had their guns pointed at the sky.

I yelled out, "I can walk. I can walk."

Somebody said, "No, sir. You will not walk."

I slumped back. And two guys got on my right side. Two guys got on my left side. One held me under the head. One more lifted my feet. Then they held me high above their shoulders, like I was a Viking or some kind of hero. They formed a perimeter around me. They told me my feet would never touch ground there again. And they held me high up in the air until the chopper came.

I really don't know what I was put in for. I was told maybe the Navy Cross. Maybe the Medal of Honor. It came down to the Silver Star. One of those guns is at Quantico in the Marine Aviation Museum. And the other is at Fort Sill in Oklahoma. And they look just as horrible today as they did when we attacked them.

Rome lost his leg. From what I'm told, they gave him a puppy sired by Hobo. So Hobo survived Dewey Canyon. They wanted to destroy him at first, but he got back to the kennel. If anybody would've destroyed that dog, it would have been me.

But Hobo didn't get back to the States. Those dogs that were used in Vietnam were not brought back. The Air Force destroyed all those dogs. They were afraid of what they might do here.

If I had Hobo right now, he wouldn't have to worry about nothing the rest of his life. He was a hell of a dog. He could sense right and wrong. I would have trusted Hobo with my own children. If somebody got wrong or was an enemy of my family, Hobo would have brought his ass to me. There ain't no doubt about it. Yet he was a nice dog. He would give me a kiss on the jaw. I loved that dog.

But the thing that really hurt me more than anything in the world was when I came back to the States and black people considered me as a part of the establishment. Because I am an officer. Here I was, a veteran that just came back from a big conflict. And most of the blacks wouldn't associate with me. You see, blacks are not supposed to be officers. Blacks are supposed to be those guys that take orders, and not necessarily those that give them. If you give orders, it means you had to kiss somebody's rear end to get into that position.

One day I wore my uniform over to Howard University in Washington to help recruit officer candidates. Howard is a black school, like the one I went to in Texas, Jarvis Christian College. I thought I would feel at home. The guys poked fun at me, calling me Uncle Sam's flunky. They would say the Marine Corps sucks. The Army sucks. They would say their brother or uncle got killed, so why was I still in. They would see the Purple Heart and ask me what was I trying to prove. The women wouldn't talk to you either.

I felt bad. I felt cold. I felt like I was completely out of it.

20
Nursing and Disillusionment
LYNDA VAN DEVANTER

I went up-country with two other second lieutenants, Michelle Neuman and Coretta Jones, flying in a six-passenger single-engine plane to Nha Trang and hopping a supply helicopter from there to Pleiku. Michelle was a petite blonde, with blue eyes, a pageboy haircut, and the face of an elf. From the time she was an infant, everyone had called her Mickie, a name that seemed to fit perfectly her bubbly personality. She had been raised near Boston, but had gone to a nursing school in San Jose, California, to get away from home. When she laughed, it sounded more like a giggle. She was a whirlwind of undirected energy, and she was one of the most fun people I'd every known. She was forever trying to tell jokes and usually forgetting the punch lines. Even when she remembered them, she would giggle so hard that she wouldn't be able to get the words out. Of course, Mickie's punch lines never mattered. Her giggle was so infectious that it would be impossible not to laugh with her. If I didn't know better, I would have sworn that she had invented the word "cute." Everybody liked her immediately.

Coretta was far more subdued than her outgoing friend. She had gone to the same nursing school as Mickie, but since Coretta was two years ahead, they hadn't got to know each other until recently, as the result of a one in a million coincidence. Ten days earlier, they had found themselves the only women on the same plane out of Travis, headed for Vietnam. Coretta was three years older than Mickie and two years older than I. She had worked in the emergency room of a hospital in Oakland, California, her hometown, before deciding to join the Army to "find something better." She was tall and black, with a body that was slightly overweight but very attractive. Although at that point, I thought of myself as a girl, there was no question in my mind that Coretta was a woman. She carried herself with a quiet confidence and seemed to be one of the few people who really listened when others talked. However, the thing that stood out the most was her compassion. There wasn't anything about her that you could point to and say made her compassionate, but her concern for others always came through. Maybe it was an expression given off by those big brown eyes or from her warm smile. Whatever it was, I knew instinctively that she was a person who could be counted on in a crunch.

When we arrived at the 71st Evac Hospital, we were met with an enthusiasm that was hard to believe. I don't think I've ever felt so welcome anywhere. But everyone had a strange habit of referring to us as "turtles" or "FNGs."

"Why turtles?" I asked.

"Because it took so long for you to get here," one of the nurses said. "The people you're replacing have waited a whole year."

"And what's an FNG?"

"What else?" she said. "A Fucking New Guy. Welcome to the war. We could use some new blood around here."

There was a list in the emergency room [ER] that had the name of every person assigned to the hospital. Next to each name was the person's blood type. When the hospital ran out of blood, someone would go immediately to that list. As a result, replacements were more than just people who could take over some of the workload; they were, literally, new blood.

We all experienced a degree of shock when we saw the hospital compound for the first time. Coretta made her evaluation less than five minutes after we had left the helicopter. "This is the damnedest hospital I've ever seen," she said. That was probably an understatement.

After signing in at headquarters, we got an abbreviated tour. The 71st consisted of a group of ramshackle wooden buildings and metal Quonset huts, all covered with a layer of red dust and protected by a fence, barbed wire, bored guards, and Vietnamese soldiers in tanks. The ER was about fifty yards from the helipad and was connected to the post-op/intensive care unit and the operating room [OR]—actually six operating cubicles, three on each side of an open hallway and divided from each other by five-and-a-half-foot-tall cabinets. The building housing them was called the surgical-T, because of its shape. Next door to the surgical-T was the morgue. As we walked past it, a nurse wheeled a gurney through its double doors. I felt like I wasn't supposed to look.

Our guide was a six-foot-four-inch hulk of a man who must have weighed 250 pounds and who looked like he could lift a tank with one arm. He wore dirty, wrinkled fatigues and his jungle boots were coated with a layer of red dust. His clothes hung on him. I had the feeling that he was the kind of man who would have looked sloppy even in a tux. He appeared to enjoy the role of tour guide, and he seemed to like the three of us instantly, although he didn't bother to tell us his name.

When we were finished with the business part of the tour, our guide offered to show us the "important sights," which were the park, the banana trees, and the pool. The park was a narrow strip of ground behind the headquarters building and between a couple of other buildings he referred to as hooches. It was called the Bernard J. Piccolo Memorial Peace Park, in honor of the popular commander who had just left. The banana trees were a couple of scrawny things near the commanding officer's trailer. The signs in front of them identified them as the Bernard J. Piccolo Memorial Banana Tree and the Elizabeth L. Piccolo Memorial Banana Tree. He said both names fully, as if to combine them into the Bernard J. and Elizabeth L. Piccolo Trees would have been highly irreverent. And God pity anyone who had the nerve to call them Bernie and Liz. Such sacrilege would never be permitted. It was important to always respect Bernard J. because he had been "a truly wonderful man," and Elizabeth L., because she had waited faithfully back in the world while her husband "did his duty for God, apple pie, and country. Amen."

Our last stop was the pool. "Only evac hospital in-country with our very own pool," he said proudly.

"Don't tell us," I said. "You call it the Bernard J. Piccolo Memorial Swimming Pool."

He laughed. "No, actually the people around here were thinking of calling it the Captain Bubba L. Kominski Memorial Swimming pool, in honor of just possibly the second best neurosurgeon on the entire continent of Asia, with perhaps the exception of Upper Mongolia. But Bubba Kominski is far too modest to allow anything like that."

"Why Bubba L. Kominski?" I asked.

"Because the good captain just happened to save the life of an infantry lieutenant who just happened to be the son of an engineer colonel who just happened to be grateful enough to the 71st to donate some men and machinery to our noble effort to make life on this planet more meaningful. In short, Captain Bubba L. Kominski, gentleman, scholar, neurosurgeon of distinction, and father of the six-month-old Glenda Lee Kominski, just happened to be the man responsible for getting this pool built."

"Sounds impressive," I said teasingly. "And when do we just happen to get to meet this wonderful Captain Bubba L. Kominski?"

Our guide smiled broadly, put his enormous, meaty hands around my waist, and lifted me more than a foot off the ground until I was at eye level with him. "You're looking at the man," he said. "Captain Bubba L. Kominski at your service."

Bubba got us temporarily set up with cots in the living room of Colonel Bernard J. Piccolo's trailer, which was vacant until a new commander arrived. "They're gonna have to kick a couple of doctors out of a hooch so you girls can have more permanent quarters," he said.

The next day, Mickie, Coretta, and I started to work. Coretta was assigned to the emergency room. Mickie and I joined the operating room staff. None of us was quite ready for duty at the 71st.

That first shift was a shock. There were *only* fifteen wounded soldiers who needed surgery. I saw young boys with their arms and legs blown off, some with their guts hanging out, and others with "ordinary" gunshot wounds. In addition, at least another twenty-five DPCs—delayed primary closures—were scheduled for the OR. These were guys who had been brought in with wounds a few days earlier. Since wounds coming into the 71st were usually dirty, and the possibilities of infection high, doctors would stop the bleeding, remove the metal fragments or bullets, and clean the wound during the initial surgery. Then, rather than close the outer skin immediately, they would leave the wound covered with sterile fine mesh gauze and antibiotics for a few days to make sure infections didn't get a chance to start. Later, when the risk of infection was lessened, the guy would be brought back into the OR for a DPC.

My first case was a D & I, debridement and irrigation, with Bubba Kominski. "I bet you thought us world-renowned neurosurgeons were above mere donkey work like this," he said. "Well, Van, lesson number one is that everybody around this death factory is a jack of all trades." The D & I was probably the most common operation in Vietnam. When a soldier got a frag wound, he would usually have little holes all over his body, where fragments had broken the skin. Our job, after we stopped the bleeding, was to remove the metal fragments and cut away any dead skin—debridement—and then to clean the wound with sterile saline solution to reduce the risk of infection—irrigation. Bubba called it, "making big holes out of little holes." He said our kid had stepped on a Bouncing Betty.

"A Bouncing Betty?" I asked.

"It's a land mine," he answered. "An explosive charge bounces up to about waist level before going bang. The V.C. like it because it tends to deprive our upstanding young men of a part of their anatomy that usually spends a lot of time at attention when it's in the presence of unclothed beautiful women. Fortunately, this young trooper had his back to the charge. Family jewels all in place, but it sure took a bite out of his ass."

The next lesson that Bubba taught me was to forget most of the things I had learned in nursing school and at the OR school, starting with the arrangement of my instrument tray. "You can always tell the FNGs by the way they set up their Mayo stands," he said. In almost every OR, there are specific ways to organize the instruments. Every item has a place, and the best scrub nurses can find things blindfolded. The system is based on the idea that the only person using the tray will be the scrub. She normally hands the surgeon what he needs. If he forgets this rule, he is usually reminded with a quick rap across his knuckles.

However, as Bubba quickly pointed out, we had neither the time nor personnel for us to follow these standards. Stateside operations are usually performed by a surgeon with at least one assistant plus a scrub. In Vietnam, I would be expected to be both scrub nurse and assistant, and sometimes would find myself without a free hand with which to give instruments. He proved his point immediately. "Get on the other side of the table," he said. "You're going to start cutting with me."

"I don't know how to cut," I said.

"That's why I'm going to teach you, Van. Welcome to med school."

Bubba was an excellent teacher and I learned quickly. From that case, we went to a neuro case, one in which a nineteen-year-old boy had gotten a bullet lodged in his back, pressing against his spinal cord. As Bubba cut down to the vertebrae and started working his way to the spinal cord, I saw another facet of his personality. He became very intense, and concentrated every ounce of his being on the delicate work that had to be done. It would have been obvious to even an untrained observer that Captain Bubba L. Kominski was a virtuoso with a knife. He may very well have been accurate in calling himself "the second best neurosurgeon in Asia."

The wounded soldier had been brought in paralyzed, but Bubba hadn't been quite sure if it was because the spinal cord had been cut or only bruised. Although a bruise could also be serious enough to cause permanent paralysis, it would leave some hope.

It turned out that our kid's spinal cord was moderately bruised, with the bullet lodged against it. "No question about it," Bubba said. "We got us some damage here." He used his tiny instruments to slowly and meticulously cut away pieces of vertebrae and remove the bullet, taking special care not to do any further damage to the spinal cord. "Hey, Van, we got a bleeder that let loose. Could you give me some suction while I tie it off?" I was extremely nervous. One mistake could end whatever small chances this guy might have to walk again. Finally, Bubba dropped a bullet into the specimen bowl.

As he finished the surgery, I asked, "Do you think he'll walk again?"

"Hard to tell," he said. "But if he does or doesn't we'll never know. We just patch them up and send them away. We never hear what happens after they're gone."

"Isn't it frustrating?"

"You'll get used to it, Van. This is an assembly line, not a medical center."

One thing I knew I'd never get used to was something I encountered later in the day when I had to work with another doctor on my first serious burn case. The soldier, whose entire body had been charred beyond recognition, had been at the 71st for the past three days. His patrol had been accidentally attacked by one of our own helicopters. Of the ten men, he was the only survivor. In spite of the work that was being done to keep him alive, he was undoubtedly going to die. Almost his entire body, except for his feet, had been seared by napalm, a jellied petroleum substance that oozes down the skin and into the pores, carrying flames with it. By now, he was covered with a sickly blue-green slime, called pseudomonas, a common bacterial infection among severely burned patients. I could barely look at the kid while we scraped away the infected dead tissue, trying to get down to a viable area so he might have some chance of healing. Long after we were finished with him, I was unable to get the smell of pseudomonas and napalm out of my nose. I seemed to be in my clothes, my hair, and even the pores of my skin. I would live with that smell for the next year. It was disgusting.

When I went to the mess hall that night, all the food smelled like the burned soldier. I had managed to control my stomach during the surgery, but twice that evening, when I thought about it, I retched. . . .

Once Carl [a Vietnam boyfriend] was gone, I tried to bury my loneliness in work. I missed him, probably more than I've ever missed anyone in my life. A few times, I thought of breaking my promise and writing him a letter. But I didn't want to interfere in his other life. He was back in the real world with his wife and kids, where all of us wanted to be. What could I possibly offer him now?

I checked that mail each day for a card, a letter, some sort of reminder that I was not forgotten. Carl never sent a word. Maybe it was best that way.

However, I could still hear his voice telling me I had to be tough to survive. And as each day passed, I found myself developing a harder shell to protect my emotions. For the first few weeks after he went home, I drank heavily and used more grass. But after a while, I started avoiding them because they lowered my defenses. Before, they had effectively deadened all pain and kept me from feeling the suffering of others. Now, they only made me feel it more. I was getting tired. This war was beginning to look different than the one I had believed in only a few weeks earlier. I started listening to the local discontents who railed against Nixon, Congress, the Joint Chiefs of Staff, and the whole U.S. government. Every time another person died on my table, I came one step closer to agreeing with them. I still tried to remind myself that we were in Vietnam to save people who were threatened by tyranny, but that became more and more difficult to believe as I heard stories of corrupt South Vietnamese officials, U.S. Army atrocities, and a population who wanted nothing more than to be left alone so they could return to farming their land. I saw kids—American eighteen- and nineteen-year-olds and little Vietnamese and Montagnard kids—who were dying of diseases that I thought had been eliminated from the face of the earth. There were cases of malaria, polio, typhoid, cholera, and tetanus. One day, I saw some dead American soldiers lying outside the morgue. The had been ambushed by an NVA unit. The butchers had cut off our soldiers' penises and stuffed them into the GIs' mouths. I was outraged by the scene, but not as outraged as I became when I later saw a similar scene, only this time with dead Viet Cong. It was the first time I realized that our clean-cut, wholesome American boys could be as brutal as the "godless Communists."

Neither group was as bad as the ROKs, The ROKs were soldiers from the Republic of Korea. They were part of a token international force that had been assembled in South Vietnam so the U.S. need not claim this as a solely American war. The ROKs handled most of the interrogations in our area and were some of the hardest soldiers there. They practiced every conceivable kind of torture, and often the interrogations ended in death regardless of whether the person was a V.C. or just an innocent Vietnamese who happened into the wrong place at the wrong time. One of the favorite forms of torture was referred to as the "Bell Telephone Hour." They would connect electrical wires from a field telephone set to the victim's testicles or vagina. If presented with an answer they didn't like, they would crank the phone to produce a shock. The pain must have been excruciating. Yet that wasn't the worst type of interrogation.

The preferred technique was far more gruesome. I saw the results of that method on a night when we received an unconscious V.C. suspect for surgery. He had been scalped. It wasn't a quick scalping. It had taken place over a number of hours, a little at a time, to bring about the maximum amount of suffering. They had made the man stand on his toes while they attached his flesh to a hook. Each time he moved an inch, he was in agony.

By the time we got that case, I was already insensitive enough to the suffering to laugh when one of our own surgeons lifted the flap of scalp and said, "No sense wasting this. Know any bald guys?"

During those months after Carl left, I lost my direction and found myself becoming a person I would never have been before Vietnam. Maybe he would have said I was merely getting tough. Like thousands of Americans, I began calling the Vietnamese—both friendly and enemy—"gooks." I would have thought I was above that sort of racism; after all, hadn't I marched in the United States for civil rights like a good Catholic girl who believed all oppression was wrong? I began to understand how many of my friends had felt during my early months there. I had looked down on them for displaying just the kind of attitude I was beginning to develop. Now, I saw the Vietnamese as nothing more than a group of thieves and murderers. It was especially difficult because V.C. looked the same as anyone else. Rather than try to distinguish between the friends and enemies, I learned to hate all of them. They were the ones who kept killing American soldiers. Why should we bother saving them?

Once, in the middle of a push, I was directed to scrub on a belly case. When I looked at the chart, I realized I would be working on a prisoner of war, an NVA lieutenant colonel. I was furious. I stormed up to the nurse in charge. "We still have GIs out there," I said. "What the fuck are we doing this guy for?"

"We're following triage protocol," she said. "This soldier is next."

"But twenty minutes ago, this jerk was out there trying to blow us away."

"And now he's wounded and needs our help, Van. Get to work."

"If you're such a gook lover, why don't you scrub on the case?"

"Because I've ordered you to do it."

In addition to being upset, I was extremely confused by the whole episode. I could understand that as a human being, he had a right to proper care, but every bone in my body told me that he wasn't worth the effort. In fact, he could have been the officer who had ordered Father Bergeron's execution, or the battalion commander who was responsible for every single case we got that day. I wanted to spit in his face. Instead, I spit in my hands. That was how I scrubbed for the case before donning sterile gloves. If he died of an infection, fuck him.

A part of me knew that after it was over, I would be ashamed. I had taken a vow as a nurse to help all human beings no matter what race, creed, color, or sex. According to that vow, they were all entitled to quality care. But my bitterness far outweighed any vows I had spoken in a graduation ceremony. I did what I had to do for that POW and not one bit more. All the time we worked on him, I wished that he would die.

But he didn't.

When we were finished and it was apparent that the NVA colonel would live, the surgeon suggested we literally charge an arm and a leg for the operation. I offered to get the saw and we all laughed hysterically. Some day, I would hate myself for having laughed. But not now. . . .

When the soldiers of World War II came home, they were met by brass bands, ticker-tape parades, and people so thankful for their service that even those who had never heard a shot fired in anger were treated with respect. It was a time when words like honor, glory, and duty held some value, a time when a returning GI was viewed with esteem so high it bordered on awe. To be a veteran was to be seen as a person of courage, a champion of democracy, an ideal against which all citizens could measure themselves. If you had answered your country's call, you were a hero. And in those days, heroes were plentiful.

But somewhere between 1945 and 1970, words like bravery, sacrifice, and valor had gone out of vogue. When I returned to my country in June of 1970, I began to learn a very bitter lesson. The values with which I had been raised had changed; in the eyes of most Americans, the military services had no more heroes, merely babykillers, misfits, and fools. I was certain that I was neither a babykiller nor a misfit. Maybe I was a fool.

There are those among the poets, philosophers, and psychologists who believe that the root of all unhappiness is unfulfilled expectation. Many people, they argue, have unrealistic expectations. If you learn not to expect too much, their logic goes, you won't be disappointed. Therefore, you'll be happier. Perhaps they're right. Perhaps if I hadn't expected anything at all when I returned to the States, I would not have been disappointed. Maybe I would have been contented simply to be on American soil. Maybe all of us who arrived at Travis Air Force Base on June 16 had unrealistic expectations.

But we didn't ask for a brass band. We didn't ask for a parade. We didn't even ask for much of a thank you. All we wanted was some transportation to San Francisco International Airport so we could hop connecting flights to get home to our families. We gave the Army a year of our lives, a year with more difficulties than most Americans face in fifty years. The least the Army could have done was to give us a ride.

At Travis we were herded onto buses and driven to the Oakland Army Terminal where they dumped us around 5 A.M. with a "so long, suckers" from the driver and a feeling that we were no more than warm bodies who had outlived their usefulness. Unfortunately, San Francisco International was at least twenty miles away. Since most of us had to get flights from there, wouldn't it have been logical to drop us at the airport? Or was I expecting too much out of the Army when I asked it to be logical?

I checked into commercial buses and taxis, but none were running. There was a transit strike on, and it was nearly impossible to get public transportation of any kind. So I hung one of my suitcases from my left shoulder, hefted my duffel bag onto my right shoulder, grabbed my overnight case with my left hand and my purse with my right, and struggling under the weight, walked out to the highway, where I stuck out my thumb and waited. I was no stranger to hitchiking. It was the only way to get around in Vietnam. Back in 'Nam, I would usually stand on the flight line in my fatigues, combat boots, jungle hat, pigtails, and a smile. Getting a ride there was a cinch. In fact, planes would sometimes reach the end of the runway, then return to offer me a lift.

But hitchhiking in the real world, I was quickly finding out, was nowhere near as easy—especially if you were wearing a uniform. The cars whizzed past me during rush hour, while I patiently waited for a good Samaritan to stop. A few drivers gave me the finger. I tried to ignore them. Some slowed long enough to yell obscenities. One threw a carton of trash and another nearly hit me with a half-empty can of soda. Finally, two guys stopped in a red and yellow Volkswagen bus. The one on the passenger side opened his door. I ran to the car, dragging the duffel bag and other luggage behind me. I was hot, tired, and dirty.

"Going anywhere near the airport?" I asked.

"Sure am," the guy said. He had long brown hair, blue eyes framed by wire-rimmed glasses, and a full curly beard. There were patches on his jeans and a peace sign on his T-shirt. His relaxed, easy smile was deceptive.

I smiled back and lifted my duffel bag to put it inside the van. But the guy slammed the door shut. "We're going past the airport, sucker, but we don't take Army pigs." He spit on me. I was stunned.

"Fuck you, Nazi bitch," the driver yelled. He floored the accelerator and they both laughed uncontrollably as the VW spun its wheels for a few seconds, throwing dirt and stones back at me before it roared away. The drivers of other passing cars also laughed.

I looked down at my chest. On top of my nametag sat a big gob of brownish-colored saliva. I couldn't touch it. I didn't have the energy to wipe it away. Instead, I watched as it ran down my name tag and over a button before it was absorbed into the green material of my uniform.

I wasn't angry, just confused. I wanted to know why. Why would he spit on me? What had I done to him? To either of them? It might have been simple to say I had gone to war and they blamed me for killing innocent people, but didn't they understand that I didn't want this war any more than the most vocal of peace marchers? Didn't they realize that those of us who had seen the war firsthand were probably more antiwar than they were? That we had seen friends suffer and die? That we had seen children destroyed? That we had seen futures crushed?

Were they that naive?

Or were they merely insensitive creeps who used the excuse of my uniform to vent their hostility toward all people?

I waited a few more hours, holding my thumb out until I thought my arm would fall off. After awhile, I stopped watching people as they hurled their insults. I had begun noticing the people who didn't scream as they drove by. I soon realized they all had something in common. It was what I eventually came to refer to as "the look." It was a combination of surprise at seeing a woman in uniform, and hatred for what they assumed I represented. Most of them never bothered to try to conceal it. "The look" would start around the eyes, as if they were peering right through me. Their faces would harden into stone. I was a pariah, a nonperson so low that they believed they could squash me underfoot; I was as popular as a disease and as untouchable as a piece of shit.

While I stood there alone, I almost wished I was back in 'Nam. At least there you expected some people to hate you. That was a war. But here, in the United States, I guess I wanted everything to be wonderful. I thought that life would be different, that there would be no more pain. No more death. No more sorrow. It was all going to be good again. It had to be good again. I had had enough of fighting, and hatred, and bitterness.

Around 10:30 A.M., when I had given up hope and was sitting on my duffel bag, a passing driver shouted three words that perfectly illustrated my return to the world:

"Welcome home, asshole!"

A few minutes later, an old black man in a beat-up '58 Chevy stopped and got out of his car. He walked with a limp and leaned forward as if he couldn't stand straight. His clothes were frayed and his face deeply lined. He ran his bony fingers through his gray-black hair, then shook his head and smiled. "I don't know where you're going, little girl," he said. "But I been by here four times since early morning and you ain't got a ride yet. I can't let you spend your whole life on this road." He was only headed for the other side of Oakland, but he said he'd rather go out of his way than see me stranded. He even carried my duffel bag to the trunk. As we drove south on 101, I didn't say much other than thank you, but my disillusionment was obvious.

"People ain't all bad, little girl," he said. "It's just some folks are crazy mixed up these days. You keep in mind that it's gotta get better, 'cause it can't get any worse."

21
"They Did Not Know Good from Evil"
TIM O'BRIEN

"*LUI LAI, LUI LAI!*" Stink would scream, pushing them back. "*Lui lai*, you dummies. . . . Back up, move!" Teasing ribs with his rifle muzzle, he would force them back against a hootch wall or fence. "*Coi Chung!*" he'd holler. Blinking, face white and teeth clicking, he would kick the stragglers, pivot, shove, thumb flicking the rifle's safety catch. "Move! *Lui lai*. . . . Move it, go, go!" Herding them together, he would watch to be sure their hands were kept in the open, empty. Then he would open his dictionary. He would read slowly, retracing the words several times, then finally look up. "*Nam xuong dat,*" he'd say. Separating each word, trying for good diction, he would say it in a loud, level voice. "Everybody . . . *nam xuong dat.*" The kids would just stare. The women might rock and moan, or begin chattering among themselves like caged squirrels, glancing up at Stink with frazzled eyes. "Now!" he'd shout. "*Nam xuong dat.* . . . Do it!" Sometimes he would fire off a single shot, but this only made the villagers fidget and squirm. Puzzled, some of them would start to giggle. Others would cover their ears and yap with the stiff, short barking sounds of small dogs. It drove Stink wild. "*Nam xuong* the fuck down!" he'd snarl, his thin lips curling in a manner he practiced while shaving. "Lie down! *Man len*, mama-san! Now, goddamn it!" His eyes would bounce from his rifle to the dictionary to the cringing villagers. Behind him, Doc Peret and Oscar Johnson and Buff would be grinning at the show. They'd given the English-Vietnamese dictionary to Stink as a birthday present, and they loved watching him use it, the way he mixed languages in a kind of stew, ignoring pronunciation and grammar, turning angry when words failed to produce results. "*Nam thi xuong dat!*" he'd bellow, sweating now, his tongue sputtering over the impossible middle syllables. "*Man len*, pronto, you sons of bitches! Haul ass!" But the villagers would only shake their heads and cackle and mill uncertainly. This was too much for Stink Harris. Enraged, he'd throw away the dictionary and rattle off a whole magazine of ammunition. The women would moan. Kids would clutch their mothers, dogs would howl, chickens would scramble in their coops. "*Dong* fuckin' *lat thit!*" Stink would be screaming, his eyes dusty and slit like a snake's. "*Nam xuong dat!* Do it, you ignorant bastards!" Reloading, he would keep firing and screaming, and the villagers would sprawl in the dust, arms wrapped helplessly around their heads. And when they were all down, Stink would stop firing. He would smile. He would glance at Doc Peret and nod. "See there? They understand me fine. *Nam xuong dat.* . . . Lie down. I'm gettin' the hang of it. You just got to punctuate your sentences."

Not knowing the language, they did not know the people. They did not know what the people loved or respected or feared or hated. They did not recognize hostility unless it was patent, unless it came in a form other than language; the complexities of tone and tongue were beyond them. Dinkese, Stink Harris called it: monkey chatter, bird talk. Not knowing the language, the men did not know whom to trust. Trust was lethal. They did not know false smiles from true smiles, or if in Quang Ngai a smile had the same meaning it had in the States. "Maybe the dinks got things mixed up," Eddie once said, after the time a friendly-looking farmer bowed and smiled and pointed them into a minefield. "Know what I mean? Maybe . . . well, maybe the gooks cry when they're happy and smile when they're sad. Who the hell knows? Maybe when you

215

smile over here it means you're ready to cut the other guy's throat. I mean, hey . . . didn't they tell us way back in AIT that this here's a different culture?" Not knowing the people, they did not know friends from enemies. They did not know if it was a popular war, or, if popular, in what sense. They did not know if the people of Quang Ngai viewed the war stoically, as it sometimes seemed, or with grief, as it seemed other times, or with bewilderment or greed or partisan fury. It was impossible to know. They did not know religions or philosophies or theories of justice. More than that, they did not know how emotions worked in Quang Ngai. Twenty years of war had rotted away the ordinary reactions to death and disfigurement. Astonishment, the first response, was never there in the faces of Quang Ngai. Disguised, maybe. But who knew? Who ever knew? Emotions and beliefs and attitudes, motives and aims, hopes—these were unknown to the men in Alpha Company, and Quang Ngai told nothing. "Fuckin' beasties," Stink would croak, mimicking the frenzied village speech. "No shit, I seen hamsters with more feelings."

But for Paul Berlin it was always a nagging question: Who were these skinny, blank-eyed people? What did they want? The kids especially—watching them, learning their names and faces, Paul Berlin couldn't help wondering. It was a ridiculous, impossible puzzle, but even so he wondered. Did the kids *like* him? A little girl with gold hoops in her ears and ugly scabs on her brow—did she feel, as he did, goodness and warmth and poignancy when he helped Doc dab iodine on her sores? Beyond that, though, did the girl *like* him? Lord knows, he had no villainy in his heart, no motive but kindness. He wanted health for her, and happiness. Did she know this? Did she sense his compassion? When she smiled, was it more than a token? And . . . and what *did* she want? Any of them, what did they long for? Did they have secret hopes? His hopes? Could this little girl—her eyes squinting as Doc brushed the scabs with iodine, her lips sucked in, her nose puckering at the smell—could she somehow separate him from the war? Even for an instant? Could she see him as just a scared-silly boy from Iowa? Could she feel sympathy? In it together, trapped, you and me, all of us: Did she feel that? Could she understand his own fear, matching it with hers? Wondering, he put mercy in his eyes like lighted candles; he gazed at the girl, full-hearted, draining out suspicion, opening himself to whatever she might answer with. Did the girl see the love? Could she understand it, return it? But he didn't know. He did not know if love or its analogue even existed in the vocabulary of Quang Ngai, or if friendship could be translated. He simply did not know. He wanted to be liked. He wanted them to understand, all of them, that he felt no hate. It was all a sad accident, he would have told them—chance, high-level politics, confusion. He had no stake in the war beyond simple survival; he was there, in Quang Ngai, for the same reasons they were: the luck of the draw, bad fortune, forces beyond reckoning. His intentions were benign. By God, yes! He was snared in a web as powerful and tangled as any that victimized the people of My Khe or Pinkville. Sure, they were trapped. Sure, they suffered, sure. But, by God, he was just as trapped, just as injured. He would have told them that. He was no tyrant, no pig, no Yankee killer. He was innocent. Yes, he was, He was innocent. He would have told them that, the villagers, if he'd known the language, if there had been time to talk. He would have told them he wanted to harm no one. Not even the enemy. The enemy! A word, a crummy word. He *had* no enemies. He had wronged no one. If he'd known the language, he would have told them how he hated to see the villages burned. Hated to see the paddies trampled. How it made him angry and sad when . . . a million things, when women were frisked with free hands, when old men were made to drop their pants to be searched, when, in a ville called Thin Mau, Oscar and Rudy Chassler shot down ten dogs for the sport of it. Sad and stupid. Crazy. Mean-spirited and self-defeating and wrong. Wrong! He would have told them this, the kids especially. But not me, he would have told them. The others, maybe, but not me. Guilty perhaps of hanging on, of letting myself be dragged along, of falling victim to gravity and obligation and events, but not—not!—guilty of wrong intentions.

After the war, perhaps, he might return to Quang Ngai. Years and years afterward. Return to track down the girl with gold hoops through her ears. Bring along an interpreter. And then, with the war ended, history decided, he would explain to her why he had let himself go to war. Not because of strong convictions, but because he didn't know. He didn't know who was right, or what was right; he didn't know if it was a war of self-determination or self-destruction, outright aggression or national liberation; he didn't know which speeches to believe, which books, which politicians; he didn't know if nations would topple like dominoes or stand separate like trees; he didn't know who really started the war, or why, or when, or with what motives; he didn't know if it mattered; he saw sense in both sides of the debate, but he did not know where truth lay; he didn't know if Communist tyranny would prove worse in the long run than the tyrannies of Ky or Thieu or Khanh—he simply didn't know. And who did? Who really did? He couldn't make up his mind. Oh, he had read the newspapers and magazines. He wasn't stupid. He wasn't uninformed. He just didn't know if the war was right or wrong. And who did? Who really *knew*? So he went to the war for reasons beyond knowledge. Because he believed in law, and law told him to go. Because it was a democracy, after all, and because LBJ and the others had rightful claim to their offices. He went to the war because it was expected. Because not to go was to risk censure, and to bring embarrassment on his father and his town. Because, not knowing, he saw no reason to distrust those with more experience. Because he loved his country and, more than that, because he trusted it. Yes, he did. Oh, he would rather have fought with his father in France, knowing certain things certainly, but he couldn't choose his war, nobody could. Was this so banal? Was this so unprofound and stupid? He would look the little girl with gold earrings straight in the eye. He would tell her these things. He would ask her to see the matter his way. What would *she* have done? What would *anyone* have done, not knowing? And then he would ask the girl questions. What did she want? How did she see the war? What were her aims—peace, any peace, peace with dignity? Did she refuse to run for the same reasons he refused—obligation, family, the land, friends, home? And now? Now, war ended, what did she want? Peace and quiet? Peace and pride? Peace with mashed potatoes and Swiss steak and vegetables, a full-tabled peace, indoor plumbing, a peace with Oldsmobiles and Hondas and skyscrapers climbing from the fields, a peace of order and harmony and murals on public buildings? Were her dreams the dreams of ordinary men and women? Quality-of-life dreams? Material dreams? Did she want a long life? Did she want medicine when she was sick, food on the table and reserves in the pantry? Religious dreams? What? What did she *aim* for? If a wish were to be granted by the war's winning army—any wish— what would she choose? Yes! If LBJ and Ho were to rub their magic lanterns at war's end, saying, "Here is what it was good for, here is the fruit," what would Quang Ngai demand? Justice? What sort? Reparations? What kind? Answers? What were the questions: What did Quang Ngai want to know?

In September, Paul Berlin was called before the battalion promotion board.

"You'll be asked some questions," the first sergeant said. "Answer them honestly. Don't for Chrissake make it complicated—just good, honest answers. And get a fuckin' haircut."

It was a three-officer panel. They sat like squires behind a tin-topped table, two in sunglasses, the third in skintight tiger fatigues.

Saluting, reporting with his name and rank, Paul Berlin stood at attention until he was told to be seated.

"Berlin," said one of the officers in sunglasses. "That's a pretty fucked-up name, isn't it?"

Paul Berlin smiled and waited.

The officer licked his teeth. He was a plump, puffy-faced major with spotted skin. "No bull, that's got to be the weirdest name I ever run across. Don't sound American. You an American, soldier?"

"Yes, sir."

"Yeah? Then where'd you get such a screwy name?"

"I don't know, sir."

"Sheeet." The major looked at the captain in tiger fatigues. "You hear that? This trooper don't know where he got his own name. You ever promoted somebody who don't know how he got his own fuckin' name?"

"Maybe he forgot," said the captain in tiger fatigues.

"Amnesia?"

"Could be. Or maybe shell shock or something. Better ask again."

The major sucked his dentures halfway out of his mouth, frowned, then let the teeth slide back into place. "Can't hurt nothin'. Okay, soldier, one more time—where'd you find that name of yours?"

"Inherited it, sir. From my father."

"You crappin' me?"

"No, sir."

"And just where the hell'd he come up with it . . . your ol' man?"

"I guess from his father, sir. It came down the line sort of." Paul Berlin hesitated. It was hard to tell if the man was serious.

"You a Jewboy, soldier?"

"No, sir."

"A Kraut! Berlin . . . by jiminy, that's a Jerry name if I ever heard one!"

"I'm mostly Dutch."

"The hell, you say."

"Yes, sir."

"Balls!"

"Sir, it's not—"

"Where's Berlin?"

"Sir?"

The major leaned forward, planting his elbows carefully on the table. He looked deadly serious. "I asked where Berlin is. You heard of fuckin' Berlin, didn't you? Like in East Berlin, West Berlin?"

"Sure, sir. It's in Germany."

"Which one?"

"Which what, sir?"

The major moaned and leaned back. Beside him, indifferent to it all, the captain in tiger fatigues unwrapped a thin cigar and lit it with a kitchen match. Red acne covered his face like the measles. He winked quickly—maybe it wasn't even a wink—then gazed hard at a sheaf of papers. The third officer sat silently. He hadn't moved since the interview began.

"Look here," the major said. "I don't know if you're dumb or just stupid, but by God I aim to find out." He removed his sunglasses. Surprisingly, his eyes were almost jolly. "You're up for Spec Four, that right?"

"Yes, sir."

"You want it? The promotion?"

"Yes, sir, I do."

"Lots of responsibility."

Paul Berlin smiled. He couldn't help it.

"So we can't have shitheads leadin' men, can we? Takes some brains. You got brains, Berlin?"

"Yes, *sir*."

"You know what a condom is?"

Paul Berlin nodded.

"A condom," the major intoned solemnly, "is a skullcap for us swingin' dicks. Am I right?"

"Yes, sir."

"And to lead men you got to be a swingin' fuckin' dick."

"Right, sir."

"And is that you? You a swingin' dick, Berlin?"

"Yes, sir!"

"You got guts?"

"Yes, sir. I—"

"You 'fraid of gettin' zapped?"

"No, sir."

"Sheeet." The major grinned as if having scored an important victory. He used the tip of his pencil to pick a speck of food from between his teeth. "Dumb! Anybody not scared of gettin' his ass zapped is a dummy. You know what a dummy is?"

"Yes, sir"

"Spell it."

Paul Berlin spelled it.

The major rapped his pencil against the table, then glanced at his wristwatch. The captain in tiger fatigues was smoking with his eyes closed; the third officer, still silent, stared blankly ahead, arms folded tight against his chest.

"Okay," said the major, "we got a few standard-type questions for you. Just answer 'em truthfully, no bullshit. You don't know the answers, say so. One thing I can't stand is wishy-washy crap. Ready?"

"Yes, sir."

Pulling out a piece of yellow paper, the major put his pencil down and read slowly.

"How many stars we got in the flag?"

"Fifty," said Paul Berlin.

"How many stripes?"

"Thirteen."

"What's the muzzle velocity of a standard AR-15?"

"Two thousand feet a second."

"Who's Secretary of the Army?"

"Stanley Resor."

"Why we fightin' this war?"

"Sir?"

"I say, why we fightin' this fuckin'-ass war?"

"I don't—"

"To win it," said the third, silent officer. He did not move. His arms remained flat across his chest, his eyes blank. "We fight this war to win it, that's why."

"Yes, sir."

"Again," the major said. "Why we fightin' this war?"

"To win it, sir."

"You sure of that?"

"Positive, sir." His arms were hot. He tried to hold his chin level.

"Tell it loud, trooper: Why we fightin' this war?"

"To win it."

"Yeah, but I mean *why*?"

"Just to win it," Paul Berlin said softly. "That's all. To win it."

"You know that for a fact?"

"Yes, sir. A fact."

The third officer made a soft, humming sound of satisfaction. The major grinned at the captain in tiger fatigues.

"All right," said the major. His eyes twinkled. "Maybe you aren't so dumb as you let on. *Maybe*. We got one last question. This here's a cultural type matter . . . listen up close. What effect would the death of Ho Chi Minh have on the population of North Vietnam?"

"Sir?"

Reading slowly from his paper, the major repeated it. "What effect would the death of Ho Chi Minh have on the population of North Vietnam?"

Paul Berlin let his chin fall. He smiled.

"Reduce it by one, sir."

In Quang Ngai, they did not speak of politics. It wasn't taboo, or bad luck, it just wasn't talked about. Even when the Peace Talks bogged down in endless bickering over the shape and size of the bargaining table, the men in Alpha Company took it as another bad joke—silly and sad—and there was no serious discussion about it, no sustained outrage. Diplomacy and morality were beyond them. Hardly anyone cared. Not even Doc Peret, who loved a good debate. Not even Jim Pederson, who believed in virtue. This dim-sighted attitude enraged Frenchie Tucker. "My God," he'd sometimes moan in exasperation, speaking to Paul Berlin but aiming at everyone, "it's your *ass* they're negotiating. Your ass, my ass. . . . Do we live or die? That's the issue, by God, and you blockheads don't even talk about it. Not even a lousy *opinion*! Good Lord, doesn't it piss you off, all this Peace Talk crap? Round tables, square tables! Idiotic diplomatic etiquette, power plays, maneuvering! And here we sit, suckin' air while those mealy-mouthed sons of bitches can't even figure out what kind of table they're gonna sit at. Jesus!" But Frenchie's rage never caught on. Sometimes there were jokes, cynical and weary, but there was no serious discussion. No beliefs. They fought the war, but no one took sides.

They did not know even the simple things: a sense of victory, or satisfaction, or necessary sacrifice. They did not know the feeling of taking a place and keeping it, securing a village and then raising the flag and calling it a victory. No sense of order or momentum. No front, no rear, no trenches laid out in neat parallels. No Patton rushing for the Rhine, no beachheads to storm and win and hold for the duration. They did not have targets. They did not have a cause. They did not know if it was a war of ideology or economics or hegemony or spite. On a given day, they did not know where they were in Quang Ngai, or how being there might influence larger outcomes. They did not know the names of most villages. They did not know which villages were critical. They did not know strategies. They did not know the terms of the war, its architecture, the rules of fair play. When they took prisoners, which was rare, they did not know the questions to ask, whether to release a suspect or beat on him. They did not know how to feel. Whether, when seeing a dead Vietnamese, to be happy or sad or relieved; whether, in times of quiet, to be apprehensive or content; whether to engage the enemy or elude him. They did not know how to feel when they saw villages burning. Revenge? Loss? Peace of mind or anguish? They did not know. They knew the old myths about Quang Ngai—tales passed down from old-timer to newcomer—but they did not know which stories to believe. Magic, mystery, ghosts and incense, whispers in the dark, strange tongues and strange smells, uncertainties never articulated in war stories, emotion squandered on ignorance. They did not know good from evil.

June 9, 1970. Maj. Gen. Glenn D. Walker, commanding general of the 4th Infantry Division, is briefed at Fire Base Nutmeg. OFFICIAL U.S. ARMY PHOTO

CHAPTER 7

The Military

Above the battlefield, off the line, or back in the Pentagon, the war looked very different. There is an old cliché that generals are always fighting the last war, and in Vietnam there was something to this saying. Suffusing the writings of military leaders during the 1960s and 1970s is a quiet confidence that, with enough manpower and firepower, the Americans could defeat the Asian enemy (like the Japanese in 1945), or at least halt his aggression (as in Korea, 1950–1953). At the same time, the military establishment was quick to embrace new and sophisticated weaponry that made the Vietnam War unlike any other in history. The Americans used napalm, chemical defoliants, laser-guided "smart" bombs, and electronic troop-detection devices disguised as pieces of mud. Although these weapons took an enormous toll on the NLF and North Vietnamese, they were not enough to win the war.

Commentators vary in their assessments of the military's performance. Gen. Bruce Palmer, Jr., was intimately involved in military decision making during the 1960s, both in Washington and Vietnam. He is not uncritical of command practices, but, as he writes in the preface to the book from which this piece is excerpted, mistakes made in Vietnam were "honest mistakes, and many were mistakes only in hindsight." Loren Baritz, a historian, offers a more penetrating indictment of military practice. Unlike Palmer, Baritz places the performance of the military in the larger context of American culture and draws a sharp distinction between the behavior of the "grunts" on the ground and the officers living in relative safety some distance from the front. In the third reading, Michael Bilton and Kevin Sim reconstruct the terrible events in the hamlet of My Lai on the morning of March 16, 1968. The slaughter of innocents began early that day in the war.

22
Assessing the Military's Performance
BRUCE PALMER, JR.

American direction and conduct of the war and the operational performance of our armed forces, particularly during the 1962–1969 period, generally were professional and commendable. Performance continued to be of a high quality until the 1969–1970 period, when dissent at home began to be reflected in troop attitudes and conduct in Vietnam. From 1969 until the last U.S. combat troops left in August 1972, a decline in performance set in; the discovery of widespread drug use in Vietnam in the spring of 1970 signalled that more morale and disciplinary troubles lay ahead. The so-called "fraggings" of leaders that began in 1969–1970 were literally murderous indicators of poor morale and became a matter of deep concern.

Extremely adverse environmental conditions and very trying circumstances contributed to this decline in performance. Particularly galling to our forces in the field were the widely publicized statements of highly placed U.S. officials, including senators, against American involvement. Such statements were perceived to support the enemy and badly damaged the morale of our troops. The deteriorating climate at home also affected the conduct of American prisoners of war (mostly airmen) held in North Vietnamese POW camps; this was reflected in the increasing number of men who were accused of collaborating with the enemy in the 1969–1971 period, as compared to the very few during the earlier years of the war.

For the ground combat troops, Vietnam was a light infantry war of small units, mostly rifle platoons and companies, rarely of formations larger than a battalion. The Army tailored its basic fighting units of infantry and direct support artillery to the terrain and the peculiar nature of combat in Vietnam. Rifle companies, for example, were reduced in strength and lightened up by eliminating some of the heavier supporting weapons and equipment found in the normal organization. As a result, American infantry could move more swiftly and easily over the ground, and the tactical airmobility of the modern assault helicopter could be fully exploited.

Before Vietnam, the Army was primarily geared to fighting a highly sophisticated, mechanized war in Europe. Although a few relatively light divisions existed, most of the Army divisions were heavy armor or mechanized divisions either already deployed in Germany or earmarked for service in Europe. Thus, the Army's problem of adjusting to a much different kind of warfare in Vietnam on terrain far different from the European scene was a complex one. The Army had to maintain a ready capability to fight in Europe even while conducting a major war in Vietnam. The questions of priorities between the two theaters were never answered satisfactorily.

The military helicopter truly came of age in Vietnam, where the Army, at times opposed by its sister services, never lost its faith in this remarkable instrument. Clearly the single most outstanding military innovation in the Vietnam War was the development and introduction into combat of the "chopper" in various forms—the troop-carrying assault helicopter, the helicopter gunship for escort and close fire support missions, the attack helicopter with a tank-killing capability, and the scout helicopter for performing classic but still essential cavalry missions.

The contribution of the Army's organic aviation arm, rotary and fixed wing, cannot be overstated. These aircraft were involved in practically every military function—

command and control, reconnaissance, firepower, mobility, medical evacuation, and supply, as well as utility missions of every conceivable description. But it was the airmobile divisions (1st Cavalry and 101st Airborne) and air cavalry squadrons that brought the airmobile concept to the pinnacle of its potential. In these units the helicopter literally substituted for ground vehicles of every kind and totally freed the fighting elements from the tyranny of surface obstacles to movement. "Owning" their own helicopters and possessing a field maintenance capability that could accompany the forward assault forces, these units gave the theater commander a "Sunday punch" of unequalled flexibility and versatility.

Army aviators were committed in combat in the early 1960s, providing aviation support to South Vietnamese troops and developing battle-tested airmobility tactics and techniques long before the first Army ground combat forces arrived on the scene. In Vietnam these pioneer flying men earned a permanent place among the Army's elite—the combat arms. These men and their wondrous flying machines are here to stay in the Army—they will more than pay their way on future battlefields.

Although it was essentially a light infantry war, armor played a valuable role and did it well. The 11th Armored Cavalry Regiment was the largest armor unit in Vietnam and performed a variety of important reconnaissance, security, and offensive combat missions. The regiment was often employed on independent missions with decisive results. Each Army division had its own organic armored cavalry squadron, and at least one of its infantry battalions was mechanized; that is, its infantry was normally transported in armored personnel carriers. Armored units fought numerous key battles in every corps tactical zone: their heavy firepower and high ground mobility were well known to and respected by the enemy. In the dry monsoon they could operate almost anywhere, penetrating some of the most rugged and densely covered enemy war zones and base areas in Vietnam and Cambodia.

Army field artillery performed extremely well in Vietnam. In the American artillery system the ubiquitous forward observer, accompanying his supported infantry rifle company wherever it moves, is the key to the optimum functioning of the entire system. Despite the unusual terrain encountered—thick jungle foliage, rugged mountains, and land like the Mekong Delta, so flat and unvarying that determining troop positions was especially difficult—our forward observers performed effectively. Quick response was often a problem when operating near populated areas because of the necessity to make checks and even double checks to insure safety and accuracy. On the other hand, in a situation such as the defense of Khe Sanh, rounds were on the way in forty seconds after fire was requested.

Vietnam also brought out the need for fire support coordinators in modern battle, even in counterinsurgency situations, because of the proliferation of weapons systems available to support ground troops. The high density of aircraft in the battle area—Air Force, Marine, and Army—further complicated fire coordination. Overlapping control of airspace brought on by the legitimate claims of each service to control the use of airspace, required by its forces, was often a potential problem. Nevertheless overall fire support coordinators in Vietnam performed generally in an outstanding manner.

At Khe Sanh, the Air Force (that is, MACV's [Military Assistance Command, Vietnam] component air command, the 7th Air Force) was designated as the overall manager of airspace, and although the Marine Corps objected vehemently to the arrangement, it worked well. Indeed, the close and skillful coordination of Marine light artillery fires, Army long-range (175 mm) artillery fires, Air Force B-52 strikes, and Air Force and Marine tactical air strikes resulted in devastating casualties among attacking enemy troops.

The most common military term, and certainly one of the major tactical innovations, to come out of the Vietnam War was the "fire support base," or simply "fire base." The fire base was not just a defensive position but also the firepower element integral to any offensive effort. The concept developed partly because of the vulnerability of artillery firing batteries in unsecured areas to close-in mass enemy assault and hence the need to protect them with infantry. Thus, a position jointly occupied by supporting artillery and defending infantry became known as a fire base. Normally the fire base was also the location of the forward command post of the infantry battalion conducting operations in the area and providing for the defense of the base. This arrangement insured that the artillery firing units would always be effective, day or night, when called upon to support offensive operations with indirect fire. Infantry and artillery units located on a fire base came in close, intimate contact with each other, and when the fire base was attacked infantrymen and artillerymen soon learned to value highly the mutual support they could give each other. There were many variations of fire bases according to their location, the ground available for defense, the units and weapons involved, and the like. In short, the organization of a fire base reflected the flexibility and ingenuity of the American soldier and his leaders.

Battalion, brigade, and division commanders generally showed considerable professional skill in maneuvering their units and employing their combined arms. The 4th Infantry Division, for example, operating in the vast Kontum-Pleiku plateau region of the Highlands, time and again outwitted, outmaneuvered, and outfought its NVA foes despite the latter's inherent advantages—the enemy's ability to decide when to leave the sanctuary of Cambodia, where to cross the border, and what objectives to attack in South Vietnam.

Having addressed the performance of U.S. troops in action, I would be very remiss if I did not include at least a brief word about the selfless service of our advisers. Their performance—Army, Navy, Air Force, and Marine—generally was outstanding throughout the war, from the earliest days in the 1950s to the end. The great majority were U.S. Army officers and NCOs who served from the palace level to the ARVN battalion and the district/subdistrict level in the field. As ARVN advisers, they shared the hardships and dangers of infantry combat; as CORDS advisers, the equally risky and austere environment of a South Vietnamese district chief in a Viet Cong-infested area; and as Special Forces advisers, the lonely, perilous life in a CIDG [Civilian Irregular Defense Group] camp on the border. In the vast majority of cases they never complained, asked for very little, and literally gave their all for their South Vietnamese counterparts. The American people should be very proud of them.

These comments on the performance of our ground forces have been made basically with the U.S. Army in mind. Marine and Army ground combat elements, because of the commonality of their primary task—combat on the ground—have many similar interests, characteristics, organizational patterns, and operational modes. Recognizing that comparisons can be odious, and usually are, I hesitate to make any. Nevertheless, having had some close experience with U.S. Marines in various operational theaters in the past, I will venture one major observation, a difference between the Marine Corps and the Army that I have found striking. Marines traditionally place far more responsibility and authority on their noncommissioned officer corps. Inherently this is a sound principle, and I fault the Army for the converse—not giving NCOs sufficient authority and responsibility, and instead putting too great a load on company grade officers. But as a result of this Marine emphasis on NCOs, I have repeatedly noted two general shortcomings—inadequate supervision of NCOs by the Marine officer corps, and marine officers, especially the more senior ones, not always knowing what is going on at the troop level and consequently not taking adequate care of their men.

The offensive air war, controlled by CINCPAC [Commander-in-Chief, Pacific] more or less independently of the war in South Vietnam conducted by COMUSMACV [U.S. Commander, MACV], was conducted by and large in a very commendable manner. These air operations consisted of two different but concurrent campaigns—the offensive against North Vietnam itself, and the interdiction campaign along inland and coastal routes in North Vietnam and inland routes through the panhandle of Laos.

The two air campaigns, frequently overlapping in a geographical sense, were conducted primarily by the land-based aircraft of the 7th U.S. Air Force located in South Vietnam and Thailand, and by U.S. Navy carrier-based aircraft located in the South China Sea. CINCPAC assigned to MACV the responsibility for air operations in Laos, basically an interdiction mission; MACV in turn delegated control of these operations to MACV's air component, 7th Air Force. But for air strikes against North Vietnam, CINCPAC decentralized operations to the Pacific Air Forces and the Pacific Fleet, coordinating their operations principally by geographic assignment of targets, the Navy taking targets generally more accessible by attack from the sea, and the Air Force taking targets further inland. But true unity of air operations against North Vietnam was never fully achieved; B-52 operations in the region, for example, remained under the control of SAC [Strategic Air Command] throughout the war.

CINCPAC's geographic assignment of targets nevertheless worked well primarily because it avoided the inherently far more difficult task of coordinating the operations of aircraft from two different services. Such coordination would have been quite difficult because the Navy and the Air Force have different doctrine and operating procedures, their communications systems and equipment are different, and they do not normally train and operate together. These are basic facts of life which are all too often overlooked by ardent proponents of joint operations.

Combat aircraft pilots and crews performed exceptionally well under very tough conditions. As I have already observed, enemy air defenses were the heaviest and most formidable ever encountered by our air and naval forces in history. The advent of the "smart bomb" in later stages of the war was a great boon, but the losses of U.S. aircraft and crews continued to be heavy. Adverse weather and rugged terrain were also major handicaps. Finally, our incredibly complicated rules of engagement, which varied from country to country and even from area to area, were often too much for pilots to handle. These rules, imposed by the U.S. government, were simply unreasonable for men flying at 500 knots, trying to stay alive and yet close on their targets. Near the end of American involvement, when Chinese territory was unintentionally violated by our aircraft, the Chinese seemed to understand the problem better than our own statesmen.

One lesson that seems rather apparent has emerged from these operations. Sustained air operations during a long, difficult war are more readily conducted by land-based aircraft with their land-based support, a system designed for the long haul. Carrier-based aircraft and their carriers, on the other hand, are not designed to remain on station for prolonged periods. As a result, our carrier task groups took a terrific beating and fell far behind in their ship overhaul schedules. The impact of this extraordinary strain is felt even today [early 1970s] in the Navy.

In terms of tactical air support in South Vietnam, Army-Air Force relations were close, cordial, and mutually satisfying, and the Air Force's performance was generally outstanding. Emergency tactical air support was available on short notice, day or night, in almost any kind of weather. B-52 support was more than impressive—when a B-52 saturation attack occurred, the ground nearby literally shook and our own troops well understood why the enemy was terrified. Aerial resupply reached new levels of reliability, accuracy, and volume in Vietnam. Various parachute drop techniques, including low-level parachute extraction, were extensively used and successfully demonstrated. Medical air evacuation was also well executed.

Organic Marine aviation support of their own Marine forces on the ground was likewise outstanding. The Marine system, whereby the Marine division commander has full control of the Marine Air Wing associated with his division, works well for their purposes. The only area where the Marines seemed to come up short lay in airmobility, that is, the exploitation of the helicopter's unique capabilities. Because of the relatively larger size of their assault helicopters (compared to the Army's squad-carrying-sized "Huey") and their centralized control of helicopters under the Air Wing commander, the Marines, in my opinion, did not fully achieve the tactical advantages of integrated airmobility.

The overall control of air operations involving more than one service caused a major problem only once in South Vietnam—during the siege of Khe Sanh in western I CTZ [Corps Tactical Zone] in the winter of 1968. General William Momyer, commanding the 7th Air Force, insisted that his headquarters, under the overall command of General Westmoreland, be assigned the responsibility, with commensurate authority, for controlling all air operations, regardless of the services involved, in support of the besieged Marines at Khe Sanh. The Marines strongly objected and carried their case through Marine channels all the way to the JCS. Westmoreland agreed with and supported Momyer's position, which the JCS carefully considered and finally approved. But the matter left some bitterness in the Marines, who understandably resist any attempt to interpose external control between their ground and supporting air elements.

Very few joint Army-Air Force operations, other than normal tactical air support missions, were undertaken in Vietnam. Only one sizable airborne (parachute assault) operation was conducted, but it was not of major consequence. Nevertheless, countless American paratroopers served with distinction in practically every combat unit in Vietnam, although the nature of the war was not conducive to airborne operations.

But there was one major joint operation, the Son Tay POW camp raid of November 1970. The main effort of this raid was made by a joint Army-Air Force task force, with the Air Force providing large troop-carrying helicopters, air cover, and air support, and the Army providing the assault ground force. The Navy and Marines flew major air attacks in other areas of North Vietnam as diversionary efforts designed to deceive the enemy as to the true location, direction, and nature of the main attack. The plan worked well, the enemy was confused, and surprise was achieved. Unfortunately, our POWs had been removed from the camp before the operation was launched and the mission was unsuccessful—an intelligence failure but an operational success.

This raid also raised the morale of the families of our prisoners of war and of our men missing in action. These gallant relatives never gave up hope and very properly kept the pressure on the State and Defense departments to do everything humanly possible to determine the status of their men. Fortunately, too, the raid resulted in noticeably improved treatment of our POWs in North Vietnam. Unfortunately, the situation of many of our men lost, missing, or captured in Laos, Cambodia, and South Vietnam has never been satisfactorily established, and the agony of uncertainty about the fate of their loved ones continues in some American families to this day.

But even sustained, outstanding operational performance can go for naught if the intelligence that guides operations and generates the thrust of operational efforts is lacking in quality. Accordingly, let us turn to a brief examination of the performance of American intelligence at the national level as well as in the theater of operations.

For the president and other U.S. policymakers in Washington, there was a plethora of intelligence studies and estimates about the Vietnam War originating from a wide variety of official organizations, ranging from the U.S. Embassy, the CIA station chief, and HQ MACV in Saigon, as well as HQ CINCPAC in Honolulu, to the proliferation of intelligence agencies in Washington. Most of the Washington-level wartime studies were produced by a single agency, some by two agencies working together, and only relatively few by the whole intelligence community.

The Washington players making up the community were: (1) The director of Central Intelligence (DCI), his Central Intelligence Agency, and the now-defunct Board of National Estimates, reporting through the DCI to the president and the National Security Council. (2) From the Pentagon, the Defense Intelligence Agency (DIA), responsible to the secretary of defense and the JCS; and the intelligence organizations of the services, each reporting to its own service chief. (3) From the Department of State, the Bureau of Intelligence and Research (INR), responsible to the secretary of state. And (4) the cryptological community, consisting of the National Security Agency (NSA), responsible to the secretary of defense; and the service security agencies each reporting to its service chief.

The DCI presided over this basically loose confederation and chaired the U.S. Intelligence Board, now known as the National Foreign Intelligence Board, whose principal members are the heads of the CIA, DIA, INR, and NSA. Obviously, the DCI's authority over this board is somewhat attenuated, inasmuch as three of the four other principals are responsible to a cabinet member.

In wartime the theater commander, usually a unified commander, normally assumes control of all intelligence assets, including the CIAs, in his area of responsibility. The Vietnam War was a unique case, however, and this wartime takeover was not invoked. So the CIA station chief in Saigon continued his regular peacetime function as the senior intelligence adviser to the U.S. ambassador. As a consequence, unity of U.S. intelligence effort was not achieved in Vietnam and, despite coordination and cooperation between the CIA and the MACV J-2, undesirable duplication and competition did take place. Unfortunately, this jurisdictional problem spilled over into combined U.S.-South Vietnamese intelligence activities, resulting in such unhelpful consequences as having separate CIA-South Vietnamese and MACV J-2-South Vietnamese interrogation centers operating in the same provincial and district capitals.

While the CIA station chief in Saigon, MACV, and CINCPAC naturally concentrated on the more immediate aspects of the conflict, the national-level intelligence organs focused on the longer-term strategic aspects. The latter included such matters as the assessment of opposing U.S./allied and North Vietnamese strategies; North Vietnamese perceptions of the U.S. war effort; the effectiveness of the U.S. air war against North Vietnam; North Vietnamese capacity to wage a prolonged war and their dependence on the Soviet Union and China; and the prospects for survival over the longer term of a free and independent South Vietnam.

During the earlier years of the direct American military involvement in Vietnam, up until the time of the enemy's Tet offensive of 1968, the military held the center of the intelligence stage. MACV, CINCPAC, and DIA were the dominant voices and had the ear of the president and his NSC staff. But beginning a few months after the start of the sustained American air offensive in March 1965, the CIA, at the request of Defense Secretary McNamara, played an active intelligence role, initially evaluating the effectiveness of U.S. air attacks against North Vietnam and later judging the progress of the war and the prospects of allied success. After Tet 1968 and the turn-about in the

Johnson administration's attitude toward the war, the intelligence clout in Washington shifted more in favor of the CIA.

On balance, the Agency did a good job in assessing the situation in Southeast Asia during the 1965–74 period. Its overall intelligence judgments were generally sound and its estimates were mostly on the mark. Several facts illustrate the truth of this statement. First, the Agency, in evaluating the effectiveness of U.S. air attacks, consistently concluded that the attacks did not reduce North Vietnamese logistic capabilities to sustain the war, that North Vietnam could afford to take the punishment, that Hanoi's will was not shaken, and that the material cost of the resulting damage to North Vietnam was simply passed on to the USSR and China, while Hanoi's constantly improving air defense system (provided by the USSR and China) inflicted rising air losses on the United States.

Second, with respect to North Vietnam's ability to wage a prolonged war, the Agency consistently estimated that Hanoi would continue to base its strategy on a war of attrition, since North Vietnam had the manpower base as well as an assured source of adequate arms and supplies to continue such a grinding war indefinitely, and that Hanoi's leaders believed they possessed more staying power than the United States and South Vietnam, and would ultimately prevail. Because of redundant land routes linking North Vietnam to China and the Soviet Union, the Agency did not judge North Vietnam to be vulnerable to a U.S. naval blockade.

Finally, as South Vietnam's fortunes waned and U.S. support faltered in late 1973 and in 1974, the Agency consistently warned that the South Vietnamese situation was becoming parlous and that the North Vietnamese would exploit their military advantage to gain their long-sought final victory. The Agency did not, however, anticipate that this victory would come as early as the spring of 1975. As South Vietnam's security posture deteriorated in 1975, especially after Hanoi's final offensive was launched early that year, the military situation on the ground became the preeminent factor in deciding the country's fate. Thereafter, overall strategic-political assessments of South Vietnam's longer-term viability were simply not possible.

One particularly complex and contentious problem plagued the intelligence community throughout the war—estimating enemy troop strength and determining the composition of his major units, the so-called order of battle. These are among the most difficult military intelligence judgments of all to make in wartime, especially in a people's war like Vietnam in which regular troops (so-called main force and local force units), their administrative and logistic support forces, part-time guerrillas and militia, and political cadres are often intermingled. Enemy ground combat casualties are particularly difficult to estimate as a result of battles involving civilians, regular soldiers, and local guerrillas and militiamen.

The CIA's estimates were probably more accurate overall than MACV's. As time went by, CIA and MACV estimates moved much closer together in the category of regular combat units but were never fully reconciled with respect to guerrilla strengths. In this latter category, the differences were partly conceptual, partly philosophical, and partly methodological. Basically, MACV held to a conservative approach in recognizing military capabilities that resulted in an underestimation of guerrilla forces. Likewise, MACV's conservative approach to estimates of enemy units and personnel infiltrating from the North led to a time lag in MACV's acceptance of new infiltrators, and hence higher total infiltration figures.

Estimating enemy casualties—the "body count" syndrome—is not a new problem; it has been a complicating factor in past wars. More than one example of highly exaggerated body counts resulting in inflated enemy loss estimates can be found in the

American campaign records of World War II and the Korean War. In both Korea and Vietnam, the United States was faced with the very different and complex problems of fighting a major war but in a limited manner—limited in terms of objectives, geography, means employed, and resources committed. In both wars there was no territorial objective other than to defend the status quo ante; thus it was not possible to demonstrate or assess progress in terms of territory gained and held. Leaders quite naturally turned to other indicators of how the war was going, among them the number of enemy battle casualties. At one point in the Korean War, the explicit, if crudely stated, military objective was to kill as many Chinese ("Chinks") as possible. In Vietnam a similar objective of attriting enemy forces was present. Moreover, the difficulty of distinguishing regular and irregular forces from noncombatants tended to break down normal inhibitions against causing civilian casualties. Such incentives were invitations for fighting units to exaggerate claims of "enemy" killed. Unfortunately, a few small-unit commanders condoned or even encouraged padded reports, further exacerbating the "body count" syndrome.

Higher headquarters, nonetheless, have ways to judge the validity of unit claims; for example, by weighing the intensity of the fighting by comparing friendly and enemy casualties and by noting the number of weapons captured in comparison with the number of enemy reported killed. Comparatively low friendly casualties and few enemy weapons captured should arouse the suspicions of the higher headquarters and call for a check on the intensity of fighting when a high "body count" is reported.

In Vietnam, especially in the Delta, some units were inclined to exaggerate claims of enemy killed and were careless about avoiding civilian casualties. But by and large the great majority of American units tried to submit factual reports based on actual evidence rather than estimations, and conscientiously sought to limit casualties among noncombatants. In addition, field force headquarters and HQ MACV, whenever feasible, checked the overall circumstances of the battle reported before accepting the enemy casualty figures submitted.

Even when heavy enemy battle losses are substantiated, one must be careful not to judge their psychological effect on the enemy on the basis of occidental values. Indeed, American military professionals who fought in the Pacific in World War II or in Korea became acutely aware of differing oriental values with respect to human life, and knew the pitfalls of putting too much store in the impact of heavy casualties on the morale of a determined foe or on the will of a ruthless totalitarian government.

In Vietnam, the factual evidence concerning the enemy's manpower capacity seemed pretty clear to our leaders in the field. We realized that the enemy decided where and when he would do battle and could therefore control his casualty rate. We repeatedly saw specific, identified enemy fighting units decimated in combat only to return a few months later from their base sanctuaries at full strength, ready to fight again. These facts, coupled with what theater intelligence told us about the rate of infiltration of enemy troop units and replacements down the Ho Chi Minh Trail, timed with planned enemy "high points" (offensives), constituted positive indications that the enemy could fight this kind of war indefinitely. Raw manpower did not seem to be a limitation. Moreover, frightful enemy casualties, which, had they been American would have had major repercussions in our society, seemed to have no effect on the leadership in Hanoi or on the North Vietnamese people. Thus, one might conclude with some reason that U.S. officials should not have been misled by faulty estimates of enemy losses and of the enemy's effective troop strength.

One might well ask why senior U.S. policymakers in Washington, with the exception of Defense Secretary McNamara, did not pay more attention to CIA views and to the disagreements within the intelligence community. There is no simple answer to this complex question. As already indicated, given the nature of the intelligence community it would be unreasonable to expect unanimous views, especially when matters of great import are involved. Moreover, the exposure of differing views, particularly on major issues, can be considered a strength rather than a weakness, because to paper over or submerge them runs the risk of badly misleading policymakers. International relations are difficult to judge even in normal times, but when examining them through the fog of war, policymakers are entitled to know what honest differences of opinion may exist before making judgments. With respect to Vietnam, the head of the CIA was up against a formidable array of senior policymakers, including the president, the secretary of state, the secretary of defense, the chairman of the JCS, and the national security adviser to the president—all strong personalities who knew how to exercise the clout of their respective offices. It is not surprising then that the director of Central Intelligence, Richard Helms (from 30 June 1966 to 2 February 1973), who served under both Presidents Johnson and Nixon, was reportedly content to let the responsible policy officials make up their own minds. No doubt Helms was also determined to protect and preserve the traditional objectivity of intelligence vis-a-vis policy. But, as alluded to above, McNamara was not entirely satisfied with his intelligence from the Defense Department and beginning in late 1965 relied more and more on the CIA for what he believed were more objective and accurate intelligence judgments.

At this point, several comments in the realm of tactics and techniques should be underscored. First, let us look at the matter of surprise. Whether the North Vietnamese achieved truly strategic surprise in an overall political-military sense during the Vietnam War is arguable. But unquestionably they achieved surprise in a tactical sense in two notable cases before the January 1973 cease-fire. These were their Tet offensive of 1968 and their March 1972 "Easter" offensive across the eastern part of the DMZ. The NVA also achieved major tactical surprise after the cease-fire when it attacked Ban Me Thuot in II CTZ in March 1975 at the beginning of the final offensive against South Vietnam.

Examining the question of why this came about, one must conclude that a major factor was our overreliance on signal intelligence, from which we derived most of our strategic and tactical information pertaining to Southeast Asia. This kind of intelligence can be very misleading and is also subject to manipulation by the enemy. It is more suitable for judgments of a longer-term strategic nature, and is not always reliable or appropriate for short-term tactical purposes. Identifying and, by direction-finding techniques, locating a radio transmitter belonging to a specific NVA regiment, for example, does not necessarily mean that the regiment is there too, although it is a good indication that elements of the regiment are in the vicinity. But in actuality, a small forward communications detachment might be the only element of the regiment present. One obvious conclusion is that we did not put enough emphasis on direct human sources of intelligence, as opposed to those of the electronic variety.

We were also weak in counterintelligence, that is, an organized, disciplined effort to deny information about our own plans, operations, and other military matters to the enemy. U.S. communications security, for example, was not satisfactory in Southeast Asia; we never achieved even a reasonably good posture. Because of our careless habits, talking in clear (uncoded) text over insecure phone or voice radio, and our frequent failure to use truly secure codes, the enemy all too often knew our planned moves well in advance, even strikes by the Strategic Air Command, and took action to alert their units and people. As a consequence we deprived ourselves of numerous opportunities to surprise the enemy, a prized advantage.

At times we used more military force than was called for by the situation, especially when fighting near or in populated areas. Since heavy firepower and area-type weapons, such as tactical air support, artillery, and mortars, are not discriminating enough, their use risks civilian casualties and material damage which can be self-defeating in pacification efforts. Unobserved "H & I" (harassing and interdiction) artillery fire and air strikes, often based on dubious intelligence reports, were at times directed into areas (sometimes designated by South Vietnamese officials as "free fire zones") believed to be occupied only by enemy forces. This practice was not really effective militarily and was generally a waste of ammunition. Moreover, it ran the unnecessary risk of inflicting casualties on civilians and being counterproductive politically and psychologically, whether the people concerned were helping the enemy or not.

Related to the foregoing, American and South Vietnamese troops during the period when U.S. troops were still present in strength (1966–71) often became too accustomed to an abundance of externally provided heavy firepower and neglected their own organic capabilities that were more discriminating. This habit can also result in less capable infantry troops who come to rely on massive externally provided firepower rather than on the skillful use of fire and maneuver on their own.

In later years (1971–75), however, after most U.S. ground forces had been withdrawn, massive U.S. airpower was needed to make up for South Vietnam's principal shortcomings: the lack of enough forces overall (in particular armor and artillery), an inadequate strategic reserve, and an inability to shift forces from one region to another. After the cease-fire in January 1973, when U.S. airpower was no longer available, a new situation existed wherein the South Vietnamese simply lacked enough airpower, armor, and larger caliber artillery of their own to handle the numerous large, modern NVA formations arrayed against them.

The helicopter can be both an asset and liability. This is a costly resource requiring considerable logistic and maintenance support that must be used wisely. Airmobile operations require tactical skill and intensive training by both aviation and infantry elements; a poorly conducted operation can be disastrous. U.S. and allied forces at times became too heavily dependent on helicopter support. The "chopper" is a versatile machine which accords great advantages of mobility, logistic support, fire support, and medical evacuation. But there is still no substitute for lean, tough troops who can march long distances on foot and can survive with minimum support. The availability of the helicopter makes it too easy to overfly trouble on the ground or to withdraw troops from difficult positions. The latter action in particular can undermine the tenacity and willingness of troops to fight to the finish that must characterize first-class infantry.

The helicopter also allows senior officials to visit their people operating on the ground more readily, but this is a double-edged sword. It can lead to oversupervision of junior officials and can make senior leaders believe they know more about the situation on the ground than they actually do.

Logistic support of American forces was generally outstanding. Americans tend to be profligate, however, and our armed forces are no exception. Amassing huge quantities of all kinds of supplies in Vietnam on the grounds that supply lines might be interrupted was an example of overly cautious logistic planning. Similarly, administrative support and base facilities were too comfortable for some American headquarters and personnel in Vietnam. This had bad psychological effects, set a poor example for our own fighting soldiers as well as those of our allies, and lent an air of unreality at times to the American military presence. A more spartan existence would have been better for all.

Overall, our troops had little, if anything, to complain about. Communications support, logistic support of all kinds, medical care which made miracles seem commonplace, and engineer support—all without exception were outstanding. Even the military police earned the respect if not affection of the "GI" in Vietnam. Nevertheless, a more efficient logistic system could have conserved precious resources without hurting overall troop performance.

The Army's most serious problems were in the manpower and personnel area. Basically they stemmed from the failure to mobilize and the decision to hold to a one-year tour in Vietnam. Without at least a partial mobilization the Army was denied the use of the trained, experienced units and personnel present in the National Guard and organized reserves. This meant that, as the Army expanded from roughly 950,000 in 1964 to about 1,550,000 in 1968 to meet the requirements of Vietnam, the additional men and women entering the service were mostly very young, untrained, and inexperienced, resulting in the dilution of overall experience in the Army, particularly in the leadership ranks, the officers and noncommissioned officers. The failure to mobilize or to declare an emergency also meant that personnel would flow in and out of the armed forces on a peacetime basis rather than being held in the service for the duration of the emergency. Thus, draftees conscripted for two years could serve at the most about sixteen months overseas. This factor, coupled with a judgment that all personnel (career and noncareer) serving in Vietnam would perform better if on a known, fixed tour, led to the one-year rotation policy, a very bad mistake in my view. Finally, as its troop strength built up in Vietnam, the Army reached the point at which almost as many soldiers (about 725,000) were serving overseas as in the continental United States (about 825,000). Of those overseas, more than half were serving in Vietnam and Korea and had to be replaced every year. The number of replacements required in Vietnam steadily grew, of course, as the fighting intensified and battle losses and noncombat casualties rose. Moreover, about 250,000 soldiers in the United States (almost one-third of the total on duty there) were undergoing basic training and were not available for assignment to units.

For the Army the overall simple arithmetic was that its so-called sustaining rotation base in the continental United States was not large enough to furnish the large number of trained replacements required each year for Vietnam and Korea, to maintain the forces in Europe on a three-year tour, and to give career soldiers much of a breathing spell between repetitive tours in Vietnam. The length of the tour in Europe had to be progressively shortened and in the end the proud, combat-ready Seventh Army ceased to be a field army and became a large training and replacement depot for Vietnam. For political reasons ("guns and butter" and the demands of "The Great Society"), Defense Secretary McNamara would not recognize the legitimate manpower shortfalls of the Army and disapproved Army requests for increases in its authorized strength to meet worldwide demands. The principal cumulative effects of these misguided policies on the Army's posture in Vietnam are discussed below.

Although new units, with very few exceptions, arrived in Vietnam with a reasonably high level of unit proficiency, and incoming replacement personnel likewise generally possessed the required individual skills, the problem was to maintain unit efficiency and cohesion, and develop teamwork in the face of a high personnel turnover rate. Because of battle casualties, injuries, sickness, and other personnel losses, and the steady loss of soldiers returning home at the end of their one-year tour, the average rifle company, for example, became an entirely different outfit in terms of individual men every nine or ten months.

Maintaining a high standard of leadership in Vietnam was another major problem. The Army simply was unable to provide an adequate replacement flow of leaders, officers, and NCOs with experience commensurate with their responsibilities. The one-year tour, as well as the failure to mobilize, stretched the experienced leadership available from career personnel very thin throughout the Army worldwide. Moreover, many career and noncommissioned officers, after completing two or three tours in Vietnam and coming under increasing pressure from their families, decided to retire, thus further increasing the loss of experience. The end result was a slow, steady deterioration of experienced leadership in Vietnam that hurt the continuity of our effort and eroded our dedication to assigned missions.

Without mobilization, the one-year rotation policy was logical for our two-year draftees. But the tour for the career officer and NCO should have been two to three years. Proponents of the one-year tour for careerists argued that the high tempo of combat operations and the severe, constant strain on leaders dictated the shorter tour in the combat zone. They pointed out that helicopter operations could keep troops in almost constant contact with the enemy and that combat units could be shifted suddenly from the relatively safe environment of a base camp into a hot fire fight in a matter of minutes. This is a telling point, but such a problem could have been alleviated by in-country rotation between combat jobs and more secure noncombat positions.

Vietnam uncovered a major deficiency in the training of American military personnel, both officer and enlisted. This weakness lay in the area of the Geneva Conventions and their applicability to unconventional, guerrilla warfare. Our armed forces did not do an effective job—either in the United States or in Southeast Asia—of orienting their uniformed personnel, particularly ground combat troops, to what they would face in this kind of war. As a result, our troops were not prepared for this ambiguous, complex type of warfare and did not fully understand how the internationally accepted rules of warfare applied to Vietnam. One can make the case that the tragic My Lai aberration largely stemmed from inadequate orientation and training on the Geneva Conventions, further aggravated by the scarcity of mature, experienced leadership among lower ranking American officers and noncommissioned officers. As a result of My Lai, while American soldiers were still in combat in Vietnam, the Army inaugurated a massive orientation program to correct this deficiency.

Having examined the performance of American forces, U.S. intelligence, some of our tactical and logistic shortcomings, and the serious weaknesses of our manpower system, we might well ask whether any significant improvements in U.S. performance would have made any difference in the outcome. The answer is probably "no." The war was lost primarily at strategic, diplomatic, and domestic political levels, although the final defeat of South Vietnamese forces on the ground was more tactical and military in nature. Nevertheless, we American military professionals have much to learn from the tragic experience of Vietnam, because heeding those lessons could mean the difference between winning and losing in a future conflict.

23
Military Mismanagement
LOREN BARITZ

The moral decay and increasing incompetence of the army's senior officers in Vietnam was minimally caused by personal failures of individuals. . . . The corruption in Vietnam was systemic and was caused by procedures within the army that had been borrowed from other American bureaucratic institutions, primarily industry.

When the army adopted the "up or out" model of personnel management soon after World War II, it assumed that if an employee is not promotable, he is not employable. That meant that individuals with long and useful experience, who had found their right rung on the bureaucratic ladder, could not be retained. Up or out always devalues experience and always demands change at the price of stability. Americans seem unable to imagine an individual being satisfied by doing a job for which he is suited. We insist that job advancement must be perpetual. This constant upward swimming produced the bends, maybe not for the individuals concerned, but for the army as an institution.

Although the industrial bureaucratization of the army began in the 1940s, the extent of its corrosive damage was first made undeniable in Vietnam. What had happened was that a system of rewards was imposed on the military that changed the senior officer from a military leader into a bureaucratic manager. Many senior officers in other times and places led their men into battle, shared their risks, and were respected if not loved. Vietnam proved that men cannot be "managed" into battle.

Why should a bureaucrat risk his life to manage his men? When the code of the military was replaced with that of the bureaucracy, personal risk became not only meaningless, but stupid. If the point was promotion, not victory, risk was, as they say, counterproductive. The details of the army's definition of career management assaulted military logic, morale, and honor. The My Lai slaughter was a consequence of this deformation.

The bureaucratization of the army led to a definition of officers as personnel managers and troops as workers. It was not clear why the "workers" should have risked their lives to follow the orders of the "boss" who was not at risk himself. This sort of corruption invariably starts at the top, with the big boss. In 1966, General [William] Westmoreland reported in unashamed industrial language and with apparent pride, "[My troops] work, and they work hard. It has been my policy that they're on the job seven days a week, working as many hours as required to get the job done."[1] Perhaps his bureaucratic instincts, as deep as any man's could be, had been reinforced by his stint at the Harvard Business School. Vice Admiral James B. Stockdale wrote that "our business school-oriented elite tried to manipulate rather than fight the Vietnam War."[2]

General Westmoreland was America's senior personnel manager in-country, and that is how he thought of himself. He reported to the National Press Club that by 1967 the armed forces of South Vietnam had made progress. The first reason for this good news was: "Career management for officers, particularly infantry officers, has been instituted." The second reason was: "Sound promotion procedures have been put into effect." As a consequence of these and other "improvements," he concluded, "the enemy's hopes are bankrupt."[3]

The peculiar swagger of Americans, as John Wayne personified it, had been changed from confidence born of competence and courage to confidence wrung from ignorance. Bureaucrats are planners, and they must always believe, or pretend very hard to believe, or at least insist they believe, in the effectiveness and wisdom of their plans. The result is the sort of arrogance that drains the oxygen from a room, that makes the bureaucrat-in-chief light-headed. For example, General Westmoreland had not one doubt: "We're going to out-guerrilla the guerrilla and out-ambush the ambush . . . because we're smarter, we have greater mobility and firepower, we have endurance and more to fight for. . . . And we've got more guts."[4]

It is written that one should know one's enemy, that pride precedes failure. The general had insulated himself from reality, was unable to hear criticism, and seemed quite pleased with himself. He was America's perfect manager of a war. As a result he was more interested in procedures and public relations than content. He wanted to engineer appearances, not substance. Every reporter who listened to his Saigon briefings understood that it was a shell game. Evidently, he himself had no idea that this was so.

Under the leadership of General Westmoreland and the rotating Chiefs of Staff, the military bureaucracy became so top-heavy that it lost its balance. There was a higher percentage of officers in the field during the Vietnam War than in other American wars, and higher than in the armies of other nations. At its peak the percentage of officers in Vietnam was almost double what it had been in World War II. In 1968, there were 110 generals in the field in Vietnam. In absolute terms there were about as many generals, admirals, colonels, and navy captains in Vietnam as there were at the height of World War II. There was a lower ratio of officer deaths than was true earlier and elsewhere. Of the seven generals who died, five lost their lives in their helicopters. There was a higher ratio of medals distributed to officers, especially as the combat began to wind down, than ever before.

Colonel John Donaldson's Vietnam career is illustrative. In 1968, he was given command of the Americal Division's 11th Brigade, which a few months earlier had sent Lieutenant Calley's platoon into My Lai. The colonel replaced Colonel Oran Henderson, who would be acquitted of the charge of a My Lai cover-up. In his first six months of command, Colonel Donaldson "earned" an "average of about one medal a week: two Distinguished Flying Crosses, two Silver Stars, a Bronze Star Medal for Valor, twenty Air Medals, a Soldier's Medal, and a Combat Infantryman Badge." He was soon promoted to brigadier general and won nine additional Air Medals and two Legions of Merit, and was transferred to the Pentagon as a strategist.[5] During the My Lai investigation it was thought that to protect his predecessors he had destroyed key documents needed by the investigators. He denied this. In 1971, he was the first American general charged with a war crime since about 1900. He was accused of "gook hunting," shooting Vietnamese from his helicopter. He was acquitted.

In 1962, military promotion decisions had been centralized under the Chiefs of Staff. Thereafter, the military became a bureaucratic promotion machine. Meanwhile, the grunts continued to slog through the paddies and jungles. Many of them knew that something was rotten. By 1967, combat troops made up 14 percent of the troops in Vietnam; in World War II it was 39 percent; 34 percent at the end of the Korean War; and, 29 percent in 1963.[6] Approximately 86 percent of the military in Vietnam was not assigned to combat. At the height of the buildup in 1968, when there were about 540,000 military personnel in Vietnam, 80,000 were assigned to combat. The rest, the other 460,000, constituted the grunts' enormous category of REMFs [rear echelon mother fuckers].

It is probably true that never before, in the military or anywhere, had bureaucratic officials so enthusiastically served their own interests to the detriment of the objective they were supposed to accomplish. The managerial corps finally lost to dedicated troops in black pajamas.

As the officers blamed the politicians, many grunts blamed the officers. Bruce Lawlor, a CIA case officer, knew what was happening: "The only thing the officers wanted to do was get their six months in command and then split back to the States and be promoted and go on to bigger and better things. It doesn't take long for the average guy out in the field to say, 'Fuck it!' "[7] Or, as another example, a colonel sent troops into action without telling them (to make sure they would not evade a fight) that they would encounter an enemy base camp. Herb Mock, an infantryman who walked point on that mission, later went to find the colonel: "You made us walk right into the ambush. That's a sorry goddamn thing to do. You ain't worth shit as an officer."[8] Herb Mock's best friend was killed in the ambush.

The army itself recognized that something was wrong. In 1970, General Westmoreland ordered the Army War College to conduct an analysis of the officer corps. The study was so damaging that he at first had it classified. What had happened, in the language of the Army War College study, was that, "careerism" in the officer corps had replaced the ethic of the officer. Careerism means that personal advancement replaces the desire to get the job done. In fact, the "job" *is* personal advancement. (This helps to explain the cheating scandals at the service academies.) Bureaucratic employees get paid to get promoted.

In April General Westmoreland ordered the commandant of the Army War College to study the moral and professional climate of the army. Although he did not believe that the army was suffering a "moral crisis," he directed the study to focus "on the state of discipline, integrity, morality, ethics, and professionalism in the Army."[9]

In the study's preface, Major General G. S. Eckhardt, Commandant, simply stated, "This study deals with the heart and soul of the Officer Corps of the Army."[10] The study involved interviewing about 420 above-average officers, an extensive questionnaire, and many group discussions. As a result, the study concluded that "prevailing institutional pressures" had created a divergence between the ideals and the current practices of the officers corps. "These pressures seem to stem from a combination of self-oriented, success-motivated actions, and a lack of professional skills on the part of middle and senior grade officers."[11] The officers participating in the study described the typical Vietnam commander: "an ambitious, transitory commander—marginally skilled in the complexities of his duties—engulfed in producing statistical results, fearful of personal failure, too busy to talk with or listen to his subordinates, and determined to submit acceptably optimistic reports which reflect faultless completion of a variety of tasks at the expense of the sweat and frustration of his subordinates."[12]

Many of the officers involved in the study agreed that the cause of this breakdown was that the army itself had "generated an environment"[13] that rewarded trivial and short-run accomplishments to the neglect of significant achievement and the longer-term health of the army. The cause was not the "permissive society"[14] at home, or the antiwar and antimilitary protests, but the army itself.

The study reported that junior officers were better officers than their own commanders, and that the younger men "were frustrated by the pressures of the system, disheartened by those seniors who sacrificed integrity on the altar of personal success, and impatient with what they perceived as preoccupation with insignificant statistics." A captain was quoted: "Many times a good soldier is treated unfairly by his superiors for maintaining high standards of professional military competence." A colonel said,

"Across the board the Officer Corps is lacking in their responsibilities of looking out for the welfare of subordinates."[15]

An important conclusion of the study was that moral failure and technical incompetence was closely connected. Incompetence seemed to come first and the need to cover it up created the thousand techniques for lying, passing the buck, and avoiding responsibility. The study acknowledged that such behavior was army-wide: "signing of false certificates; falsification of flight records; condoning of the unit thief or scrounger; acceptance by middle and upper grade officers of obviously distorted reports; falsification of . . . trips for self gain and the attendant travel pay; hiding of costs under various programs; hiding AWOLs by placing them on leave to satisfy commander's desire for 'Zero Defect' statistics."[16]

The army's emphasis on quantification (a disease it caught when Secretary McNamara sneezed) meant that success was defined only by what could be measured. This was partly caused by the computer craze and resulted in the application to the army of "the commercial ethic."[17] This contributed to two unfortunate consequences: ignoring characteristics that could not easily be expressed in numbers, such as leadership, and emphasizing activities that could be measured, such as "savings bond scores and the reenlistment rate."[18] Officers were promoted for doing well in these "programs," while they were not reprimanded for failures in areas that the computers could not be programmed to measure, such as duty, honor, country. One captain complained: "The fact that my leadership ability is judged by how many people in my company sign up for bonds or give to the United Fund or Red Cross disturbs me."[19] (One noncom told me that his superior in Vietnam always forced him to buy bonds, but encouraged him to cancel as soon as the good report went out.)

This definition of what mattered to the army as an institution suited the careerist officers who were in "the business" to make a good living. One captain described his battalion commander as a man who "had always his mission in mind and he went about performing that mission with the utmost proficiency. His mission was getting promoted."[20] A major exploded: "The only current decorations I admire are the DSC and the Medal of Honor, all others are tainted by too often being awarded to people who do not deserve them. . . . Duty, Honor, Country is becoming—me, my rater, my endorser, make do, to hell with it."[21] Another major was a little more relaxed: "My superior was a competent, professional, knowledgeable military officer that led by fear, would double-cross anyone to obtain a star, drank too much and lived openly by no moral code."[22] This "superior" was soon promoted and got his first star.

The Army War College study revealed how the officers derived bureaucratic lessons even from My Lai. Officers got into trouble at My Lai because they found no AK-47s, Soviet-made rifles carried by both the guerrillas and by the North's army; that made it difficult to claim that all the villagers were combatants. "This exposure to My Lai . . . it has driven some of the units to carry AK-47s around with them so that if they did kill someone they've got a weapon to produce with the body."[23]

When General Westmoreland read the study he proclaimed it a "masterpiece," and restricted its distribution to generals only. As a group they had quite substantial reservations about its conclusions. General Westmoreland did, however, write a number of letters to inform the officer corps that integrity was important. That was the most significant result of this remarkable study. Young Pentagon officers formed a group called GROWN: Get Rid of Westmoreland Now.

Vietnam was the only available war for upwardly mobile officers, and if they failed to get an assignment in Vietnam, called getting their ticket punched, their careers would be thwarted. This infected the officer corps from top to bottom, beginning even before the West Point cadets graduated. For example, James Lucian Truscott IV arrived at West Point in 1965, where he hoped to follow his family's tradition of soldiering:

> When I was 22 years old I was pretty well convinced from having officer after officer after officer—major, lieutenant colonel, full colonel—come and tell me, personally or in front of a class, "You've got to go to Vietnam and get your fucking ticket punched. The war sucks. It's full of it. It's a suck-ass war. We're not going to win it. We're not fighting it right, but go and do it." You know, "Duty, Honor, Country" had suddenly become "Self-Duty, Honor, Country."[24]

A year after he graduated from West Point, Mr. Truscott resigned his commission rather than go to Vietnam.

For the office warriors, Vietnam was a marvelous opportunity to get ahead in the world. According to marine General David Shoup, some of the generals and admirals hoped to deepen America's involvement in Vietnam to speed promotions.[25] But such motivation was not a sufficient reason to risk getting hurt or killed, or even to suffer through the war in more discomfort than was absolutely necessary.

Among the Vietnam generals he surveyed, Brigadier General Kinnard found that 87 percent believed that careerism was "somewhat of a problem" or "a serious problem."[26] Careerist officers would not take risks in combat or in their relations with their superiors. Risk could lead to error, and a single mistake noted on an officer's efficiency report could ruin his career. This produced an equivalence of error, from incorrect table manners at "the Club" to a failure of judgment in combat. An instructor at the Command and General Staff College, said this of the rating procedure: "The system demands perfection at every level—from potatoes to strategy. It whittles away at one's ethics."[27]

When every glitch, however petty, might end up as a black mark on the rating sheet, officers of course trained themselves to be passive, to keep quiet, and to worry more about pleasing those above them than those below. Carried to an extreme in Vietnam, the rating system produced an even conformity of thought, a religion of pleasing superiors, a very high price on dissent, and a comfortable tour for the three- and four-star generals who were not rated. Careerism inevitably forced officers to think of their subordinates as their most important resource for making them look good, to protect their "image" on paper.

Career management and sound promotion procedures, as General Westmoreland described them, motivated the bureaucratic colonels and generals who observed the war, if they observed it all, safe in their helicopter offices fifteen hundred feet above the danger. They claimed they needed to be in the air to see the bigger picture, so as not to lose perspective by the more limited horizons of the earthbound warriors. Sometimes this was true, but the grunts hated it. Whether it was necessary or not, the chopper always gave the officers an opportunity to have the desired combat experience without the risks of combat. The availability of helicopters meshed perfectly with the imperatives of ticket-punching. Field commanders, especially lieutenants and captains, resented it also, but for obvious reasons they were less outspoken. For the grunts, the appearance of the colonel's chopper was a reminder that they and not he might get blown away. He would not be late for the happy hour at the Club, while they would remain in the field with another meal of C-rats. It reinforced a class hatred that was, in its pervasiveness, probably unique to the Vietnam War. Mike Beamon, a navy anti-guerrilla scout—he called himself a terrorist—said it all: "I was more at war with the officers there than I was with the Viet Cong."[28]

The length of time an officer in Vietnam served in a combat assignment was not a matter of established military doctrine. It was a rule of thumb of the commanders in the field. Although there were exceptions, and although some officers served more than one tour, the expectation of a twelve-month tour, even for officers, set the outer limit of a combat assignment. In 1968, the systems analysts in the Office of the Secretary of Defense studied the length of time officers served in combat. They found that the typical combat command of a maneuver battalion or a rifle company was "surprisingly short."[29] More than half the battalion commanders, usually lieutenant colonels, were rotated out of combat command in less than six months. More than half the company commanders, usually captains, were relieved before they completed four months. One of the reasons for so short a command tour was reported in a secret document prepared in the Office of the Deputy Chief of Staff for Personnel in 1970: "Career personnel have greater opportunity for career development and progression. . . ."[30] With short assignments more officers could get their tickets punched.

After 1970, 2,500 lieutenant colonels each hoped to command one of the 100 battalions, 6,000 colonels wanted a command of one of the 75 brigades, and 200 major generals wanted to get one of the 13 divisions.[31] The competition for one of these assignments was fierce, and the office politicking was everywhere. As they got the right punches, the right assignments, the officers' careers flourished. Of the men who were considered for promotion to major, 93 percent succeeded, as did 77 percent to lieutenant colonel, and 50 percent to colonel. Colonel David Hackworth understood what was happening:

> We had all the assets to win this war we had half a million troops, unlimited amounts of money and the backing of the administration. No doubt we could have won if we'd had commanders who knew how to use these assets, instead of these amateurs, these ticket punchers, who run in for six months, a year, and don't even know what the hell it's all about.[32]

There were two important consequences of these short command assignments: Officers did get the "experience" required for their promotions; and the men under their command were killed in higher numbers because of their commanders' inexperience. The systems analysts discovered that a maneuver battalion under a commander with more than six months experience suffered only two thirds the battle deaths of battalions commanded by officers with less than six months of experience. The average command lasted 5.6 months. The analysts discovered that a battalion commander with less than six months experience lost an average of 2.5 men a month; those with more experience lost 1.6 men a month. In their technocratic, economistic, dehydrated view of the world, the analysts explained that "the rate of battle deaths is a measure of the cost of success." They wanted a "cheaper price."[33]

The analysts also found that the length of experience of a company commander reduced the battle deaths of his troops. The average command was just under four months. These officers were themselves killed at a higher rate than more experienced officers, a rate that rose in each of the first four months, and that dramatically dropped by two thirds in the fifth month, from which point it remained low and stable. In the first four months, about 4 percent of these officers were killed; afterward, 2.5 percent were killed. "This implies," the systems analysts concluded, "that a company commander could be left in office 6 more months, for a total of 10, without incurring an additional risk as great as that to which he was exposed during his first 4 months in command."[34] Nonetheless, they were "relieved" (perhaps in several senses of that word)

in four months so that another green commander could step onto the promotion esca-
lator, and two thirds of them were sent out of combat to staff positions. The typical
captain in Vietnam had three different "jobs" during his twelve-month tour in Vietnam. The companies commanded by officers with less than five months' experience
had an average of .8 killed in action each month; those with more than four months
lost .6 KIA, a drop of 25 percent.

As usual, the military was not delighted by the work of the Whiz Kids. As usual,
the military argued that the systems analysts did not understand war. The deputy chief
of staff for operations concluded, "Our commanders in the field can best judge the
length of time an officer should remain in command of a unit in combat."[35] The brass
on the spot had not "arbitrarily" set the average command assignments at six months
and four months. These periods of time were selected because "we know from experience that a commander begins to 'burn out' after a period in this hazardous and exact-
ing environment." After the typical time in command, and after burnout, "the commander
is not fighting his unit as hard as he did during the first few months of command when
he was full of snap, zest and aggressiveness and eager to destroy the enemy."[36]

The analysts were unimpressed by the Pentagon's argument. They claimed there
was "no data" to prove that commanders burn out. Their conclusion was ominous: "We
cannot prove its existence and we suspect that the present rotation policy may be based
more on considerations of providing a wide base of combat experience than on the
'burn out' factor."[37]

The military headquarters in Saigon obviously had to join this argument, to "re-
but" the analysts. MACV acknowledged that there was a "learning curve" for battle
commanders, contested the statistical reliability of the figures used, and insisted that
the analysts had failed to understand that battles vary in intensity. The analysts agreed
about varying intensity, but added that "regrettably, data are not available," presumably unavailable in Saigon as well as Washington. They did not believe this was a
serious point because their study covered so many areas of combat that differences
would cancel each other out. They agreed that more information would always be helpful
and might have produced different results. "But we doubt it. It was our view (and
MACV confirms this) that more experienced battalion commanders are more effective: on the average fewer of their men get killed in combat."[38]

The American military establishment took pride in its effective adoption of "sound
business practices." But, on the question of the duration of command, the military
borrowed from no one. There is no other institution that transfers its leaders before
they can learn their jobs. There is also no other institution in which the price of ignorance is the death of other people. One scholar compared the time in office between
military officers and business executives and found that military officers with less
than one year's experience was 46 percent of all officers; the comparable figure for
executives was 2 percent. Military officers with five or more years of experience were
6 percent of the total; 88 percent of business executives had that much experience.[39]
There were reasons why the military moved its people so quickly, but the development
of competence and the safety of the troops were not among them.

General Westmoreland uncharacteristically said, "It may be that I erred in Vietnam in insisting on a one-year tour of duty. . . ." But, as he reconsidered the possibility
of an error, he concluded that longer tours would have been "discrimination against
officers" and would have added to his difficulties in getting enough junior officers
from OCS and ROTC. Perhaps, he said, an eighteen-month tour would have been "a
workable compromise."[40] He did not mention the fate of the GIs.

Yet, every sane observer of the rotation system agreed that it interfered with conducting the war. The Army War College study of the careerism of officers cited the short tour as a major factor in the deformation of the code of officers. Careerism, it said, can be diminished "by building mutual trust and confidence, and loyalty that comes from being in one assignment long enough to be able to recover from mistakes; and to have genuine concern—as a practical matter—about the impact which expedient methods will have on the unit next year."[41] After questioning and interviewing hundreds of officers, this study pointed out that the army had not questioned its promotion policy "for some time," and had simply continued to make the assumption that moving officers through the wide variety of jobs required for promotion was a sound policy. "The implications of this assumption," the study said, "are so far-reaching that possibly no single personnel management concept—save that of the uninhibited quest for the unblemished record—has more impact on the future competence of the Officer Corps."[42]

Before a company commander learned his job he was sent elsewhere. Before an intelligence officer could establish all his contacts he was sent elsewhere. There was no way the military could learn from its experience. That is what John Paul Vann, a distinguished officer who had resigned in disgust from the military, meant when he said that America did not fight a ten-year war, but rather ten one-year wars. For the officers the spin was even faster. Experience obviously could not accumulate. Lessons could not be learned. It was not only a teenage war, but a war in which no one had time to become seasoned or wise. There was no institutional memory, and with every year's rotation, the war began anew, with staff trying to hold up "the old man" who always had the power of command.

It was thus a teenage war led by amateurs. The GIs did not complain, of course, about serving "only" one year, but some of them knew, as Thomas Bird, a grunt with the 1st Cavalry, admitted:

> Toward the end of my tour, when I started knowing what I was doing in the jungle and started knowing what to do under fire, it was just about time to go home. I'm going to be replaced by a guy who is as green as I was when I got here, and by the time he gets good at it he's going to be replaced by a guy who is green. It's no wonder we never got a foothold in the place.[43]

Keeping the war's score by counting bodies, an index imposed by Washington, was made to order for careerist officers. They could and did distinguish themselves by reporting more bodies than their competitors. One general later concluded that the body count was "gruesome—a ticket punching item."[44] Another said, "Many commanders resorted to false reports to prevent their own relief," that is, to prevent someone else from replacing them and getting ahead by filing more acceptable reports. Another general said, "I shudder to think how many of our soldiers were killed on a body-counting mission—what a waste."[45]

When a career depends on the reported height of a pile of bodies, several sorts of decay result. Once, when the men of Charlie Company engaged the enemy, their lieutenant called for a helicopter to evacuate the wounded. "To hell with the wounded, *get those gooks*,"[46] the lieutenant colonel radioed back from his helicopter above the action. The lieutenant turned to see his machine gunner firing at the commander's chopper.

Having instituted a process that rewarded cheating, the bureaucratic bosses simply denied that it could have happened. Most (61 percent) of the generals in Vietnam knew that the statistics were snake oil,[47] but none complained in public. They were wedded to the system. For example, in 1973, some of the majors at the army's Command and General Staff College at Leavenworth asked the commandant to permit a discussion of the ethics of officers in Vietnam. According to a reporter:

> One general was saying that he was right on top of things in his units, that no one would dare submit a falsified report there. A young major stood up and said, General, I was in your division, and I routinely submitted falsified reports. The General's response was, When you speak to a general officer, stand at attention.[48]

The most senior officers, "Old Bulls," then at Leavenworth rejected what they called this "moralistic streaking." It is an iron law of bureaucracy that the higher one is in the organization, the more optimistic one is. How could it be otherwise? If one is in charge, things must be working well. A corollary is that the more senior one is, the more one is subject to the disease of being hard-of-listening. This law and its corollary may also partly explain General Westmoreland's constant assurances that things were working out satisfactorily, and that a solution would come soon. It seems reasonably clear that he really believed his own crooning. It is extremely difficult for the chief administrative officer of an organization to think that someone else would have done a better job. The Old Bulls at Leavenworth were not different from senior supervisors in Saigon, Washington, or anywhere else where bureaucracy is a settled fact of life.

Some defenders of the bureaucratic army argue that the problem in Vietnam was caused by the disorganization of American society at the time. They say that the pool of men from which the military had to draw was inadequate for military purposes. The "permissive society," the availability and use of drugs, and, most of all, the collapse of respect for authority throughout American culture apparently produced some officers who were not up to the military's legitimate expectations of correct conduct. The conclusion to this argument is that something did go wrong in Vietnam, but it was the fault of American culture, not the military.

The most careful work on this subject was done by two former officers, Richard Gabriel and Paul Savage. They argue that it was the army itself, not permissive American society, that produced the Vietnam officers' conduct. They show that earlier armies had always enforced conduct separate from contemporary fashions. That is what the military must do, and formerly had done, because it is a unique institution. It cannot function if its style of command, leadership, and even management is responsive to changing social fashions. The necessary characteristics for an officer in combat has no useful civilian analogy. Combat is unique. The army must train soldiers to perform specific functions regardless of any set of social circumstances.

The Army War College study itself asserts that the failures were inside the military and not a result of any "defects" in American society. It also concluded that the antiwar movement had no discernible impact on the quality or motivation of "officer material." If the crisis was, and is, internal to the army, the solution must also be. Yet, those who rose to the most senior levels of military command were precisely the bureaucrats who benefited by the corruption. The army's own study, in stunning bureaucratic language, acknowledged that for this very reason, reform was unlikely: "The fact also that the leaders of the future are those who survived and excelled within the rules of the present system militates in part against any self-starting incremental return toward the practical application of ideal values."[49] That is to say, reform must and cannot be internal.

The grunts understood that they were endangered by the guerrillas, the regular army of North Vietnam, and their own temporary, rotating officers, in no particular order of threat. They knew that the home front did not support what they were doing. If no one cared about them, they could not care about the rules or established authority. Occasionally, around 1970, grunts would scribble UUUU on their helmets: the unwilling, led by the unqualified, doing the unnecessary, for the ungrateful. Other helmets proclaimed POWER TO THE PEOPLE, KILL A NONCOM FOR CHRIST or NO GOOK EVER CALLED ME NIGGER. It was finally as if all that they could believe and remember were pain and death. One young man from the Bronx, for example, was cited for heroism:

> They gave me a Bronze Star and they put me up for a Silver Star. But I said you can shove it up your ass. I threw all of the others away. The only thing I kept was the Purple Heart, because I still think I was wounded.[50]

A wound is the most intimate souvenir.

It cannot be surprising that the grunts found ways to resist corrupt officers in a war that could not be understood. Desertions, excluding AWOLs, in the army alone rose from 27,000 in 1967 to 76,634 in 1970, a rate increase of 21 per thousand to 52 per thousand.[51] The marines were even worse with 60 desertions per thousand.[52] According to the Department of Defense, the rate of desertion in Vietnam was higher than in either Korea or World War II, and the rate increased as the intensity of the fighting declined and absurdity increased. As President Nixon began withdrawing troops, many of the grunts remaining on the ground lost even more conviction about why they should stay and fight. The desertion rate from 1965 to 1971 increased by 468 percent.[53]

Fragging, defined as an attempt to murder by using a grenade, reached astonishing levels in Vietnam. It was usually a result of the fear and hatred felt by the workers toward their bosses. For example, marine Private Reginald Smith testified in a court-martial that his lieutenant was so slow in setting up a listening post that by the time he sent three marines out, the NLF was waiting and killed two of them. The troops were discussing the incompetence of this lieutenant just before he was killed by a fragmentation grenade.[54] It was frequently said that combat squads raised a bounty to be awarded to anyone who would "waste" a particularly hated officer. The Criminal Investigating Department of the Third Marine Amphibious Force said there were more than 20 fraggings in eight months of 1969, according to the transcript of a court-martial. The Defense Department admits to 788 fraggings from 1969 to 1972.[55] This figure does not include attempts to kill officers with weapons other than "explosive devices," such as rifles. Richard Gabriel calculated that "as many of 1,016 officers and NCOs may have been killed by their own men,"[56] but he points out that this figure includes only men who were caught and tried. There is no precedent in American military history for violence against officers on anything like this scale.

Another response of the "workers" was to "strike," that is, to disobey a combat order, that is, to commit mutiny. The Pentagon kept no records of mutinies, but Senator Stennis of the Senate Armed Forces Committee said that there were 68 mutinies in 1968 alone.[57]

Yet another form of resistance by grunts was the pandemic use of hard drugs. In the spring of 1970, 96 percent pure white heroin appeared in Saigon; by the end of the year it was everywhere, sold in drugstores and by Vietnamese children on street corners. This junk was so pure and cheap that the troops smoked or sniffed, with only a minority reduced to injection. Its use was not remarkable in Vietnam because smoking was usually a group activity, accepted by almost everyone, and common for clean-cut Midwestern boys as well as for city kids. Nothing in all of military history even nearly resembled this plague. About 28 percent of the troops used hard drugs, with more than half a million becoming addicted.[58] This was approximately the same percentage of high school students in the States who were using drugs, but they were using softer stuff. In Vietnam, grass was smoked so much it is a wonder that a southerly wind did not levitate Hanoi's politburo.

The failure of senior officers is partly reflected in the fact that they knew what was going on and did nothing to stop it, and did not protest. Richard Gabriel and Paul Savage concluded that "the higher officer corps was so committed to expedience that the organized distribution of drugs was accepted as necessary to the support of the South Vietnamese government, which often purveyed the drugs that destroyed the Army that defended it."[59] The CIA and the diplomatic corps in Vietnam prevented other governmental agencies from getting at the truth, while individuals with the CIA, if not the Agency itself, helped to fly drugs into Vietnam from Laos.

Despite an occasional attempt to do something—usually punishing the troops—about the blizzard of skag, neither the U.S. government nor the military ever accomplished anything worth mentioning. The much advertised urine testing (to be conducted in what the GIs called The Pee House of the August Moon) was ineffective because the tests were unreliable, the troops who were not hooked could flush their bodies before the tests, and no one was prepared actually to help the soldiers who were addicts. One scholar concluded that "in not rooting out the sources of heroin in Laos and Thailand, the government had simply made a calculation that the continued political and military support of those groups profiting from the drug traffic was worth the risk of hooking U.S. soldiers."[60] General Westmoreland, as usual, blamed everyone but his own senior officers: "The misuse of drugs . . . had spread from civilian society into the Army and became a major problem. . . . A serious dilution over the war years in the caliber of junior leaders contributed to this. . . ."[61]

Racial conflict was suffused throughout the war, from 1968 until the end. Every service, including the previously calm air force, had race riots of varying magnitude. As some of America's cities burned, or rather as the ghettos in some cities burned, the domestic rage found its counterpart in the military. Fraggings were sometimes racially motivated. One battalion commander said, "What defeats me is the attitude among the blacks that 'black is right' no matter who is right or wrong." One black soldier said, "I'd just as soon shoot whitey as the VC."[62] In one incident that is what actually happened: Two white majors were shot trying to get some black GIs to turn down their tape recorder.

White officers were sometimes offended by expressions of black solidarity, including ritual handshakes, the closed fist, swearing, black jargon, and, especially, blacks arguing that they were being forced to fight "a white man's war." (The North Vietnamese and the NLF often tried to exploit that theme through various forms of psychological warfare.) The weight of the military justice system was lowered on black GIs far out of proportion to their numbers. The congressional Black Caucus did a study in 1971 that showed that half of all soldiers in jail were black.[63] The next year, the Defense Department learned that blacks were treated more harshly than whites for identical offenses. The occasional race riots were invariably triggered by the increasing militance of American blacks in general, the peculiarly obtuse social attitudes of many older military officers, the frustrated hopes of the Great Society, the sense of an unfair draft, and an unfair shake in Vietnam.

Notes

1. "General Westmoreland Reports on Vietnam War," *U.S. News & World Report*, Nov. 28, 1966, p. 48.
2. James B. Stockdale, Foreword in Richard A. Gabriel, *To Serve with Honor* (Westport, Conn.: Greenwood Press, 1982), p. xiv.
3. William C. Westmoreland, "Progress Report on the War in Viet-Nam," Nov. 21, 1967, *Department of State Bulletin*, Dec. 11, 1967, p. 788.
4. Cincinnatus, *Self-Destruction*, p. 112.
5. Maureen Mylander, *The Generals* (New York: Dial Press, 1974), p. 12.
6. Starr, *The Discarded Army*, p. 12.
7. Bruce Lawlor in Al Santoli, *Everything We Had: An Oral History of the Vietnam War* (New York: Ballantine Books, 1985), p. 176.
8. Herb Mock in Ibid., p. 183.
9. William C. Westmoreland, "Analysis of Moral and Professional Climate in the Army," April 18, 1970, in U.S. Army War College, "Study on Military Professionalism," Carlisle Barracks, Pa., June 30, 1970, p. 53.
10. Ibid., p. i.
11. Ibid., p. iv.
12. Ibid., pp. 13–14.
13. Ibid., p. v.
14. Ibid., p. B44.
15. Ibid., pp. 12, 15.
16. Ibid., p. B29.
17. Ibid., p. 20.
18. Ibid., p. 21.
19. Ibid., pp. B1, B5.
20. Ibid., p. 25.
21. Ibid., pp. B1–2.
22. Ibid.
23. Ibid., pp. B1–14.
24. A. D. Home, ed., *The Wounded Generation* (Englewood Cliffs, N.J.: Prentice-Hall, 1981), pp. 143–44.
25. David Shoup, "The New American Militarism," *The Atlantic Monthly*, April 1969, pp. 51–56.
26. Douglas Kinnard, *The War Managers* (Hanover, N.H.: University Press of New England, 1977), p. 174.
27. Cincinnatus, *Self-Destruction*, p. 144.
28. Santoli, *Everything We Had*, p. 219.
29. Office of Systems Analysis, Office of the Secretary of Defense, "Experience in Command and Battle Deaths," January 1968, p. 24; Center of Military History, Department of the Army.
30. Office of the Deputy Chief of Staff for Personnel, Department of the Army "Study of the 12-Month Vietnam Tour," June 29, 1970, Appendix: "Advantages and Disadvantages of 12-Month Hostile Fire Area Tour," p. 1; Center of Military History, Department of the Army.
31. Mylander, *The Generals*, p. 74.
32. Haynes Johnson and George C. Wilson, *Army in Anguish* (New York: Pocket Books, 1972), p. 76.
33. Office of Systems Analysis, "Experience in Command," p. 25.
34. Ibid., p. 27.
35. Ibid., p. 29.
36. Ibid.
37. Ibid., p. 30.

38. Ibid., "MACV Rebuttal," p. 15.
39. Oscar Grutsky, "The Effects of Succession," in Morris Janowitz, ed., *The New Military* (New York: Russell Sage Foundation, 1964), p. 89.
40. William C. Westmoreland, *A Soldier Reports* (New York: Da Capo Press, 1989), p. 417.
41. Army War College, "Study on Military Professionalism," p. 23.
42. Ibid., p. 26.
43. Santoli, *Everything We Had*, p. 43.
44. Kinnard, *The War Managers*, p. 75.
45. Ibid.
46. Peter Goldman and Tony Fuller, *Charlie Company* (New York: William Morrow, 1983), p. 98.
47. Kinnard, *The War Managers*, p. 172.
48. James Fallows, *National Defense* (New York: Random House, 1981), p. 121.
49. Army War College, "Study on Military Professionalism," p. 29.
50. Robert J. Lifton, *Home from the War* (New York: Simon & Schuster, 1973), p. 178.
51. Richard A. Gabriel and Paul L. Savage, *Crisis in Command* (New York: Hill and Wang, 1978), p. 182.
52. William Hauser, *America's Army in Crisis* (Baltimore: Johns Hopkins University Press, 1973), p. 94.
53. Gabriel and Savage, *Crisis in Command*, p. 42.
54. Charles J. Levy, *Spoils of War* (Boston: Houghton Mifflin Co., 1974), p. 46.
55. Gabriel and Savage, *Crisis in Command*, p. 183.
56. Richard A. Gabriel, *To Serve with Honor* (Westport, Conn.: Greenwood Press, 1982), p. 4.
57. Gabriel and Savage, *Crisis in Command*, p. 45.
58. Gabriel, *To Serve with Honor*, p. 3.
59. Gabriel and Savage, *Crisis in Command*, p. 48.
60. Starr, *The Discarded Army*, p. 114.
61. Westmoreland, *A Soldier Reports*, p. 371.
62. Baskir and Strauss, *Chance and Circumstance*, p. 137.
63. Ibid., p. 138.

24
My Lai: The Killing Begins
MICHAEL BILTON AND KEVIN SIM

Soon after first light, Charlie Company lined up on the landing field inside the defended perimeter of LZ [Landing Zone] Dottie, waiting for the "Dolphins" and the "Sharks" to appear out of the sky.* Some of the men were bleary-eyed. They had talked long into the night about what the next day would be like, before finally snatching a few hours' sleep, only to be ushered from their bunks before dawn, at 5:30 A.M., and told to gather up their gear.

Platoon commanders distributed ammunition. More than a hundred men and several tons of fighting gear were about to be shipped 11 miles in an operation they hoped would take the enemy completely by surprise. The target of their first full-scale combat assault was less than fifteen minutes' flying time away. The troops could hear the distant *whop-whop-whop-whop* of the nine liftships and gunships from the 174th Helicopter Assault Company before the aircraft emerged from behind the tree line. They landed close by, kicking up clouds of fine dust from the downdraft of spinning rotors.

The "Slicks," the troop-carrying helicopters, were to move the company in two lifts. First they would take [Capt. Ernest] Medina's command group, the 1st Platoon, and as many of the 2nd Platoon as they could manage. These would then secure the landing zone for the remainder of the company. Also to be carried on the second lift were a few additional men from other brigade units temporarily assigned to Charlie Company for the Pinkville operation. They included Lieutenant Dennis Johnson, a military intelligence officer, and his Vietnamese interpreter. Demolition engineers Jerry "Hotrod" Hemming and Calvin Hawkins had volunteered for the operation only the day before. Finally, an Army photographer and a reporter from the public information outfit were being taken along as well.

Weighed down by extra clips of ammunition, machine-gun bandoleers, grenades, flak jackets, water canteens, ropes, flashlights, .45 pistols, medical bandages, grenade launchers, and K-rations, the men on the first lift waited at the departure point. The additional equipment they needed for battle meant an extra heavy load for the liftships. Radio operators stuck close to their platoon command groups; ammo bearers were joined as if by an umbilical cord to the machine-gun teams. When the choppers touched down, the men in the first lift clambered into the vibrating compartments of the doorless cargo holds. Waiting for them on either side of the aircraft were two gunners, crouched beneath a metal covering enclosing the helicopter's transmission and hydraulic system, directly beneath the rotor mast.

The pilots sat in heavily armored seats of half-inch-thick steel wrapped in an aluminum frame. They throttled every last percent of available power on the gauge, making mental notes against checklists of radio call signs and frequencies. They had already made their calculations of the likely weight they were carrying, judging down to the last few hundred pounds how high and how fast they could fly the aircraft, men, and equipment. Behind them turbine fans spun gases from a jet engine and caused the machines to shudder violently. The pilots waited for the point when the 48-foot-long

*"Dolphins" and "Sharks": liftships and gunships of the 174th Helicopter Assault Company as well as their radio call signals.

rotors were spinning fast enough to give the aircraft lift. They then pulled on the control stick, adjusted the rotor wings, and allowed the aircraft to rise slowly off the ground.

Watching this at a distance, the remnants of Charlie Company left behind on the ground inhaled the sweet smell of kerosene filtering from engine exhausts. Finally the "Dolphins" and "Sharks" staggered from their parking slots and gradually lifted into the air. They lumbered, nose tilted forward, along the ground until the pilots judged they had enough power to climb higher. Rising above the tree line, they gathered up into a "V" formation before heading south, hugging the edge of Highway One.

On the ground the Army photographer began work. Ron Haeberle had been in the fourth year of college as a photography major in his home town of Cleveland, Ohio, when he was drafted. The Army quickly recognized his talent with a camera and assigned him to the Public Information Detachment at brigade headquarters at Duc Pho. Haeberle and Jay Roberts, a . . . reporter from Arlington, Virginia, were assigned to write a morale-boosting piece on Task Force Barker's campaign to root out the Viet Cong from the Batangan Peninsula. Their usual procedure, developed after similar missions with other outfits, was to prepare a press release and photograph that would be used in *Stars and Stripes* and many other Army newspapers. The MACV [Military Assistance Command, Vietnam] information office in Saigon circulated their stories, and often they made it onto the AP [Associated Press] wire and into the papers back home. Now, Haeberle's service-issue Leica, with its black-and-white film, stayed unused as he focused his own 35-mm Nikon on the slowly rising helicopters. He had captured the first image of the day on Ektachrome color film.

Several hundred feet above, the pilots lined up behind the aircraft they were designated to follow in the formation. By 7:22 A.M. the first lift of troops had left Dottie behind and was well on its way. "Coyote Six," Frank Barker's command-and-control helicopter, was already on station. "Skeeter," a tiny bubble helicopter, was *en route* from Chu Lai. During the battle it would skip low over the trees, reconning the battle ground, ferreting out the enemy positions, drawing fire for the high and low gunships to engage. Off the coastline away out to the east on the South China Sea, *News Boy India Two Zero*, a high-powered Swift Boat of the "Brown Water Navy," which operated among South Vietnam's inshore waters and rivers, moved into position. It was all going like clockwork.

In the hamlet, which the Americans had labeled My Lai 4 on their military maps, the day had begun several hours earlier with the lighting of fires. This was women's work. Every household had a fire in their dirt yard, sheltered from the wind and shared with dogs, pigs, ducks, and chickens. With luck the dying embers from the night before were enough to give a flame to a freshly applied handful of dried twigs. A pan of water was boiled constantly on the lighted fire and replaced only when a meal was to be heated up. It was an early morning routine which had gone on for generation after generation. Most of the farmers, who were heads of households, were already out in the fields. Some of the older children had gone to fetch water from wells, or check how many fish they had netted in the river.

Seven kilometers away, the pilots swung their aircraft round in a long semicircle and made their final run-in to approach the landing zone from the southwest. They scanned the horizon, looking for smoke: not the fine wisps of blue smoke from household fires, but thick, heavy, white smoke, the kind that accompanied the booming sounds of surface detonating rounds as high explosive and white phosphorus shells whumped and burst onto the western edge of the settlement. For three minutes, just before

7:30 A.M., a small group of artillerymen sweated and strained to deliver their first barrage of the day from four 105-mm guns. D company, 6/11th Artillery Battalion, had fired thousands of rounds into Quang Ngai Province during its time at the fortified fire base at LZ Uptight, across the Diem Diem River only 6 miles north of My Lai 4. To the artillerymen firing the guns the target was merely a set of coordinates, though they knew perfectly well that when the shells landed they would kill anything within a radius of 35 meters on unobstructed flat ground.

The impact of the artillery fire was being monitored that morning by Lieutenant Dennis Vasquez, an observer aboard Frank Barker's "Charlie Charlie" aircraft. Covering a similar route to the one they had taken on their fly-by recce the day before, Barker's observation team were still several miles away from the LZ. In the distance Vasquez could see smoke popping around what he took to be the landing zone. When the shells thundered in toward their target the people of My Lai 4 fled underground into crude bomb shelters or tunnels dug beneath their homes.

Virtually unobserved, the artillery barrage was tantamount to blind firing. No spotter was close enough to adjust the fire away from the village. What was intended as an artillery preparation for the paddy fields 400 meters northwest of the village turned instead into something else. In those three minutes 120 rounds fell not only among the dikes and fields but also very close to the fragile dwellings spread out around the hamlet. Eventually they strayed over into the inhabited area itself, sending shrapnel flying, snapping trees like twigs, causing terror and panic.

Blind firing was nothing new to the province of Quang Ngai. Hundreds of thousands of rounds had been lobbed across the region, from the mountains in the west right down to the wide coastal plain. Mostly it was harassment and interdiction fire intended to unsettle the Viet Cong and to keep them on their toes at night. Some of these barrages were fired by an artillery unit at a fire base perched on top of a mountain overlooking the Song Ve Valley. In August the previous year, B Battery of the 2nd Battalion of the 320th Artillery celebrated the firing of its 250,000th round with a brief ceremony, complete with pennants flying and a color guard standing to attention.

In his command-and-control chopper, the "Charlie Charlie" ship, Barker sat at a homemade console of radios. At the flick of a switch he could contact the ground troops and the gunships. Sitting next to Barker, Lt. Vasquez didn't bother to adjust the artillery fire which was intended to clear the drop zone for the helicopters. Barker was keen to keep down the heads of any Viet Cong defensive positions. Every one and a half seconds a shell exploded close to the village. So powerful was the roar of the artillery it could be clearly heard several miles away by the members of Charlie Company who remained waiting on the ground at Dottie.

At LZ Uptight, where the rounds of the preparatory artillery barrage were being fired the mortar platoon members left behind manning the direction-finding radar listened in on their radios. Over in Task Force Barker's tactical operations center at Dottie, and further to the south in the operations room of the brigade headquarters at Duc Pho, more radio operators waited to monitor news of the battle.

As the liftships neared their arrival point, the men of Charlie Company were shaken by the sudden fusillade of machine guns pouring tracer fire down onto the landing zone. Martin Fagan, with Medina's command group in the fourth helicopter, sat next to the port door gunner. The deafening clatter as the machine gun opened up scared the hell out of him. To Dennis Conti, who was with Lt. [William] Calley's command group, the gunner nearest him appeared to be firing almost straight down as they dropped through thick smoke low over the landing zone.

The paddy field was bone dry. As they hit the ground Calley shouted: "Let's go!" and everyone but Conti jumped out. He had caught his mine sweeper in the seats behind him. Eventually freeing himself, he jumped down into the long elephant grass. Conti was considered by everyone in the platoon to be a street-smart Italian. Joe Cool. Ladies' man. But now, with the smoke from the fires still drifting around, he became disoriented. He couldn't tell which way the rest of the platoon had gone. To his right he heard a machine gun open up and saw what he thought was a farmer running with his cattle. He fired a round from an M-79 grenade launcher—but the man was too far away.

Machine gunners Robert Maples and James Bergthold jumped out of their "slick" when it was still six feet off the ground. Hitting the paddy, Maples stumbled under the weight of the machine gun he was carrying and lost his helmet. He scrambled around trying to find the steel pot and then ran to the irrigation dike. Bergthold, carrying a .45 pistol, three hand grenades, his pack, and about six hundred rounds of machine-gun ammunition, struggled along behind. Hemming and Hawkins, the demo men from the engineering battalion, also made a dash for the safety of the dike. Hawkins then had to run back to find a roll of detonation cord his partner dropped when jumping out of the liftship. He found the cord and rejoined Hemming.

The "Dolphins" took off again and the leadship announced over the air the landing zone was "cold." The "Sharks" continued pouring all kinds of fire onto the fringes of the village with machine guns, grenade launchers, and rockets. Barker acknowledged the message from "Dolphin Lead" and relayed it back to the operations center at Dottie. The information surprised him. Against all the odds the LZ was cold. There was no enemy fire. Just then the "Warlord" aeroscouts took up a chase of several armed men in black pajamas running below them. "We got a couple of dinks with weapons," the pilot of the lead ship radioed as another chopper headed off to block an escape route. From different parts of My Lai 4 villagers were trying to get to safety a few hundred yards away down a road which led in one direction to Quang Ngai City and in the other to the coast. The rest of the villagers stayed hiding in their bunkers or simply took shelter in their homes.

The next twenty minutes saw intense aerial activity as the helicopters continued searching for signs of enemy positions. The fifty troops on the ground spread out and secured defensive positions, running to the bank of an irrigation ditch. Out in the fields another farmer frantically raised his hands by way of both greeting and to show he had no weapon. He was immediately felled by a burst from a machine gun. The first lift held their defensive positions and waited for the rest of the 2nd and 3rd platoons to join them.

The second lift had a quicker journey across country to the LZ. There was no longer any reason to follow a circuitous route; the element of surprise had only been required for the first lift. John Smail, a squad leader with the 3rd Platoon, nearly didn't make it at all. His assigned chopper on the landing field at Dottie quickly filled up. He approached to get on board but there was no room for him and he had a few anxious moments as he quickly raced round searching for another ship to board. As they lifted off at 7:38 A.M., the other men began joking with him about almost being left behind before the start of Charlie Company's most important mission.

Soon they were over the landing zone. The door gunners in the "slick" carrying Diego Rodriguez, of the 2nd Platoon, opened up with yet more tracer fire. Already nervous about what lay ahead, Rodriguez sat by the starboard door. Suddenly spent shells flew up from the machine gun and struck him in the face. In another ship, meanwhile, Haeberle took a couple of more shots with his Nikon of the approach to the landing zone.

When the second lift hit the LZ they too quickly spread out as they ran to take up defensive positions with the others. Mortars were set up and a 3rd Platoon squad led by Steven Grimes was sent to recover a VC weapon spotted by one of the aeroscouts who had marked it with a smoke canister. Other members of the platoon saw a woman carrying a child in the brush some distance away. A tall soldier from Chicago named Charles West stood up and with his M-16 on full automatic began loosing off a burst of fire from the hip. Smail, his squad leader, got angry and shouted out how stupid the soldier had been to fire in the direction of where Grimes's men had gone searching for the VC weapon. He could have killed their own men.

To Michael Bernhardt what was happening already confirmed his worst fears about Medina's instructions the night before. Along with the gunships, almost everyone in the 1st and 2nd platoons were firing their weapons, and now the 3rd Platoon was joining in. The moment a Vietnamese was spotted, volleys of fire were loosed off, and the "enemy" fell wounded or dying. It was apparent to Bernhardt, as it was to virtually everyone gathered there on the ground, that they were receiving no return fire at all. There was no incoming.

The 1st and 2nd platoons got ready to move into the village in separate groups. Spread out "on line" in a typical infantry formation, they moved forward, over the dike, through another paddy, and entered the village firing from the hip. The 3rd Platoon and Medina's command group stayed behind, forming a defensive perimeter on the western edge of the village, about 150 meters from the tree line. Twenty minutes after they arrived Medina wanted Bernhardt to check out a suspicious-looking ammo box someone had found. Among his equipment Bernhardt carried a long rope. To make sure it wasn't booby-trapped he tied the rope round the box and jerked it several times. When it failed to explode, he opened the lid and found inside a small Sony radio and various pieces of a medical kit. Bernhardt kept hold of the box for the rest of the day.

Shortly before 8 A.M., Medina radioed the operations center via the "Charlie Charlie" ship that they had fifteen confirmed VC killed. It was his first lie of the day. It was impossible to have a battle and not have enemy killed.

Over the course of the next three hours Charlie Company moved through My Lai 4 and also entered several other subhamlets, small pockets of homes grouped together and known in the neighborhood by a particular local name. The place the Americans called My Lai 4 was in fact called Tu Cung by the Vietnamese who lived there. It had a number of subhamlets—including Binh Tay and Binh Dong. Tu Cung, along with three other hamlets—My Lai, Co Luy, and My Khe—spread over two or three square kilometers as far as the coast to the west and the Tra Khuc River to the south. Collectively this formed an area the locals called Son My village. The whole of Son My was the target for Task force Barker over the next three days.

The totality of what happened in My Lai 4 that morning was not known to any single individual who took part in Charlie Company's combat operation. As they assaulted the village each platoon split into separate squads and soon these too became broken down, as numerous groups of men, often in ones and twos, moved through the hamlet. Occasionally they crossed each other's paths and squads from different platoons intermingled. At the end of the day a number of soldiers remarked that it had been a miracle none of them was caught in any crossfire. Parts of the village were covered in thick foliage, bamboo trees, banana trees, and other vegetation. No single group of GIs had the opportunity to see what everyone else was doing. But they could all hear firing, often long bursts of automatic fire from M-16s and machine guns.

Hand grenades were thrown and the M-79 launchers hurled small bomblets 100 meters or more through the air.

A few geographical features gave Charlie Company some sense of direction. A main trail ran approximately north–south for the whole of the village. Another ran west–east forming a "T" junction of sorts where the two trails met almost in the middle of the settlement. An irrigation ditch formed in a discontinuous semicircle around the furthest southern fringes of the village several hundred meters beyond the tree line, separated from the inhabited area by rice paddies.

Lt. Col. Barker's plan provided for two platoons initially to sweep through the village, quickly taking out any enemy opposition they encountered. Half an hour later the 3rd Platoon would come in behind, mopping up, killing the livestock, and burning hootches. Capt. Medina and his command group would direct operations from the rear.

Calley's 1st Platoon edged into the southern portion of My Lai 4 in three separate squads, line abreast. Calley and his radio operator, Charles Sledge, held back, maintaining a discreet distance from the troops advancing in front of them. Prisoners or Viet Cong suspects were to be sent back to the platoon commander for screening.

Greg Olsen fired his M-60 machine gun as they moved forward, trying to hit a man running away. The weapon suddenly jammed while Lenny Lagunoy was feeding him a belt of ammunition. Lagunoy grabbed the gun from Olsen, recocked it so as to clear the obstruction, and fired once more on the fleeing villager. All around them troops were firing on anything that moved. Olsen shot at animals, pigs, chickens, ducks, and cows. Soldiers yelled inside small dwellings for people to come out, using hand signals if they appeared. If there was no answer, they threw grenades into the shelters and bunkers. Others didn't bother to find out if the bunkers were empty and threw the grenades in regardless. Small clusters of people were being gathered into one larger group of fifty or sixty old men, women, children, and babies in arms, some so badly wounded they could hardly walk. Olsen noticed one elderly woman shot in the hip. Several of the troops saw their buddies behaving in ways which shocked them.

For Robert Maples it was not the first time he had seen things he disapproved of, but this was something altogether different. A quiet, mild-mannered, and thoughtful Negro from Englishtown, a rural area of New Jersey, he had enlisted almost two years before out of a sense of curiosity about Vietnam instead of waiting to be drafted. Not long after he arrived in the country, Maples and some of the other men saw a personnel carrier with twenty human ears strung like trophies on its radio antenna. Everyone in the company soon heard about it. Then, on one of their first patrols up in the mountains, they discovered they were being followed. A couple of the guys set up an ambush and killed those shadowing them. To prove it, they cut off their ears and brought them back for the rest to see. Maples was disgusted. He thought the episode gross and unwarranted. Now, minutes after they entered My Lai 4, he and Bergthold came across a hut which had been raked with bullets. Inside, Bergthold discovered three children, a woman with a flesh wound in her side, and an old man squatting down, hardly able to move. He had been seriously wounded in both legs. From six feet Bergthold aimed his .45 pistol and pulled the trigger, causing the top of the man's head to fly off. It was a sight that would be forever etched in Maples's memory. Bergthold claimed to have shot the old man as an act of mercy.

Two other members of the same squad, Roy Wood and Harry Stanley, were taken by surprise when a woman came out of a bamboo hut. Wood whirled and fired, creasing the woman in the side, slightly injuring her. The woman had two children, one a baby in arms, the other only just able to walk. They sent her back to Calley for screening. In another hut they found a man, his wife, a teenage girl, and a younger girl. Wood grabbed the terrified man and shouted: "VC?" Holding his hands in the air, as if to plead for his life, the man replied: "No VC." Then Wood saw the pitiful sight of an elderly woman who had been wounded, staggering down a path toward them. She had been shot with an M-79 grenade which had failed to explode and was still lodged in her stomach. An old man wearing a straw coolie hat and no shirt was with a water buffalo in a paddy 50 meters away. He put his hands in the air. Several members of the platoon opened fire as Calley watched. Harry Stanley saw that the fleeing villagers were offering no resistance. His friend Allen Boyce, who lived in New Jersey only a couple of miles from Maples, came up behind him with a Vietnamese farmer, aged between 40 and 50 years, in custody. He wore black pajamas and his shirt hung open so that Stanley could see his chest. Boyce pushed the man forward to where Stanley was standing beside the trail. Suddenly, and for no reason, Boyce stabbed the man with the bayonet attached to the end of his rifle. He fell to the ground gasping for breath. Boyce killed him and then grabbed another man being detained, shot him in the neck, and threw him into a well, lobbing an M-26 grenade in after him.

"That's the way you gotta do it," he told [Varnado] Simpson, who had considered Boyce a close friend during jungle training in Hawaii. This sort of deranged behavior profoundly affected many of those who witnessed it and refused to take part. Maples, who was standing nearby, said to Stanley: "That Boyce has gone crazy."

Even Robert Lee, the platoon medic, joined in the frenzy but confined his efforts to slaughtering animals. He killed a cow that had been injured. Lee was from a farming community and "didn't want to see the beast suffer." Up in front, he and the platoon sergeant, Isaiah Cowan, could see women and children being slain. They were stunned by what was happening all around them. The further they went into the village, the more bodies they found.

Dennis Conti stayed for a while with Calley's command group but occasionally wandered off on his own, zigzagging across the path which ran west to east through the village as far as the main trail. He stuck close to Calley in case the platoon leader needed the mine sweeper. He helped round up people for questioning, a normal procedure when they searched villages. He gave his mine sweeper to an old man to carry while he moved some of the Vietnamese toward the platoon command group. To Conti the men appeared all psyched up when they landed. The shooting, once it began, created almost a chain reaction. He joined in, without killing anyone. Inside the village his comrades appeared out of control. Families had huddled together for safety in houses, in the yards and in bunkers only to be mown down with automatic weapon fire or blown apart by fragmentation grenades. Women and children were pushed into bunkers and grenades thrown in after them. But if Conti discovered anyone alive he brought them back to the trail. He and Paul Meadlo collected a group of about twenty-five people—mostly women and children. Still more were brought over by other members of the platoon. At one point, wandering off on his own, Conti found a woman aged about 20 with a 4-year-old child. He forced her to perform oral sex on him while he held a gun at the child's head, threatening to kill it. Just at that moment Calley happened along and angrily told him to pull on his pants and get over to where he was supposed to be.

Amid all this mayhem the first and second platoons overlapped on occasions when the right flank of Lieutenant Stephen Brooks's 2nd Platoon crossed paths with the left flank of the 1st Platoon. Half a dozen people from both platoons then witnessed a stocky, blond-haired 2nd Platoon soldier from Kansas City called Gary Roschevitz become hysterical when troops from the 1st Platoon were walking a small group of villagers back for screening. Roschevitz, aged 25, was older than most of the grunts in the company. Standing almost six feet tall and weighing close to 230 pounds, he made a surprise grab for Roy Wood's M-16 and demanded the weapon as a trade for his M-79. But Wood wasn't having any.

"Don't turn them over to the company," Roschevitz appealed to those gathered there. "Kill them!"

Wood, who was physically by far the smaller of the two men, held tightly onto his rifle. Roschevitz then snatched hold of Varnado Simpson's M-16, turned, and shot a Vietnamese farmer in the head. Wood began feeling sick at the sight of the man's brains spilling onto the ground and turned away. Roschevitz shot two more peasants in the head before handing the gun back to Simpson.

As far as the outside world knew, a firefight against a large Viet Cong force was underway in the village. Barker and [Col. Oran] Henderson were back on the scene briefly in their respective helicopters. By about 8:30 A.M., Barker had checked once more with Medina to find out how things were going. Medina told him that the body count was 84 enemy killed, and Barker relayed the additional 69 KIA [killed in action] to the tactical operations center. In fact the death toll was far higher, but still no shots had been fired at Charlie Company and they had yet to kill a single enemy soldier.

In the northern portion of the village the 2nd Platoon had also run berserk. Employing the routine combat assault technique used by Calley, Stephen Brooks's men also approached line abreast in three squads. Firing as they moved, they came to dwellings and yelled out "Lai Dai" in Vietnamese ("Come here") at the villagers sheltering in homemade shelters or bunkers. Fragmentation grenades were tossed inside; homes were sprayed with automatic fire. Children aged only 6 or 7 came toward them with their hands outstretched, saying "Chop chop." They asked for the food and candy they had received from other American soldiers on two previous visits to the village. The soldiers scythed them down. After one group of Vietnamese were killed in front of a hut, the first squad leader, Sergeant Kenneth Scheil, began telling the men with him that he didn't like what they were all doing but that he had to obey orders. The villagers had huddled together for safety, but the Americans poured fire into them, tearing their bodies apart, one man firing a machine gun at random, others using their M-16s on automatic.

Dennis Bunning informed his squad leader, Sgt. [Kenneth] Hodges, he wasn't going to fire on women and children. Hodges ordered him to get right out on the far left flank, beyond the tree line and into the rice paddies. Brooks's radio operator, Dean Fields, witnessed Varnado Simpson shoot a woman with a baby from a distance of about 25 meters. Her right arm was shot almost completely off at the wrist. All that held it on was a fragile piece of flesh. She ran into a hootch and someone yelled an order for her and the baby to be killed.

Max Hutson, the weapons squad leader, formed a machine-gun team with Floyd Wright. As soon as they passed the tree line they were confronted less than 30 feet away by a middle-aged woman climbing out of a tunnel using both hands. She was unarmed but they opened fire and she fell back into the tunnel. Hutson and Wright took turns on the machine gun. Whenever they came across any Vietnamese they opened fire, killing them. Hutson could see people firing all around him—the whole scene was one of chaos and confusion, with people moving, yelling, and shouting. Some of the troops were afraid they would be shot by their own men.

The other machine-gun team, Charles Hutto and Esequiel Torres, were also firing at everything that moved—Hutto with the M-60 and Torres with his rifle. After thirty minutes Tores demanded they swap. By this time Hutto, growing weary of all the killing, was glad to hand over the heavier and more powerful weapon.

Jay Buchanon, the platoon sergeant, was also over on the extreme left flank of the platoon, almost on the edge of the tree line. He quickly realized the whole assault was a complete mess. Amid the thick undergrowth he knew there was no opposition but it sounded like a pitched battle was going on. He yelled: "Keep moving, keep moving—fire when fired upon. Stay on line, keep moving. If you receive fire, return it."

Away to his right, closer to where Brooks was moving forward, a slaughter was taking place. Thomas Partsch, a sensitive soul who made regular entries in his diary whenever the platoon took a break, could see that Brooks had totally lost control. As soon as villagers emerged with their hands held up, the troops shot them down. Partsch and Gary Crossley came to a building. It was a well-made house, 20 feet by 10 with a small extension on the side measuring about 8 feet by 6, which gave it an L-shaped appearance. The dwelling was of good quality, a permanent structure made of mud and clay. It had an elevated floor about one step up from the ground and a roof which overhung the house by about two feet over the entrance door, with bamboo windows either side, providing shade from the tropical sun. An old man appeared dressed in black pajamas. Without hesitating Crossley shot the old man in the left arm, just below the elbow. The shot severed the arm, causing it to hang down. Attempting to put his hands in the air, the old man yelled: "No VC! No VC!" A woman wearing black pajama bottoms and a white shirt came out carrying a baby. She frantically shouted in Vietnamese at the two Americans, then proceeded to drag the man inside. Partsch noticed that Crossley looked physically pale and was shaking nervously. He hadn't fired again. When Partsch asked him why, he said that he didn't know.

"Why didn't you finish the job?" Partsch asked again. Crossley replied that he just couldn't bring himself to pull the trigger a second time, he only wanted to see what it was like to shoot someone. Just then two men—Hutson, the weapons squad leader, and Wright, carrying the machine gun—went in after the Vietnamese couple and opened up with a burst of fire.

Occasionally Partsch was close enough to Lt. Brooks and his radio operator to hear Medina calling: "What the hell is going on over there?" At times the static was so bad that Brooks couldn't make contact. After receiving one such message the platoon leader ushered Partsch away from the radio. Overhead, Partsch saw Frank Barker flying low over the treetops in his helicopter—clearly recognizable in his white flying helmet, sitting in his normal position, right near the edge of the door next to the machine gunner.

When he sat down for a rest, Partsch got out his diary and wrote in pencil his account of the day's proceedings so far:

> Got up at 0530 and we left 0715. We had nine choppers, two lifts. We started to move slowly through the village, shooting everything in sight, children, men, women, and animals. Some was sickening. Their legs were shot off and they were still moving. They were just hanging there. I think their bodies are made of rubber. I didn't fire a single round yet and didn't kill anybody, not even a chicken. I couldn't. We are now supposed to push two more villages. It is about 10.00 hours and we are taking a rest before going in. We also got two weapons, one M-1 and a carbine.

Those in My Lai 4 that day had a choice whether or not to take part in what was happening. Many followed what they believed were their orders. Some appeared even to enjoy the activity. Only a handful offered any real help or compassion to the Vietnamese. The platoon medic, a Mexican-American named George Garza, found a little boy aged 6 or 7 with an arm injury and bandaged it. Harry Stanley and another Negro, Herbert Carter, the 1st Platoon tunnel rat, located a second child. Carter admired Stanley, describing him often as a "sharp dude." He believed he cared more for the Vietnamese than his fellow Americans. Stanley urged the boy to keep quiet and stay hidden.

Another who refused to take part in the slaughter, Leonard Gonzalez, was also assigned to the extreme left flank of the 2nd Platoon, beyond the tree line. He patrolled in a rice paddy at the far northwest corner of the village. On the edge of the field Gonzalez discovered a young girl aged 11 or 12, wounded in the chest. She was lying on her back, dressed in black pajamas with a white top, crying and moaning with pain. Gonzalez got his canteen and poured water on the girl's forehead and tried to get her to drink some water. There was little more he could do for her and he got up to leave. Gonzalez had only gone a few paces when he heard a shot; he turned to see that she had been killed.

An order came telling the squad to close up. This meant that Gonzalez and Bunning, who was about 25 meters away, had to move over out of the paddy, through the trees and into the village itself. In a clearing near a small hootch a group of fifteen Vietnamese had been gathered, four women in their thirties, three in their fifties, three girls in their late teens and five children aged between 3 and 14. Standing around were seven or eight soldiers from two different squads including Hutto, Torres, and Roschevitz. Gonzalez heard someone yell that if anyone was behind the Vietnamese to take cover because they were going to open fire. A shot rang out and a bullet penetrated the head of a young child being carried by its mother, blowing out the back of its skull. Others began firing also until the entire group was dead. Gonzalez could stand no more; he turned away and vomited. Few words were spoken until someone said: "Let's move out."

Roschevitz later fired two rounds from his M-79 grenade launcher at a group of Vietnamese sitting on the ground. The first bomblet missed; the second landed among them with devastating effect, but against the odds it failed to kill them all. Someone finished off those left alive. A soldier stopping over a tunnel yelled for the occupants to come out. Gonzalez moved closer and could hear people responding as if they were about to comply, whereupon the soldier threw in a grenade and yelled: "Fire in the hole!"—telling everyone to stand clear.

Behind the 1st and 2nd platoons Medina's command group had formed a security line out in the paddy fields beyond the western perimeter of My Lai 4. Some forty-five minutes had elapsed since the first troops entered the village and Medina was waiting to send in the 3rd Platoon, led by a recent arrival, a young lieutenant named Geoffrey LaCross. This was LaCross's very first combat mission. From Lake Leelanau, Michigan, he had joined the company and taken command of the platoon only three weeks before, on February 26. . . . Medina hoped the savvy of the platoon sergeant, Manuel Lopez, would make up for LaCross's inexperience. It helped that the 3rd Platoon had been given the less taxing role of mopping up.

For Medina, the best way to clear a village was to send a sweep team through very rapidly, clearing people out of the hootches as quickly as possible. The search teams would then go from hootch to hootch, checking bunkers and tunnels looking for any enemy who might be hiding. One added refinement today was that LaCross's men were also to burn the village. Medina received the instruction to let the Zippo squads loose from Frank Barker directly. Barker said he had arranged for this to be cleared with the Vietnamese authorities in Quang Ngai through the senior district advisor to the 2nd ARVN Division. The truth was that since the area was controlled by the Viet

Cong the government officials didn't care what happened to people in the villages. Medina knew Barker regularly met with the Vietnamese and the American province advisors. The burning of villages was supposed to be strictly controlled. As far as Medina was concerned, the burning of villages was always carried out with the approval of the South Vietnamese.

Some distance away Sergeant Grimes's squad from the 3rd Platoon searched for Viet Cong weapons. They set off through the paddy fields and then followed the line of the irrigation ditch which ran around the village. Grimes's men crossed over a bamboo footbridge and saw a tiny bubble aeroscout reconning low over the ground drop a smoke grenade. They recrossed the bridge, moved toward a clump of foliage, and found an M-1 and a rifle.

More rifles were found when the 2nd Platoon located the bodies of two VC killed by the gunships and marked with smoke. The VC, each about 20 years old, were not in uniform but carried an American pack, pistol belts, and ammo pouches. They had been armed with an M-1 and a carbine, which was now full of mud and still loaded.

Deeper into the village the 1st Platoon collected a large group of about sixty Vietnamese. They were made to squat down. An alert Conti spotted a 4-year-old child running away toward a hootch. Dropping his gear, he sprinted after the child, which managed to escape him. He discovered a woman with a baby in a hootch and a much older female he took to be the grandmother in a nearby underground shelter. Conti escorted the young woman and her child back to the holding point and then returned for the old woman who had refused to move. He then teamed up with Meadlo. Once more they guarded the squatting Vietnamese. Calley appeared with his radio operator, Charles Sledge.

Calley had been called twice that morning on the radio by an anxious Medina. "What is happening over there?" Medina demanded to know, challenging the slow progress of the 1st Platoon. He wanted Calley to get his men back on line and keep moving. This made the young platoon commander nervous. Throughout his time with the company he had frequently been made the butt of Medina's jokes. Medina knew Calley couldn't command the respect of his men. Now, under pressure, Calley replied that the large groups of civilians they had gathered were slowing the platoon down. Never one to accept excuses, Medina told Calley simply to get rid of them. So when Calley came across Meadlo and Conti in the clearing and said: "Take care of them," his intention was clear. It was his way of getting Medina off his back.

Conti thought nothing of the implications of Calley's request when he replied simply: "OK." Like many in the company he regarded the man as a joke and resented the way Calley tried to suck up to the men one minute, calling them by their first names, and then shouted and bawled at them the next. Conti felt his platoon commander had absolutely no leadership ability.

Among the squatting Vietnamese were ten to fifteen men with beards and ten women, as well as a handful of very elderly, gray-haired women who could hardly walk. The rest were children of all ages—from babies up to early teens.

Calley, who was carrying a bandolier of ammunition around one shoulder, said: "I thought I told you to take care of them."

Meadlo somewhat naively responded: "We are. We're watching over them."

"No," riposted Calley. "I want them killed." He moved over to where Conti was standing beside Meadlo. "We'll get on line and fire into them."

Conti and Meadlo looked at each other and backed off, neither of them wanting a part in what was about to happen. Calley, losing his temper, beckoned them toward him: "Come here . . . come here. Come on, we'll line them up; we'll kill them."

Conti, searching for an excuse, pointed out that he was carrying a grenade launcher and he didn't want to waste ammunition. Perhaps he should keep guard over by the tree line in case anyone tried to get away, he suggested.

Calley turned to Meadlo: "Fire when I say 'Fire.' "

Conti stood behind them as Calley and Meadlo, standing side by side, blazed away. They stood only ten feet from their hapless victims, changing magazines from time to time. The Vietnamese screamed, yelled, and tried to get up. It was pure carnage as heads were shot off along with limbs; the fleshier body parts were ripped to shreds. Meadlo had taken twenty-three fully loaded magazines for his M-16 in his pack when they left Dottie. He fired in a spraying motion. He noticed one man dressed in red fall dead as he fired the rifle on automatic until the magazine was exhausted. Then he reloaded. He then switched to semiautomatic fire and loaded the third magazine.

After a minute or so Meadlo couldn't continue. Tears flooded down his cheeks. He turned, stuck his rifle in Conti's hand, and said: "You shoot them." Conti pushed the weapon back: "If they are going to be killed, I'm not doing it. Let him do it," he said, pointing at Calley, By this time Conti could see that only a few children were left standing. Mothers had thrown themselves on top of the young ones in a last desperate bid to protect them from the bullets raining down on them. The children were trying to stand up. Calley opened fire again, killing them one by one. Conti swore at him. Finally, when it appeared to be all over, Calley calmly turned and said: "OK, let's go." Suddenly someone yelled out that more Vietnamese, five women and six children some distance away, were making a break for the tree line. Calley burst out: "Get them, get them! Kill them!" Conti waited until they reached the tree line before letting loose with his grenade launcher, firing above them into the top of the trees. He asked Calley if he should pursue the fleeing villagers, but Calley replied no.

The urgency now was to push on to the far end of the village. Calley cajoled his men forward. They split up once more and continued to come across still more Vietnamese hiding in bunkers, shelters, and their fragile homes, terrified. Gathered in groups they were marched to the far side of the village, toward the paddy fields and the irrigation ditch. By the time Conti arrived at the edge of the ditch there were already a number of Vietnamese standing there, guarded by some of the soldiers, who squatted down and took a rest. Conti approached Charles Hall, from Chicago, a Negro soldier in the first squad who was standing near a small wooden bridge which crossed the ditch. The Italian boasted how Calley had earlier caught him with his pants down and his penis out trying to get a blow job from the Vietnamese woman, while threatening her child with a gun. Nothing surprised any of them about Conti. He and a half a dozen members of the company were notorious for fooling with the local women—so much so that medics administered shots of penicillin to him while they were on operations in the field. Nick Capezza, the company medic, used to joke how he nearly exhausted his supplies of the antibiotic drug giving Conti his shots for venereal disease.

Meadlo's face was flushed. His eyes were still full of tears when he arrived with Grzesik at the ditch site and found Calley sitting down. "We've got another job to do," he said looking up at them. About ten members of the platoon were guarding forty to fifty Vietnamese. Babies were crying and crawling around. James Dursi, a heavy-set Irish-Italian from Brooklyn, was looking at a man in white robes with a goatee beard, whom he took to be a Buddhist monk, praying over an elderly woman. She was seriously ill and had been carried through the village on a narrow wooden platform which the Vietnamese use as a bed. Calley was now on his feet. Harry Stanley appeared on the scene and tried to question the monk, who was crying and bowing as he tried to make himself understood. Calley couldn't understand him. Grzesik, who had attended

Vietnamese language classes in Hawaii, tried more questions and got nowhere. Calley was getting more and more impatient. Where had the Viet Cong gone? Where were the weapons? Where were the NVA?

When the man shook his head, Calley struck him in the mouth with his rifle butt.

Just then a child, aged about 2 years and parted from its mother, managed to crawl up to the top of the ditch. Dursi watched horrified as Calley picked the child up, shoved it back down the slope, and shot it before returning to question the monk. The villagers pleaded for the holy man's life. Stanley asked the bearded man the same questions in Vietnamese that Calley was asking in English in an effort to defuse the situation. But the monk vainly replied that there were no North Vietnamese soldiers in the village. There were no weapons. Stanley translated these replies. Immediately Calley grabbed the monk, pulled him round, hurled him into the paddy, and opened fire with Meadlo's M-16. As the elderly *mama-san* lying prostrate tried to get up, she too was killed.

More Vietnamese shepherded by soldiers were arriving on the scene, and Calley indicated to Meadlo and Boyce he wanted everyone killed. He began pushing the peasants into the irrigation channel. Others joined in, using their rifle butts to shove the wailing Vietnamese down the steep slope. Some jumped in by themselves; others sat down on the edge, moaning and crying, clearly aware that disaster was imminent. It was a pitiful sight.

Up until the time all the firing started, Herbert Carter had been kneeling beside Dursi, quietly playing with a couple of children. Dursi said incredulously: "I think Calley wants them all killed." Carter said: "Oh, no."

"He can send me to jail but I am not going to kill anybody," said Dursi, beginning to move away, wondering what would happen to him for refusing to fire. Dursi was another one who liked to play with the children. Earlier in the day he had been devastated after he opened fire and killed someone running from the village. It turned out to be a woman carrying a baby and Dursi was horrified and ashamed by what he had done. Olsen had seen he was really cut up about it.

A woman standing next to Robert Maples showed him a bullet wound in her left arm. He felt helpless. There was nothing he could do for her. Calley shoved her in the ditch and told Maples: "Load your machine gun and shoot these people."

Maples shook his head and replied: "I'm not going to do that." Calley turned his M-16 on Maples as if to shoot him there and then. Maples was surprised and relieved when some of the other soldiers interposed to protect him. Calley backed off. Seconds later he and Meadlo began firing. A machine gun opened up and one of the squad leaders tried to usher the men into line so they could all fire simultaneously. Dursi stood completely frozen, watching disbelievingly, as the Vietnamese tried frantically to hide under one another, mothers protecting babies. Screaming at Dursi above the sounds of M-16s on full automatic, Meadlo continued pouring shells into the ditch. Crying hysterically once more, he stopped for a second: "Why aren't you firing?" he pleaded with Dursi, "Fire, why don't you fire?" The onlookers saw the remnants of shredded human beings, hundreds of pieces of flesh and bone, flying up in the air as the shallow ravine was repeatedly sprayed with bullets. Magazine after magazine was reloaded during the mass execution.

THREE

CONTROVERSIES AND CONSEQUENCES OF AMERICAN INVOLVEMENT

Kompong Cham, Cambodia. Cambodian soldier wearing a helmet with a message describing his feelings. UPI/CORBIS-BETTMANN

CHAPTER 8

Laos and Cambodia

French Indochina included not just Vietnam but its neighbors to the west, Laos and Cambodia. For brief periods—Laos in 1960–61, Cambodia in 1969–70—these places made front-page news in the United States when the Kennedy and Nixon administrations tried, with decidedly limited success, to keep them out of Communist hands. Otherwise, Laos and Cambodia were the sites of the sideshow war, an adjunct to the conflict on the main stage. Part of the Ho Chi Minh Trail ran through Laos; Communist war matériel transited Cambodia on its way to South Vietnam, and Communist troops sheltered there. Both places had their own Communist movements: the Pathet Lao in Laos, the Khmer Rouge in Cambodia. And both places were vigorously bombed by the United States.

The readings in this chapter shed light on the sideshow wars. Historian Timothy Castle summarizes and evaluates U.S. policy toward Laos from 1955 to 1975. While the Americans were committed to keeping some kind of anti-Communist force in the field, Ho Chi Minh and his generals were equally determined to maintain Laos as a conduit for North Vietnamese troops and supplies heading south. The other two readings are excerpts from books by British scholar William Shawcross and former National Security Adviser and Secretary of State Henry Kissinger, offering strikingly different interpretations of the Nixon administration's secret decision to bomb North Vietnamese sanctuaries inside Cambodia in 1969. The Shawcross-Kissinger debate remains one of the most bitter from the period and raises troubling questions. Was bombing Cambodia a risk worth taking, or did it expand and prolong the war? Was the secrecy of the bombing justified? And finally, does the Nixon administration bear any responsibility for the ultimate victory of the Khmer Rouge, and is it therefore tainted by the unspeakable crimes of the Communist regime in Cambodia from 1975 to 1978?

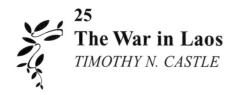

25
The War in Laos
TIMOTHY N. CASTLE

The American military aid program in Laos began as an adjunct to other U.S. security initiatives in the region. Rejecting the 1954 Geneva settlement as inadequate to preclude communist aggression in Southeast Asia, the Eisenhower administration orchestrated the creation of the Southeast Asia Treaty Organization. When the United States succeeded France in training the South Vietnamese armed forces, it also began providing military assistance to the French Military Mission in Laos. America's "can do" spirit was, however, inconsistent with the lax French colonial work ethic and the United States moved immediately to take charge of Lao military training.

Initial U.S. efforts at Lao military assistance, which began in 1955, fell miserably short. The Programs Evaluations Office was encumbered by a staff of military retirees and former or would-be military personnel; it lacked direction, experienced great difficulty with the French military, and was hampered by the convoluted Lao political situation. Nevertheless, Washington allowed the PEO to muddle along for more than three years before deciding that the program required the attention of a senior active-duty military officer. The arrival of Brigadier General [John A.] Heintges in February 1959 signaled Washington's decision to begin a full-fledged military aid program and, therefore, an even greater departure from the 1954 agreements.

Although it was not planned, General Heintges's assignment coincided with Prime Minister Phoui Sananikone's announcement that the Royal Lao government viewed the 1954 Geneva Agreements as fully implemented. This declaration, and the recent replacement of Pathet Lao cabinet members by right-wing army officers, touched off increased military contact between the Pathet Lao and the Lao army. The Royal Lao Army acquitted itself in its usual desultory fashion, evidence that the PEO had accomplished little, and the Phoui government publicly requested greater U.S. military aid.

Washington responded quickly to the Lao request and Heintges soon had several hundred U.S. Army Special Forces trainers and Filipino contract technicians assigned to the PEO. The arrival of these additional personnel and an increased budget still did not markedly improve the fighting capabilities of the Royal Lao Army. The Green Berets were frustrated by the short length of their tours in Laos and the refusal of Lao officers to take part in any training programs. And, while the integration of Filipino technicians into the Lao military seemed expedient at the time, it inculcated a reliance on foreigners that stifled later efforts to make the Lao armed forces more self-sufficient.

The expanded American presence in Laos provided opportunities for enormous graft and malfeasance within the royal government. Pathet Lao propagandists rightly pointed to suddenly wealthy civil servants, while the Lao people waited futilely for promised roads, schools, and clinics. The Lao army's enlisted force was exploited by their officers, who often short-changed the men in their pay and food rations and sold newly arrived U.S. military equipment. A sincere, but naive attempt by Captain Kong Le to redress these injustices and end foreign influence in his country elevated the Laotian civil war into a confrontation of superpowers.

Kong Le's 1960 coup and the installation of Souvanna Phouma as prime minister were immediately and firmly opposed by the United States and Thailand. Since the

1954 signing of the Manila Pact, Washington and Bangkok had been united in their efforts to oppose the inclusion of the Pathet Lao in any Lao coalition government. This anticommunist fervor caused the United States and Thailand to overlook the copious shortcomings of General Phoumi [Nosavan]'s military leadership and his financial misdeeds, while precipitously dismissing anyone who considered involving the Pathet Lao in a political settlement.

The Thai blockade of Vientiane, the suspension of American military aid to Souvanna's government, and blatant PEO assistance to General Phoumi's forces only exacerbated the situation. For five years the U.S. had enjoyed the advantage of resupplying the Lao military through Thailand by air transport and highway shipment. In contrast, support for the Pathet Lao from China and North Vietnam had to make its way into Laos via time-consuming truck convoys. When Souvanna countered these actions by accepting Soviet military aid he dramatically balanced the military assistance scales. Suddenly, the United States and its new president were faced with an unprecedented Soviet airlift and the realization that the Russians had decided to test America's resolve in Southeast Asia.

The Laotian crisis, escalating in the first days and months of the Kennedy administration, threatened to undercut the young president's international credibility, his foreign policy agenda, and force the United States into a war with the Soviets. Kennedy insisted that he would not be "humiliated" by the Soviets, but the president and his advisors knew enough about the land and people of Laos to decide that the United States should avoid, if possible, a conventional war in Laos. The White House decided to pursue a strategy of tough military "signaling" to the Soviets, while expanding the Lao military assistance program and ordering the development of a secret and unconventional military force in Laos.

Earlier U.S. military assistance efforts in Laos were covert in deference to the 1954 Geneva Accords and mostly focused on the training and support of a conventional army. The Kennedy administration, beginning in 1961, greatly expanded America's involvement in Laos. Since the Royal Lao Army had repeatedly shown its ineptitude, the United States simply recruited a group that would fight. Emphasizing the dangers the communists posed to the Hmong way of life, the CIA was able to develop a surrogate army for the lowland Lao. Determined to make Laos a bastion of freedom, Washington chose to ignore the consequences of supporting a government that was often reluctant to shed blood in its own defense. Although diplomatic maneuvering would prompt a brief respite in U.S. military activity, America's covert Lao war policy was set.

The 1962 Geneva Agreements allowed the United States and the Soviet Union to back away from military confrontation, but the diplomats did little to solve the Lao kingdom's security concerns. President Kennedy, despite the knowledge that North Vietnamese forces remained in Laos, complied with the Geneva terms and ordered a complete withdrawal from Laos of the U.S. Military Assistance Advisory Group. The president acted at the urging of Ambassador W. Averell Harriman, who firmly believed the Soviets could ensure North Vietnamese adherence to the accords. Harriman's faith was misplaced, and perhaps the Kremlin truly misjudged its sway over Hanoi. In any case, Ho Chi Minh never had any intention of abandoning his Laotian highway to South Vietnam.

In addition to Harriman's Soviet "guarantee," there was also a State Department judgment that Hanoi's forces would be circumspect in their violations of Laotian neutrality. This is a critical point in understanding America's Lao policy.

Because the North Vietnamese were transiting Laos en route to make war in South Vietnam, the White House was now conceding that American intervention, if necessary, should occur in South Vietnam and not Laos. In addition, the administration believed that as long as the North Vietnamese denied their presence in Laos, the U.S. could also undertake "nonattributable" military action in the kingdom without fear of international condemnation. Accordingly, Washington could then move its focus to Vietnam where, administration experts predicted, the U.S. could more easily defend the region against communist expansion.

The CIA experienced little difficulty in implementing this covert war policy. Vang Pao and his Hmong clans, driven off their mountains by continuing communist pressure and facing hostility in the lowlands, had little choice but to fight. Air America's experienced pilots and unparalleled repair facilities promised professional and durable air support. Once USAID [Agency for International Development] was directed by the president to assist the CIA with refugee relief and "cover" for agency operatives, the team was complete. The training of the lowland Lao army was left to DEPCHIEF [Deputy Chief, Joint U.S. Military Advisory Group, Thailand], the U.S. military attachés in Laos, and the USAID Requirements Office.

Without Thai air bases and Thai manpower the United States could not have supported a meaningful covert war in Laos. Bangkok, anxious to see the United States stem communism on the far side of the Mekong, allowed the basing of hundreds of American aircraft—which flew missions over Laos, Cambodia, and the Vietnams—and established "Headquarters 333" to work in concert with the CIA. At no financial cost the astute Thais were able to gain increased border security and hundreds of millions of dollars in military and economic aid. Moreover, the American presence guaranteed the Thai a powerful and immediate buffer against any large-scale communist aggression.

The political implications of the United States conducting a secret war in a neutral country left no doubt that the American ambassador to Laos would have to have strict control over the operation. Even though the "Kennedy letter" enunciated the ambassador's authority over the embassy's "Country Team," the State Department was quite judicious in the selection of its senior Vientiane diplomat. Leonard Unger became the first ambassador to undertake the extraordinarily difficult job of publicly proclaiming American adherence to Lao neutrality, while secretly directing a prohibited military assistance program. Ambassador Unger was more than equal to the task and was subsequently posted to Bangkok where he continued to be an active participant in arranging Thai support for the Lao war.

Ambassador William Sullivan was the most important and influential man in the twenty-year history of America's military assistance program in Laos. For more than four years Sullivan ran the Vientiane Country Team and the Lao war with virtual impunity. His experience in Geneva and support in Washington provided Sullivan with formidable foreign policy insight and political clout. Ambassador Sullivan established himself as the supreme and unquestioned arbiter of all U.S. activities in Laos. His personal attention and involvement in every aspect of the American Mission insured its smooth and professional operation; Sullivan's flaw was an undisguised distrust of the American military.

Ambassador Sullivan believed that U.S. policy objectives in Laos dictated that the U.S. military presence there be minimal. As the war in Vietnam intensified, Sullivan was under increasing pressure from the U.S. military command in Saigon to ease these restrictions. The ambassador was correct in refusing to delegate all of his military authority to COMUSMACV [Commander of the U.S. Military Assistance Command,

Vietnam]. America's announced respect for the 1962 Geneva Accords would have looked foolish, indeed, if Laos had been designated a part of COMUSMACV's theater of operations. Nonetheless, Sullivan could have allowed COMUSMACV, through the 7/13th Air Force, a much greater role in the direction of the air war. Professional military advice on aerial operations would not have exposed America's true military involvement in Laos and it might have improved the air campaign.

Sullivan's decision to exclude COMUSMACV and the 7/13th Air Force from almost all decision making elevated the military role of the CIA. In particular, through the ambassador, the CIA exercised considerable control over American military air power. As evidenced by the recollections and writings of many senior U.S. Air Force officers, CIA officers were mostly untrained in the employment of sophisticated bomber aircraft. Also questionable was the Agency's direction of Air America and U.S. Air Force helicopters in the insertion and extraction of large numbers of troops. In defense of the CIA role, William Sullivan and William Colby have both pointed to the Agency's long experience in Laos as compared to the usual one-year U.S. military tour of duty. Still, Sullivan could have directed a closer association between the CIA and the 7/13th AF that might have capitalized on the expertise of both organizations. It is obvious the CIA wanted air power on demand, with no outside interference.

Ambassador Sullivan also insisted that DEPCHIEF play a minor role in Lao operations. The USAID Requirements Office was staffed by dedicated people, mostly former military men. But the RO, even with the addition of Project 404 personnel, was able neither to gauge the effectiveness of the Lao military nor adequately supervise Lao use of American aid. The results were sloppy training, abuse of military equipment, opportunities for wholesale malfeasance, and an ineffective army. If the DEPCHIEF commander had been given a responsible place on the embassy Country Team, the RO workers and their colleagues in Thailand might well have developed more effective training programs. Such a collaboration offered the chance of some real improvement in the Lao military.

The military situation in Laos began to change in the late 1960s. America's covert paramilitary war in Laos was fast escalating into a conventional conflict with enormous human and financial costs. The increased aggressiveness of the North Vietnamese dry-season campaigns, a new administration in Washington, and a growing antiwar feeling in the American Congress brought change, albeit slowly, to America's Lao policy.

Ambassador G. McMurtrie Godley, who enjoyed close associations within the CIA, initially retained most of William Sullivan's management policies. The CIA station chief continued to serve as the ambassador's principal military advisor and DEPCHIEF and the 7/13th AF were largely ignored. As the war in Laos accelerated, Godley and his Country Team found themselves increasingly involved in large-scale military operations. The Hmong, who for years had effectively served as guerilla fighters, were now regularly employed against sizable North Vietnamese forces. Marginally equipped and poorly suited for conventional combat, the Hmong suffered horrific casualties. The kingdom's defense began to depend almost entirely on massive aerial bombing and the infusion of additional Thai artillery and infantry units. Nevertheless, Godley clung to the policies of the past and allowed his staff to dictate military requirements to a wholly exasperated 7/13th AF and COMUSMACV.

After years of effort, in 1972 the Pentagon convinced the State Department that DEPCHIEF required the attention of a general officer. Brigadier General [John] Vessey's performance quickly won Godley's confidence, and, for the first time since the departure of Major General [Reuben] Tucker in October 1961, there was a professional military leader in Laos. Vessey's expertise and recommendations led the way for much improved relations between the U.S. Embassy in Vientiane and senior U.S. military officials in Thailand and South Vietnam. Visits to Laos by U.S. general officers, unthinkable in the past, began to occur with some frequency. Increased understanding, on both sides of the Mekong, measurably improved cooperation on military matters.

However, public revelations about the true extent of America's involvement in the kingdom brought about stiff reductions, mandated by the U.S. Congress, in Lao military aid. By late 1972 there was little question that the United States would soon disengage from the war in Vietnam. The U.S. military had "joined" the Vientiane Country Team a little late.

The war in Laos was always fought in the shadow of Vietnam, so when Hanoi and Washington concluded a settlement there was no doubt that the Lao conflict would soon end. Dr. [Henry] Kissinger's recollections notwithstanding, the Royal Lao government had no choice but to complete a cease-fire agreement with the Pathet Lao. Nevertheless, Prince Souvanna Phouma was hardly an unwitting victim of American foreign policy. By late 1964 the prince was fully aware of America's covert Lao ground and air campaigns. For more than eight years Souvanna had accepted, and often requested, U.S. military activity in Laos. During much of this period, the prince also maintained close contact with his brother, Prince Souphanouvong. The prime minister and Henry Kissinger might well have enjoyed a mutual discussion on Metternich.

The February 1973 Vientiane Agreement stopped U.S. bombing in Laos and, once a new Lao coalition government was formed, mandated the expulsion of Air America and the Thai SGUs [Special Guerrilla Units]. Although some in Washington hoped that the new Lao government would allow the retention of a small U.S. military assistance program, America's covert war in Laos was at an end.

Over the next year, as the Pathet Lao and the royalists attempted to form a new government, the United States continued to supply the Royal Lao Army with military aid. It was a wasted effort. For too many years, with U.S. acquiescence, the Lao military had been content to sit out the war and allow the Americans to pay the Hmong and Thais to defend the kingdom. Now, even with the imminent cancellation of the U.S. military aid program, there was no sense of urgency. Some senior Lao military officers believed Souvanna and Souphanouvong would come to a compromise and, as before, the communists would only be part of a new government. Others, reflecting a traditional Lao perspective, were resigned to their fate. The Lao were not, and could never be, "Turks."

The formation of the Lao Provisional Government of National Union resulted in the complete withdrawal by late May 1974 of the remaining Thai SGUs and the departure of all nonaccredited U.S. military personnel from Laos. The United States had fully complied with the Vientiane Agreement, even though President Nixon, like President Kennedy in 1962, knew that the North Vietnamese remained in Laos. Unlike Kennedy, however, Nixon was not thinking about a future U.S. covert return to Laos. On May 9, 1974, the U.S. House Judiciary Committee had opened impeachment hearings on the president of the United States. Regardless of North Vietnamese duplicity, U.S. military involvement in Laos and the rest of Indochina had come to an end.

When the North Vietnamese forces entered Saigon on April 30, 1975, the Pathet Lao knew their victory was also near. Plans for any future U.S. military aid program in Laos completely evaporated, and the U.S. embassy in Vientiane was drawn down to a skeleton staff. The military assistance program in Laos was ended.

This study began with a basic question: Why was Laos of importance to the United States? The answer inheres in the geopolitical foundation of the containment strategy. The engine that drove America's overall post–World War II involvement in Southeast

Asia was its determination to halt communist expansion before it consumed the entire continent. Laos, which uniquely bordered all the region's other states, was a key component of any successful communist movement in South Vietnam, Thailand, and Cambodia. The preservation of a truly neutral Laos, which would deny communist trespass of the kingdom, therefore figured prominently in the U.S. containment strategy. This examination has shown, however, that Laotian neutrality was never achieved. Communist violations of the 1954 and 1962 Geneva Agreements were countered by the establishment of a covert U.S. military assistance program for Laos, also a clear violation of Laotian neutrality.

Was American policy toward Laos, therefore, a failure? The answer depends upon one's criteria. State Department official Roger Hilsman, in *To Move a Nation*, has called President Kennedy's containment stratagem of neutralizing Laos a "triumph of statecraft." Hilsman and successive White House advisors discerned the political, military, and physical tangle of Laos; the chaotic, land-locked country was no place to fight another Asian ground war. To this end, America's objective of shifting the conventional military confrontation with the communists to Vietnam was both pragmatic and adept. For more than a decade the United States successfully maintained the façade of Laotian neutrality and focused its armed forces on winning the public war in Vietnam.

The geographic imperative of Laos nevertheless remained. Official neutrality notwithstanding, Laos was essential to the spread of communism in Southeast Asia. The kingdom's eastern provinces were Hanoi's critical avenues to the south. In response, U.S.-controlled Hmong and Thai ground forces worked hard to disrupt these resupply activities. Increasingly, American bombers rained the Ho Chi Minh Trail with tons of bombs. Yet, both sides wisely avoided a full-scale war in Laos. The North Vietnamese army and their Pathet Lao allies could have struck at many of the important Laotian river cities, including Luang Prabang. Washington could have ordered American troops inserted into Laos and placed along the Trail. In either case the result would have been an immediate and bloody escalation of the war. Both countries refrained from direct confrontation and precipitous military action, so that "nonattributable war" exacted relatively few American casualties.

By avoiding direct military intervention in Laos, America also relinquished an opportunity to sever Hanoi's pipeline to South Vietnam. Despite harassment by the "secret army" and massive American bombing, the North Vietnamese continued to make their way south. The United States, unwilling to commit American ground forces to Laos, constrained by a war-weary and disillusioned public, and allied with an ineffective South Vietnamese military, could not defeat the North Vietnamese. Ultimately, Laotian "neutrality" worked to the advantage of Hanoi and doomed U.S. objectives.

Washington could take some solace in the fact that relatively few American lives were lost in Laos, and the majority of the Lao Lum and their cities escaped the fighting, but one Laotian group suffered greatly. For the Hmong of northeastern Laos there was no neutrality. Their horrific casualties were payment in advance for the promise of a better life, free of communist or lowland Lao controls. Americans solicited these highland guerilla fighters; still, U.S. policymakers cannot be held completely responsible for the Hmong losses. The elite of Vientiane and Luang Prabang, who openly viewed the mountain people as little more than savages, were quite willing to sit back and allow their Hmong surrogates to fight the communist trespassers. After all, the lowland Lao army rarely possessed the determination to stand and fight effectively against the North Vietnamese. Moreover, communist proscriptions were anathema to the Hmong way of life. U.S. involvement increased the level of violence, but even without American assistance most of Vang Pao's Hmong clans would have resisted the North Vietnamese.

A final legacy of America's Laotian policy is that it cemented Thai-U.S. relations. A major confrontation in Laos would have quickly spread across the long and porous Thai-Lao border. Anxious to assist in the containment of communism, Bangkok permitted the United States to build critical air facilities and to recruit manpower for the "secret army." As the war expanded, these nominally Royal Thai Air Force bases became the cornerstone of the American bombing campaigns in Laos, Cambodia, and North Vietnam. The U.S.-paid Thai forces increasingly took the place of the decimated Hmong guerrillas. Thailand acquired enormous economic and military benefits from the American presence, and the Untied States obtained what some observers have termed an "unsinkable aircraft carrier."

America's war in Laos, hidden from public view for so long, deserves greater study. The unique relationships, among the Departments of State, Defense, and the Central Intelligence Agency, along with the cooperation of the Royal Thai government, and the sacrifices of the Hmong people, all merit further examination. America's longest war cast a long shadow and, [over] twenty years later, there is still much to be learned.

26
Bombing Cambodia: A Critique
WILLIAM SHAWCROSS

The first request was unpretentious. On February 9, 1969, less than a month after the inauguration of Richard Nixon, General Creighton Abrams, commander of United States forces in South Vietnam, cabled General Earle G. Wheeler, Chairman of the Joint Chiefs of Staff, to inform him that "recent information, developed from photo reconnaissance and a rallier gives us hard intelligence on COSVN HQ facilities in Base Area 353."

COSVN HQ was the acronym for the elusive headquarters—"Central Office for South Vietnam"—from which, according to the United States military, the North Vietnamese and Viet Cong were directing their war effort in South Vietnam. Until then, Abrams remarked, the military had placed COSVN in Laos. Now he was certain the headquarters was much farther south, in one of neutral Cambodia's border states which were being used by the Communists as bases and sanctuaries from the fighting in Vietnam. Abrams wanted to attack it.

> The area is covered by thick canopy jungle. Source reports there are no concrete structures in this area. Usually reliable sources report that COSVN and COSVN-associated elements consistently remain in the same general area along the border. All our information, generally confirmed by imagery interpretation, provides us with a firm basis for targeting COSVY HQs.

Already Abrams had been instructed by the new administration to discuss United States troop withdrawals with the South Vietnamese. Now he reminded Wheeler that he had predicted a large-scale enemy offensive around Saigon in the near future. An attack on COSVN, he argued, "will have an immediate effect on the offensive and will also have its effect on future military offensives which COSVN may desire to undertake." An appropriate form of assault would be "a short-duration, concentrated B-52 attack of up to 60 sorties, compressing the time interval between strikes to the minimum. This is more than we would normally use to cover a target this size, but in this case it would be wise to insure complete destruction."

Abrams seems to have understood some of the implications of this request. Prince Norodom Sihanouk, Cambodia's ruler, had long been trying to keep his country out of the war in Vietnam. Abrams assured Wheeler that "there is little likelihood of involving Cambodian nationals if the target boxes are placed carefully. Total bomber exposure over Cambodian territory would be less than one minute per sortie." (Put another way, sixty sorties would take about one hour.) The general also thought it necessary to point out that "the successful destruction of COSVN HQs in a single blow would, I believe, have a very significant impact on enemy operations throughout South Vietnam." He asked for authority for the attack.

The Joint Chiefs sent Abrams's memo up to Melvin R. Laird, a former Wisconsin Republican Congressman, who was the new Secretary of Defense. Laird passed it to the White House, where it received the immediate attention of the new President and his National Security Affairs adviser, Dr. Henry Kissinger.

Two days later General John P. McConnell, the acting chairman in Wheeler's absence, sent a reply that must have cheered Abrams; it indicated that Washington was taking the idea even more seriously than Abrams himself. His request to Wheeler had not been highly classified, but simply headed "Personal for Addressees." McConnell's answer, however, was routed so that almost no one but he and Abrams could see it and was plastered with classifications: "Top Secret"—"Sensitive"—"Eyes Only"—"Delivery during Waking Hours"—"Personal for Addressee's Eyes Only."

McConnell told Abrams that his request had been presented to "the highest authority." In the conventions of cable language, this meant that President Nixon himself had seen it. The President had not rejected the idea; Abrams was told that "this matter will be further considered." The cable went on:

> 2. The highest authority desires that this matter be held as closely as possible in all channels and in all agencies which have had access to it.
>
> 3. The highest authority also wants your estimate on the number of Cambodian civilians who might become casualties of such an attack.
>
> 4. It will not, repeat not, be necessary for you to send a briefing team to Washington. However, it will be important for you to keep me informed on any further developments from your viewpoint. Warm regards.

Despite McConnell's advice, Abrams did send a briefing team to Washington. Two colonels arrived at the Pentagon, and a special breakfast meeting was arranged at which they could explain Abrams' proposals to a number of senior officials. These included Melvin Laird, General Wheeler, Colonel Robert Pursley, Laird's military assistant, and Lieutenant General John Vogt, then the Air Force's Assistant Deputy Chief of Staff for Plans and Operations. The meeting was also attended by a representative from Dr. Kissinger's National Security Council staff, Colonel Alexander Haig.

The colonels outlined their argument with conviction. This time, they claimed, it really was true: Viet Cong and North Vietnamese headquarters had been located. Base Area 353 was in the so-called Fish Hook, a corner of Cambodia that jutted into South Vietnam, northwest of Saigon. Even without COSVN, it was considered one of the most important Communist sanctuaries in Cambodia. Several regiments were based there and it also contained military hospitals and large caches of food and arms.

Over the next five weeks Abrams's request was frequently discussed by the National Security Council staff and at Presidential meetings in the Oval Office of the White House. Understandably perhaps, the Joint Chiefs were enthusiastic in support of the proposal. Melvin Laird was more skeptical. But he acknowledged that if COSVN had really been discovered it should be destroyed and argued that it could be publicly justified as an essential precondition to troop withdrawal. Nixon and Kissinger, however, were adamant that if it were done, it had to be done in total secrecy. Normal "Top Secret" reporting channels were not enough. Later, General Wheeler recalled that the President said—"not just once, but either to me or in my presence at least half a dozen times"—that nothing whatsoever about the proposal must ever be disclosed.

Before a final decision was made, the Chiefs cabled Abrams to tell him that he could make tentative plans for launching the strike on the early morning of March 18. He was told of the demands for secrecy and was given a code name for the operation— "Breakfast," after the Pentagon briefing.

The cable set out in detail the way in which the raids were to be concealed. The planes would be prepared for a normal mission against targets in Vietnam. If the Joint Chiefs sent the signal "Execute repeat Execute Operation Breakfast," they would then be diverted to attack the Cambodian base area. No announcement would be made. "Due to sensitivity of this operation addressees insure that personnel are informed only on a strict need-to-know basis and at the latest feasible time which permits the operation to be conducted effectively."

Abrams made the necessary dispositions, and on March 17 Wheeler cabled him: "Strike on COSVN headquarters is approved. Forty-eight sorties will be flown against COSVN headquarters. Twelve strikes will be flown against *legitimate* targets of your choice in SVN not repeat not near the Cambodian border." (Emphasis added)

The strikes were to take place almost at once, between three o'clock and seven o'clock on the morning of March 18, unless Abrams received a priority "Red Rocket" message "Cancel repeat Cancel Operation Breakfast."

The cable described how the press was to be handled. When the command in Saigon published its daily bombing summary, it should state that, "B-52 missions in six strikes early this morning bombed these targets: QUOTE Enemy activity, base camps, and bunker and tunnel complexes 45 kilometers north-east of Tay Ninh City. UNQUOTE. Following the above, list two or more other B-52 targets struck (12 sorties)."

Wheeler continued:

> In the event press inquiries are received following the execution of the Breakfast Plan as to whether or not U.S. B-52s have struck in Cambodia, U.S. spokesman will confirm the B-52s did strike on routine missions adjacent to the Cambodian border but state that he has no details and will look into this question. Should the press persist in its inquiries or in the event of a Cambodian protest concerning U.S. strikes in Cambodia, U.S. spokesman will neither confirm nor deny reports of attacks on Cambodia but state it will be investigated. After delivering a reply to any Cambodian protest, Washington will inform the press that we have apologized and offered compensation.

Finally, Wheeler reminded Abrams and the B-52 commanders, "Due to the sensitivity of this operation all persons who know of it, who participate in its planning, preparation or execution should be warned not repeat not to discuss it with unauthorized individuals."

Many of the B-52s used in Indochina were based at Anderson Air Force Base in Guam. The planes had been built in the 1950s as an integral part of the United States' nuclear deterrent, but since 1965 more than a hundred of them had been adapted to carry dozens of conventional 750-lb. bombs in their bellies and under their wings. They were still controlled by Strategic Air Command but were at the disposition of the Commander of U.S. Forces in South Vietnam. Abrams could call upon sixty planes a day. Each plane could carry a load of approximately thirty tons of bombs.

Before takeoff, the crews of the B-52s were always briefed on the location of their targets in South Vietnam. After Wheeler's March 17 "Execute Operation Breakfast" order was received, the pilots and navigators of the planes to be diverted were taken aside by their commanding officer and told to expect the ground controllers in Vietnam to give them the coordinates of new targets—they would be bombing Cambodia.

That evening the heavily laden planes rumbled off the long runway, rose slowly over the Russian trawlers, which almost always seemed to be on station just off the island, and climbed to 30,000 feet for the monotonous five-hour cruise to Indochina. There was little for the six-man crew to do—except watch for storm clouds over the Philippines and refuel in mid-air—until they were above the South China Sea approaching the dark line of the Vietnamese coast.

At this point they entered the war zone and came under control of the ground radar sites in South Vietnam. But even now there was little reason for concern. There were no enemy fighter planes to harass and chivvy them, no antiaircraft fire, no ground-to-air missiles. A ground radar controller gave the navigator the coordinates of the final bomb run. Then the controller watched on his radar screen as the planes in cells of three, approached the target; as they did so he counted down the bombardiers with the words "Five—four—three—two—one—*hack*."

Twenty times that night the ground controllers, sitting in their air-conditioned "hootches" in South Vietnam, cans of Coke or 7-Up by their elbows, called out *hack*. Sixty long strings of bombs spread through the dark and fell to the earth faster than the speed of sound. Each plane load dropped into an area, or "box," about half a mile wide by two miles long, and as each bomb fell, it threw up a fountain of earth, trees and bodies, until the air above the targets was thick with dust and debris, and the ground itself flashed with explosions and fire. For the first time in the war, so far as is known, forty-eight of such boxes were stamped upon neutral Cambodia by the express order of the President.

One group of men was especially delighted by the event. Since May 1967, when the U.S. Military command in Saigon became concerned at the way the North Vietnamese and Viet Cong were evading American "search and destroy" and air attacks in Vietnam by making more use of bases in Laos and Cambodia, the U.S. Special Forces had been running special, highly classified missions into the two countries. Their code name was Daniel Boone.

The Daniel Boone teams entered Cambodia all along its 500-mile frontier with South Vietnam from the lonely, craggy, impenetrable mountain forests in the north, down to the well-populated and thickly reeded waterways along the Mekong River. There was a quality of fantasy about the missions. They usually contained two or three Americans and up to ten local mercenaries, often recruited from the hill tribes of the area. All the Americans were volunteers, and they were enjoined to the strictest secrecy; the release they had to sign subjected them to a $10,000 fine and up to ten years' imprisonment for disclosing details of the forays. Because the missions were supposed to be what the Army called "sterile," the Americans either wore uniforms that could not be traced to any American unit or were disguised in the black pajamas of the Viet Cong. They carried what had become by the middle '60s the universal symbol of revolution, the Soviet-designed AK-47 automatic rifle made in China. Deaths were reported to relatives as having occurred "along the border."

These and other precautions helped conceal the work from the American press and the Congress. But black pajamas do not really hide well-fed Caucasians prowling around Southeast Asian jungles. Teams often found that, within two hours of being "inserted" by helicopter (parachutes were not used, because the Americans fell so much faster than the Vietnamese), their opponents had put trackers onto them. Their reconnaissance mission abandoned, they had to flee through the jungle or crawl through the thick fifteen-foot grass, evading their stalkers until they could find a suitable clearing to call helicopter support for rescue.

Randolph Harrison, who saw himself then as a "gung-ho lieutenant," arrived at the Special Forces headquarters in Ban Me Thuot, in the Central Highlands, in August 1968. He was given command of one of the reconnaissance companies, and he made his first mission into Cambodia on November 17, 1968, just after the American people, in the hope of peace, narrowly elected Nixon. At this time there was no consensus within the United States' intelligence establishment on the extent to which the North Vietnamese and Viet Cong were using Cambodia as a sanctuary or as a supply route, but Harrison was shocked by the evidence he saw of the enemy's insouciance just across the border from his own camp.

"There were hard-surface roads, those concrete reinforced bunkers. I personally found some abandoned base camps that were acres in size," he said later. "When you get an opportunity to see that blatant an example of their presence there, you scream and beg and do everything you can to get somebody to come in there and blast them." What he and his friends wanted most of all, he said, were B-52 "Arclight" strikes— "We had been told, as had everybody . . . that those carpet bombing attacks by B-52s [were] totally devastating, that nothing could survive, and if they had a troop concentration there it would be annihilated." They were enthusiastic when, on the morning of March 18, Major Michael Eiland, the Daniel Boone Operations officer, came up from Saigon to tell them of Operation Breakfast. He ordered a reconnaissance team into Area 353 by helicopter to pick up any possible Communist survivors. "We were told that . . . if there was anybody still alive out there they would be so stunned that all [we would] have to do [was] walk over and lead him by the arm to the helicopter."

Captain Bill Orthman was chosen to lead this team; he was given a radio operator named Barry Murphy and eleven Vietnamese. All were confident and rather excited. They were flown over the border and landed in rubble and craters. After the helicopters had taken off, the Daniel Boone men moved toward the tree line in search of their dead or dazed enemy. But within moments they were, in Harrison's words, "slaughtered."

The B-52 raid had not wiped out all the Communists as the Special Forces men had been promised. Instead, its effect, as Harrison said, had been "the same as taking a beehive the size of a basketball and poking it with a stick. They were mad."

The Communists fired at them from behind the trees on three sides. Three of the Vietnamese soldiers were immediately hit and Orthman himself was shot both in the leg and in the stomach. The group split apart and Orthman stumbled toward a bomb crater. Then a C.S. gas grenade in his rucksack burst into flames, searing the flesh of his back and his left arm. Barry Murphy threw himself into another crater and radioed frantically for the helicopters to return. Back at base they heard his call, "This is Bullet. We've got four wounded and are taking fire from all directions. We don't . . . Oh god! I'm hit!, hit! I'm hit! My leg! Ow! I'm . . . again! My back ahh can't move!" His last scream was indecipherable.

Eventually one helicopter managed to come back down through the automatic-weapons fire to pick up the survivors. Orthman was saved because a friend jumped out and rushed across the ground to carry him aboard. Three of the Vietnamese made it to the helicopter; Barry Murphy's body was not recovered.

Despite the setback, another reconnaissance team was immediately ordered to take off for Cambodia to gather "dazed" Viet Cong. Their earlier enthusiasm for the mission was now gone and in a rare breach of discipline the Daniel Boone men refused. Three of them were arrested. "You can't be court-martialed for refusing to violate the neutrality of Cambodia," Randolph Harrison reassured them. They were not.

As the night fell over Indochina, day was beginning in Washington. In his basement office in the White House, Henry Kissinger was discussing a point of policy with Morton Halperin, a young political scientist who had worked in the Pentagon during the previous administration and was now Kissinger's assistant for planning.

As the two men were talking, Colonel Alexander Haig came into the room and handed Kissinger a paper. As he read it, Halperin noticed, Kissinger smiled. He turned to Halperin and said that the United States had bombed a base in Cambodia and the first bomb-damage assessment showed that the attack had set off many secondary explosions. What did Halperin think of that? Halperin, who knew nothing of Breakfast, made a noncommittal answer. Kissinger told him that he was placing great trust in him and he must respect the confidence; almost no one else knew about the attack and no one else must know.

In his February 9 cable, Abrams had asked for a single attack to destroy COSVN headquarters. But once the decision had been made in principle that Communist violations of Cambodia's neutrality justified aggressive reciprocal action, it was not difficult to repeat the performance. The first mission had not been discovered by the press, nor had Cambodia protested. Indeed, it would now have been hard for the White House to insist on only one attack: Base Area 353 was, according to Abrams's headquarters, the Military Assistance Command, Vietnam (MACV), only one of fifteen Communist sanctuaries.

Over the next fourteen months 3,630 B-52 raids were flown against suspected Communist bases along different areas of Cambodia's border. Breakfast was followed by "Lunch," Lunch by "Snack," Snack by "Dinner," Dinner by "Dessert," Dessert by "Supper," as the program expanded to cover one "sanctuary" after another. Collectively, the operation was known as "Menu."

In 1973, after the bombing was finally discovered, both Nixon and Kissinger maintained, and still maintain, that the secrecy was necessary to protect Sihanouk, who was variously described as "acquiescing in," "approving," "allowing" or even "encouraging" the raids, so long as they were covert. They maintained that the areas were unpopulated and that only Vietnamese Communist troops, legitimate targets, were there. When he was confirmed as Secretary of State in 1973, for example, Kissinger declared that "It was not a bombing of Cambodia, but it was a bombing of North Vietnamese in Cambodia," and "the Prince as a minimum acquiesced in the bombing of unpopulated border areas." In 1976 he stated that "the government concerned [Sihanouk's] never once protested, and indeed told us that if we bombed unpopulated areas they would not notice." In fact, the evidence of Sihanouk's "acquiescence" is at least questionable, and the assertion that no Cambodians lived in these areas not only was untrue, but was known to be untrue at the time. The Joint Chiefs themselves informed the administration as early as April 1969 that many of the sanctuary areas were populated by Cambodians who might be endangered by bombing raids. The White House was to ignore this reservation.

The Chiefs' description of the bases is contained in a memorandum of April 9, 1969, written for the Secretary of Defense, in which they advocated invasion as well as bombing of Cambodia. Its conclusions were based on "Giant Dragon" high-altitude overflights, "Dorsal Fin" low-level aerial surveys and the Daniel Boone ground forays, among other evidence. It described the military purpose as well as the nature of each of the fifteen bases they had identified, and went on to estimate the number of Cambodians they contained. The figures are worth considering.

Base Area 353, Breakfast, covered 25 square kilometers and had a total population of approximately 1,640 Cambodians, of whom the Joint Chiefs reckoned 1,000 to be peasants. There were, according to the Chiefs, thirteen Cambodian towns in the area. (Villages would be a more accurate description.)

Base Area 609, Lunch, was north, near the Laotian border, in wild country without any towns. The Chiefs asserted that there were an estimated 198 Cambodians there, all of them peasants.

Base Area 351, Snack, covered 101 square kilometers and had an estimated 383 Cambodians, of whom 303 were considered peasants. There was one town in the area.

Base Area 352, Dinner, had an estimated Cambodian population of 770, of whom 700 were peasants. It contained one town.

Base Area 350, Dessert, had an estimated Cambodian population of 120, all peasants.

The Chiefs believed that all these "sanctuaries" should be attacked. They attempted to estimate how many Cambodians would be killed; they maintained that, as the Cambodians lived apart from the Vietnamese troops, their casualties would be "minimal." But they conceded that such calculations depended on many variables and were "tenuous at best." There was no pretense that the raids could occur without danger to the Cambodians—"some Cambodian casualties would be sustained in the operation." And they agreed that "the surprise effect of attacks could tend to increase casualties, as could the probable lack of protective shelters around Cambodian homes to the extent that exists in South Vietnam." Cambodian peasants, unlike the Vietnamese, had little experience of being bombed.

Some scruples, however, were brought to bear. Three of the fifteen sanctuaries—base areas 704, 354, and 707, which had "sizeable concentrations of Cambodian civilian or military population" in or around them—were not recommended for attack at all. (The definition of "sizeable" is not known; presumably it was higher than the 1,640 Cambodians living in the Breakfast site, which they had approved.) The Chiefs' warning seems to have made no difference. Base Area 704 appeared on the White House's Menu as Supper. In the course of events, 247 B-52 missions were flown against it.

Because of Nixon's repeated insistence on total secrecy, few senior officials were told about Menu. The Secretary of the Air Force, Dr. Robert Seamans, was kept in ignorance; since he is not in the chain of command, this was not illegal, but General Wheeler later said that, if necessary, he would have lied to him and denied that the raids were taking place. The Chief of Staff of the Air Force, General John Ryan, was not informed; nor were the Cambodian desk officers on Abrams's intelligence arm in Saigon, the Office of Strategic Research and Analysis. None of the Congressional committees, whose duty it is to recommend appropriations and thus enable the Congress to fulfill its constitutional function of authorizing and funding war, was notified that the President had decided to carry war into a third country, whose neutrality the United States professed to respect. Instead, only a few sympathetic members of Congress, who had no constitutional authority to approve this extension of war, were quietly informed.

But if Congress and the public were easily kept in ignorance, the official record-keeping system required more sophisticated treatment. The Pentagon's computers demanded, for purposes of logistics, a complete record of hours flown, fuel expended, ordnance dropped, spare parts procured. In response to Nixon's demands for total and unassailable secrecy, the military devised an ingenious system that the Joint Chiefs liked to describe as "dual reporting."

Whether they flew from Guam, from Okinawa, or from Thailand, most B-52 missions over South Vietnam were guided to their targets by the "Skyspot" ground radar controllers at one of four radar sites in the country. The controllers received details—known as the "frag"—of the proposed strike after it had been approved in Washington. From the "frag," they calculated the range and bearing of the target from the radar site and the altitude, airspeed and ballistics of the bomb load. They then guided the planes down a narrow radar beam to target.

After missions were completed, B-52 crews reported what primary or secondary explosions they had seen to their debriefing officer at base, and the ground controllers sent their own poststrike reports to Saigon. Both reports entered the Pentagon computers and the official history of the war.

The procedures for Menu were modeled on Operation Breakfast. After a normal briefing on targets in Vietnam, the pilots and navigators of the planes that were to be diverted that night were told privately to expect the ground controllers to direct them to drop their bombs on a set of coordinates that were different from those they had just received. It was not a wide diversion; the South Vietnamese cover targets were usually selected so that the planes could simply fly another few kilometers beyond, until they were over the Cambodian target.

Major Hal Knight of Memphis was, for much of 1969, supervisor of the radar crews for the region of Vietnam that lay between Saigon and the Cambodian border. Every afternoon before a Menu mission, a special Strategic Air Command courier flight came to Bien Hoa airbase, where he worked, and he was handed a plain manila envelope containing an ordinary poststrike report form on which target coordinates had already been filled in. He locked it in his desk until evening and then, when the shift had assembled, gave the coordinates to his radar crew. They fed them through their Olivetti 101 computers to produce the details of the final bombing run for the new Cambodian target. These were called to the navigators when the B-52s arrived on station overhead in the early-morning dark.

After the bombs were released, the plane's radio operator—who was not supposed to know of the diversion—called his base by high-frequency radio to say that the mission had been accomplished. At base, the intelligence division, which also knew nothing of the change, entered the original South Vietnamese coordinates on the poststrike report. When the crews landed and were debriefed they were asked routine questions about malfunction, bomb damage and weather. The pilots and navigators were to make no mention of the new target—they had, after all, been forewarned, so it did not really count as a diversion.

At Bien Hoa itself Knight was under instructions to gather up every scrap of paper and tape with which the bombing had been plotted and lock them in his desk until daybreak. Only then (his superiors were afraid that pieces of paper might be dropped in the dark) was he to take the documents to an incinerator behind the hut and very carefully burn them. He was then to call a Saigon number he had been given—it was at Strategic Air Command Advanced Echelon—in order to tell the unidentified man who answered the telephone that "the ball game is over." The normal poststrike reports from the radar site were filled out with the coordinates of the original South Vietnamese cover target and sent, in the ordinary way, to Saigon by security mail. The night's mission over Cambodia entered the records as having taken place in Vietnam. The bombing was not merely concealed; the official, *secret* records showed that it had never happened.

The system worked well by the book, but it took no account of the attitudes of the men who were expected to implement it. Hal Knight, for example, accepted the military logic of bombing Cambodia but intensely disliked this procedure. Strategic Air Command is responsible for the nation's nuclear defense, and falsification of its reporting process was for him, alarming; Knight had been trained to believe that accurate reporting was "pretty near sacred." He was especially concerned that he was violating Article 107 of the Military Code of Justice, which provides that any one "who, with intent to deceive, signs any false record, return regulation, order or other official document, knowing the same to be false . . . shall be punished as a court-martial may direct."

Red tape protects as well as restricts, and Knight feared that the institutional safeguards and controls that are integral to the maintenance of discipline and of a loyal, law-abiding army were being discarded. He did not know at what level the bombing had been authorized or whom these unprecedented procedures were supposed to deceive; but he did appreciate, to his dismay, that the practice gave him horrifying license.

A normal target was known to many people at the radar site, to the entire B-52 crew, to the intelligence unit at the plane's base and to dozens of Pentagon officials; a Menu mission was known only to him and a very few others. There was nothing to stop him from choosing the coordinates of a town in South Vietnam or Cambodia and having it bombed. Indeed, "if someone could have punched the right number into the right spot they could have had us bombing China," he observed later.

Knight discussed the falsification with other radar operators on other sites; they too found it hard to explain. If confidentiality were so important, why not simply raise the classification from "Secret" to "Top Secret"? He asked his commanding officer, Lieutenant Colonel David Patterson about it; he was told not to do so.

"So I said, well, what is the purpose of it?"

Patterson replied "Well, the purpose is to hide these raids."

"Who from?" asked Knight.

He was apparently told, "Well, I guess the Foreign Relations Committee."

The Foreign Relations Committee did not find out about the unauthorized and illegal extension of the war into a neutral country until 1973, when Knight himself wrote to Congress to complain. But even under the restrictions imposed, the campaign was, to paraphrase Dean Rusk, known to the President, two members of the NSC, a couple of State Department officials and three hundred colonels in the Pentagon.

One evening soon after the raids began, the pilot of a Forward Air Control plane (FAC), which guided fighter bombers to their targets in South Vietnam, was sitting outside his hootch at An Loc, a few miles from the Cambodian border. "We saw beacons going overhead to the West," said Captain Gerald Greven later. "We saw the flames in the distance and the trembling of the ground from what appeared to be B-52 strikes." He was surprised, because he knew of no targets in that area. The next morning he flew to find the craters, and "to my astonishment they were on the West side of the river separating the borders of South Vietnam and Cambodia."

Greven was impressed by the amount of destruction the raids had caused, but puzzled. "I went back to my commander and he said he had no knowledge of the strike and why it had taken place." He spoke to the regional commander for the Forward Air Controllers— "he also declared to have no knowledge." He then went on to Air Support headquarters at Bien Hoa and spoke to the commanding officer. "I was told, with a slight smile, that obviously my 'maps were in error.'" Greven correctly took that to mean that he "did not have a need to know." He asked no more questions. But eventually he, too, contacted Congress.

William Beecher was the *New York Times* Pentagon correspondent, a diligent reporter. After Nixon's victory in November 1968, Beecher asked his contacts in the Defense Department how they would advise the new President to extricate American troops from Vietnam. He was told that one possible way of "buying time" would be to bomb the sanctuaries. Beecher noted this hypothesis and by April 1969 began to suspect that it was being carried out. The Pentagon was reporting its bombing strikes in South Vietnam near the Cambodian border, but he knew that no targets were there. And, despite the special "security precautions," information began to leak almost at once. On March 26, one week after the Breakfast mission, the *New York Times* reported briefly but accurately that Abrams had requested B-52 strikes against the sanctuaries. Ronald Ziegler, the White House Press Secretary, was quoted as giving a "qualified denial" to the reports. "He said that to his knowledge no request had reached the President's desk." This story was followed by comments—in *U.S. News & World Report* and by columnist C. L. Sulzberger in the *New York Times*—urging that Nixon do what he had in fact already begun. But only Beecher took the trouble to follow the obvious lead that any "qualified denial" offers. He revisited those to whom he had talked at the end of 1968, and on May 9 he revealed in the *Times* that "American B-52 bombers have raided several Viet Cong and North Vietnamese supply dumps and base camps in Cambodia for the first time, according to Nixon Administration sources, but Cambodia has not made any protest."

Beecher wrote that the bombing had started because of the increase in supplies reaching South Vietnam by sea and through Cambodia, supplies that "never have to run any sort of bombing gauntlet before they enter South Vietnam." He claimed that Prince Sihanouk had dropped hints that he would not oppose American pursuit of Communist forces which he was himself unable to dislodge. Perhaps most important, Beecher stated that the bombing was intended "to signal" Hanoi that the Nixon administration, "while pressing for peace in Paris, is willing to take some military risks avoided by the previous Administration . . . to demonstrate that the Nixon Administration is different and 'tougher.' . . ."

The revelation aroused no public interest. Four years later, this same account was to cause at least a short-lived uproar and spark demands for impeachment, but at the time it had little obvious effect. There was no press follow-up, and no members of the Senate Foreign Relations Committee, the Senate Armed Services Committee or the Appropriations committees voiced concern. In Key Biscayne, however, where Nixon and Kissinger and their staffs were working on the first of Nixon's major Vietnam speeches, the article provoked reactions that verged on hysteria.

After reading the story with Nixon, Kissinger spent much of his morning on the telephone with FBI Director J. Edgar Hoover. According to Hoover's detailed memoranda of the conversations, Kissinger asked him, in his first call at 10:35 A.M., to make "a major effort to find out where [the story] came from." A half hour later Kissinger telephoned again to say that while the FBI was about it they should try to find the sources of previous Beecher stories as well. Hoover replied that he would call back the next day with any information they had managed to gather. But within two hours Kissinger was on the line again, this time to ask Hoover to be sure he was discreet "so no stories will get out." Just how the Director liked being told how to protect his beloved FBI is not recorded, but Hoover assured Kissinger that discretion would be maintained; he had decided, he said, not to contact Beecher directly but to try to divine the source of the story from other reporters.

That afternoon, relaxing by the swimming pool with other members of the National Security Council staff, Kissinger invited his aide Morton Halperin to walk with him down the beach. Strolling along the sand, Kissinger told him of the great concern he felt over the Beecher leak. Halperin knew Kissinger well; they had been together at Harvard. He recalls that Kissinger assured him of his personal trust in him but reminded him that there were others in the Nixon administration who were suspicious of Halperin's New York and Harvard background and the fact that he had worked in [Robert] McNamara's Pentagon. It was he who was suspected of leaking to Beecher. Halperin replied that he could not have been the source; after all, it was only by chance (and Kissinger's indiscretion) that he knew anything about the bombing. Kissinger apparently agreed that this was so, but said that he was under great pressure from other members of the administration and the White House.

Kissinger now proposed an ingenious way of justifying his confidence in Halperin to the others. So that he could not possibly be held responsible for any future leaks, Kissinger suggested that he be taken off the distribution list for highly classified material. Then when a leak next occurred, he would be above suspicion and also retroactively cleared.

Halperin did not find the arrangement amusing; he had been dealing with classified materials for years and had never been asked to prove his loyalty. But Kissinger was such an old friend and presented his case with such charm and solicitousness, Halperin recalls, that he agreed to the proposal.

Kissinger and Hoover talked once more that day. At 5:05 P.M. the FBI director telephoned to report his progress. To judge by Hoover's memo, it was a bizarre conversation.

Hoover told Kissinger that Beecher "frequented" the Pentagon press office (hardly a surprising piece of information, in view of the fact that he was a Pentagon correspondent). There were still many pro-Kennedy people in the Pentagon, Hoover remarked, and they all fed Beecher with information. But on this occasion he was convinced that Morton Halperin was the culprit. According to FBI files, Halperin believed the United States had "erred in the Vietnam commitment"; moreover, the Canadian Mounted Police had discovered that he was on the mailing list of a Communist publication, "Problems of Peace and Socialism." Both Halperin and Beecher were members of the "Harvard clique" (as, of course, was Kissinger), and it was clear where the blame must lie. At the end of his memo Hoover noted, in words which resonate down the years, "Dr. Kissinger said he appreciated this very much and he hoped I would follow it up as far as we can take it, and they will destroy whoever did this if we can find him, no matter where he is."

That same afternoon the FBI placed a wiretap on Halperin's home in Bethesda, a bedroom suburb of Washington. This tap was immediately followed by others. In important, specific detail, these taps infringed the limits of the law. They marked the first of the domestic abuses of power now known as Watergate.

Night after night through the summer, fall, and winter of 1969 and into the early months of 1970 the eight-engined planes passed west over South Vietnam and on to Cambodia. Peasants were killed—no one knows how many—and Communist logistics were somewhat disrupted. To avoid the attacks, the North Vietnamese and Viet Cong pushed their sanctuaries and supply bases deeper into the country, and the area that the B-52s bombarded expanded as the year passed. The war spread.

27
Bombing Cambodia: A Defense
HENRY A. KISSINGER

The 1968 understanding with the North Vietnamese that led to the bombing halt in-cluded the "expectation" that there would be no attacks on major cities or across the DMZ [Demilitarized Zone]. When we took office, however, enemy infiltration was mounting, which strongly indicated that a new offensive was in the offing.

The only plan we found for such a contingency was for renewal of bombing of the North. On November 24, 1968, Secretary of Defense Clark Clifford had declared on ABC-TV's "Issues and Answers": "If they, at some time, show us that they are not serious and that they are not proceeding with good faith, I have no doubt whatsoever that the President will have to return to our former concept and that is to keep the pressure on the enemy and that would include bombing if necessary." Averell Harriman made the same point in a White House briefing on December 4, 1968. General Earle Wheeler, Chairman of the Joint Chiefs, was only following inherited doctrine when he told Nixon at the NSC [National Security Council] meeting of January 25, 1969, that everything possible was being done in Vietnam "except the bombing of the North."

No one in the new Administration, however, could anticipate a resumption of the bombing of the North with anything but distaste. We were savoring the honeymoon that follows the Inauguration of a new President; Nixon had never previously enjoyed the approval of the media. None of us had the stomach for the domestic outburst we knew renewed bombing would provoke—even if it were the direct result of North Viet-namese betrayal of the understandings that had led to the bombing halt. Above all, we had not yet given up hope, in the first month of the new Presidency, of uniting the nation on an honorable program for settlement of the war.

Unfortunately, alternatives to bombing the North were hard to come by. On Janu-ary 30, I met in the Pentagon with [Melvin] Laird and Wheeler to explore how we might respond should there be an enemy offensive in South Vietnam. Wheeler reiter-ated that American forces within South Vietnam were already fully committed; the only effective riposte would be operations in the DMZ or renewed bombing of the North. Laird demurred at the latter suggestion, emphasizing that the bombing halt had encouraged public expectations that the war was being wound down. Nor did I favor it, because I was eager to give negotiations a chance. On February 1, Nixon sent me a note: "I do not like the suggestions that I see in virtually every news report that 'we anticipate a Communist initiative in South Vietnam.' I believe that if any initiative occurs it should be on our part and not theirs." But my request to the Joint Chiefs for suggestions elicited the now familiar response outlining various levels of air or naval attacks on North Vietnamese targets and Mel Laird's (and my) equally standard reluc-tance to accept the recommendation.

Thought then turned to bombing of the North Vietnamese sanctuary areas in Cam-bodia, for reasons exactly the opposite of what has been assumed; it was not from a desire to expand the war, but to avoid bombing North Vietnam and yet to blunt an unprovoked offensive which was costing 400 American lives a week.

Revisionists have sometimes focused on the Nixon Administration's alleged as-sault on the "neutral" status of a "peaceful" country. These charges overlook that the issue concerned territory which was no longer Cambodian in any practical sense. For four years as many as four North Vietnamese divisions had been operating on Cambodian soil from a string of base areas along the South Vietnamese border. In 1978 the Communist victors in Cambodia put the uninvited North Vietnamese presence in northeastern Cambodia in 1969–1970 at 300,000, which far exceeded our estimates. Cambodian officials had been excluded from their soil; they contained next to no Cambodian population.* They were entirely controlled by the North Vietnamese. From these territories North Vietnamese forces would launch attacks into South Vietnam, inflict casualties, disrupt government, and then withdraw to the protection of a formally neutral country. It requires calculated advocacy, not judgment, to argue that the United States was violating the neutrality of a peaceful country when with Cambodian encouragement we, in self-defense, sporadically bombed territories in which for years no Cambodian writ had run, which were either minimally populated or totally unpopulated by civilians, and which were occupied in violation of Cambodian neutrality by an enemy killing hundreds of Americans and South Vietnamese a week from these sanctuaries.

The first suggestion came from General Wheeler. When Laird on January 30 had expressed doubt that a renewed bombing of the North was politically supportable, Wheeler proposed, as an alternative, attacks on the complex of bases that the North Vietnamese had established illegally across the border in Cambodia. On February 9, General [Creighton] Abrams cabled General Wheeler from Saigon that recent intelligence from a deserter, as well as photo reconnaissance, showed that the Communist headquarters for all of South Vietnam was located just across the Cambodian border. (As a novice I was more impressed by such seemingly definitive evidence than I would be later on. As it turned out, the Communist leaders in Phnom Penh eight years later also confirmed that the deserter's information had been accurate on that score.) Abrams requested authority to attack the headquarters from the air with B-52s. Ambassador [Ellsworth] Bunker endorsed the idea in a separate cable through State Department channels.

These recommendations fell on fertile ground. In the transition period on January 8, 1969, the President-elect had sent me a note: "In making your study of Vietnam I want a precise report on what the enemy has in Cambodia and what, if anything, we are doing to destroy the buildup there. I think a very definite change of policy toward Cambodia probably should be one of the first orders of business when we get in." General [Andrew J.] Goodpaster had drafted a reply for my signature with detailed information about the North Vietnamese base areas along the Cambodian border. He reported that "our field command in South Vietnam is convinced that the vast bulk of supplies entering Cambodia come in through Sihanoukville. . . . What we are doing about this is very limited. . . . The command in the field has made several requests for authority to enter Cambodia to conduct pre-emptive operations and in pursuit of withdrawing forces that have attacked us. All such requests have been denied or are still pending without action."

The importance of Sihanoukville was one of the contested issues in the NSSM [National Security Study Memorandum] 1 study. The US military command in Saigon was convinced that between October 1967 and September 1968 some ten thousand tons of arms had come in through Sihanoukville. But CIA and State disputed this. According to them the flow of supplies down the Ho Chi Minh Trail through Laos was

---

*The Communist deserter who helped pinpoint the location of the North Vietnamese headquarters reported that no Cambodians were permitted in the headquarters area. General [Creighton] Abrams reported this to the President in February along with an assurance that the target was at least a kilometer distant from any known Cambodian hamlets.

more than adequate to take care of the external requirements of *all* Communist forces in South Vietnam. At stake in this analysts' debate, of course, was whether the Cambodian sanctuaries were so crucial a target that they should be attacked; as happens all too frequently, intelligence estimates followed, rather than inspired, agency policy views. Those who favored attacks on the sanctuaries emphasized the importance of Sihanoukville; those who were opposed depreciated it. (When U.S. and South Vietnamese forces moved into these sanctuaries in April 1970, documents in Communist storage dumps indicated that shipments through Cambodia far exceeded even the military's highest estimates.)

But whatever the dispute about whether the matériel traveled through Sihanoukville or down the Ho Chi Minh Trail, there was no dispute about the menace of the North Vietnamese bases in Cambodia to American and South Vietnamese forces. On February 18, I received a briefing by a two-man team from Saigon, together with Laird, Deputy Secretary [David] Packard, General Wheeler, and Laird's military assistant, Colonel Robert E. Pursley. I reported to the President the conviction of General Abrams that no Cambodian civilians lived in the target area. Nevertheless, I advised against an unprovoked bombing of the sanctuaries. We should give negotiations a chance, I argued, and seek to maintain public support for our policy. We could review the situation again at the end of March—the classic bureaucratic stalling device to ease the pain of those being overruled. Nixon approved that recommendation on February 22, the day before he was to leave on his trip to Europe.

On the very day of Nixon's decision to defer action against the sanctuaries, the North Vietnamese transformed vague contingency planning into a need to deal with a crisis. After weeks of preparation antedating the new Administration, Hanoi launched a countrywide offensive. Americans killed in action during the first week of the offensive numbered 453, 336 in the second week, and 351 in the third; South Vietnamese casualties were far heavier, averaging over 500 a week. It was an act of extraordinary cynicism. No substantive negotiating sessions had been held in Paris with our new delegation, headed by Henry Cabot Lodge; the new Administration could hardly have formed its policy. Whether by accident or design, the offensive began the day before a scheduled Presidential trip overseas, thus both paralyzing our response and humiliating the new President. It occurred despite the fact that Nixon had communicated with the North Vietnamese in the transition period (as we shall see below), emphasizing his commitment to settle the war on the basis of the self-respect and honor of all parties involved. Without even testing these professions of intent, the first major move of Hanoi was to step up the killing of Americans. I noted in a report to the President that the North Vietnamese had been "able to achieve a relatively high casualty rate among US and South Vietnamese forces while not exposing their own main units."

Nixon received a military briefing on the enemy offensive in the Oval Office surrounded by piles of loose-leaf briefing books compiled by my staff and the State Department for each country he was about to visit. (Nixon later came to use the Oval Office mostly for ceremonial occasions; he usually preferred to work in his informal office in the Executive Office Building.) Nixon was going through the books, committing them to memory, grumbling about the effort he had to make to do so. He was also seething. All his instincts were to respond violently to Hanoi's cynical maneuver. For years he had charged his predecessors with weakness in reacting to Communist moves. But he was eager also that his first foreign trip as President be a success. American retaliation might spark riots in Europe; passivity might embolden our adversary. He did not resolve this dilemma immediately. The only White House reaction on the day the offensive started was a phone call by me to Soviet Ambassador [Anatoly] Dobrynin. The President wanted Moscow to understand, I said, that if the North Vietnamese offensive continued we would retaliate.

But the next day, on February 23, while in the air en route from Washington to Brussels, Nixon made up his mind; he suddenly ordered the bombing of the Cambodian sanctuaries. It seemed to me that a decision of this magnitude could not be simply communicated to Washington and to Saigon by cable from *Air Force One* without consulting relevant officials or in the absence of a detailed plan for dealing with the consequences. I therefore recommended to Nixon to postpone the final "execute" order for forty-eight hours and sent a flash message to Colonel Alexander Haig, then my military assistant in Washington, to meet me in Brussels, together with a Pentagon expert. I wanted to go over the military operations once again and to work out a diplomatic plan.

Haig, [H. R.] Haldeman (representing Nixon, who could not attend without attracting attention), the Pentagon planning officer, and I met on board *Air Force One* at Brussels airport on the morning of February 24, just before the president spoke at NATO headquarters. The plane that Nixon used had been built to Johnson's specifications. Directly behind a stateroom for the President was a conference area with an oversized chair fitting into a kidney-shaped table; both the chair and the table were equipped with buttons that enabled them to develop a life of their own. The chair could assume various positions; the table could move hydraulically up and down. If one pressed the wrong button the table would slowly sink, pinning one helplessly in the chair; the situation could turn critical if the chair was rising at the same time. In this awesome setting we worked out guidelines for the bombing of the enemy's sanctuaries: The bombing would be limited to within five miles of the frontier; we would not announce the attacks but acknowledge them if Cambodia protested, and offer to pay compensation for any damage to civilians. In the short time available, we developed both a military and a diplomatic schedule as well as guidance for briefing the press. Haig and the Pentagon expert left immediately for Washington to brief Laird. Nixon later in London gave [William P.] Rogers a cryptic account of his thinking but no details.

Before the day was out, Laird cabled his reservations from Washington. He thought that it would be impossible to keep the bombing secret, the press would be difficult to handle, and public support could not be guaranteed. He urged delay to a moment when the provocation would be clearer. It was symptomatic of the prevalent mood of hesitation, the fear to wake the dormant beast of public protest. In retrospect, it is astonishing to what extent all of us focused on the legal question of whether the understanding had been violated, and not on the four hundred American deaths a week by which Hanoi sought to break our will before we could develop any course of action. Even more astonishing now is that during this entire period no serious consideration was given to resuming the bombing of North Vietnam: the bombing halt, entered to speed a settlement, was turning into an end in itself.

I agreed with Laird's conclusions about the Cambodian bombing, if not with his reasoning. I thought that a failure to react to so cynical a move by Hanoi could doom our hopes for negotiations; it could only be read by Hanoi as a sign of Nixon's helplessness in the face of domestic pressures; it was likely to encourage further military challenges, as North Vietnam undertook to whipsaw Nixon as it had succeeded with Johnson. But the timing bothered me. I did not think it wise to launch a new military operation while the President was traveling in Europe, subject to possible hostile demonstrations and unable to meet with and rally his own government. I also did not relish the prospect of having Vietnam the subject of all our European press briefings or of privately trying to offer explanations to allied governments not always eager to reconcile their private support of our Vietnam efforts with their public stance of dissociation. I said as much to the President. The following day, while we were in Bonn, Nixon canceled the plan.

The so-called mini-Tet exposed the precariousness of our domestic position. The enemy offensive surely must have been planned over many months. It occurred when we were barely four weeks in office and before the enemy could possibly know what we intended—since we did not know ourselves. Yet the *New York Times* on March 9 blamed the new Administration for having provoked Hanoi by presuming to spend a month in studying the options in a war involving an expeditionary force of over 500,000 men: "The sad fact is that the Paris talks have been left on dead center while Ambassador Lodge awaits a White House go-ahead for making new peace proposals or for engaging in private talks out of which the only real progress is likely to come. Everything has been stalled while the Nixon Administration completes its military and diplomatic review." This theme soon was repeated in the Congress.

The President adopted a restrained posture in public while champing at the bit in private. At a news conference on March 4 he declared:

> We have not moved in a precipitate fashion, but the fact that we have shown patience and forbearance should not be considered as a sign of weakness. We will not tolerate a continuation of a violation of an understanding. But more than that, we will not tolerate attacks which result in heavier casualties to our men at a time that we are honestly trying to seek peace at the conference table in Paris. An appropriate response to these attacks will be made if they continue.

On March 4, I passed on to the President without comment a Laird memo recommending against proposals by the Joint Chiefs to attack North Vietnam. Laird was far from a "dove"; in normal circumstances his instincts were rather on the bellicose side. He would have preferred to aim for victory. But he was also a careful student of the public and Congressional mood. He was a finely tuned politician and as such he had learned that those who mount the barricades may well forgo a future in politics; he was not about to make this sacrifice. He therefore navigated with great care between his convictions, which counseled some military reaction, and his political instinct, which called for restraint. He opposed bombing North Vietnam; he became a strong supporter of the attack on the Cambodian sanctuaries. (His only disagreement had to do with public relations policy; he did not think it possible to keep the bombing secret, on practical, not on moral, grounds.) The President, following a similar logic, ordered a strike against the Cambodian sanctuaries for March 9. On March 7, Rogers objected because of prospects for private talks in Paris.

Nixon retracted his order a second time. With each time he marched up the hill and down again, Nixon's resentments and impatience increased. Like Laird he kept saying that he did not want to hit the North, but he wanted to do "something." On March 14, Nixon was asked at a news conference whether his patience was wearing thin. He replied:

> I took no comfort out of the stories that I saw in the papers this morning to the effect that our casualties for the immediate past week went from 400 down to 300. That is still much too high. What our response should be must be measured in terms of the effect on the negotiations in Paris. I will only respond as I did earlier. . . . We have issued a warning. I will not warn again. And if we conclude that the level of casualties is higher than we should tolerate, action will take place.

Next day the North Vietnamese fired five rockets into Saigon—a further escalation and violation of the understanding. There were thirty-two enemy attacks against major South Vietnamese cities in the first two weeks of March. At 3:35 P.M. the day the rockets hit Saigon I received a phone call from the President. He was ordering an immediate B-52 attack on the Cambodian sanctuaries. Capping a month of frustration, the President was emphatic: "State is to be notified only after the point of no return. . . . The order is not appealable." ("Not appealable" was a favorite Nixon phrase, which to those who knew him grew to mean considerable uncertainty; this, of course, tended to accelerate rather than slow down appeals.)

I told the President that such a decision should not be taken without giving his senior advisers an opportunity to express their views—if only to protect himself if it led to a public uproar. No time would be lost. A detailed scenario would have to be worked out in any event, and to prepare instructions would require at least twenty-four hours. A meeting was therefore scheduled for the following day in the Oval Office. I consulted Laird, who strongly supported the President's decision. To prepare for the meeting, I wrote a memo for the President listing the pros and cons. The risks ranged from a pro forma Cambodian protest to a strong Soviet reaction; from serious Cambodian opposition to explicit North Vietnamese retaliation—though it was hard to imagine what escalation Hanoi could undertake beyond what it was already doing. Finally, there was the risk of an upsurge of domestic criticism and new antiwar demonstrations. I recommended that our Paris delegation ask for a private meeting on the day of the bombing so as to emphasize our preference for a negotiated solution. I urged the President to stress to his associates that the proposed bombing was *not* to be a precedent. What my checklist did not foresee (what none of our deliberations foresaw) is what in fact happened: no reaction of any kind—from Hanoi, Phnom Penh, Moscow, or Peking.

The meeting on Sunday afternoon, March 16, in the Oval Office was attended by Rogers, Laird, Wheeler, and myself. It was the first time that Nixon confronted a concrete decision in an international crisis since becoming President; it was also the first time that he would face opposition from associates to a course of action to which he was already committed. He approached it with tactics that were to become vintage Nixon. On the one hand, he had made his decision and was not about to change it; indeed, he had instructed me to advise the Defense Department to that effect twenty-four hours before the meeting. On the other hand, he felt it necessary to pretend that the decision was still open. This led to hours of the very discussion that he found so distasteful and that reinforced his tendency to exclude the recalcitrants from further deliberations.

The Oval Office meeting followed predictable lines. Laird and Wheeler strongly advocated the attacks. Rogers objected not on foreign policy but on domestic grounds. He did not raise the neutral status of Cambodia; it was taken for granted (correctly) that we had the right to counter North Vietnam's blatant violation of Cambodia's neutrality, since Cambodia was unwilling or unable to defend its neutral status. Rogers feared that we would run into a buzz saw in Congress just when things were calming down. There were several hours of discussion during which Nixon permitted himself to be persuaded by Laird and Wheeler to do what he had already ordered. Having previously submitted my thoughts in a memorandum, I did not speak. Rogers finally agreed to a B-52 strike on the base area containing the presumed Communist headquarters. These deliberations are instructive: A month of an unprovoked North Vietnamese offensive, over a thousand American dead, elicited after weeks of anguished discussion exactly *one* American retaliatory raid within three miles of the Cambodian border in an area occupied by the North Vietnamese for over four years. And this would enter the folklore as an example of wanton "illegality."

After the meeting, the Joint Chiefs sought to include additional attacks on North Vietnamese troop concentrations violating the Demilitarized Zone. Laird and I agreed that it was more important to keep Rogers with us and the proposal was not approved.

The B-52 attack took place on March 18 against North Vietnamese Base Area 353, within three miles of the Cambodian border. For this strike the Pentagon dug into its bottomless bag of code names and came up with "Breakfast"—as meaningless as it was tasteless. When an air attack hits an ammunition or fuel depot, there are always secondary explosions that provide nearly conclusive evidence of a successful raid. The initial assessment by the crew of the March 18 Breakfast strike reported "a total of 73 secondary explosions in the target area ranging up to five times the normal intensity of a typical secondary."

Originally the attack on Base Area 353 was conceived as a single raid. Nixon ordered another strike in April 1969 partly because there had been no reaction from either Hanoi or Phnom Penh to the first, partly because the results exceeded our expectations, but above all because of an event far away in North Korea. Nixon had wanted to react to the shooting down of an unarmed American reconnaissance plane by bombing North Korea. (He had severely criticized Johnson for his failure to take forceful measures in response to the capture by North Korea of the electronic ship *Pueblo*.) Nixon had refrained, primarily because of the strong opposition of Rogers and Laird. But as always when suppressing his instinct for a jugular response, Nixon looked for some other place to demonstrate his mettle. There was nothing he feared more than to be thought weak; he had good foreign policy reasons as well for not letting Hanoi believe that he was paralyzed.

In May, Nixon ordered attacks on a string of other Cambodian base areas, all unpopulated and within five miles of the border. The strike on Base Area 350 was given the code name of "Dessert"; Base Area 351 was "Snack," Base Area 740 was "Supper," Base Area 609 was "Lunch," and Base Area 352 was "Dinner." On the theory that anything worth doing is worth overdoing, the whole series was given the code name of "Menu." From April through early August 1969 attacks were intermittent; each was approved specifically by the White House. Afterward, general authority was given; raids were conducted regularly. The map, defining the narrow strip of base areas within a few miles of the border, refutes the charges of "massive bombing of neutral Cambodia" that impelled twelve members of the House Judiciary Committee in 1974 to propose an article of impeachment on the theory that Nixon had concealed from Congress this "presidential conduct more shocking, and more unbelievable than the conduct of any president in any war in all of American history," as Representative Robert Drinan imagined it. Neither Cambodia nor North Vietnam ever claimed that there were Cambodian or civilian casualties. The statistics of tonnage dropped during these raids, so often invoked as an example of Administration barbarity, conveniently omit this salient fact or that it was confined to a strip only a few miles wide along the border. The series continued until May 1970, when strikes began openly in support of U.S. and South Vietnamese ground operations against the North Vietnamese bases.

Periodic reports on the Menu strikes were sent to the President. In November 1969, he wrote on one, "continue them." In December 1969 and February 1970, he asked for an evaluation of their usefulness. Each time, Laird reported that General Abrams and Ambassador Bunker were convinced (as he reported on one occasion) that "Menu has been one of the most telling operations in the entire war." General Abrams credited the Menu operations with disrupting enemy logistics, aborting several enemy offensives, and reducing the enemy threat to the whole Saigon region. Laird endorsed the Joint Chiefs' and General Abrams's view that the Menu strikes "have been effective and can continue to be so with acceptable risks."

The original intention had been to acknowledge the Breakfast strike in response to a Cambodian or North Vietnamese reaction, which we firmly anticipated. For example, the CIA predicted in memoranda of February 20 and March 6 that Hanoi would "certainly" or "almost certainly" seek to derive propaganda advantages from charging an American expansion of the conflict. The Defense Department doubted that the attacks could be kept secret; my own view on that subject was agnostic. In a conversation with Nixon on March 8, I said: "Packard and I both think that if we do it, and if silence about it doesn't help, we have to step up and say what we did." The President agreed. A formal acknowledgment was prepared for the contingency of a Cambodian protest. It offered to pay damages and asked for international inspection.

Our initial reticence was to avoid *forcing* the North Vietnamese, Prince Sihanouk of Cambodia, and the Soviets and Chinese into public reactions they might not be eager to make. A volunteered American statement would have obliged Hanoi to make a public response, perhaps military retaliation or interruption of the peace talks. It would have required Sihanouk to take a public stand, tilting toward Hanoi as he tried to walk a tightrope of neutrality. It could have prompted reactions from the Soviet Union and China in the midst of our serious pursuit of triangular diplomacy.

But Hanoi did *not* protest. In fact, its delegation in Paris accepted Lodge's proposal for private talks on March 22 within seventy-two hours of our request. And Sihanouk not only did not object; he treated the bombing as something that did not concern him since it occurred in areas totally occupied by North Vietnamese troops and affected no Cambodians; hence it was outside his control and even knowledge.

In fact, our relations with Cambodia improved dramatically throughout the period of the bombing. Sihanouk's subtle and skillful balancing act between domestic and foreign pressures had been a cause of wonderment for a decade. An hereditary prince, Norodom Sihanouk had managed to obtain a mass support among the population that appeared to make him unassailable. He had established his country's independence and acquired the aura of indispensability. He had maneuvered to keep his country neutral. After the Laos settlement of 1962, he had concluded that the Communists, whom he hated, would probably prevail in Indochina. He adjusted to that reality by acquiescing in the North Vietnamese establishment of base areas in his country. In 1965 he found a pretext to break diplomatic relations with us. Yet his collaboration with the Communists was reluctant; Hanoi was encouraging the Khmer Rouge (Cambodian Communists), who began guerrilla activity long before there was any American action in Cambodia; Sihanouk sentenced the Communist leaders to death in absentia. For all these reasons I strongly supported a Rogers recommendation to the President in February 1969 that we approach Sihanouk with a view to improving relations.* These overtures were eagerly received. Our Embassy in Phom Penh reopened, headed by a chargé d'affaires.

---

*Interestingly enough, these diplomatic overtures to Cambodia were opposed by the Department of Defense and the Joint Chiefs of Staff, who feared that they might interfere with possibilities of bombing the Cambodian sanctuaries. I received a memorandum from Defense warning against such "diplomatic action which implies a restraint or inhibition in any expansion of current operating authorities designed to protect our forces in South Vietnam." This was signed by Paul Warnke, then still Assistant Secretary of Defense for International Security Affairs.

Sihanouk's acquiescence in the bombing should have come as no surprise. As early as January 10, 1968, during the previous Administration, he had told Presidential emissary Chester Bowles:

> We don't want any Vietnamese in Cambodia. . . . We will be very glad if you solve our problem. We are not opposed to hot pursuit in uninhabited areas. You would be liberating us from the Viet Cong. For me only Cambodia counts. I want you to force the Viet Cong to leave Cambodia. In unpopulated areas, where there are not Cambodians,—such precise cases I would shut my eyes.

On May 13, 1969, nearly two months after the bombing had begun, Sihanouk gave a press conference which all but confirmed the bombings, emphatically denied any loss of civilian life, and to all practical purposes invited us to continue:

> I have not protested the bombings of Viet Cong camps because I have not heard of the bombings. I was not in the know, because in certain areas of Cambodia there are no Cambodians. . . .
>
> Cambodia only protests against the destruction of the property and lives of Cambodians. All I can say is that I cannot make a protest as long as I am not informed. But I will protest if there is any destruction of Khmer [Cambodian] life and property.
>
> Here it is—the first report about several B-52 bombings. Yet I have not been informed about that at all, because I have not lost any houses, any countrymen, nothing, nothing. Nobody was caught in those barrages—nobody, no Cambodians. . . .
>
> That is what I want to tell you, gentlemen. If there is a buffalo or any Cambodian killed, I will be informed immediately. But this is an affair between the Americans and the Viet Cong–Viet Minh without any Khmer witnesses. There have been no Khmer witnesses, so how can I protest? But this does not mean—and I emphasize this—that I will permit the violation by either side. Please note that.

On August 22, 1969, Sihanouk said the same to Senator [Mike] Mansfield* (according to the reporting cable):

> there were no Cambodian protests of bombings in his country when these hit only VC's and not Cambodian villages or population. He declared that much of his information regarding U.S. bombings of uninhabited regions of Cambodia came from U.S. press and magazine statements. He strongly requested the avoidance of incidents involving Cambodian lives.

And on July 31, 1969, after four and a half months of bombing of North Vietnamese sanctuaries inside Cambodia, Sihanouk warmly invited President Nixon to visit Cambodia to mark the improvement of U.S.–Cambodian relations. Relations continued to improve until Sihanouk was unexpectedly overthrown.

No one doubted the legality of attacking base areas being used to kill American and friendly forces, from which all Cambodian authority had been expelled and in which, according to Sihanouk himself, not even a Cambodian buffalo had been killed. We saw no sense in announcing what Cambodia encouraged and North Vietnam accepted. The reason for secrecy was to prevent the issue from becoming an international crisis, which would almost certainly have complicated our diplomacy or war effort. The war had been expanded into Cambodia four years earlier by the North Vietnamese, who occupied its territory. The war had been escalated within Vietnam from

---

* Senator Mansfield did not know of the Menu program and undoubtedly assumed Sihanouk was speaking of accidental bombings.

February 22 on, with North Vietnamese attacks on cities in violation of the 1968 understandings. To bomb base areas from which North Vietnamese soldiers had expelled all Cambodians so that they could more effectively kill Americans—at the rate of four hundred a week—was a minimum defensive reaction fully compatible with international law. It would surely have been supported by the American public. It was kept secret because a public announcement was a gratuitous blow to the Cambodian government, which might have forced it to demand that we stop; it might have encouraged a North Vietnamese retaliation (since how could they fail to react if we had announced we were doing it?). The North Vietnamese kept silent because they were not eager to advertise their illegal presence on Cambodian soil. Our bombing saved American and South Vietnamese lives.

This is why the press leaks that came from American sources struck Nixon and me as so outrageous. Accounts of B-52 or other air strikes against sanctuaries in Cambodia appeared in the *New York Times* (March 26, April 27) and *Washington Post* (April 27); a detailed story by William Beecher appeared in the *New York Times* on May 9; there was another in the *Wall Street Journal* on May 16; a widely disseminated UPI [United Press International] story appeared in the *Washington Post* on May 18; *Newsweek* reported it on June 2.

The conviction that press leaks of military operations were needlessly jeopardizing American lives, which I shared, caused the President to consult the Attorney General and the Director of the FBI about remedial measures. J. Edgar Hoover recommended wiretaps, which he pointed out had been widely used for these (and other much less justified) purposes by preceding administrations. The Attorney General affirmed their legality. Nixon ordered them carried out, in three categories of cases: officials who had adverse information in their security files; officials who had access to the classified information that had been leaked; and individuals whose names came up as possibilities in the course of the investigation according to the first two criteria. On the basis of these criteria, seventeen wiretaps were established by the FBI on thirteen officials and also four newsmen, lasting in some cases only a few weeks and in other cases several months. (My office was not aware of all of them.) Contrary to malicious lore, senior officials did not spend time pruriently reading over lengthy transcripts of personal conversations. What was received were brief summaries (usually about a page in length) of what the FBI considered discussions of sensitive military or foreign policy matters. The FBI's threshold of suspicion tended to be much lower than the White House's. In May 1971, Nixon cut off the reports sent to my office; thereafter, they went only to Haldeman, who had been receiving them all along. . . .

I wish to record that I went along with what I had no reason to doubt was legal and established practice in these circumstances, pursued, so we were told, with greater energy and fewer safeguards in previous administrations. The motive, which I strongly shared, was to prevent the jeopardizing of American and South Vietnamese lives by individuals (never discovered) who disclosed military information entrusted to them in order to undermine policies decided upon after prayerful consideration and in our view justified both in law and in the national interest. I believe now that the more stringent safeguards applied to national security wiretapping since that time reflect an even more fundamental national interest—but this in no way alters my view of the immorality of those who, in their contempt for their trust, attempted to sabotage national policies and risked American lives.

At the same time, we were wrong, I now believe, not to be more frank with Congressional leaders. To be sure, President Nixon and I gave a full briefing in the Oval Office on June 11, 1969, to Senators John Stennis and Richard Russell, Chairmen of the Senate Armed Services and Appropriations committees. Senate Minority Leader Everett Dirksen was also informed. In the House, Representatives Mendel Rivers and Leslie Arends, the Chairman and a ranking minority member of the House Armed Services Committee, as well as Minority Leader Gerald Ford, were briefed. Laird briefed key members of the Armed Services and Appropriations committees of both houses. Not one raised the issue that the full Congress should be consulted. This was at that time the accepted practice for briefing the Congress of classified military operations. Standards for Congressional consultation, too, have since changed, and this is undoubtedly for the better.*

Nor is it true that the bombing drove the North Vietnamese out of the sanctuaries and thus spread the war deep into Cambodia. To the extent that North Vietnamese forces left the sanctuaries it was to move back into Vietnam, not deeper into Cambodia—until after Sihanouk was unexpectedly overthrown a year later. Then, North Vietnamese forces deliberately started to overrun Cambodian towns and military positions in order to isolate Phnom Penh and topple Sihanouk's successor.† And the widened war caused by that new act of North Vietnamese aggression, while searing and tragic, was not secret. It was fully known by our public, debated in the Congress, and widely reported in the press. Our air operations then were conducted under strict rules of engagement, supervised by our Ambassador in Phnom Penh and aided by aerial photography, designed to avoid areas populated by Cambodian civilians to the maximum extent possible. The "secret" bombing concerned small, largely uninhabited territories totally occupied by the North Vietnamese. The picture of a warlike, bloodthirsty government scheming to deceive is a caricature of the reality of harassed individuals, afraid alike of capitulation on the battlefield and more violent escalation, choosing what they considered a middle course between bombing North Vietnam and meekly accepting the outrage of a dishonorable and bloody offensive. The attacks on the enemy sanctuaries in Cambodia were undertaken reluctantly, as a last resort, as a minimum response, when we were faced with an unprovoked offensive killing four hundred Americans a week. We attacked military bases unpopulated by civilians and at most only five miles from the border. We would have been willing to acknowledge the bombing and defend it had there been a diplomatic protest. There was no protest; Cambodia did not object, nor did the North Vietnamese, nor the Soviets or the Chinese. Proceeding secretly became, therefore, a means of maintaining pressure on the enemy without complicating Cambodia's delicate position, without increasing international tensions in general, and without precipitating the abandonment of all limits.

---

*The Pentagon's double-bookkeeping had a motivation much less sinister than that described in revisionist folklore. To preserve the secrecy of the initial (originally intended as the only) raid, Pentagon instructions were kept out of normal channels. The purpose was not to deceive Congress (where key leaders were informed) but to keep the attack from being routinely briefed to the Saigon press. The procedure was continued by rote when bombing became more frequent two months later. When Congressional committees asked for data four years later, new Pentagon officials, unaware of the two reporting channels, unwittingly furnished data from the regular files. This was a bureaucratic blunder, not deliberate design.

†Sihanouk in a conversation with me on April 25, 1979, in front of witnesses denied that our bombing had had any effect in pushing the North Vietnamese to move westward. Our bombing "did not impress them," he said jovially.

CHAPTER 9

Interpreting the War

Students of history eventually must try to explain why the United States became involved in Vietnam and why it stayed so long in the war; there are no more fundamental and important questions than these. Even as the war was going on, policymakers, scholars, and journalists were offering their interpretations of U.S. intervention. At first, some concluded that the United States had been sucked into Vietnam step by unthinking step: the well-intentioned but naive Americans had walked into a quagmire. Others, such as Frances FitzGerald, assert that American values and assumptions were inappropriate in Vietnam's cultural landscape and inescapably led to tragedy. James Thomson, Jr., who served as an adviser on East Asian affairs in the Kennedy and Johnson administrations, argues that the United States fought on in Vietnam for a variety of reasons, many of them having to do with the Washington bureaucracy's inability to change course when change seemed warranted—especially in the absence of Southeast Asia experts in the Department of State. This viewpoint was a liberal's critique of the war. Radicals, among them the distinguished linguist Noam Chomsky, indicted neither culture nor bureaucracy but American ideology. The Vietnam War, they claimed, was the awful but logical result of U.S. imperialism, undertaken by the state and authorized by liberal intellectuals. In the late 1970s and early 1980s a "revisionist" interpretation of the war emerged. Led by Norman Podhoretz, the revisionists criticized the opponents of the war and generally defended the most determined policymakers and military officials. Content with none of these arguments, James William Gibson confronts the war at what he says was its most basic level: Americans saw the Vietnamese Communists as their technological and racial inferiors—unnatural "foreign Others" who defied prevailing modern "regimes" of knowledge and power.

Historical interpretation is always difficult, and the passions that continue to surround the Vietnam War make the work of its chroniclers particularly hazardous. The various schools of thought on the U.S. intervention have different approaches to evidence, different disciplinary perspectives, and different ideas about how to weigh the importance of personality against that of the institutions or systems of policymaking. It may be frustrating to confront the multiplicity of interpretations of the U.S. involvement in Vietnam, but it is also the highest responsibility of historians.

South Vietnam. A U.S. Marine displays a Communist flag found on patrol just south of the Demilitarized Zone (DMZ). OFFICIAL U.S. MARINE CORPS PHOTO

28
A Clash of Cultures
FRANCES FITZGERALD

Somewhere, buried in the files of the television networks, lies a series of pictures, ranging over a decade, that chronicles the diplomatic history of the United States and the Republic of Vietnam. Somewhere there is a picture of President Eisenhower with Ngo Dinh Diem, a picture of Secretary McNamara with General Nguyen Khanh, one of President Johnson with Nguyen Cao Ky, and another of President Nixon with President Thieu. The pictures are unexceptional. The obligatory photographs taken on such ceremonial occasions, they show men in gray business suits (one is in military fatigues) shaking hands or standing side-by-side on a podium. These pictures, along with the news commentaries, "President Nixon today reaffirmed his support for the Thieu regime," or "Hanoi refused to consider the American proposal," made up much of what Americans knew about the relationship between the two countries. But the pictures and news reports were to a great extent deceptions, for they did not show the disproportion between the two powers. One of the gray-suited figures, after all, represented the greatest power in the history of the world, a nation that could, if its rulers so desired, blow up the world, feed the earth's population, or explore the galaxy. The second figure in the pictures represented a small number of people in a country of peasants largely sustained by a technology centuries old. The meeting between the two was the meeting of two different dimensions, two different epochs of history. An imagined picture of a tributary chieftain coming to the Chinese court represents the relationship of the United States to the Republic of Vietnam better than the photographs from life. It represents what the physical and mental architecture of the twentieth century so often obscures.

At the beginning of their terms in office President Kennedy and President Johnson, perhaps, took full cognizance of the disproportion between the two countries, for they claimed, at least in the beginning, that the Vietnam War would require only patience from the United States. According to U.S. military intelligence, the enemy in the south consisted of little more than bands of guerrillas with hardly a truck in which to carry their borrowed weapons. The North Vietnamese possessed antiaircraft guns and a steady supply of small munitions, but the United States could, so the officials promised, end their resistance with a few months of intensive bombing. In 1963 and 1965 few Americans imagined that a commitment to war in Vietnam would finally cost the United States billions of dollars, the production of its finest research and development laboratories, and fifty-five thousand American lives. They did not imagine that the Vietnam War would prove more politically divisive than any foreign war in the nation's history.

In one sense Presidents Kennedy and Johnson had seen the disproportion between the United States and Vietnam, but in another they did not see it at all. By intervening in the Vietnamese struggle the United States was attempting to fit its global strategies into a world of hillocks and hamlets, to reduce its majestic concerns for the containment of Communism and the security of the Free World to a dimension where governments rose and fell as a result of arguments between two colonels' wives. In going to Vietnam the United States was entering a country where the victory of one of the great world ideologies occasionally depended on the price of tea in a certain village or the outcome of a football game. For the Americans in Vietnam it would be difficult to make this leap of perspective, difficult to understand that while they saw themselves as building world order, many Vietnamese saw them merely as the producers of garbage from which they could build houses. The effort of translation was too great.

The televised pictures of the two chiefs of state were deceptive in quite another way: only one of the two nations saw them. Because of communications, the war was absurd for the civilians of both countries—but absurd in different ways. To one people the war would appear each day, compressed between advertisements and confined to a small space in the living room; the explosion of bombs and the cries of the wounded would become the background accompaniment to dinner. For the other people the war would come one day out of a clear blue sky. In a few minutes it would be over: the bombs, released by an invisible pilot with incomprehensible intentions, would leave only the debris and the dead behind. Which people was the best equipped to fight the war?

The disparity between the two countries only began with the matter of scale. They seemed, of course, to have come from the same country, those two figures in their identical business suits with their identical pronouncements: "The South Vietnamese people will never surrender to Communist tyranny," "We are fighting for the great cause of freedom," "We dedicate ourselves to the abolition of poverty, ignorance, and disease and to the work of the social revolution." In this case the deception served the purposes of state. The Chinese emperor could never have claimed that in backing one nomad chieftain against another he was defending the representative of Chinese civilization. But the American officials in supporting the Saigon government insisted that they were defending "freedom and democracy" in Asia. They left the GIs to discover that the Vietnamese did not fit into their experience of either "Communists" or "democrats."

Under different circumstances this invincible ignorance might not have affected the outcome of the war. The fiction that the United States was defending "freedom and democracy" might have continued to exist in a sphere undisturbed by reality, a sphere frequented only by those who needed moral justification for the pursuit of what the U.S. government saw as its strategic interests. Certain "tough-minded" analysts and officials in any case ignored the moral argument. As far as they were concerned, the United States was not interested in the form of the Vietnamese government—indeed, it was not interested in the Vietnamese at all. Its concerns were for "containing the expansion of the Communist bloc" and preventing future "wars of national liberation" around the world. But by denying the moral argument in favor of power politics and "rational" calculations of United States interests, these analysts were, as it happened, overlooking the very heart of the matter, the issue on which success depended.

The United States came to Vietnam at a critical juncture of Vietnamese history— a period of metamorphosis more profound than any the Vietnamese had ever experienced. In 1954 the Vietnamese were gaining their independence after seventy years of French colonial rule. They were engaged in a struggle to create a nation and to adapt a largely traditional society to the modern world. By backing one contender—by actually creating that contender—the United States was not just fighting a border war or intervening, as Imperial China so often did, in a power struggle between two similar contenders, two dynasties. It was entering into a moral and ideological struggle over the form of the state and the goals of the society. Its success with its chosen contender would depend not merely on U.S. military power but on the resources of both the United States and the Saigon government to solve Vietnamese domestic problems in a manner acceptable to the Vietnamese. But what indeed were Vietnamese problems, and did they even exist in the terms in which Americans conceived them? The unknowns made the whole enterprise, from the most rational and tough-minded point of view, risky in the extreme.

In going into Vietnam the United States was not only transposing itself into a different epoch of history; it was entering a world qualitatively different from its own. Culturally as geographically Vietnam lies half a world away from the United States. Many Americans in Vietnam learned to speak Vietnamese, but the language gave no more than a hint of the basic intellectual grammar that lay beneath. In a sense there was no more correspondence between the two worlds than that between the atmosphere of the earth and that of the sea. There was no direct translation between them in the simple equations of x is y and a means b. To find the common ground that existed between them, both Americans and Vietnamese would have to re-create the whole world of the other, the whole intellectual landscape. The effort of comprehension would be only the first step, for it would reveal the deeper issues of the encounter. It would force both nations to consider again the question of morality, to consider which of their values belong only to themselves or only to a certain stage of development. It would, perhaps, allow them to see that the process of change in the life of a society is a delicate and mysterious affair, and that the introduction of the foreign and the new can have vast and unpredictable consequences. It might in the end force both peoples to look back upon their own society, for it is contrast that is the essence of vision.

The American intellectual landscape is, of course, largely an inheritance from Europe, that of the Vietnamese a legacy from China, but in their own independent development the two nations have in many respects moved even further apart from each other. As late as the end of the nineteenth century Americans had before them a seemingly unlimited physical space—a view of mountains, deserts, and prairies into which a man might move (or imagine moving) to escape the old society and create a new world for himself. The impulse to escape, the drive to conquest and expansion, was never contradicted in America as it was in Europe by physical boundaries or by the persistence of strong traditions. The nation itself seemed to be less of a vessel than a movement. The closing of the frontier did not mean the end to expansion, but rather the beginning of it in a new form. The development of industry permitted the creation of new resources, new markets, new power over the world that had brought it into being. Americans ignore history, for to them everything has always seemed new under the sun. The national myth is that of creativity and progress, of a steady climbing upward into power and prosperity, both for the individual and for the country as a whole. Americans see history as a straight line and themselves standing at the cutting edge of it as representatives for all mankind. They believe in the future as if it were a religion; they believe that there is nothing they cannot accomplish, that solutions wait somewhere for all problems, like brides. Different though they were, both John Kennedy and Lyndon Johnson accepted and participated in this national myth. In part perhaps by virtue of their own success, they were optimists who looked upon their country as willing and able to right its own wrongs and to succor the rest of the world. They believed in the power of science, the power of the will, and the virtues of competition. Many Americans now question their confidence; still, the optimism of the nation is so great that even the question appears as a novelty and a challenge.

In their sense of time and space, the Vietnamese and the Americans stand in the relationship of a reversed mirror image, for the very notion of competition, invention, and change is an extremely new one for most Vietnamese. Until the French conquest of Vietnam in the nineteenth century, the Vietnamese practiced the same general technology for a thousand years. Their method of rice culture was far superior to any other in Southeast Asia; still it confined them to the river-fed lowlands between the Annamite cordillera and the sea. Hemmed in by China to the north and the Hindu kingdom of Champa to the south, the Vietnamese lived for the bulk of their history within the closed circle of the Red River Delta. They conquered Champa and moved south down the narrow littoral, but by American or Chinese standards they might have been standing still, for it took them five centuries to conquer a strip of land the length of Florida. The Vietnamese pride themselves less on their conquests than on their ability to resist and to survive. Living under the great wing of China, they bought their independence and maintained it only at a high price of blood. Throughout their history they have had to acknowledge the preponderance of the great Middle Kingdom both as the power and as the hub of culture. The Vietnamese knew their place in the world and guarded it jealously.

For traditional Vietnamese the sense of limitation and enclosure was as much a part of individual life as of the life of the nation. In what is today northern and central Vietnam the single form of Vietnamese settlement duplicated the closed circle of the nation. Hidden from sight behind their high hedges of bamboos, the villages stood like nuclei within their surrounding circle of rice fields. Within the villages as within the nation the amount of arable land was absolutely inelastic. The population of the village remained stable, and so to accumulate wealth meant to deprive the rest of the community of land, to fatten while one's neighbor starved. Vietnam is no longer a closed economic system, but the idea remains with the Vietnamese that great wealth is antisocial, not a sign of success but a sign of selfishness.

With a stable technology and a limited amount of land the traditional Vietnamese lived by constant repetition, by the sowing and reaping of rice and by the perpetuation of customary law. The Vietnamese worshiped their ancestors as the source of their lives, their fortunes, and their civilization. In the rites of ancestor worship the child imitated the gestures of his grandfather so that when he became the grandfather, he could repeat them exactly to his grandchildren. In this passage of time that had no history the death of a man marked no final end. Buried in the rice fields that sustained his family, the father would live on in the bodies of his children and grandchildren. As time wrapped around itself, the generations to come would regard him as the source of their present lives and the arbiter of their fate. In this continuum of the family "private property" did not really exist, for the father was less of an owner than a trustee of the land to be passed on to his children. To the Vietnamese the land itself was the sacred, constant element: the people flowed over the land like water, maintaining and fructifying it for the generations to come.

Late in the war—about 1968—a Vietnamese soldier came with his unit to evacuate the people of a starving village in Quang Nam province so that the area might be turned into a "free fire zone." While the villagers were boarding the great American helicopters, one old man ran away from the soldiers shouting that he would never leave his home. The soldiers followed the old man and found him hiding in a tunnel beside a small garden planted with a few pitiful stunted shrubs. When they tried to persuade him to go with the others, he refused, saying, "I have to stay behind to look after this piece of garden. Of all the property handed down to me by my ancestors, only this garden now remains. I have to guard it for my grandson." Seeing the soldiers look askance, the old man admitted that his grandson had been conscripted and that he had not heard from him in two years. He paused, searching for an explanation, and then said, "If I leave, the graves of my ancestors, too, will become forest. How can I have the heart to leave?"

The soldiers turned away from the old man and departed, for they understood that for him to leave the land would be to acknowledge the final death of the family—a death without immortality. By deciding to stay he was deciding to sacrifice his life in postponement of that end. When the soldiers returned to the village fourteen months later, they found that an artillery shell had closed the entrance to the tunnel, making it a grave for the old man.[1]

Many American officials understood that the land and the graves of the ancestors were important to the Vietnamese. Had they understood exactly why, they might not have looked upon the wholesale creation of refugees as a "rational" method of defeating Communism. For the traditional villager, who spent his life immobile, bound to the rice land of his ancestors, the world was a very small place. It was in fact the village or *xa*, a word that in its original Chinese roots signified "the place where people come together to worship the spirits." In this definition of society the character "earth" took precedence, for, as the source of life, the earth was the basis for the social contract between the members of the family and the members of the village. Americans live in a society of replaceable parts—in theory anyone can become President or sanitary inspector—but the Vietnamese lived in a society of particular people, all of whom knew each other by their place in the landscape. "Citizenship" in a Vietnamese village was personal and untransferable. In the past, few Vietnamese ever left their village in times of peace, for to do so was to leave society itself—all human attachments, all absolute rights and duties. When the soldiers of the nineteenth-century Vietnamese emperors came to the court of Hué, they prayed to the spirits of the Perfume River, "We are lost here *[dépaysés]* and everything is unknown to us. We prostrate ourselves before you [in the hope that] you will lead us to the good and drive the evil away from us."[2] The soldiers were "lost" in more than a geographical sense, for without their land and their place in the village, they were without a social identity. To drive the twentieth-century villager off his land was in the same way to drive him off the edges of his old life and to expose him directly to the political movement that could best provide him with a new identity.

During the war the village *dinh* or shrine still stood in many of the villages of the south as testimony to the endurance of the traditional political design of the nation. In prehistoric times, before the advent of national government, the *dinhs* referred to the god of the particular earth beneath the village. In assuming temporal power, the emperors of Vietnam took on the responsibility to perform the rites of the agriculture for all the Vietnamese villages and replaced the local spirits with the spirits of national heroes and genii. Under their reign the *dinh* contained the imperial charter that incorporated the village into the empire, making an ellision between the ideas of "land," "Emperor," and "Vietnamese." The French brushed away the sacred web of state, but they did not destroy this confluence of ideas. The Vietnamese call their nation *da nuoc*, "earth and water"—the phrase referring both to the trickle of water through one rice field and the "mountains and rivers" of the nation.

Like the Celestial Empire of China, the Vietnamese empire was in one aspect a ritual state whose function was to preside over the sacred order of nature and society. At its apex the emperor stood as its supreme magician-god endowed with the responsibility to maintain the harmonious balance of the *yin* and the *yang*, the two related forces of the universe. His success in this enterprise (like that of the villagers in the rites of ancestor worship) depended upon the precision with which he followed the elaborate set of rituals governing his relations with the celestial authorities and the people of the empire. To act in conformity with the traditional etiquette was to insure harmony and prosperity for the entire nation. In A.D. 1129 the Emperor Ly Than Tong proclaimed to the court: "We have little virtue; we have transgressed the order of Heaven, and upset the natural course of events; last year the spring was blighted by a long rain; this year there is a long drought. . . . Let the mandarins examine my past acts in order to discover any errors or faults, so that they may be remedied."[3] In analyzing these disasters the emperor blamed them on his deviation from Tao, the traditional way, which was at once the most moral and the most scientific course.

As Americans are, so to speak, canted towards the future, the traditional Vietnamese were directed towards the past, both by the small tradition of the family and the great tradition of the state. Confucianism—the very foundation of the state—was not merely a "traditional religion," as Judaism and Christianity are the traditional religions of the West. Originating in a society of ancestor worshipers, it was, like ancestor worship itself, a sacralization of the past. Unlike the great Semitic prophets, Confucius did not base his teachings on a single, contemporary revelation. "I for my part am not one of those who have innate knowledge," he said. "I am simply one who loves the past and is diligent in investigating it."[4] According to tradition, Confucius came to his wisdom through research into the great periods of Chinese civilization—the Chou empire and its predecessors in the distant past. Tradition presents the Master not as a revolutionary but as a true reactionary. Arriving at certain rules and precepts for the proper conduct of life, he did not pretend to have comprehended all wisdom, but merely to have set up guideposts pointing towards the Tao or true way of life. For him the Tao was the enlightened process of induction that led endlessly backwards into the past of civilization. The Tao may have been for him a secular concern, a matter of enlightened self-interest. ("The Master never spoke of the spirits," reported his disciples, leaving the question moot.) But for later Confucians it had a sacred weight reinforced by magic and the supernatural.

For traditional Vietnamese, formal education consisted of the study of the Confucian texts—the works of the Master and the later commentaries. To pass beyond the small tradition of the family and the village was therefore not to escape the dominion of the past, but to enter into it more fully. The mandarins, the literate elite, directed all their scholarship not towards invention and progress, but towards a more perfect repetition of the past, a more perfect maintenance of the status quo. When a French steamship was sighted off the shores of Vietnam in the early nineteenth century (or so the story goes) the local mandarin-governor, instead of going to see it, researched the phenomenon in his texts, concluded it was a dragon, and dismissed the matter.[5]

As long as Vietnamese society remained a closed system, its intellectual foundations remained flawless and immobile. Quite clearly, however, they could not survive contact with the West, for they were based on the premise that there was nothing new under the sun. But the coming of the French posed a terrible problem for the Vietnamese. Under the dominion of the old empire the Vietnamese were not members of a religious community (like the Christians of Byzantium or the Muslims of the Abbasid caliphate) but participants in a whole, indivisible culture. Like the Chinese, they considered those who lived outside of its seamless web to be by definition barbarians. When the Vietnamese conquered peoples of other cultures—such as the Chams—they included these people within the structure of empire only on condition of their total assimilation. The peoples they could not assimilate, they simply surrounded, amoeba-like, and left them to follow their own laws. The various montagnard tribes that lived beyond the zone of wet-rice cultivation retained their own languages, customs, and governments for thousands of years inside Vietnam. But with the arrival of the French forces in the nineteenth century the Vietnamese confronted a civilization more powerful than their own; for the first time since the Chinese conquest in the second century B.C. they faced the possibility of having to assimilate themselves. Confucianism was, after all, not merely a religion or an arbitrary morality, but a science that operated inside history. Confucius said, "If it is really possible to govern countries by ritual and yielding, there is no more to be said. But if it is not really possible, of what use is ritual?"[6] The rituals and the way of life they confirmed did not help the Vietnamese defend themselves against the French, and thus certain mandarins concluded they had to be abandoned. As the French armies swept across the Mekong Delta, Phan Thanh Giang, the governor of the western provinces, reconciled this logic with his loyalty to the nation by committing suicide and ordering his sons not to serve the French but to bring up their children in the French way.[7]

Similarly, those mandarins who decided to resist the French saw the foreign armies as a threat not only to their national sovereignty and to their beliefs, but to their entire way of life. The southern patriots warned their people:

> Our country has always been known as a land of deities; shall we now permit a horde of dogs and goats to stain it?
>
> The moral obligations binding a king to his subjects, parents to their children, and husbands to their wives were highly respected. Everyone enjoyed the most peaceful relationships.
>
> Our customs and habits were so perfect that in our country, in our ancestors' tombs, and in our homes, all things were in a proper state.
>
> But from the moment they arrived with their ill luck, happiness and peace seem to have departed from everywhere.[8]

And the mandarins were correct: the French occupation changed the Vietnamese way of life permanently. Since the Second World War the Vietnamese have been waging a struggle not merely over the form of their state but over the nature of Vietnamese society, the very identity of the Vietnamese. It is the grandeur of the stakes involved that has made the struggle at once so intense and so opaque to Westerners.

Just before the fall of the Diem regime in 1963 the American journalists in Vietnam wrote long and somewhat puzzling analyses of the Buddhist demonstrations, in which they attempted to explain how much the rebellion against Diem owed to "purely religious" motives, how much to "purely political" ones. Like most Westerners, these journalists were so entrenched in their Western notion of the division of church and state that they could not imagine the Vietnamese might not make the distinction. But until the arrival of the European missionaries there was never such a thing as a church in Vietnam. Shaped by a millennium of Chinese rule and another of independence within the framework of Southeast Asia, the "Vietnamese religion" was a blend of Confucianism, Taoism, and Buddhism sunken into a background of animism. More than a "religion" in any Western sense, it was the authority for, and the confirmation of, an entire way of life—an agriculture, a social structure, a political system. Its supernatural resembled one of those strange metaphysical puzzles of Jorge Luis Borges: an entire community imagines another one which, though magical and otherworldly, looks, detail for detail, like itself. In the courts of Hué and Thanglong, organization-minded genii presided over every government department and took responsibility for the success or failure of each mandarin's enterprise. (During a long period of drought in the seventeenth century the Emperor Le Thai Ton ordered his mandarins: "Warn the genii on my behalf that if it doesn't rain in three days, I will have their tablets boiled and thrown in the river so as to prevent my people from uselessly throwing away their money on them.")[9] In the villages the peasants recognized hosts of local spirits and ghosts as well as the official genii delegated by the mandarins. In Paul Mus's words, religion was the "spiritualization of the community itself" and "the administration of Heaven." The "religion," in some sense, was the state and vice versa—except that the emperor was not the representative of God on earth, but rather a collective moral personality, a representation of the sacred community to itself.

For the Vietnamese today as in centuries past, each regime—each state or political movement—has its own "virtue," its own character, which, like that of a human being, combines moral, social, and political qualities in a single form. Whether secular parties or religious sects, all modern Vietnamese political movements embrace a total design for the moral life of the individual and the social order of the nation. With Ngo Dinh Diem, for instance, this spherical Confucian universe showed up continually through the flat surfaces of Western language. He spoke of himself as the chosen of Heaven, the leader elected to defend Vietnamese morality and culture. The Buddhist leaders had much the same pretensions, and even for the Vietnamese Communists, the heirs to nineteenth-century Western distinctions between church and state, between one class and another, the society retains its moral impulse, its balanced Confucian design.

Never having known a serious ideological struggle in their history, many Americans persisted in thinking of the Vietnamese conflict as a civil war, as a battle between two fixed groups of people with different but conceivably negotiable interests. But the regional conflict existed only within the context of a larger struggle that resembled a series of massive campaigns of conversion involving all the people in the country and the whole structure of society. Owing to the nature of the old society, the struggle was even more all-encompassing than the European revolutionary wars. Americans, and indeed most Westerners, have lived for centuries with a great variety of institutions—with churches, with governments, with a patriarchal family, with industrial concerns, trade unions and fraternities, each of which offered a different kind of organization, different kinds of loyalties—but the Vietnamese have lived with only three: the family, the village, and the state.[10] As the family provided the model for village and state, there was only one type of organization. Taken together, the three formed a crystalline world, geometrically congruent at every level. The mandarins, for instance, were known as the "fathers of the people," and they stood in the same relationship to the emperor (himself the "son of Heaven") as the Vietnamese son stood to his father. Recruited by competitive examination, they moved closer to the emperor, that is, higher in the great imperial family, as they passed through the grades of the examination system. The village was a more informal organization—a Vietnamese deviation from the orthodox Chinese model—but it reflected a similar hierarchical design. The "government" of the family, the village, and the empire derived from one single set of instructions. Thus, a change in one implied a change in all the others.[11]

To American officials throughout the war it seemed absolutely unreasonable that the non-Communist sects and political factions could not come to some agreement, could not cooperate even in their opposition to the Communists. But then the Americans had been brought up in a pluralistic world, where even the affairs of the family are managed by compromise between its members. In the traditional Vietnamese family—a family whose customs survived even into the twentieth century—the father held absolute authority over his wife (or wives) and children. The Vietnamese woman by custom wielded a great deal more power than her Chinese sister, but the traditional

Chinese-based law specified that the patriarch governed his wife and children as he governed his rice fields. In theory, though not by customary practice, he could dispose of them as he wished, and they had no recourse against him.[12] The emperor held a similar power over the great family of the empire. By law the trustee of all the rice lands,[13] he held them for the villages on condition of their productivity and good behavior. Without a priesthood or independent feudal aristocracy to obstruct the unified field of his power, he exercised authority through a bureaucracy of mandarins totally dependent on him. Though Vietnam was often divided between warlord families, the disputes were never resolved by a sharing of power—by treaties such as the dukes of Burgundy made with the kings of France—but always by the restoration of an absolute monarch. Even after Vietnam had been divided for two centuries between the Trinh dynasty in the north and the Nguyen in the south, the Vietnamese would not acknowledge the legitimacy of both sovereigns. To do so would have been to assert that the entire moral and social fabric of the community had dissolved. As a family can have only one father, so the nation could have only one emperor to preside over its one Tao or way of life.

> Good conduct, then contentment; thus calm prevails. Hence there follows the hexagram of PEACE. Peace means union and interrelation.

In the *I Ching*, the ancient Chinese Book of Changes, lie all the clues to the basic design of the Sino-Vietnamese world. As the commentary to the verse explains, the Chinese character translated as "peace" implies not only the absence of conflict, but a positive union conducive to prosperity and contentment. To the Vietnamese of the twentieth century "peace" meant not a compromise between various interest groups and organizations, but the restoration of a single, uniform way of life. The Vietnamese were not interested in pluralism, they were interested in unanimity.

Since the Second World War one of the main reasons for the hostility of American intellectuals to Communism has been the suppression of intellectual freedom by Communist leaders in the Soviet Union and the Eastern European countries. In an attempt to rally Americans to the Vietnam War U.S. officials and their sympathizers took pains to argue that the Vietnamese Communists came from the same totalitarian mold. The difficulty with their argument was, however, that the non-Communist Vietnamese leaders believed in intellectual freedom no more than the Communists—a fact that would seem to indicate that their attitudes were founded not in ideology but in culture.

Intellectual freedom, of course, implies intellectual diversity. Westerners tend to take that diversity for granted, for the Western child, even of the narrowest background, grows up with a wide variety of authorities—parents, teachers, clergy, professional men, artists, scientists, and a host of other experts. The traditional Vietnamese child, however, grew up into a monolithic world composed of the family and its extensions in the state. For him there was no alternative to the authority of the father and no question of specialized knowledge. The education of a mandarin was greater, but hardly more diverse, than that of the rice farmer, for the Confucian tradition provided a personal philosophy, a religion, a technology, and a method of managing the state. For the mandarin there was no such thing as "pure science" or "knowledge for its own sake." There was (somewhere) a single correct answer to every question; the mandarin therefore studied in order to learn how to act.

The Vietnamese have lived with diversity for over a century, but the majority—including many of those brought up with French education—still perceive the intellectual world as uniform and absolute. While teaching at the Saigon university in 1957 one young American professor discovered at the second session of his course on comparative government that several students had memorized large sections of their first reading assignment. Pleased but somewhat bewildered, he asked them to finish their work on Machiavelli and turn to Montesquieu. The next day after class the students came to him in open rebellion. "What do you mean?" they asked angrily. "What do you mean by teaching us one thing one day and one thing the next?" The students could not conceive that government could be a matter of opinion. Either a government had worked or it had not, and if it had not worked, then it was not a proper subject for study. Ho Chi Minh said in answer to the question "What is the aim of study?": "One must study in order to remould one's thinking . . . to foster one's revolutionary virtues. . . . Study is aimed at action: the two must go hand in hand. The former without the latter is useless. The latter without the former is hard to carry through."[14]

In trying to teach comparative government, the American professor had, of course, assumed that his Vietnamese students possessed certain analytical tools: a conceptual framework, for instance, that allowed them to abstract the idea "government" from all the various instances of government that have existed in the world. In his course he would often be working from the general to the particular by a process of deductive logic. (A republic has certain characteristics, this state has the same characteristics, therefore it must be a republic.) What he did not realize was that his logic was hardly more universal than the forms of government he was discussing, and that most Vietnamese have an entirely different organization of mind.

The Chinese system of orthography, used by the Vietnamese until the mid-nineteenth century,[15] was not, like the Roman alphabet, composed of regular, repeatable symbols. It was built of particulars. The ideograms for such abstract notions as "fear" or "pleasure" were composed of pictures of concrete events (the pictures of a man, a house, and so on) and to the highly literate these events were always visible within the larger word. The writing was therefore without abstraction, for each word has its own atmosphere, impossible to translate into Western languages and irreducible to categories. Each word was a thing-in-itself.[16] Traditional Vietnamese education accorded with its medium. The child did not learn "principles" from his parents, he learned how to imitate his father in his every action. Confucius said, "When your father is alive, discover his project and when he is dead, remember his actions. If in three years you have not left the road followed by your father, you are really a son full of filial piety."[17] In his formal education the child encountered not a series of "disciplines" but a vast, unsystematized collection of stories and precepts. In the Confucian texts instructions on how to dress and write poetry were juxtaposed with injunctions to such virtues as patience and humility. Each precept, independently arrived at by a process of induction (the Confucian researches into the past), had its own absolute importance for the proper conduct of life. Phrased, perhaps, as a moral absolute, the precept still depended for authority on the success it was thought to have conferred in the past. Confucian logic was, in a sense, pure pragmatism applied over a vast distance in time. In reading the Confucian precepts the child arrived not at a theory of behavior but at a series of clues to the one true way of life.

At the end of his scholarly book, *Viet Cong*, Douglas Pike, an American official and the leading government analyst of the National Liberation Front, breaks out of his neutral tone to conclude: "The NLF and the people it influenced lived in a muzzy, myth-filled world of blacks and whites, good and evil, a simplistic world quite out of character with the one to which the Vietnamese was accustomed. . . . Here, one felt, was tomorrow's society, the beginning of 1984, where peace is war, slavery is freedom, the nonorganization is the organization."[18] American officials might, perhaps, legitimately criticize the National Liberation Front, but they have had, as in this instance, a curious tendency to criticize what is most typically and essentially Vietnamese. A world where there is no clear air of abstraction, no "principles" and no "theories," cannot but seem "muzzy" and "myth-filled" to Westerners. The Vietnamese Communist leaders differ from the non-Communists only in that they have successfully assimilated the Western conceptual framework and translated it into a form of intellectual organization that their less educated compatriots can understand. Like Mao's *Thoughts*, the NLF's "Three Silences" and "Six Duties of a Party Member" correspond exactly to the Confucian precepts. Taken together, they do not form an "ideology" in the Western sense, but the elements of a Tao, or, as the Vietnamese now call it, a "style of work," a "style of life." As for the NLF being "tomorrow's society, the beginning of 1984, where peace is war, slavery is freedom," it is not perhaps so different from the United States government—at least on the subject of Vietnam. In 1970, for instance, President Nixon called the American invasion of Cambodia a "step towards peace" and his firm stand behind President Thieu a firm stand "for the right of all the South Vietnamese people to determine for themselves the kind of government they want."[19] The difference between the two is simply that Americans have traditionally distinguished between objective truth and political persuasion, description and project, whereas the Vietnamese have not—at least not in the same manner.

Westerners naturally look upon it as sinister that the children of North Vietnam and the NLF zones of the South learn to read and do arithmetic from political material. But "politics," or "government" in the widest sense of the word, was also the basis for the traditional education. Confucianism was, first and foremost, a philosophy of social organization. The Confucian texts, for instance, provided the foundation for the imperial law. ("Is not the law . . . true virtue?" asked one of the nineteenth-century intellectuals. "In the law we can . . . find complete expositions of the three duties [of a prince, a father, and a husband] and of the five constant virtues [benevolence, righteousness, propriety, knowledge, and sincerity] as well as the tasks of the six ministries [of the central government].")[20] As one historian has pointed out, the texts established a social contract between the government and the governed, for in order to claim legitimacy the emperor would have to echo Confucius's "I invent nothing, I transmit," thus acknowledging the limitations on his personal power. To learn how to read was therefore already to learn the management of the state. Because the Confucian texts formed the whole of civil education, the bias of the intellectuals was towards these "human sciences," towards practical instruction in the governing of society. To the traditional Confucian scholars all knowledge led back into the political and moral world of man. Mathematics and the physical sciences were no exceptions for, as scientists, the Confucians understood the universe as a unified "field" in which the movements of heaven and earth directly affect human society. The aim of the physical sciences was to plot these movements, these changes, so that man might put himself in tune with the world and with his fellow men. The mandarins, for instance, studied astrology in order to learn the political outlook for the nation: the appearance of comets or the fall of meteorites presaged the smaller disturbances of man. While man could do nothing by himself, he could with intelligence discern the heavenly movements and put his own smaller sphere in accord with the larger one. In China, after a dynastic struggle, the new emperor coming to power would break the instruments of the court musicians in the conviction that they, like the old dynasty, were out of tune with the universe— that they had in some sense caused the rebellion. Similarly, the new emperor would initiate the "rectification of names" so that the words he used for the affairs of state should (unlike those of his predecessor) perfectly accord with the magical etiquette governing the relations of man and nature.

At the time of the Buddhist struggle in 1966 the Buddhist leaders claimed, "Ninety percent of the Vietnamese are Buddhists . . . the people are never Communists," while the NLF leaders claimed by contrast, "The struggle of the religious believers in Vietnam is not separate from the struggle for national liberation." The two statements were mutually contradictory, and an American might have concluded that one or both of their proponents was telling an untruth. But neither the Buddhists nor the NLF leaders were actually "lying," as an American might have been under similar circumstances. Both groups were "rectifying the names" of the Vietnamese to accord with what was no longer the "will of Heaven" but "the laws of history" or "the spirit of the times." They were announcing a project and making themselves comprehensible to their countrymen, for whom all knowledge, even the most neutral observation, is to be put to use.[21]

With this intellectual framework in mind it is perhaps easier to see why the pilots of the People's Republic of China should read Mao's *Thoughts* in order to learn how to fly an airplane. The Vietnamese Communists look upon technology as an independent discipline in certain respects, but they insist that political education should be the basis for using it. During the period of conflict and change in their society, this emphasis on politics is not, perhaps, as unreasonable as it seems to most Americans. Without political education it proved useless or destructive for the cadets of the Saigon air force to learn how to fly airplanes.

For Americans the close relationship the Vietnamese draw between morality, politics, and science is perhaps more difficult to understand now than at any other time in history. Today, living in a social milieu completely divided over matters of value and belief, Westerners have come to look upon science and logic alone as containing universal truths. Over the past century Western philosophers have worked to purge their disciplines of ethical and metaphysical concerns; Americans in particular have tended to deify the natural sciences and set them apart from their social goals. Under pressure from this demand for "objective truth," the scholars of human affairs have scrambled to give their own disciplines the authority and neutrality of science. But because the social scientists can rarely attain the same criteria for "truth" as physicists or chemists, they have sometimes misused the discipline and taken merely the trappings of science as a camouflage for their own beliefs and values. It is thus that many American "political scientists" sympathetic to American intervention in Vietnam have concluded that the NLF's subordination of science and "objective truth" to politics has its origins in Communist totalitarianism.

For Westerners who believe in the eternal verity of certain principles the notion of "brainwashing" is shocking and the experience is associated with torture. But in such societies as those in Indonesia, China, and Vietnam, it is in one form or another an activity of every political movement. Under the traditional Vietnamese empire there was only one truth, only one true way. And all modern Vietnamese parties have had to face the task of changing the nature of the "truth." Among people with an extremely pragmatic cast of mind, for whom values depend for their authority upon success, the task has implied a demonstration that the old ways are no longer useful, no longer adapted to the necessities of history. During the course of the war both the Saigon government and the NLF held "reeducation" courses for defectors and prisoners, with varying degrees of success. Those Americans who objected to the process (and most

Americans singled out the NLF) saw it in European terms as the forcible destruction of personality, a mental torture such as Arthur Koestler described in *Darkness at Noon*. But to the Vietnamese, Communist and non-Communist, it did not imply torture at all, for the reason that they have a very different kind of commitment to society than do Westerners.

And it is this commitment that lies at the basis of intellectual organization. Unlike the Westerner, the Vietnamese child is brought up not to follow certain principles, but to accept the authority of certain people. The "Three Net Ropes" of the traditional society consisted in the loyalty of the son to his father, of the wife to her husband, and the mandarin to his emperor. The injunctions to filial piety and conjugal obedience were unconditional. Traditional Vietnamese law rested not upon the notion of individual rights, but the notion of duties—the duty of the sovereign to his people, the father to his son, and vice versa. Similarly, the Confucian texts defined no general principles but the proper relationship of man to man. Equal justice was secondary to social harmony. This particular form of social contract gave the individual a very different sense of himself, of his own personality. In the Vietnamese language there is no word that exactly corresponds to the Western personal pronoun I, *je, ich*. When a man speaks of himself, he calls himself "your brother," "your nephew," "your teacher," depending upon his relationship to the person he addresses. The word he uses for the first person *(toi)* in the new impersonal world of the cities originally denoted "subject of the king."[22] The traditional Vietnamese did not see himself as a totally independent being, for he did not distinguish himself as acutely as does a Westerner from his society (and by extension, the heavens). He did not see himself as a "character" formed of immutable traits, eternally loyal to certain principles, but rather as a system of relationships, a function of the society around him. In a sense, the design of the Confucian world resembled that of a Japanese garden where every rock, opaque and indifferent in itself, takes on significance from its relationship to the surrounding objects.

In central Vietnam, where the villages are designed like Japanese gardens, a young Vietnamese district chief once told this writer that he had moved a group of villagers from a Liberation village to his headquarters in order to "change their opinions." He had not lectured the villagers on the evils of Marxism and he did not plan to do so; he would simply wait for them to fall into relationship with his political authority. Had the villagers, of course, received an adequate political education, his waiting would be in vain. A "hard-core" NLF cadre would understand his community to include not only the village or the district but all of Vietnam. His horizons would be large enough in time and space to encompass a government-controlled city or years of a harsh, inconclusive war. But with regard to his refugees, the district chief was probably right: the old people and the children had left their NLF sympathies behind them in the burning ruins of a village only two miles distant.

In the old society, of course, a man who moved out of his village would find in his new village or in the court of Hué the same kind of social and political system that he had left behind him. During the conflicts of the twentieth century, however, his movement from one place to another might require a change of "ideology," or of way of life. In 1966 one American official discovered an ARVN soldier who had changed sides five times in the war, serving alternately with three NLF units and three GVN battalions. Clearly this particular soldier had no political education to speak of and no wider sense of community. But even for those that did, the possibility of accommodation and change remained open. When asked by an American interviewer what he thought of the GVN, one Front defector found it necessary to specify that "with the mind of the other regime" (i.e., that of the NLF) he felt it was bad for the people. At that point he was preparing himself to accept a new interpretation.

Such changes of mind must look opportunistic or worse to Westerners, but to the Vietnamese with their particular commitment to society it was at once the most moral and the most practical course. Indeed, it was the only course available, for in such situations the Vietnamese villager did not consider an alternative. In the old language, a man depended upon the "will of Heaven"; it was therefore his duty to accommodate himself to it as well as possible. In a letter to his subordinates of the southern provinces Phan Thanh Giang described this ethic of accommodation in the most sophisticated Confucian terms:

> It is written that he who lives according to Heaven's will is in the right way; he who departs from Heaven's will is wrong. To act according to Heaven's will is to act according to one's reason. Man is an intelligent animal created by Heaven. Each animal lives according to its proper nature, like water which seeks its own level or fire which spreads in dry places. . . . Man to whom Heaven has given reason should endeavor to live according to that reason.[23]

In conclusion Phan Thanh Giang requested that his officials surrender without resistance to the invading French forces. "The French," he wrote, "have huge battleships, full of soldiers and armed with powerful cannons. . . . It would be as senseless for you to assail [them] as for the fawn to attack the tiger. You would only draw suffering upon the people whom Heaven has entrusted to your care."[24] Loyal to the Vietnamese emperor, Phan Thanh Giang could not so easily accommodate himself to necessity. Branding himself as a traitor, he chose the same course that, throughout history, his predecessors had taken at the fall of dynasties. Suicide was the only resolution to the unbearable conflict between loyalty to the emperor and obligation to what he saw as the will of Heaven, to the will of the community as a whole.

But such protests against the will of Heaven were only for the mandarins, the moral leaders of the community. They were not for the simple villager, for as Confucius said, "The essence of the gentleman is that of wind; the essence of small people is that of grass. And when a wind passes over the grass, it cannot choose but bend."[25] In times of political stability the villager accommodated himself to the prevailing wind that clearly signaled the will of Heaven. Only in times of disorder and uncertainty when the sky clouded over and the forces of the world struggled to uncertain outcome, only then did the peasant take on responsibility for the great affairs of state, and only then did the leaders watch him carefully, for, so went the Confucian formula, "The will of Heaven is reflected in the eyes and ears of the people."

This ancient political formula clarified the basis on which twentieth-century Vietnamese, including those who no longer used the old language, would make their political decisions. Asked which side he supported, one peasant from a village close to Saigon told a Front cadre in 1963: "I do not know, for I follow the will of Heaven. If I do what you say, then the Diem side will arrest me; if I say things against you, then you will arrest me, so I would rather carry both burdens on my shoulders and stand in the middle." Caught between two competing regimes, the peasant did not assert his right to decide between them, rather he asked himself where his duty lay. Which regime had the power to claim his loyalty? Which would be the most likely to restore peace and harmony to his world? His decision might be based on personal preference (a government that considered the wishes of the people would be more likely to restore peace on a permanent basis). But he had, nonetheless, to make an objective analysis of the situation and take his gamble, for his first loyalty lay neither with the Diem regime nor the

NLF but with the will of Heaven that controlled them both. At certain periods *attentisme* was the most moral and the most practical course.

As a warning to Westerners on the difficulties of understanding the twentieth-century conflict in Vietnam, Paul Mus told an ancient Chinese legend that is well known to the Vietnamese. There was trouble in the state of Lu, and the reigning monarch called in Confucius to ask for his help. When he arrived at the court, the Master went to a public place and took a seat in the correct way, facing south, and all the trouble disappeared.[26]

The works of Vo Nguyen Giap are but addenda to this legend, for the legend is the paradigm of revolution in Vietnam. To the Vietnamese it is clear from the story that Confucius was not taking an existential or exemplary position, he was actually changing the situation. Possessed of neither godlike nor prophetic authority, he moved an entire kingdom by virtue of his sensitivity to the will of Heaven as reflected in the "eyes and ears of the people." As executor for the people, he clarified their wishes and signaled the coming—or the return—of the Way that would bring harmony to the kingdom. For the Hoa Hao and the Cao Dai, the traditionalist sects of the south that in the twentieth century still believed in this magical "sympathy" of heaven and earth, political change did not depend entirely on human effort. Even the leaders of the sects believed that if they, like Confucius, had taken "the correct position," the position that accorded with the will of Heaven, all Vietnamese would eventually adopt the same Way, the same political system that they had come to.

Here, within the old spiritualist language, lies a clue as to why the Vietnamese Communists held their military commanders in strict subordination to the political cadres. Within the domestic conflict military victories were not only less important than political victories, but they were strictly meaningless except as reflections of the political realities. For the Communists, as for all the other political groups, the vehicle of political change was not the war, the pitch of force against force, but the struggle, the attempt to make manifest that their Way was the only true or "natural" one for all Vietnamese.* Its aim was to demonstrate that, in the old language, the Mandate of Heaven had changed and the new order had already replaced the old in all but title. When Ho Chi Minh entered Hanoi in August 1945, he made much the same kind of gesture as Confucius had made in facing south when he said (and the wording is significant, for he was using a language of both East and West), "We, members of the Provisional Government of the Democratic Republic of Viet-Nam solemnly declare to the world that Viet-Nam has the right to be a free and independent country—and in fact it is so already. The entire Vietnamese people are determined to mobilize all their physical and mental strength, to sacrifice their lives and property in order to safeguard their independence and liberty."[27] His claims were far from "true" at the time, but they constituted the truth in potential—if he, like Confucius, had taken the "correct position." For the Confucians, of course, the "correct position" was that which accorded with the will of Heaven and the practice of the sacred ancestors. For Ho Chi Minh the "correct position" was that which accorded with the laws of history and the present and future judgment of the Vietnamese people.

*"The English word 'struggle,' a pale translation of the Vietnamese term *dau tranh*, fails to convey the drama, the awesomeness, the totality of the original." (Douglas Pike, *Viet Cong*, p. 85.)

Notes

1. Viet Hoai, "The Old Man in the Free Fire Zone," in *Between Two Fires: The Unheard Voices of Vietnam*, ed. Ly Qui Chung, pp. 102–105.
2. Léopold Cadière, *Croyances et pratiques religieuses des viêt-namiens*, vol. 2, p. 308.
3. Nghiem Dang, *Viet-Nam: Politics and Public Administration*, p. 53.
4. Confucius, *The Analects of Confucius*, p. 127.
5. Conversation with Paul Mus.
6. Confucius, *Analects*, p. 104. According to Waley, "The saying can be paraphrased as follows: If I and my followers are right in saying that countries can be governed solely by correct carrying out of ritual and its basic principle of 'giving way to others,' there is obviously no case to be made out for any other form of government. If on the other hand we are wrong, then ritual is useless. To say, as people often do, that ritual is all very well so long as it is not used as an instrument of government, is wholly to misunderstand the purpose of ritual."
7. Charles Gosselin, *L'Empire d'Annam*, p. 149.
8. Truong Buu Lam, *Patterns of Vietnamese Response to Foreign Intervention: 1858–1900*, p. 77. From an anonymous appeal to resist the French (1864).
9. Paul Mus, "Les Religions de l'Indochine," in *Indochine*, ed. Sylvain Lévi, p. 132.
10. There were also handicraft guilds and Buddhist and Taoist priesthoods, but these are details. The generalization is true enough for the purposes of contrast.
11. For the French, the emperor's persecution of French Catholic missionaries (though there were relatively few cases) served as a pretext for intervention in Vietnam. But to the French emperors conversion to Catholicism signified not just a religious apostasy but alienation from the state itself.
12. The Gia Long code, promulgated by the early nineteenth-century founder of the Nguyen dynasty, was a much more exact copy of the Chinese codes than the Le code that governed Vietnam from the fifteenth to the nineteenth centuries.
13. Le Thanh Khoi, *Le Viêt-Nam*. According to the French historian, Henri Maspero, the land did not belong to the emperor, but to the people, whose will was expressed by the mouth of the sovereign. This reflexive relation between the people and the sovereign is typical of the Vietnamese political philosophy derived from Mencius.
14. Truong Chinh, *President Ho Chi Minh*, p. 68.
15. In the seventeenth century a French missionary, Alexandre de Rhodes, transcribed the Vietnamese language into the Roman alphabet, using diacritical marks to indicate the different tones. His aim was to render the Bible and other Christian texts into Vietnamese. The first people to use *quoç ngu*, as his system was called, were therefore the Vietnamese Catholics. The Latin alphabet came into general use only after the French conquest.
16. A hypothesis: the spoken language with its five tones may also be more concrete (more allusive, less abstract) than Western languages because of the element of music in it. In the way that people recall particular situations and particular people from the sound of a familiar tune, so the Vietnamese may associate words more directly with particular events than do Westerners. Cf. A. R. Luria, *The Mind of a Mnemonist* (New York: Basic Books, 1968).
17. Gosselin, *Empire*, p. 27.
18. Douglas Pike, *Viet Cong*, pp. 379, 383.
19. *New York Times*, 8 October 1970.
20. Nguyen Truong To, "Memorials on Reform," in *Patterns of Response*, ed. Truong Buu Lam, p. 98.
21. If the Buddhists were, for instance, to be proved wrong in the end, then their statement would be both untrue and useless.
22. Phan Thi Dac, *Situation de la personne au Viet-Nam*, pp. 137–156.
23. Phan Thanh Giang, "Letter on His Surrender," in *Patterns of Response*, ed. Truong Buu Lam, pp. 87–88.

24. Ibid., p. 88. Phan Thanh Giang may have been wrong in his assessment of the military situation. Other mandarins had behaved differently, many of them resisting the French to the last. Given his assessment, however, there was little else for him to do.

25. Confucius, *Analects*, p. 168.

26. Paul Mus, "Cultural Backgrounds of Present Problems," p. 13. In the *Analects* the Master recounts this story about one of the divine sages of the past.

27. Ho Chi Minh, *Ho Chi Minh on Revolution*, p. 145.

29
A Bureaucratic Tangle
JAMES C. THOMSON, JR.

As a case study in the making of foreign policy, the Vietnam War will fascinate historians and social scientists for many decades to come. One question that will certainly be asked: How did men of superior ability, sound training, and high ideals—American policymakers of the 1960s—create such costly and divisive policy?

As one who watched the decision-making process in Washington from 1961 to 1966 under Presidents Kennedy and Johnson, I can suggest a preliminary answer. I can do so by briefly listing some of the factors that seemed to me to shape our Vietnam policy during my years as an East Asia specialist at the State Department and the White House. I shall deal largely with Washington as I saw or sensed it, and not with Saigon, where I have spent but a scant three days, in the entourage of the Vice President, or with other decision centers, the capitals of interested parties. Nor will I deal with other important parts of the record: Vietnam's history prior to 1961, for instance, or the overall course of America's relations with Vietnam.

Yet a first and central ingredient in these years of Vietnam decisions does involve history. The ingredient was *the legacy of the 1950s*—by which I mean the so-called "loss of China," the Korean War, and the Far East policy of Secretary of State Dulles.

This legacy had an institutional by-product for the Kennedy Administration: in 1961 the U.S. government's East Asian establishment was undoubtedly the most rigid and doctrinaire of Washington's regional divisions in foreign affairs. This was especially true at the Department of State, where the incoming Administration found the Bureau of Far Eastern Affairs the hardest nut to crack. It was a bureau that had been purged of its best China expertise, and of farsighted, dispassionate men, as a result of McCarthyism. Its members were generally committed to one policy line: the close containment and isolation of mainland China, the harassment of "neutralist" nations which sought to avoid alignment with either Washington or Peking, and the maintenance of a network of alliances with anti-Communist client states on China's periphery.

Another aspect of the legacy was the special vulnerability and sensitivity of the new Democratic Administration on Far East policy issues. The memory of the McCarthy era was still very sharp, and Kennedy's margin of victory was too thin. The 1960 Offshore Islands TV debate between Kennedy and Nixon had shown the President-elect the perils of "fresh thinking." The Administration was inherently leery of moving too fast on Asia. As a result, the Far East Bureau (now the Bureau of East Asian and Pacific Affairs) was the last one to be overhauled. Not until Averell Harriman was brought in as Assistant Secretary in December, 1961, were significant personnel changes attempted, and it took Harriman several months to make a deep imprint on the bureau because of his necessary preoccupation with the Laos settlement. Once he did so, there was virtually no effort to bring back the purged or exiled East Asia experts.

There were other important by-products of this "legacy of the fifties":

The new Administration inherited and somewhat shared *a general perception of China-on-the-march*—a sense of China's vastness, its numbers, its belligerence; a revived sense, perhaps, of the Golden Horde. This was a perception fed by Chinese intervention in the Korean War (an intervention actually based on appallingly bad communications and mutual miscalculation on the part of Washington and Peking; but the careful unraveling of that tragedy, which scholars have accomplished, had not yet become part of the conventional wisdom).

The new Administration inherited and briefly accepted a *monolithic conception of the Communist bloc*. Despite much earlier predictions and reports by outside analysts, policymakers did not begin to accept the reality and possible finality of the Sino-Soviet split until the first weeks of 1962. The inevitably corrosive impact of competing nationalisms on Communism was largely ignored.

The new Administration inherited and to some extent shared *the "domino theory" about Asia*. This theory resulted from profound ignorance of Asian history and hence ignorance of the radical differences among Asian nations and societies. It resulted from a blindness to the power and resilience of Asian nationalisms. (It may also have resulted from a subconscious sense that, since "all Asians look alike," all Asian nations will act alike.) As a theory, the domino fallacy was not merely inaccurate but also insulting to Asian nations; yet it has continued to this day to beguile men who should know better.

Finally, the legacy of the fifties was apparently compounded by an uneasy sense of a worldwide Communist challenge to the new Administration after the Bay of Pigs fiasco. A first manifestation was the President's traumatic Vienna meeting with Khrushchev in June, 1961; then came the Berlin crisis of the summer. All this created an atmosphere in which President Kennedy undoubtedly felt under special pressure to show his nation's mettle in Vietnam—if the Vietnamese, unlike the people of Laos, were willing to fight.

In general, the legacy of the fifties shaped such early moves of the new Administration as the decisions to maintain a high-visibility SEATO (by sending the Secretary of State himself instead of some underling to its first meeting in 1961), to back away from diplomatic recognition of Mongolia in the summer of 1961, and most important, to expand U.S. military assistance to South Vietnam that winter on the basis of the much more tentative Eisenhower commitment. It should be added that the increased commitment to Vietnam was also fueled by a new breed of military strategists and academic social scientists (some of whom had entered the new Administration) who had developed theories of counterguerrilla warfare and were eager to see them put to the test. To some, "counter-insurgency" seemed a new panacea for coping with the world's instability.

So much for the legacy and the history. Any new Administration inherits both complicated problems and simplistic views of the world. But surely among the policymakers of the Kennedy and Johnson Administrations there were men who would warn of the dangers of an open-ended commitment to the Vietnam quagmire?

This raises a central question, at the heart of the policy process: Where were the experts, the doubters, and the dissenters? Were they there at all, and if so, what happened to them?

The answer is complex but instructive.

In the first place, the American government was sorely *lacking in real Vietnam or Indochina expertise*. Originally treated as an adjunct of Embassy Paris, our Saigon embassy and the Vietnam Desk at State were largely staffed from 1954 onward by French-speaking Foreign Service personnel of narrowly European experience. Such diplomats were even more closely restricted than the normal embassy officer—by cast of mind as well as language—to contacts with Vietnam's French-speaking urban elites. For instance, Foreign Service linguists in Portugal are able to speak with the peasantry if they get out of Lisbon and choose to do so; not so the French speakers of Embassy Saigon.

In addition, the *shadow of the "loss of China"* distorted Vietnam reporting. Career officers in the Department, and especially those in the field, had not forgotten the fate of their World War II colleagues who wrote in frankness from China and were later pilloried by Senate committees for critical comments on the Chinese Nationalists. Candid reporting on the strengths of the Viet Cong and the weaknesses of the Diem government was inhibited by the memory. It was also inhibited by some higher officials, notably Ambassador Nolting in Saigon, who refused to sign off on such cables.

In due course, to be sure, some Vietnam talent was discovered or developed. But a recurrent and increasingly important factor in the decision-making process was *the banishment of real expertise.* Here the underlying cause was the "closed politics" of policymaking as issues become hot: the more sensitive the issue, and the higher it rises in the bureaucracy, the more completely the experts are excluded while the harassed senior generalists take over (that is, the Secretaries, Undersecretaries, and Presidential Assistants). The frantic skimming of briefing papers in the back seats of limousines is no substitute for the presence of specialists; furthermore, in times of crisis such papers are deemed "too sensitive" even for review by the specialists. Another underlying cause of this banishment, as Vietnam became more critical, was the replacement of the experts, who were generally and increasingly pessimistic, by men described as "can-do guys," loyal and energetic fixers unsoured by expertise. In early 1965, when I confided my growing policy doubts to an older colleague on the NSC staff, he assured me that the smartest thing both of us could do was to "steer clear of the whole Vietnam mess"; the gentleman in question had the misfortune to be a "can-do guy," however, and is now [late 1960s] highly placed in Vietnam, under orders to solve the mess.

Despite the banishment of the experts, internal doubters and dissenters did indeed appear and persist. Yet as I watched the process, such men were effectively neutralized by a subtle dynamic: *the domestication of dissenters.* Such "domestication" arose out of a twofold clubbish need: on the one hand, the dissenter's desire to stay aboard; and on the other hand, the nondissenter's conscience. Simply stated, dissent, when recognized, was made to feel at home. On the lowest possible scale of importance, I must confess my own considerable sense of dignity and acceptance (both vital) when my senior White House employer would refer to me as his "favorite dove." Far more significant was the case of the former Undersecretary of State, George Ball. Once Mr. Ball began to express doubts, he was warmly institutionalized: he was encouraged to become the inhouse devil's advocate on Vietnam. The upshot was inevitable: the process of escalation allowed for periodic requests to Mr. Ball to speak his piece; Ball felt good, I assume (he had fought for righteousness); the others felt good (they had given a full hearing to the dovish option); and there was minimal unpleasantness. The club remained intact; and it is of course possible that matters would have gotten worse faster if Mr. Ball had kept silent, or left before his final departure in the fall of 1966. There was also, of course, the case of the last institutionalized doubter, Bill Moyers. The President is said to have greeted his arrival at meetings with an affectionate, "Well, here comes Mr. Stop-the-Bombing. . . ." Here again the dynamics of domesticated dissent sustained the relationship for a while.

A related point—and crucial, I suppose, to government at all times—was *the "effectiveness" trap*, the trap that keeps men from speaking out, as clearly or often as they might, within the government. And it is the trap that keeps men from resigning in protest and airing their dissent outside the government. The most important asset that a man brings to bureaucratic life is his "effectiveness," a mysterious combination of training, style, and connections. The most ominous complaint that can be whispered of a bureaucrat is: "I'm afraid Charlie's beginning to lose his effectiveness." To preserve your effectiveness, you must decide where and when to fight the mainstream of policy; the opportunities range from pillow talk with your wife, to private drinks with your friends, to meetings with the Secretary of State or the President. The inclination to remain silent or to acquiesce in the presence of the great men—to live to fight another day, to give on this issue so that you can be "effective" on later issues—is overwhelming. Nor is it the tendency of youth alone; some of our most senior officials, men of wealth and fame, whose place in history is secure, have remained silent lest their connection with power be terminated. As for the disinclination to resign in protest: while not necessarily a Washington or even American specialty, it seems more true of a government in which ministers have no parliamentary back-bench to which to retreat. In the absence of such a refuge, it is easy to rationalize the decision to stay aboard. By doing so, one may be able to prevent a few bad things from happening and perhaps even make a few good things happen. To exit is to lose even those marginal chances for "effectiveness."

Another factor must be noted: as the Vietnam controversy escalated at home, there developed a *preoccupation with Vietnam public relations as opposed to Vietnam policymaking.* And here, ironically, internal doubters and dissenters were heavily employed. For such men, by virtue of their own doubts, were often deemed best able to "massage" the doubting intelligentsia. My senior East Asia colleague at the White House, a brilliant and humane doubter who had dealt with Indochina since 1954, spent three quarters of his working days on Vietnam public relations: drafting presidential responses to letters from important critics, writing conciliatory language for presidential speeches, and meeting quite interminably with delegations of outraged Quakers, clergymen, academics, and housewives. His regular callers were the late A. J. Muste and Norman Thomas; mine were members of the Women's Strike for Peace. Our orders from above: keep them off the backs of busy policymakers (who usually happened to be nondoubters). Incidentally, my most discouraging assignment in the realm of public relations was the preparation of a White House pamphlet entitled *Why Vietnam*, in September, 1965; in a gesture toward my conscience, I fought—and lost—a battle to have the title followed by a question mark.

Through a variety of procedures, both institutional and personal, doubt, dissent, and expertise were effectively neutralized in the making of policy. But what can be said of the men "in charge"? It is patently absurd to suggest that they produced such tragedy by intention and calculation. But it is neither absurd nor difficult to discern certain forces at work that caused decent and honorable men to do great harm.

Here I would stress the paramount role of *executive fatigue.* No factor seems to me more crucial and underrated in the making of foreign policy. The physical and emotional toll of executive responsibility in State, the Pentagon, the White House, and other executive agencies is enormous; that toll is of course compounded by extended service. Many of today's Vietnam policymakers have been on the job for from four to seven years. Complaints may be few, and physical health may remain unimpaired, though emotional health is far harder to gauge. But what is most seriously eroded in the deadening process of fatigue is freshness of thought, imagination, a sense of possibility, a sense of priorities and perspective—those rare assets of a new Administration in its first year or two of office. The tired policymaker becomes a prisoner of his own narrowed view of the world and his own cliched rhetoric. He becomes irritable and defensive—short on sleep, short on family ties, short on patience. Such men make bad policy and then compound it. They have neither the time nor the temperament for new ideas or preventive diplomacy.

Below the level of the fatigued executives in the making of Vietnam policy was a widespread phenomenon: *the curator mentality* in the Department of State. By this I mean the collective inertia produced by the bureaucrat's view of his job. At State, the average "desk officer" inherits from his predecessor our policy toward Country X; he regards it as his function to keep that policy intact—under glass, untampered with, and dusted—so that he may pass it on in two to four years to his successor. And such curatorial service generally merits promotion within the system. (Maintain the status quo, and you will stay out of trouble.) In some circumstances, the inertia bred by such an outlook can act as a brake against rash innovation. But on many issues, this inertia sustains the momentum of bad policy and unwise commitments—momentum that might otherwise have been resisted within the ranks. Clearly, Vietnam is such an issue.

To fatigue and inertia must be added the factor of internal confusion. Even among the "architects" of our Vietnam commitment, there has been persistent *confusion as to what type of war we were fighting* and, as a direct consequence, *confusion as to how to end that war*. (The "credibility gap" is, in part, a reflection of such internal confusion.) Was it, for instance, a civil war, in which case counter-insurgency might suffice? Or was it a war of international aggression? (This might invoke SEATO or UN commit-ment.) Who was the aggressor—and the "real enemy"? The Viet Cong? Hanoi? Peking? Moscow? International Communism? Or maybe "Asian Communism"? Differing en-emies dictated differing strategies and tactics. And confused throughout, in like fash-ion, was the question of American objectives; your objectives depended on whom you were fighting and why. I shall not forget my assignment from an Assistant Secretary of State in March, 1964: to draft a speech for Secretary McNamara which would, *inter alia*, once and for all dispose of the canard that the Vietnam conflict was a civil war. "But in some ways, of course," I mused, "it *is* a civil war." "Don't play word games with me!" snapped the Assistant Secretary.

Similar confusion beset the concept of "negotiations"—anathema to much of offi-cial Washington from 1961 to 1965. Not until April, 1965, did "unconditional discus-sions" become respectable, via a presidential speech; even then the Secretary of State stressed privately to newsmen that nothing had changed, since "discussions" were by no means the same as "negotiations." Months later that issue was resolved. But it took even longer to obtain a fragile internal agreement that negotiations might include the Viet Cong as something other than an appendage to Hanoi's delegation. Given such confusion as to the whos and whys of our Vietnam commitment, it is not surprising, as Theodore Draper has written, that policymakers find it so difficult to agree on how to end the war.

Of course, one force—a constant in the vortex of commitment—was that of *wish-ful thinking*. I partook of it myself at many times. I did so especially during Washington's struggle with Diem in the autumn of 1963 when some of us at State believed that for once, in dealing with a difficult client state, the U.S. government could use the lever-age of our economic and military assistance to make good things happen, instead of being led around by the nose by men like Chiang Kai-shek and Syngman Rhee (and, in that particular instance, by Diem). If we could prove that point, I thought, and move into a new day, with or without Diem, then Vietnam was well worth the effort. Later came the wishful thinking of the air-strike planners in the late autumn of 1964; there were those who actually thought that after six weeks of air strikes, the North Vietnam-ese would come crawling to us to ask for peace talks. And what, someone asked in one of the meetings of the time, if they don't? The answer was that we would bomb for another four weeks, and that would do the trick. And a few weeks later came one instance of wishful thinking that was symptomatic of good men misled: in January, 1965, I encountered one of the very highest figures in the Administration at a dinner, drew him aside, and told him of my worries about the air-strike option. He told me that I really shouldn't worry; it was his conviction that before any such plans could be put into effect, a neutralist government would come to power in Saigon that would politely invite us out. And finally, there was the recurrent wishful thinking that sustained many of us through the trying months of 1965–1966 after the air strikes had begun: that surely, somehow, one way or another, we would "be in a conference in six months," and the escalatory spiral would be suspended. The basis of our hope: "It simply can't go on."

As a further influence on policymakers I would cite the factor of *bureaucratic detachment.* By this I mean what at best might be termed the professional callousness of the surgeon (and indeed, medical lingo—the "surgical strike" for instance—seemed to crop up in the euphemisms of the times). In Washington the semantics of the military muted the reality of war for the civilian policymakers. In quiet, air-conditioned, thick-carpeted rooms, such terms as "systematic pressure," "armed reconnaissance," "targets of opportunity," and even "body count" seemed to breed a sort of games-theory detachment. Most memorable to me was a moment in the late 1964 target planning when the question under discussion was how heavy our bombing should be, and how extensive our strafing, at some midpoint in the projected pattern of systematic pressure. An Assistant Secretary of State resolved the point in the following words: "It seems to me that our orchestration should be mainly violins, but with periodic touches of brass." Perhaps the biggest shock of my return to Cambridge, Massachusetts, was the realization that the young men, the flesh and blood I taught and saw on these university streets, were potentially some of the numbers on the charts of those faraway planners. In a curious sense, Cambridge is closer to this war than Washington.

There is an unprovable factor that relates to bureaucratic detachment: the ingredient of *crypto-racism.* I do not mean to imply any conscious contempt for Asian loss of life on the part of Washington officials. But I do mean to imply that bureaucratic detachment may well be compounded by a traditional Western sense that there are so many Asians, after all; that Asians have a fatalism about life and a disregard for its loss; that they are cruel and barbaric to their own people; and that they are very different from us (and all look alike?). And I *do* mean to imply that the upshot of such subliminal views is a subliminal question whether Asians, and particularly Asian peasants, and most particularly Asian Communists, are really people—like you and me. To put the matter another way: would we have pursued quite such policies—and quite such military tactics—if the Vietnamese were white?

It is impossible to write of Vietnam decision-making without writing about language. Throughout the conflict, words have been of paramount importance. I refer here to the impact of *rhetorical escalation* and to the *problem of oversell.* In an important sense, Vietnam has become of crucial significance to us *because we have said that it is of crucial significance.* (The issue obviously relates to the public relations preoccupation described earlier.)

The key here is domestic politics: the need to sell the American people, press, and Congress on support for an unpopular and costly war in which the objectives themselves have been in flux. To sell means to persuade, and to persuade means rhetoric. As the difficulties and costs have mounted, so has the definition of the stakes. This is not to say that rhetorical escalation is an orderly process; executive prose is the product of many writers, and some concepts—North Vietnamese infiltration, America's "national honor," Red China as the chief enemy—have entered the rhetoric only gradually and even sporadically. But there is an upward spiral nonetheless. And once you have *said* that the American Experiment itself stands or falls on the Vietnam outcome, you have thereby created a national stake far beyond any earlier stakes.

Crucial throughout the process of Vietnam decision-making was a conviction among many policymakers: that Vietnam posed a *fundamental test of America's national will*. Time and again I was told by men reared in the tradition of Henry L. Stimson that all we needed was the will, and we would then prevail. Implicit in such a view, it seemed to me, was a curious assumption that Asians lacked will, or at least that in a contest between Asian and Anglo-Saxon wills, the non-Asians must prevail. A corollary to the persistent belief in will was *a fascination with power* and an awe in the face of the power America possessed as no nation or civilization ever before. Those who doubted our role in Vietnam were said to shrink from the burdens of power, the obligations of power, the uses of power, the responsibility of power. By implication, such men were soft-headed and effete.

Finally, no discussion of the factors and forces at work on Vietnam policymakers can ignore the central fact of *human ego investment*. Men who have participated in a decision develop a stake in that decision. As they participate in further, related decisions, their stake increases. It might have been possible to dissuade a man of strong self-confidence at an early stage of the ladder of decision; but it is infinitely harder at later stages since a change of mind there usually involves implicit or explicit repudiation of a chain of previous decisions.

To put it bluntly: at the heart of the Vietnam calamity is a group of able, dedicated men who have been regularly and repeatedly wrong—and whose standing with their contemporaries, and more important, with history, depends, as they see it, on being proven right. These are not men who can be asked to extricate themselves from error.

The various ingredients I have cited in the making of Vietnam policy have created a variety of results, most of them fairly obvious. Here are some that seem to me most central:

Throughout the conflict, there has been *persistent and repeated miscalculation* by virtually all the actors, in high echelons and low, whether dove, hawk, or something else. To cite one simple example among many: in late 1964 and early 1965, some peace-seeking planners at State who strongly opposed the projected bombing of the North urged that, instead, American ground forces be sent to South Vietnam; this would, they said, increase our bargaining leverage against the North—our "chips"—and would give us something to negotiate about (the withdrawal of our forces) at an early peace conference. Simultaneously, the air-strike option was urged by many in the military who were dead set against American participation in "another land war in Asia"; they were joined by other civilian peace-seekers who wanted to bomb Hanoi into early negotiations. By late 1965, we had ended up with the worst of all worlds: ineffective and costly air strikes against the North, spiraling ground forces in the South, and no negotiations in sight.

Throughout the conflict as well, there has been *a steady give-in to pressures for a military solution* and only minimal and sporadic efforts at a diplomatic and political solution. In part this resulted from the confusion (earlier cited) among the civilians—confusion regarding objectives and strategy. And in part this resulted from the self-enlarging nature of military investment. Once air strikes and particularly ground forces were introduced, our investment itself had transformed the original stakes. More air power was needed to protect the ground forces; and then more ground forces to protect the ground forces. And needless to say, the military mind develops its own momentum in the absence of clear guidelines from the civilians. Once asked to save South Vietnam, rather than to "advise" it, the American military could not but press for escalation. In addition, sad to report, assorted military constituencies, once involved in Vietnam, have had a series of cases to prove: for instance, the utility not only of air power (the Air Force) but of supercarrier-based air power (the Navy). Also, Vietnam policy has suffered from one ironic by-product of Secretary McNamara's establishment of civilian control at the Pentagon: in the face of such control, interservice rivalry has given way to a united front among the military—reflected in the new but recurrent phenomenon of JCS unanimity. In conjunction with traditional congressional allies (mostly Southern senators and representatives) such a united front would pose a formidable problem for any President.

Throughout the conflict, there have been *missed opportunities, large and small, to disengage ourselves from Vietnam on increasingly unpleasant but still acceptable terms.* Of the many moments from 1961 onward, I shall cite only one, the last and most important opportunity that was lost: in the summer of 1964 the President instructed his chief advisers to prepare for him as wide a range of Vietnam options as possible for post-election consideration and decision. He explicitly asked that all options be laid out. What happened next was, in effect, Lyndon Johnson's slow-motion Bay of Pigs. For the advisers so effectively converged on one single option—juxtaposed against two other, phony options (in effect, blowing up the world, or scuttle-and-run)—that the President was confronted with unanimity for bombing the North from all his trusted counselors. Had he been more confident in foreign affairs, had he been deeply informed on Vietnam and Southeast Asia, and had he raised some hard questions that unanimity had submerged, this President could have used the largest electoral mandate in history to de-escalate in Vietnam, in the clear expectation that at the worst a neutralist government would come to power in Saigon and politely invite us out. Today, many lives and dollars later, such an alternative has become an elusive and infinitely more expensive possibility.

In the course of these years, another result of Vietnam decision-making has been *the abuse and distortion of history.* Vietnamese, Southeast Asian, and Far Eastern history has been rewritten by our policymakers, and their spokesmen, to conform with the alleged necessity of our presence in Vietnam. Highly dubious analogies from our experience elsewhere—the "Munich" sellout and "containment" from Europe, the Malayan insurgency and the Korean War from Asia—have been imported in order to justify our actions. And more recent events have been fitted to the Procrustean bed of Vietnam. Most notably, the change of power in Indonesia in 1965–1966 has been ascribed to our Vietnam presence; and virtually all progress in the Pacific region—the rise of regionalism, new forms of cooperation, and mounting growth rates—has been similarly explained. The Indonesian allegation is undoubtedly false (I tried to prove it, during six months of careful investigation at the White House, and had to confess failure); the regional allegation is patently unprovable in either direction (except, of course, for the clear fact that the economies of both Japan and Korea have profited enormously from our Vietnam-related procurement in these countries; but that is a costly and highly dubious form of foreign aid).

There is a final result of Vietnam policy I would cite that holds potential danger for the future of American foreign policy: *the rise of a new breed of American ideologues who see Vietnam as the ultimate test of their doctrine.* I have in mind those men in Washington who have given a new life to the missionary impulse in American foreign relations: who believe that this nation, in this era, has received a threefold endowment that can transform the world. As they see it, that endowment is composed of, first, our unsurpassed military might; second, our clear technological supremacy; and third, our allegedly invincible benevolence (our "altruism," our affluence, our lack of territorial aspirations). Together, it is argued, this threefold endowment provides us with the opportunity and the obligation to ease the nations of the earth toward modernization and stability: toward a full-fledged *Pax Americana Technocratica*. In reaching toward this goal, Vietnam is viewed as the last and crucial test. Once we have succeeded there, the road ahead is clear. In a sense, these men are our counterpart to the visionaries of Communism's radical left: they are technocracy's own Maoists. They do not govern Washington today. But their doctrine rides high.

Long before I went into government, I was told a story about Henry L. Stimson that seemed to me pertinent during the years that I watched the Vietnam tragedy unfold—and participated in that tragedy. It seems to me more pertinent than ever as we move toward the election of 1968.

In his waning years Stimson was asked by an anxious questioner, "Mr. Secretary, how on earth can we ever bring peace to the world?" Stimson is said to have answered: "You begin by bringing to Washington a small handful of able men who believe that the achievement of peace is possible.

"You work them to the bone until they no longer believe that it is possible.

"And then you throw them out—and bring in a new bunch who believe that it is possible."

30
An Act of Imperialism
NOAM CHOMSKY

At 8 A.M. on April 30, 1975, the last U.S. Marine helicopter took off from the roof of the American Embassy in Saigon. Less than five hours later, General Minh made the following announcement over the Saigon radio: "*I, General Duong Van Minh, President of the Saigon Government, appeal to the armed forces of the Republic of Vietnam to lay down their arms and surrender to the forces of the NLF unconditionally. I declare that the Saigon Government, from central to local level, has been completely dissolved.*"[1]

For the United States, these events signaled the end of a quarter-century effort to maintain Western domination over all or part of Indochina. For the Vietnamese, it meant that the foreign invaders had finally been repelled and their colonial structures demolished, after more than a century of struggle.

With fitting symmetry, history had come full circle. "The first act of armed intervention by a Western power in Vietnam," according to the Vietnamese historian Truong Buu Lam, "is generally held to have been perpetrated in 1845 by a ship of the United States Navy, the *Constitution*," in an effort to force the release of a French bishop.[2] The skipper of "Old Ironsides" was Commander John Percival, known as "Mad Jack." Sailors under his command "disembarked at Danang and proceeded to terrorize the local population . . . United States sailors fired on an unresisting crowd and several dozens were killed" before Mad Jack withdrew in failure.[3] A few years later the French navy returned and took Da Nang, and in the years that followed, established their imperial rule over all of Indochina, bringing misery and disaster. The agronomist Nghiem Xuan Yem wrote in 1945 that under French colonization "*our people have always been hungry . . .* so hungry that the whole population had not a moment of free time to think of anything besides the problem of survival."[4] In the northern parts of the country, two million people are reported to have died of starvation in a few months in 1945.[5]

Throughout this period, resistance never ceased. Early French eyewitnesses reported that

> We have had enormous difficulties in imposing our authority in our new colony. Rebel bands disturb the country everywhere.[6] The fact was that the centre of resistance was everywhere, subdivided to infinity, almost as many times as there were Annamese. It would be more exact to consider each farmer busy tying up a sheaf of rice as a centre of resistance.[7]

Meanwhile, the French complained, the only collaborators are

> intriguers, disreputable or ignorant, whom we had rigged out with sometimes high ranks, which became tools in their hands for plundering the country without scruple . . . Despised, they possessed neither the spiritual culture nor the moral fibre that would have allowed them to understand and carry out their task.[8]

A century later, the imperial overlords had changed, but their complaints never varied. The resistance, however, did significantly change its character over the years:

At first, the partisans fought to recover the independence of their country to avenge their king, and to safeguard their traditional pattern of life. By the 1900s, as the occupation developed into a systematic exploitation of the colony's economic resources, creating in its wake large-scale social disruptions, slogans of explicit social and political values were added to the original calls for independence from the French. The spontaneous reaction against foreigners, the armed struggle to oust them, had grown into a demand for revolutionary—political and later social—changes.[9]

The August revolution of 1945, led by the Viet Minh, was the culmination of a struggle of revolutionary nationalism. On September 2, President Ho Chi Minh proclaimed the independence of Vietnam:

Our people have broken the chains which for a century have fettered us, and have won independence for the Fatherland. Viet Nam has the right to be free and independent and in fact it is so already. The entire Vietnamese people are determined to mobilize all their physical and mental strength, to sacrifice their lives and property, in order to safeguard their freedom and independence.[10]

. . . It is important to bear in mind that the United States Government was never in any doubt as to the basic facts of the situation in Vietnam. Intelligence reports describe the "intense desire on the part of the Annamese for independence and thorough hatred by them of the French and any other white people who happen to be in any way supporting or sympathizing with the French."[11] The Headquarters of the OSS, China Theatre, reported to the Chief of the Intelligence Division on September 19, 1945, that Emperor Bao Dai, in an interview, "stated that he had voluntarily abdicated, and was not coerced by the Provisional Government," because he approved "the nationalistic action of the Viet Minh" and preferred to "live as a private citizen with a free people than rule a nation of slaves." On the same date, the same source reported an interview with Ho Chi Minh, "the President of the Provisional Government of Viet Nam," in which Ho assured him that "his people are prepared for a long struggle of ten or twenty years, and are willing to fight for the freedom, not of their own, but of future generations." He reported his personal opinion that "Mr. Ho Chi Minh is a brilliant and capable man, completely sincere in his opinions," and that "when he speaks, he speaks for his people, for I have travelled throughout Tonkin province, and found in that area people of all classes are imbued with the same spirit and determination as their leader." The new government, he reported, "is an outgrowth of the controlling forces in the military resistance"; "Viet Nam looks to America for moral support in their struggle, almost expect it." A "personal observation" of October 17 certifies "to the fact that the great mass of the population supports Ho Chi Minh and his party, and to the anti-Japanese action in which they have engaged . . . In travelling through Tonkin, every village flew the Viet Minh flag . . . The women and children were also organized, and all were enthusiastic in their support." The report continues that American observers "saw how well the majority of the people follow the orders of Ho Chi Minh and the Provisional Government," apart from "some of the wealthy merchants and former high Annamese officials."

As for those at the receiving end of these communications, the State Department's assessment of Ho Chi Minh and the Provisional Government of Vietnam was summed up this way by Abbot Low Moffat, the Chief of the Division of Southeast Asian Affairs:

I have never met an American, be he military, OSS, diplomat, or journalist, who had met Ho Chi Minh who did not reach the same belief: that Ho Chi Minh was first and foremost a Vietnamese nationalist. He was also a Communist and believed that Communism offered the best hope for the Vietnamese people. But his loyalty was to his people. When I was in Indochina it was striking how the top echelon of competent French officials held almost unanimously the same view. Actually, there was no alternative to an agreement with Ho Chi Minh or to a crushing of the nationalist groundswell which my own observations convinced me could not be done. Any other government recognized by the French would of necessity be puppets of the French and incapable of holding the loyalty of the Vietnamese people.[12]

Thus, the United States committed itself with its eyes open and with full knowledge of what it was doing to crush the nationalist forces of Indochina. "Question whether Ho as much nationalist as Commie is irrelevant," Secretary of State Dean Acheson explained. Quite the contrary, he urged in May 1949, that "no effort should be spared" to assure the success of the French Quisling government, since there seemed to be "no other alternative to estab Commie pattern Vietnam." And on the eve of the Korean war, in March 1950, Acheson observed that French military success "depends, in the end, on overcoming opposition of indigenous population"; we must help the French "to protect IC [Indochina] from further COMMIE encroachments."[13]

Two years earlier, a State Department Policy Statement of September 1948 had spelled out the fundamental "dilemma" which the United States faced in Indochina. It was a "dilemma" which would never cease to haunt American policymakers. The "dilemma" was this. The Communists under Ho Chi Minh had "captur[ed] control of the nationalist movement," thus impeding the "long-term objective" of the United States, namely, "to eliminate so far as possible Communist influence in Indochina." The State Department analysis added that "our inability to suggest any practicable solution of the Indochina problem" was caused by "the unpleasant fact that Communist Ho Chi Minh is the strongest and perhaps the ablest figure in Indochina and that any suggested solution which excludes him is an expedient of uncertain outcome." But to the very end, the United States continued to back former agents of French colonialism, who easily transferred their allegiance to the successor imperial power, against the nationalist movement "captured" (by implication, illegitimately) by the Viet Minh and its successors.

This "dilemma" is absolutely central to the understanding of the evolution of American policy in Indochina. The *Pentagon Papers* historian, considering the situation after the Tet offensive of 1968, asks whether the United States can "overcome the apparent fact that the Viet Cong have 'captured' the Vietnamese nationalist movement while the GVN has become the refuge of Vietnamese who were allied with the French in the battle against the independence of their nation." It does not occur to him to ask whether the United States *should* attempt to "overcome" this fact. Rather, the problem is a tactical one: how can the fact be overcome? In this analysis, the historian reflects quite accurately the tacit assumptions that were unquestioned in the extensive documentary record.

For propaganda purposes, the issue was reformulated. It was our noble task to protect Indochina from "aggression." Thus, the *Pentagon Papers* historian, in the musings just cited, continues by observing that the question he raises is "complicated, of course, by the difficult issue of Viet Cong allegiance to and control by Communist China." Again, the historian accurately reflects the mentality revealed in the documents. He does not try to *demonstrate* that the Viet Cong owed allegiance to Communist China or were controlled by Peking. Rather, he adopts the premise as an *a priori* truth, untroubled by the fact that no evidence was ever brought forth to substantiate it.

Not that intelligence didn't try. Elaborate attempts were made to demonstrate that the Viet Minh and its successors were merely the agents of some foreign master. It was, in fact, a point of rigid doctrine that this must be true, and no evidence to the contrary served to challenge the doctrine. Depending on date and mood, the foreign master might be the Kremlin or "Peiping," but the principle itself could not be questioned.

The function of the principle is transparent: it served to justify the commitment "to defend the territorial integrity of IC and prevent the incorporation of the ASSOC[iated] States within the COMMIE-dominated bloc of slave states" (Acheson, October 1950), or to safeguard Vietnam from "aggressive designs Commie Chi" (Acheson, May 1949) by support for the French puppet regime. One of the most startling revelations in the *Pentagon Papers* is that in the twenty-year period under review, the analysts were able to discover only one staff paper (an intelligence estimate of 1961) "which treats communist reactions primarily in terms of the separate national interests of Hanoi, Moscow, and Peiping, rather than primarily in terms of an overall communist strategy for which Hanoi is acting as an agent."

Intelligence labored manfully to provide the evidence required by the doctrine. But their failure was total. It was impossible to establish what had to be true, that Ho Chi Minh was a puppet of the Kremlin or "Peiping."[14] Faced with this problem, American officials in Saigon reached the following casuistic conclusion: "It may be assumed that Moscow feels that Ho and his lieutenants have had sufficient training experience and are sufficiently loyal to be trusted to determine their day-to-day policy without supervision." In short, the absence of evidence that Ho was a puppet was held up as conclusive proof that he "really" was an agent of international communism after all, an agent so loyal and trustworthy that no directives were even necessary.

The whole amazing story gives a remarkable indication of how effective are the controls over thought and analysis in American society. It is a gross error to describe the *Pentagon Papers*, as is commonly done, as a record of government lies. On the contrary, the record reveals that the top policy planners and, for the most part, the intelligence agencies were prisoners of the ideology of our highly ideological society. No less than "independent intellectuals" in the press and the universities, they believed precisely those doctrines that had to be believed in order to absolve the United States of the charge of aggression in Indochina. Evidence was—and remains—beside the point.

Not only were the Viet Minh necessarily agents of a foreign power, they were also literally "aggressors." The National Security Council, in February 1950, held that France and the native armies it had assembled "is now in armed conflict with the forces of communist aggression." A presidential commission of early 1954 added that France was fighting "to defend the cause of liberty and freedom from Communism in Indochina" while the cause of the Viet Minh is "the cause of colonization and subservience to Kremlin rule as was the case in China, in North Korea and in the European satellites." Later internal documents refer generally to the VC aggression in the South and describe the Pathet Lao in Laos as "aggressors." Indeed, the Joint Chiefs of Staff went so far as to characterize "political warfare, or subversion" as a form of aggression. And Adlai Stevenson informed the United Nations Security Council that "the United States cannot stand by while Southeast Asia is overrun by armed aggressors," adding that "the point is the same in Vietnam today as it was in Greece in 1947," where the United States was also defending a free people from "internal aggression," a marvelous new Orwellian construction.

By and large the New Frontiersmen were quite at home with this rhetoric. With "aggression checked in Vietnam," writes Arthur Schlesinger, "1962 had not been a bad year."[15] In fact, 1962 was the first year in which U.S. military forces were directly engaged in combat and combat support, the bombing of villages, the gunning down of peasants from helicopters, defoliation, etc. Only three years later, in April 1965, did U.S. intelligence report the presence of the first North Vietnamese battalion in the south.

It is important to recognize that these ridiculous rationalizations for American aggression in Indochina were accepted in their essentials within the American "intellectual community." Left-liberal opinion, regarding itself as "opposing the war," called for a peace settlement between South and North Vietnam with American troops in place in the South; in short, a victory for American imperialism.[16] The war is described in retrospect as a "tragic error," where worthy impulse was "transmuted into bad policy," a case of "blundering efforts to do good." Such assessments are offered even by people who became committed opponents of the war in its latter phases. The plain and obvious fact that the United States was guilty of aggression in Indochina is rejected with horror and contempt; or, to be more accurate, it is simply dismissed as beyond the bounds of polite discourse by liberal commentators. These facts give an important insight into the nature of the liberal opposition to the war which later developed, largely on "pragmatic" grounds, when it became obvious that the costs of the war to us (or, for the more sensitive, to the Vietnamese as well) were too great for us to bear.[17]

The fundamental dilemma, perceived from the start, permitted only two outcomes to the American involvement in Indochina. The United States government might on the one hand choose to come to terms with the Vietnamese nationalist movement, or it might bend its efforts to the destruction of the Viet Minh and its successors. The first course was never seriously contemplated. Therefore, the United States committed itself to the destruction of the revolutionary nationalist forces in Indochina. Given the astonishing strength and resiliency of the resistance, the American intervention in Vietnam became a war of annihilation. In every part of Indochina, the pattern was repeated. As in the days of the early French conquest, "each farmer busy tying up a sheaf of rice" might be "a centre of resistance." Inevitably, the United States undertook to destroy the rural society.

American intellectuals dutifully supplied the rationale. We were engaged in a process of "urbanization and modernization," they explained, as we drove the peasants out of their villages by bombs, artillery and search-and-destroy operations, simultaneously destroying the countryside to ensure that return would be impossible. Or, the United States was helping to control "village thugs" in violent peasant societies where "terrorists can operate largely unmolested whether or not the local population supports them" (Ithiel de Sola Pool). More generally:

> In the Congo, in Vietnam, in the Dominican Republic, it is clear that order depends on somehow compelling newly mobilized strata to return to a measure of passivity and defeatism from which they have recently been aroused by the process of modernization. At least temporarily, the maintenance of order requires a lowering of newly acquired aspirations and levels of political activity, [as] we have learned in the past thirty years of intensive empirical study of contemporary societies.[18]

By the end, even the more cynical and sadistic were driven to silence as the horrendous record of the achievements that they had sought to justify for many years was slowly exposed to public view.

The terminology of the "behavioral sciences" was continually invoked in an effort to delude the public and the colonial administrators themselves. "Counterinsurgency theorists" explained in sober terms that "all the dilemmas are practical and as neutral in an ethical sense as the laws of physics."[19] It is simply a matter of discovering the appropriate mix of aversive conditioning (B-52 raids, burning of villages, assassination, etc.) and positive reinforcement (the detritus of the American presence) so as to overcome the unfair advantage of the revolutionaries—revolutionaries who in fact had won popular support by virtue of their constructive programs,[20] much to the dismay of the social scientists who persisted to the end with claims to the contrary based on "empirical studies" which they never produced.

In a report to President Kennedy after a 1962 study mission in Southeast Asia, Senator Mike Mansfield discussed the "widespread support of the peasants for the Vietcong," and remarked that any "reorientation" of peasant attitudes "involves an immense job of social engineering." He anticipated the unpleasant need of "going to war fully ourselves against the guerrillas—and the establishment of some form of neocolonial rule in South Vietnam," which he "emphatically" did not recommend. Others, however, took up the task of social engineering with zeal and enthusiasm. The Australian social psychologist Alex Carey, who has studied the matter in some detail, concludes that the American pacification program was "neither more nor less than a nation-sized sociological experiment in bringing about changes, desired by American policy, in the attitudes and values of a physically captive population."[21] The more sophisticated analysts went further still. They derided the concern for popular attitudes—such mysticism has no place in a scientific civilization such as ours— and urged instead that we concern ourselves solely with more objective matters, that is, with controlling behavior. This advance to the higher stages of applied science was necessitated by the miserable failure of the colonial agents in their efforts to mimic native revolutionaries.[22]

I cannot survey here the techniques that were attempted. Perhaps the mentality of the "scientists" is sufficiently indicated in one minor experiment in operant conditioning reported in *Congressional Hearings*.[23] An American psychiatrist working in a mental hospital in Vietnam subjected one group of patients to "unmodified electroconvulsive shock" which "produces systemic convulsions similar to a grand mal epileptic seizure and in many patients is very terrifying." Others were offered work "including tending crops for American Special Forces—Green Berets—in Viet Cong territory 'under the stress of potential or actual VC attack or ambush.'" Asked about the "research value" of this amusing study, one witness testified that "the entire field of behavior conditioning is of great interest in the treatment of mental patients as well as prisoners." This example, insignificant in context, reveals very clearly who was insane, the patients or the "scientists," just as academic studies on "control of village violence" leave no doubt as to who are the violent individuals who must be somehow controlled in a civilized society.

Commenting on the "experiment" just cited, Alex Carey observes that "To be mentally ill and Asian deprives a man of most of his humanity; to be a communist and Asian deprives him of all of it." He goes on to show how this experiment exhibits in microcosm the major features of the program of social engineering devised by the American descendants of [Heinrich] Himmler's SS and the Nazi physicians as they sought to design a more appropriate culture for the benighted Vietnamese once control had been gained over the population by violence and terror.

While studying the American pacification program, Carey interviewed John Paul Vann, field operations coordinator of the U.S. Operations Mission, who was generally regarded as the most important American official in Vietnam after the Ambassador and the chief military commander.[24] Vann provided him with a remarkable 1965 memorandum, since privately circulated, "in response to a request for material on the concepts and theory that had guided the pacification programme."[25] In this memorandum, Vann noted that a social revolution was in process in South Vietnam, "primarily identified with the National Liberation Front," and that "a popular political base for the government of South Vietnam does not now exist." But it is "naïve" to expect that "an unsophisticated, relatively illiterate, rural population [will] recognize and oppose the evils of Communism." Therefore, the United States must institute "effective political indoctrination of the population," under an American-maintained "autocratic government."

Vann was not a brutal murderer of the style of those who designed the military operations. He objected strongly to the ongoing destruction of the civilian society by American terror. His view was that of the benevolent imperialist, the bearer of the White Man's Burden, who urged that "we should make it clear [to the Vietnamese villagers] that we continue to represent that permanent revolution of mankind which the American revolution advanced; and that only the principles of that revolution can ultimately produce the results for which mankind longs." We must overcome "the pseudo-science of communism" by the techniques of the behavioral sciences, "psywar," firm in our conviction that "our system . . . is more in keeping with the fundamentals of human nature," as John F. Kennedy once explained.[26] If the Vietnamese are too stupid to comprehend these well-known facts, then we must drill them in by force—with the most benevolent of intentions. Indeed, it would be immoral to do otherwise, just as we do not permit children of retardates to injure themselves in their innocence.

The United States Government and its agents in the field had to carry out two essential tasks. The first and most crucial was to destroy the society in which the resistance was rooted—the society "controlled by the Viet Cong," in the terminology of the propagandists. In South Vietnam, the primary victim of American aggression, a vast expeditionary force was let loose to accomplish this task. But by the late 1960s, Washington came to understand why earlier imperial aggressors—the French in Indochina, for example—had relied primarily on hired killers or native forces organized under colonial management to conduct a war against a resisting civilian population. To its credit the invading American army had begun to disintegrate, necessitating its withdrawal.[27] The disintegration was in part due to revulsion against its tasks, and in part to the indirect influence of the peace movement at home, which—as apologists for state violence lamented—was "demoralizing American public opinion."[28] Washington's response was to assign the job of destruction to more impersonal agencies—helicopter gunships, bombers, and artillery. American technology devised fiendish devices to maximize the damage done to "enemy personnel.". . .

The task of destruction was accomplished with partial success. In South Vietnam, the society was virtually demolished, though the resistance was never crushed. But the aggressors faced a second and more difficult job: to construct a viable Quisling regime out of the wreckage, and to rebuild the society in accordance with the imperial vision. This effort was a dismal failure. Like the French before them, the American conquerors were able to assemble "a crew of sychophants, money-grubbers and psychopaths,"[29] but rarely more. Efforts were made to integrate the ruined societies into the "free world economy" by encouraging American and Japanese investment. Academic studies explained how foreign investment "must be liberated from the uncertainties and obstacles that beset it" so that it might take advantage of the cheap labor offered by a society of rootless atomized individuals driven from their villages by American urbanization, a virtually ideal labor market.[30] It was hoped that with the vast flow of arms and the expansion of the police, the merry crew of torturers and extortionists placed into power by the United States would somehow manage to control the population.

To the very end, the American government was committed to victory, at least in South Vietnam. To fend off liberal criticism, [Henry] Kissinger and his press entourage spoke vaguely of a "decent interval," but there is no evidence that they looked forward to anything short of total victory for the American client regime. Nonetheless, success was beyond their grasp. When Washington was no longer able to call forth the B-52's, the whole rotten structure collapsed from within, virtually without combat. Symbolic of the American failure in its second task—reconstruction of the society it had demolished—was the "fall of Danang," where the foreign aggression began more than a century before. Three intact ARVN divisions with more than 100,000 men and enough ammunition for a six-month siege were stationed in Danang, as of March 26. "Thirty-six hours later, without a single shot having been fired, the ARVN ceased to exist as a fighting unit." What happened is described by a French teacher who remained:

> The officers fled by air taking with them the ground crews so that the pilots that had stayed on could not get their planes started. Left without leaders the army fell apart. On March 28 widespread looting started. The rice stocks were sacked and in the hospitals the army and the local staff stole all the drugs in order to sell them on the black market. Then the army started shooting civilians at random, often to steal their motorcycles. By then half of the army was in civilian clothes, which they had stolen. For 36 hours, with the Vietcong nowhere in sight but with rumors of their arrival constantly spreading, the city became a nightmare. By that time the population had but one hope: that the Vietcong would arrive as quickly as possible to restore order, any order.

Many civilians fled, "because the Americans told us the Communists would kill us," as they explained to reporters. America "left behind in Danang . . . an empty shell and a good deal of hatred, which will probably endure."[31]

The fact of the matter is that there never was any hope for the population of Indochina apart from a victory for the forces of revolutionary nationalism. . . .

The Nazi-like brutality of the American assault on Indochina is the most searing memory of these terrible years. Even though the ideologists and propagandists will labor to erase it, I cannot believe that they will succeed. Nonetheless, it must be understood that the savage programs put into operation by the Government and justified or ignored by much of the intelligentsia did not merely result from some sadistic streak in the American character. To be sure, the element of racism cannot be dismissed. One may doubt whether such maniacal "experiments in population control" would have been conducted—at least, with such self-satisfaction and lack of guilt—on a white population. But in a deeper sense, the savagery of the American attack was a necessary and unavoidable consequence of the general policy that was adopted in the late 1940s— the policy of crushing a revolutionary nationalist movement that was deeply rooted in the population, and that gained its support because of the appeal of its commitment to independence and social reconstruction.

This policy remained in force until the final collapse of the Saigon regime. During the 1950s, the United States hoped to regain control over all of Indochina. The National Security Council in 1956 directed all U.S. agencies in Vietnam to "work toward the weakening of the Communists in North and South Vietnam in order to bring about the eventual peaceful reunification of a free and independent Vietnam under anti-Communist leadership." Policy for Laos was stated in similar terms: "In order to prevent Lao neutrality from veering toward pro-Communism, encourage individuals and groups in Laos who oppose dealing with the Communist [bloc]—Support the expansion and reorganization of police, propaganda and army intelligence services, provided anti-Communist elements maintain effective control of these services—Terminate economic and military aid if the Lao Government ceases to demonstrate a will to resist internal Communist subversion and to carry out a policy of maintaining its independence."[32] In Cambodia as well, the United States made significant efforts (in part, through the medium of its Thai, South Vietnamese and Philippine subordinates) to reverse the commitment to neutralism.[33] A few years later, it was recognized that Viet Minh control over North Vietnam was irreversible, and the imperial managers lowered their sights. The goal was now a "non-Communist South Vietnam" instituted and guaranteed by American military force (since there was no other way), and a Western-oriented Laos and Cambodia.

Given this continuity of policy, it is hardly surprising that many Vietnamese saw the Americans as the inheritors of French colonialism. The *Pentagon Papers* cites studies of peasant attitudes demonstrating that "for many, the struggle which began in 1945 against colonialism continued uninterrupted throughout [Ngo Dinh] Diem's regime: in 1954, the foes of nationalists were transformed from France and Bao Dai, to Diem and the U.S. . . . . but the issues at stake never changed." By early 1964, even the U.S.-backed generals were warning of the "colonial flavor to the whole pacification effort," noting that the French in their worst and clumsiest days never tried to control the local society as the Americans were planning to do. But the American leadership saw no alternative, and rejected the objections of their clients as "an unacceptable rearward step." A Systems Analysis study concluded that unless the Viet Cong infrastructure ("the VC officials and organizers") "was destroyed, U.S.-GVN military and pacification forces soon degenerated into nothing more than an occupation army." They did not add that if this "infrastructure" was destroyed, the U.S.-GVN forces would be nothing but a gang of murderers. Both conclusions are, in fact, correct, and reflect the natural consequences of the implementation of the Indochina policy first mapped out in the late nineteen-forties.

It was only after the Tet offensive that American terror was unleashed against South Vietnam in its full fury. What was to come was indicated by the tactics employed to reconquer the urban areas that quickly fell into the hands of Vietnamese resistance forces in January–February 1968. The events in Hué were typical. Here, thousands of people "were killed by the most hysterical use of American firepower ever seen," and then designated "as the victims of a Communist massacre."[34] The "accelerated pacification program" that followed was a desperate effort to reconstruct the shattered American position. It had some success. Describing the "massive" increase in population which had been achieved by August 1970, John Paul Vann estimated that "we control two million more people than we controlled two years ago," although he added that "occupation is only the first step in pacification." As for that second step—the "willing cooperation of the people with the Government and the overt rejection of the enemy"—contrary to the pretense of ignorant social scientists, that step had not been and never would be achieved.[35]

Many people think of My Lai when recalling the post-Tet terrorism. But this is misleading. In fact, My Lai was just one of many such massacres. Some of these massacres, including My Lai, took place during "Operation Wheeler Wallawa." In this campaign, over 10,000 "enemy" were reported killed, including the victims of My Lai, who were listed in the official body count. Speaking of "Wheeler Wallawa," Kevin Buckley, head of the *Newsweek* bureau in Saigon, observed that an examination of that whole operation would have revealed the incident at My Lai to be a particularly gruesome application of a wider policy which had the same effect in many places at many times. Of course, the blame for that could not have been dumped on a stumblebum lieutenant. Calley was an aberration, but "Wheeler Wallawa" was not.

The real issue concerning this operation was not the "indiscriminate use of firepower," as often is alleged.[36] Rather, "it is charges of quite discriminating use—as a matter of policy, in populated areas."*

One can gain a better understanding of American post-Tet strategy—strategy brought to its culmination under the management of Henry Kissinger—by considering such operations as "Speedy Express." This campaign was conducted by the U.S. 9th Infantry Division in the Mekong Delta province of Kien Hoa in early 1969. Studied in detail by Alex Shimkin and Kevin Buckley, a partial description of it appeared in *Newsweek* for June 19, 1972. What follows is based on notes supplied to me by Buckley.

For many years, the province had been "almost totally controlled" by the NLF:

> For a long time there was little or no military activity in the delta. The 9th Division did not even arrive until the end of 1966. Front activities went far beyond fighting. The VC ran schools, hospitals and even businesses. A pacification study revealed that an NLF sugar cane cooperative for three villages in the Mo Cay district of Kien Hoa produced revenue in 1968 which exceeded the entire Saigon government budget that year for Kien Hoa.

But the "aggressive military effort carried out by the U.S. 9th Infantry Division" had succeeded in establishing some degree of government control. In the six months of Operation Speedy Express, "a total of some 120,000 people who had been living in VC controlled areas" came under government control. To achieve this result, the 9th Division applied "awesome firepower," including "3,381 air strikes by fighter bombers, dropping napalm, high explosives and antibombs," B-52's and artillery shelling "around the clock" at a level that "it is impossible to reckon." Armed helicopters "scour[ed] the landscape from the air night and day," accounting for "many and perhaps most of the enemy kills." The 9th Division reported that "over 3,000 enemy troops were killed in March, 1969, which is the largest monthly total for any American division in the Vietnam War." All told, 10,899 people were killed and 748 weapons were captured. From these figures alone one can make a fair judgment as to the nature of the "enemy troops" who were killed by bombing and shelling, much of it at night. In the single month of March, the Ben Tre hospital reported 343 people wounded by "friendly" fire as compared with 25 by "the enemy." And as a U.S. pacification official noted, "Many people who were wounded died on their way to the hospitals" or were treated elsewhere (at home, in VC hospitals, or ARVN dispensaries). A senior pacification official estimated that "at least 5,000" of those killed "were what we refer to as non-combatants."

---

*The director of the nearby Canadian hospital, Dr. Alje Vennema, reports that he knew of the My Lai massacre at once but did nothing because it was not at all out of the ordinary; his patients were constantly reporting such incidents to him.[37]

In fact, the military panel investigating My Lai discovered that a similar massacre had taken place only a few miles away at the village of My Khe. Proceedings against the officer in charge were dismissed on the grounds that he had carried out a perfectly normal operation in which a village was destroyed and its population was forcibly relocated.[38] The panel's decision tells us all we need to know about "Wheeler Wallawa."

Interviews in the "pacified" areas confirm the grim picture. One VC medic reported that his hospital took care of at least 1,000 people in four villages in early 1969. "Without exception the people testified that most of the civilians had been killed by a relentless night and day barrage of rockets, shells, bombs and bullets from planes, artillery and helicopters." In one area of four villages, the population was reduced from 16,000 to 1,600. Every masonry house was in ruins. Coconut groves were destroyed by defoliants. Villagers were arrested by U.S. troops, beaten by interrogators, and sent off to prison camps. The MACV [Military Assistance Command, Vietnam] location plots for B-52's show that the target center for one raid was precisely on the village of Luong Phu. In the neighboring village of Luong Hoa, village elders estimated that there were 5,000 people in the village before 1969 but none in 1970 "because the Americans destroyed every house in the village with artillery, air strikes or by burning them down with cigarette lighters." About 100 people were killed by bombing, they report. Pounding from the air was "relentless." Helicopters chased and killed people working in fields. Survival was possible in deep trenches and bunkers, but many small children "were killed by concussion from the bombs which they could not withstand even though they were in bunkers," villagers report. An experienced American official compared My Lai and the operations of the 9th Division as follows:

> The actions of the 9th Division in inflicting civilian casualties were worse. The sum total of what the 9th did was overwhelming. In sum, the horror was worse than Mylai. But with the 9th, the civilian casualties came in dribbles and were pieced out over a long time. And most of them were inflicted from the air and at night. Also, they were sanctioned by the command's insistence on high body counts.

He also stated that "the result was an inevitable outcome of the unit's command policy."

While the 9th division was at work in the field, others were doing their job at home. One well-known behavioral scientist, who had long deplored the emotionalism of critics of the war and the inadequacy of their empirical data, wrote this as the campaign ground on: "the only sense in which [we have demolished the society of Vietnam] is the sense in which every modernizing country abandons reactionary traditionalism."[39]

Operation Speedy Express was regarded as a "stunning success." Lauding the commanding General—one must assume, without irony—upon his promotion, General Creighton Abrams spoke of "the great admiration I have for the performance of the 9th Division and especially the superb leadership and brilliant operational concepts you have given the Division." "You personify the military professional at his best in devotion and service to God and country," rhapsodized Abrams, referring specifically to the "magnificent" performance of the 9th Division, its "unparalleled and unequaled performance," during Speedy Express. . . .

Again, it is important to bear in mind that the character of the American war cannot be attributed solely to a sadistic military leadership or to incompetent or deranged civilian advisers. It was a calculated and rational enterprise undertaken to realize goals that could be achieved in no other way: namely, the goal, stated clearly in the 1940s, of preventing Communist domination in a region where, it was always understood, the Communists had "captured" the national movement. Furthermore, the tactics employed were by no means novel. To cite only the most obvious analogy, recall the air war in Korea, and significantly, the manner in which it was later analyzed. . . .

Why feign surprise at the bombing of dikes in 1972 when 12,000 peasants (including, it seems, the remnants of My Lai) were driven from their homes in the Batangan

Peninsula in January 1969, after having lived in caves and bunkers for months in an effort to survive constant bombardment, and were then shipped to a waterless camp near Quang Ngai over which floated a banner which said, "We thank you for liberating us from communist terror"?[40] Just another episode in which this "modernizing country abandons reactionary traditionalism" under the guidance of its benevolent big brother.

The same fundamental "dilemma" that made inevitable the savagery of the war always compelled the United States to evade any serious moves towards a negotiated settlement, and to reject the "peaceful means" that are required by the "supreme law of the land." In the second Mansfield Report (December 1965), it is explained that:

> negotiations at this time, as a practical matter, would leave the Viet Cong in control of the countryside (much of which, by the way, they have controlled for many years and some of it since the time of the Japanese occupation). The Nationalists (and only with our continued massive support) would remain in control of Saigon, provincial capitals and the coastal base-cities. The status of the district seats would be in doubt.[41]

This conclusion was based on the reasonable assumption that "negotiations merely confirm the situation that exists on the ground."

Thus, despite the massacre of some 200,000 people in the preceding decade, despite the direct engagement of American military forces for four years, and despite the massive invasion and aerial bombardment of 1965, a political settlement was unthinkable, because the National Liberation Front controlled the countryside.[42]

Similar reasoning had impelled the United States to undertake overt aggression earlier in the year. Throughout 1964, the NLF made repeated efforts to arrange a negotiated settlement based on the Laos model, with a neutralist coalition government. But the United States rejected any such "premature negotiations" as incompatible with its goal of maintaining a non-Communist South Vietnam under American control. The reason was quite simple. As American officials constantly reiterated, the NLF was the only significant political force and the U.S.-imposed regime had virtually no popular base. Only the politically organized Buddhists could even conceive of entering into a coalition with the NLF, and the Buddhists, as General [William] Westmoreland sagely observed, were not acting "in the interests of the Nation." Ambassador [Henry Cabot] Lodge later regarded them as "equivalent to card-carrying Communists," according to the Pentagon historian. Thus, the U.S. Government position was that only General Westmoreland and Ambassador [Maxwell] Taylor understood "the interests of the Nation," all political groupings in South Vietnam thereby being automatically excluded from any possible political settlement. To be sure, as William Bundy explained, we might be willing to consider the peaceful means required by law "after, *but only after*, we have established a clear pattern of pressure" (i.e., military force; his emphasis). As noted earlier, pacification specialist Vann took the same view, as did all other knowledgeable observers.

The United States therefore supported General [Nguyen] Khanh and the Armed Forces Council. But by January 1965, even that last hope went up in smoke. As Ambassador Taylor explained in his memoirs,[43] the United States government "had lost confidence in Khanh" by late January 1965. He lacked "character and integrity," added Taylor sadly. The clearest evidence of Khanh's lack of character was that by late January he was moving towards "a dangerous Khanh-Buddhist alliance which might eventually lead to an unfriendly government with which we could not work." Moreover, as we now know from other sources, he was also close to a political agreement with the NLF.[44] Consequently, Khanh was removed. And in late January, according to the *Pentagon Papers*, Westmoreland "obtained his first authority to use U.S. forces for combat within South Vietnam." The systematic and intensive bombing of South Vietnam (accompanied by a more publicized but less severe bombing of the North) began a few weeks later, to be followed by the open American invasion.

At every other period, much the same was true. The 1954 Geneva Accords were regarded as a "disaster" by the United States. The National Security Council met at once and adopted a general program of subversion throughout the region to ensure that the political settlement envisioned in the Accords would not be achieved.[45] In October 1972, just prior to the U.S. Presidential election, the DRV offered a peace proposal that virtually recapitulated the Geneva Accords and also incorporated the central positions in the founding documents of the NLF. Nixon and Kissinger could not openly reject this offer just prior to the elections, but they indicated clearly that the proposal was unacceptable while claiming deceitfully that "peace was at hand." Abetted by the subservient press, they were able to carry out this charade successfully, but when their later efforts to modify the proposals (including the Christmas bombings) failed utterly, they were compelled to accept the very same offer (with trivial changes in wording) in January 1973.

As in the case of Geneva 1954, this agreement was purely formal. Even before the Paris Agreements of January 1973 were signed, Kissinger explained to the press that the United States would reject every essential principle in the Agreements. And in fact, the United States at once committed itself to subverting these agreements by intensifying the political repression in South Vietnam and by launching military actions against PRG [Provisional Revolutionary Government (of South Vietnam)] territory through the medium of its client regime, massively supplied with arms. Again, the treachery of the mass media served to delude the public with regard to these events, helping to perpetuate the slaughter.[46]

By mid-1974, U.S. Government officials were reporting enthusiastically that their tactics were succeeding. They claimed that the [Nguyen Van] Thieu regime had conquered about 15 percent of the territory of the PRG, exploiting its vast advantage in firepower, and that the prospects for further successes were great. As in the 1950s, the whole structure collapsed from within as soon as the Communists were so ungracious as to respond.

The point of this brief résumé has been to illustrate the complete refusal of the United States to consider any political settlement. The reason was always the same. It was always understood that there was no political base for the U.S. aggression, so that a peaceful political settlement would constitute a defeat. This was precisely the dilemma of 1948, and it was never resolved. . . .

As I noted earlier, it was after the Tet offensive of early 1968 that the American murder machine really went into high gear in South Vietnam. The reasons were essentially two. It was feared that a political settlement of some sort would be inescapable, given the mounting pressures within the U.S. and in the international arena to limit or terminate the American war. And with the American military forces disintegrating in the field, it was evident that they would soon have to be withdrawn and replaced by native mercenaries. Given all this, it was decided to carry out the maximum amount of destruction possible in South Vietnam in the time remaining. The hope was that a U.S.-imposed regime might maintain control over a sufficiently demoralized and shattered society. As noted, American officials like Vann felt that the post-Tet accelerated pacification campaigns had been partially successful in bringing the population under American "occupation," though "pacification" would, of course, still require substantial efforts.

Imperialist ideologues in the academic community generally shared this analysis. Henry Kissinger, in his last contribution to scholarship before ascending to high office, outlined "the thrust for American policy in the next phase" as follows: "the United States should concentrate on the subject of the mutual withdrawal of external forces and avoid negotiating about the internal structure of South Vietnam for as long as possible."[47] Putting aside his irrelevant rationalizations, the meaning of this prescription is obvious. If American terrorism could succeed in at last demolishing the southern resistance, an American client regime might be able to maintain itself. This would, however, only be possible if the North Vietnamese could be compelled to withdraw (the war planners had always expected that the bombing of the North and the direct American invasion of the South would draw the DRV into the Southern conflict). Then, with North Vietnam out of the way, the United States could bring to bear the socio-economic programs mentioned earlier to maintain the stable, non-Communist South Vietnam it had always sought. Of course, Kissinger's prescription required that the southern resistance be smashed before the withdrawal of American troops. This is why it was under his regime that such operations as Speedy Express were launched against the South Vietnamese, while the air war was stepped up in Laos and Cambodia.

It is not surprising that Kissinger was, for a time, the great hope of American liberals. As I have already noted, left-liberal "opponents" of the war had themselves urged that the solution was a peaceful settlement between South and North Vietnam with American military forces remaining in the South. Indeed, to this day they feel that their proposals to this effect might have occasionally been questionable in "nuance," but nothing more.[48] Thus, it was perfectly natural that Kissinger should have been able to pacify much of the liberal opposition with his analysis of how an American military victory over the South Vietnamese might yet be attained.

To be sure, Kissinger was fully aware of the fundamental dilemma that had always plagued America policymakers. His way of phrasing the problem was as follows:

> The North Vietnamese and Viet Cong, fighting in their own country, needed merely to keep in being forces sufficiently strong to dominate the population after the United States tired of the war. We fought a military war; our opponents fought a political one . . . our military operations [had] little relationship to our declared political objectives. Progress in establishing a political base was excruciatingly slow . . . In Vietnam—as in most developing countries—the overwhelming problem is not to buttress but to develop a political framework . . . One ironic aspect of the war in Vietnam is that while we profess an idealistic philosophy, our failures have been due to an excessive reliance on material factors. The Communists, by contrast, holding to a materialistic interpretation, owe many of their successes to their ability to supply an answer to the question of the nature and foundation of political authority.[49]

Translating to simple prose: our problem is that the Vietnamese live there and we do not. This has made it difficult for us to develop a viable Vietnamese regime, whereas the Viet Minh and their successors had long ago created a functioning and successful social order in which they gained their support. There is no "irony" here. Rather, the problem is one that all imperial aggressors confront when faced with stubborn resistance, magnified in this case by the appeal of the social revolution.

Given the fundamental commitment to destroy the national movement, the United States was compelled to conduct a war of annihilation in South Vietnam and the surrounding region, and to reject any political settlement of the conflict. The question, however, remains: why was it always regarded as necessary to pursue this course? As noted earlier, the fundamental "dilemma" was clearly perceived in 1948, when State

Department analysts explained that the "long-term objective" of the United States was "to eliminate so far as possible Communist influence in Indochina." The rationalization offered was that we must "prevent undue Chinese penetration and subsequent influence in Indochina" because of our deep concern "that the peoples of Indochina will not be hampered in their natural developments by the pressure of an alien people and alien interests." Therefore, the United States attempted to restore French rule, in accordance with another "long-term objective": "to see installed a self-governing nationalist state which will be friendly to the U.S. and which . . . will be patterned upon our conception of a democratic state," and will be associated "with the western powers, particularly with France, with whose customs, language and laws [the peoples of Indochina] are familiar, to the end that those peoples will prefer freely to cooperate with the western powers culturally, economically and politically" and will "work productively and thus contribute to a better balanced world economy," while enjoying a rising standard of income.

The subsequent history in Indochina (and elsewhere) reveals just how deep was the American commitment to self-government, to democracy, and to a rising standard of living for the mass of the population. We may dismiss this as the usual imperialist tommyrot.

But the concern that Indochina "contribute to a better balanced world economy" was real enough. There is compelling documentary evidence, from the *Pentagon Papers* and other sources, that this and related concerns dominated all others and impelled the United States on its course in Indochina. As the record clearly demonstrates, American planners feared that the success of revolutionary nationalism would cause "the rot to spread" to the rest of mainland Southeast Asia and beyond to Indonesia and perhaps South Asia, ultimately impelling Japan, the workshop of the Pacific, to seek an accommodation with the Communist powers. Should this all happen, the United States would in effect have lost the Pacific phase of the Second World War, a phase which was fought in part to prevent Japan from constructing "new order" closed to American penetration.

The mechanism by which the rot would spread was never clearly spelled out. But there is ample evidence that the planners understood that it would not be by military conquest. Rather, the danger was seen to lie in what they sometimes called "ideological successes," the demonstration effect of a successful revolution in Indochina (as in China). To counter this danger, pressure was put on Japan to reject "accommodation" with China. Access to Southeast Asia was promised as a reward for good behavior. And access was granted. By 1975, "Japanese commercial interests in Southeast Asia account for one-third of its U.S. $100,000 million annual trade, more than 90% of the total $4,000 million 'yen credits' and a substantial share of the $10,000 million overseas investment balance,"[50] transactions which "have tended to enrich only a privileged few in Southeast Asia and their business and political counterparts in Japan." It is no surprise, then, "that Japan was the only major country which had fully supported the American war policy in Indochina, including all-out bombing of North Vietnam in [1972]."[51]

In spite of the fact that there is now substantial documentary evidence to support this analysis of American intentions,[52] it cannot be accepted by ideologists.[53] Instead, they emphasize other, peripheral factors—the need to gain French support for American programs in Europe, concern for some mystic "image," etc. To be sure, these factors were real enough. Thus, restoration of European capitalism was the primary objective of American post-war policy, and it was achieved in a manner which (not coincidentally) supported an immense expansion of overseas investment by American-based corporations. And there is no doubt that the United States was concerned to reinforce the image of a grim destroyer that would tolerate no challenge to its global order. But the primary reason why the long-term objective of destroying the Communist-led nationalist movement could not be abandoned is precisely the one that is repeatedly and clearly stressed in the documentary record: the United States could not tolerate the spreading of the rot of independence and self-reliance over Southeast Asia, with its possible impact upon Japan, the major industrial power of the Pacific region.

The precise weight of the motives that led American planners to commit themselves to the destruction of the Vietnamese nationalist movement may be debated, but the extensive documentary record now available, and briefly surveyed here, leaves no doubt that the commitment was undertaken in full awareness of what was at stake. This fact is difficult for many American intellectuals to accept, even those who opposed the war. To cite one striking and not untypical example, Professor John K. Fairbank of Harvard argues that a "factor of ignorance" lies at the source of what he called "our Vietnam tragedy." Lacking "an historical understanding of the modern Vietnamese revolution," we did not "realize that it was a revolution inspired by the sentiment of nationalism while clothed in the ideology of communism as applied to Vietnam's needs. . . . The result was that in the name of being anti-Communist, vague though that term had become by 1965, we embarked on an anti-nationalist effort." We misconceived "our role in defending the South after 1965," conceiving it as aimed at blocking aggression from North Vietnam and "forestalling a southward expansion of Chinese communism."[54] As we have seen, this analysis is refuted at every point by the historical record. The top planners knew from the start that the revolution was inspired by nationalism while clothed in the ideology of communism, and consciously embarked on an effort to destroy the national movement. They always understood that intervention from the North was a response to American aggression (which they, like Fairbank, called "defending the South"). "Chinese expansion" was fabricated to provide a propaganda cover for American aggression in Indochina. At the very moment when they were planning the 1965 escalation, William Bundy and John McNaughton noted that unless the United States expanded the war, there would probably be "a Vietnamese-negotiated deal, under which an eventually unified Communist Vietnam would reassert its traditional hostility to Communist China."

As to why scholars choose to ignore the factual record, one may only speculate. We may note that it is convenient to blame the American "failure" on ignorance—a socially neutral concept—thus deflecting analysis of the systematic and institutional factors that brought about the American war.

A study group sponsored by the Woodrow Wilson Foundation and the National Planning Association once defined the primary threat of "communism" as the economic transformation of the Communist powers "in ways which reduce their willingness and ability to complement the industrial economies of the West";[55] American hegemony in "the West" was naturally assumed. The comment is accurate and astute. The United States, as the dominant power in the global capitalist system (the "free world"), will use what means it can muster to counter any move towards independence that will tend to "reduce" this "willingness and ability."

Three-quarters of a century ago, Brooks Adams proclaimed that "Our geographical position, our wealth, and our energy pre-eminently fit us to enter upon the development of Eastern Asia and to reduce it to part of our own economic system."[56] As Oliver Wendell Holmes admiringly commented, Adams thought that the Philippine War "is the first gun in the battle for the ownership of the world."[57] American victory in the Pacific War of 1941–45 appeared to lay the basis for success in achieving this "long-term objective." The United States Government was not prepared to see its vision—which, in the familiar manner, was presented as utterly selfless and benign—threatened by a nationalist movement in a small and unimportant country where the peasants were too naïve to understand what was in their best interests. The policy planners and intellectuals, who stood by quietly while hundreds of thousands were slaughtered in Indonesia as the "Communist menace" was crushed and the country's riches again flowed towards the industrial powers, or who watched with occasional clucking of tongues as countries of the Western hemisphere fell under the rule of American-backed fascist torturers, could hardly have been expected to react differently in the case of Indochina. Nor did they, until the domestic costs of the war mounted beyond tolerable levels, and a spontaneous movement of protest and resistance threatened to shatter domestic tranquility and authority.

Notes

1. *Far Eastern Economic Review*, May 23, 1975.
2. Truong Buu Lam, *Patterns of Vietnamese Response to Foreign Intervention: 1858–1900*, Monograph Series No. 11, Southeast Asia Studies, Yale University, 1967.
3. Helen B. Lamb, *Vietnam's Will to Live*, New York, Monthly Review Press, 1972.
4. Cited by Ngo Vinh Long, *Before the Revolution*, Cambridge, MIT Press, 1973; emphasis in original.
5. *Viet Nam: A Historical Sketch*, Foreign Languages Publishing House, Hanoi, 1974.
6. Paulin Vial, cited by Lam, *op. cit.*
7. Léopold Pallu, cited by Lamb, *op. cit.*
8. French resident minister Muselier, 1897, cited in *Vietnam: Fundamental Problems*, Vietnamese Studies no. 12, Foreign Languages Publishing House, Hanoi, 1966.
9. Lam, *op. cit.*
10. Cited in *Viet Nam: A Historical Sketch*.
11. Major F. M. Small, memorandum of Strategic Services Unit, War Department, 25 October 1945, cited in Frank M. White, *Causes, Origins, and Lessons of the Vietnam War*, Hearings before the Committee on Foreign Relations, U.S. Senate, 92nd Congress, 2nd session, May 1972, U.S. Government Printing Office, 1973. The intelligence reports cited below are from the same source.
12. Congressional testimony, May 11, 1972. In *Causes*.
13. Cited from the Government edition of the *Pentagon Papers* in my *For Reasons of State*, New York, Pantheon, 1973, p. 128. Unless otherwise indicated, citations from the *Pentagon Papers* are given with precise sources here.
14. For a review of the intelligence record as presented in the *Pentagon Papers*, see *For Reasons of State*, pp. 51f.
15. Arthur M. Schlesinger, Jr., *A Thousand Days*, 1965; Fawcett Crest Books, New York, p. 695.
16. See note 48 below.
17. For some discussion, see my article in *Ramparts*, July 1975.
18. Ithiel de Sola Pool, formerly chairman of the Council on Vietnamese Studies of SEADAG and chairman of the Political Science department at MIT, cited, with some discussion, in my *American Power and the New Mandarins*, Pantheon, New York, 1969, p. 36. For further discussion of his contributions and those of his colleague, Samuel Huntington, also past chairman of the Council on Vietnamese Studies and chairman of the Department of Government at Harvard, see my *At War with Asia*, Pantheon, New York, 1970, pp. 54–63, and *For Reasons of State*. It was Huntington who first explained how "In an absent-minded way the United States in Vietnam may well have stumbled upon the answer to 'wars of national liberation,'" namely, "forced-draft urbanization and modernization"

by application of military power "on such a massive scale as to produce a massive migration from countryside to city."

19. George K. Tanham and Dennis J. Duncanson, "Some dilemmas of counterinsurgency," *Foreign Affairs*, vol. 48, no. 1, 1969.

20. For evidence on this matter, cf. Jeffrey Race, *War Comes to Long An*, University of California Press, Berkeley, 1971; Robert L. Sansom, T*he Economics of Insurgency in the Mekong Delta*, MIT Press, Cambridge, 1970; Georges Chaffard, *Les Deux Guerres du Vietnam*, La Table Ronde, Paris, 1969; David Hunt, *Organizing for Revolution in Vietnam, Radical America*, vol. 8, nos. 1 & 2, 1974. Race and Sansom were associated with the U.S. military; Hunt's study is based on material released from the RAND Corporation's "Viet Cong Motivation and Morale" project; Chaffard was a French journalist with many years experience in Vietnam. There are many other sources. For the "Mansfield Reports," cited below, see *Two Reports on Vietnam and Southeast Asia*, Dec. 18, 1962 and Dec. 17, 1965, U.S. Government Printing Office, April 1973. For a despairing assessment of the success of the guerrillas and the popularity of the Hanoi government, see Konrad Kellen, "1971 and beyond: the view from Hanoi," June 1971; paper delivered at SEADAG meeting, May 8, 1971. Kellen is a RAND analyst.

21. Alex Carey, "Clockwork Vietnam: psychology of pacification (i)," mimeographed, 1972. See *Meanjin Quarterly*, Australia, 1973 for parts of this and subsequent sections of his "Clockwork Vietnam." Carey is lecturer in Psychology of International Relations at the University of New South Wales. His investigations are based in part on several months research in South Vietnam in 1970.

22. See, for example, Charles Wolf, *United States Policy and the Third World*, Boston, Little, Brown and Co., 1967. For discussion of this and other similar contributions, see *American Power and the New Mandarins*, chapter 1, my *Problems of Knowledge and Freedom*, Pantheon, New York, 1972, chapter 2, and *For Reasons of State*, pp. 98f.

23. Hearings before the Subcommittee on Health of the Committee on Labor and Public Welfare, U.S. Senate, 93rd Congress, First Session. February 21 and 22, 1973, Part 1, U.S. Government Printing Office, 1973, p. 268. For the original study, see Dr. Lloyd Cotter, *American Journal of Psychiatry*, July 1967.

24. See the obituary in *Newsweek*, June 19, 1972.

25. Carey, "Clockwork Vietnam: the social engineers take over (2)," *Meanjin Quarterly*.

26. Quotes in Carey, "Clockwork Vietnam: psychology of pacification (i)." From Colonel Reuben Nathan, "Psychological warfare: key to success in Vietnam," *Orbis*, Spring 1967. Nathan was director of U.S. psychological warfare in Vietnam.

27. On the collapse of the military forces, see David Cortright, *Soldiers in Revolt*, New York. Doubleday, 1975.

28. Ithiel de Sola Pool, Introduction to his privately printed "Reprints of publications on Vietnam: 1966–1970," May 1971.

29. David G. Marr, "The rise and fall of 'counterinsurgency,' " in Chomsky and Zinn, eds. *op. cit.*, p. 208. Marr was a U.S. Marine Corps intelligence officer, the only Vietnamese-speaking American in the first marine helicopter squadron sent to Vietnam by President Kennedy.

30. For a review of such programs, see *For Reasons of State*, chapter 4.

31. "Max Austerlitz," pseudonym of a journalist who remained in Danang after its "fall." "After the Fall of Danang," *New Republic*, May 17, 1973.

32. NSC Memorandum 5612/1, 5 September 1956. Volume 10 of *United States-Vietnam Relations, 1945–67*, U.S. Government Printing Office, 1971: the government edition of the *Pentagon Papers*.

33. On this period in Cambodia, see D. R. SarDesai, *Indian Foreign Policy in Cambodia, Laos, and Vietnam, 1947–1964*, Berkeley, University of California Press, 1968. Also Malcolm Caldwell and Lek Tan, *Cambodia in the Southeast Asian War*, New York, Monthly Review Press, 1973. See also references cited in *For Reasons of State*, chapter 2.

34. Philip Jones Griffiths, *Vietnam Inc.*, New York, Macmillan, 1971, p. 137. Griffiths is a British journalist-photographer who was in Hué at the time. For more on the massacres at

Hué, both the actual and fabricated ones, see *For Reasons of State*, pp. 230f; N. Chomsky and E. S. Herman, *Counterrevolutionary Violence*, Warner Modular Inc., 1973; and references cited in these sources. For a recent summary, see E. S. Herman and D. G. Porter, "The myth of the Hué massacre," *Ramparts*, May–June 1975.

35. Interview with Vann in Carey. "Clockwork Vietnam: psychology of pacification (i)." On the great progress allegedly being made on all fronts by the Saigon government, as revealed by "applied social science." cf. Pool, *op. cit.* His final conclusion: "Not that South Viet Nam will fall after American combat troops are withdrawn: it seems too strong for that."

36. Cable from Buckley and Shimkin to *Newsweek* U.S. offices, January 18, 1972.

37. Cf. his interview in the *Ottawa Citizen*, January 12, 1970; cited in *For Reasons of State*, p. 222.

38. See references in *For Reasons of State*, p. xx; also the two studies by Seymour Hersh: *My Lai Four*, Random House, New York, 1970; *Cover-up*, Random House, 1972.

39. Ithiel de Sola Pool, letter, *New York Review of Books*, February 13, 1969. For news reports on the exploits of the 9th Division in early 1969, cf. *At War with Asia*, pp. 99f.

40. For references and further details, see *At War with Asia*, p. 104; *For Reasons of State*, p. 225. For additional comment on this military operation ("Bold Mariner," reportedly the largest American amphibious operation since World War II), which coincided with "Speedy Express," see the statement by Martin Teitel of the American Friends Service Committee, Hearing before the Subcommittee to Investigate Problems Connected with Refugees and Escapees (Kennedy Subcommittee) of the Committee on the Judiciary, U.S. Senate, 92nd Congress, Second Session, May 8, 1972, U.S. Government Printing Office, 1972. Teitel also describes the U.S.-GVN atrocities of April 1972 in the same area subsequent to the bloodless liberation by the NLF-NVA.

41. Cf. note 20.

42. On the relative U.S.-DRV troop levels, as revealed by the *Pentagon Papers*, see my article "The Pentagon Papers as propaganda and as history," in Chomsky and Zinn, eds., *op. cit.*; also *For Reasons of State*, pp. 82 (and note 147), 239f.

43. General Maxwell D. Taylor, *Swords and Plowshares*, New York, Norton, 1972.

44. Speaking in Paris, January 26, 1965, Khanh released correspondence with Huynh Tan Phat, then Vice-President of the Central Committee of the NLF, from late January 1965, indicating that agreement was close. Cf. my article in *Ramparts*, July 1975, for further details. There is, incidentally, also evidence that the Diem regime may have been approaching a negotiated settlement just prior to the U.S.-backed coup in which Diem was murdered. Cf. Chaffard, *op. cit.*, chapter 8 and Mieczyslaw Maneli, *War of the Vanquished*, New York, Harper and Row, 1971. John P. Roche, an unreconstructed hawk, claims that he had furnished evidence to the Pentagon historians, which they ignored, that the Kennedy Administration had decided not to permit a deal between Diem and Ho Chi Minh. Cf. his "Pentagon Papers," *Political Science Quarterly*, vol. 87, no. 2, 1972.

45. For details on this important document misrepresented beyond recognition in the *Pentagon Papers* history, see *For Reasons of State*, pp. 100f.

46. For details on these matters see my "Endgame: the tactics of peace in Vietnam," *Ramparts*, April 1973; and "Reporting Indochina: the news media and the legitimization of lies," *Social Policy*, September/October 1973.

47. On United States intervention in Laos, see the articles by Haney and Chomsky in Chomsky and Zinn, eds., *op. cit.*; also *At War with Asia*, chapter 4, and *For Reasons of State*, chapter 2, and the references cited there.

48. See the comment by the editors in *Dissent*, Spring 1975, in response to a letter of mine correcting a wholly fabricated version of my criticisms of their earlier editorial position. As indicated in their response, they prefer to restrict attention to the fabrication rather than attending to the entirely different original, which suggests that they perhaps do have some reservations about their long-held position. For further details, see the interchange in the *New Republic* referred to in this exchange.

49. *Op. cit.*, pp. 104–06.

50. Koji Nakamura, "Japan: a new face for Asia," *Far Eastern Economic Review*, May 23, 1975.

51. Correspondent, "Putting Washington before ASEAN," *ibid*. The text gives the date 1968 instead of 1972, presumably an error.

52. Cf. *At War with Asia*, chapter 1; *For Reasons of State*, chapter 1, section V; the articles by John W. Dower, Richard B. Du Boff and Gabriel Kolko in Chomsky and Zinn, eds., *op. cit.*

53. For discussion of some misunderstandings of this critique by Richard Tucker, Charles Kindelberger and others, cf. *For Reasons of State*, pp. 42–46, 56–58.

54. John K. Fairbank, "Our Vietnam tragedy," *Newsletter*, Harvard Graduate Society for Advanced Study and Research, June 1975. Fairbank also remarks that our "greatly accelerating the urbanization of Vietnam" after 1965 was "not necessarily to our credit or to the benefit of South Vietnam." Scholarly caution, perhaps appropriate in an issue of the *Newsletter* that announced a new professorship of Vietnamese Studies named for Kenneth T. Young, formerly Chairman of SEADAG and Director of Southeast Asian Affairs in the State Department in 1954–58, when the United States took over direct responsibility for repression and massacre in South Vietnam. Young was one of those to urge publicly that the United States and its local subordinates "should deliberately increase urbanized markets and the town groupings coupled with fewer remote villages and fewer dispersed hamlets outside the modernizing environment" to "outmatch and outclass the Viet Cong where they are weak" (cf. note 18), thus making "a virtue out of necessity." *Asian Survey*, August 1967. At that time, no rational person could be deceived as to how "urban realignment," as Young called it, was being and must be effected by the American Expeditionary Force.

　　　Perhaps some day the University of Berlin will institute an Eichmann chair of Jewish Studies.

55. William Y. Elliott, ed., *The Political Economy of American Foreign Policy*, New York, Holt, 1955, p. 42.

56. Quoted in Akire Iriye, *Across the Pacific*, New York, Harcourt, Brace and World, 1967, p. 77.

57. Cited by Frank Freidel, in *Dissent in Three American Wars*, Cambridge, Harvard University Press, 1970.

31
A Defense of Freedom
NORMAN PODHORETZ

Here then we arrive at the center of the moral issue posed by the American intervention into Vietnam.

The United States sent half a million men to fight in Vietnam. More than 50,000 of them lost their lives, and many thousands more were wounded. Billions of dollars were poured into the effort, damaging the once unparalleled American economy to such an extent that the country's competitive position was grievously impaired. The domestic disruptions to which the war gave rise did perhaps even greater damage to a society previously so self-confident that it was often accused of entertaining illusions of its own omnipotence. Millions of young people growing to maturity during the war developed attitudes of such hostility toward their own country and the civilization embodied by its institutions that their willingness to defend it against external enemies in the future was left hanging in doubt.

Why did the United States undertake these burdens and make these sacrifices in blood and treasure and domestic tranquillity? What was in it for the United States? It was a question that plagued the antiwar movement from beginning to end because the answer was so hard to find. If the United States was simply acting the part of an imperialist aggressor in Vietnam, as many in the antiwar movement professed to believe, it was imperialism of a most peculiar kind. There were no raw materials to exploit in Vietnam, and there was no overriding strategic interest involved. To Franklin Roosevelt in 1941, Indochina had been important because it was close to the source of rubber and tin, but this was no longer an important consideration. Toward the end of the war, it was discovered that there was oil off the coast of Vietnam and antiwar radicals happily seized on this news as at last providing an explanation for the American presence there. But neither Kennedy nor Johnson knew about the oil, and even if they had, they would hardly have gone to war for its sake in those pre-OPEC days when oil from the Persian Gulf could be had at two dollars a barrel.

In the absence of an economic interpretation, a psychological version of the theory of imperialism was developed to answer the maddening question: *Why are we in Vietnam?* This theory held that the United States was in Vietnam because it had an urge to dominate—"to impose its national obsessions on the rest of the world," in the words of a piece in the *New York Review of Books*,[1] one of the leading centers of antiwar agitation within the intellectual community. But if so, the psychic profits were as illusory as the economic ones, for the war was doing even deeper damage to the national self-confidence than to the national economy.

Yet another variant of the psychological interpretation, proposed by the economist Robert L. Heilbroner, was that "the fear of losing our place in the sun, of finding ourselves at bay, . . . motivates a great deal of the anti-Communism on which so much of American foreign policy seems to be founded." This was especially so in such underdeveloped countries as Vietnam, where "the rise of Communism would signal the end of capitalism as the dominant world order, and would force the acknowledgment that America no longer constituted the model on which the future of world civilization would be mainly based."[2]

All these theories were developed out of a desperate need to find or invent selfish or self-interested motives for the American presence in Vietnam, the better to discredit it morally. In a different context, proponents of one or another of these theories— Senator Fulbright, for example—were not above trying to discredit the American presence politically by insisting that no national interest was being served by the war. This latter contention at least had the virtue of being closer to the truth than the former. For the truth was that the United States went into Vietnam for the sake not of its own direct interests in the ordinary sense but for the sake of an ideal. The intervention was a product of the Wilsonian side of the American character—the side that went to war in 1917 to "make the world safe for democracy" and that found its contemporary incarnations in the liberal internationalism of the 1940s and the liberal anti-Communism of the 1950s. One can characterize this impulse as naïve: one can describe it, as Heilbroner does (and as can be done with any virtuous act), in terms that give it a subtly self-interested flavor. But there is no rationally defensible way in which it can be called immoral.

Why, then, were we in Vietnam? To say it once again: because we were trying to save the Southern half of that country from the evils of Communism. But was the war we fought to accomplish this purpose morally worse than Communism itself? Peter L. Berger, who at the time was involved with Clergy and Laymen Concerned About Vietnam (CALCAV), wrote in 1967: "All sorts of dire results might well follow a reduction or a withdrawal of the American engagement in Vietnam. Morally speaking, however, it is safe to assume that none of these could be worse than what is taking place right now." Unlike most of his fellow members of CALCAV, Berger would later repent of this statement. Writing in 1980, he would say of it: "Well, it was not safe to assume. . . . I was wrong and so were all those who thought as I did." For "contrary to what most members (including myself) of the antiwar movement expected, the peoples of Indochina have, since 1975, been subjected to suffering far worse than anything that was inflicted upon them by the United States and its allies."[3]

To be sure, the "bloodbath" that had been feared by supporters of the war did not occur—not in the precise form that had been anticipated. In contrast to what they did upon taking power in Hanoi in 1954 (when they murdered some 50,000 landlords), or what they did during their brief occupation of Hué during the Tet offensive of 1968 (when they massacred 3,000 civilians), the Communists did not stage mass executions in the newly conquered South. According to Nguyen Cong Hoan, who had been an NLF agent and then became a member of the National Assembly of the newly united Communist Vietnam before disillusionment drove him to escape in March 1977, there were more executions in the provinces than in the cities and the total number might well have reached into the tens of thousands. But as another fervent opponent of the war, the *New York Times* columnist Tom Wicker was forced to acknowledge, "what Vietnam has given us instead of a bloodbath [is] a vast tide of human misery in Southeast Asia—hundreds of thousands of homeless persons in United Nations camps, perhaps as many more dead in flight, tens of thousands of the most pitiable forcibly repatriated to Cambodia, no one knows how many adrift on the high seas or wandering the roads."[4]

Among the refugees Wicker was talking about here were those who came to be known as "the boat people" because they "literally threw themselves upon the South China Sea in small coastal craft. . . ."[5] Many thousands of these people were ethnic Chinese who were being driven out and forced to pay everything they had for leaky boats; tens of thousands more were Vietnamese fleeing voluntarily from what Nguyen

Cong Hoan describes as "the most inhuman and oppressive regime they have ever known."[6] The same judgment is made by Truong Nhu Tang, the former Minister of Justice in the PRG who fled in November 1979 in a boat loaded with forty refugees: "Never has any previous regime brought such masses of people to such desperation. Not the military dictators, not the colonialists, not even the ancient Chinese overlords."[7]

So desperate were they to leave that they were willing to take the poor chance of survival in flight rather than remain. Says Nguyen Cong Hoan: ". . . Our people have a traditional attachment to their country. No Vietnamese would willingly leave home, homeland, and ancestors' graves. During the most oppressive French colonial rule and Japanese domination, no one escaped by boat at great risk to their lives. Yet you see that my countrymen by the thousands and from all walks of life, including a number of disillusioned Vietcongs, continue to escape from Vietnam; six out of ten never make it, and for those who are fortunate to make it, they are not allowed to land."[8] Adds one of the disillusioned who did make it, Doan Van Toai: "Among the boat people who survived, including those who were raped by pirates and those who suffered in the refugee camps, nobody regrets his escape from the present regime."[9]

Though they invented a new form of the Communist bloodbath, the North Vietnamese (for, to repeat, before long there were no Southerners in authority in the South, not even former members of the NLF and the PRG) were less creative in dealing with political opposition, whether real or imagined. The "re-education camps" they had always used for this purpose in the North were now extended to the South, but the result was not so much an indigenous system of Vietnamese concentration camps as an imitation of the Soviet Gulag. (*The Vietnamese Gulag*, indeed, was the name Doan Van Toai gave to the book he published about the camps in 1979.) The French journalist Jean Lacouture, who had supported the Communists during the war to the point (as he now admitted) of turning himself into a "vehicle and intermediary for a lying and criminal propaganda, [an] ingenuous spokesman for tyranny in the name of liberty,"[10] now tried to salvage his integrity by telling the truth about a re-education camp he was permitted to visit by a regime that had good reason to think him friendly. "It was," he wrote, "a prefabricated hell."[11]

Doan Van Toai, who had been in the jails over which so much moral outrage had been expended in the days of Thieu, describes the conditions he himself encountered when he was arrested by the Communists: "I was thrown into a three-foot-by-six-foot cell with my left hand chained to my right foot and my right hand chained to my left foot. My food was rice mixed with sand. . . . After two months in solitary confinement, I was transferred to a collective cell, a room 15 feet wide and 25 feet long, where at different times anywhere from 40 to 100 prisoners were crushed together. Here we had to take turns lying down to sleep and most of the younger, stronger prisoners slept sitting up. In the sweltering heat, we also took turns snatching a few breaths of fresh air in front of the narrow opening that was the cell's only window. Every day I watched my friends die at my feet."[12]

Toai adds: "One South Vietnamese Communist, Nguyen Van Tang, who was detained 15 years by the French, eight years by Diem, six years by Thieu, and who is still in jail today, this time in a Communist prison, told me . . . 'My dream now is not to be released; it is not to see my family. My dream is that I could be back in a French prison 30 years ago.' "[13]

No one knows how many people were sent to the Vietnamese Gulag. Five years after the fall of Saigon, estimates ranged from 150,000 to a million. Prime Minister Pham Van Dong, who so impressed Mary McCarthy with his nobility in 1968, told a

French magazine ten years later that he had "*released* more than one million prisoners from the camps,"[14] although according to the figures of his own government he had arrested only 50,000 in the first place.

These prisoners naturally included officials of the former government of South Vietnam, but many opponents of the Thieu regime could also be found among them, some of whom were by 1981 known to have died in the camps. One such was Thic Thien Minh, "the strategist of all the Buddhist peace movements in Saigon, . . . who was sentenced to 10 years in jail by the Thieu regime, then released after an outpouring of protest from Vietnamese and antiwar protesters around the world," and who died after six months of detention by the Communists in 1979. Another was Tran Van Tuyen, a leader of the opposition to Thieu in the Saigon Assembly. A third was the philosopher Ho Huu Tuong, "perhaps the leading intellectual in South Vietnam," who died in a Communist prison in 1980. All these—along with other opponents of Thieu possibly still alive, like Bui Tuong Huan, former president of Hué University; Father Tran Huu Thanh, a dissident Catholic priest; and Tran Ngoc Chau, whose own brother had been a North Vietnamese agent—were arrested (and of course held without trial) "in order," says Toai, "to preempt any possible opposition to the Communists."[15]

Before the Communist takeover, there had been a considerable degree of political freedom in South Vietnam which manifested itself in the existence of many different parties. After the North Vietnamese conquest, all these parties were dissolved: as for the NLF, "they buried it," in the bitter words of Truong Nhu Tang, "without even a ceremony," and "at the simple farewell dinner we held to formally disband the NLF in late 1976 neither the party nor the government sent a representative." The people of Vietnam, who "want only the freedom to go where they wish, educate their children in the schools they choose and have a voice in their government" are instead "treated like ants in a colony. There is only the opportunity to follow orders strictly, never the opportunity to express disagreement. Even within the [Communist] party, the principle of democracy has been destroyed in favor of the most rigid hierarchy. Stalinism, discredited throughout most of the Communist world, flourishes under the aged and fanatic Vietnamese leadership."[16]

Reading these words, one recalls Susan Sontag, Mary McCarthy, and Frances FitzGerald expending their intellectual energies on the promulgation of theories of Vietnamese culture calculated to deny that the people of Vietnam cared about freedom in the simple concrete terms set forth by Tang. One recalls Sontag saying that "incorporation" into a society like that of North Vietnam would "greatly improve the lives of most people in the world." One also recalls that both Sontag and McCarthy were troubled by the portraits of Stalin they saw all over the North; they were there, Sontag thought, because the Vietnamese could not bear to waste anything. Perhaps that is also how she would explain why portraits of Soviet leaders began appearing in public buildings, schools, and administrative offices throughout South Vietnam after 1975, and why the following poem by To Huu, president of the Communist Party Committee of Culture and a possible successor to Pham Van Dong,[17] was given a prominent place in an anthology of contemporary Vietnamese poetry published in Hanoi in the seventies:

> *Oh, Stalin! Oh, Stalin!*
> *The love I bear my father, my mother, my wife, myself*
> *It's nothing beside the love I bear you.*
> *Oh, Stalin! Oh, Stalin!*
> *What remains of the earth and of the sky*
> *Now that you are dead.?*[18]

Written on the occasion of Stalin's death, this poem no doubt earned its place in an anthology twenty years later by virtue of its relevance to the spirit of the new Communist Vietnam. For if the Vietnamese Communist party is Stalinist, so is the society over which it rules. "Immediately after the fall of Saigon, the Government closed all bookshops and theaters. All books published under the former regimes were confiscated or burned. Cultural literature was not exempt, including translations of Jean-Paul Sartre, Albert Camus and Dale Carnegie [!]. . . . The new regime replaced such books with literature designed to indoctrinate children and adults with the idea that the 'Soviet Union is a paradise of the socialist world.' "[19]

As with books, so with newspapers. Under the old regime, under constant attack throughout the world for its repressiveness, there had been *twenty-seven* daily newspapers, three television stations, and more than twenty radio stations. "When the Communists took over," writes the political analyst Carl Gershman, "these were all closed down, and replaced by two official dailies, one television channel, and two radio stations—all disseminating the same government propaganda."[20]

All the other freedoms that existed, either in full or large measure, under the Thieu regime were also eliminated by the Communists. Freedom of movement began to be regulated by a system of internal passports, and freedom of association was abolished to the point where even a large family gathering, such as a wedding or a funeral, required a government permit and was attended by a security officer.

Freedom of religion, too, was sharply curtailed. The Buddhists, who were so effective an element in the opposition to Diem, soon learned that there were worse regimes than his. A Human Rights Appeal drafted by the Unified Buddhist Church and smuggled out by the Venerable Thich Manh Giac when he escaped by boat, charged that the government, "pursuing the policy of shattering the religious communities in our country, . . . has arrested hundreds of monks, confiscated hundreds of pagodas and converted them to government administration buildings, removed and smashed Buddha and Bodhisattva statues, prohibited celebration of the Buddha's birthday as a national holiday, . . . and forbidden monks to travel and preach by ordering restrictions in the name of 'national security.' "[21]

Unlike demonstrations by Buddhists in 1963, this appeal fell on deaf ears; whereas a raid on a Buddhist temple led directly to the overthrow of Diem, a similar raid by the Communist police in April 1977 went unnoticed; and whereas the self-immolation of a single Buddhist monk in 1963 attracted the horrified attention of the whole world, the self-immolation of twelve Buddhist nuns and priests on November 2, 1975, in protest against Communist repression, received scarcely any notice either in the United States or anywhere else.

When all this is combined with the terrible economic hardships that descended upon Vietnam after 1975—hardships that were simultaneously caused by the new regime and used by it to justify resettling millions of people in the so-called New Economic Zones, remote jungle areas where they worked "in collective gangs at such tasks as clearing land and digging canals,"[22] under primitive living conditions with little food and rampant disease—it is easy to see why a sense of despair soon settled over the country. Truong Nhu Tang: "The fact is that today Communism has been rejected by the people and the even many party members are questioning their faith. Members of the former resistance, their sympathizers and those who supported the Vietcong are disgusted and filled with bitterness. These innocent people swear openly that had they another chance their choice would be very different. The commonly heard expression is: I would give them not even a grain of rice. I pull them out of their hiding holes and denounce them to the authorities."[23]

The Buddhist human-rights appeal conveyed much the same impression: "Since the liberation thousands have committed suicide out of despair. Thousands have fled the country in small boats. Hospitals are reserved for cadres: civilians hardly have a chance to be hospitalized in case of sickness, while more than 200 doctors remain in detention. Schoolchildren under fourteen have been assigned to collect pieces of scrap material in big garbage heaps and other places during the summer vacation. . . . A country that used to export rice has no rice to eat, even though the number of 'laborers' has now increased about ten times." The government, the appeal went on to say, prohibits "creative thinking and participation of independent groups. Totalitarianism destroys all possibility of genuine national reconciliation and concord."[24]

Some years after these words were written, a great and angry dispute broke out in the United States over the question of whether there was any practical validity or moral point in the distinction between authoritarianism and totalitarianism. Not surprisingly, those who dismissed the distinction as academic were in general veterans of the antiwar movement, who still refused to see that (as Gershman said in 1978) "for the Vietnamese, the distinction between a society that is authoritarian . . . and one that is totalitarian" turned out to be anything but academic.[25]

Peter L. Berger, one of the few former members of the antiwar movement who recognizes that "the transformation of Saigon into Ho Chi Minh City now offers a crystal-clear illustration of the difference between authoritarianism and totalitarianism, both in terms of political science and political morality," expresses amazement at "the persistent incapacity of even American professors to grasp a difference understood by every taxi driver in Prague." He believes that this incapacity derives in large part from a strong ideological interest in hiding "the fact that totalitarianism today is limited to socialist societies"—a fact that "flies in the face of the socialist dream that haunts the intellectual imagination of the West. . . ."[26]

I have no doubt that Berger is right about this. But where Vietnam in particular is concerned, there is a strong interest not only in protecting the socialist dream in general but, more specifically, in holding on to the sense of having been on the morally superior side in opposing the American struggle to prevent the replacement of an authoritarian regime in the South with a totalitarian system. The truth is that the antiwar movement bears a certain measure of responsibility for the horrors that have overtaken the people of Vietnam; and so long as those who participated in that movement are unwilling to acknowledge this, they will go on trying to discredit the idea that there is a distinction between authoritarianism and totalitarianism. For to recognize the distinction is to recognize that in making a contribution to the conquest of South Vietnam by the Communists of the North, they were siding with an evil system against something much better from every political and moral point of view.

Some veterans of the antiwar movement have protected themselves from any such acknowledgment of guilt by the simple expedient of denying that there is any truth in the reports by refugees like Toai, Coan, and Tang or journalists like Lacouture. Noam Chomsky, for example, speaks of "the extreme unreliability" of these reports,[27] and he is echoed by William Kunstler, Dave Dellinger, and other inveterate apologists for the Vietnamese Communists. Peter Berger compares such people to "individuals who deny the facts of the Holocaust" and rightly considers them "outside the boundaries of rational discourse."[28]

There are, however, others—like the editors of the Socialist magazine *Dissent,* Irving Howe and Michael Walzer—who are fully aware of the horrors that have followed the American withdrawal and the Communist conquest, and who are at least willing to ask, "Were We Wrong about Vietnam?" But of course their answer to this question is No. They were right because they were against both Saigon *and* Hanoi: they were right "in refusing to support the imperial backers of both." What then did they support? "Some of us . . . hoped for the emergence of a Vietnamese 'third force' capable of rallying the people in a progressive direction by enacting land reforms and defending civil liberties." But since, as they admit, there was very little chance of any such alternative, to have thrown their energies into opposing the American effort was tantamount to working for the Communist victory they say they did not want. Nevertheless, they still congratulate themselves on being against the evils on both sides of the war: "Those of us who opposed American intervention yet did not want a Communist victory were in the difficult position of having no happy ending to offer—for the sad reason that no happy ending was possible any longer, if ever it had been. And we were in the difficult position of urging a relatively complex argument at a moment when most Americans, pro- and antiwar, wanted blinding simplicities."[29] This is not moral choice; this is moral evasion—irresponsible utopianism disguised as moral realism. Given the actual alternatives that existed, what did the urging of "a relatively complex argument" avail for any purpose other than to make those who urged it feel pleased with themselves? If it served any purpose at all for the people of South Vietnam, it was to help deliver them over to the "blinding simplicities" of the totalitarianism Howe and Walzer so piously deplore and whose hideous workings they are now happy to denounce and protest against, even though there is no one in Ho Chi Minh City or Hanoi to listen or to hear.

Another veteran of the antiwar movement, Professor Stanley Hoffmann of Harvard, who also sees "no reason not to protest the massacres, arbitrary arrests, and persecutions perpetrated by the regimes that have taken over after our exit," nevertheless urges "those who condemned the war . . . to resist all attempts to make them feel guilty for the stand they took against the war." It was not, says Hoffmann, the antiwar movement that contributed to these horrors, but rather the people (led by Nixon and Kissinger) who were supposedly fighting to prevent them. True as this was of Vietnam—where "a monstrously disproportionate and self-destructive campaign" only added "to the crimes and degradation of eventual Communist victory"—it was even truer of Cambodia. "All those who, somehow, believe that the sufferings inflicted on the Cambodian people, first by the Pol Pot regime, and now by the Vietnamese, retrospectively justify America's attempt to save Phnom Penh from the Reds" were instructed by Hoffmann in 1979 to read a new book "showing that the monsters who decimated the Cambodian people were brought to power by Washington's policies."[30]

The book Hoffmann was referring to, *Sideshow: Kissinger, Nixon and the Destruction of Cambodia*, by the English journalist William Shawcross, sought to demonstrate that those Americans who fought to stop the Communists from coming to power in Cambodia were responsible for the crimes the Communists committed when the fight against them was lost. They can be held responsible, not as one might imagine because they did not fight as hard as they should have, or because in the end they deserted the field, but on the contrary because they entered the field in the first place. By attacking—first by bombing, then by invading—the North Vietnamese sanctuaries in Cambodia, the Americans (that is, Nixon and Kissinger) not only drove the Communists deeper into Cambodia, thereby bringing the war to areas that had previously been at peace. They also intensified the rage and bitterness of the Khmer Rouge (as the Cambodian Communists under Pol Pot were called), thereby turning them into perhaps the most murderous rulers ever seen on the face of the earth.

Sideshow is a brilliantly written and argued book. Indeed, not since Hannah Arendt's *Eichmann in Jerusalem*—which shifts a large measure of responsibility for the murder of six million Jews from the Nazis who committed the murders to the Jewish leaders who were trying to save as many of their people as they could—has there been so striking an illustration of the perverse moral and intellectual uses to which brilliance can be put.

There are, for example, the clever distortions and omissions that enable Shawcross to charge the Nixon Administration with having destabilized the neutral government of Prince Norodom Sihanouk by bombing the sanctuaries (when in fact Sihanouk welcomed these attacks on the Communist military bases within his own country which he himself was not powerful enough to banish) and with causing large numbers of civilian casualties by the indiscriminate pattern of the bombing raids (when in fact care was taken to minimize civilian casualties). But what is fully on a par of perversity with Hannah Arendt's interpretation of the Jewish role in the genocidal program of the Nazis against them is the idea that Pol Pot and his followers needed the experience of American bombing and the "punishment" they subsequently suffered in the war against the anti-Communist forces of Cambodia to turn them into genocidal monsters.

This idea about the Khmer Rouge can easily enough be refuted by the simple facts of the case. Thus, according to Kenneth Quinn, who conducted hundreds of interviews with refugees from Cambodia, the Khmer Rouge began instituting the totalitarian practices of their revolutionary program in areas they controlled as early as 1971.[31] So too Father François Ponchaud, who was in Phnom Penh when the Communists arrived and whose book *Cambodia: Year Zero* Shawcross himself calls "the best account of Khmer Rouge rule":[32] "The evacuation of Phnom Penh follows traditional Khmer revolutionary practice: ever since 1972 the guerrilla fighters had been sending all the inhabitants of the villages and towns they occupied into the forests to live, often burning their homes so they would have nothing to come back for."[33]

Indeed, as Shawcross himself points out, this revolutionary program was outlined in uncannily clear detail in the thesis written at the University of Paris in 1959 by Khieu Samphan, who would later become the Khmer Rouge commander in chief during the war and the head of state afterward. But Shawcross, in line with his own thesis that it was the war that made "the Khmer Rouge . . . more and more vicious,"[34] stresses that "the methods this twenty-eight-year-old Marxist prescribed in 1959 for the transformation of his country were essentially moderate."[35] In support of the same thesis, he quotes Quinn to the effect that "the first steps to change radically the nature of Khmer society" that the Khmer Rouge took in 1971 were "limited."[36]

What Shawcross fails or refuses to see is what Ponchaud understands about such moderate methods and limited steps—namely, that they remained moderate and limited only so long as the Khmer Rouge lacked the power to put them into practice. "Accusing foreigners cannot acquit the present leaders of Kampuchea," Ponchaud wrote (before the Vietnamese invaded Cambodia and replaced the Khmer Rouge Communists with a puppet Communist regime of their own); "their inflexible ideology has led them to invent a radically new kind of man in a radically new society." Or again: "On April 17, 1975, a society collapsed: another is now being born from the fierce drive of a revolution which is incontestably the most radical ever to take place in so short a time. It is a perfect example of the application of an ideology pushed to the furthest limits of its internal logic."[37]

The blindness to the power of ideas that prevents Shawcross from recognizing ideology as the source of the crimes committed against their own people by the Khmer Rouge is his greatest intellectual sin. It is a species of philistinism to which many contemporary intellectuals (who, as intellectuals, might be expected to attribute a disproportionate importance to the role of ideas) are paradoxically prone, and it takes the form of looking for material factors to account for historical developments even when, as in this case, the main causal element is clearly located in the realm of ideas.

But this sin is exceeded in seriousness by the moral implications of Shawcross's book. As Peter W. Rodman (who has been an aide to Henry Kissinger both in and out of government) says in concluding a devastating critique of Shawcross's scholarship: "By no stretch of moral logic can the crimes of mass murderers be ascribed to those who struggled to prevent their coming into power. One hopes that no craven sophistry will ever induce free peoples to accept the doctrine that Shawcross embodies: that resistance to totalitarianism is immoral."[38]

Yet it is just this "craven sophistry" that Stanley Hoffmann reaffirms in the very face of the horrors that have befallen the peoples of Indochina under Communist rule: "As Frances FitzGerald put it," he writes, "our mistake was in creating and building up 'the wrong side,' and we were led by that mistake to a course of devastation and defeat."[39] One can almost forgive Anthony Lewis for asking "What future possibility could be more terrible than the reality of what is happening to Cambodia now?"[40] since he asked this question before the Khmer Rouge took over. One can almost forgive the *New York Times* for the headline "Indochina without Americans: For Most, a Better Life" on a piece from Phnom Penh by Sydney H. Schanberg[41] since it was written before the Khmer Rouge had begun evacuating the city and instituting a regime that led to the death of nearly half the population of the country. Such writers should have known enough about the history of Communism to know better, and they should now be ashamed of their naïvete and of the contribution they made to the victory of forces they had a moral duty to oppose. Nevertheless, they were not yet aware of what Hoffmann already knew when he *still* described the Communists as the right side in Indochina and still denounced those who resisted them as immoral and even criminal. This is almost impossible to forgive.

In May 1977, two full years after the Communist takeover, President Jimmy Carter—a repentant hawk, like many members of his cabinet, including his Secretary of State and his Secretary of Defense—spoke of "the intellectual and moral poverty" of the policy that had led us into Vietnam and had kept us there for so long. When Ronald Reagan, an unrepentant hawk, called the war "a noble cause" in the course of his ultimately successful campaign to replace Carter in the White House, he was accused of having made a "gaffe." Fully, painfully aware as I am that the American effort to save Vietnam from Communism was indeed beyond our intellectual and moral capabilities, I believe the story shows that Reagan's "gaffe" was closer to the truth of why we were in Vietnam and what we did there, at least until the very end, than Carter's denigration of an act of imprudent idealism whose moral soundness has been so overwhelmingly vindicated by the hideous consequences of our defeat.

Notes

1. Jason Epstein, "The CIA and the Intellectuals," *New York Review of Books*, Apr. 20, 1967.
2. Robert L. Heilbroner, "Counterrevolutionary America," *Commentary*, Apr. 1967.
3. "Indochina and the American Conscience," *Commentary*, Feb. 1980.
4. Tom Wicker, *New York Times*, July 8, 1979. Quoted in Charles Horner, "America Five Years After Defeat," *Commentary*, Apr. 1980.
5. Carl Gershman, "After the Dominoes Fell," *Commentary*, May 1978.
6. Nguyen Cong Hoan, Hearings before the Subcommittee on International Organizations of the House Committee on International Relations, July 26, 1977, pp. 145–67.

7. Truong Nhu Tang, "Vietnam, the Myth of a Liberation," unpublished ms., 1981.

8. See note 6 above.

9. Doan Van Toai, "A Lament for Vietnam," *New York Times Magazine*, Mar. 29, 1981.

10. Jean Lacouture, interview with François Fejto, in *Il Giornale Nuovo* (Milan), quoted in Michael Ledeen, "Europe—The Good News and the Bad," *Commentary*, Apr. 1979.

11. Jean Lacouture, quoted in "After the Dominoes Fell," *Commentary*, May 1978.

12. "A Lament for Vietnam," *New York Times Magazine*, Mar. 29, 1981.

13. Ibid.

14. Quoted in "A Lament for Vietnam," *New York Times Magazine*, Mar. 29, 1981.

15. "A Lament for Vietnam," *New York Times Magazine*, Mar. 29, 1981; "After the Dominoes Fell," *Commentary*, May 1978.

16. Truong Nhu Tang, "Vietnam, the Myth of a Liberation," unpublished ms., 1981.

17. *Foreign Report*, July 16, 1981.

18. To Huu, quoted in "A Lament for Vietnam," *New York Times Magazine*, Mar. 29, 1981.

19. "A Lament for Vietnam," *New York Times Magazine*, Mar. 29, 1981.

20. "After the Dominoes Fell," *Commentary*, May 1978.

21. Quoted in "After the Dominoes Fell," *Commentary*, May 1978.

22. "After the Dominoes Fell," *Commentary*, May 1978.

23. Truong Nhu Tang, "Vietnam, the Myth of a Liberation," unpublished ms., 1981.

24. Quoted in "After the Dominoes Fell," *Commentary*, May 1978.

25. "After the Dominoes Fell," *Commentary*, May 1978.

26. "Indochina and the American Conscience," *Commentary*, Feb. 1980.

27. Quoted in "After the Dominoes Fell," *Commentary*, May 1978.

28. "Indochina and the American Conscience," *Commentary*, Feb. 1980.

29. Irving Howe and Michael Walzer, "Were We Wrong about Vietnam?," *New Republic*, Aug. 18, 1979.

30. Stanley Hoffmann, "The Crime of Cambodia," *New York Review of Books*, June 28, 1979.

31. Peter W. Rodman, "Sideswipe," *American Spectator*, Mar. 1981.

32. William Shawcross, "Shawcross Swipes Again," *American Spectator*, July 1981.

33. François Ponchaud, *Cambodia: Year Zero*, New York: Holt, Rinehart & Winston, 1978, p. 21. Quoted in "Sideswipe," *American Spectator*, Mar. 1981.

34. "Shawcross Swipes Again," *American Spectator*, July 1981.

35. William Shawcross, *Sideshow*, New York: Pocket Books, 1979, p. 243.

36. Kenneth Quinn, quoted in "Shawcross Swipes Again," *American Spectator*, July 1981.

37. *Cambodia: Year Zero*, pp. xvi, 192. Quoted in "Sideswipe," *American Spectator*, Mar. 1981.

38. "Sideswipe," *American Spectator*, Mar. 1981.

39. "The Crime of Cambodia," *New York Review of Books*, June 28, 1979.

40. Anthony Lewis, *New York Times*, Mar. 17, 1975. Quoted in "Sideswipe," *American Spectator*, Mar. 1981.

41. *New York Times*, Apr. 13, 1975. Quoted in "Sideswipe," *American Spectator*, Mar. 1981.

32
A Perfect Technowar
JAMES WILLIAM GIBSON

If you are setting up an ambush, you must first pick a place where men are likely to walk. A well-trodden path is an excellent choice since most Americans are averse to slower, more difficult movement in a dimly lit jungle. Having selected a frequently used trail, you then position your mines and grenades and automatic weapons to achieve overlapping or intersecting "fields of fire." The area where the fields of fire are the most dense is known as the "killing zone."

Search-and-destroy sent many Americans down the trail to the killing zone. Over 80 percent of the firefights were initiated by the enemy.[1] Although high command eventually came to know this, military practice never changed. The old trails continued to be used. "There it is," as the grunts used to say.

Similarly, conventional paths in search of war lead only to destruction of serious intellectual inquiry. War as mistake, war as failure of nerve, war as collection of dates and statistics that are somehow supposed to make it rational and compact enough to readily talk about—none of these definitions can account for the paradox of the ambush that is known lurking, but rarely avoided.

It must be recognized that knowledge neither falls from heaven nor grows on trees, but is instead created in specific social contexts involving political and economic power. Politically and economically powerful people make decisions on the basis of studies produced by professional economists, systems analysts, and political scientists, and they utilize more informal kinds of knowledge, such as the reports created by bureaucracies. It is best, then, not to think of a political and economic power structure making decisions about Vietnam and intellectual knowledge about the war as two separate categories, but instead to approach the search for war in terms of how power and knowledge operate together at a deep structural level of logic. As the French philosopher and historian Michel Foucault indicated, the study of modern societies is best approached as a study of "regimes" of power and knowledge, since the two can no longer be thought separate.[2]

In thinking about Vietnam, two specific relationships must be considered immediately. First, the United States *lost*. The tendency to displace Vietnam into political or literary contexts that never really confront the war represents a flight from recognizing the final outcome. American defeat seems "unreal" to Americans; thus the war itself becomes "unreal." Since previous knowledge about Vietnam provided neither the conceptual frameworks nor the information necessary to comprehend the defeat of the power structure, the war has remained invisible. Displacement hides intellectual bankruptcy. Displacement hides the political and military failure of the power structure.

Second, much primary knowledge about the war was produced by military and other governmental bureaucracies. Bureaucracies produce knowledge for utilization by bureaucracies. Military bureaucracies have no interest, for example, in estimating civilian casualties caused by bombing and air strikes. Civilian casualties detract from their efficiency as military units, and military units are rewarded for efficiency. High civilian casualties also make the actions of military commanders *illegitimate* to the public. There are many other absences of knowledge. Some are simply blank spaces; others indicate places where knowledge about the war was discounted and ignored for various reasons. Such absences constitute problems only if one takes current structures of power and knowledge to be sacrosanct, as having a monopoly on defining reality. Ultimately, though, questioning the definition of reality provided by the United States leads the way out of the tunnel.

The search for war begins in this country, at a time when defeat anywhere appeared *unthinkable*—the end of World War II. The United States emerged from that war as the only true victor, by far the greatest power in world history. Although the other Allies also won, their victories were much different. Great Britain's industrial strength was damaged and its empire was in disarray. France had been defeated and occupied by Nazi Germany. Much French industry had either been bombed by Britain and the United States or looted by Germany. The Soviet Union "won," but over twenty million of its people were killed and millions more wounded. Many of its cities and large areas of countryside were nothing but ruins. China "won," but despite American funding, the warlord Chiang Kai-shek and his subordinate warlords lost to the peasant communist revolution led by Mao Tse-tung. Even before Chiang Kai-shek's defeat, post-World War II China was largely a wasteland, suffering from famine and civil war. In other words, the United States won World War II and everyone else lost.

It is important to comprehend the changes that occurred *within* the United States that made its success overseas possible. Before World War II, both the world economy and the American economy had been in severe crisis. Unemployment was extremely high. Many factories and other businesses closed; those that remained open had underutilized production capabilities. Compared to 1986, the economy was decentralized. Even as late as 1940, some 175,000 companies produced 70 percent of all manufactured goods, while the hundred largest companies produced 30 percent.

Relationships between the economy and the state changed during the Depression. The United States had long practiced "free market" capitalism. Franklin Roosevelt and the Democratic-controlled Congress attempted to regulate capitalism in their "New Deal" program. Some endeavors, such as the minimum wage, Social Security, and laws making it easier for labor unions to organize, had impact and became enduring features of advanced capitalism. Federal efforts to organize the economy, however, did not succeed. The Supreme Court declared the National Recovery Act to be unconstitutional; the Court in effect ruled that state powers to regulate and organize the economy were limited. In any case, the New Deal did not succeed in its economic revitalization program. Unemployment levels in 1940 were close to what they had been in 1932, when Roosevelt was first elected.

Then came Pearl Harbor and the Second World War. Phenomenal changes occurred within a few short years. By 1944, the hundred largest manufacturing firms produced 70 percent of the nation's manufactured goods, while all the rest produced only 30 percent.[3] Economic mobilization for war necessitated radical state intervention in the economy. State war-managers favored awarding huge contracts to the largest industrial firms. These administrators thought that only the largest firms had truly "scientific" production lines and that only the largest firms had managerial expertise to produce huge quantities of goods. By the end of the war leading manufacturers had received billions of dollars from the state. Contracts were awarded on a "cost-plus" basis, meaning that the state financed machinery and other production facilities, as well as the costs of labor, and beyond that guaranteed specific profit rates. The federal government thus violated the customary operations of the "free market" and created a state-organized and -financed, highly centralized form of capitalism in which a few firms dominated the economy. The gross national product increased from $91 billion in 1939 to $166 billion in 1945. Such tremendous economic expansion was unprecedented in world history.

Science had always been involved in the production process; you can't produce steel without detailed knowledge of physics, chemistry, metallurgy, and so forth. But in some ways, during the prewar period, science was not fully integrated into the economy. During World War II, however, thousands of scientists were hired by the government and large corporations. As Gerald Piel, a former editor of *Scientific American,* says, "The universities transformed themselves into vast weapons laboratories. Theoretical physicists became engineers, and engineers forced solutions at the frontiers of knowledge."[4] Science was enlisted in the economic production process and military destruction process to an unprecedented degree.

So-called managerial science also was incorporated into the war effort. The original master of "scientific management," Frederick Taylor, had won many adherents among businessmen in the 1920s and 1930s, especially among larger industrial firms confronted by massive unionization. For workers, scientific management meant progressive dissolution of their control over work processes.[5] By the 1940s, management had become a more esoteric discipline. For example, during World War II, Professor Robert McNamara of the Harvard University Business School developed statistical techniques of systems analysis for the War Department as management tools in controlling large organizations. McNamara became famous for organizing flight patterns of bombers and fighters in the air war against Germany. After the war, in the 1950s, he served as general manager and vice president of Ford Motor Company. In 1960, President Kennedy chose him as secretary of defense. Advanced "scientific" methods thus took root in both government and business.

This radical shift from a capitalist economy organized around small to medium-sized firms to an advanced capitalist economy organized around relatively few firms with high-technology production thus occurred through federal government intervention and was directed toward war production. Politics, economics, and science were now united in a new way. Just as the state changed capitalism and changed the practice of science, so too did the now vastly expanded economy and scientific apparatus change the nature and practice of politics, particularly the conduct of foreign policy. As the possessor of an advanced technological system of war production, the United States began to view political relationships with other countries in terms of concepts that have their origin in physical science, economics, and management. A deeply mechanistic world view emerged among the political and economic elite and their intellectual advisers.

The writings of Dr. Henry Kissinger provide a good introduction to modern power and knowledge relationships as they shaped American foreign policy in the post-World War II era. Kissinger was national security adviser to President Richard Nixon from 1969 through 1972 and was later secretary of state under Nixon and then Gerald Ford from 1973 through 1976. Before his ascension to formal political power, he was an important adviser to Nelson Rockefeller and a key intellectual in the foreign-policy establishment. His books and essays were held in great esteem.

Kissinger writes that since 1945, American foreign policy has been based "on the assumption that *technology plus managerial skills* gave us the ability to reshape the international system and to bring domestic transformations in 'emerging countries.' "[6] He indicates that there are virtually no limits to this technical intervention in the world: "A scientific revolution has, for all practical purposes, removed technical limits from the exercise of power in foreign policy."[7] Power thus becomes measured solely in technical terms: political power becomes physically embedded in the United States' large, efficient economy, its war production system capable of creating advanced war machines, and its economic-managerial science for administering these production systems. By this standard the United States had virtually unlimited power to control the world.

Moreover, since these physical means of power were created in large part through science, the United States also maintains a highly privileged position of *knowledge*. The United States knows more about "reality" itself, reality being defined in terms of physical science. Power and knowledge thus go together. Knowing "reality" is also "hard work." The West, in Kissinger's view, had been committed to this hard epistemological work since Sir Isaac Newton first formulated his laws of physics. Although Kissinger never speaks of "virtues" in connection with the hard work of the West, such connotations are implicit in his writings—Max Weber's *Protestant Ethic and Spirit of Capitalism* is tacitly enlisted in his program.[8] Power, knowledge, and virtue all accrue to the United States. Its foreign-policy endeavors are thus blessed. From this perspective Kissinger discusses the differences between the Third World and the West. Ultimately, he claims that the West knows reality and the underdeveloped countries live only in their own delusions:

> As for the difference in philosophical perspective, it may reflect the divergence of the two lines of thought which since the Renaissance have distinguished the West from the part of the world now called underdeveloped (with Russia occupying an intermediate position). The West is deeply committed to the notion that the real world is external to the observer, that knowledge consists of recording and classifying data— the more accurately the better. Cultures which have escaped the early impact of Newtonian thinking have retained the essentially pre-Newtonian view that the real world is almost entirely internal to the observer.
>
> Although this attitude was a liability for centuries—because it prevented the development of the technology and consumer goods which the West enjoyed—it offers great flexibility with respect to the contemporary revolutionary turmoil. It enables the societies which do not share our cultural mode to alter reality by influencing the perspective of the observer—a process which we are largely unprepared to handle or even perceive. And this can be accomplished under contemporary conditions without sacrificing technological progress. Technology comes as a gift; acquiring it in its advanced form does not presuppose the philosophical commitment that discovering it imposed on the West. Empirical reality has a much different significance for many of the new countries because in a certain sense they never went through the process of discovering it (with Russia again occupying an intermediate position).[9]

By this theory, American intervention in the Third World not only brings technology and consumer goods into play but also brings *reality* to the Third World. In claiming the West's radical monopoly on knowing reality, the Third World becomes *unreal*. Those who live there and have retained "the essentially pre-Newtonian view that the real world is almost entirely internal to the observer" are therefore totally unlike the West and its leading country. Those who are totally unlike us and live in their own delusions are conceptualized as foreign Others. The foreign Other can be known only within the conceptual framework of technological development and production systems. For instance, the Other may have bicycles. Bicycles can be readily comprehended by the West as a form of "underdeveloped" transportation, as opposed to the trucks and automobiles found in the "developed" West. Bicycles are "less" than cars by definition. In this sense the Other can be known. Insofar as he is like us, he is far down on the scale of power and knowledge; insofar as he is not like us, he remains the foreign Other living his self-delusions in an unreal land.

Who defeated the most powerful nation in world history? Who defeated several hundred thousand troops equipped with the most advanced weaponry that the most ethnologically sophisticated nation had to offer? Who defeated a war budget of more than one trillion dollars? For the most part, peasants of underdeveloped agricultural economies defeated the United States. The insurgents of what was called "South Vietnam" were peasants. What was called "North Vietnam" was also a relatively primitive, agricultural economy with little industrial base.

How could a nation of peasants with bicycles defeat the United States? By Kissinger's theory such a defeat is *unthinkable*. Kissinger's claim to a monopoly of true knowledge for the West turns into its opposite. Classifying nations and peoples purely on the basis of their possession, or lack, of technologically advanced production and warfare systems leads only to radical reduction of what can be considered as valid knowledge about the world. This regime of power and knowledge thus creates a world that is "almost entirely internal to the observer." Kissinger writes that "the West is deeply committed to the notion that the real world is external to the observer, that knowledge consists of recording and classifying data—the more accurately the better." He calls this the "Newtonian" view of the world, after the eighteenth-century theoretical physicist Sir Isaac Newton.

However, Newtonian mechanics is a theory about nature. It says nothing about society, about human social relationships. Newtonian mechanics says nothing about societies where millions of peasants are dominated by a few hundred landlords; it says nothing about countries where the population may be yellow or brown or black in skin color, but their rulers have white skins and come from distant lands. It says nothing about social conflict, about social relationships of domination and subordination; and in particular, Newtonian mechanics says nothing about social revolution.

Instead, the deeply mechanistic view of the world can see bicycles of the Third World only as compared to the cars of the West. Bicycles cannot "beat" cars and trucks and planes and railroads. But in 1954, the Vietnamese beat the French in a battle at Dien Bien Phu. Thousands of peasants cut trails through jungles and across mountains; thousands more dug tunnels close to French fortifications; thousands more walked alongside bicycles loaded with supplies for the Vietminh army. Social relationships between the Vietminh soldiers and the peasantry were such that thousands of peasants could be mobilized for the war effort. Social relationships that are rendered invisible by the modern regime of power and knowledge can defeat a system of power that conceives the world only in terms of technological-production systems. At the time, the French were amazed at their loss. The Americans were similarly amazed years later. They did not learn from the French because they thought that the French simply did not have enough tools of war; the United States had many more.

What is at issue concerns conceptually mapping "nature" onto society, of rendering the social world invisible. This false scientific project has historical precedent in the theory of capitalism, the famous nature-like "laws of supply and demand" that govern the market. Adam Smith, eighteenth-century author of *The Wealth of Nations*, is usually awarded credit for positing capitalism as economic nature, the true discovery of the actual order of things, the social organization that imitates nature best. Viewing capitalism as nature, this theory of immutable laws of supply and demand, was later criticized by Karl Marx.

Marx contended that the production process constituted a social relationship between those who owned the means of production (the capitalist) and those who were employed by capitalists as laborers (the working class). The working class collectively produced all wealth, but received only a fraction back as wages; the rest went to the capitalists. Capitalism was based on a specific kind of class domination, not a "natural" order. However, structural relationships of class domination are rendered invisible by the phenomenal form of capitalist production, the commodity. Everything *appears* as a commodity to be bought and sold, even the workers. A loaf of bread appears as an object to be eaten, which is sold in a store for a price. No relationships of class structure are written on the package cover. "The commodity is a mysterious thing," wrote Marx. "In it definite social relationships among men assume the fantastic form of relationships among things." Marx called this project of mapping nature onto society "commodity fetishism."[10]

Ironically, Marx thought that the phenomenal force of commodity fetishism would be attenuated when *science* became a *"direct force of production*, integral to the operation of all basic industry."[11] Science to Marx represented the collective knowledge of society. Although individual bits of knowledge could be privately owned—as in patents—basic scientific advancement resulted from social "poolings" of thousands of individual efforts to know the world. Thus, when science became a "direct force of production, integral to the operation of all basic industry," the relationship of knowledge to the production process would make the social character of production more evident.

Men and women could more readily see that since knowledge was a collective product of the human species, then the goods produced by privately owned industry (using scientific knowledge in the production process) rightfully belonged to society as a whole, not only to the capitalist class. People would see both the moral right and logical necessity for collective ownership and control of the society. Because people would be organizing economic activity together, the goods produced would not appear as independent entities obeying naturelike laws of supply and demand. Collective social organization and decision-making about social development and resource allocation replaces the market. No longer do "definite social relationships among men assume the fantastic form of relationships among things." With the transition to socialism, commodity fetishism and other forms of falsely mapping a model of nature onto society would end. Scientific rationalization of capitalist production was thus a crucial stage in Marx's theory of the transition from capitalism toward socialism.

The prediction for radical social change in advanced capitalist countries did not come true. Instead, a new kind of fetishism came into existence in the post-World War II period. The scientific rationalization and expansion of the production process occurred during wartime; it was directed by the state toward the *production of war*. The largest industrial firms became quantum levels larger, and their owners and top executives entered into new relationships with the government. Privately owned production facilities still dominated the economy, but these firms were state financed to a considerable degree and their products were used by the state to wage war and conduct foreign policy. C. Wright Mills called this new social organization rule by "the power elite."[12] Seymour Melman has used the term "the permanent war economy."[13] Both men have written works of great merit, but neither fully conveys the transformations of power and knowledge that mark American foreign policy since World War II.

Whereas Marx saw the locus of fetishism and naturalization as structurally situated in the system of commodity production, this new fetishism involved rationalized capitalist production as it was organized for war production. Political and social power became conceptualized and practiced solely in terms of how high societies ranked in their ability to produce high-technology warfare. To those in command of the system, the world's international political and economic relationships appeared as a series of technical or physical problems to be solved by the correct, scientifically determined administration of force: how much war production or threat of war production was necessary to achieve American policy objectives in other nations.

This new fetishism is thus a kind of social physics, a metaphorical transposition of Sir Isaac Newton's world of physical forces and mechanical interactions onto the social world. War-production systems become the units of this social physics. To appropriate Marx's phrasing, in this new fetishism definite social relationships among men assume the fantastic form of relationships among high-technology production systems for producing warfare. And when relationships appear as warfare systems, then social relationships disappear from view just as they do with the system of simple commodity production. For example, how can complex social revolutions be understood by war-managers, when for them the highest form of political power is an atomic bomb that could literally vaporize the revolution? At best, war-managers can only translate social revolution into their own fetishized, technical categories of control and production. How many weapons does the revolution have? What is its structure of command, control, and communication? How do enemy war-managers instrumentally manipulate their people? In this way, Kissinger's claim that the West in general and the United States in particular have an epistemological monopoly on "the notion that the real world is external to the observer" turns back on itself. The question must be asked, who is the foreign Other for whom "the real world is almost entirely internal to the observer"?

The Other is the man mesmerized by his own system of production, his own system for the production of destruction, his own "technology plus managerial skills," which creates the possibility of bringing "domestic transformations in 'emerging countries.'" The Other is the man who writes, "A scientific revolution has, for all practical purposes, removed technical limits from the exercise of power in foreign policy." The history of modern foreign policy is the history of this power and knowledge regime. It is the history of a system totally enclosed upon itself, the history of a regime whose basic assumptions of knowledge are never questioned by those in power. At the same time, these men legitimate their decisions and subsequent actions in terms of a radical monopoly of knowledge: they have a scientific right to intervene in the Third World.

Kissinger is but one man. He has been cited both because of his position and fame and because his writings are so clearly concerned with the questions at hand. Still, he is not solely responsible for the modern regime of power and knowledge. To the contrary, the basic assumptions about power and knowledge articulated by Kissinger were shared by thousands of academics and policymakers. Much of the literature on international relations and development or "modernization" of the Third World shares these same mechanistic assumptions. Fetishism is not an individual problem; it is a characteristic of particular social structures and how those social structures are conceived by members of the society.

In the 1950s, there was one contradiction in the regime of power and knowledge that worried political elites and defense intellectuals. The problem had to do with using the atomic bomb, especially the difficult situation created when both the United States and the Soviet Union had the bomb. Using the atomic bomb became more dangerous to the United States, because the Soviet Union could retaliate in kind. In this event, the vast systems of production on both sides would be destroyed. During the 1950s, this projected scenario was called mutually assured destruction. The scenario placed limits on American ability to intervene militarily in the world. Much effort was expended in attempting to solve this contradiction of virtually limitless technical power that now seemed highly limited.

The most renowned scholar who helped solve this problem was, again, Dr. Henry Kissinger. His book on the subject was entitled *Nuclear Weapons and Foreign Policy* (1957). Kissinger was opposed to all-out nuclear war because such war destroyed the American advantage: "We have seen . . . that the power of modern weapons reduces the importance of our industrial potential in an all-out war because each side can destroy the industrial plant of its opponent with its forces-in-being at the very outset. With modern weapons [atomic weapons], industrial potential can be significant only in a war in which it is not itself the target."[14] From the necessity to preserve American industrial potential, Kissinger derives a strategic doctrine in which this potential can be best used. By virtue of its tehnological production system, the United States can achieve its foreign-policy objectives by *limited wars* fought as *wars of attrition:*

> As a result, limited war has become the form of conflict which enables us to derive the greatest strategic advantage from our industrial potential. It is the best means for achieving a continuous drain of our opponent's resources without exhausting both sides. The prerequisite for deriving a strategic advantage from industrial potential is a weapons system sufficiently complex to require a substantial production effort, but not so destructive as to deprive the victor of any effective margin of superiority. Thus the argument that limited war may turn into a contest of attrition is in fact an argument in favor of a strategy of limited war. A war of attrition is the one war that Soviet block could not win.[15]

Kissinger even said that the purpose of limited war was to demonstrate the capacity for destruction by our advanced war-production system, not literally to destroy an enemy: "Strategic doctrine must never lose sight that its purpose is to affect the will of the enemy, not to destroy him, and that we can be limited only by presenting the enemy with an unfavorable calculus of risks."[16] In another formulation of the same theoretical point, Kissinger wrote: "In a limited war the problem is to apply graduated amounts of destruction for limited objectives and also to permit the necessary breathing spaces for political contacts."[17]

All that remained necessary was to reorganize the American military so that it could fight limited wars of attrition. Kissinger gave great priority to preparing the military for this new kind of warfare: "One of the most urgent tasks of American military policy is to create a military capability which can redress the balance in limited wars and which can translate our technological advantage into local superiority."[18]

For the army these were golden words. When preparing for nuclear war during the 1950s, the air force had received most of the money allocated to the Department of Defense; the navy came second and the army got what was left. Prospects for a new mission involving a capital-intensive, technologically sophisticated army were exciting! Now the army, too, could speed up its transformation in organization and doctrine to fit smoothly into modern warfare. This transition had started in the Second World War with Chief of Staff George C. Marshall's decision to adopt the corporate model of organization as a means of managing military logistics. Corporatization of the military continued in the fifties. Close association with business and science in preparing new weapons systems accentuated the trend.

However, the full implications of this transformation go far beyond matters of management and weaponry considered as just *parts* of the American military. The same "fetishism" of technological production systems found in foreign policy similarly occurs within the military. The *social relationships* within the military disappear and all that remain are technological-production systems and ways of managing them. In the early 1950s, Morris Janowitz, a military sociologist, detected conflict between the traditional idea of the officer corps as being composed of "heroic" combat leaders or "gladiators," and the emerging career path of the "military manager."[19] Combat leaders inspire troops to fight in dangerous battle; social relationships of loyalty from top to bottom and bottom to top are crucial. Managers allocate resources. As two other military sociologists, Richard Gabriel and Paul Savage, say, "no one expects anyone to die for IBM or General Motors."[20]

Second, in a world where only technology and production count, the enemy begins to be seen *only* in those terms. The bicycle example in Vietnam was no joke. Limited war fought as a war of attrition means that only information about technological-production systems will count as valid knowledge about the enemy. For the military as well as civilian policymakers, the enemy becomes a mirror image of ourselves, only "less" so. Military strategy becomes a one-factor question about technical forces; success or failure is measured quantitatively. Machine-system meets machine-system and the largest, fastest, most technologically advanced system will win. Any other outcome becomes *unthinkable*. Such is the logic of *Technowar*.

The search for war now leads to the enemy. The enemy, of course, is communism. Although it is self-evident that Communist countries, particularly the Soviet Union, have been the enemy of American foreign policy in the post-World War II era, this same self-evidence tends to obscure just *how* this Communist enemy is conceptualized. Much debate could well ensue: the merits of "private property" capitalism versus "state-planning" of the economy; "representative democracy" versus "democratic centralism" in the Communist party; a privately owned "free press" versus a state-owned and state-censored press. All of these issues are worthy of great scrutiny, research, and debate. Only one subject will be considered here, though, and that is the question of Communist "expansion."

By the end of World War II, the Soviet Union's army occupied Eastern Europe. In most countries except Yugoslavia and Czechoslovakia, the preexisting *internal* Communist movements were relatively weak. The invading Red Army with its accompanying Communist party political officers proceeded to establish a series of "puppet" or "satellite" governments, all under relatively firm control by the Soviet Union. In Yugoslavia, a large Communist movement, led by Marshal Tito, had fought a guerrilla war against the Nazis and had much popular support. Yugoslavia consequently did not become a "puppet" regime of the Soviet Union. Czechoslovakia did not retain its independence.

The original American concept of Communist expansion comes from Soviet occupation and control of Eastern Europe. Expansion meant "foreign" Communists occupying a country and ruling it without any consent of the native population. This original concept of Communist expansion thus had great historical truth. But historical truth is sometimes detached from its historical context. Communism as the ultimate foreign Other had a theoretical position already prepared for it by the capitalist West.

Capitalists, both the old variant called "laissez-faire" and the new capitalist order coming into existence during the war, understood themselves as being modeled on *nature*. If capitalism was nature, then communism by definition had to be *antinature*. By logical extension, if capitalism represented the natural economic structure of all nations, then by definition a Communist movement could only be *foreign*; it had to come from the *outside* because nature itself occupied the *inside*. In this way the historical truth of the Soviet conquest of Eastern Europe moved into a theoretical position of communism as the inevitable foreign Other.

This fetishized concept of communism as foreign Other, antinature itself, did not permit the United States to comprehend the Chinese revolution in 1949. Parts of China had long been occupied by the capitalist West. Its sovereignty as a nation had been diminished by imperialist conquest. Where the West did not rule, feudal landlord-warlords governed. The United States had special "trade agreements" with China, and sent troops and gunboats to maintain its economic position. Communist-led peasant revolution began in the 1920s in this milieu. Peasants wanted land for themselves and sovereignty from foreign governments.

Japan displaced Western powers in 1939 when it invaded China; the country now became subject to Japanese imperialism. When the United States entered World War II, it supported those Chinese political factions that had benefited from previous business arrangements with the West. These forces, led by Chiang Kai-shek, were known in the United States as the *Nationalist Chinese.* The very semantic construction of the phrase meant that the Communists were "unnational," and therefore "foreign," not a real Chinese movement by any means. Consequently, the internal social dynamics of the Chinese revolution disappeared. When the Communist-led peasant revolution won in 1949, it appeared to the United States not as an internal social revolution, but as another instance of external Communist expansion ultimately controlled by the Soviet Union. Ironically, the Chinese Communist party had long been in severe conflict with the Soviet Union. Joseph Stalin had not supported the revolution during the war because it conflicted with his own policy of a "united front" with the West against fascism! Some members of the United States State Department knew about the internal dynamics of the Chinese revolution, but they were purged during the 1950s because they were held responsible for the "loss of China" to communism.

In 1950, war began in Korea. The country had been provisionally divided into a Communist northern region and a right-wing military regime in the south. After a long period of military probes by both sides along the provisional boundary, North Korea invaded South Korea. The Korean War will not be explored in depth here; it is sufficient to say that the Korean War consolidated the notion that all Communist movements inevitably come from outside a country's borders and are ultimately controlled by Moscow. Subsequently the United States began massive funding to the French to help them retain their colony, Vietnam, against internal national and social revolution led by Communists. When the French were defeated in 1954, the United States announced a doctrine which would make Vietnam contested ground for decades.

The domino theory has been much discussed, but rarely scrutinized. "Domino" is a metaphor, but the *nature* of that metaphor has not been seen. On April 7, 1954, the original dominoes—the nations of Southeast Asia—stood up to be counted. President Dwight D. Eisenhower said: "You have a row of dominoes set up, and you knock over the first one, and what will happen to the last one is the certainty that it will go over very quickly, so you could have the beginning of a disintegration that would have the most profound influences."[21]

The falling dominoes were soon joined by a *popping cork.* On April 26, Eisenhower said that Indochina resembled "a sort of cork in the bottle, the bottle being the great area that includes Indonesia, Burma, Thailand, all the surrounding areas of Asia." Secretary of State [John Foster] Dulles added his verse a few days later in an address to a

Senate and House Committee: "If Indochina should be lost, there would be a *chain reaction* throughout the Far East and Southeast Asia."[22]

"Falling dominoes," "cork in the bottle," "chain reaction"—what theory is being proposed here? According to one radical historian, Gabriel Kolko, the domino theory constitutes a theory of modern history: "Translated into concrete terms, the domino theory was a counterrevolutionary doctrine which defined modern history as a movement of Third World and dependent nations—those with strategic value to the United States or its capitalist associates—away from colonialism or capitalism and toward national revolution and forms of socialism."[23]

The failure of Kolko's analysis concerns *translation*. He has translated the domino theory into the Marxist theory of society, a theory in which concreteness, history, national revolution, and forms of socialism—emphasis on the plurality—exist as elements of a conceptual framework for understanding the social world. However, in the domino theory, none of these concepts exists: the domino theory effectively abolishes the possibility of history, national revolution, and forms of socialism. The conceptual order it elaborates is entirely different.

"Falling dominoes," "cork in the bottle," "chain reaction"—these terms find their theoretical reference not in the social world of history, where men live and die, but in the lifeless world of Newtonian mechanics. The foreign Other, Communist antinature, invades and destroys the natural order of Vietnam (capitalism). If Vietnam "falls" to communism, then the rest of Asia will surely follow, each fall from grace faster than its predecessor—an inevitable, inexorable mechanical process. Countries no longer have real histories, culture, and social structures. The names of Asian countries become just that—names marking undifferentiated objects. And these names are inscribed upon a vast ledger, debit or credit, Communist or anti-Communist.

It is now time to name this ledger, to tie together constituent elements of the domino theory and other ideas that conceptualize the social world in terms of nature. The universe of post-World War II American foreign policy will be called *mechanistic anticommunism*. The demonic machine that lives outside of the natural capitalist order is the *foreign Other*. *Technowar* or the *production model of war* designates the military mode of strategy and organization in which war is conceptualized and organized as a high-technology, capital-intensive production process. The military and civilian executives who command the foreign policy and military apparatus are *war-managers*. History for them becomes a series of static points, each point measuring the balance of technological forces between the United States and the foreign Other. Some countries belong on the "credit" or capitalist side of the ledger; other countries belong to the "debit" or socialist side of the ledger. And still other countries, particularly Third World countries, become abstract sites for confrontation. No movement of a Third World country into the "debit" column is ever permanent: the ledger can be transformed by the introduction of more forces. To the war-managers, the policy of mechanistic anticommunism and Technowar against the foreign Other will ultimately produce victory. Since the United States has the most technologically advanced economy and warfare production system, then defeat by a nationalist social revolution in a peasant society becomes *unthinkable*.

There were no "mistakes" made during the Vietnam War. Nor was there a failure of will; the "self-imposed restraints" were only on official paper, not in Technowar practice. Instead, the Vietnam War should be understood in terms of the deep structural logic of how it was conceptualized and fought by American war-managers. Vietnam represents the perfect functioning of this closed, self-referential universe. Vietnam was *The Perfect War*.

Notes

1. Alain C. Enthoven and Wayne K. Smith, *How Much Is Enough? Shaping the Defense Program, 1961–1969* (New York: Harper & Row, 1971), p. 297.

2. For an introduction to Foucault's work see *Power/Knowledge: Selected Interviews and Other Writings*, edited by Colin Gordon (New York: Pantheon Books, 1980).

3. John Morton Blum, *V Was for Victory: Politics and American Culture during World War II* (New York: Harcourt Brace Jovanovich, 1976), p. 123.

4. *Ibid.*, pp. 144–145.

5. For an analysis of "scientific management" and the rationalization of production in the United States see Harry Braverman, *Labor and Monopoly Capital* (New York: Monthly Review Press, 1976).

6. Henry A. Kissinger, *American Foreign Policy*, expanded edition (New York: W. W. Norton, 1974), p. 57.

7. *Ibid.*, p. 54.

8. Max Weber, *The Protestant Ethic and the Spirit of Capitalism*, translated by Talcott Parsons (New York: Charles Scribner, 1958).

9. Kissinger, *American Foreign Policy*, pp. 48–49.

10. Karl Marx, *Capital: A Critique of Political Economy,* vol. 1: *The Process of Capitalist Production*, edited by Frederick Engels (New York: International Publishers, 1967), p. 72.

11. Karl Marx, *Grundrisse: Foundation of the Critique of Political Economy*, translated by Martin Nicholas (Middlesex, England: Penguin Books in association with New Left Review, 1973), p. 706.

12. C. Wright Mills, *The Power Elite* (New York: Oxford University Press, 1956).

13. Seymour Melman, *The Permanent War Economy: American Capitalist in Decline* (New York: Simon and Schuster, 1974).

14. Henry A. Kissinger, *Nuclear Weapons and Foreign Policy*, published for the Council on Foreign Relations (New York: Harper and Brothers, 1957), p. 155.

15. *Ibid.*, p. 155.

16. *Ibid.*, p. 126.

17. *Ibid.*, pp. 156–157.

18. *Ibid.*, pp. 154–155.

19. Morris Janowitz, *The Professional Soldier: A Social and Political Portrait* (Glencoe, Ill.: Free Press, 1960).

20. Richard A. Gabriel and Paul L. Savage, *Crisis in Command* (New York: Hill and Wang, 1978), p. 20.

21. Quoted by F. M. Kail, *What Washington Said: Administration Rhetoric and the Vietnam War, 1949–1969* (New York: Harper & Row, 1973), p. 66.

22. *Ibid.*, p. 85.

23. Gabriel Kolko, "The American Goals in Vietnam," in *The Pentagon Papers: Critical Essays*, edited by Noam Chomsky and Howard Zinn, vol. 5 of *The Pentagon Papers: The Senator Gravel Edition* (Boston: Beacon Press, 1972), p. 1.

CHAPTER 10

The War at Home

The Vietnam War was not the first American conflict to attract domestic pro-test, but by the late 1960s it had almost certainly become the most unpopular war in the nation's history. (The slight qualification is needed because there were no public opinion polls at the time of the War of 1812 or the Civil War.) Americans opposed the war for a variety of reasons. Some people thought that the United States was immorally engaged in imperialism in Vietnam. Oth-ers continued to have faith in the rectitude of American foreign policy overall but held that the intervention in Vietnam was a terrible mistake—a departure from the necessary (or generally benign) foreign involvements of the past. And surely some marched in antiwar demonstrations in fear that if the war dragged on, they or someone whom they loved would be sent off to fight.

The readings in this chapter address these and other concerns. Christian Appy underscores the importance of social class in determining who went to war and who did not; Vietnam, as he puts it, was a "working-class war." The genesis of the opposition to the war is the focus of Tom Wells's piece. He examines the tensions created when a group with a multifaceted reform agenda leaps onto a bandwagon playing just one song; and he describes the onset of protest, and the Johnson administration's response, in the early part of 1965. The chapter concludes with a look at women who resisted the war: an excerpt from Myra MacPherson's *Long Time Passing*. Implicit in the selection of this excerpt is the question of whether gender conditioned an individual's reaction to the war.

Washington, DC, November 17, 1965. Peace demonstrators march along Pennsylvania Avenue, in front of the White House. UPI/BETTMANN NEWSPHOTOS

33
Working-Class War
CHRISTIAN G. APPY

"We all ended up going into the service about the same time—the whole crowd." I had asked Dan Shaw about himself, why *he* had joined the Marine Corps; but Dan ignored the personal thrust of the question. Military service seemed less an individual choice than a collective rite of passage, a natural phase of life for "the whole crowd" of boys in his neighborhood, so his response encompassed a circle of over twenty childhood friends who lived near the corner of Train and King Streets in Dorchester, Massachusetts—a white, working-class section of Boston.

Thinking back to 1968 and his streetcorner buddies, Dan sorted them into groups, wanting to get the facts straight about each one. It did not take him long to come up with some figures. "Four of the guys didn't go into the military at all. Four got drafted by the army. Fourteen or fifteen of us went in the Marine Corps. Out of them fourteen or fifteen"—here he paused to count by naming—"Eddie, Brian, Tommy, Dennis, Steve: six of us went to Nam." They were all still teenagers. Three of the six were wounded in combat, including Dan.

His tone was calm, almost dismissive. The fact that nearly all his friends entered the military and half a dozen fought in Vietnam did not strike Dan as unusual or remarkable. In working-class neighborhoods like his, military service after high school was as commonplace among young men as college was for the youth of upper-middle-class suburbs—not welcomed by everyone but rarely questioned or avoided. In fact, when Dan thinks of the losses suffered in other parts of Dorchester, he regards his own streetcorner as relatively lucky. "Jeez, it wasn't bad. I mean some corners around here really got wiped out. Over off Norfolk Street ten guys got blown away the same year."

Focusing on the world of working-class Boston, Dan has a quiet, low-key manner with few traces of bitterness. But when he speaks of the disparities in military service throughout American society, his voice fills with anger, scorn, and hurt. He compares the sacrifices of poor and working-class neighborhoods with the rarity of wartime casualties in the "fancy suburbs" beyond the city limits, in places such as Milton, Lexington, and Wellesley. If three wounded veterans "wasn't bad" for a streetcorner in Dorchester, such concentrated pain was, Dan insists, unimaginable in a wealthy subdivision. "You'd be lucky to find three Vietnam veterans in one of those rich neighborhoods, never mind three who got wounded."

Dan's point is indisputable: those who fought and died in Vietnam were overwhelmingly drawn from the bottom half of the American social structure. The comparison he suggests bears out the claim. The three affluent towns of Milton, Lexington, and Wellesley had a combined wartime population of about 100,000, roughly equal to that of Dorchester. However, while those suburbs suffered a total of eleven war deaths, Dorchester lost forty-two. There was almost exactly the same disparity in casualties between Dorchester and another sample of prosperous Massachusetts towns—Andover, Lincoln, Sudbury, Weston, Dover, Amherst, and Longmeadow. These towns lost ten men from a combined population of 100,000. In other words, boys who grew up in Dorchester were four times more likely to die in Vietnam than those raised in the fancy suburbs. An extensive study of wartime casualties from Illinois reached a similar conclusion. In that state, men from neighborhoods with median family incomes under

$5,000 (about $15,000 in 1990 dollars) were four times more likely to die in Vietnam than men from places with median family incomes above $15,000 ($45,000 in 1990 dollars).

Dorchester, East Los Angeles, the South Side of Chicago—major urban centers such as these sent thousands of men to Vietnam. So, too, did lesser known, midsize industrial cities with large working-class populations, such as Saginaw, Michigan; Fort Wayne, Indiana; Stockton, California; Chattanooga, Tennessee; Youngstown, Ohio; Bethlehem, Pennsylvania; and Utica, New York. There was also an enormous rise in working-class suburbanization in the 1950s and 1960s. The post-World War II boom in modestly priced, uniformly designed tract housing, along with the vast construction of new highways, allowed many workers their first opportunity to purchase homes and to live a considerable distance from their jobs. As a result, many new suburbs became predominantly working class.

Long Island, New York, became the site of numerous working-class suburbs, including the original Levittown, the first mass-produced town in American history. Built by the Levitt and Sons construction firm in the late 1940s, it was initially a middle-class town. By 1960, however, as in many other postwar suburbs, the first owners had moved on, often to larger homes in wealthier suburbs, and a majority of the newcomers were working class. Ron Kovic, author of one of the best-known Vietnam memoirs and films, *Born on the Fourth of July*, grew up near Levittown in Massapequa. His parents, like so many others in both towns, were working people willing to make great sacrifices to own a small home with a little land and to live in a town they regarded as a safe and decent place to raise their families, in hope that their children would enjoy greater opportunity. Many commentators viewed the suburbanization of blue-collar workers as a sign that the working class was vanishing and that almost everyone was becoming middle class. In fact, however, though many workers owned more than ever before, their relative social position remained largely unchanged. The Kovics, for example, lived in the suburbs but had to raise five children on the wages of a supermarket checker and clearly did not match middle-class levels in terms of economic security, education, or social status.

Ron Kovic volunteered for the marines after graduating from high school. He was paralyzed from the chest down in a 1968 firefight during his second tour of duty in Vietnam. Upon returning home, after treatment in a decrepit, rat-infested VA [Veterans' Administration] hospital, Kovic was asked to be grand marshal in Massapequa's Memorial Day parade. His drivers were American Legion veterans of World War II who tried unsuccessfully to engage him in a conversation about the many local boys who had died in Vietnam:

> "Remember Clasternack? . . . They got a street over in the park named after him . . . he was the first of you kids to get it. . . . There was the Peters family too . . . both brothers. . . . Both of them killed in the same week. And Alan Grady. . . . Did you know Alan Grady? . . .
>
> "We've lost a lot of good boys. . . . We've been hit pretty bad. The whole town's changed."

A community of only 27,000, Massapequa lost 14 men in Vietnam. In 1969, *Newsday* traced the family backgrounds of 400 men from Long Island who had been killed in Vietnam. "As a group," the newspaper concluded, "Long Island's war dead have been overwhelmingly white, working-class men. Their parents were typically blue collar or clerical workers, mailmen, factory workers, building tradesmen, and so on."

Rural and small-town America may have lost more men in Vietnam, proportionately, than did even central cities and working-class suburbs. You get a hint of this simply by flipping through the pages of the Vietnam Memorial directory. As thick as a big-city phone book, the directory lists the names and hometowns of Americans who died in Vietnam. An average page contains the names of five or six men from towns such as Alma, West Virginia (pop. 296), Lost Hills, California (pop. 200), Bryant Pond, Maine (pop. 350), Tonalea, Arizona (pop. 125), Storden, Minnesota (pop. 364), Pioneer, Louisiana (pop. 188), Wartburg, Tennessee (pop. 541), Hillisburg, Indiana (pop. 225), Boring, Oregon (pop. 150), Racine, Missouri (pop. 274), Hygiene, Colorado (pop. 400), Clayton, Kansas (pop. 127), and Almond, Wisconsin (pop. 440). In the 1960s only about 2 percent of Americans lived in towns with fewer than 1,000 people. Among those who died in Vietnam, however, roughly four times that portion, 8 percent, came from American hamlets of that size. It is not hard to find small towns that lost more than one man in Vietnam. Empire, Alabama, for example, had four men out of a population of only 400 die in Vietnam—four men from a town in which only a few dozen boys came of draft age during the entire war.

There were also soldiers who came from neither cities, suburbs, nor small towns but from the hundreds of places in between, average towns of 15,000 to 30,000 people whose economic life, however precarious, had local roots. Some of these towns paid a high cost in Vietnam. In the foothills of eastern Alabama, for example, is the town of Talladega, with a population of approximately 17,500 (about one-quarter black), a town of small farmers and textile workers. Only one-third of Talladega's men had completed high school. Fifteen of their children died in Vietnam, a death rate three times the national average. Compare Talladega to Mountain Brook, a rich suburb outside Birmingham. Mountain Brook's population was somewhat higher than Talladega's, about 19,500 (with no black residents of draft age). More than 90 percent of its men were high school graduates. No one from Mountain Brook is listed among the Vietnam War dead.

I have described a social map of American war casualties to suggest not simply the geographic origins of U.S. soldiers but their class origins—not simply where they came from but the kinds of places as well. Class, not geography, was the crucial factor in determining which Americans fought in Vietnam. Geography reveals discrepancies in military service primarily because it often reflects class distinctions. Many men went to Vietnam from places such as Dorchester, Massapequa, Empire, and Talladega because those were the sorts of places where most poor and working-class people lived. The wealthiest youth in those towns, like those in richer communities, were far less likely either to enlist or to be drafted.

Mike Clodfelter, for example, grew up in Plainville, Kansas. In 1964 he enlisted in the army, and the following year he was sent to Vietnam. In his 1976 memoir, Clodfelter recalled, "From my own small home town . . . all but two of a dozen high school buddies would eventually serve in Vietnam and all were of working class families, while I knew of not a single middle class son of the town's businessmen, lawyers, doctors, or ranchers from my high school graduating class who experienced the Armageddon of our generation."

However, even a sketchy map of American casualties must go farther afield, beyond the conventional boundaries of the United States. Although this fact is not well known, the military took draftees and volunteers from the American territories: Puerto Rico, Guam, the U.S. Virgin Islands, American Samoa, and the Canal Zone. These territories lost a total of 436 men in Vietnam, several dozen more than the state of Nebraska. Some 48,000 Puerto Ricans served in Vietnam, many of whom could speak only a smattering of English. Of these, 345 died. This figure does not include men who were born in Puerto Rico and emigrated to the United States (or whose parents were born in Puerto Rico). We do not know these numbers because the military did not make a separate count of Hispanic-American casualties either as an inclusive category or by country of origin.

Guam drew little attention on the American mainland during the war. It was only heard of at all because American B-52s took off from there to make bombing runs over Vietnam (a twelve-hour round-trip flight requiring midair refueling) or because a conference between President Johnson and some of his top military leaders was held there in 1967. Yet the United States sent several thousand Guamanians to fight with American forces in Vietnam. Seventy of them died. Drawn from a population of only 111,000, Guam's death rate was considerably higher even than that of Dorchester, Massachusetts.

This still does not exhaust the range of places we might look for "American" casualties. There were, of course, the "Free World forces" recruited by and, in most cases, financed by the United States. These "third country forces" from South Korea, Australia, New Zealand, Thailand, and the Philippines reached a peak of about 60,000 troops (U.S. forces rose to 550,000). The U.S. government pointed to them as evidence of a united, multinational, free-world effort to resist communist aggression. But only Australia and New Zealand paid to send their troops to Vietnam. They had a force of 7,000 men and lost 469 in combat. The other nations received so much money in return for their military intervention that their forces were essentially mercenary. The Philippine government of Ferdinand Marcos, for example, received the equivalent of $26,000 for each of the 2,000 men it sent to Vietnam to carry out noncombat, civic action programs. South Korea's participation was by far the largest among the U.S. sponsored third countries. It deployed a force of 50,000 men. In return, the Korean government enjoyed substantial increases in aid, and its soldiers were paid roughly 20 times what they earned at home. More than 4,000 of them lost their lives.

The South Vietnamese military was also essentially the product of American intervention. For twenty-one years the United States committed billions of dollars to the creation of an anticommunist government in southern Vietnam and to the recruitment, training, and arming of a military to support it. Throughout the long war against southern guerrillas and North Vietnamese regulars, about 250,000 South Vietnamese government forces were killed. The United States bears responsibility for these lives and for those of third country forces because their military participation was almost wholly dependent on American initiatives.

In this sense, perhaps we need to take another step. Perhaps all Vietnamese deaths, enemy and ally, civilian and combatant, should be considered American as well as Vietnamese casualties. To do so is simply to acknowledge that their fates were largely determined by American intervention. After all, without American intervention (according to almost all intelligence reports at the time and historians since), Vietnamese unification under Ho Chi Minh would have occurred with little resistance.

However one measures American responsibility for Indochinese casualties, every effort should be made to grasp the enormity of those losses. From 1961 to 1975, 1.5 to 2 million Vietnamese were killed. Estimates of Cambodian and Laotian deaths are even less precise, but certainly the figure is in the hundreds of thousands. Imagine a memorial to the Indochinese who died in what they call the American, not the Vietnam, War. If similar to the Vietnam Memorial, with every name etched in granite, it would have to be forty times larger than the wall in Washington. Even such an enormous list of names would not put into perspective the scale of loss in Indochina. These are small countries with a combined wartime population of about 50 million people. Had the United States lost the same portion of its population, the Vietnam Memorial would list the names of 8 million Americans.

To insist that we recognize the disparity in casualties between the United States and Indochina is not to diminish the tragedy or significance of American losses, nor does it deflect attention from our effort to understand American soldiers. Without some awareness of the war's full destructiveness we cannot begin to understand their experience. As one veteran put it: "That's what I can't get out of my head—the bodies . . . all those bodies. Back then we didn't give a shit about the dead Vietnamese. It was like: 'Hey, they're just gooks, don't mean nothin.' You got so cold you didn't even blink. You could even joke about it, mess around with the bodies like they was rag dolls. And after awhile we could even stack up our own KIAs [killed in action] without feeling much of anything. It's not like that now. You can't just put it out of your mind. Now I carry those bodies around every fucking day. It's a heavy load, man, a heavy fucking load."

Presidents Kennedy, Johnson, and Nixon sent 3 million American soldiers to South Vietnam, a country of 17 million. In the early 1960s they went by the hundreds—helicopter units, Green Beret teams, counterinsurgency hotshots, ambitious young officers, and ordinary infantrymen—all of them labeled military advisers by the American command. They fought a distant, "brushfire war" on the edge of American consciousness. Beyond the secret inner circles of government, few predicted that hundreds of thousands would follow in a massive buildup that took the American presence in Vietnam from 15,000 troops in 1964 to 550,000 in 1968. In late 1969 the gradual withdrawal of ground forces began, inching its way to the final U.S. pullout in January 1973. The bell curve of escalation and withdrawal spread the commitment of men into a decade-long chain of one-year tours of duty.

In the years of escalation, as draft calls mounted to 30,000 and 40,000 a month, many young people believed the entire generation might be mobilized for war. There were, of course, many ways to avoid the draft, and millions of men did just that. Very few, however, felt completely confident that they would never be ordered to fight. Perhaps the war would escalate to such a degree or go on so long that all exemptions and deferments would be eliminated. No one could be sure what would happen. Only in retrospect is it clear that the odds of serving in Vietnam were, for many people, really quite small. The forces that fought in Vietnam were drawn from the largest generation of young people in the nation's history. During the years 1964 to 1973, from the Gulf of Tonkin Resolution to the final withdrawal of American troops from Vietnam, 27 million men came of draft age. The 2.5 million men of that generation who went to Vietnam represent less than 10 percent of America's male baby boomers.

The parents of the Vietnam generation had an utterly different experience of war. During World War II virtually all young, able-bodied men entered the service—some 12 million. Personal connections to the military permeated society regardless of class, race, or gender. Almost every family had a close relative overseas—a husband fighting in France, a son in the South Pacific, or at least an uncle with the Seabees, a niece in the WAVES, or a cousin in the Air Corps. These connections continued well into the 1950s. Throughout the Korean War years and for several years after, roughly 70 percent of the draft-age population of men served in the military; but from the 1950s to the 1960s, military service became less and less universal. During the Vietnam years, the portion had dropped to 40 percent: 10 percent were in Vietnam, and 30 percent served in Germany, South Korea, and the dozens of other duty stations in the United States and abroad. What had been, in the 1940s, an experience shared by the vast majority gradually became the experience of a distinct minority.

What kind of minority was it? In modern American culture, *minority* usually serves as a code word for nonwhite races, especially African Americans. To speak of American forces in Vietnam as a minority invites the assumption that blacks, Hispanics, Asian Americans, and Native Americans fought and died in numbers grossly disproportionate to their percentage of the total U.S. population. It is a common assumption, but not one that has been sufficiently examined. For that matter, the whole experience of racial minorities in Vietnam has been woefully ignored by the media and academics. For Hispanics, Asian Americans, and Native Americans, even the most basic statistical information about their role in Vietnam remains either unknown or inadequately examined.

We know how many black soldiers served and died in Vietnam, but the more important task is to interpret those figures in historical context. Without that context, racial disproportions can be either exaggerated or denied. To simplify: At the beginning of the war blacks comprised more than 20 percent of American combat deaths, about twice their portion of the U.S. population. However, the portion of black casualties declined over time so that, for the war as a whole, black casualties were only slightly disproportionate (12.5 percent from a civilian population of 11 percent). The total percentage of blacks who served in Vietnam was roughly 10 percent throughout the war.

African Americans clearly faced more than their fair share of the risks in Vietnam from 1965 to 1967. That fact might well have failed to gain any public notice had the civil rights and antiwar movements not called attention to it. Martin Luther King was probably the most effective in generating concern about the number of black casualties in Vietnam. King had refrained from frequent public criticism of the war until 1967, persuaded by moderates that outspoken opposition to the war might divert energy from the cause of civil rights and alienate prowar politicians whose support the movement sought (President Johnson, for example). By early 1967, however, King believed the time had come to break his silence. As for diverting energy and resources from domestic social reform, King argued, the war itself had already done as much. More importantly, he could not in good conscience remain silent in the face of a war he believed unjust.

King's critique of the war was wide ranging, based on a historical understanding of the long struggle in Vietnam for national independence, on a commitment to nonviolence, and on outrage over the violence the United States was inflicting on the land and people of Indochina. Always central in King's criticism of the war, however, was its effect on America's poor, both black and white. "The promises of the Great Society," he said, "have been shot down on the battlefield of Vietnam." The expense of the war was taking money and support that could be spent to solve problems at home. The war on poverty was being supplanted by the war on Vietnam. Beyond that, King stressed, the poor themselves were doing much of the fighting overseas. As he put it in his famous speech at Riverside Church in New York City (April 1967), the war was not only "devastating the hopes of the poor at home," it was also "sending their sons and their brothers and their husbands to fight and to die in extraordinarily high proportions relative to the rest of the population."

While King focused attention on the economic condition of white and black soldiers, he emphasized the additional burden on blacks of fighting overseas in disproportionate numbers while being denied full citizenship at home: "We have been repeatedly faced with the cruel irony of watching Negro and white boys on TV screens as they kill and die together for a nation that has been unable to seat them together in the same schools. So we watch them in brutal solidarity burning the huts of a poor village, but we realize that they would never live on the same block in Detroit." In another speech he added, "We are willing to make the Negro 100 percent of a citizen in warfare, but reduce him to 50 percent of a citizen on American soil. Half of all Negroes live in substandard housing and he has half the income of white. There is twice as much unemployment and infant mortality among Negroes. [Yet] at the beginning of 1967 twice as many died in action—20.6 percent—in proportion to their numbers in the population as a whole."

In his postwar apologia for U.S. intervention, *America in Vietnam*, Guenter Lewy accused King of heightening racial tension by making false allegations about black casualties in Vietnam. After all, Lewy argued, black casualties for the whole war were 12.5 percent, no higher than the portion of draft-age black males in the total U.S. population. Lewy's charge falls apart, however, as soon as one points out that black casualties did not drop to the overall figure of 12.5 until well after King was assassinated. During the period King and others were articulating their criticisms of the war, the disproportions were quite significant. To attack the antiwar movement for failing to use postwar statistics is not only unfair, it is ahistorical. Moreover, King was by no means the first prominent black to criticize the war or the disproportionate loss of black soldiers. Malcolm X, Muhammad Ali, Adam Clayton Powell, Dick Gregory, John Lewis, and Julian Bond were among those who spoke out repeatedly well before 1967. In fact, had the civil rights movement not brought attention to racial disproportions in Vietnam casualties, those disproportions almost certainly would have continued. According to Commander George L. Jackson, "In response to this criticism the Department of Defense took steps to readjust force levels in order to achieve an equitable proportion and employment of Negroes in Vietnam." A detailed analysis of exactly what steps were taken has yet to be written. It is clear, however, that by late 1967, black casualties had fallen to 13 percent and then to below 10 percent in 1970–72.

Blacks were by no means united in opposition to the war or the military. For generations blacks had been struggling for equal participation in all American institutions, the military included. In World War II the struggle had focused on integration and the "right to fight." Aside from some all-black combat units, most blacks were assigned to segregated, rear-area duty. The military was officially desegregated in 1948, and most blacks served in integrated units in the Korean War. It was the Vietnam War, though, that was hailed in the mass media as America's first truly integrated war. In 1967 and 1968 several magazines and newspapers ran major stories on "the Negro in Vietnam." While disproportionate casualties were mentioned, they were not the target of criticism. Instead, these articles—including a cover story in *Ebony* (August 1968)—emphasized the contributions of black soldiers, their courageous service, and the new opportunities ostensibly provided by wartime duty in an integrated army. The point was often made that blacks had more civil rights in the military than at home. In *Harper's* magazine (June 1967), Whitney Young of the Urban League wrote, "In this war there is a degree of integration among black and white Americans far exceeding that of any other war in our history as well as any other time or place in our domestic life." As Thomas Johnson put it in *Ebony* giving the point an ironic turn, "The Negro has found in his nation's most totalitarian society—the military—the greatest degree of functional democracy that this nation has granted to black people."

Whitney Young justified disproportionate black casualties as the result not of discrimination but of "the simple fact that a higher proportion of Negroes volunteer for hazardous duty." There was some truth to this. In airborne units—the training for which is voluntary—blacks were reported to comprise as much as 30 percent of the combat troops. Moreover, blacks had a reenlistment rate three times higher than whites. It fell dramatically as the war went on, but it was always much higher than that of white soldiers. These points surely suggest that many blacks were highly motivated, enthusiastic troops.

That enthusiasm itself does not prove that the military had equal opportunities for blacks or an absence of discrimination. After all, presumably the same blacks who volunteered for airborne (for which they received additional pay) might just as eagerly have volunteered for officer candidate school had they been offered the chance. Only 2 percent of the officers in Vietnam were black. Blacks might have taken advantage of opportunities to fill higher-paying noncombat positions, had they been offered. The military's response was that blacks were disproportionately enlisted combat soldiers because they were simply not qualified to fill other jobs. Of course, qualifications are determined by the crudest measurement—standardized tests—and black soldiers scored significantly lower than whites. In 1965, for example, 41 percent of black soldiers scored in the lowest levels of the Armed Forces Qualification Test (categories IV and V), compared to 10 percent of the white soldiers.

These scores account for much of the disproportion. To that extent they reflect the relationship of race and class in civilian society. Poor and working-class soldiers, whether black or white, were more likely to be trained for combat than were soldiers economically and educationally more advantaged. While enlisted men of both races were primarily from the bottom half of the social structure, blacks were considerably poorer. One study found that 90 percent of black soldiers in Vietnam were from working-class and poor backgrounds. This is a large part of the reason why more blacks reenlisted. Men who reenlisted were given bonuses of $900 to $1,400, equivalent to one-third of the median family income for black families in the mid-1960s. However, the military's assignment of blacks to low-ranking positions was not simply a reflection of the economic and racial inequalities of civilian society. The military contributed its own discrimination. In the first years of American escalation, even those blacks who scored in the highest test category were placed in combat units at a level 75 percent higher than that of whites in the same category.

Though racial discrimination and racist attitudes surely persisted in the military, class was far more important than race in determining the overall social composition of American forces. Precisely when the enlisted ranks were becoming increasingly integrated by race, they were becoming ever more segregated by class. The military may never have been truly representative of the general male population, but in the 1960s it was overwhelmingly the domain of the working class.

No thorough statistical study has yet been conducted on the class origins of the men who served in Vietnam. Though the military made endless, mind-numbing efforts to quantify virtually every aspect of its venture in Vietnam, it did not make (so far as anyone has discovered) a single study of the social backgrounds of its fighting men. Quantitative evidence must be gathered from a variety of disparate studies. Probably the most ambitious effort to gather statistical information about the backgrounds of Vietnam-era soldiers was conducted just prior to the large-scale American escalation. In 1964 the National Opinion Research Center (NORC) surveyed 5 percent of all active-duty enlisted men.

According to NORC's occupational survey (Table 1) roughly 20 percent of American enlisted men had fathers with white-collar jobs. Among the male population as a whole more than twice that portion, 44 percent, were white-collar workers. Of course, not all white-collar jobs are necessarily middle class in the income, power, and status they confer. Many low-paying clerical and sales jobs—typically listed as white collar—are more accurately understood as working-class occupations. While the white-collar label exaggerates the size of the middle class, it nonetheless encompasses almost all privileged Americans in the labor force. Thus, the fact that only 20 percent of U.S. soldiers came from white-collar families represents a striking class difference between the military and the general population.

Table 1. Occupations of Fathers of Enlisted Men, by Service, 1964 (Percent)

Father's Occupation	Army	Navy	Air Force	Marines
White-collar	17.0	19.8	20.9	20.4
Blue-collar	52.8	54.5	52.0	57.2
Farmer	14.8	10.7	13.3	9.1
Military	1.8	2.1	1.8	2.0
Father absent	13.6	12.9	12.0	11.3
(Approx. N)	(28,000)	(17,500)	(28,000)	(5,000)

Source: 1964 NORC survey, in Charles C. Moskos, *The American Enlisted Man: The Rank and File in Today's Military* (New York: Russell Sage Foundation, 1970), p. 195.

The high portion of farmers in the sample is a further indication of the disproportionate number of soldiers from rural small towns. In the 1960s only about 5 percent of the American labor force was engaged in agriculture. In the NORC survey, more than twice as many, 12 percent, came from farm families. Though the survey does not reveal the economic standing of this group, we should avoid an American tendency to picture all farmers as independent proprietors. At the time of the survey about two-thirds of the workers engaged in agricultural labor were wage earners (farm laborers or migrant farmworkers) with family incomes less than $1,000 per year.

There is also a good reason to believe that most of the men with absent fathers grew up in hard-pressed circumstances. In 1965, almost two-thirds of the children in female-headed families lived below the census bureau's low-income level. All told, the NORC survey suggests that on the brink of the Vietnam escalation at least three-quarters of American enlisted men were working class or poor. . . .

The inclusion of officers would not dramatically raise the overall class backgrounds of the Vietnam military. Officers comprised 11 percent of the total number of men in Vietnam, so even if many of them were from privileged families, the statistical impact would be limited. Furthermore, though we need further studies of the social backgrounds of the Vietnam-era officer corps, it may well have been the least privileged officer corps of the twentieth century. For example, in his study of the West Point class of 1966, Rick Atkinson found a striking historical decline in the class backgrounds of cadets. "Before World War I, the academy had drawn nearly a third of the corps from the families of doctors, lawyers, and other professionals. But by the mid 1950s, sons of professionals made up only 10 percent of the cadets, and links to the upper class had been almost severed. West Point increasingly attracted military brats and sons of the working class." Also, as the war dragged on, the officer corps was depleted of service school and ROTC [Reserve Officers' Training Corps] graduates and had to rely increasingly on enlisted men who were given temporary field commissions or sent to officer candidate school. These officers, too, probably lowered the class background of the officer corps.

Class inequality is also strikingly revealed in the most important post-war statistical study of Vietnam veterans, *Legacies of Vietnam*. Commissioned by the Veterans' Administration in 1978, about two-thirds of the *Legacies* sample of Vietnam veterans was working class or below. That figure is remarkable because the survey used sampling techniques designed to produce the widest possible class spectrum; that is, in choosing people for the study it sought a "maximum variation in socioeconomic context." Even so, the sample of Vietnam veterans was well below the general population in its class composition. When measured against backgrounds of nonveterans of the same generation, Vietnam veterans came out on the bottom in income, occupation, and education.

The key here is disproportion. The point is not that *all* working-class men went to Vietnam while everyone better off stayed home. Given the enormous size of the generation, millions of working-class men simply were not needed by the military. Many were exempted because they failed to meet the minimum physical or mental standards of the armed forces. However, the odds of working-class men going into the military and on to Vietnam were far higher than they were for the middle class and the privileged.

The *Legacies* study also suggests an important distinction between black and white soldiers. The black veterans, at least in this sample, were significantly more representative of the entire black population than white veterans were of the white population. This reflects the fact that whites and blacks have different class distributions, with blacks having a much larger portion of poor and working people and a much smaller middle class and elite. In the *Legacies* sample, 82 percent of black nonveterans were working class and below, compared with 47 percent of the white nonveterans. In other words, while black soldiers were still, as a group, poorer than white soldiers, in relationship to the class structure of their respective races, blacks were not as disproportionately poor and working class as whites. This is, I think, one reason why black veterans seem to have less class-based resentment than white veterans toward the men of their race who did not serve in Vietnam.

Table 2. Educational Attainment of Vietnam Veterans at Time of Separation from the Armed Forces, 1966–1971 (Percent)

Fiscal year	Less than 12 Years of School	12 Years of School	1 to 3 Years of College	4 or More Years of College
1966	22.9	62.5	8.3	6.3
1967	23.6	61.8	9.0	5.6
1968	19.6	65.5	9.7	6.2
1969	18.3	60.0	15.9	5.8
1970	17.5	56.9	17.0	8.6
1971	14.7	55.4	19.4	10.5
Total, 1966–71	19.4	60.3	13.2	7.2

Source: Reports and Statistics Service, Office of Controller, Veterans' Administration, 11 April 1972, in John Helmer, *Bringing the War Home: The American Soldier in Vietnam and After* (New York: Free Press, 1974), p. 303.

Education, along with occupation and income, is a key measure of class position. Eighty percent of the men who went to Vietnam had no more than a high school education (Table 2). This figure would compare well to statistics of some previous wars. After all, at the time of the Civil War and well into the twentieth century, only a small minority of Americans had high school educations. However, if considered in historical context, the low portion of college educated among American soldiers is yet another indication of the disproportionately working-class composition of the military. The 1960s was a boomtime for American education, a time when opportunities for higher education were more widespread than ever before. By 1965, 45 percent of Americans between eighteen and twenty-one had some college education. By 1970 that figure was more than 50 percent. Compared with national standards, American forces were well below average in formal education. Studies matching school enrollments to age and class show that the educational levels of American soldiers in Vietnam correspond roughly to those of draft-age, blue-collar males in the general population (Table 3). Of course, many veterans took college courses after their military service. However, the *Legacies* study found that by 1981 only 22 percent of veterans had completed college compared with 46 percent of nonveterans.

Table 3. Percentage of Males Enrolled in School, 1965–1970

Age	Blue-Collar	White-Collar
16–17	80	92
18–19	49	73
20–24	20	43

Source: Andrew Levison, *The Working-Class Majority* (New York: Penguin Books, 1974), p. 121.

The portion of soldiers with at least some college education increased significantly in the late 1960s as draft calls increased and most graduate school deferments ended. By 1970 roughly 25 percent of American forces in Vietnam had some college education. Impressive as this increase was, it still fell well below the 50 percent for the age group as a whole, and it came as American troop levels in Vietnam were beginning to drop. Moreover, college education per se was no longer so clear a mark of privilege as it had been prior to World War II. Higher education in the post-World War II era expanded enormously, especially among junior and state colleges, the kinds of schools that enrolled the greatest number of working-class students. Between 1962 and 1972, enrollments in two-year colleges tripled. College students who went to Vietnam were far more likely to come from these institutions than from elite, four-year, private colleges. A survey of Harvard's class of 1970, for example, found only two men who served in Vietnam. College students who did go to Vietnam usually secured noncombat assignments. Among soldiers in Vietnam, high school dropouts were three times more likely to experience heavy combat than were college graduates.

Young men have fought in all wars, but U.S. forces in Vietnam were probably, on average, the youngest in our history. In previous wars many men in their twenties were drafted for military service, and men of that age and older often volunteered. During the Vietnam War most of the volunteers and draftees were teenagers; the average age was nineteen. In World War II, by contrast, the average American soldier was twenty-six years old. At age eighteen young men could join or be drafted into the army. At seventeen, with the consent of a guardian, boys could enlist in the Marine Corps. Early in the war, hundreds of seventeen-year-old marines served in Vietnam. In November 1965 the Pentagon ordered that all American troops must be eighteen before being deployed in the war zone. Even so, the average age remained low. Twenty-two-year-old soldiers were often kidded about their advanced age ("hey, old man") by the younger men in their units. Most American troops were not even old enough to vote. The voting age did not drop from twenty-one to eighteen until 1971. Thus, most of the Americans who fought in Vietnam were powerless, working-class teenagers sent to fight an undeclared war by presidents for whom they were not even eligible to vote.

No statistical profile can do justice to the complexity of individual experience, but without these broad outlines our understanding would be hopelessly fragmented. A class breakdown of American forces cannot be absolutely precise, but I believe the following is a reasonable estimate: enlisted ranks in Vietnam were comprised of about 25 percent poor, 55 percent working class, and 20 percent middle class, with a statistically negligible number of wealthy. Most Americans in Vietnam were nineteen-year-old high school graduates. They grew up in the white, working-class enclaves of South Boston and Cleveland's West Side; in the black ghettos of Detroit and Birmingham; in the small rural towns of Oklahoma and Iowa; and in the housing developments of working-class suburbs. They came by the thousands from every state and every U.S. territory, but few were from places of wealth and privilege.

34
Seeds of a Movement
TOM WELLS

In late December [1964] members of the Young Socialist Alliance (YSA), the youth group of the Socialist Workers Party, met in Chicago for their national convention. The YSA and SWP would come to play major roles in the anti-Vietnam War movement in the years ahead. At this time, however, the YSA "paid no special attention to Vietnam." It would continue to emphasize "general socialist education" focused on, as the YSA leader Lew Jones later remembered, "whatever issue we could get our hands on." Many of the conventioneers knew little about the war in any event. Some may not even have known where Vietnam was.

Simultaneously, the National Council (NC) of the Students for a Democratic Society, a politically diverse left-leaning organization, was gathered in the venerable meeting hall of the Cloakmakers' Union in New York. Before getting to the tasks at hand, the SDSers seized a large portrait of Lyndon Johnson gawking at them from a wall and turned it around. It was late afternoon by the time Todd Gitlin, SDS's co-point man on international issues with Paul Booth, proposed that the organization write and circulate a "We Won't Go" antidraft statement to protest the growing U.S. intervention in Vietnam. The war was not the main political issue on Gitlin's mind at this time (he was more concerned with U.S. funding of South African apartheid), but he felt *something* had to be done about it, and he and Booth had even invited the progressive journalist I. F. Stone to speak to the NC the evening before to rouse indignation over the issue.

Gitlin's proposal failed to take hold, as did another to send medical supplies to the National Liberation Front (NLF) in South Vietnam. They seemed a bit too radical to some, even pro-communist. Jim Brook, a liberal SDSer, weighed in with a proposal to hold an April march against the war in Washington. The objections came fast and steady. Despite the fact that they were licking their wounds from a sobering summer in the ghettos, the many SDSers then bent on building "community unions" of the urban poor argued vehemently that antiwar protest was too centered on a single issue and not where the radical action was. Furthermore, it might alienate their constituents, more than a few of whom seemed hawkish on Vietnam. SDSers also opposed Brook's proposal on tactical grounds. Impressed by the grass-roots organizing in the South of the Student Nonviolent Coordinating Committee (SNCC), many felt large marches tended to stall local political motion, usurp inordinate amounts of time, energy, and resources, leave no lasting impact on their participants, and bring paltry political returns. "The past few years . . . have shown the government to be increasingly unresponsive to public mass protest," wrote two SDSers. "Even when concessions in legislation or public policy are granted, the concessions are generally sufficient to make the marcher, but not the grievances or problems, go away." The result, often enough, was "demoralization." SDSers also maintained that national marches tended to target specific government policies without challenging the "undemocratic" manner in which those policies were made. As Clark Kissinger, who was then SDS's national secretary, would recall, "There was a tendency to write national marches off on the basis of just the nature of the tactic alone without coming to grips with the political content of them and the role that they can play if they're done right." The 1963 March on Washington for Jobs and Freedom led by the Reverend Martin Luther King, Jr., was responsible for much of the antimarch sentiment inside SDS. It seemed to many activists to have been little more than an Establishment-led legislative exercise that had derailed local civil rights activity. "There was a real bad taste coming off the 1963 march," Kissinger said.

Come late evening, during a lull in the NC debate—and when a number of community organizers were out of the room—Brook's proposal squeaked by. The march's public appeal, the NC decided, would be gut-level: "SDS advocates that the U.S. get out of Vietnam for the following reasons: (a) the war hurts the Vietnamese people, (b) the war hurts the American people, (c) SDS is concerned about the Vietnamese and American people." SDS would be the event's sole organizational sponsor, but any group was welcome to participate. The first national action against the war was now in the works.

Carl Oglesby was a newcomer to SDS at the time of the group's meeting. When I met him years later, he was a freelance writer in Cambridge, Massachusetts. A slender, bespectacled man with gray-brown hair, a rough complexion, and a short beard, he looked younger than his fifty-one years. He spoke eloquently and effusively. In the fall of 1964, Oglesby was running the technical publications department of a major military contractor in Ann Arbor, Michigan. He commanded a sizable army of workers and was leading "a very high-powered bourgeois life-style." "I had a little red car, and my wife had a little blue car, and we jollied around town," Oglesby recalled. That November, an open letter he had written beseeching a newly elected local congressman to denounce the war was published in the University of Michigan's literary magazine. It quickly caught the alert eyes of local SDSers. Wondering why they had never heard of this guy Oglesby before, this articulate critic of the war living smack dab in their own backyard (surely they knew all the radicals around), they called him up. Two SDSers then "came out on a motorcycle in a couple of minutes and we wound up rapping the whole evening about SDS and change and politics and the country," Oglesby remembered. "I right away felt a real kinship with SDS people."

Oglesby was turned on by these "whippersnapper middle-class white kids" and decided to go to an SDS meeting. He was impressed by what he observed there:

> That was the best debate I ever heard. . . . That was an amazing meeting. I had never been around a bunch of people who were so smart and who were so sincere, in the sense that they listened to each other and they actually tried to meet one another's points. You could even see people have their minds changed because somebody showed them a reason or a fact that they hadn't known about. . . . And I was personally persuaded at that meeting, by that debate, that instead of coming into SDS as a director of research or some such thing, I should come into SDS as a community organizer and come with my wife and kids to live in Boston, in Roxbury, where we had a project.

Why community organizing? The "analysis," as Oglesby reconstructed it, was relatively simple. Since the path to change was through the Democratic Party, argued Tom Hayden and other SDSers, student activists had to build a base inside the party by organizing a new constituency. The urban poor were a logical target group for radicals inspired by SNCC's work among the downtrodden, particularly those convinced that economic trends would soon bloat the ranks of the poor. If impoverished whites and blacks could be mobilized together, the theory went, they would overcome the racial anxieties and hostilities then restraining the growth of a powerful "interracial movement of the poor." Many SDSers contended that such a movement was the only vehicle capable of wielding the political clout necessary to stop the war. SDS would halt "the seventh war from now," one offered.

Ghetto organizing also had romantic appeal. Many SDSers sentimentalized poverty. Whenever a community organizer would rise from his indigent element and drift into a meeting—soiled t-shirt, jeans, work boots, Marlboros, and all—"there would always be 'ooohhs' and 'aaahhs' and great deference, as though we were being visited by royalty," Oglesby recalled. " 'Hey, a real person is coming in.' . . . You could tell he was real, he pinched all the girls' asses, and the girls would put up with it from the working-class guy because they knew he didn't know any better, right?, whereas from their true class brothers they would never tolerate this kind of behavior." SDS's "cult of the ghetto" was "slightly sick," one SDSer deduced.

According to the community organizers, then, SDS had to leave the campuses behind. Oglesby:

> The Tom Hayden program . . . meant students are not really that important. Students are debaters and debate is not important. Tom always is an anti-intellectual. He is now and he was then. He never had respect for the academic situation as such. To him it was in certain respects a necessary way station—you had to go there, you had to pass through it—but if you were going to grow as a person and mature as a political figure you had to put it behind you. You couldn't play around in the sandbox. . . . [Hayden] wanted to get students to drop out of school and go off to some ghetto in a big city far from home, live with cockroaches and racial torment and the agonies of poverty, and in that way try to blend into the community—in which they would, in fact, stand out like so many sore thumbs.

Although poised to mingle with cockroaches, Oglesby was a bit skeptical about the returns. The poor's "alienation" from the American political process struck him as more of an "obstacle" than a spur to political action. "They weren't people who tended to think of themselves as involved anyway," he said. "It wasn't their city, it wasn't their state, it wasn't their America—it was somebody else's." But middle-class people, Oglesby thought, "identified with the state or the government, they saw it as theirs, they felt like it should be responsive to them." Their expectations seemed to him "a powerful source of resistance to an administration that lied and deceived."

SDS's veteran community organizers were by then pessimistic themselves. During gloomy meetings in early January, they conceded that no interracial movement of the poor was going to arise soon. By late summer SDS's community organizing venture had proven "a failure."

Preparations for the spring peace march began immediately after the December NC meeting. Most SDSers were not expecting an earthshaking event. [Clark] Kissinger remembered that when he took the liberty of chartering a train to transport people to Washington "everybody else on the national committee almost had a fit, because they thought we'd be paying it off for the rest of our lives." Two to three thousand might show up if things went well. Todd Gitlin was feeling "doomed." Given the government's "enormous commitment to the war" and "so little opposition to it," he brooded, the fighting in Vietnam would probably drag on "for a very long time." "It felt to me simply a matter of existential ethics to do what you could [to stop the war], but without any great expectations," he recalled.

SDS sent out letters inviting all progressive political organizations to join the march. Most hedged. America's prominent peace groups—SANE [Committee for a Sane Nuclear Policy], Student Peace Union, Women's International League for Peace and Freedom, Turn Toward Peace, Committee for Nonviolent Action, War Resisters League, Fellowship of Reconciliation—simply ignored this bid to protest their government's violence in Vietnam. They were irritated that SDS had assumed sole sponsorship and failed to offer alternative U.S. policies in Vietnam. Most disturbing, its non-exclusionary policy meant that communists would be on the scene (including the Communist Party's youth group, the Du Bois Clubs, whose name sounded so much like the Boys Club that the vigilant Richard Nixon called it "an almost classic example of communist deception and duplicity"); amid continuing Cold War fever at home, the antiwar groups perceived, cavorting with communists would be the peace movement's "kiss of death." The Du Bois Clubs and May 2nd Movement immediately expressed interest in the march, however. So did the Socialist Workers Party—in more ways than one.

Peter Camejo was then a major SWP leader. In 1986, when I met him, he was the president of Progressive Asset Management, a broker-dealership in Oakland, California, specializing in "socially responsible" investments. He had remained a radical and was still active in various political causes. Camejo left the SWP in 1981 after a nearly thirty-year association because of growing "sectarian" and "dogmatic" behavior by the organization. "I began to have doubts about our ability to work with anybody," he told me, likening his SWP days to living in a religious sect. "I *totally* believed that the SWP had all the answers to all questions. I was a *cultist* of the SWP." Camejo said SDS's call for the April peace march was the "decisive turning point" in the SWP's political trajectory during the war. The SWP promptly began flooding existing local antiwar committees and organizing new ones. "Our position was to go into the antiwar committees . . . and propose that they declare against both the Democrats and Republicans," Camejo remembered. "This was very sectarian, because that wasn't the issue—the issue was to unite people who opposed the war."

The SWP sensed that a national movement might take hold and wanted to build it not only for the purpose of stopping the war but also to radicalize the American people as a stepping-stone on the path to socialist revolution, its ultimate goal. Since the Democratic and Republic parties were both "parties of the ruling class" that sold the capitalist system to the public according to the SWP, they had to be attacked. A national movement would also be fertile ground for recruiting new SWP members. "You know, we can build an organization of eight hundred to a thousand people off of this," Camejo told himself, gazing out a window in the SWP's national office in New York and licking his chops over the march's enlistment possibilities. ("That's how small we were thinking at the time," he would exclaim years later.) In Clark Kissinger's words, the SWP "perceived immediately when we said we were willing to do [the march] on a nonexclusionary basis that this was their big opportunity."

The SWPers' naked recruitment goals would soon anger large segments of the peace movement and fuel internal tensions. "They clearly put the recruiting of members above the issue of ending the war," the War Resister League Leader David McReynolds recalled.

Several months later, the SWP dropped its insistence that local antiwar committees denounce America's two bourgeois parties. Instead, they should simply demand "U.S. Out of Vietnam Now!" More significant, the SWP decided that by far the most effective antiwar activity was organizing large, legal demonstrations. Since most Americans were more likely to join a legal demonstration than more militant forms of protest, the SWP reasoned, that tactic would maximize the movement's size. "Our whole approach was focused on trying to find forms of activity that could be understood by the average working person and would seem possible for them to participate in when they reached the point of beginning to question the war," the later YSA leader Don Gurewitz remembered.

The SWP also believed that large demonstrations would be most likely to convince silent skeptics about the war that they were not alone; many would then voice their concerns. "Most people hear the media and think, 'I'm the only one who's doubting,' or, 'There's very few of us,'" Camejo explained. "And people in governmental power, from Johnson all the way to Nixon, continuously tried to emphasize that the opposition was a tiny minority. Our theory was that if a million people went into the streets that you would break that." The SWP also felt the government was more likely to respond to large protests than small ones. They demonstrated broader public opposition and threatened widespread upheaval. With small protests, officials "don't feel the pressure," Camejo said.

The SWP's robotlike promotion of mass demonstrations was to become its main badge of identity in the peace movement. Inside the SWP, the position assumed divine truth. Camejo remembered:

> It became like fundamental religious dogma that you were for single-issue, peaceful, legal demonstrations. And there were very few questioning it. We would pound away at this inside the SWP. Because, you see, it was the cutting edge. When new people came around to be in the Vietnam War movement in general, SWPers would explain why this is the key, and on that basis they would recruit. . . . So that was *a, b, c, d.* I mean, that was pounded away over and over and over again. . . . You wouldn't join the SWP unless you agreed with that. It was sort of like a definition of membership.

It was a definition other activists would come to know all too well. . . .

Three weeks before the Marines were turned loose [in March 1965 to engage in offensive operations rather than merely guard base areas], thirty faculty members at the University of Michigan gathered to plan an expression of opposition to the war. Present were many familiar faces, "veterans of a string of advertisements for the test ban, for a fair housing ordinance, for the election of Lyndon B. Johnson." They felt "betrayed." Their peace candidate, the man who had promised no wider war, had blood all over his hands. And they felt desperate. Despite preparing countless newspaper advertisements and letters to government officials protesting the bombings, the horror in Vietnam had only mounted. The State Department had had the gall to treat them like children: it answered their letters with pamphlets explaining the diabolical nature of communism illustrated by a leering [Nikita] Khrushchev.

The sociology professor William Gamson rose to speak. The situation in Vietnam was too grave to continue treading the old tired ground, he said. Ads and letters just wouldn't do anymore. Gamson proposed that the group organize a one-day faculty moratorium on teaching-as-usual and transform the university into a massive classroom on the war. Nearly fifty faculty members signed a petition supporting the plan.

On March 16, a group of nervous signers met to reconsider. Michigan's faculty senate was discussing censure, deans were up in arms, the governor and legislators were hollering for disciplinary action. The anthropologist Marshall Sahlins suggested that, instead of holding a strike, teachers conduct their classes during the day and hold sessions on the war at night—all night. The Michigan organizers ultimately agreed on the all-night format, although some believed "that we were making a very bad mistake." The detractors felt that the time for polite academic give-and-take was gone; to them the move reeked of retreat. Worse, they thought few would show up for a nocturnal educational experience. "We thought, 'Sure, a few hundred, that would be good,'" Carl Oglesby recalled. With the switch to the evening design, however, university administrators, relieved that the brouhaha was over, virtually began promoting the event.

"They fell all over themselves trying to cooperate with us," Oglesby remembered. Faculty and student interest skyrocketed.

On the evening of March 24, over three thousand people showed up on the Ann Arbor campus for the nation's first "teach-in" on the war. Lectures and debates ran until 8 A.M., despite a midnight bomb threat that temporarily forced people outside into 20° F weather (where they held a rally). Exchanges were both reasoned and passionate. "Facts were demanded and assumptions were exposed," one participant wrote. "On that night, people who really cared talked of things that really mattered." Hierarchical relations between faculty and students received a stiff jolt; students locked horns with professors whose classes they had hardly spoken in. Opponents of the war gained valuable social support, inciting many to plan future protests. Prowar participants were asked to explain their positions; some began questioning their allegiances. "It was such a powerful event," Oglesby fervently recalled. The campus was now alive with debate on Vietnam. It was impossible to avoid the controversy whether one wanted to or not.

During the rest of the spring, teach-ins spread like wildfire across America's campuses. Over a hundred took place. The "stroke of genius out there in Michigan . . . put the debate on the map for the whole academic community," Oglesby said. "And you could not be an intellectual after those teach-ins and not think a lot and express yourself and defend your ideas about Vietnam." With the surprising success of the Michigan teach-in, his own "faith in students and the academic situation and the importance of directly organizing on Vietnam was switched back, it came alive again, and from that time on there was never any real thought of my . . . coming to Boston to do community organizing."

The grandest of the teach-ins took place at the University of California in Berkeley. Two graduate students, Jerry Rubin and Barbara Gullahorn, had initially proposed the event to Stephen Smale, a mathematics professor and teachers' union activist. "The idea was to do something really big and exciting and very exceptional," Smale would recall. "To make it a very memorable kind of event." More than thirty thousand people participated in the 36-hour marathon, perhaps twelve thousand at one time. Some barely missed a beat. "I arrived there at the beginning and didn't leave until it was over," Marilyn Milligan recounted. "I was just totally taken by that teach-in, totally engaged. . . . I just didn't want to leave at all. We were there and that was it." Before wearily trudging home, Milligan signed up to work with the teach-in's sponsor, the Vietnam Day Committee. She would shortly assume a leadership role in that organization.

The escalation of the war also fueled interest in the April SDS march. Besieged with requests for information on it, SDS organizers shifted into high gear. "We just rolled over the whole antiwar movement," Paul Booth said afterward—"they had never seen anything like this." Even activists with the old peace groups expressed interest. Estimates of attendance surged toward fifteen thousand.

The White House was less enthusiastic about the protest. Thousands of peaceniks parading around Washington would hardly keep the war out of the public spotlight, officials knew. The march might also give the North Vietnamese the wrong impression about the American public's enthusiasm for the war, thereby encouraging them. On April 14, McGeorge Bundy mentioned the upcoming "left-wing student protest" to Johnson and counseled, "A strong peaceloving statement tomorrow or Friday might help cool them off ahead of time." No statement was forthcoming.

April 17 was a gorgeous spring day. By early afternoon, twenty thousand people were gathered at the Washington Monument. Most were students. There were also many adults, including Communist Party members marching under their own banner for the first time since the birth of McCarthyism. The highlight of the afternoon was a moving closing speech by SDS's 25-year-old president, Paul Potter. The war, Potter declared, "has provided the razor, the terrifying sharp cutting edge that has finally severed the last vestige of illusion that morality and democracy are the guiding principles of American foreign policy." "What kind of system" allowed "good men" to work such evil? he asked. "We must name that system. We must name it, describe it, analyze it, understand it and change it." Despite pleas from the crowed to go ahead and name that system, Potter abstained. SDS's leaders feared that using the word *capitalism* would provoke more red-baiting and had earlier decided "to leave it as a mystery as to whether or not there was a capitalist system in the United States," Booth wryly recalled.

Not everyone in the crowd was enraptured by Potter's testimony. In fact, not everyone was there to protest the war. The sun was shining, the cherry trees were blossoming—love was in the air. Daniel Ellsberg, a Defense Department official, arrived on the scene with his attention focused on one Patricia Marx. Ellsberg had been admiring Marx for some time now and several days earlier had gathered the fortitude to call her up to ask for a date. He was thinking about Saturday, he had said, the first Saturday he would have off since staring work at the Pentagon the previous August. Unfortunately, Marx responded, she already had plans to go to the SDS demonstration, partly because she opposed the war, but also to conduct interviews for her public radio program in New York. She had plans to interview I. F. Stone, for instance. But she would be pleased if he would accompany her. Ellsberg suddenly felt a little dizzy. He *supported* America's "commitment" in Vietnam and had even helped produce the White Paper that Stone had so mercilessly demolished. "You *can't* ask me to take my first day off from the Pentagon to go to an antiwar rally!" he stammered, incredulous. Yes, she could. Ellsberg donned marching shoes. He even lugged Marx's bulky tape recorder around for the day. Ellsberg later made no bones that he "never would have gone" to the demonstration had it not been for the lure of romance. He married Marx in 1970.

Following Potter's speech, the crowd swept down the mall toward the Capitol. Youths wearing gas masks led the charge. Despite SDS's dislike of marches as a pressure tactic, the protesters planned to deliver to Congress a petition demanding an end to the war. Along the way, their exuberant mood began to hint of "something darker." Reaching a wall of police near the Capitol steps, a barrier through which only a few were ticketed to pass, a chorus of voices rang out, "Let's all go. LET'S ALL GO." According to one marcher, "it seemed that the great mass of people would simply flow on through and over the marble buildings, that our forward motion was irresistibly strong, and that even had some been shot or arrested, nothing could have stopped that crowd from taking possession of its government."

But it was not to be. No more than several hundred demonstrators proceeded up the Capitol steps. Many went home frustrated. The war makers would not heed legal demonstrations, they believed; militant civil disobedience was required to move murderers.

The feeling would grow.

Lyndon Johnson avoided the protest by spending the weekend at his ranch in Texas. In the face of a 400-strong picket led by SDSers at the front gate, he undoubtedly took solace from an earlier note from an aide, Marvin Watson, that twenty-two Secret Service agents would be on hand to protect him from the "so-called demonstrators."

The sudden outpouring of antiwar protest in the spring of 1965 struck a nerve in the American Establishment. James Reston, that titan of U.S. journalism, complained that many teach-ins had rejected "serious intellectual inquiry" for "propaganda of the most vicious nature. . . . This is no longer a casual form of campus spring fever." C. L. Sulzberger, a foreign affairs columnist for the *New York Times*, detected "a strange lemming instinct" among the protesters; they "refuse," he lamented, "to see the struggle in its true meaning as advertised quite openly by the Communists themselves: a showdown with global implications." In the early fall, Senator Thomas Dodd (D-Conn.) apprised the nation that the peace movement was under the control of "pseudo-Americans," soldiers in a "massive psychological warfare attack" on the war by the global "Communist apparatus." Dodd expressed the hope that his revelations would "assist loyal critics of Administration policy to purge their ranks of the Communists and crypto-Communists" so that debate on Vietnam could be restricted to "honest men."

Administration officials were the most agitated. On April 23, Dean Rusk abruptly departed from a prepared speech to take a shot at the war's opponents. "I continue to hear and see nonsense about the nature of the struggle" in Vietnam, commented the secretary of state. "I sometimes wonder at the gullibility of educated men and the stubborn disregard of plain facts by men who are supposed to be helping our young to learn." When a group of religious demonstrators publicly voiced their dissatisfaction with a meeting they'd held with Robert McNamara, Assistant Secretary Arthur Sylvester muttered angrily, "Only church people would do what you are doing." Johnson hit the roof when the poet Robert Lowell announced in early June that he was boycotting the White House Festival of the Arts to protest the war. "The roar in the Oval Office could be heard all the way into the East Wing," one White House staffer recorded. After other prominent American writers and artists declared their support for Lowell's stand, the president ranted about the "sonsofbitches" who had turned his perfectly decent cultural celebration into a goddamn platform on Vietnam. "None of us realized . . . the tawdry lengths that some people would go to in impoliteness and incivility," Jack Valenti, a White House aide, remarked later. Valenti exclaimed that he'd "never met a man with less civility, with less sense of good judgment about how you handle yourself when you're a guest in somebody's house" than the writer Dwight MacDonald, who circulated an antiwar petition at the festival. MacDonald, he gibed, "needed to gargle with Lavoris." Following the festival, Johnson determined that all future White House guests would have to receive FBI clearances. This type of thing led the presidential aides Richard Goodwin and Bill Moyers to conclude in alarm that Johnson was literally suffering from "paranoid disintegration." The war, public opposition to it and other developments seemingly out of Johnson's control were triggering frequent "irrational outbursts" and "unacceptable orders," Goodwin recalled. Listening to one bizarre tirade from the president, Moyers "felt weird, almost felt as if he wasn't really talking to a human being at all."

McGeorge Bundy, a former Harvard dean, exhibited an icy disdain for antiwar academics. "I cannot honestly tell you that I think your letter reflects great credit on its authors, either as a piece of propaganda or as a serious effort to engage in discussion," he told one correspondent from the teach-in movement. "If your letter came to me for grading as a professor of government, I would not be able to give it high marks." To a critic from the *Harvard Crimson*, Bundy acidly commented, "No useful purpose is served by assuming that Dr. Strangelove is in charge here."

Years later, Bundy was a professor of history at New York University, having received his professorship in 1979 over the objection of two dozen professors there that he had helped prosecute a war of "genocide" against the Vietnamese people. He subsequently said "I wish we had quit" the war before he left the government in 1966. A haughty man of privileged lineage, with a flint-sharp mind, caustic tongue, and little patience for lesser beings, Bundy could be particularly frosty on the subject of Vietnam, often refusing even to discuss the issue (although one journalist who interviewed him on the arms race, forewarned that he wouldn't touch Vietnam, got him talking about it after "a couple of tall Scotches"). When I interviewed him, Bundy was visibly defensive about the war, answering many queries with curt statements of little substantive content. He also exhibited remarkably persistent memory lapses. When asked about his expectations in early 1965 about future domestic opposition to the war, however, Bundy acted like a man eager to make an admission. He acknowledged that the spring upsurge in antiwar sentiment caught the administration off guard:

> I think that we were not paying a great deal of attention to what one thinks of now, looking back on it, as the "protest," or the people who were against the war from the beginning, largely out of their own perceptions of who were the good guys and who were the bad guys. And I think we underestimated the degree to which there had been a revival of what called itself the "New Left." So I think we weren't thinking very much about that. And I remember myself being somewhat surprised by the level of student and academic protest in the spring and summer of 1965. . . .
>
> My own encounter with direct opposition to the war came in [two teach-ins in June]. . . . It was all very sober and careful and well-behaved on both sides, but it did represent a kind of opposition that, even then was, I think, stronger than I would have predicted six months earlier. And in that sense . . . I think we were not fully alert to the way the country was going to see the matter.

William Bundy emphasized that administration officials were "very definitely . . . concerned about" the spring antiwar protests. Sitting in a barren room at the Council on Foreign Relations' New York office, the tall, drawn, proud Bundy recalled, "What the arguments of that period revealed—and we should have acted on it much sooner than we did—was how much of the past history was understood in . . . a misleading fashion." For example, teach-in speakers were claiming that the United States had reneged on the 1954 Geneva Peace Accords on the war by refusing to implement their provision for democratic elections in South Vietnam in 1956; Bundy and other officials knew the United States had only *pledged* to uphold the Accords, however, not actually signed them. The protesters were also arguing that the revolution in South Vietnam was home-grown, but Bundy and his colleagues were persuaded by intelligence reports that Hanoi was pulling the strings. And the protesters were alleging that Ngo Dinh Diem, the mystic whom the United States installed as president of South Vietnam in 1954 after it assumed France's colonial role in Vietnam and who died in a U.S.-backed coup in 1963, was "a terrible character," Bundy derisively recalled, who had tortured and killed his political opponents; yet officials had no doubt worse nastiness would be in store if the communists took over. "A great deal of arguments that we had long known existed and discarded and never thought needed to be reargued suddenly came to the surface," Bundy said. The White Paper and other administration propaganda just "hadn't made the case" for the war, he lamented. "We discovered tremendous weaknesses in the way the thing was understood. People really hadn't focused on it before we started the bombing. An awful lot of people hadn't been paying any attention and hadn't seen how critical the situation was becoming. This was true of somebody like Arthur Schlesinger, for example, who spent 1964 and 1965 writing his book on Kennedy and, as it were, came out of the cave and looked around and said, 'Gee whiz, look what happened'—and turned into an opponent of the war."

Feeble or not, however, realized officials, the protesters' arguments were influencing others. "Articulate critics" of the war from the universities and churches "have stimulated extensive worry and inquiry in the nation as a whole," McGeorge Bundy apprised Johnson in June. Dean Rusk was concerned the protests might be affecting Congress. Something had to be done to stem the onslaught. "We simply aren't doing our propaganda job right in this country," Jack Valenti told the president in April.

In early May, the government dispatched a four-person "truth team" to six midwestern universities to discuss "the facts of life in Vietnam" (as one official put it). The team included "young, articulate" representatives of the State Department, Agency for International Development, and U.S. Army, all "just back from Vietnam," Valenti informed Johnson. Although the officials evoked much sympathy from their audiences, they typically ended up on the defensive, with some forums turning into "hooting sessions" when students felt their intelligence had been insulted.

The University of Wisconsin in Madison was the scene of a particularly trying encounter for the administration's propagandists. Students laughed at the truth-team leader Thomas Conlon's assertion that the United States was fighting to defend South Vietnam's freedom. When he denied the United States "runs the show" there, shouts erupted from all over the room, "Aw, c'mon. Let's be honest." Conlon's angry directives to students to "Sit down!" and mail their questions to Washington did nothing to boost his popularity. As the official was leaving the wreckage, Arnold Lochlin, a bio-chemistry student, blocked his path. "Get this straight, sweetie," Lochlin taunted. "We're not going to fight your filthy fascist war. Go fight it yourself."

Other government spokesmen tried a different tack. Daniel Ellsberg was among the "bright young men" (as Valenti called them) that the administration sent out to campuses to explain the facts of life in Vietnam when requests for speakers came in. He used a "soft-sell" approach when talking to teach-in audiences:

> I conceded a great deal of the opponent's position. For instance, if they started telling me about Diem, I would say "I'm not here to talk about Diem. Diem is everything you say. Diem is dead. That was two years ago." And that was totally disarming, see, because they were all there prepared to talk about the GVN. . . . They were so amazed to hear a government official knock Diem that they didn't know what to say next. And my general case was not unlike that: "The GVN has its faults, but let's look at the VC. . . . Are we sure to win? No. But should we quit without trying?" . . . And I really talked about negotiations right then.

Ellsberg's teach-in career was not a long one, however. He was privy to the "inside story" of the U.S. invasion of the Dominican Republic in late April and wasn't eager to face opponents of the action in a public forum. "We were 100 percent lying about what we were doing in the Dominican Republic," he recalled. Although Johnson claimed the invasion was necessary to fend off another spate of communist aggression, Ellsberg knew the Dominican Republic was "one of the few communist-free environments in the whole world. And so the explanation of why you were sending twenty thousand Marines was a little difficult." Ellsberg called the government office responsible for scheduling officials' appearances on campuses and demanded, "Take me off the list *now*. I ain't going out there to face questions about the Dominican Republic. You can screw that."

As the government's truth teams were taking to the road, the Inter-University Committee for a Public Hearing on Vietnam (IUCPHV), a national antiwar body, was planning a national teach-in in Washington, D.C., on May 15–16. Many IUCPHV organizers lusted for a "confrontation" with a senior government official. They felt it would discredit the administration's justifications for the war in front of a wide audience. Other organizers argued that supporters of the war should not be part of the program; officials already had ready access to podiums for expressing their nonsense, they asserted, and the teach-ins' value lay in surfacing antiwar sentiment. The IUCPHV eventually decided on a confrontation. It solicited McGeorge Bundy's participation.

Bundy agreed to do battle—but only under certain conditions. He vetoed the IUCPHV's choice of Hans Morgenthau, a famous political scientist, as his main debating foe, citing "personal reasons." Bundy found Senator Wayne Morse unsuitable for that role as well. The national security adviser and his aides also required that the moderator of the teach-in establish a "high tone of discussion . . . ruling out of order any heckling, rudeness, or other unseemly conduct"; he would have to field questions alternately from pro- and antiwar audience members "to inhibit a stream of hostile questioning," and questioners could not make "speeches." In short, Bundy's presence required that the teach-in be conducted on a "non-emotional level." In addition, neither Bundy nor other officials would participate in a closing session on alternative policies in Vietnam. As the White House aide Chester Cooper warned Bundy, the IUCPHV organizers planned to issue "a climactic call for a Congressional investigation" of the war at the session, which might facilitate a "psychological victory" by the peace movement.

Bundy got his way on these points and signed on the dotted line. The administration's advance men then swung into action. State Department researchers prepared detailed analyses of the views the obviously feared Morgenthau (accepted as one of three antiwar panelists) had held on the war from 1962 on (he had been "essentially consistent," they reported), William Bundy and other officials briefed pro-administration participants in, according to Cooper, a "thorough and effective" manner. "There are excellent possibilities that our speakers, who have been doing their homework, will prevail in rational debate" with the "highly emotional" antiwar panelists, Cooper wrote Bundy. The White House snatched up a thousand tickets to the event (out of an audience capacity of five thousand) and made "a careful distribution" of them to ensure that "knowledgeable" questioners would be present. One hundred tickets were channeled to the Young Democrats, "who," Cooper knew, were "quite interested in supporting the President." The administration rented a nearby hotel room to house researchers in case the need for rapid-fire responses to troubling disclosures arose. Cooper advised Bundy that he had "underplayed the nature and extent of our advance preparations" in discussions with the media.

Based on his contacts with "alienated and semi-alienated" academics, James Thomson, a national Security Council staffer, counseled Bundy on appropriate behavior. The "growing and potentially dangerous chasm" between many ("often naïve") professors and government could "be bridged," analyzed Thomson, if Bundy demonstrated "reasonableness, good humor, patience, warmth," and "concern" for his critics at the teach-in. This would help "discredit" protesters' "caricature" of officials as "computerized, hard-nosed monsters," a chief reason for the chasm between them. Although "silliness and ignorance and fraud" should not "go unchallenged," Thomson recommended, "the education of our critics" was best considered "a secondary objective" at the event; it was a "less promising" one anyway. "In sum, if you do nothing more on Saturday than convey a clear image of the humaneness, reasonableness, and intelligence of top policymakers—whatever the provocation—you will do much to begin to bridge the chasm."

As curtain time approached, the government's star performer abruptly pulled out of the production. Tight-lipped officials initially refused to explain Bundy's absence. They later stated that Johnson had whisked him off to deal with the crisis in the Dominican Republic. Bundy subsequently explained that he "had a lot of differences with the president" over whether he should participate in the teach-in. "He felt I shouldn't go and there shouldn't be any such encounter between the administration and [its critics]. He may well have been right. But I had undertaken to have a debate—and then I got sent to the Dominican Republic." Johnson evidently threatened to fire him for "disloyalty." Bundy released a written apology to the teach-in that reflected his contempt for protesters. When it was read, many in the audience of several thousand groaned.

A speech by Arthur Schlesinger, Jr., whom Bundy had asked to serve as his replacement, also irked many at the teach-in. Schlesinger advocated sending more troops to Vietnam, cutting back on [Operation] Rolling Thunder, and negotiating. He also maintained that the United States was fighting partly to preserve Americans' right to free speech. When Schlesinger finished his remarks, audience members, "bursting with impatience," queued up to give him a piece of their minds. By the time he had stepped down from the stage, Schlesinger was badly shaken. "What kind of audience is this?" he murmured. Two decades later, Schlesinger called his recommendation of additional troops "a mistake I regret" and said that he was "quite rightly" attacked at the teach-in.

As a holding action, Walt Rostow wrote Dean Rusk afterward, the administration's participation in the event was "a good idea. . . . On a one-shot basis it defused quite a lot of tension on our flank." Rostow opined that "the only truly objectionable feature of the occasion was the sanctimonious assumption of higher virtue among the critics"—a curious statement coming from a man known among his colleagues for an unhealthy attachment to his own ideas. Rostow was not eager to set up additional encounters with the IUCPHV, though. "We should not encourage a regular relation between this group and the U.S. government," he advised.

Nagged by his hasty trip to the Dominican Republic, however, Bundy arranged to participate in two public "debates" on the war in June. He and his staff again secured favorable formats. With CBS, they planned a televised "dialogue" on June 21 moderated by their "preferred choice," Eric Sevareid. Believing the "rigid procedures of a debate . . . in which participants are primarily interested in attacking, defending, or scoring debaters' points" a "poor" arrangement for gaining "acceptance and support of present policies," Bundy and his aides insisted the event have an "informal" and "reasoning together" tone. Sevareid should concentrate on "keeping the discussion moving and pertinent" rather than mediating between sides. The administration knew the IUCPHV would be "less than pleased" with this format; "as a sop," it agreed to accept Morgenthau as Bundy's opponent.

During the CBS dialogue, Sevareid posed four questions central to the government's case on Vietnam. The questions allowed a scholarly looking Bundy, dipping heavily into classified material, to lay out the administration's arguments with studied precision (nonetheless, many viewers found his performance arrogant and shallow). Morgenthau weakly advocated peace "with honor." When Bundy attacked Morgenthau's "pessimism" on the war by noting mistaken political forecasts he had made in the past, the political scientist responded. "I admire the efficiency of Mr. Bundy's office." "I do my own [research]," Bundy lied. For teach-in activists, it was an agonizingly placid affair.

Over that spring and summer, the Johnson administration took other measures to counteract the growing peace movement. Following a talk with the president, who had "no doubt" that communists were behind the dissent, J. Edgar Hoover directed the FBI to prepare a memorandum linking SDS with communism. FBI agents infiltrated SDS chapters. Administration officials drafted speeches with the protesters' criticisms "in mind" and provided propaganda "kits" to friendly nongovernmental speakers. They recruited supportive students to tour the country and flew thirty such students to Vietnam to advance their expertise on the war. The administration suggested prowar youth come to Washington ("at their own expense") to meet officials, thereby receiving a few stimulative strokes ("it wouldn't take too much massaging to do the trick," predicted Cooper in advocating the visits). Compliant South Vietnamese intellectuals were flown to the United States to further educate Americans. The administration moved to get the Young Democrats "into the picture" too. And it shot a film entitled *Why Vietnam?* that was later distributed to the Army. Vietnam veteran David Cortright recalled that the film began with a southern Army officer wailing, "Whhhyyy Veeetnam?" followed by "five minutes of bullshit," followed by another "Whhhyyy Veeetnam?" then five more minutes of bullshit, and so on. "This was at basic training, and people were hooting and hollering," Cortright amusedly recounted. The film evoked "mixed feelings" inside the administration.

35
Women at the Barricades, Then and Now
MYRA MacPHERSON

Women in the antiwar movement became media stars—from singer Joan Baez and actress Jane Fonda to extreme radicals and anarchists who advocated violent revolution, like Weathermen Bernardine Dohrn and Kathy Boudin. Others, less visible among the bomb throwers, like Jane Alpert, blew up their buildings, then became wanted fugitives who traveled underground and surfaced in the eighties to write about their experiences. Yet all along there were other women—nameless and faceless to the press—who threw themselves into the antiwar movement with dedicated passion. They were the reasonable, the caring, who did not make headlines. Like many veterans, some feel they were war casualties who lost time. They got off the track, but the train kept going. Curiously, while veterans feel they were discriminated against for having gone to war, many of these women feel they were also discriminated against because of their far-left credentials—especially as the country moved more to the right.

For most involved in antiwar work, writing a résumé in the mid-seventies became a game of artful dodging. "Only the top leaders landed jobs with the Carter administration. On the West Coast, the welcome mat was not out," recalls a former activist who wants to remain anonymous. "Frankly, I'm not at all anxious to portray myself as the agitator I was." She is in her late thirties and has been "trying to get legitimate for three years." Friends told her to rewrite her résumé when she came to Washington. She played up her skills—she was a superb editor of a sizable magazine—but deemphasized that they were acquired on a left-wing publication. She told her prospective bosses, "You might not agree with the content, but you have to admit I have the skills and experience." She attended both Harvard and Berkeley graduate schools but never acquired a master's, dropping out for antiwar work. She is now overqualified for her current researcher's job. "I'm doing the kind of work I used to *assign*," she says ruefully.

In many ways, she epitomizes the best of the women of her generation. Intelligent, gentle, thoughtful, she pursued antiwar activism with passionate and sincere intensity. She uses the constant phrase of many who sided with the NLF: "We were naïve. We idealized the 'noble Vietnamese.' " She sighs. " 'If America was wrong, then they *must* be right.' There was no in-between. There was a real lack of ambiguity. Still, even if we had known it would turn out *exactly* as it did, our job was to get the U.S. *out*."

Some of her friends still work with causes. One female friend slogged through years of postwar schooling to catch up and become a doctor. Others, like herself, had not reckoned with either the shifting tides of conservatism or the heavy psychological toll of being an outsider all those years. "A lot have never left. The more their vision of the world isn't validated, the more they are convinced they are right. Getting an establishment job is still viewed as anathema to them."

During the war there had been a wrenching separation from parents and a brother in the Army. If her brother went to Vietnam and she continued to march in the streets, her mother warned she would not be welcome at home. She told her daughter, "I will never speak to you again." There was intense conflict; *she* could not understand how her mother could let a son go to Vietnam. Her brother did not go, but it took years to reunite the family.

For her, a demonstration was no Saturday-night revelry. "I took it terribly seriously." There is a touch of envy for those younger, less committed, who went on with their lives. "Even now, in their early thirties, they are young enough to start careers and families." She is approaching forty and knows that she will never have children. A marriage she has had, though not a documented one. She lived for a decade with an antiwar activist. When they parted it was, for her, like a divorce.

For women like her, Vietnam put her personal life on hold. "It didn't just interrupt your career, it could screw it up." During the early part of the seventies, she continued to speak out against the war—for a leftist radio network, newsletters, magazines—and became a foreign-policy analyst. By the late seventies, leftist views were out of fashion; few places would give her the benefit of believing she could separate her expertise from her beliefs. "Dropping out and spending ten years of your life very *actively* against the war doesn't seem the best resume for a job."

She lacks both a strident self-promotion and the arrogance of some in her age group. "You talk about people who thought we acted superior. I'm sure we *acted* that way—but I felt I was the 'enemy.' "

They were the outsiders—the hunted, the chased, the beaten. The women would dress for demonstrations; would wear heavy work boots and jackets to catch the blows, wetted handkerchiefs to cover the face and eyes when the tear gas came. It was an experience women in the generation before and those in college now, with their designer labels and sorority pins, could never know.

Polls consistently show that demonstrators had little backing in the country. Middle America eventually tired of the war, but they disliked student demonstrators even more. Those who viewed them as troublemakers seldom saw the confrontation through the eyes of students. Some drove police to a frenzy, true, but many of the dedicated rank and file were victims of nonprovoked attacks—chased into corners of alleys or buildings and then beaten. Many still recall the terror of being trapped by police swinging wildly with their clubs.

"I remember a demonstration when Dean Rusk was speaking at the Mark Hopkins [Hotel, in San Francisco]. It was the first time the police used *attack* techniques to stop us. They just started chasing us. *Anyone caught was beaten.*" The concept of free speech and assembly was gone. "They chased us into a little chapel. I knew they could get in and beat the crap out of us, and we couldn't get out. A priest came out and talked to the police, and they let us out. They shot a demonstrator in People's Park. At Berkeley, they had to rotate the National Guard constantly. They were our age, and they didn't want them fraternizing with us." The police on attack were fearsome to this woman, barely 5'2". "They wore masks, helmets, and came down fiercely."

Mollie Ivins recalls the same reaction, the unleashed rage. "I had great admiration for good cops and great loathing for bad cops. There was that whole class thing, that generational hostility. Older cops would eye these long-haired kids, certain they were 'getting a lot of pussy.' I saw some ugly stuff—cops deliberately going after women. It happened to me in a couple of demonstrations."

Being an "enemy" of the establishment provoked a sense of lawlessness in the California activist who was clubbed and chased into the chapel. "Why was I bothering to stop at a red light? Why do I obey the law when they would beat the crap out of me if they could? We were outlaws in America. We assumed our phones were tapped, assumed half our friends were agents. It affected me for a long, long time."

Reentry into the establishment world was frightening. A wariness remains. It is vastly ironic that veterans and some women who fought so hard against the war would turn up in the eighties as survivors. They lived through a searing period as unwanted outsiders.

"I'm not saying it is anything as bad as veterans who can't find jobs, but believe me it has been hard. For a lot of people, taking up your life again was not easy. *Almost no one talks about it!* Imagine what we believed! For a long time we thought and were told, 'You're all privileged. You can do this and pop back in, whenever you want.' It just wasn't true. You had to be almost irresponsible—turn away from your personal goals."

After the war, she staked everything on a nonestablishment magazine that might have remained rewarding if it had ever become solvent.

She realizes now that she "never thought through what I was going to do with the rest of my life. The movement was an all-absorbing thing. I didn't stop to think ever what plans I should have. *Thinking personally wasn't highly regarded.* Living in a commune, working on the war . . . There wasn't much time for yourself." Her voice gets a bit firmer. "I feel I gave a whole bunch of the best years of my life to that. Now I do not think of myself as an activist or an organizer. Now I have to put my own life together."

Jane Fonda remains the point-woman for the wrath of many veterans. The right, incorrectly, blame the whole antiwar movement for her actions. In any gathering of veterans there will always be an expletive for her. Even some who turned antiwar cannot forgive her for embracing Hanoi, for posing on one of their tanks. Dean Phillips, a much-decorated antiwar veteran, explodes, "Fonda did irreparable damage to the antiwar movement. She pissed off 80 percent of Americans not on the fringes. People needed to hear it from the guy who fought it—not those assholes at Yale whose biggest decision was getting Daddy's Mercedes and Fonda, who was not in danger of starving to death. There she was criticizing the capitalistic system—which is the hallmark of hypocrisy."

In the late seventies, Fonda further created discord by refusing to join Joan Baez and other antiwar activists in lending her name to an ad decrying the fate of Vietnam's boat people and those oppressed in Vietnam.

Today Fonda has moved on to making more millions as she deflabs the overweight women of America with her "Work-Out" books, records, and videocassettes. Most of the women who went through her regimen in 1982 have no idea that they were in fact subsidizing the political career of former SDS leader Tom Hayden. Fonda contributed handsomely to her husband's 1982 million-dollar-plus campaign for an insignificant state assemblyman seat.

When Hayden was deriving fame and power through antiwar leadership, women were discovering a cruel truth. Lip service to equality did not mean they joined the council of decision makers. Often excluded from meaningful roles at the top, many turned to the feminist movement. The civil rights and antiwar movements emphasized a heightened sense of injustice and—at least in rhetoric—created a more receptive climate for the women's movement. The rebirth of feminism was a welcome niche for those who had been burned by chauvinism in male antiwar ranks.

Margery Tabankin was a University of Wisconsin activist from 1965 to 1969 and later visited Hanoi. The first woman president of the National Student Association since 1947, she was elected on an antiwar platform. She recalls that "Hayden was my hero. We revered these guys. It was like 'what could we do for them?' When Hayden got off the plane to make a speech in Wisconsin, the first thing he handed me was his dirty laundry and asked if I would do it for him. I said, 'I'll have it for you by tonight.' "

Tabankin became one of the few women organizers, joined SDS, and helped coordinate the 1969 Moratorium. "Part of being a woman was this psychology of proving I was such a good radical, 'better than the men.' We felt we were motivated by something higher because we didn't have to go to war ourselves. Most guys didn't take women seriously, however. They were things to fuck. We once did a questionnaire to check reasons why students were drawn to antiwar rallies and demonstrations. One reason frequently checked was 'to make social contacts.' You went through this intense experience, and you went back and had sex." People forget that the women's movement was fledgling at the time. "It [sex] was much more on men's terms."

Despite such aspects of second-class citizenship, the antiwar movement gave Tabankin a sense of heightened consciousness: "You had the right to have opinions about anything—including your government."

"I got beaten up badly covering one of my first civil disobedience rallies for the University of Wisconsin paper. Seventy people were hospitalized," says Tabankin. "We were protesting Dow Chemical on campus. Kids were sitting in a building, refusing to move, and the cops walked in and shouted, 'Everybody out—we'll give you three seconds.'

"They started busting heads, and everyone just totally freaked out, running to get out, clustering in panic at two doors. I got hit in the stomach with a club. Because I was injured, I was the only reporter to get into the emergency room. I ended up being the person the *New York Times* was calling in the hospital to tell them what was going on, how many were injured." Her eyes still shine, recalling the moment. "I was, like, ecstatic—but on the other hand, my friends were hurt." The experience radicalized her. "I remember saying, 'I've had it with writing about things. I'm going to do it.' "

Tabankin abandoned everything for antiwar work. There are great gaps in her education. "For two semesters I literally never went to classes. Borrowed notes and took the tests. We were really self-righteous. We knew a better world, and we were going to make it. That wasn't even negotiable. Our demands were to stop the war, to guarantee the poor an annual income and racial equality. We really created in our minds what the world should be like. *It was my whole reason to live.* I found a passion in my life I never knew was there. Realistically, there were about 100 major activists out of 40,000 on campus. The rest were like soldiers who marched."

Like some other women who threw themselves totally into the movement, she is somewhat envious of those who did not. "They had a much more integrated life. They still came to the demonstrations, but they were graduating and going on. The guy I was in love with—I really think one reason he would not marry me was because of my Vietnam politics—went on to law school and is with a very establishment firm. He really changed."

Tabankin recognized the less committed for what they were. "People get emotional when self-interest is at stake. Young people didn't care enough when their lives weren't on the line. I'd say 5 percent felt intensely passionate about the issue."

She recognizes the deep schisms between some antiwar leaders and the radical left. She agrees with those who view Sam Brown and Tom Hayden as pragmatic manipulators thrust into prominence by the movement. "Some were only for stopping the war, but one faction of SDS got so caught up in being against the system and for economic and racial change. They saw this as totally interrelated. Then you had crazies splitting off, anarchists, and terrorists. I was between the SDS and the student government type. Although a little more to the left of student government, I wasn't totally an SDS person. Many in the Mobe viewed Sam Brown and Al Lowenstein as sell-out pigs. We just didn't see it, the polarization, then. We were so caught up, we didn't see how destructive it was."

Tabankin was arrested seven times and finally became a burned-out casualty. She dropped out of activism and went home. "The greatest luxury was having my mother's housekeeper do my laundry." She became a community organizer for youth projects, raised money for foundations, worked on two union-reform efforts for miners, and became head of VISTA when Sam Brown became Carter's director of the Action agency. She defends the activists of the sixties and sees ongoing commitment. "The same 5 percent *then* are the same 5 percent of our generation still working for causes—toxic waste, nuclear freeze, trying to get progressives elected. Much of it is grassroots."

The attempt of some in the media to lump "the generation" as idealistic causists was a mistake. "There never was a 'generation' that really meant it. Many didn't give a shit, then and now. Most got caught up in the time period—but it wasn't based on ideology, it was based on events. They weren't socialized then and they aren't now."

Today Tabankin, in her mid-thirties, is herself opting for profits while working for causes on the side. In 1981 Tabankin and Bill Danoff, author of the song "Country Roads," formed Danoff Music Company. They represent twenty-four Washington-area songwriters, plugging them to Los Angeles and Nashville producers and singers. They also manage a few bands. Tabankin's biggest coup was selling a song by Jon Carroll, Washington rock musician and songwriter, to Linda Ronstadt. Carroll's "Get Closer" became the title track of an album that went gold in 1982. The single made the Top Twenty. Tabankin tries to make a vague connection between yesteryear's activism and today's entrepreneurship. You need "commonsense networking skills" in both fields, she says—whom to contact and how, what will be effective. One difference, however, is the "profit motive."

Tabankin feels she acquired strength and self-confidence during the sixties and has been able to transfer organizing skills into business. The negatives? "It became my whole life, and I lost out on normal, lasting personal relationships."

The negatives for the generation? "People want to make it more than it was. Civil rights didn't change the fact that blacks still have problems, the women's movement doesn't mean women have equal rights, the antiwar movement doesn't mean our foreign policy isn't going to go totally crazy in the near future."

As women activists recall that era, it is striking how negatively they regarded American soldiers. "As we turned against the government, we turned against them as symbols," said Tabankin. "That was our biggest mistake. That was stupid tactically. The compassion wasn't there; the expressed view was that 'I don't want to get killed, and I don't think *they* should go do that.' Instead of the government, we blamed the foot soldier. If I have any regret, it's the way we treated them." At the time, reviling soldiers was part of the tactic—such as war-crime tribunals—to heighten the perception that the war had to be stopped. "You had to be for the North if you wanted the people to win."

Tabankin looks back with some chagrin at her naïveté. In 1972, as part of a delegation to Hanoi, she was imbued with the concept that the war was nationalistic in origin and had remained so. "I was witnessing destruction of civilian life. I saw their hospital forty-five minutes after it had been totally demolished. The ambulance was taking out the dead and living. That was in May 1972—the scariest time of my life. There were bombing attacks at all times of day and night. We brought the first footage out of North Vietnam and sold it to '60 Minutes.'"

"The North Vietnamese didn't want us to meet with POWs. We pushed and pushed and made ourselves obnoxious, and we saw ten of them," recalls Tabankin. "They looked pale but healthy. One black had heard that [George] Wallace had been shot and was interested in that. Another asked me to go back and tell his wife he was all right."

The prisoners said little about their treatment; it did not even occur to Tabankin at the time that they would have major difficulty expressing themselves with North Vietnamese officials in the room. The accounts of torture that emerged after the POWs' return demolished reports of those who had seen them under such carefully controlled conditions. We talked of Susan Sontag's ecstatic descriptions of the "gentle captors" of the North. Tabankin winces slightly, then reiterates, "It was so easy to be naïve."

The range of opinions among those twenty-seven million women who came of age during the Vietnam Generation was clearly vast.

Some dropped the sixties with a vengeance, like those who populate Jerry Rubin's Manhattan mix-and-mingle salons. Rubin, yesteryear's Yippie trying to make it in the eighties as an example of the "Me" Decade Meets Wall Street phenomenon, is a "networking" party giver. He talks about money, power, and "leveraged" women. "Leverage in financial terms is when a small amount of money controls a larger amount of money. Leverage is therefore power. I'm into leverage. Now Barbara Walters is leveraged. She speaks, you know, and people listen. Right? Huh? You get it? The leveraged woman."

Those serious in the movement always viewed Rubin as a member of the comic fringe, much overplayed by the media. They are not surprised that he shed his antiwar activism like an old worn overcoat and speaks without a scintilla of idealism about past motivation. "I get very nervous talking about the sixties. Who wants to live in the past?" More than anyone from the sixties antiwar, antiauthoritarian movement, Rubin epitomizes the view of one cynical observer: "Money is the long hair of the eighties." One evening incipient leveraged men and women—eager imitations of high-fashion gloss—moved around at one of his "networking" salons, handing out business cards as they used to pass around joints. Pat Frazer, who said she is a "commercial actress," spoke in a super-modulated voice and seemed to epitomize the women present. What was she doing? "Anything I can."

In the sixties, "Jerry was my ideal. At college I was involved. Now I'm involved in the eighties. You're on your own—and all of a sudden it's 'getting for yourself.' I'm interested in taxes." She had no quarrel with cutting social programs for the poor and disadvantaged. "That's okay. My priorities are now in defense and space." And in the sixties? "Then I was anti-American." Because it was chic? "Partly."

Of course there are other sixties women who wouldn't spend a minute at Rubin's mixers or embrace his values. They may be involved in careers or motherhood rather than issues—but they do not negate their past. Others remain active in causes. For some, a need for personal peace followed radical commitment. In 1983 a bright college graduate in Washington summed up the feeling of many taking time off to be a full-time mother. "I gave my *all* to the movement, but now it is time for myself." . . .

The class division of the war created friction between some in the emerging women's movement and resuming veterans. Leaders in the women's movement had little or no firsthand experience with anyone who went to Vietnam. For them it was simple to cavalierly dismiss veterans' preference in civil service as discriminatory. In the early seventies, when returning veterans needed all the help they could get, various women's groups, particularly NOW [National Organization for Women], opposed laws which gave extra points to wartime veterans applying for civil service jobs. For example, the Federal Women's Program Committee of the Denver Federal Executive Board questioned whether the law was consistent with equal-employment rulings—acknowledging that those who were drafted "may have suffered disruptions in their normal lifestyles." That understatement enraged combat veterans since draftees comprised 60 percent of U.S. Army dead from 1967 through 1970.

Dean Phillips, special assistant to the VA director (1977–81), said, "Women were not beating down doors to demand entrance into the armed services during Vietnam." Phillips noted that women who served did not make up the 2 percent quota then established for females. They too would have been entitled to veterans' preference if they had entered the service. "Treatises on sex discrimination often ignore perhaps the most blatantly sexist policy in our country's history," said Phillips, "the limitation of the drafting of those who will die and be crippled in combat exclusively to the male sex. At no time during the war did any women's organization file any lawsuit claiming that restrictive draft or enlistment laws injured female employment opportunities by making it more difficult for women to serve in the armed forces. After virtually ignoring the issue of the male-only draft during the veterans' preference debate in the late seventies, NOW president Ellie Smeal made a fool out of herself in 1981 by claiming that past exclusion from the draft had discriminated *against women*. Feminists, who *avoided* service during Vietnam, were now saying that their younger sisters are discriminated against by not being included in draft registration—something *they* wanted no part of during Korea or Vietnam."

Phillips, an ex-paratrooper who went on long-range patrols in enemy-controlled areas with the 101st Airborne Division in 1967–78, won numerous decorations, including the Silver Star, Purple Heart, and two Bronze Stars. During law school in Denver in the early seventies, he had a compatible relationship with NOW. He even received letters of appreciation from them for his active support of the ERA [Equal Rights Amendment]. That union was shattered when NOW refused to alter its 1971 position of opposing *any* and *all* government laws or programs giving special preference to veterans, even those badly maimed in combat. Phillips points to a letter from NOW's national headquarters confirming in 1979 that the 1971 resolution—with no modifications—was still their official position. Phillips assisted in the defense of the constitutionality of veterans' preference, which was ultimately upheld by the Supreme Court in June of 1979.

Phillips contends that NOW's opposition to all forms of veterans' preference was a tactical error that helped defeat the ERA in several crucial states. "The two-million-member VFW [Veterans of Foreign Wars] passed a resolution opposing the ERA in *direct* response to the NOW resolution opposing all forms of veterans' preference. Then VFW people worked effectively against the ERA through their contacts with state legislators. Sure, they would not have been *for* the ERA in any case—but they wouldn't have even gotten involved to oppose it if it hadn't been for NOW's position."

Other veterans, less active than Phillips, also felt that the women's movement should have left veterans' preference alone. "In one way I felt the government was back to pitting all of us minorities against one another in a fight for jobs," said one combat veteran, "but we felt the women didn't understand what we had been through."

Today, in urban centers like Boston, New York, and Washington, there are curious permutations of friendships from the Vietnam Generation. Ann Zill, who helps spend millions in liberal causes for Stewart Mott, had a brother who was injured in Vietnam. One of her closet friends is a Marine combat veteran who argues vehemently that the United States should have been in Vietnam and could have won. Zill herself was an antiwar activist.

Ann Broderick Zill, the oldest of four children, grew up in a small town in Maine. Her father was a "corporate mogul" who worked for Chevrolet. At Barnard College in New York, she was among the early war protesters. Zill had violent arguments with her brother, Peter Broderick, five and a half years younger, about the war, and was devastated when he joined the Army in 1968 and became an officer. Two months into Vietnam, he was "literally blown up" and spent nearly fifteen months recuperating. "He lost a whole lot of his intestines and had a colostomy for a while and has 60 percent permanent disability, and he basically does nothing with his life," Zill said in 1981. "He's a town janitor and plays a lot of tennis." For a man loaded still with shrapnel, she says, "He's in very good shape."

The wounded brother and the "knee-jerk peacenik" sister were forced to confront each other's views. There was a night in 1981 when their mother died. The Irish Catholic family had always been able to drink and fight and laugh together. The drinks came heavily that night. "Peter was sobbing and reliving the Vietnam War, and this is 1981." Did he come to a political point of view? "He views it through a very small slit of consciousness. He does not deal with the larger moral questions. Yet I suspect that if pressed to the wall now he would be able to say some things were fundamentally wrong with the war—but he's never been able to in the past. He's scarred by the war."

"We don't fight now, but we used to back then. He was a young kid, and I could not believe that he believed in this war. I argued that it was stupid and wrong for us to be involved."

All the time her brother was in Vietnam, all the time he lay in the hospital, Zill marched and worked for peace. "I felt very conflicted. I watched this man of six feet two, who now weights 190, go to something just over 100 pounds. Skin and bones and could barely walk. He kept getting pneumonia." His agony reinforced her feeling that the war was wrong. "But I couldn't talk about that with Peter. He didn't want to hear that. He liked to tell war stories and make us laugh, and I had to laugh at the damn fucking war stories whether I wanted to or not. I will *always* believe that war was senseless."

Her brother tells a story of a marine whose injuries were so overwhelming that he was encased in a plaster cast. For nights he kept begging for a knife. Broderick was convinced the man wanted to commit suicide. Then one night the marine, whose face was bandaged except for his face and mouth, yelled, "I can't see, I'm caught in a net and can't get out." Broderick felt "deep elation. He *didn't* want to kill himself." He was trying to see. "I sensed a great pride in that marine; he hadn't given up. He didn't let my faith down. He was a fighter . . . never quitting the struggle or relenting an inch. . . . I never saw him again, although he remains with me forever."

It is this emphasis on personal bravery and courage that fills the memory of many veterans, not the ideological rights and wrongs of the war. Ann Zill, unlike many women in the movement, was able to broaden her perspective through her brother, to understand the motivation of some who went. "He was a very good antidote for my overall sense that if you were for the war, you were crazy. He forced me to realize that a lot of perfectly reasonable people had been trained to believe it was your patriotic duty to defend your country—and that they believed this war was about protecting Vietnam from the Communists."

Zill is now divorced from the husband who "used to joke that he made love, not war, because that's how he got out. By having babies." As a father he was deferred. In 1981 she was dating a Mexican American who was too young for Vietnam and now organizes against the draft, arguing that blue-collar and lower-class youths would still be the ones to go. "The inequities would still be there."

Zill loved growing up in the sixties. "The spirit of liberation and of questioning authority. Vietnam shaped my life. One of my closest friend's lifework grew out of war protest. She now does analytical think-pieces about Indochina and Southeast Asia. And I haven't changed my basic view—although I like to think I'm more effective now. I work for a man who gives away about a million a year, and his first interest is to prevent nuclear annihilation. Trying to prevent another going-to-war exercise is a very sobering, humbling exercise. The peace movement today is *meshuggina*. It's a terrible failure, completely inadequate. The selling of the Pentagon was brilliant. They played to the psychological needs of this country to be strong and protected after Vietnam—even as life is crumbling all around." Zill was talking in 1981, before public sentiment had shifted to some degree against the government's excessive defense budget.

She is asked to assess the sixties movement.

"I'm somewhat critical by nature. There were a lot of arrogant kids. Sam Brown so turned me off that I have never been able to like him to this day, and I used to run into him at the same parties when he ran Action." Like many dedicated antiwar activists, she tried to overlook personalities. "My allegiance remained with the people who were trying to stop the war. And my efforts in that regard got more sensible as time went on. It never occurred to me to side with the North, but I can't blame those who did. Still, that is part of my brother's story. He was really rejected when he showed up on campus in his Army outfit one day because he had to wear it to get some discount on the cost of something—I've forgotten what. But how vilified he was!" She points up an important psychological reaction of many veterans in similar situations. "That made him cling to the *need* to defend that war longer, I think, than he would otherwise have done. And so that's an example of one of those great ironies about how much campus condemnation exacerbated and helped polarize an already tough situation. Yet I understand those people who did it."

Zill is not too optimistic about generational reconciliation. "You need to bring the extremes together, and I'm not sure that can happen. I doubt that I would ever to able to say that my sympathies are with my brother, who believed in it as he did. On the other hand, I will defend to the death his right to think that way. Maybe if more people can understand someone like I can my brother, there *will* be a coming together."

One of the problems of the Vietnam Generation was a tendency to stereotype, to divide into monolithic clumps of "them" and "us." Vestiges of that thinking remain. One female antiwar activist enjoys a close friendship with a veteran—but irreconcilable differences cloud it.

"We all viewed each other back then as some faceless mass. To the veterans, we were a faceless mass who treated them like shit. Just as I criticize people for not seeing us as individuals, we didn't see *soldiers* as people. We just wanted to stop the war. We felt so defensive, a minority of college kids clustered together. I remember being angry at the soldiers. It was good to say, 'Fuck you,' to let them know people didn't like it—that there were people who passionately *did not want this war*. We had a real macro view—do anything to stop it. We were more oblivious than arrogant about the classness."

She pauses to reflect. "We were lucky to live in a time when there was a social movement. As a generation it set us apart in an irreconcilable way—even as it caused huge divisions within the generation. Maybe as time goes by, and people don't know where Vietnam is once again, maybe it will bring us together. The fact that we lived through it, on one hand, is all of our touchstone with reality. For us it will always be—and for the veterans it will always be. And yet on another level, we are on opposite sides."

She sighs. "I'm still emotional about it, and so are they. One friend thinks he's better because he faced death and we haven't. I think there is something more important to life than being on a battlefield—I don't see it as the highest value of life, and yet I appreciate his feeling.

"People who fought and people who fought against the war were at loggerheads—but it changed our lives forever." She sighs. "Still, there is no settling of accounts. No one can lay it to rest."

CHAPTER 11

The Legacy of the War

This chapter offers a necessarily sketchy view of a huge subject: the impact of the war on both Vietnam and the United States. When North Vietnamese and National Liberation Front forces captured Saigon in April 1975, they faced the daunting tasks of unifying and rebuilding their shattered country. Neil Sheehan, the perceptive reporter who covered the war for the *New York Times*, returned to Vietnam with his wife, Susan, in 1989. In Saigon, he revisited places he had known well, and he heard the stories of Vietnamese who had coped with the staggering changes that had occurred over the past twenty-five years. One such person who spoke to Sheehan was Nguyen Van Linh, the general secretary of the Vietnamese Communist Party, who, despite his position, endorsed the benefits of a mixed economy.

In the United States, the results of the war were hardly as cataclysmic, but many people were deeply affected by the experience. There were those who deserted from the military because they could not tolerate what they believed to be the moral enormity of the war. One of these was Richard Perrin, whose story is told here by Gloria Emerson. And, of course, there were those who did go to war, and who came back with wounds both physical and psychological. Emmett, a character in Bobbie Ann Mason's novel *In Country*, is one of these. At the end of the novel (and this excerpt), Emmett goes to visit the Vietnam Veterans' Memorial—the Wall—in Washington. With him are his niece, Sam Hughes, and Mamaw, Sam's paternal grandmother, whose son Dwayne—Sam's father—was killed in Vietnam. The last scene is a reminder of the pain caused by the war, but it carries with it the hope of redemption.

Photograph taken of the traveling Vietnam Veterans' Memorial at Houston, Texas, on May 21, 1987. UPI/BETTMANN NEWSPHOTOS

36
Returning to South Vietnam
NEIL SHEEHAN

In 1965, Saigon's Tan Son Nhut Airport had been busier than Chicago's O'Hare. One waited forty-five minutes to take off, strung out in a bizarre gaggle that had a Pan American jetliner bound for Hong Kong behind a propeller-driven A-I "Skyraider" laden with bombs and shiny aluminum canisters of napalm for some unfortunate hamlet in the countryside. Now, of course, the mad bustle was gone. Our plane from Hanoi was probably the only aircraft, including the occasional military flight, to land in an hour, and it landed at the old destination with a different name—Ho Chi Minh City, as Saigon and its environs were renamed after 1975. (In the relaxation of *doi moi* [economic reform], however, people were starting to call the city Saigon again.) My journey to the North had been a voyage of discovery; almost everything I had encountered there had been new. In the South I was beginning another journey, a voyage of rediscovery through the kaleidoscope of the past and the emotions it aroused. As was to be the case wherever I went through a changed but familiar land, something inevitably called the past to mind.

At Tan Son Nhut it was the archaeology of our American empire—rows of half-moon-shaped concrete shelters, erected at considerable expense, to safeguard U.S. warplanes from Communist mortar and rocket attacks. The shelters were empty, and weeds were growing among them. On the drive into the city it was the coils of rusting concertina wire on top of the compound walls that had protected the homes of former Saigon government officials and buildings rented to Americans. The Vietnamese who lived in them now apparently found the barbed wire a deterrent to burglars and, as with much else the Americans had left behind, no one had gotten around to removing it.

The street signs along the main avenue from the airport said "Nguyen Van Troi" where before they had said "Cach Mang," but the new name evoked a memory too. At a small bridge about halfway into town, Nguyen Van Troi, a twenty-four-year-old electrician, had tried to set off a bomb under a car carrying Robert McNamara, secretary of defense during the Kennedy and Johnson administrations, on one of McNamara's periodic visits to assess the war. Nguyen Van Troi had died before a firing squad in Saigon's Chi Hoa Prison in 1964 shouting "Long live Ho Chi Minh."

We checked into the Rex, scene of the "Five O'Clock Follies" during the war, the derisive nickname the press corps had coined for the military briefing each afternoon. Thanks to the determination of its director, Dao Huu Loan, an enterprising Northerner who had emigrated to the South in 1975, to turn it into the best hotel in town, the Rex had come a long way from its days as a propaganda mill downstairs and a bachelor officers' quarters on the upper floors. A marble lobby had replaced the mundane side entrance that once led to the offices of JUSPAO, or Joint U.S. Public Affairs Office. The ground floor at the front of the hotel where the briefings were held had become a bar and an expanse of souvenir shops, but I could still see the rows of seats filled with reporters and the podium where the briefing officer had stood to announce how many sorties had been flown, how many "structures" had been destroyed, how many "contacts" had been made with the enemy.

Nixon's strategy to win the war in its final years had been to gain public support in the United States by gradually withdrawing American troops, while shifting the burden of the fighting in Vietnam to the Saigon regime's forces. He had called his policy "Vietnamization." Ironically, Saigon was being "Vietnamized" because his policy had failed. The Rex was an example of what was happening to the city. For the first time since the French seized permanent control in 1861, Saigon was becoming a Vietnamese place. The Vietnamese really were in charge now, and they were gradually putting to their own use what the French and Americans had built and left behind. In the process the past could sometimes be difficult to find even if one searched for it consciously.

During the war everyone had known the location of the grand emporium of American civilization, the main PX [post exchange] in Cholon, the Chinese section of the city. Susan had bought the ornaments for our first Christmas tree there on a steamy day in August 1965. The air conditioning had been turned up high, and Bing Crosby was singing "White Christmas" over the stereo system. "Buy them now, lady," a Pfc. serving as salesclerk had admonished her when he spotted her looking at the ornaments. "They'll be gone in a week." Twenty-four years later we met an older Chinese businessman who remembered where the PX had been and drew a sketch of the intersection. We still had trouble finding it. Numerous people on nearby streets had no recollection.

Thang [Duong Quang] and I finally discovered it by peering over the gate of an abandoned compound. The Vietnamese had turned the site into a dump for the scrap they sell to dealers from Southeast Asian neighbors like Singapore and the Philippines. The yard in front was filled with the carcasses of trucks and other cast-off military vehicles, piles of worn-out tires, and rusted shipping containers with "U.S. Army" still visible in white on the weathered green paint. The whitewashed stucco buildings behind, once beckoning with cornucopias of Scotch whisky and filter cigarettes, hi-fis and television sets, room air conditioners, lipstick and hair spray to tempt Vietnamese women, were abandoned and gray with moss.

Then, at a moment when one least expected it, the past was there. At the Ho Chi Minh City Arts and Literature Association the conversation moved from trying to stem the showing of pornographic and violent videotapes in a city where there were an estimated 20,000 VCRs, to the travails of self-sufficiency brought on by *doi moi*. Parked in the courtyard was a ten-wheel Soviet military truck, freshly painted in bright yellow but otherwise old enough to have come down the Ho Chi Minh Trail, that the association had bought in a so far money-losing enterprise to haul logs to sawmills from the rain forests of Tay Ninh. The vice-chairman, a writer of short stories named Vien Phuong, mentioned that the association's headquarters had previously belonged to the mother-in-law of General Nguyen Van Thieu, the last American strongman. Would we like to see a safe in which he had found two million Saigon government piastres? Mr. Phuong asked.

He had discovered the safe in a bedroom he was currently using as an office after the house had been seized in 1975 and had sent for a welder to cut it open with an acetylene torch. Mr. Phuong said he had used the cash to support fellow writers during the months immediately following the fall of Saigon because the former government's currency, although worthless outside the country, had remained legal tender with considerable purchasing power for quite a while. There were five more safes in the house, but Mr. Phuong had found them already opened and cleaned out by Thieu's mother-in-law before she fled. One still stood bizarrely on a stair landing, somehow dragged there in the panic at the end, the symbol of a society so corrupt that it had finally collapsed of its own moral emptiness.

The Vietnamese had bestowed the best-known foreign residence in the city on their Soviet benefactors. The Russian consul general slept in the two-story villa where Ellsworth Bunker, the longest-serving U.S. ambassador in Saigon, had lived from 1967 to 1973. Like his Vietnamese hosts, the consul general had not taken the trouble to remove the accoutrements of the past, and so he had a house that might have been better appreciated by a Russian diplomat in Afghanistan—a spiked grille along the top of the front compound wall, floodlights, a reinforced concrete tower where Marine guards in battle gear had once crouched when the Viet Cong had attempted a surprise attack through the old Mac Dinh Chi cemetery at the end of the street.

The tombstones the guerrillas hid behind were gone because of a postwar policy of turning urban cemeteries into parks. The remains of the two most famous occupants of the cemetery, Ngo Dinh Diem, the Catholic mandarin installed in power by the United States in 1954 and then overthrown and assassinated in an American-sponsored coup in 1963 after he had become a liability, and those of his brother and virtual co-ruler, Ngo Dinh Nhu, assassinated with him, were not claimed by relatives, and so were cremated and placed with other unclaimed remains in a mausoleum north of the city. Now rock bands played on weekend nights on the open-air stage in the park. There was an outdoor coffee shop. A park guard in a blue uniform blew a whistle at two young people riding a forbidden bicycle along one of the shrub-lined walks.

General [William] Westmoreland's house had been less fortunate in its heir. The Ho Chi Minh City branch of the Vietnamese Women's Federation was doing nothing to keep the place up. A traditional colonial mansion in ochre with white trim and lou-vered green shutters, the house had been elegant, particularly during the early 1960s in the time of Westmoreland's predecessor as commander in chief, General [Paul D.] Harkins, when the war had still been a countryside affair that did not seem to threaten the city. General Harkins had occasionally invited reporters to the house to meet some distinguished visitor from Washington. An Army sergeant in starched khakis who served as the butler would greet us under the covered doorway off the circular drive. The Vietnamese servants had worn white uniforms.

Now a sign on the street outside, in front of a cage where a sentry had stood, advertised bus tours to the seaside resort of Vung Tau and to Da Lat in the moun-tains—the equivalent for the Women's Federation of the log-hauling enterprise launched by the Arts and Literature Association. Four tour buses were parked inside the walled grounds where Jeeps and staff cars and General Westmoreland's black Chrysler Impe-rial had come and gone. Radio aerials lingered on the red tile roof, no longer commu-nicating with anyone

Other former American buildings had been placed on hold toward the hoped-for day when Washington would end its economic embargo and establish diplomatic rela-tions. The buildings were being kept under official or semiofficial ownership so that they could easily be vacated. I had already noticed the pattern in Hanoi. The villa there that had been the U.S. Consulate during the French years was awaiting possible con-version into the first U.S. Embassy in Vietnam's national capital. In the meantime it was serving as a headquarters for the Fatherland Front, the government-controlled political and civic organization to encourage national unity.

The fortresslike building of seven stories with a helicopter pad on the roof that had been the U.S. Embassy in Saigon was temporarily serving as offices for Vietnam's petroleum bureaucracy until it could be reopened as the first U.S. Consulate in Ho Chi Minh City. The consulate would need more office space than the embassy in Hanoi. It would have to handle the concerns of the largest Vietnamese community overseas, the more than a million Vietnamese who at present live in the United States, a community constantly growing because of immigration, illegally as "boat people" and legally through the Orderly Departure Program run by both governments. Virtually all are from the South, the largest number from the Saigon-Cholon area, and most have relatives in Vietnam. Since the reformers within the Party gained the upper hand in 1986, thousands have begun to return each year for family visits during Tet and to explore business opportunities.

The property of the losers on the Vietnamese side was another matter. During the war one of the most closely watched streets in the city was a short one in Cholon called Ngo Quyen, where Gen. Cao Van Vien, chief of the Saigon government's Joint General Staff, lived in three adjacent houses with his family, aides, and guards. An area across the street was cleared out for his helicopter to land on. General Vien fled to the United States a few days before the end in 1975. His three houses and the helicopter pad were initially seized and turned into the headquarters for a supply unit, and then, as the Vietnamese Army began demobilizing in the 1980s, given to the unit's officers. Three retired senior colonels of the unit got the three houses. The helicopter pad went to lesser-ranking officers, who managed to build enough new apartments on it to shelter twenty-one families with shops in front to boot.

One of the three houses came with a garden. The retired colonel to whom it was given, Tran Vu Hoa, a sixty-two-year-old native of Hanoi who had spent fifteen years of the American war in the South after being sent down at the beginning in 1960, converted the garden into a café to supplement his pension. The lights of such "garden cafés" could be seen all over the city at night as every family fortunate enough to have extra space tried to turn it into money.

A genial man who said he had fought for the independence of Vietnam and friendship between the American and Vietnamese peoples, Colonel Hoa invited us inside to see the house. His wife was also retired from service during the war as an official in the Ministry of Transportation. The Hoas shared their house with one unmarried daughter, three married daughters, their husbands, and six grandchildren. In addition, Mrs. Hoa kept six cats. General Vien had been helpful to me during the war because he was an affable man and, in a contradiction that was common to the ARVN officer corps, could be perceptive and honest in private about military matters. The last time Susan and I had been to the house had been for dinner with him and his wife. It had not been crowded then. . . .

It was a Sunday morning in July, and we were standing in the living room of what used to be the British ambassador's residence in Saigon at 261 Dien Bien Phu. Thang, Tien [Tran Le], Ambassador Vu Hac Bong, the chief of the Ho Chi Minh City Service of External Relations, two officials from his press office, and an interpreter we had not met before, whose English was unusually fluent, were there too. We were awaiting the arrival of Nguyen Van Linh, general secretary of the Vietnamese Communist Party, a man who had survived twelve years of French prisons, thirty years of war and manhunts in the South, and a decade of internecine political struggle after the Communist victory in 1975 to ultimately start his country down a new path amidst the new turmoil of peace.

There was no customary roar of engines from the security escort cars when Mr. Linh did arrive. Such emblems of status were not his style, and having lived so much of his life with danger he did not seem concerned about it. When he was chosen general secretary in 1986, he had dismissed the security escorts of his predecessor, Le Duan. The car that pulled into the driveway was a modest one called a Lada, the Soviet version of a Fiat, with Mr. Linh in the back and a single bodyguard up front beside the driver.

In Hanoi, Vietnamese leaders of Mr. Linh's generation, men in their seventies, normally dressed in one of two ways for semiformal occasions like an interview: a short-sleeved blouse and slacks in extremely hot weather, or a high-collar tunic like the one Ho had worn, often referred to as a "Mao jacket" in the West because the Chinese leader had also favored it. They usually did not wear the preferred dress of younger officials, a safari shirt and slacks, which the Vietnamese called *bo ky gia*, literally "correspondent's suit," for the American television correspondents who had introduced it to the country. The choice had to do with outlook rather than age. Despite his national office, Mr. Linh spent more time in Saigon than he did in Hanoi, and on this Sunday morning he wore a *bo ky gia* neatly cut of gray-green cotton.

Until he emerged from the jungle in 1975, little was known of Nguyen Van Linh, and a decade and a half afterward little is still known of him outside of Vietnam. Although he was an important Viet Minh figure in the South during the French war and one of the handful of ranking Communist leaders there throughout the American conflict, the United States Information Service noted in a biographical sketch published as late as April 1973 that there was "insufficient information available from which to construct a proper profile" of him. Strangely enough, the profile that was published, based on CIA and military intelligence reports, identified him as Nguyen Van Cuc, his real name at birth in Hanoi on July 1, 1915, but lacked the early alias, Nguyen Van Linh, that he had long since adopted as his name. The number of lesser *noms de guerre* Mr. Linh employed over the years to confuse the intelligence services of France and America—Muoi, Muoi Cuc, Muoi Ut, Buu Cuc, Rau, Bay—understandably made it difficult to determine precisely who he was.

He was always different. Ho Chi Minh and most of the original generation of revolutionaries who followed him—like Pham Van Dong, prime minister of the North for many years, who polished Linh's French when they were prisonmates on the penal island of Poulo Condore off the coast southeast of Saigon during the 1930s—were from mandarin families with nationalist sympathies. Mr. Linh was not. "My parents were well-paid civil servants of the French administration," he said. His father was a professor in a lycée in Hanoi. Linh does not recall the subject his father taught because his father died when he was eight and he went to live with an uncle in Haiphong who was a minor official in the colonial legal system. The uncle enrolled him in a lycée there for a proper French education.

The nationalist sentiment spreading among young Vietnamese caught him just the same. He joined a clandestine youth organization, and in 1929, at the age of fourteen, he was arrested with two classmates while distributing anti-French leaflets. He got eighteen months in jail. The following year a series of uprisings in the North frightened the colonial authorities. Special tribunals were set up with the power to condemn dissidents to the guillotine or impose life imprisonment. Although French law said that Linh should be tried as a juvenile, he was taken before a tribunal at the end of the eighteen months and resentenced as an adult to ten years on Poulo Condore.

Victor Hugo and *Les Misérables*, not Karl Marx and *Das Kapital*, pointed him toward Communism. He had given no thought to social issues until one day not long before his arrest. Several older members of the clandestine youth organization, whom he later discovered were already versed in Communist beliefs, posed a question to him: After they had driven the foreigner from the country, would he be satisfied to live in a Vietnam ridden by the social injustice he could see around him? "At this moment I had started reading *Les Misérables* and the image of Jean Valjean was very striking to me—a poor man, so poor he had to beg for his daily bread," Mr. Linh said in his expressive way, smiling, frowning, gesturing with his small hands as he spoke, switching from Vietnamese to French, to the consternation of the interpreter. He had also read a novel by Hector Malot, another nineteenth-century French romanticist, about an orphan boy named Rémi. "He had to travel with a circus all over Europe to earn his living." But Victor Hugo was the decisive influence on him, and *Les Misérables* remains his favorite novel. "It touched the strings of my heart very directly—I was very moved," Mr. Linh said. So he gave his answer: "I could not be satisfied with a society where there is an enormous gap between rich and poor." Then he would have to struggle for two goals, the older students said: national independence and social revolution.

Penal servitude on Poulo Condore (the island was renamed Con Dao after 1975), a "University of the Revolution," as Mr. Linh remarked in a common but apt Vietnamese description of the French prison system, furthered his political education. Pham Van Dong, seven years older and a founding member of the Vietnamese Communist Party, was more than Linh's "professeur de français" on the island. He was also one of Linh's instructors in Marxism-Leninism. When Linh was released in 1936 in an amnesty by the Popular Front government in France, he joined the Party and went to work in Haiphong organizing cells among laborers. He did not stay free for long. The outbreak of World War II returned Indochina to normalcy—repression. The French police picked him up in Vinh in Central Vietnam, where he had been dispatched to try to rescue a newly shattered Party apparatus, and shipped him back to Poulo Condore.

The reason Mr. Linh remained a twilight figure until 1975 was simple: He never left the South. Liberation from Poulo Condore in 1945, when Japan, which had conquered Indochina, surrendered and the first war for Vietnamese independence broke out, meant for him thirty years of never having a safe place to sleep. Others fought the French in the South and regrouped to the North after the Geneva Agreements of 1954. Mr. Linh was assigned to be one of the "stay-behinds," as the CIA labeled them, who were kept in the South to lead a political struggle for the 1956 all-Vietnam election that had been provided for at Geneva, an election that was never to take place. He became the leading "stay-behind," the ranking Communist in South Vietnam, when Le Duan, another of Mr. Linh's prisonmates on Poulo Condore, was summoned to the North in 1956 and Mr. Linh replaced him as Party secretary for the South.

The Vietnamese have a special term for those like Mr. Linh who stayed in 1954. They are known as "winter cadres" because they survived the winter of the terror Diem and the CIA launched to track them down. The trials of the American war that was to follow were grim, and Mr. Linh recalled them vividly. "I remember very well when the first waves of B-52s came to Vietnam," he said. "I was in Cu Chi at the time. It happened at seven P.M. We were meeting in an underground room. Everything was shaking around us." Yet nothing that occurred during the American war had the harrowing quality of the guillotinings and shootings and prison camps of Diem's Denunciation of Communists campaign. Those were the worst years, Mr. Linh said, "a ferocious time."

Of the 8,000 to 10,000 ordered to stay in the South in 1954, only about 2,000 to 2,500 survived. "I was nearly arrested many times," Mr. Linh said. "Had I been arrested, I would not be talking to you now," ("Our lives were counted in days and hours," one of Mr. Linh's fellow winter cadres remembered.) It was a relief, Mr. Linh said, when guerrilla warfare resumed at the end of the 1950s and they could shoot back.

In the meantime Ho Chi Minh and the other Communist leaders had let loose a horror of their own in the North in the mid-1950s—a Chinese-style land reform campaign orchestrated by Truong Chinh, then general secretary and chief ideologue of the

Party. Thousands of real and purported landlords were tried before kangaroo courts and shot, and their families left to starve.

Somehow, Nguyen Van Linh emerged in 1975 from prisons and manhunts and wars with an open mind, a sense of humor, and an enterprising spirit—and they quickly got him into trouble. His stature was so high with Le Duan, now general secretary, and other members of the old guard in Hanoi like Pham Van Dong that in 1978 he was appointed chairman of the government body that was to oversee the absorption of the South, the so-called Socialist Transformation Commission for South Vietnam. He surprised and angered his mentors by advocating a mixed economy in which "patriotic capitalists," that is, those who had stayed and were willing to coooperate with the new rulers, would be allowed to keep their factories and businesses. He also argued against the collectivization of agriculture. "The correct way would have been to help the peasants in the South to cultivate their own land as farmers do in the United States," Mr. Linh said. Southern farmers would then have had "all the incentives to increase production and be efficient."

He was denounced for "right-wing" thinking and his proposals rejected. Le Duan and the old guard went ahead with their plan to impose on the South the same centralized economy that prevailed in the North by seizing all privately owned factories and businesses and forcing Southern farmers into state cooperatives. A dour authoritarianism prevailed. Mr. Linh was appalled. "Socialism does not equal austerity and cannot be identified with a soldier's camp where there is a uniform and the same meals for everyone," he said.

Mr. Linh had not abandoned the concern for social justice first aroused in him by *Les Misérables*. "As a Communist I should always think of the interests of working people," he said. Rather, he had decided that orthodox socialism did not serve those interests because it was a foolish dream that would bankrupt the country. The touchstone of his thinking was, ironically, the lesson he had learned fighting the United States in the South: nothing worked unless it was firmly grounded in reality.

"The war against the Americans was not a war between equals; the U.S. Army was stronger than we were and had more weapons." Mr. Linh said. The Vietnamese would have lost had they simply traded blows. They had to devise a means within their grasp of wearing down the strength of their American opponent. "My comrades and I could not afford to be subjective in our conclusions. Had we been subjective, we would immediately have been crushed by reality," Mr. Linh said. "So I continued to think according to that pattern when I shifted to peaceful restructuring."

By 1982, when Mr. Linh's persistence in his odd-man-out stance had exhausted the patience of Le Duan and other senior Party figures and he was ejected from the inner circle by being kicked out of the Politburo, he was ready to leave Hanoi and the Politburo anyway. He was offered a return to a post he had previously held, Party secretary for Ho Chi Minh City, as a way of easing him into retirement. Mr. Linh did not see the job as a tombstone: "Ho Chi Minh City was a very useful testing ground for my ideas." There were men and women in Saigon with whom he had shared the experience of the American war, who had also learned from it to think in the creative, unorthodox way he did, and who would support him. "That's why I left the Politburo with a light heart," he said.

From Saigon, Mr. Linh began waging economic guerrilla warfare against Hanoi. He encouraged state factory managers in the Ho Chi Minh City area to act on their own initiative; he authorized private business ventures as well. "Inspection delegations" were sent down from Hanoi to record Mr. Linh's misdeeds. The confrontation became extremely tense.

He got away with his defiance because the man and the moment were unique. In an age of monumental slaughters to settle scores, the Vietnamese Communists behaved with comparative restraint toward their defeated opponents after the victory in 1975. The much-feared "bloodbath" did not occur. Instead, nearly 100,000 persons, almost all of them former Saigon army officers and government officials, were imprisoned for years (the number of years depended on the individual's rank and record) in "reeducation camps." Conditions were grim, but the reeducation camps were not like Nazi death camps or the Japanese prison camps of World War II in which half of the inmates perished. Ninety-four thousand of the reeducation camp prisoners survived and were released.

The explanation for the restraint was complicated. The leadership feared a repetition of the bloody excesses of the land reform campaign of the 1950s. The thirty years of war since 1945 had pitted neighbor against neighbor and family member against family member, and trials and executions would only have added to the bitterness. There also seems to be an element of forbearance and proportion in Vietnamese culture, suppressed during the years of war, that reemerged in its aftermath. (The one group to which the Vietnamese Communists did exhibit great cruelty during the postwar years was the Chinese minority in Vietnam. Fearing that the Chinese might become a fifth column for Beijing, the Vietnamese authorities expelled many of them, and, as "boat people," thousands perished on the sea.)

For all his tyrannical dogmatism, Le Duan never attempted to acquire the personal power of Mao Tse-tung and purge those who opposed him in a Vietnamese version of China's Cultural Revolution. As a "veteran of the Party" with an impeccable revolutionary and war record, Mr. Linh had a standing in the postwar politics of Vietnam that could not be denied. He could be fired as Party secretary for Ho Chi Minh City, just as he had been thrown out of the Politburo, but he could not be arrested and imprisoned or executed.

The relentless deterioration in Vietnam's economic and social conditions created enough doubt in Hanoi to keep him from being fired. Mr. Linh reinforced the doubt by inviting members of the old guard like Pham Van Dong to Ho Chi Minh City to look at factories and enterprises there and see that his way worked. By 1986, when Le Duan died, the reform movement was in the ascendancy. In yet another irony, Truong Chinh, the fanatic of the 1950s who had been disgraced by the land reform campaign and not permitted to hold an executive office until he became interim general secretary on Le Duan's death, promoted Mr. Linh's candidacy for the post at the Sixth Party Congress that year. In a speech to the congress he attacked the postwar attempt to create an orthodox Marxist state as a colossal error. He too had been invited to Ho Chi Minh City by Mr. Linh to see a different way. "Nothing is stronger than reality," Mr. Linh said.

Mr. Linh has often been called the Vietnamese [Mikhail] Gorbachev, and up to a point there is some aptness in the comparison. He is a man of the system without being a captive of the system. The difference was that Mr. Linh seemed to have a firmer grasp of the end result he wanted and to be prepared to risk drastic economic change to achieve it. "Socialism is prosperity," he said. And while not abandoning his earlier principles, he was willing to compromise on them. The free enterprise element of the mixed economy he envisioned meant social inequities; it also meant jobs Vietnamese so desperately needed: "We have to accept a certain level of exploitation."

The predicament was how to achieve the end result. It was obvious that until Vietnam could obtain enough foreign business investment and financing from the international lending institutions to build the infrastructure necessary for a modern economy, the country was going to remain poor. The process could not begin to occur on a major scale until the American embargo was lifted, and then the task of bringing it to fruition would take years. Vietnam came to terms with China in the fall of 1991 and the two countries resumed peaceable relations, but the United States continued its boycott. In the meantime the radical measures adopted by Mr. Linh and his adherents could improve the country's lot but not genuinely stabilize a fragile economy. The inflation they held in check during 1989 began to rise again during 1990 and was exceeding 100 percent a year by the end of 1991.

Time had also run out on Mr. Linh in his mid-seventies. The vitality of this trim man, with his steel gray hair combed straight, his alert eyes under the salt-and-pepper brows, was deceptive. He had an episode of colon cancer in 1988 and underwent surgery in Russia. There had been no recurrence, but his health was precarious. He was not the boss in Vietnam; rather, the first among equals. The element of restraint that protected him when he was a dissident worked against him after he became general secretary.

Decision making in Vietnam is by consensus. To act, the general secretary has to convince the other twelve members of the Politburo to go along with him. The naysayers can always slow him down by failing to agree. When I saw him, Mr. Linh was attempting to place protégés, men in their fifties and sixties whom he trusted to carry on his ideas, in positions of authority. Because of his age and health he was determined to retire at the Seventh Party Congress in 1991, when he would be seventy-six. "You cannot resist nature. I shall be a wrongdoer if I remain at my post," he said. The other old men also had their protégés and sometimes blocked his appointments. Yet he was convinced he had made a start, and events seemed to bear him out. When the Seventh Party Congress came, he did retire and was succeeded as general secretary by a Northerner he had converted to his thinking, Do Muoi, and he maneuvered into the prime ministership his friend and subordinate in the jungle, Vo Van Kiet.

His conviction that he had set his country on a course from which there was no full turning back and the simplicity of his life gave one the impression of a man who is at peace with himself. Mr. Linh's home in Saigon is an unpretentious house where he and his wife encourage the presence of their grandchildren. Does he still play Ping-Pong, as I had heard he liked to do? "No more Ping-Pong . . . well, perhaps from time to time. I do every day a kind of gymnastics appropriate for old people," he explained. He laughed as he mimicked himself at these exercises, breathing rhythmically and rotating his hands through the air. The exercises were called *tai chi*. Mr. Linh performed them for a half hour after he woke at 5 A.M., the same time he had gotten up every day in the jungle.

The main Communist headquarters where Mr. Linh had served as deputy during the war was called the Central Office for South Vietnam. The U.S. military, with its love of acronyms, shortened this to COSVN, and "COSVN" became synonymous with "mystery" because the American generals were constantly trying to find it and never succeeding. Richard Nixon announced on national television that he was going to destroy it during his sweep into Cambodia in 1970; he did not find COSVN either. I had heard that the final location of the headquarters was being preserved in the jungle. Could Susan and I go there? I asked Mr. Linh. "Of course you can," he said. Then he left as he had come, in the back of the off-white Lada, with just one security guard up front, to spend the rest of that Sunday with his family.

37
A Deserter and His Family
GLORIA EMERSON

Rennie Perrin, a middle-aged Vermont barber, was sound asleep when his wife, a nurse, came home from her shift at the Veterans Administration Hospital, so she thought it wiser to wait until the morning to tell him their son, Richard, had deserted. Mrs. Perrin heard it on the radio at the hospital, where she had night duty. The next day—it was in September 1967—Mr. Perrin had to be told, for there was a story on their son, a nineteen-year-old private, in the local paper, the Springfield *Times-Reporter*. Mr. Perrin, a veteran of World War II who had been discharged after a year in the Army because he had tuberculosis, listened to his wife, Betty. Then he began to cry. She stayed very calm.

"Somebody had to," Mrs. Perrin said.

Five years after Richard Perrin made that choice, his parents were still anxious and shy about talking about the son who had so much changed their lives, as if they still feared he might be hurt. For quite some time Mrs. Perrin thought certain Americans might go to Canada and try to kill the deserters living there.

The couple live in a mobile home in Sharon, Vermont, off Route 14, about ten miles north of White River Junction. They moved here in 1972 from North Springfield, where they lived for fifteen years and raised three children. Springfield is a factory town with not more than ten thousand people, known for its machine tools and often called "precision valley," Mr. Perrin said. He had his own barbershop, called Ray's, but he left it at the age of sixty-three. He only says of all this that business was slow because men were letting their hair grow longer and that he wasn't trained to do the hair styling that younger customers wanted. He does not give his son's notoriety as a reason for leaving. They moved to Sharon to be nearer the V.A. hospital where Mrs. Perrin has worked since 1966 in the orthopedic and neurosurgical wards.

It was in December 1973 when I saw them. They are not cheerful now at Christmas. Mr. Perrin speaks with effort, as if his words were little roots that had to be pulled up carefully from hard ground.

"We had a terrible time for a long time," Mr. Perrin said. "As long as he is in Canada, it will never really be over for us." He thought that people whose sons had been killed in Vietnam might find it easier to accept their loss, find it easier to go on with life, than he and his wife did. Their boy was always missing. "You make up your mind they're gone now and you can't bring them back," he said. "But with Dick, he's alive and can't come back."

The unspoken fear of Mr. and Mrs. Perrin was quite clear. It was that one of them—he at sixty-four, or she at fifty—might fall ill and not be able to see Richard before death. The other children would come to them, of course, but without Richard there was always a space and a longing.

"You'd be surprised at how fast things can happen to people," Mrs. Perrin said, meaning the heart-can-go, the lungs-can-go, the-kidneys-or-liver-can-go, just like that. She looked at Mr. Perrin; he looked at her. They did not want to complain about how they had been treated or tell me the names of people who had snubbed or wounded them. They did not want to be considered whiners.

Mr. Perrin was still a member of the American Legion because he paid his dues, but he had stopped going to their meetings. Mrs. Perrin was a member of the Daughters of the American Revolution.

I've never been back because I know how they would feel. It would be hard for me to listen to them talk—oh, I know how they talk." Mr. Perrin said, "You know they all went to war, and anybody who doesn't do that—well, I feel I'm just as good a legionnaire as they are. I believe in this country. I love this country. Even if Dick did desert, he said himself that he loved this country. There was the time when they asked him if he wanted to become a C.O. and he said no. He wasn't against all wars, just this one. If someone came to attack this country, he'd fight for the defense of it. . . .

In the beginning it was terrible for us. I was very patriotic, like most men are. I used to make statements like those I've heard people say in front of me since Dick deserted. People saying "Anyone who deserts should be shot." It's awful hard for people to understand. When this first happened we didn't go along with Dick because we didn't understand it. Like most people don't. But when you're involved in it you start asking yourself questions, why all this happened. Now that we know, we feel a lot better. In the beginning it was terrible.

Mr. Perrin was born in France, in Vosges above Nancy; he remembered his parents talking, with bitterness, about World War I. He came to Vermont as a child, growing up in Barre, but no one could pronounce his real first name, René. They called him Re-en, or Rinay, or Rin, so he called himself Rennie, for everyone could pronounce that.

Richard Perrin was nineteen, a tank mechanic in the 1st Battalion of the 64th Armored Brigade stationed in Kitzingen, West Germany, when he deserted and went to Paris to begin an organization called RITA, which stood for "Resist Inside the Army." It was an underground antiwar group of GIs trying to encourage dissension. Perhaps the most shocking time for his parents was December 11, 1967, when they saw their son on CBS television from Paris with the black radical Stokely Carmichael, who had recently called for the defeat of the United States in Vietnam.

I remember the deserters who came to Paris. A very tall boy from Florida who liked scrambled eggs slept on my living-room floor for three nights, but we thought it better if I did not know his last name. He went on to Sweden, he could not bear being in Paris. None of them were sure if the French government would not turn them over to the Americans, if there would not be a knock on the door at midnight, and the door kicked down. The deserters had pledged that they would engage in no political activity while in France, but their existence was a political act, their being in a room meant the war and the Army were in the room too.

The notorious interview took place at midnight in Paris after long, secret arrangements which took the CBS television crew and a *New York Times* reporter to a middle-class apartment. White bedsheets were hung in one room to shield a Dutch activist who had arranged everything. He stayed behind the sheets as he spoke of increasing desertions. Private Perrin walked through the sheets to sit down and face the camera, which rested on him like a huge, unblinking eye. He was calm and spoke quietly of his life, recalling how at fifteen he had joined a march in Chicago in 1964 led by the Reverend Dr. Martin Luther King, Jr.

"About this time I began thinking that, maybe, everything I was told in school, maybe, wasn't all like that," the private said.

In Springfield, Vermont, his parents were horrified. Mr. Perrin told a reporter: "We don't go along with what this boy did but we realize he has been brainwashed."

He insisted that his son had been a "good soldier" when he first enlisted. Local people, who considered Carmichael a Communist if not something even more evil, were very critical and let their opinions be known. A picture of Richard Perrin appeared on the front page of the town newspaper with the headline AWOL GI RECALLED AS AVERAGE STUDENT.

Mrs. Perrin was worried that the two younger children, David and Nancy, would be bullied or taunted. "That day when I sent them off to school—it was David's twelfth birthday—I remember telling the kids to hold your head high," she said. "When David went in his classroom one of the kids said 'Is that your brother?' and David said 'Shut your big fat mouth.' That's the way he handled it."

She is dark-haired, small, quicker to smile than her husband. Both speak softly. Their son once said of them, in an interview with another American in exile, that his parents were outwardly conservative people but more liberal than their Vermont friends.

"With my folks there is a sort of basic humanism which stuck in my head," Richard Perrin said. "They wouldn't tolerate me saying nigger, Polack, anything like that . . . I was always truthful with them, anything I did, I would always go home and tell them about it."

The word "deserter"—the ancient, horrid word with its dreadful picture of a cringing, failing man who flees—made them feel sick. It is a word they still do not like. It makes most Americans nervous, too, for they think of a battlefield and a soldier running from it, leaving other men in a lurch. No one thinks of courage or convictions.

It took Mr. and Mrs. Perrin nearly three years to accept what Richard had done and to see his reasons, although they always defended him even when they disapproved. Her husband was ahead of her on that, Mrs. Perrin said.

After graduating from high school, Richard had been unable to find a job because of his draft status. He went to California to visit his half brother, Ronald, the child of Mr. Perrin's first marriage, who was fifteen years older and always had a stunning and gentle influence on the younger boy. It was he who had worked for civil rights and made Richard see its importance. That year Ronald, who was teaching at the University of California, was in the antiwar movement, but nothing about Vietnam seemed to reach Richard Perrin until after he enlisted and was in advanced infantry training.

While sitting in a PX cafeteria at Fort Leonard Wood, Private Perrin, an E-2 squad leader at the armored vehicles repair shop, overheard two sergeants reminiscing about Vietnam. One described how he had gotten a confession from a captured Vietnamese by pushing the naked prisoner against the very hot engine of a tank so his genitals would burn. The sergeant was talking in a normal voice, not as if he was telling a secret. From then on, Richard Perrin began to pay attention to everything about the war. At the end of June 1967 he was sent to Fort Sill, Oklahoma. Ronald, who had earlier told him not to desert, had heard that a Private Andy Stapp, also at Fort Sill, was organizing GIs to protest the war. Richard later described his good friend Andy, who formed the American Servicemen's Union, as "anticapitalist, antiimperialist" while saying of himself that at Fort Sill he was just "antiwar." But he was that, and he worked hard.

"He was learning and reading about Vietnam. He was really tore up. He called home, very upset, and begged us to see it the way he did," Mr. Perrin said.

"But of course we didn't," Betty Perrin added, "we believed what we were reading in the papers at that time. We wanted him to just get the three years over and get home."

At Fort Sill, during a press conference of antiwar GIs, Private Perrin handed out his own statement, which received considerable attention in the press. He was eighteen.

"I was being trained as a truck mechanic and was on my way to Fort Sill to work on armored trucks and self-propelled artillery," the statement said. "I realized I was being trained to support these atrocities. At this point I decided to find out for myself whether there was any justification for the war. Everyone said there was, but they couldn't tell me what it was."

He ended the statement by saying that he hoped the people in the United States would wake up to the fact that they were being led through a period that would one day "be called the darkest in our history."

For his failure one night to sign out on the pass register, shortly after the press conference, Private Perrin was arrested, handcuffed and taken to the city jail in Lawton, before being turned over to the military authorities. He was charged with an article 15, nonjudicial punishment, which he refused to sign. He demanded a court-martial. It was clear to him he was only being punished for his antiwar activities, not for neglecting to sign the pass register.

Mr. and Mrs. Perrin were flown down to see their son and told by officers to try to bring the boy around to a reasonable point of view, that the military only wanted to straighten him out. They talked to a captain, then to a general, who explained the domino theory to them and the importance of South Vietnam being protected. When they saw Richard, who was in the stockade, they could hardly believe it.

"It was an awful shock," Mrs. Perrin said. "His head had been shaved but they wouldn't let him shave his face or change his clothes."

"He didn't look like our boy," Mr. Perrin said.

"He said he was ashamed to wear the uniform," Mrs. Perrin said.

Richard Perrin said later that when the Army assumed he repented, they offered to shorten his sentence of thirty days' hard labor. If he stopped his antiwar work, the Army said, they would send him to Germany, not Vietnam. Perrin agreed, but in Germany the racism on the bases— much more acute than in the United States—the memory of the stockade, his fatigue and disgust with the military led him to desert. He refused, in all ways, to be a soldier any more. In Paris he wanted RITA to inspire soldiers to challenge and harass the military.

"I was sort of hanging on to the old liberal myth: There's nothing wrong with the U.S. . . . The war is just a mistake. . . . We can stop this and elect a new administration," Richard Perrin said of himself in 1968.

In Springfield nothing was quite the same for his parents, or ever could be. Some people wrote letters to the paper protesting what Richard Perrin had done.

"One letter, I remember, said that we or the schools had failed in not having the Perrin boy read the story *The Man without a Country*," Mrs. Perrin said. A disabled World War II veteran wrote in his letter that deserters like their son should be shot. The man's wife was a friend of Mrs. Perrin's; they were both nurses. "We never talked about it, we just never even mentioned it," she said.

A lot of people asked his parents about Richard, including some whose own sons had been in Vietnam.

"You've heard me say this, Betty, but sometimes I had the feeling that some people, not all of them, would ask me about Dick because some of them were pumping me and that deep down they were probably hoping he was having a hard time," Mr. Perrin said, shaking his head.

But there were a few people who tried to tell him when he was still puzzled and sorrowful, that his son had done the right thing. The couple were encouraged to keep in touch with their son, not to turn their backs on him, by Phillips B. Henderson, pastor of the North Springfield Baptist Church, who had known Richard and had liked him.

Mrs. Perrin felt as if she and her husband had lost a child. "If they were mean, it made me mad. If they were kind, it almost brought me to tears," she said.

She was more often on the verge of tears. When Richard wrote from Canada for a grade transcript, the Springfield school board refused to send it to him. One board member was the father of Richard's closest friends in high school. He told his own children never to associate with their classmate again and he forbid them to write the deserter. When I asked them about the reaction of relatives in Vermont and New Hampshire, Mr. and Mrs. Perrin looked at each other but said nothing.

Richard moved to Canada in January 1969, working for a year and a half operating two hostels and a counseling service for the Union of American Deserters in Regina, Saskatchewan. He married a Canadian girl and both worked at a center for retarded children in Moose Jaw. At twenty-two Richard Perrin said that he did not think he would plan on returning to the United States and that he would be of no use there. At twenty-five he was in Regina working as a garage mechanic. He had always loved working on cars, that was one reason he never let his hair grow long, for he couldn't stand having it get in his eyes when he worked. His two-year-old son was named Shayne.

"He was the quietest of the children," Mrs. Perrin said. "There was a wide streak of idealism in Richard, together with an impatience with hypocrisy. Richard was the most quiet, I didn't always know what he was thinking because he didn't talk much, but when he did open up to talk you'd better be ready to listen. . . ."

They are stubborn people, refusing to give in to the strain and isolation they had felt for so long. Perhaps they had not even known how taxing it had been until the Perrins went to an amnesty conference in Vermont in the fall of 1973. It was so new for them to be surrounded by people like themselves, people who were proud of their sons for escaping the draft or leaving the Army. One young man went up to Mr. Perrin to shake his hand because he had a son in Canada. It was a man who had gone to jail rather than to Vietnam. Mr. Perrin spoke of that handshake, and the encounter, as if he had suddenly received an award.

"Even if they did let them come back, maybe it wouldn't be very pleasant for them—there would always be someone saying something and pointing them out as deserters," Mr. Perrin said. "Dick wouldn't want to come back to live."

The couple had visited their son and his family five times in Saskatchewan. The visits had been happy. David, the youngest son, had spoken often of the brother who went to Canada, for he was proud of him. Richard did not become a ghost. Mrs. Perrin showed me some color photographs of their reunions in Canada; there was Richard Perrin, a tall dark-haired man with a face that was a little blurred in the photographs.

"He doesn't look like a criminal, does he?" Mrs. Perrin asked.

38

Agent Orange, and the Wall at Home
BOBBIE ANN MASON

Sam had seen a bumper sticker in town: SPRAYED AND BETRAYED. When she told Emmett, he grunted and kept digging. He had Clearasil on his face. She realized that not every soldier who came back from Vietnam was as weird as Emmett. She knew of veterans—relatives of classmates—who had adjusted perfectly well. They had nice houses and wives and kids. They didn't wear skirts, even for a joke, and they didn't refuse to get a job or buy a car. Allen Wilkins was one of them. He owned a men's wear store and coached Little League. His daughter was a teen model in a Glamor Barn TV ad on Channel 6. Sam wondered if it was just her own crazy family rather than Vietnam.

The next morning, she decided to go along with Emmett to McDonald's instead of taking her usual run. She was curious about the veterans he hung around with. She had known them for years but had never thought much about them as vets.

At McDonald's, Emmett's buddies weren't there yet. A small bald man who worked with Lonnie's father at the hardware store stopped at their booth and teased Emmett about his "new girlfriend." He meant Sam.

"She keeps me in line," Emmett said, elbowing Sam.

"Emmett, I heard they're hiring at the cookie factory," the man said.

"Fuck the cookie factory," Emmett said, with his mouth full of Egg McMuffin.

The man winked at Sam. "Do you let him use that language at home, Sam?"

She shrugged. "It's on HBO."

"Does he let you watch HBO?"

"He don't care," she said, irritated.

"If I had HBO, I wouldn't let my wife watch it."

"Don't pay no attention to him, Sam," Emmett said as the man walked away. "He's got shit for brains."

Pete Simms and Tom Hudson joined them then. They had Cokes and little apple pies. Pete worked on a highway crew, and Tom was an auto mechanic with his own body shop. Sam knew Tom had been wounded in the war, but she couldn't tell, except that his posture was a little stiff. He sat down beside Emmett.

"Do you care if I set next to you, Sam?" asked Pete. "I won't bite."

"I'll let you set here if you show me your tattoo," Sam said impulsively. Emmett had once told her about Pete's tattoo. When Pete was in Vietnam, he had had a map of the Jackson Purchase region of western Kentucky tattooed on his chest.

"You want me to show you right here?" Pete asked flirtatiously. "I might get arrested. Come on out to my truck and I'll show you."

"What kind of truck you got?"

"A Ford Ranger. Why?"

"I need a car," Sam said.

"You need a hole in the head," said Emmett.

"I wonder if anybody ever tattooed his own face on his chest," Sam said. "Like a face on a T-shirt."

"I tell you one thing," Pete said. " I wish I had a goddamn T-shirt with this map on it instead of having it on my chest." He ate a bite of apple pie. "Ow! That's hot! Emmett, how come this long-legged little niece of yours is here? What's her trouble?"

"She's got ants in her pants," said Emmett.

"*He's* got Agent Orange," said Sam."Look at his face."

"I got Agent Orange," said Pete jokingly. "In the head." He laughed and blew on his pie. "I had a place come on my leg, all brown and funny? But it went away. Reckon it ate on down to the bone?"

"Nothing can hurt you, Pete," said Tom. "You're like that guy on TV that ate a bicycle."

"That was on *That's Incredible*," said Sam. "I saw that."

"Don't you know that was bound to mess that guy up?" Pete said with a grin.

"Did either one of you get sprayed with Agent Orange?" Sam asked point-blank.

Pete and Tom sucked their Coke straws simultaneously.

"I don't think so," Tom said slowly. He tapped a cigarette from a wrinkled pack.

Emmett snapped his Egg McMuffin box shut. "Sam's got Nam on the brain," he said. "She's been reading a bunch of history books and pestering me."

"What do those books tell you, Sam?" asked Tom, staring at her.

"Nothing. They're just dull history books." She was embarrassed. The books didn't say what it was like to be at war over there. The books didn't even have pictures.

Pete said, "Hell, I remember when they used to spray it. They'd tell us to get inside because they were going to spray, but it wasn't any big deal. It smelled sweet. It smelled like oranges."

"Buddy Mangrum can't even drink half a beer without getting sick," Tom said. "They say that's Agent Orange."

There was a racket in the back of McDonald's. A kid's birthday party was beginning. Sam tried to imagine these men fighting in the jungle. She had never been able to picture Emmett with a gun, but Granddad had talked offhandedly about shooting the dog. Emmett had told her Granddad wasn't serious.

"I think my problem's I might be allergic to fleas," Emmett said with a shiver. "My cat's got fleas. And he sleeps right on my head."

"If I had a car, I'd take you to the V.A.," Sam said. "I'd march you right in there and show them your face. Boy, I'd give anything for a car."

"Tom's got a car he wants to sell," Pete said.

"That bug? Yeah, I'll sell you my VW bug." Tom and Pete looked at each other and laughed. "I'll have to fix it up some, but you can have it for six thousand dollars."

Pete laughed. "Don't let him rip you off, Sam. It's a seventy-three."

"I'll give you a bargain," Tom said. "You can have it for six hundred. It runs good. I just have to fix it up a little."

"I don't have that much." She had three hundred dollars in the bank, but she had to live on it for the summer.

"You can come and see it."

Tom was looking straight into her eyes, and she looked away, punching her straw in her drink. Something about him excited her, but she didn't know what it was. He looked at her as though he really wanted her to have that car. She knew her face must be red.

Emmett flattened his Egg McMuffin box and went to the men's room.

"Do you want to see my tattoo, Sam?" Pete said with a wink.

"Sure."

"That's my street," Pete said, lifting his T-shirt and pointing to his chest. "And that little red thing that looks like a ladybug is my old Corvette. My wife sold it while I was gone. It would be a classic now."

Hairs sprouted from the heart of the Jackson Purchase. The tattoo was the size of a *National Geographic*, outlined in blue, with the towns in red.

He said, "I look at it upside down, and in the mirror it's backwards. This was maybe the stupidest thing I ever did in my life." He laughed.

Tom laughed with him. "When you're that age, you do some of the stupidest things you could ever think of, and you think, Oh, wow, ain't this the funniest thing in the world!" He shrugged. He wasn't bad-looking, Sam thought. He was about Emmett's age.

"You think about that car, Sam," Tom said when he left. "Come over and see it if you want to."

On the way home, Sam asked Emmett, "Are your friends always that goofy?"

"They just like to have fun. They're good guys."

"I wish I had that Volkswagen," she said. Her mother used to have one, and Sam had learned to drive on it.

"I don't think you can buy a car. You're underage."

"I could if you sign for me."

"Since I'm so responsible and have so much money? Yeah, anybody suing me would strike it rich!"

"Would you sign for me if I bought a car?"

"You get the money first and ask me again."

Sam saw a blue Volkswagen Beetle down the street, in front of a funeral parlor. She wouldn't mind having a VW bug.

Sam suddenly remembered something she had heard about Pete. Cautiously, she asked, "Hey, Emmett, is it true that Pete chased his wife out of the house once with a shotgun?"

"No, she was chasing him. He was out in the yard shooting—not at her. He was just shooting. Cindy wouldn't put up with his foolishness, though. She told him he had to quit it or she was walking."

"What was Pete shooting at?"

They crossed the street before he would answer. On the corner was the dental clinic where her mother used to be a receptionist. Sam asked him again, "What was Pete shooting at?"

"He said it was just an urge that come over him, and he got rid of it by going out and shooting off his gun."

When they were a block from the house, Emmett said suddenly, "He had a map of Vietnam in the den, and his wife tore it down because it didn't fit her decorating scheme. It sounds crazy, but I think he'd rather be back in Nam."

"Did you ever wish that?"

"No. Hell, no! Are you kidding?"

At the corner of their block, Emmett paused to look at something off in the field down by the waterworks, perhaps a bird, but he seemed to be listening for something, and Sam thought of the way Radar O'Reilly on M*A*S*H could always hear the choppers coming in with wounded before anyone else could.

Emmett could look at anything—a rosebush, a stop sign, an ordinary bird, or even a circular from Kroger's—and get absorbed in it as though it were the most fascinating thing on earth. That was how he was so good at *Pac-Man*, and it was the way he watched his birds, stalking them and probably imagining a full-feathered bird based on nothing more than a glimpse of wing, a bright patch of crest or throat. Emmett reminded Sam of James Stewart in *Harvey*, an old movie they had seen on Channel 7's Midnight Theatre. Harvey was an imaginary rabbit who went everywhere with James Stewart.

Sometimes it seemed that Emmett had somebody invisible along with him, too, some presence that guided him. But it probably wasn't a rabbit. It was probably a cat.

When Sam was seven or eight, she and Emmett had a stamp collection. They spent hours together poring over cellophane packets of exotic stamps sent on trial each month from stamp companies. Their stamp album was old and the countries were wrong—old colonial countries like Ceylon and the Belgian Congo. Vietnam was Indochine. While they played with the stamps, Emmett told Sam war stories, sprinkled with M-60s and grenade launchers and C-130 transport planes, and Sam's favorite—the amtrac, which Emmett laughingly described as a "yellow submarine." Sam had a picture of Vietnam in her mind from Emmett's stories—a pleasant countryside, something like Florida, with beaches and palm trees and watery fields of rice and green mountains. The sky was crowded with wonderful aircraft—C-47s with Gatling guns, Hueys, Chinooks, Skytrains, Bird Dogs. Emmett even made plastic models of helicopters and jet fighters, and he used them to act out his stories.

Irene stopped the stories. It upset her to be reminded of the war, but the reality of it didn't register on Sam until one day soon after they got their first color TV set. She was eight or nine. On the evening news, a report from Vietnam—it was during the fall of Saigon, in 1975, she thought—showed some people walking along a road with bundles on their backs. Some were carrying babies in their arms. Army jeeps chugged along the road. The landscape was believable—a hill in the distance, a paved road with narrow dirt shoulders, a field with something green planted in rows. The road resembled the old Hopewell road that twisted through the bottomland toward Paducah. For the first time, Vietnam was an actual place. As Sam watched, a child in a T-shirt and no pants ran down the road, and its mother called after it, scolding it. . . .

As they drive into Washington . . . Sam feels sick with apprehension. She has kept telling herself that the memorial is only a rock with names on it. It doesn't mean anything except they're dead. It's just names. Nobody here but us chickens. Just us and the planet Earth and the nuclear bomb. But that's O.K., she thinks now. There is something comforting about the idea of nobody here but us chickens. It's so intimate. Nobody here but us. Maybe that's the point. People shouldn't make too much of death. Her history teacher said there are more people alive now than dead. He warned that there were so many people alive now, and they were living so much longer, that people had the idea they were practically immortal. But everyone's going to die and we'd better get used to the notion, he said. Dead and gone. Long gone from Kentucky.

Sometimes in the middle of the night it struck Sam with sudden clarity that she was going to die someday. Most of the time she forgot about this. But now, as she and Emmett and Mamaw Hughes drive into Washington, where the Vietnam Memorial bears the names of so many who died, the reality of death hits her in broad daylight. Mamaw is fifty-eight. She is going to die soon. She could die any minute, like that racehorse that keeled over dead, inexplicably, on Father's Day. Sam has been so afraid Emmett would die. But Emmett came to Cawood's Pond looking for her, because it was unbearable to him that she might have left him alone, that she might even die.

The Washington Monument is a gleaming pencil against the sky. Emmett is driving, and the trafffic is frightening, so many cars swishing and merging, like bold skaters in a crowded rink. They pass cars with government license plates that say FED. Sam wonders how long the Washington Monument will stand on the Earth.

A brown sign on Constitution Avenue says VIETNAM VETERANS MEMORIAL. Emmett can't find a parking place nearby. He parks on a side street and they walk toward the Washington Monument. Mamaw puffs along. She has put on a good dress and stockings. Sam feels they are ambling, out for a stroll, it is so slow. She wants to break into a run. The Washington Monument rises up out of the earth, proud and tall. She remembers Tom's bitter comment about it—a big white prick. She once heard someone say the U.S.A. goes around fucking the world. That guy who put pink plastic around those islands should make a big rubber for the Washington Monument, Sam thinks. She has so many bizarre ideas there should be a market for her imagination. These ideas are churning in her head. She can hardly enjoy Washington for these thoughts. In Washington, the buildings are so pretty, so white. In a dream, the Vietnam Memorial was a black boomerang, whizzing toward her head.

"I don't see it," Mamaw says.

"It's over yonder," Emmett says, pointing. "They say you come up on it sudden."

"My legs are starting to hurt."

Sam wants to run, but she doesn't know whether she wants to run toward the memorial or away from it. She just wants to run. She has the new record album with her, so it won't melt in the hot car. It's in a plastic bag with handles. Emmett is carrying the pot of geraniums. She is amazed by him, his impressive bulk, his secret suffering. She feels his anxiety. His heart must be racing, as if something intolerable is about to happen.

Emmett holds Mamaw's arm protectively and steers her across the street. The pot of geraniums hugs his chest.

"There it is," Sam says.

It is massive, a black gash in a hillside, like a vein of coal exposed and then polished with polyurethane. A crowd is filing by slowly, staring at it solemnly.

"Law," says Sam's grandmother quietly. "It's black as night."

"Here's the directory," Emmett says, pausing at the entrance. "I'll look up his name for you, Mrs. Hughes."

The directory is on a pedestal with a protective plastic shield. Sam stands in the shade, looking forward, at the black wing embedded in the soil, with grass growing above. It is like a giant grave, fifty-eight thousand bodies rotting here behind those names. The people are streaming past, down into the pit.

"It don't show up good," Mamaw says anxiously. "It's just a hole in the ground."

The memorial cuts a V in the ground, like the wings of an abstract bird, huge and headless. Overhead, a jet plane angles upward, taking off.

"It's on Panel 9E," Emmett reports. "That's on the east wing. We're on the west."

At the bottom of the wall is a granite trough, and on the edge of it the sunlight reflects the names just above, in mirror writing, upside down. Flower arrangements are scattered at the base. A little kid says, "Look, Daddy, the flowers are dying." The man snaps, "Some are and some aren't."

The walkway is separated from the memorial by a strip of gravel, and on the other side of the walk is a border of dark gray brick. The shiny surface of the wall reflects the Lincoln Memorial and the Washington Monument, at opposite angles.

A woman in a sunhat is focusing a camera on the wall. She says to the woman with her, "I didn't think it would look like this. Things aren't what you think they look like. I didn't know it was a wall."

A spraddle-legged guy in camouflage clothing walks by with a cane. Probably he has an artificial leg, Sam thinks, but he walks along proudly, as if he has been here many times before and doesn't have any particular business at that moment. He seems to belong here, like Emmett hanging out at McDonald's.

A group of schoolkids tumble through, noisy as chickens. As they enter, one of the girls says, "Are they piled on top of each other?" They walk a few steps farther and she says, "What are all these names anyway?" Sam feels like punching the girl in the face for being so dumb. How could anybody that age not know? But she realizes that she doesn't know either. She is just beginning to understand. And she will never really know what happened to all these men in the war. Some people walk by, talking as though they are on a Sunday picnic, but most are reverent, and some of them are crying.

Sam stands in the center of the V, deep in the pit. The V is like the white wings of the shopping mall in Paducah. The Washington Monument is reflected at the center line. If she moves slightly to the left, she sees the monument, and if she moves the other way she sees a reflection of the flag opposite the memorial. Both the monument and the flag seem like arrogant gestures, like the country giving the finger to the dead boys, flung in this hole in the ground. Sam doesn't understand what she is feeling, but it is something so strong, it is like a tornado moving in her, something massive and overpowering. It feels like giving birth to this wall.

"I wish Tom could be here," Sam says to Emmett. "He needs to be here." Her voice is thin, like smoke, barely audible.

"He'll make it here someday. Jim's coming too. They're all coming one of these days."

"Are you going to look for anybody's name besides my daddy's?"

"Yeah."

"Who?"

"Those guys I told you about, the ones that died all around me that day. And that guy I was going to look up—he might be here. I don't know if he made it out or not."

Sam gets a flash of Emmett's suffering, his grieving all these years. He has been grieving for fourteen years. In this dazzling sunlight, his pimples don't show. A jet plane flies overhead, close to the earth. Its wings are angled back too, like a bird's.

Two workmen in hard hats are there with a stepladder and some loud machinery. One of the workmen, whose hat says on the back NEVER AGAIN, seems to be drilling into the wall.

"What's he doing, hon?" Sam hears Mamaw say behind her.

"It looks like they're patching up a hole or something." *Fixing a hole where the rain gets in.*

The man on the ladder turns off the tool, a sander, and the other workman hands him a brush. He brushes the spot. Silver duct tape is patched around several names, leaving the names exposed. The names are highlighted in yellow, as though someone has taken a Magic Marker and colored them, the way Sam used to mark names and dates, important facts, in her textbooks.

"Somebody must have vandalized it," says a man behind Sam. "Can you imagine the sicko who would do that?"

"No," says the woman with him. "Somebody just wanted the names to stand out and be noticed. I can go with that."

"Do you think they colored Dwayne's name?" Mamaw asks Sam worriedly.

"No. Why would they?" Sam gazes at the flowers spaced along the base of the memorial. A white carnation is stuck in a crack between two panels of the wall. A woman bends down and straightens a ribbon on a wreath. The ribbon has gold letters on it, "VFW Post 7215 of Pa."

They are moving slowly. Panel 9E is some distance ahead. Sam reads a small poster propped at the base of the wall: "To those men of C Company, 1st Bn. 503 Inf., 173rd Airborne who were lost in the battle for Hill 823, Dak To, Nov. 11, 1967. Because of their bravery I am here today. A grateful buddy."

A man rolls past in a wheelchair. Another jet plane flies over.

A handwritten note taped to the wall apologizes to one of the names for abandoning him in a firefight.

Mamaw turns to fuss over the geraniums in Emmett's arms, the way she might fluff a pillow.

The workmen are cleaning the yellow paint from the names. They sand the wall and brush it carefully, like men polishing their cars. The man on the ladder sprays water on the name he has just sanded and wipes it with a rag.

Sam, conscious of how slowly they are moving, with dread, watches two uniformed marines searching and searching for a name. "He must have been along here somewhere," one says. They keep looking, running their hands over the names.

"There it is. That's him."

They read his name and both look abruptly away, stare out for a moment in the direction of the Lincoln Memorial, then walk briskly off.

"May I help you find someone's name?" asks a woman in a T-shirt and green pants. She is a park guide, with a clipboard in her hand.

"We know where we are," Emmett says. "Much obliged, though."

At panel 9E, Sam stands back while Emmett and Mamaw search for her father's name. Emmett, his gaze steady and intent, faces the wall, as though he were watching birds; and Mamaw, through her glasses, seems intent and purposeful, as though she were looking for something back in the field, watching to see if a cow had gotten out of the pasture. Sam imagines the egret patrolling for ticks on a water buffalo's back, ducking and snaking its head forward, its beak like a punji stick.

"There it is," Emmett says. It is far above his head, near the top of the wall. He reaches up and touches the name. "There's his name, Dwayne E. Hughes."

"I can't reach it," says Mamaw. "Oh, I wanted to touch it," she says softly, in disappointment.

"We'll set the flowers here, Mrs. Hughes," says Emmett. He sets the pot at the base of the panel, tenderly, as though tucking in a baby.

"I'm going to bawl," Mamaw says, bowing her head and starting to sob. "I wish I could touch it."

Sam has an idea. She sprints over to the workmen and asks them to let her borrow the stepladder. They are almost finished, and they agree. One of them brings it over and sets it up beside the wall, and Sam urges Mamaw to climb the ladder, but Mamaw protests. "No, I can't do it. You do it."

"Go ahead, ma'am," the workman says.

"Emmett and me'll hold the ladder," says Sam.

"Somebody might see up my dress."

"No, go on, Mrs. Hughes. You can do it," says Emmett. "Come on, we'll help you reach it."

He takes her arm. Together, he and Sam steady her while she places her foot on the first step and swings herself up. She seems scared, and she doesn't speak. She reaches but cannot touch the name.

"One more, Mamaw," says Sam, looking up at her grandmother—at the sagging wrinkles, her flab hanging loose and sad, and her eyes reddened with crying. Mamaw reaches toward the name and slowly struggles up the next step, holding her dress tight against her. She touches the name, running her hand over it, stroking it tentatively, affectionately, like feeling a cat's back. Her chin wobbles, and after a moment she backs down the ladder silently.

When Mamaw is down, Sam starts up the ladder, with the record package in her hand.

"Here, take the camera, Sam. Get his name." Mamaw has brought Donna's Instamatic.

"No, I can't take a picture this close."

Sam climbs the ladder until she is eye level with her father's name. She feels funny, touching it. A scratching on a rock. Writing. Something for future archaeologists to puzzle over, clues to a language.

"Look this way, Sam," Mamaw says. "I want to take your picture. I want to get you and his name and the flowers in together if I can."

"The name won't show up," Sam says.

"Smile."

"How can I smile?" She is crying.

Mamaw backs up and snaps two pictures. Sam feels her face looking blank. Up on the ladder, she feels so tall, like a spindly weed that is sprouting up out of this diamond-bright seam of hard earth. She sees Emmett at the directory, probably searching for his buddies' names. She touches her father's name again.

"All I can see here is my reflection," Mamaw says when Sam comes down the ladder. "I hope his name shows up. And your face was all shadow."

"Wait here a minute," Sam says, turning away her tears from Mamaw. She hurries to the directory on the east side. Emmett isn't there anymore. She sees him striding along the wall, looking for a certain panel. Nearby, a group of marines is keeping a vigil for the POWs and MIAs. A double row of flags is planted in the dirt alongside their table. One of the marines walks by with a poster: "You Are an American, Your Voice Can Make the Difference." Sam flips through the directory and finds "Hughes." She wants to see her father's name there too. She runs down the row of Hughes names. There were so many Hughes boys killed, names she doesn't know. His name is there, and she gazes at it for a moment. Then suddenly her own name leaps out at her.

SAM ALAN HUGHES PFC AR 02 MAR

49 02 FEB 67 HOUSTON TX 14E 104

Her heart pounding, she rushes to panel 14E, and after racing her eyes over the string of names for a moment, she locates her own name.

SAM A HUGHES. It is the first on a line. It is down low enough to touch. She touches her own name. How odd it feels, as though all the names in America have been used to decorate this wall.

Mamaw is there at her side, clutching at Sam's arm, digging in with her fingernails. Mamaw says, "Coming up on this wall of a sudden and seeing how black it was, it was so awful, but then I came down in it and saw that white carnation blooming out of that crack and it gave me hope. It made me know he's watching over us." She loosens her bird-claw grip. "Did we lose Emmett?"

Silently, Sam points to the place where Emmett is studying the names low on a panel. He is sitting there cross-legged in front of the wall, and slowly his face bursts into a smile like flames.

CHAPTER 12

Afterword

This excerpt from a book written by a Vietnamese woman, Le Ly Hayslip, is a memoir of her life in Vietnam, from her birth in 1949 to her departure for the United States (with an American husband) in 1969. The memoir is intercut with a description of Le Ly's return to Vietnam in 1986, an attempt to come to terms with her past. Hers was a harrowing life: she joined the NLF when she was twelve, was jailed and tortured several times by representatives of the South Vietnamese government, and then was falsely accused of treachery and raped by two of her comrades. She fled her village for Saigon and Danang, had a child out of wedlock, and became thickly involved in the black market, selling "souvenirs," including marijuana, to Americans. Her father committed suicide. Determined to leave Vietnam for a better life in the United States, Le Ly fell into a series of unhappy relationships with Americans, who feigned tenderness but exploited her mercilessly. Finally, she met Ed Munro, a lonely old man who wanted "a good Oriental wife who knows how to take care of her man." Practicality overcomes romance in the following melancholy passage.

Hong Kong, August 13, 1987. Two of the refugees—"boat people"—who have fled Vietnam in the years since liberation, this ethnic Chinese woman and her child wait at a processing center. REUTERS/BETTMANN NEWSPHOTOS

39
Letting Go
LE LY HAYSLIP

I found it very hard to concentrate at work after Ed made his proposal. He said that in return for marrying him and coming to America and taking care of him as his wife, he would see to it that I would never have to work again; that my little boy, Jimmy, would be raised in a nice neighborhood and go to an American school; and that neither of us would have to face the dangers and travails of war again. It was the dream of most Vietnamese women and the answer to my prayers—except—

I was still a young woman. The proper time to care for a sixty-year-old husband is at the end of a long and happy marriage, not the beginning. I knew I was attractive to young men and wanted a husband my own age—as my mother and Ba Xuan and Sister Hai all had. On the other hand, I did not especially want to wind up like my sister Lan, who had many lovers, both Vietnamese and American (and now a child by one of them) and no prospects for marriage and a better life at all. Those friends in whom I confided about this problem weren't much help. Some were jealous of my golden opportunity to flee the war, or at least to enjoy the easy life of an American housewife. Others only ridiculed me for even considering a union with someone old enough to be my father. It seemed an unsolvable dilemma.

Of course, Ed was as persistent as he was kind. Because I did not want to be disrespectful, I kept putting him off by saying. "It's too far away," meaning the idea was "so distant" that I didn't even want to think about it, although he took it to mean that I thought America was too far away, so he redoubled his efforts to assure me that it was a wonderful place to live. At the core of my problem, I knew, was the Vietnamese distinction between *duyen* and *no*—the components of marriage that every child learns when he or she becomes engaged. *Duyen no* together denotes a married couple's karma—the destiny they share and what they owe to each other to achieve it. *Duyen* means love—physical attraction and affection; *no* means "debt"—the duty that goes with the office of husband or wife. In a marriage without *no*, the flames of emotion run too high and the couple risks burning up in too much passion or despair. In a marriage without *duyen*, which is the union I would face with Ed, there would be no passion at all—no affection beyond good manners—and nothing to look forward to but the slow chill of a contract played out through all its clauses. Worse, marriages of *no*—quite common in Vietnam—often led to the abuse of one spouse by the other, through extramarital affairs, wife-beating, and the thousand other games perfected by cheated souls.

It took me many months to come to grips with this problem and learn my own mind. Young men, I decided, were for marriageable young women—not unwed mothers, black marketeers, and Viet Cong fugitives. By trying to do my duty to everyone in my life—parents, Communist cadremen, rich employers, corrupt officials—I had wound up failing in my duty to myself and the child of my breast, who depended on me. I decided to read the handwriting on the wall. Younger men valued me as a companion, an ornament, and a plaything—that was true enough; but not as a partner for their lives. And why should they? For any American to want me for a wife, he would have to have an extraordinary need—not for a party girl or bedmate or crutch to support his weaknesses, or for someone to help him pretend the times were normal when they were not—but as a companion for the completion of his own life's circle. For me to trust myself again to an American, that man must be such an extraordinary person. In Ed Munro, who was completely unlike the other men I had met in my life, perhaps I— and my fatherless son—had discovered such a man.

In August 1969, when Ed's contract in Vietnam was into its final year, I agreed to become his wife. It was a decision that turned out to be filled with many unexpected costs.

For example, instead of rejoicing wholeheartedly with me, my friends began to warn me about the many legal and practical roadblocks established to discourage Vietnamese-American marriages and emigration to the United States. To make matters worse, the detailed investigations that went into certifying every applicant for a visa made it almost inevitable that my previous arrests (for everything from aiding the Viet Cong to selling illegal drugs) would be discovered and I would quickly be branded an "undesirable alien." What such revelations might mean to my fiancé, I couldn't even think about.

Fortunately, Ed was a man of the world as well as a man of his word. He didn't ask about my past and said that as far as he was concerned, our new life began on the day we met and I could make of it anything I chose; that nothing in my past should stand between us and our future happiness. He said he would be willing to pay whatever was necessary to ensure that our paperwork was approved. Because he had never before dealt with the corrupt Republican machinery, he had no inkling of how costly this blank check might be. Because I had never tried to pull off anything this big either, I was in no position to tell him.

My first step, then, was to return to the landowner—the "dragon lady," Sister Hoa— who had helped me before. Our first meeting was not too productive because she only wanted to talk about the niceties of marriage and how wonderful life was in America; how happy she was that I had found a nice, mature American and how lucky I would be to live in Southern California. When we finally got around to talking turkey, I discovered this particular goose would take a lot of stuffing!

"What you want is very, very expensive!" she admonished me, as if she found the profit she was going to make distasteful. "You'll need permission from government agencies at the city, district, provincial, and national levels. You'll need a marriage certificate and favorable reports from both the Vietnamese and American counselors you'll have to visit. Do you plan to take your little boy with you?"

"Of course! He's my son!"

"That's too bad," she said, smiling pleasantly. "You'll need a birth certificate stating he's *con hoan*—a child without father—and we'll have to get an exit visa for him as well. Tsk!" She shook her head. "The best way to approach it is to tell me how much you and your man are prepared to spend, and I'll try to negotiate the best deal I can at each step, taking my fee from what's left over. That way, you'll know I'm not trying to cheat you."

"How much do you think all this will cost?" I asked.

"It's hard to say without knowing the problems I'll run into. When the war's going well, everything gets cheaper. When there's bad news from the front, everyone gets worried and wants more money for everything. I'd say the basic package should run about a hundred and fifty thousand *dong—*"

"I'll go to America with the caskets!" I start to get up. She was talking almost *double* the amount Ed and I had discussed. Even with my own savings, it would be impossible to pay what she asked.

"Hold on, take it easy!" She put her long-nailed fingers on my arm. "I said that's how much it *should* cost, not how much you will actually have to pay! Remember, you'll have me as your adviser. Now, let's talk things over like businesswomen, shall we? Would you care for some tea?"

By the end of the interview, we had agreed upon thirty to fifty thousand *dong* as a reasonable price—but this was for "guarantees" only, and did not include the official fees or gratuities (such as whiskey and cigarettes) that customarily went to decision makers at each level. Despite my earlier remark, I was glad I did not have to buy my way into the illegal transportation network out of the country, such as the occasional Vietnamese who, as rumors had it, rode empty American caskets to Guam or to the Philippines or Honolulu. Even an American's resources would be hard-pressed to fund such desperate and costly schemes.

While we waited for Sister Hoa to grease the proper wheels, I began to live with Ed—to become the kind of wife that he desired. At first, our jobs kept us apart a good deal of the time, which was okay with me. My shift at the Navy EM club ended about eleven, which was when Ed's night shift at the outlying camps was beginning. Although this didn't bother me at all (the idea of ministering to an old, fatherly man as a husband was still too queer to appeal to me), it was not what Ed had in mind for our relationship, so, shortly after we moved in together, he told me to quit my job. Ed's conception of a wife was not someone who worked shoulder to shoulder with her man "in the fields," which was the Vietnamese way, but a queen on a pedestal who spent her days at the beauty shop or overseeing the full-time maid he hired to do all the housework and so kept her long, red fingernails from getting broken. It was a curious role for Phung Thi women, who, for a thousand years, had never been without a day's work before them. Although I tried to please him and play the role he had in mind (idleness was infectious, I discovered—as though every day was New Year's!), I felt more guilt than pleasure. It was as if I had become Lien—an icy princess who seemed to have nothing better to do than read magazines and lord over her servants. Nevertheless, the gift of time was one I could now pass on to my son, and Jimmy began to rediscover his mother just as I began to rediscover what families were all about. Shortly after I accepted Ed's proposal, in fact, I was told by the doctor that my family was about to get a little bigger.

One Sunday, after my clothes began getting tight again at the belly, Sister Hoa came with the one-eyed policeman, an armful of papers—including a marriage certificate and a birth certificate for little Jimmy—and a justice of the peace, to the nice house Ed had rented. While we filled out the forms, Ed sent for his friends, who had agreed to be our witnesses, and told our maid to prepare for a little party to celebrate our marriage. To mark the occasion, I had borrowed one of Lan's fancy cocktail dresses, which (with a few pins and a short veil cut from a sun hat), I quickly turned into a makeshift, Western-style bridal gown.

Within an hour Ed and I were married in a civil ceremony. I had invited my sisters Ba and Lan to come, but they refused; so Hoa cried on behalf of my absent relatives. Although Lan's objections to my marriage seemed more to do with envy than principle (her American boyfriend, Robert, was a friend of Ed's and I think it nettled her that I received a marriage proposal first), Ba's complaints were more traditional. Custom demanded that a bride wait three years after the death of her father before she gives herself to a man, and even in wartime many people thought I was acting too rashly.

"*Phan boi*," Ba Xuan said one day after a particularly heated discussion of my situation. "You betray your ancestors!" She then sang a little song for my benefit, which I remembered singing myself with other girls in derision of a woman who left the village to marry a man in the city:

Da Da birds live only in Da Da trees,
They sing: Why do you marry and go far away,
Instead of loving a man nearby?
Your father gets weak;
Your mother gets old;
Who will be around
To bring them a bowl of rice,
Or serve them tea?

"Do you see now what you're doing?" Ba asked, genuinely concerned for my soul. "Americans are *thu vo thuy vo chung*—they have no beginning and no end. They don't care about their ancestors. Because they don't know what reincarnation is, they think they're free to do any cruel thing they want in this life—no matter how much it hurts others."

"Can't I be married to Ed without becoming an American myself?" I replied sincerely. "Can't I keep an altar in my house and pray to our father and to Sau Ban and to Grandma and Grandpa Phung, even if Ed doesn't believe in it himself?"

"Sure you can—of course you can—" Ba was really angry. "But secretly, he'll scorn you—and that scorn will come out later in cruelty and disrespect. I'm older than you, Bay Ly. I've been married a long time and know how men act. Why do you think all those little Amerasian bastards are shunned by our people, eh? Not because we don't think they're cute or need help, but because they're tainted with the invader's karma. You don't have to be Viet Cong to know that and hate them for it. Now you want your next child to become one of them! Honestly, Bay Ly—what gets into your head sometimes? And what will our mother think?"

That, of course, is what I regretted most: that my mother could not be with me anymore, even in spirit. Although I did not have the courage to speak to her directly about my plans, I believed the simple fact that I was marrying outside my race, let alone to an American invader, was enough to threaten her motherly love. Sadly, Lan kept me well apprised of my mother's black moods:

"*Dua con hy*, she calls you, Bay Ly," Lan told me shortly before the wedding. "A spoiled rotten child! She says you're acting ungrateful toward your parents and soiling the family name. She says that even though our father's dead, you have made him sad with your decision. It's not too late to call things off, you know."

I felt like challenging Lan—for her years of ignoring our customs herself and her own easy ways with Americans—but I knew it would be fruitless. Our mother usually sided with Lan because Lan had money and was a mature woman and was not the "baby of the family," which is how I gradually realized I would always be viewed, no matter what I did in life. Although Vietnamese are raised to respect their ancestors and love their nation, they are not above civil war. In the triangle formed by our family's sad situation—Lan's contest with me for our mother's affection, our struggle against the tide of a changing society, and our different feelings about Americans—I could almost see a fishpond version of the Viet Cong war itself. If I could not make peace with my family in such matters, how could the real fighters on both sides expect to resolve their differences?

When the short ceremony was over. Ed shook the officials' well-greased palms and complimented them on their sense of duty—working on a Sunday just to help an American get married! Their attitudes, he said innocently, were what Vietnamese-

American cooperation was all about. We then had a fine party with Ed's friends, but they, too, left quickly, as if embarrassed by their old friend's child bride. Later, my little niece Tinh, Hai's daughter, came over with sweet rice to wish me good luck and tell me that she loved me. We hugged and cried and I told her I would never forget her.

Unfortunately, our quest, which had begun so hopefully, soon bogged down in obstacles thrown up by destiny or luck—or the government.

First, there was the problem of marriage counseling, a requirement mandated by the American consulate in Danang. Now that his own child was on the way, Ed said he wanted to adopt Jimmy, which was fine with the Americans; but the Vietnamese counselor—a short, fat, greedy woman about Ed's age—raised a long list of objections. While Ed was at work, I attended sessions with this woman and negotiated a price for each objection. Unfortunately, the more I paid, the more she wanted, and each dispensation cost more than the last. After several of these "conferences," I was running out of the money Ed allotted for our paperwork. (He gave me two hundred dollars a month to run our household, fifty of which went to pay rent. The rest was to buy food and wrap up our affairs with the government.) Because Ed didn't want me to work after we were married, I had nothing to draw on for the difference but my savings—most of which I had already given to my mother. For several weeks, the officials at the chief district headquarters dined well while my mother and Jimmy and I practically starved. Still, I made sure my husband never suspected our situation. His plate was always full and our refrigerator was always stocked with cold beer. I didn't want my American savior to know the depth of corruption into which my homeland had sunk.

Finally, just when the counselor was getting ready to sign our release, she paused, and said, "Oh, yes, about my bonus—"

"What bonus are you talking about?" I asked, amazed. "I've already paid you almost every dollar to my name—including every cent my husband gives me to run our house. What more could you possibly want?"

"Oh, it's not for me," she said, as if she were asking for church donations. "It's for our 'coffee fund' here at the office. You know, we have lots of volunteers who come in and help us with our cases. We can't afford to pay them, so we offer them coffee and tea and meals when they work overtime—the way they had to work for your application. And you know how long *that's* taken us!"

I couldn't believe what I was hearing. "So—how much coffee are we talking about?" I asked guardedly.

"Well, to tell you the truth," she gazed pensively out the window, tapping her yellow teeth with the end of the pencil, "cash loses its value quickly these days, have you noticed? Even American greenbacks. I was thinking more in terms of merchandise—something that holds its value. You know, like diamonds—"

"*Diamonds!*"

"Now, don't get excited." She opened her desk drawer and produced a page torn from a Sears catalogue. "I don't mean raw gemstones or anything like that. Just something nice that will keep its value better than paper money. Like this nice diamond watch, for example"—she pointed to a pretty lady's watch on a much-handled page—"or maybe a nice dinner ring—like this!" While she shopped from the catalogue, I wondered how many other poor applicants had spent their life savings just to furnish this greedy lady's home, wardrobe, or office on the eve of their departure. We finally decided that a genuine pearl necklace would be just what the volunteers needed for breakfast, so I used up my last favors from old black market partners and obtained one for half-price. I had now completely exhausted my reserves and prayed there would be no more surprises. In the world's shortest adoption ceremony, I slid the black velvet jewelry case across her desk, received Jimmy's papers in return, and was out of the office before the price could go up again.

Unfortunately, like a frog trying to jump from a table by leaping half the distance remaining on each try, my victories always fell just short of my goal. When I brought the signed papers back to Hoa, she informed me that my plans had hit another snag.

"Of course," she said, as if it were nothing, "we'll need your mother's signature. You're still under age, and even if you're married, you'll need your parents' consent before leaving the country."

Up to this point, I had been able to avoid the whole issue of what to do about my mother. As far as she was concerned, Ed was just another American "boyfriend" (marriage to an outsider was not valid in her eyes) and my life and future, whatever they would be—as well as the life and future of my son—would always be in Vietnam. Although I knew my mother must eventually learn what was going to happen to me, I was not so sure that I had to be the one to tell her; or that she should even know before I left. Now, my procrastination had caught up to me. I would have to be either an exceptionally brave and honest daughter or a very skillful liar. Like many young girls that age, I decided to be the latter.

"Here, Mama *Du*," I said casually, shoving a form and a pen at her one day after lunch. "You have to sign this."

"What is it?" I knew she couldn't read or write, although, like many peasants, she had been taught to make her mark when it was required on legal papers.

"It's nothing; just an application for a bank account. You've probably wondered where all our savings went, right? Well, I deposited them in a safe place. What if the house burned down? All our money would go up in smoke! With my second baby on the way, I have to be more responsible."

She looked at the mysterious form a long moment, and for a guilty instant, I thought that maybe she had learned to read and would discover what I was up to. As independent as I had become over the last few years, I knew I could never stand up against my mother if she made a really big fuss over things. If the choice came down to leaving the country or destroying my mother's love for me, I knew I would have no options—even if it meant raising a hated Amerasian baby as an outcast among our people. Fortunately, I had a lifetime of peasant's habits on my side.

"Okay, if you really think it's wise." She made her mark and gave me the form. "I still wouldn't trust anyone outside the family with my money, though. Why don't you just give it to Uncle Nhu's son? He's helped us before—"

I gave her a long, tight hug and kissed the top of her graying head. "Thanks, Mama *Du*. You won't regret it!"

On February 11, 1970, my second son was born in a clean hospital run by Americans for U.S. dependents. Although Ed already had two grown sons he greeted the arrival of this new spirit like a brand-new father. He passed out cigars to his friends and told them how proud he was of "Thomas"—a good Christian name for a strong and spirited little boy. Alone in the hospital room, I sang a song of welcome to the little soul I called "Chau"—one who was destined to wander—who lay nursing at my breast:

> *Go out every day and you will learn,*
> *Each step that you take will make you wiser.*
> *Go here, go there, go eveywhere—*
> *How can you be smart by staying home?*

In the world you will find many nations
And many people all over the land;
You'll cross deep oceans and tall mountains,
And roads that crisscross the sand.
You'll find people that come in four races:
Yellow, white, red, and black;
You'll float through the sky in four directions:
East, west, north, and south.
But you will never know all these things, my son,
Unless you get out of your house.

When I got out of the hospital, my mother came to stay with us at Ed's house and help me through my period of *buon de*. Although Ed always tried to treat her kindly, she was content to behave like a servant when he was around—grunting only when spoken to and showing indifference to his favors. She was mostly concerned about how little Tommy (she always called him Chau) would get by when the war was over. If the Communists won, she knew his invader's blood—*con lai*—would put all of us in danger. If the Republicans won, she knew that same foreign blood—his light skin and American features—would cause him to be shunned in the village as soon as the Americans withdrew. As a result, she spent hours pressing his nose against his face, hoping to flatten it like a Vietnamese. she fed him dark juice and rubbed the juice on his body and kept him outdoors in hopes that his skin would darken like ours. I didn't know if these things would work or not, but I could see in them the desperation that was rising inside my mother; desperation that made it harder for me even to think about telling her the truth: that Ed and I and my two fine boys would one day step on an airliner and, very likely, never be seen by her again.

A few months after Tommy was born, Ed's overseas contract expired and it was time for him to return to the States. The plan was for Ed to go to San Diego first and prepare his home and local relatives for our arrival. After seeing him off at the airport, I moved my things to Lan's apartment where I would live until my own departure, now less than a week away.

During my last few weeks in Danang, when word of my marriage spread through the neighborhood and I dealt with people as "Mrs. Ed Munro" rather than Phung Thi Le Ly, the world around me began to change. Certainly, I was the same person I had always been, but now I was labeled in a different way. I was no longer completely Vietnamese, but I was not quite American either. Apparently, I was something much worse. Even people I had expected to understand me, to be sympathetic to my dreams, looked down on me and called me names—not always to my back: *Di lay My! Theo de quoc Ve My! Fai choi boi!* Bitch! Traitor! American whore! During many endless hours spent standing in line or sitting in waiting rooms or by desks of minor officials, I found myself on the receiving end of dirty glances from Vietnamese clerks, secretaries, errand boys, and janitors. No citizen of Danang was so poor or humble that he or she was not superior to Le Ly *Munro*—turncoat to her country. Teenagers and a few Republican soldiers who lived in our neighborhood gave me cat-calls and sang derisive songs when I passed and, on two occasions, threw stones at me when I appeared on the street alone. In one instance our home was broken into, burglarized (which was understandable), and vandalized (which was not).

Even people who forgave me my new American name could not excuse me for accepting an older man as my savior. On many occasions Ed and I were openly cheated—charged two or three times more than even the black market price for food or supplies —just so people could show us their indignation. It seemed as though the more we accepted their wrath, the more contempt they showed us. In private conversations, I was often pleasantly (and sometimes not so pleasantly) reminded that in America, people hated anyone—even other Americans—who came from Vietnam, and quoted the war protectors' slogans. They were a gallery of sullen, unforgiving faces that I often saw in my sleep: tattered victims on Vietnam's foundering ship of state watching jealously as I abandoned them for the lifeboat of America. I was experiencing, I discovered, not only what foreigners had faced in my own land for generations; but the ultimate price of my own independence. It made Sister Hoa's demands seems paltry by comparison.

In any event, after paying more bribes to obtain my passport, I was finally ready to depart Danang for Saigon; to get a visa at the American embassy—the last hurdle standing between my sons and me and our flight to a better life.

On March 20, 1970, Jimmy, Tommy, our maid, and I boarded the shuttle flight for Tan Son Nhut. All through the flight, I thought about my mother and how she would react when my maid (she drew the short straw—none of my sisters would do it!) returned to Danang and broke the news of our departure to my mother. Part of me wanted to believe she already knew the truth—learning it, perhaps, from a neighbor or by that intuition through which every mother knows her daughter—and that the truth had been in her eyes the last time I looked into her face: a benediction for my new life. Of course, unless I was to come back someday, I would probably never know.

During the two-month stay before our overseas flight, I had no trouble saying farewell to Saigon. As the capital of our country as well as Anh's home, it had become the symbol of everything I wanted to leave behind—to let go of and cut loose from my life. In the three years since I had been here, Saigon had become even bigger and noisier and dirtier and more wealthy and more wealth-driven and more cosmopolitan than it had ever been before. Rather than being less Vietnamese, which is how the Viet Cong described it, Saigon now seemed to be more and more what the Vietnamese people themselves were becoming: vicious, grasping, estranged, desperate, and dangerous—mostly to themselves. Still, I had one last piece of business to attend to before these chains were broken.

The great U.S. embassy was busy as a marketplace—full of staff and visitors. After a long wait, a junior American clerk received me only to tell me that Vietnamese citizens seeking visas were supposed to report to a different building, where such requests were processed by the Vietnamese Immigration and Naturalization Department. This distressed me greatly—not just for the extra step—but because dealing with Vietnamese bureaucrats always meant more cost and trouble.

The emigration offfice was located in a two-story white apartment building that was near the main post office and the Nha Tho Duc Ba Catholic Church. I was not encouraged when I walked through the door. Instead of a businesslike office, the apartment was the residence of a well-heeled Republican woman who had refined the art of administrative extortion to a science.

"How badly do you want to go to America?" she asked, cutting right to the heart of the matter. "You'll need documentation from the Vietnamese embassy in Washington. It's going to be expensive. How much do you have to spend?" Perhaps she phrased it this way so that if anybody ever challenged her, she could say she was simply separating the charity cases from those who could pay the government's fee.

I replied with a good, cheap guess.

"That's not enough," she said flatly. "Come into my house. We'll have to discuss your case."

After brief negotiations, accelerated by my early admission that my American husband was no longer around to pay my bills and that I could only raise more cash by selling my airline ticket, which would defeat the purpose of a visa, we agreed upon a price.

"Okay," she said, ushering me back outside. "You'll have to wait out here while I prepare your letter. My house isn't a bus station, you know. And by the way, there'll be a small surcharge for our tea fund—"

I spent the next few hours hoping that tea was cheaper than coffee—even at Saigon's inflated prices. By the end of the day, though, I went home with the all-important letter.

On May 27, 1970, my sons and I stood in line to board the big American jetliner to Honolulu. As the passengers shuffled forward, juggling their carry-on bags and jackets, they showed their tickets to one last Republican official. The Americans passed quickly. The Vietnamese, however, usually had to stop and delay the line while they fumbled through their purses or pockets. When my turn came, the official did not ask for passports or visas or certificates of any kind. He asked only a single question—the last phrase I would hear in my native tongue on the soil which held my father's bones:

"Are you carrying Vietnamese money? If so, please drop it in the basket before you go."

List of Sources

Grateful acknowledgment is made to the publishers and authors of the following selections for their permission to reprint in whole or in part.

Robert Shaplen, *The Lost Revolution: The U.S. in Vietnam, 1946–1966*, rev. ed. (New York: HarperCollins, 1966), 27–54. © 1955, 1962, 1963, 1964, 1965, and 1966 by Robert Shaplen. Reprinted by permission of HarperCollins.

George C. Herring, *America's Longest War: The United States and Vietnam, 1950–1975*, 3d ed. (New York: McGraw-Hill, 1996), 8–26. Reprinted by permission of McGraw-Hill.

David L. Anderson, ed., *Shadow on the White House: Presidents and the Vietnam War, 1945–1975* (Lawrence: University Press of Kansas, 1993), 43–62. Reprinted by permission of the University Press of Kansas.

Ellen J. Hammer, *The Struggle for Indochina, 1940–1955* (Stanford, CA: Stanford University Press, 1966), 326–37. © 1954 and 1955 by the Institute of Pacific Relations. Reprinted by permission of Stanford University Press.

Edward Geary Lansdale, *In the Midst of Wars: An American's Mission to Southeast Asia*, 2d ed. (New York: Fordham University Press, 1991), 215–27. © 1991 by Fordham University Press. Reprinted by permission of Fordham University Press.

Herbert S. Parmet, *JFK: The Presidency of John F. Kennedy* (New York: Doubleday, 1983), 325–37, 389–91. © 1983 by Herbert S. Parmet. Reprinted by permission of Doubleday, a division of Bantam Doubleday Dell Publishing Group.

Robert S. McNamara, *In Retrospect* (New York: Random House, 1995), 127–43, 471–72. © 1995 by Robert S. McNamara. Reprinted by permission of Times Books, a division of Random House, Inc.

Lloyd C. Gardner, *Pay Any Price: Lyndon Johnson and the Wars for Vietnam* (Chicago: Ivan R. Dee, 1995), 151–76. Notes omitted. © 1995 by Lloyd C. Gardner. Reprinted by permission of Ivan R. Dee, Inc.

Larry Berman, *Lyndon Johnson's War: The Road to Stalemate in Vietnam* (New York: W. W. Norton and Co., 1989), 139–49, 151–54, 213. © 1989 by Larry Berman. Reprinted by permission of W. W. Norton and Co.

George W. Ball, *The Past Has Another Pattern: Memoirs* (New York: W. W. Norton and Co., 1982), 399–409, 505–6. © 1982 by George W. Ball. Reprinted by permission of W. W. Norton and Co.

Stephen E. Ambrose, *Nixon*, vol. 2 (New York: Simon and Schuster, 1989), 525–41. Notes omitted. © 1989 by Ambrose-Tubbs. Reprinted by permission of Simon and Schuster.

Gareth Porter, *A Peace Denied: The United States, Vietnam, and the Paris Agreement* (Bloomington: Indiana University Press, 1975), 158–65, 271–78, 301–2, 316–17. © 1975 by Gareth Porter. Reprinted by permission of Indiana University Press.

William Colby, *Lost Victory* (Lincolnwood, IL: NTC/Contemporary Publishing Co.), 325–42. Reprinted by permission of NTC/Contemporary Publishing Co.

Truong Nhu Tang, with David Chanoff and Doan Van Toai, *A Vietcong Memoir* (New York: Vintage Books, 1985), 63–66, 68–80. © 1985 by Truong Nhu Tang, David Chanoff, and Doan Van Toai. Reprinted by permission of Harcourt, Brace, and Co.

Konrad Kellen, *A View of the VC: Elements of Cohesion in the Enemy Camp in 1966–1967* (Santa Monica, CA: RAND Corporation, 1969), 8–23. Reprinted by permission of RAND Corporation.

William Duiker, *Sacred War* (New York: McGraw-Hill, 1995), 251–67. Reprinted by permission of McGraw-Hill.

Tom Mangold and John Penycate, *The Tunnels of Cu Chi* (New York: Random House, 1985), 17, 19–24. © 1985 by Tom Mangold and John Penycate. Reprinted by permission of Random House.

Philip Caputo, *A Rumor of War*, 2d ed. (New York: Holt, Rinehart, and Winston, 1996), 276–85. © 1977 and 1996 by Philip Caputo. Reprinted by permission of Henry Holt and Co.

Wallace Terry, *Bloods: An Oral History of the Vietnam War by Black Veterans* (New York: Random House, 1984), 113–19. © 1984 by Wallace Terry. Reprinted by permission of Random House.

Lynda Van Devanter, with Christopher Morgan, *Home before Morning: The Story of an Army Nurse in Vietnam* (New York: Beaufort Books, 1983), 79–85, 134–37, 209–12.

Tim O'Brien, *Going after Cacciato* (New York: Delacorte Press/Seymour Lawrence, 1978), 262–73. © 1975, 1976, 1977, and 1978 by Tim O'Brien. Reprinted by permission of Delacorte Press/Seymour Lawrence, a division of Bantam, Doubleday, Dell Publishing Group.

General Bruce Palmer, Jr., *The 25-Year War: America's Military Role in Vietnam* (Lexington: University Press of Kentucky, 1984), 155–71. © 1984 by the University Press of Kentucky. Reprinted by permission of the University Press of Kentucky.

Loren Baritz, *Backfire: A History of How American Culture Led Us into Vietnam and Made Us Fight the Way We Did* (New York: William Morrow, 1985), 299–317, 375–78. © 1985 by Loren Baritz. Reprinted by permission of Loren Baritz.

Michael Bilton and Kevin Sim, *Four Hours in My Lai* (New York: Penguin Books, 1992), 102–23. © 1992 by Michael Bilton and Kevin Sim. Reprinted by permission of Viking Penguin, a division of Penguin Books USA.

Timothy N. Castle, *At War in the Shadow of Vietnam* (New York: Columbia University Press, 1993), 128–37. © 1993 by Columbia University Press. Reprinted by permission of Columbia University Press.

William Shawcross, *Sideshow: Kissinger, Nixon and the Destruction of Cambodia* (New York: Simon and Schuster, 1979), 19–26, 28–35. Reprinted by permission of William Shawcross.

Henry A. Kissinger, *White House Years* (Boston: Little, Brown and Co., 1979), 239–47, 249–54. © 1979 by Henry A. Kissinger. Reprinted by permission of Little, Brown and Co.

Frances FitzGerald, *Fire in the Lake: The Vietnamese and the Americans in Vietnam* (Boston: Little, Brown and Co., 1972), 4–27, 445–46. © 1972 by Frances FitzGerald. Reprinted by permission of Little, Brown and Co.

James C. Thomson, Jr., "How Could Vietnam Happen?: An Autopsy," *The Atlantic Monthly* (April 1968): 47–53. © 1968 by the Atlantic Monthly Co., Boston, MA.

Noam Chomsky, "U.S. Involvement in Vietnam," *Bridge: An Asian American Perspective* 4, no. 1 (October–November 1975): 4–9, 11–16, 18, 20–21. Reprinted by permission of Noam Chomsky.

Norman Podhoretz, *Why We Were in Vietnam* (New York: Simon and Schuster, 1983), 195–210, 239–40. © 1982 and 1983 by Norman Podhoretz. Reprinted by permission of Georges Borchardt, Inc., for the author.

James William Gibson, *The Perfect War: The War We Couldn't Lose and How We Did* (New York: Grove/Atlantic, 1986), 11–27, 477–78. © 1986 by James William Gibson. Reprinted by permission of Grove/Atlantic, Inc.

Christian G. Appy, *Working-Class War: American Combat Soldiers and Vietnam* (Chapel Hill: University of North Carolina Press, 1993), 11–28. Notes omitted. © 1993 by the University of North Carolina Press. Reprinted by permission of the University of North Carolina Press.

Tom Wells, *The War Within: America's Battle over Vietnam* (New York: Henry Holt and Co., 1996), 13–18, 23–33. Notes omitted. © 1996 by Tom Wells. Reprinted by permission of Henry Holt and Co.